P. D. Cranefield
Summer 1986 –
and to commemorate another year as Secretary, Walthamstow Central Baptist.

A
GENEVA
SERIES
COMMENTARY

DANIEL

A COMMENTARY ON
DANIEL

John Calvin

THE BANNER OF TRUTH TRUST

THE BANNER OF TRUTH TRUST
3 Murrayfield Road, Edinburgh EH12 6EL
PO Box 621, Carlisle, Pennsylvania 17013, USA

*

First published in Latin 1561
First translated into English 1570
This edition reprinted from the
Calvin Translation Society edition of 1852-3
First Banner of Truth edition 1966
Reprinted 1986

*

ISBN 0 85151 092 2

*Printed in Great Britain
at the University Printing House, Oxford*

TABLE OF CONTENTS

Volume I

TABLE OF CONTENTS

Volume II

INTRODUCTION

BY WILBUR M. SMITH, D.D.[1]

In the sixteenth century, the two greatest of all the reformers, Martin Luther and John Calvin, each issued a commentary on the book of Daniel. Luther's two works were published in 1524 and 1544 respectively, and carried the titles, *Der Garuss. Von dem Endchrist—aus dem Propheten Daniel*, and, *Kurtze Erclerung ober den Propheten Danielem*. The Calvin work first appeared in 1561 with the title *Praelectiones in Librum Danielis*, studio Joannis Budaei et Caroli Jonvillaei. (Calvin died three years later). This was published in Genèva. Another edition, of 1571, carried the title, *Ioannis Calvini Praelectiones in librum prophetiarum Danielis*, Ioannis Budaei & Caroli Ionuillaei labore & industria exceptae. Additus est e regione versionis Latinae Hebraicus & Chaldaicus textus. Within a year, Calvin's earlier work was translated into French, and published in 1562. A second edition followed, incorporating corrections, in 1569. The astonishing thing about the commentaries on Daniel by the two great reformers is that Luther's commentary has never been translated into English, while Calvin's commentary was translated into English within ten years after its appearance in the Latin edition, published in Geneva, and again, with massive notes, in 1852–3. With the volume you hold in your hand Calvin on Daniel is again reprinted for English readers, in the middle of the 20th century, nearly four hundred years after the original

[1]This introduction originally appeared in the 1948 edition, published in America by the William B. Eerdmans Publishing Company. With the kind permission of the author and the publishers it is included in this British edition.

edition first appeared. One wonders why Luther's rich pages have never been translated into English, but Calvin's both immediately and subsequently. It may be due to the fact that Calvin is everywhere acknowledged as the pre-eminent Biblical exegete of the Reformation, probably the greatest Biblical scholar from the time of Origen down at least to the beginning of the nineteenth century. Professor Andrew Martin Fairbairn in his chapter, "Calvin and the Reformed Church," in the *Cambridge Modern History* has some lines about our commentator that I think ought to be repeated here: "Modern oratory may be said to begin with him, and indeed to be his creation. He helped to make the vernacular tongues of Western Europe literary. He accustomed the people to hear the gravest and most sacred themes discussed in the language which they knew; and the themes ennobled the language, the language was never allowed to degrade the themes . . . He is the sanest of commentators, the most skilled of exegetes, the most reasonable of critics. He knows how to use an age to interpret a man, a man to interpret an age. His exegesis is never forced or fantastic; he is less rash and subjective in his judgments than Luther; more reverent to Scripture, more faithful to history, more modern in spirit . . . His work is inspired by a noble belief; he thought that the one way to realise Christianity was by knowing the mind of Christ; that this mind was expressed in the Scriptures; and that to make them living and credible was to make indefinitely more possible its incorporation in the thoughts and institutions of man."

I return to the earlier edition of Calvin in English (London, 1570). The title is probably important for an introduction to our new edition: "*Commentaries of that diuine Iohn Caluine, vpon the Prophet Daniell, translated into Englishe, especially for the vse of the family of the ryght honorable Earle of Huntingdon, to set forth as in a glasse, how one may profitably read the Scriptures, by consideryng the text, meditatyng the sense therof, and by prayer. Daniell 2. The stone cut foorth of the mountaine without handes, shall breake in peeces the brasse,* &c. At London. Imprinted by Iohn Daye. 1570. 4to." To this is added, an Address to the Reader by the translator (Arthur Golding). I am unable to discover anything about John Daye.

The Calvin Translation Society issued in two great volumes, of over one thousand pages, a new edition of Calvin's work on Daniel, with a new translation of the text, and a number of very scholarly dissertations, all from the pen of Thomas Myers, M.A., at that time Vicar of Sheriff Hutton, Yorkshire. Though I have sincerely tried, I have been unable to discover anything of importance concerning Thomas Myers. My correspondence directed to Great Britain has elicited no information.

Calvin himself lived in an age of ecclesiastical warfare, when many of the rulers of Europe at the time of the Reformation persecuted those who made the Word of God pre-eminent, and preached a gospel of free grace. In May 1546, Charles V, with the strong support, financial and otherwise, of Pope Paul III, began rigorously his foredoomed determination to stamp out Lutheranism in Germany. The end of that war, says Mr. A. F. Pollard, "had exhausted all classes in the nation, and an era of universal lassitude followed. Germany was a desert, and it was called a Religious Peace." Francis I attempted the same programme of fierce persecution in France, 1540-1544, during which time occurred the shameful massacre of the Waldensians. In 1545 alone, twenty-two villages were burned, over three thousand men and women slain, "while the flower of the men were sent to the galleys." Many of the survivors fled to Switzerland. The year after Calvin's work on Daniel first appeared, began the fearfully devastating Wars of Religion, eight of them, from which Europe did not recover for over two centuries. In Calvin's time, belief meant something. It was then that any true Christian might expect to endure torture and death "for His Name's sake". Calvin himself was an exile.

The experiences of Daniel and the Hebrew people in their captivity in Babylon, illustrated by such chapters in Daniel's book as the casting of the three loyal Hebrew men into the fiery furnace, and Daniel's own experience with Darius and his jealous colleagues, resulting in his being cast himself into the den of lions, gave Calvin opportunity to give expression to many things that were in his heart at this time. As he himself says in his *Dedicatory Epistle*, "I have the very best occasion of shewing you, beloved brethren, in this mirror, how God proves the faith of his people in these days by various trials; and how with wonderful wisdom he has taken care to strengthen their minds by ancient examples, that they should never be weakened by the concussion of the severest storms and tempests; or at least, if they should totter at all, that they should never finally fall away. For although the servants of God are required to run in a course impeded by many obstacles, yet whoever diligently reads this Book will find in it whatever is needed by a voluntary and active runner to guide him from the starting-post to the goal; while good and strenuous wrestlers will experimentally acknowledge that they have been sufficiently prepared for the contest . . . Here, then, we observe, as in a living picture, that when God spares and even indulges the wicked for a time, he proves his servants like gold and silver; so that we ought not to consider it a grievance to be thrown into the furnace of trial, while profane men enjoy the calmness of repose."

Out of the book of Daniel Calvin continually drew comfort and exhorted his readers. "But if ye must contend still longer (and I announce that contests more severe than ye contemplate yet remain for you) by whatsoever attack the madness of the impious bursts forth, as if it stirred up the regions below, remember that your course has been defined by a heavenly Master of the contest, whose laws ye must obey the more cheerfully, since he will supply you with strength unto the end." The best in these rich pages of this classic work are those in which Calvin sets forth in moving language the absolute sovereignty of God, and in which he draws great ethical and spiritual lessons from the experiences of Daniel and his colleagues.

As Calvin comes near to the end of his commentary, he emphasizes one great truth (commenting on Daniel 11:31, 32) which he wanted his readers in those troublesome days to understand and by which they were to be strengthened, a truth which the harassed people of God today in these stormy times need ever to remember. "It is worthy of careful observation, that the angel assigns their knowledge of God as the cause and foundation of their constancy. How then, we may ask, does it come to pass, that some few are left, when the apostates thus prostitute themselves? Because their knowledge of God shall prevail, and enable them to overcome these attacks, and bravely to repel them, and to become superior to any temptations. We see, then, the source whence our own fortitude is derived—the knowledge of God. This acknowledgment is no vain and cold imagination, but springs from that faith which spreads its living root in our hearts. Hence it follows, we do not really acknowledge God, unless we boldly contend when we are put to the test, and remain firm and stable, although Satan endeavours, by various machinations, to weaken our faithfulness. And unless we persist in that firmness which is here described, it is quite clear that God has never been truly and really acknowledged by us. The relation too is not without its weight in the phrase, *the people who shall know their God*. Here is a silent reproof, since God revealed himself to the Israelites as far as was sufficient to retain their allegiance. No one, therefore, could offer any excuse without being guilty of impiety, sacrilege, and perfidy, after being so fully instructed by the Law and the prophets."

And, who could write so helpful a paragraph, so filled with common sense, as does Calvin, in discussing the refusal of Daniel to eat the food from the king's table. He says at this point: "When we have no choice of viands, and cannot obtain what would conduce most to our health, if we are content with herbs and roots, the Lord, as I have said, can nourish us no less than if he put before us a table well supplied with every dainty. Temperance does not exist in the food itself, but in the palate—since we are equally intemperate if pleasure entices us to gratify the appetite on inferior food—so, again, we may remain perfectly temperate though feeding on the best diet. We must form the same opinion of the properties of various viands, which do not support us by their own inherent qualities, but by God's blessing, as he sees fit. We sometimes see the children of the rich very emaciated, although they may receive the greatest attention. We see also the children of the country people most beautiful in form, ruddy in countenance, and healthy in condition; and yet they feed on any kind of food, and sometimes upon what is injurious. But although they are deprived of tasty sauces, yet God gives them his blessing" (Vol. 1, p. 109).

When Calvin takes such a phrase as "break off thy sins by righteousness" (4:27) and devotes nearly six pages to its interpretation, he brings out truth that no other man at the time of the Reformation or since has unfolded. His pages on Daniel's going to his house to pray, the nearly one thousand words on the lines, "My God hath sent His angel and hath shut the lions' mouths," his words about the voice from heaven in Daniel 4:32, the significance of dreams, the deeper meaning of Belshazzar's feast—all this is done as only Calvin could do it.

A characteristic expression of Calvin in these pages, which can be duplicated in many of his other works, and is an underlying doctrine in his *Institutes*, reads, "God foresees all things, since nothing is hidden from his eyes; and he points future events, and governs the world by His will, allowing nothing to happen by chance or without His direction. . . God places before our eyes, as in a glass, the proofs of his wisdom and power, when the affairs of the world roll on, and mankind become powerful through wisdom, and some are raised on high, and others fall to the ground."

I suppose nothing on the prayer of Daniel, occupying most of the ninth chapter of his prophecy, has ever been written so rich and deep and comprehensive as the 17,000 words which Calvin devotes to the sixteen verses of this marvelous outpouring of the heart of the ancient prophet. Especially rich are the seven pages devoted to the solemn matter of the confession of sin. His remarks on fasting are sensible. When the matter of angels comes up for discussion, Calvin draws this lesson: "Since Scripture is obscure to us through the darkness in which we are involved, let us learn to reject whatever surpasses our capacity, even when some dark veil envelops it, but let us fly to the remedy which Daniel used, not to seek the understanding of God's word from angels who do not appear to us, but from Christ himself who in these days teaches us familiarly by means of pastors and ministers of the gospel."

It would be Calvin, with all of his learning, with his mastery of the Greek and Roman classics, and of most of the books of any great importance that had been written, it was Calvin who could write, "God needs no books; paper and books are but helps to our memory, which would otherwise easily let things slip; but as he never suffers from forgetfulness, hence he needs no books." (Vol. II, p. 265).

In a day like this, in which we are living, when the governments of the world are breaking up, in a day when a vast part of the earth is controlled by a merciless dictatorship, when multitudes of Christians have already known persecution, and many more will before this age ends, there is hardly any book in the Old Testament we could read with more profit than the book of Daniel, and scarcely a commentary on any portion of the Old Testament quite so profitable as Calvin's two volumes on Daniel, for as Calvin says in his dedicatory preface, "Here we observe, as in a living picture, that when God spares and even indulges the wicked for a time, he proves his servants like gold and silver; so that we ought not to consider it a grievance to be thrown into the furnace of trial, while profane men enjoy the calmness of repose. . . For God shews how all earthly power which is not founded on Christ must fall; and he threatens speedy destruction to all Kingdoms which obscure Christ's glory by extending themselves too much." As in Calvin's day, so pre-eminently in ours, "Lo! storms and tempests now flow from another fountain! Because the Rulers and Governors of the world do not willingly submit to the yoke of Christ, now even the rude multitude reject what is salutary before they even taste it. Some delight themselves in filth, like pigs, and others excited by fury rejoice in slaughter. The devil instigates by especial fury those whom he has enslaved to himself to tumults of all sorts. Hence the clash of trumpets; hence conflicts and battles."

WILBUR M. SMITH,
Professor of Apologetics,
Fuller Theological Seminary

Pasadena, California.
December 1, 1948.

TRANSLATOR'S PREFACE

THE PROPHECIES OF DANIEL are among the most remarkable Predictions of THE ELDER COVENANT. They are not confined within either a limited time or a contracted space. They relate to the destinies of mighty Empires, and stretch forward into eras still hidden in the bosom of the future. The period of their delivery was a remarkable one in the history of our race. The Assyrian hero had long ago swept away the Ten Tribes from the land of their fathers, and he in his turn had bowed his head in death, leaving magnificent memorials of his greatness in colossal palaces and gigantic sculptures. The Son of the renowned SARDANAPALUS, the worshipper of ASSARAC and BELTIS, had already inscribed his name and exploits on those swarthy obelisks and enormous bulls which have lately risen from the grave of centuries. The glory of NINEVEH had passed away, to be restored again in these our days by the marvellous excavations at KOYUNJIK, KHORSABAD, and NIMROUD. Another capital had arisen on the banks of the Euphrates, destined to surpass the ancient splendour of its ruined predecessor on the banks of the Tigris. The worshipper of the eagle-headed NISROCH—a mighty leader of the Chaldean hordes—had arisen, and gathering his armies from their mountain homes, had made the palaces and halls of NINEVEH a desert, had marched southwards against the reigning PHARAOH of Egypt—had encountered him at CARCHEMISH—hurried on to THE HOLY CITY, and carried away with him to his favourite capital the rebellious people of the Lord.   Among them was a captive of no ordinary note.   He was at that time a child, yet he lived to see this descendant of the hardy Chasdim grow great in power and fame—to hear the tale of the fall of TYRE, and "the daughter of the ZIDONIANS," and of the triumph over PHARAOH HOPHRA, whom modern researches have discovered in the twenty-sixth dynasty of Egypt's kings.   At length the haughty conqueror returns, and dreams mysteriously.   This forgotten prisoner becomes the only interpreter of wondrous visions of Empires about to arise and spread over distant centuries.   The dreamer is at length gathered to his fathers : yet the interpreter lives on through the reign of the grandson, and explains a mysterious writing on the palace wall, amidst revelry which ends in the city's overthrow.   CYRUS and his Persians, DARIUS and his Medes rise rapidly to power, and the Prophet rises with them—till envy throws the aged Seer into a lion's den.   But he perishes not till he has seen visions of the future history of mankind.   The triumphs of PERSIA and MACEDON are revealed—the division of ALEXANDER's Empire—the wars of his successors—the wide-spread dominion of ROME—the overthrow of the Sacred Sanctuary by TITUS—and THE COMING OF MESSIAH to regenerate and to rule the world when the seventy weeks were accomplished.

The Roll of the Book, containing all these surprising announcements, has naturally excited the attention of the Scholars and Divines of all ages.   Among the voluminous Comments of the laborious CALVIN, none will be received by the British public with more heartfelt interest than his LECTURES UPON DANIEL.   The various illustrations of DANIEL and THE APOCALYPSE with which the press has always teemed, display the hold which these Divine Oracles have taken of the public mind.   Various theories of interpretation have been warmly and even bitterly discussed.   The Præterist, and the Futurist, the German Neologian, and the American Divine, have each written boldly and copiously ; and the public of Christendom have read with avidity, because they have been taught that these predictions come home to our own times, and to our modern controversies.   Abstruse arguments and historical discussions have been rendered popular, through the expectation of seeing either Pope or Turk, or, perhaps, the Saracen in THE WILFUL KING, and THE LITTLE HORN. If Napoleon the First, or Napoleon the Second, if an Emperor of Russia, or a Pacha of Egypt, can be discovered in the King of the South, pushing at the King of the North —then the deep significance of the Prophecy *to us* is at once acknowledged, and the intensity of its brightness descends directly upon *our own* generation. If the "twelve hundred and ninety Days" of the twelfth Chapter be really years, then the blessing of waiting till "The Time of The End" seems to be upon us, since THE FRENCH REVOLUTION, and the waning of the Turkish sway, and the Conquests of Britain in the East, are then foretold in these "words" which have hitherto been "closed up and sealed."

Whether any of these theories be true or false, they have exercised a mighty power over the imaginations of modern Writers on Prophecy, and have so attracted the minds of Theologians to the subject, as to give force to the inquiry, What was CALVIN's view of these stirring scenes? Without anticipating his COMMENTS, it may be replied, that he disposes of the important question in a few lines. "*In numeris non sum Pythagoricus,*" is the expression of both his wisdom and his modesty. In attempting, however, a solution of these great problems in Prophecy, the opinions of THE RE-FORMERS are most important, and among them all none stands higher as a deep and original thinker than the Author of these Explanatory LECTURES. It is enough for this our Preface to remark, that the bare possibility of the contents of this Book coming home to the daily politics of Europe and the East, adds a charm and a zest to the following pages, which no infirmity in the Commentator can destroy.

In these INTRODUCTORY REMARKS, we shall allude to the present state of opinion respecting the Genuineness and Authenticity of the Book itself, touching upon some of the conjectures advanced since CALVIN's time to the present, and adverting to the scepticism of GERMAN NEOLOGY, and the bold speculations of the amiable ARNOLD. In confutation of all Infidel Objections, we shall next give a general sketch of

the History of ASSYRIA and BABYLON, as it has been lately
disentombed by the labours of MM. BOTTA and LAYARD, and
rescued from the intricacies of the Cuneiform Inscriptions
by HINCKS and RAWLINSON. By these means, the Nimroud
Obelisk in the British Museum—the palatial chambers of
KHORSABAD and KOYUNJIK—the Winged Bull of PERSEPOLIS
—the statue of CYRUS at Moorghab—and the magnificent
sculpture of DARIUS at Behistun—all become vocal proofs
of the truthfulness of DANIEL's predictions. A visit to the
East India House in London will make us acquainted with
the Standard Inscription of NEBUCHADNEZZAR, containing a
list of " all the temples built by the king in the different
towns and cities of BABYLONIA, naming the particular gods
and goddesses to whom the shrines were dedicated :¹ a
journey from Baghdad to the Bir's Nimroud, would shew us
every ruin to be of the age of NEBUCHADNEZZAR :" the testimony of experience is here decisive. " I have examined the
bricks *in situ*," says Major Rawlinson, " belonging, perhaps,
to an hundred towns and cities within this area of about
100 miles in length, and thirty or forty in breadth, and I
never found any other legend than that of Nebuchadnezzar,
the son of Nabopalassar, king of Babylon."² These interesting researches into THE TIMES OF DANIEL will be followed by
some criticism on THE BOOK OF DANIEL. Here we might enlarge to an overwhelming extent, but we are necessarily
compelled to confine our remarks to CALVIN's method of
interpreting these marvellous Prophecies. It will next be
desirable to point out how succeeding Commentators have
differed from our Reformer, while we must leave the reader
to form his own opinion of his merits when he has compared
his views with those of his successors. We shall present him,
however, with sufficient *data* for making this comparison,
and by references to some modern Writers of eminence ; and
by short epitomes of their leading arguments, we hope to
render this edition of these celebrated LECTURES as instructive and as interesting as the limit of our space will allow.

¹ Major (now Colonel) Rawlinson's Commentary on the Cuneiform Inscriptions of Babylonia and Assyria, p. 78.
² P. 76, *Ibid.*

AUTHENTICITY OF THE BOOK OF DANIEL.

THE THIRD CENTURY of Christianity had scarcely commenced, when the Authenticity of this Book was fiercely
assailed by the vigorous scepticism of PORPHYRY; and it
would be totally unnecessary to allude to so distant an opponent, had not his arguments been reproduced by the later
scholars of Germany, and adopted by one of our noble spirits,
whom in many things we delight to honour.   Although the
Jews admitted this Book into their *Hagiographa,* and our
Lord referred to its contents when predicting Jerusalem's
overthrow, yet these self-sufficient critics of our day have repeated the heathen objection which JEROME so elaborately
refuted.   If we inquire into the reason for the revival of such
obsolete scepticism, we shall find it in the pride of that carnal
mind which will not bow down submissively to the miracu-
lous dealings of the Almighty.   The Prophecies concerning
the times of the Seleucidæ and the Lagidæ are found to be
exceedingly precise and minute: hence it is argued, "they
are no prophecies at all—they are History dressed in the
garb of Prophecy, written by some pseudo-Daniel living during their supposed fulfilment."   The Sacred words of Holy
Writ become thus branded with imposture: the testimony
of the Jews and of our Lord to the integrity of the Sacred
Canon is set aside, and the simple trust of the Christian
Church both before and since the Reformation is asserted to
be a baseless delusion.   The judgment and labours of SIR
ISAAC NEWTON, the chronological acumen of FABER and HALES,
are nothing but "the foolishness of the wise," because BER-
THOLDT and BLEEK, DE WETTE and KIRMS, have repeated
the cry "*vaticinia post eventum !*"   And why this eagerness
to degrade this Book to a fabulous compilation of the Maccabæan times?   Simply because its reception as the Word
of GOD would overthrow the favourite theories of the Rationalists respecting The Old Testament.   We cannot undertake to reply to such objections in detail ; we can only furnish the reader with a few references to those Writers by
whom they have been both propagated and refuted.   We

shall first indicate and label the poison. The prœmium of ROSENMULLER furnishes us with a succinct abstract of the assertions of EICHHORN in his *Einleit. in das A. T.*,[1] of BERTHOLDT in his *Histor. krit. Einleit*,[2] of BLEEK in his *Theolog. Zeitschr.*,[3] and of GRIESINGER in his *Neue ansicht der auffatze im Buche Daniel.*[4] The antidote to these conjectures is contained in HAVERNICK'S article on DANIEL, in KITTO'S Cyclopædia of Biblical Literature, and also in his valuable "New Critical Commentary on the Book of Daniel."[5]

Professor HENGSTENBERG[6] of Berlin has ably refuted the Neologian objections of his predecessors: the American reader will find the subject ably treated in the Biblical Repertory of Philadelphia;[7] and the English student may obtain an abstract of the points in dispute from the elaborate "Introduction" of Hartwell HORNE.[8] The various theories of these Neologists imply that the Book was written during the Maccabæan period, by one or more authors who invented the earlier portions by mingling fable with history in inextricable confusion, and by throwing around the history of their own age the garb of prophetic romance! The reception of any such hypothesis would so completely nullify the whole of CALVIN'S Exposition, that we feel absolved from the necessity of entering into details. No disciple of this school will even condescend to peruse these LECTURES. It is enough for us to know, that these unworthy successors of the early German Reformers have been met with ability and research by LUDERWALD, STAUDLIN, JAHN, LACK, and STEUDEL. The unbelief of a SEMLER, a MICHAELIS, and a CORRODI, will seem to the follower of CALVIN the offspring of an unsanctified reason which has never been trained in reverential homage to the inspired Word. The keenness of this perverse criticism has attempted to explain away two important facts; first, that EZEKIEL mentions DANIEL as alive in his day, and as a model of piety and wisdom, (ch. xiv. 20, and ch.

---

[1] Pt. iii. § 615, 6—4th edit.   [2] P. 1563, &c.
[3] Pt. iii. p. 241, &c.   [4] P. 12, &c.
[5] Hamburg, 1838: an excellent treatise, in German.
[6] Die Authentie das Daniel, &c.   Berlin, 1831, 8vo.
[7] Vol. iv. *N S.*, pp. 51, &c.   [8] Vol. iv. p. 205, &c.   Edit. 8th.

xxviii. 3,[1]) and secondly, that the Canon of the Hebrew Scriptures was finally closed before the times of the Maccabæan warriors. HAVERNICK also treats with the greatest erudition the linguistic character of the Book as a decisive proof of its authenticity. He reminds us that the Hebrew language had ceased to be spoken by the Jews long before the reigns of the Seleucidæ, that the Aramæan was then the vernacular tongue, and yet still there is a difference between the Aramæan of DANIEL and the late Chaldee Paraphrasts of the Old Testament. Oriental scholars have pronounced this testimony to be decisive. Interesting as his illustrations are, the numerous subjects which demand our immediate notice will only admit of our referring the reader to the Professor's "New Critical Commentary on the Book of Daniel."[2]

Happily there exists a strong conservative protection against the injury arising from such speculations. They are perfectly harmless to us when locked up in the obscurity of a foreign language and of a forbidding theology. But it grieves the Christian mind to find a writer worthy of being classed among the boldest of Reformers giving the sanction of his authority to such baseless extravagancies. There are many points of similarity between the characters of ARNOLD and CALVIN. Both were remarkable for an unswerving constancy in upholding all they felt to be right, and in resisting all they knew to be wrong. Both were untiring in their industry, and marvellously successful in impressing the young with the stamp of their own mental vigour. Agreeing in their manful protest against the impostures of priestcraft, they differed widely respecting the Book of Daniel. Our modern interpreter, in a letter to a friend,[3] writes as follows concerning "the latter chapters of Daniel, which, if genuine, would be a clear exception to my canon of interpretation, as there can be no reasonable spiritual meaning made out of

---

[1] *Bleek, De Wette, and Kirms,* suppose some more ancient Daniel to be intended. See Rosen. Proœm., p. 6.

[2] The title is Neue critische untersuchungen uber das Buch Daniel. Hamburg, 1838, pp. 104.

[3] See the Life and Correspondence of the late Dr. Arnold of Rugby, vol. ii. p. 191, edit. 2nd. P. 195, edit. 5th.

The Kings of the North and South. But I have long thought
that the greater part of the Book of Daniel is most certainly
a very late work, of the time of the Maccabees ; and the pretended Prophecy about the Kings of Grecia and Persia, and
of the North and South, is mere history, like the poetical
prophecies in Virgil and elsewhere. In fact, you can trace
distinctly the date when it was written, because the events
up to the date are given with historical minuteness, totally
unlike the character of real prophecy, and beyond that date
all is imaginary." It is not difficult to detect the leading
fallacy of this passage in the phrase " my canon of interpretation." This original thinker, with a pertinacity equal to
that of CALVIN, had adopted his own method of explaining
Prophecy, and determined at all hazards to uphold it. As
the writings of this accomplished scholar have been very
widely diffused, it will be useful to notice the arguments
which he has employed. His " Sermons on Prophecy " contain the dangerous theory, which has been fully and satisfactorily answered by BIRKS in his chapter on " The Historical
Reality of Prophecy."[1]

Dr. ARNOLD'S statements are as follow : Sacred Prophecy
is not an anticipation of History. For History deals with
particular nations, times, places, and persons. But Prophecy
cannot do this, or it would alter the very conditions of humanity. It deals only with general principles, good and evil,
truth and falsehood, God and his enemy. It is the voice of
God announcing the issue of the great struggle between good
and evil. Prophecy then, on this view, cannot be fulfilled
literally in the persons and nations mentioned in its language,
it can only be fulfilled in the person of Christ. Thus, every
part is said to have a double sense, " one Historical, comprehended by the Prophet and his own generation, in all its
poetic features, but never fulfilled answerably to the magnificence of its language, because that was inspired by a
higher object : the other Spiritual, the proper form of which

---

[1] Chap. xx. of " The two later Visions of Daniel historically explained."
The Editor strongly recommends all the works of Mr. Birks on prophecy ;
though he differs in opinion on some points of interest, he is deeply impressed by their solid learning and their chastened piety.

neither the Prophet nor his contemporaries knew, but fulfilled adequately in Christ, and his promises to his people as judgment on his enemies." " It is History which deals with the Twelve Tribes of Israel ; but the Israel of Prophecy are God's Israel really and truly, who walk with him faithfully, and abide with him to the end." Twice the Prophecies have failed of their fulfilment, first in the circumcised and then in the baptized Church. " The Christian Israel does not answer more worthily to the expectations of Prophecy than Israel after the flesh. Again have the people whom he brought out of Egypt corrupted themselves :" and hence Predictions relating to the happiness of the Church, both before and since the times of the Messiah, have signally and necessarily failed. We cannot undertake the refutation of this general theory, we must refer the reader to the satisfactory arguments of Birks. We can only quote his clear exposition of the manner in which the Visions of Daniel confute these crude speculations:—" Instead of a mere glimpse of the sure triumph of goodness at the last, we have most numerous details of the steps of Providence which lead to that blessed consummation. The seven years' madness of NEBUCHADNEZZAR, and his restoration to the throne ; the fate of BELSHAZZAR, and the conquests of the MEDES and PERSIANS ; the rise of the Second Empire, the earlier dignity of the Medes, and the later pre-eminence of the Persians over them ; the victories of CYRUS westward in Lydia, northward in Armenia, and southward in Babylon ; the unrivalled greatness of his Empire, and the exactions on the subject provinces ; the three successors of CYRUS, CAMBYSES, SMERDIS, and DARIUS ; the accession of XERXES, and the vast armament he led against Greece, are all predicted within the time of the two earlier Empires. In the time of the Third Kingdom a fuller variety of details is given. The mighty exploits of ALEXANDER, his total conquest of Persia, the rapidity of his course, his uncontrolled dominion, his sudden death in the height of his power, the fourfold division of his kingdom, and the extinction of his posterity ; the prosperous reign of the first PTOLEMY, and of the great SELEUCUS, with the superior power of the latter before his death ; the reign of PHILADELPHUS, and the marriage of BERENICE

his daughter with ANTIOCHUS THEUS; the murder of ANTI-
OCHUS and BERENICE and their infant son by LAODICE; the
vengeance taken by EUERGETES, brother of BERENICE, on his
accession to the throne; his conquest of Seleucia, the fortress
of Syria, and the idol gods which he carried into Egypt;
the earlier death of CALLINICUS; the preparations of his
sons, SELEUCUS, CERAUNUS, and ANTIOCHUS the Great, for war
with Egypt, are all distinctly set before us. Then follows
the history of ANTIOCHUS. His sole reign after his brother's
death, his eastern conquests and recovery of Seleucia; the
strength of the two rival armies, and the Egyptian victory
at Raphia; the pride of PTOLEMY PHILOPATER and his partial conquests, with the weakness of his profligate reign;
the return of ANTIOCHUS with added strength after an interval of years, and with the riches of the East; his victories
in Judea and the capture of Sidon; the overthrow of the
Egyptian forces at Panium, the honour shewn by ANTIOCHUS
to the Temple, and his care for its completion and beauty;
his treaty with Egypt, the marriage of his daughter CLEO-
PATRA with PTOLEMY PHILOMETOR, and defection from her
father's cause; his invasion of the Isles of Greece; his rude
repulse by the Roman Consul, and the reproach of tribute
which came upon him through his defeat; his return to
Antioch and speedy death, are all described in regular order.
Then follow the reigns of SELEUCUS and ANTIOCHUS EPIPHANES,
given with an equal fulness of prophetic detail, and close the
narrative of the Third Empire. Even in the time of the
Fourth and last Kingdom, though more remote from the
days of the Prophet, the events predicted are not few. We
find there, distinctly revealed, the iron strength of the Romans, their gradual subjugation of other powers, their fierce
and warlike nature, their cruel and devouring conquests, the
stealthy policy of their empire, and its gradual advance in
the direction of the East, southward and eastward towards
the land of Israel, till it had cast down the noblest Kings,
and firmly ingrafted its new dominion on the stock of the
Greek Empire. We have next described its oppression of
the Jews, the overthrow of their City and Sanctuary by
TITUS, the Abomination of Desolation in the Holy Place,

and their arrogant pride in standing up against Messiah, the Prince of princes."[1]

If the latter portion of these predictions were really written previously to the events, they must be inspired ; and if a writer of the Maccabæan period could thus accurately predict the Conquests of Rome in the East, the whole question is decided : there is no reason whatever why the events of the Second and Third Empires should not have been foretold as clearly as those of the Fourth. Thus the very existence of the Book before the Jewish Canon was closed is a fact which proves all that is required. These Visions then become " the voice of Him who sees the end from the beginning, and pronounces in his secret council, even on the destiny of the falling sparrow. They are designed to stoop to the earthly estate of the Church, while they exalt her hopes to the glory that shall be revealed. . . . They range through everlasting ages ; but they let fall in passing a bright gleam of light that discovers to us the ass's colt, tied at the meeting of their ways, on which the Lord of glory was to ride into Jerusalem. . . . Every step in the long vista of preparation lies before them, from the seven months' reign of SMERDIS and the marriage of BERENICE with ANTIOCHUS, (ch. xi. 2-6,) to the seven months' burial of (corpses) in days to come in the land of Israel, and the marriage supper of the Lamb. . . . They touch, as with an enchanter's wand, the perplexed and tangled skein of human history, and it becomes a woof of curious and costly workmanship, that bespeaks the skill of its Divine Artificer : an outer hanging, embroidered by heavenly wisdom, for that glorious tabernacle in which the God of heaven will reveal himself for ever."[2]

THE DIVINES OF GERMANY.

Throughout this PREFACE and the subsequent DISSERTATIONS the reader will find frequent reference to THE DIVINES OF GERMANY. Some of these have proposed explanations of our

---

[1] " The two later Visions of Daniel," p. 357.　　[2] Birks. p. 359.

Prophet which appear to the English reader so manifestly erroneous, that he may fancy we have spent too much space in confuting them. But he who would keep pace with the Theological Investigations of the day, may derive improvement from
perusing the hypothesis of BERTHOLDT and DE WETTE, and rejoice that they have elicited the able replies of HAVERNICK
and HENGSTENBERG. In truth, the reader of DANIEL must put
aside for a while the laudable prejudices which he has been
taught to cherish from his earliest days, and descend into
the arena where the contest is fiercest,—whether our Prophet
was contemporary with NEBUCHADNEZZAR or ANTIOCHUS. To
many the question itself is startling, and that we may be
prepared to meet it, thoroughly furnished with available
armory, let us glance over the wide field of Continental
Rationalism as far as it concerns the Authenticity of Daniel.

The system under review is a melancholy off-shoot from
the teaching of LUTHER and his intrepid followers. They
led men away from form, and ceremony, and imposture,
to rely upon one BOOK as their Rule of Faith and Duty.
They did more—they sifted the chaff from the wheat, and
by discarding the APOCRYPHA, placed before the eager attention of mankind the pure word of heaven. LUTHER and
CALVIN held very distinct ideas about Revelation and Justification, and enforced very boldly their views of the only
Books which were written by the penmanship of the Almighty. Theirs was a work of purification and of recon-
struction on the assertion of the existence of a Divine Revelation, of its being contained in the Old and New Testaments,
and of these documents being the only Inspired Records of
what we are to believe, and how we are to live. In process of time, each Book became the subject of separate study
—its history, its criticism, and its preservation were respectively examined with intense eagerness—and a vast amount
of information was collected, which was totally unkown to
the Early Reformers. It soon became apparent that the
Reformed Churches were living under a totally different state
of things from that described in the Old Testament. The
events, for instance, of this Book of DANIEL all seemed so
mingled and so intertwined; the ordinary occurrences of

every-day life are so interlaced with marvellous dreams
and visions, and the conduct and passions of monarchs seem
so singularly controlled by an unseen Mind, that the question
occurs, Is all this literally true ?   Did it all actually come
to pass exactly as it is recorded ?   Or, Is it allegorical, or a
historical romance, or only partially inspired by Jehovah,
and tinged in its style and diction with the natural exaggeration of Oriental imagery ?   Such inquiries shew us how
the mind seeks to fathom the mysteries of what is offered to
its veneration, and have led to the conclusion, that the Sacred Books of the Hebrews are not all pure revelation, but
that they contain it amidst much extraneous matter.[1]   The
writers to whom we refer have ever since the sixteenth century been attempting to define how much of the Hebrew
Scriptures is the pure and spiritual Revelation of the Divine
Mind to us, and how much is the unavoidable impurity of
the channel through which it has been conveyed.   With the
names of some later critics, the modern Theologian is familiar.   GESENIUS, WEGSCHEIDER, and RÖHR, yet retain a powerful influence over the minds of later students, while SCHULTZ
at Breslau, GIESELER at Göttingen, ALLMANN at Heidelberg,
BRETSCHNEIDER at Gotha, DE WETTE—lately deceased—at
Basle, HARE at Jena, and WIENER at Leipsic, are writers
who worship irreverently at the shrine of human reason,
and either qualify or deny the Inspiration of Revelation.

FALSE SYSTEMS OF SCRIPTURE EXPOSITION.

An important change was necessarily made on the minds
of the successors of the Reformers, by the more general
spread of Classical Literature, and a far better acquaintance
with Hebrew philology.   Here, we must allow, that some of
the disciples of LUTHER and CALVIN were better furnished
for the work of Interpretation than their more Christian-
minded masters.   ERNESTI, the learned philologer of Leipsic,
in 1761 laid down " The Laws of a wise Interpretation," and
has ever since been considered as the founder of a scholar-

---

[1] See Töllner's *Die heilige Eingebund der heiligen Schrift.*   Linden,
1771, quoted in *Am. Saintes' Hist. Rat.*, 1849.

like system of Scriptural Exposition. His principles are now universally admitted, viz., that we must make use of history and philology of the views of the period at which each Book was written, and of all those appliances which improved scholarship has provided in the case of the Classical Authors of Greece and Rome. Every attentive reader of German Theology must perceive, that too many of their celebrated Critics have rested in this outward appeal to mere reason and research. SEMLER and TITTMANN, MICHAELIS and HENKE, have pursued this system of accommodation so far, that they have destroyed the very spirit and essence of a Divine Revelation. In the Prophets, and especially in DANIEL, whom SEMLER includes among the doubtful Books, there is a spiritual meaning only to be comprehended by the moral and religious faculties ; and except this spirit be elicited, the merely outward form of prophetic diction can effect no religious result. Let RÖHR and PAULUS sneer as they please, at the mysticism and pietism of the Evangelic Reformers, we must still contend, that without a spirituality similar to theirs, all comments are essentially lifeless and profitless to the soul of man. They may display erudition, but they will not aid the spirit which hungers and thirsts after righteousness on its way towards heaven.

Every student who desires to become familiar with these discussions, may consult with advantage the Dissertations of HENGSTENBERG, who has written fully and ably on The Genuineness of our Prophet. He has sketched, historically, the attacks which have been made, and has answered every possible objection. The impurity of the Hebrew, the words supposed to be Greek, the silence of Sirach, the disrespect shewn by the Jews, and the position in the Canon of Scripture, are all ably discussed. The miracles have been called " profuse in number and aimless in purpose ;" historical errors have been asserted, and statements called contradictory, or suspicious, or improbable ; many ideas and usages have been said to belong to later times. These and similar arguments are used to shew the Book to be the production of the times of ANTIOCHUS EPIPHANES, but they have been fully treated by this orthodox Professor at Berlin. He discusses most ably, and with the most laborious erudition, those marvellous Prophecies of this Sacred Book, which have necessarily provoked a host of assailants. He reminds us that in the earliest ages, PORPHYRY devoted his twelfth book to the assault upon this Prophet, and that we are indebted to JEROME for a knowledge of his objections as well as for their refutation. He asserted that the Book was composed during the reign of ANTIOCHUS EPIPHANES in Greek, "and that DANIEL did not so much predict future events as narrate past ones."[1] Though the imperial commands condemned his works to the flames, yet EUSEBIUS of Cæsarea, METHODIUS of Tyre, and APOLLINARIS of Laodicea, have ably refuted them. In later times, the first scholar-like attack upon the genuineness of various portions was made by J. D. MICHAELIS. COLLINS and SEMLER, SPINOZA and HOBBES, had each condemned the Book after his own manner : but it was left for EICHHORN[2] to lead the host of those later Neologians who have displayed their vanity and their scepticism, by the boastfulness of their learning and the emptiness of their conclusions. HEZEL and CORRODI treat it as the work of an impostor ; while BERTHOLDT, GRIESINGER, and GESENIUS, have each their own theory concerning its authorship and contents. Other Critics have followed the footsteps of these into paths most dangerous and delusive.

Having replied to the most subtle objections against the Genuineness of these Prophecies, HENGSTENBERG proceeds to uphold the direct arguments in its favour. He first discusses the testimony of the author himself, and then enters upon its reception into the Canon of the Sacred Writings. He comments at full length on the important passage in JOSEPHUS contra Apion. i. 8, and shews the groundlessness of every assertion which impugns its Canonical value. He next proves that the declaration of our Lord assumes the prophetical authority of the work, and traces its existence in pre-Maccabæan times. The alleged exhibition of these Writings to ALEXANDER THE GREAT and the exposition of their contents to the Grecian Conqueror of the East, form a singular

---

[1] Jerome's *Prœmium in Dan.*, Op. tom. v. p. 267.
[2] Einleitung in A. T.

episode in the midst of profound criticism. The incorrectness of the Alexandrine Version and its rejection by the
Early Church, who substituted that of Theodotion for it, is
turned into an argument against the Maccabæan origin of the
original ; for certainly, a composition of which the author
and the translators were nearly contemporary, might be better translated, than one separated by an interval of many
ages. Then the peculiar features and complexion of the
original language point out the exact period to which the
writing is to be assigned. The historical accuracy, the apparent discrepancies, and yet the real agreement with Profane Narratives, all strengthen the assertion, that the writer
lived during the times of the Babylonian and Persian Monarchies. Another argument, as strong as any of the former, is deduced from the nature of the symbolism used
throughout the Book. The reasonings of HENGSTENBERG
have now received additional confirmation from the excavations of LAYARD. The prevalence of animal imagery, rudely
grotesque and awkwardly gigantic, is characteristic of Chaldean times, and bespeaks an era previous to the Medo-Persian Sculptures at Persepolis. Summing up his reasonings,
the Professor quotes the observation of FENELON : " Lisez
DANIEL, dénonçant à Balthasar la vengeance de Dieu toute
prête a fondre sur lui, et cherchez dans les plus sublimes ori-
ginaux de l'antiquité quelque chose qu'on puisse comparer
à ces endroits là !"

ENGLISH PHILOSOPHICAL SCHOOL.

The speculations which we have hitherto discussed are
not confined within the limits of unreadable GERMAN NEO-
LOGY : they have been transfused into English Philosophy,
and presented in a popular form to the readers of our current literature. In a learned and speculative Work, entitled
" The Progress of the Intellect, as exemplified in the Religious Development of the Greeks and Hebrews," the writer [1]
has adopted the untenable hypothesis of the German Neologists. In his second section of a chapter on the " Notion of

[1] By Robert William Mackay. 2 vols. 8vo. 1850.

a supernatural Messiah," he writes as follows: "During the
severe persecution under ANTIOCHUS EPIPHANES, when the
cause of Hebrew faith in its struggle with colossal heathenism seemed desperate, and when, notwithstanding some
bright examples of heroism, the majority of the higher class
was inclined to submit and to apostatize, an unknown writer adopted the ancient name of DANIEL, in order to revive
the almost extinct hopes of his countrymen, and to exem-
plify the proper bearing of a faithful Hebrew in the presence
of a Gentile Tyrant. . . . The object of pseudo-Daniel is
to foreshow, under a form adapted to make the deepest impression on his countrymen, by a prophecy, half-allusive,
half-apocalyptic, the approaching destruction of heathenism
through the advent of Messiah.   Immediately after the overthrow of the Four Beasts, emblematic of four successive
heathen Empires, the last being the Macedonian with its
offset, the Syrian ; the 'kingdom' would devolve to the
'Saints of the Most High,' that is, to the Messianic Establishment of Jewish expectation, presided over by a being
appearing in the clouds, and distinguished, like the angels,
by his human form from the uncouth symbols of the Gentile
Monarchies."[1] He treats "Messiah" as a " title which hitherto confined to human anointed authorities, such as kings,
priests, or prophets, became henceforth, specifically appropriated to the ideal personage who was to be the Hope, the
Expectation, and the Salvation of Israel." He discusses the
Seventy Weeks as the fiction of the imaginary DANIEL, and
terms the accompanying predictions "adventurous," and as
turning out "as fallacious as all that had preceded them."
His fourth section on DANIEL'S MESSIAH is, if possible, more
wildly conjectural than the two preceding ones.   Daniel's
idea, says he, of a supernatural leader called "Son of Man,"
became afterwards "a basis of mystical Christology." Those
glowing passages of this Prophet, which fill the Christian
mind with awe and delight, are to this theorist "the earthly
or Messianic resurrection of pious Hebrews, which was all
that was originally contemplated in the prediction." In thus
attempting to overthrow the Inspired authority of DANIEL,

[1] Vol. ii. § 2, " Time of Messiah's coming," p. 307.

he mingles the Books of Esdras and the Jewish Targum, and is eager to catch at any Jewish fiction as if it were a true interpretation of ancient prophecy. He alludes to puerile Rabbinical fables as really explanatory of the Divine Records, and mingles ZOROASTER and MAIMONIDES, GFRORER and EISENMENGER, as of equal value in determining abstruse points of sound criticism! The sections with which we are concerned evince the greatest research and the crudest opinions all hurried together without the slightest critical skill or philosophical sagacity. With materials gathered together in the richest abundance, he has presented us with results which are alike baseless, futile, and injurious. TOBIT and PAPIAS, the Book of BARUCH and the Book of ENOCH, are all treated as on a level with the writings of MOSES or TACITUS, JUSTIN MARTYR or a German Mystic! The public, too, are in danger of being imposed on by a show of learning and by long Latinized words and phrases, which merely disguise, under classical forms, ideas with which the well-read Divine is already familiar; at the same time, they give such an air of scholarship to these speculations, that the unlearned may be readily deceived by their showy rationalism. The whole work utterly fails in its attempt to explain the rites and symbols of Jewish worship, and to give the slightest explanation of the " theories " and " philosophies " of the Old Testament. The tendency is to reduce it all to mysticism and symbolism, and to any other " theosophy " which leads the mind away from the Christian assurance of one God, one Faith, and one Spirit.

THE RECENT EASTERN DISCOVERIES.

The strongest of all possible arguments against these fallacious theories has lately been derived from Eastern discovery. Fresh importations of sculptured rock are daily arriving in Europe, from the sepulchres of those cities amidst which our Prophet dwelt. The more this new vein is worked, the richer it becomes. Are we to be told by BLEEK that the writer of this Book transferred the events of which he was a spectator to the more ancient times of Assyria and

Babylon ? and that NEBUCHADNEZZAR and BELSHAZZAR were but fabulous characters, of which the original types were ANTIOCHUS and ALEXANDER ?[1] Are EICHHORN and BERTHOLDT to make DANIEL another Homer, or Virgil, or Æschylus ? Then let us appeal to the testimony of MM. BOTTA and LAYARD ; let us visit the British Museum, and under the guidance of RAWLINSON and HINCKS, let us peruse, in the arrow-headed characters, the history of the Monarchs of Assyria and Babylon, and observe how exactly those memorials of antiquity illustrate the Visions of our Prophet. The assistance which these excavations afford, for the elucidation of our subject, is too important to be passed over, and we must venture upon such arguments as may properly enter into a General Preface, while they vindicate the historical accuracy of the interpretation which CALVIN has so elaborately set before us in the following LECTURES.

ANCIENT ASSYRIAN REMAINS.

The order of THE VISIONS suggests the propriety of treating, first, THE ANCIENT ASSYRIAN REMAINS ; then those of BABYLON and PERSEPOLIS, with such notices of the EGYPT OF THE PTOLEMIES as the connection of the history may require.

The earliest memorials of ASSYRIA have not been preserved in the records of literature, but by durable engravings on marble and granite. Within the last fifty years the PYRAMIDS OF EGYPT have been compelled to open their lips of stone to speak for God's Word, and the ROSETTA tablet suggested to YOUNG and CHAMPOLLION an alphabet by which they read on sarcophagus and entablature the history of the earliest dynasties of the Nile. What LEPSIUS and BUNSEN have done for Thebes and Memphis, Dendera and Edfou, LAYARD and RAWLINSON are now accomplishing for the long lost NINEVEH, the majestic BABYLON, and the elegant PERSEPOLIS. It has lately been revealed to astonished Europe, that a buried city lies, in all its pristine grandeur, beneath that huge mound which frowns over Mosul on the banks of the Tigris. KHORSABAD and KOYUNJIK, NIMROUD and BEHISTUN,

[1] Rosenmüller Procem., p. 26.

are now giving up their black obelisks, their colossal bulls,
and their eagle-headed warriors, to become " signs and wonders" to our curious generation.   In this general sketch we
must avoid details, however interesting : we can only allude
to the first Assyrian monuments discovered by M. BOTTA, in
1843,[1] as containing a line of Cuneiform Inscriptions amid
winged kings and their warlike chariots. They are deposited
in the Louvre, and form the most ancient of its esteemed
collections.   The elegant volumes of LAYARD, and the more
tangible proofs of his untiring labours, now deposited in the
British Museum, have thrown new light upon the prophetic
portion of the Elder Covenant.   Two-coned Conquerors,
winged Chiefs, carrying either the gazelle or the goat, sacred
trees, and their kneeling worshippers—

The life-like statue and the breathing bust,
The column rescued from defiling dust—

enable us to guess at the exploits of a long line of kings before the age of Saul or Priam.   The name of SARDANAPALUS
is now rescued from traditional disgrace, and ennobled in the
midst of a hardy race of ancestors and successors.   Our
progress in interpreting these arrow-headed mysteries, enables
us to assign the date 1267 B.C. for the founding of NINEVEH
as a settled point in Asiatic chronology. The earliest historical document in the world is that on the north-west palace
of NIMROUD, built by ASSAR-ADAN-PAL. He informs us of the
existence, and celebrates the exploits of TEMEN-BAR the first,
the founder of HALEH, at a time when the Hebrews were
just entering the promised land, and the Argives were colo-
nizing the virgin valleys of Hellas !   The familiar names of
SHALMANESER, SENNACHERIB, and ESARHADDON, are found in-
cised upon the enduring masonry ; and it is now possible to
ascertain who founded the MESPILA of Xenophon, who constructed the towers in the south-west palace of NIMROUD, and
who stamped his annals on the clay cylinders in the British
Museum.[2] The NIMROUD obelisk becomes a precious relic,
since it enables us to ascertain, for the first time, the events

[1] See his letters to M. Mohl in the *Journal Asiatique* for 1843; April
5, June 2, October 31, and also March 22, 1844.
[2] See Major Rawlinson's Commentary on the Cuneiform Inscriptions, p.
57, and his references to the various plates of the British Museum series.

of those nine centuries, during which NINEVEH existed from
its rise to its overthrow. We are mainly concerned with the
manner in which it confirms the truthfulness of the Prophets
of the Hebrews, and with the unanswerable arguments which
it supplies against the subtleties of German Neology. The
credibility of one Prophet is intimately bound up with that of
another. Whatever confirms either ISAIAH or EZEKIEL, throws
its reflected light upon DANIEL and HOSEA. The god NISROCH,
in whose temple SENNACHERIB was slain, (2 Kings xix. 37,
and Isaiah xxxvii. 38,) is repeatedly mentioned on the obelisk
as the chief deity of the Assyrians. The " SARGON king of
Assyria" (Isaiah xx. 1) is most probably the monarch who
founded the city excavated by M. BOTTA ; and the occurrence of the name " YEHUDA," in the 33d number of the
British Museum series, leads Interpreters to consider the
passage as alluding to the conquest of SAMARIA. The very
paintings so graphically described by EZEKIEL, (chap. xxiii.
14, 15,) have reappeared upon the walls of these palaces.
They are, perhaps, the very identical objects which this
Prophet beheld, for he dwelt at no great distance from them
on the banks of the Khabur, and wrote the passage about
thirteen years after the destruction of the Assyrian Empire.
The prophecy bears the date B.C. 593, and " the latest Assyrian sculpture on the site of NINEVEH must be as early
as B.C. 634."[1] We would gladly linger over these proofs of
the truthfulness of the ancient Prophets ; but further details
must be inserted in those DISSERTATIONS which accompany
the text, and we close this rapid sketch of these Assyrian
remains in the touching words of their enterprising Disco-
verer. " I used," says Mr. LAYARD, " to contemplate for
hours these mysterious emblems, and to muse over their intent and history. What more noble forms could have ushered
the people into the temple of their gods ? What more
sublime images could have been borrowed from nature, by
men who sought, unaided by the light of Revealed Religion,
to embody their conception of the wisdom, power, and ubiquity of a Supreme Being ? They could find no better type
of intellect and knowledge, than the head of a man ; of

---

[1] See Vaux's Nineveh and Persepolis, p. 263, edit. 2d.

strength, than the body of the lion ; of ubiquity, than the
wings of the bird. The winged-human-headed lions were
not idle creations, the offspring of mere fancy ; their meaning was written upon them. They had awed and instructed
races which had flourished 3000 years ago. Through the
portals which they guarded, kings, priests, and warriors had
borne sacrifices to their altars, long before the wisdom of the
East had penetrated to Greece, and had furnished its myth-
ology with symbols long recognised by the Assyrian vota-
ries. They may have been buried, and their existence may
have been unknown, before the foundation of the Eternal
City. For twenty-five centuries they had been hidden from
the eye of man, and they now stood forth once more in their
ancient majesty. But how changed was the scene around
them ! The luxury and civilisation of a mighty nation had
given place to the wretchedness and ignorance of a few half-
barbarous tribes ; the wealth of temples, and the riches of
great cities had been succeeded by ruins and shapeless
heaps of earth. Above the spacious hall in which they
stood, the plough had passed and the corn now waved.
Egypt had monuments no less ancient and no less wonderful, but they have stood forth for ages, to testify her early
power and renown, while those before me had but now
appeared to bear witness in the words of the Prophet, that
once ' The Assyrian was a cedar in Lebanon, with fair
branches, and with a shadowing shroud of a high stature ;
and his top was among the thick boughs. . . . His height
was exalted above all the trees of the field, and his boughs
were multiplied, and his branches became long, because of
the multitude of the waters which he shot forth. All the
fowls of heaven made nests in his boughs, and under his
branches did all the beasts of the field bring forth their
young, and under his shadow dwelt all great nations ;' for
now is ' Nineveh a desolation, and dry like a wilderness,
and flocks lie down in the midst of her ; all the beasts of the
nations, both the cormorant and the bittern lodge in the
upper lintels of it ; their voice sings in the windows, and
desolation is in the thresholds.' "[1]

[1] Vaux, p. 221.

ANCIENT BABYLONIAN REMAINS.

As we travel onwards in time, and southward in place, our attention is attracted to those Babylonian antiquities which vindicate the correctness of the Comments of CALVIN.

After centuries of extensive empire, NINEVEH yielded to a younger rival. The army of Sennacherib had been annihilated by the angel of the Lord ; ESARHADDON, his son, had planted his heathen colonists in the fertile plains of Samaria. NEBU-CHADONOSOR had won the battle of Rhagau ; PHRAORTES had been slain, and his son, CYAXARÈS in alliance with NABOPALAS-SAR, had taken NINEVEH, and destroyed for ever its place in the history of Asia. Palaces of black basalt, bas-reliefs, and hawk-headed heroes, covered with legends of unbounded triumphs, no longer rose at the bidding of the servants of Bar, and the worshippers of Assarac, Beltis, and Rimmon. No more
Her obelisks of buried chrysolite
proclaimed her far-famed majesty ; for her new masters transferred the seat of their empire to the banks of the Euphrates. The renowned son of NABOPALASSAR now commences the era of Babylonian greatness. This enterprising chieftain is no creation of poetic fancy. HERODOTUS and BE-ROSUS have recorded his exploits, and we have now the testimony of recent discovery to confirm the assertions of Daniel, and to throw fresh light upon his narrative.

" The earliest Babylonian record that we have," says Major RAWLINSON, " is, I think, the inscription engraved on a triumphal tablet at Holwan, near the foot of Mount Zagros ; it is chiefly religious, but it seems also to record the victories of a certain king named Temnin against the mountaineers. Unfortunately it is in a very mutilated state, and parts of it alone are legible. I discovered this tablet on the occasion of my last visit to Behistun, and with the help of a telescope, for there are no possible means of ascending the rock, succeeded in taking a copy of such portions of the writing as are legible. . . . I am not able at present to attempt a classification of the kings of Babylon, such as they are known from the various relics that we possess of them : nor, indeed, can I say with certainty, whether the kings recorded, with the exception of NEBUCHADNEZZAR and his father, may be anterior or posterior to the era of NABONAS- SAR. The Babylonians certainly borrowed their alphabet from the Assyrians, and it requires no great trouble or ingenuity at the present day to form a comparative table of the charac- ters."[1] "I have examined," says this enterprising traveller, "hundreds of the Hymar bricks, (near Babylon,) and have found them always to bear the name of NEBUCHADNEZZAR." Borsippa was a city in the neighbourhood of Babylon, and there is monumental "evidence of its being the capital of Shinar, as early almost as the earliest Assyrian epoch." Temenbar, the Obelisk king, conquered it in the ninth year of his reign : the bricks upon the spot are exclusively stamped with the name of Nebuchadnezzar, being at this moment tangible proofs of the reality of the words "Is not this the great Ba- bylon that I have built ?" The rebuilding of the city, and the construction and dedication of the great temple is no- ticed "in the standard inscription of Nebuchadnezzar, of which the India House slab furnishes us with the best and most perfect copy." This valuable monument gives a detail of all the temples which he built throughout the various cities of his extensive provinces, it names the particular deities to whom the shrines were dedicated, and mentions other particulars, which our present ignorance of the lan- guage enables us but partially to comprehend. The vast mound of El Kasr contains the remains of a magnificent palace, supposed to be that of NEBUCHADNEZZAR ; but as these recent excavations are more to our present purpose, it is unnecessary to refer at length to this majestic ruin.[2]

PERSIAN AND EGYPTIAN ANTIQUITIES.

Again, in commenting on the ninth chapter, CALVIN has followed the usual method of interpreting it of ALEXANDER and his successors : he naturally assumes them to be real predictions, and believes them to have been accomplished according to the utterance of their Hebrew captive. And

---

[1] Com. on Cuneif. Inscrip., p. 76.
[2] See a description of the Kasr in Kitto's Bib. Cyc., art. Babylon.

have we no traces of the foot-prints of Alexander now remaining to us ? Not long ago, a traveller, amid the barren plains of Persia, lighted unexpectedly on a magnificent ruin —alone, on a deserted plain—its polished marbles, and its chiselled columns all strewed around in wild confusion. This Chehel-Minar, or hall of forty pillars, was built by the Genii, said the Arabs, amid the desert solitudes of Merdusht. The Genii builders have lately been stripped of their disguise of fable, and the long lost Persepolis, destroyed by the mad frolic of Alexander, stands revealed to the world in the Takht-i-Jemshid. The grandeur of these pillared halls, these sculptured staircases, and fretwork fringes of horn-bearing lions, interests the reader of Daniel, through the inscriptions which they bear on their surface. The ingenuity of a Westergaard and a Lassen has been displayed in deciphering them, and has enabled us to discover the original architects. CYRUS and CAMBYSES, DARIUS HYSTASPES and XERXES, each erected his own portion. One portion can be assigned to the Achænenian dynasty, and another to the monarchs of the Sassanian family. These inscriptions also point out where the rulers of Persia formed their sepulchral repose. The tomb of Cyrus at Moorghab, his statue discovered and described by Sir R. K. PORTER, and " the thousand lines" on the sculptured rock of Behistun,[1] throw a clear and brilliant light on the statements of DANIEL, as well as on the narrative of Herodotus. These passing allusions must suffice at present—further discussions must be left for distinct dissertations—while the ninth and tenth chapters of VAUX's Nineveh and Persepolis will supply additional information to all who are inclined to search for it. Enough is introduced, if the reader is impressed with the conviction that DANIEL's Visions and CALVIN's LECTURES are no vague or cunning delusions, no skilful travestying of history, under the garb of either intentional forgery or weak credulity.

As PERSEPOLIS suggests the triumph of the He-goat, and the rising of the four horns towards the four winds of heaven, (chap. viii. 8,) so it leads us forwards towards the subsequent warfare between Asia and Egypt. The mighty

[1] Major Rawlinson in Journ. Royal Geog. Soc., vol. ix.

king stood up, and his kingdom was broken : and the king
of the south became strong and mighty, (chap. xi. 3, 4.)   An
index here points to the valley of the Nile, where there
now exists a countless host of monuments, raised by the
giants of the very earliest days of our race.   On the day
when CAMBYSES, flushed with victory, stabbed with his own
hand the living Apis, and commanded the bones of the Pharaohs to be beaten with rods, he struck to the heart the
genius of the Nile.   At that moment, the quarries were
teeming with busy sculptors, numerous as swarming bees—
massive monoliths were becoming Sphinxes and Memnons,
while architraves and propyla, worthy of the TEMPLE OF KAR-
NAK, were emerging from the living rock.   They all retired
to rest that evening, intending to renew their labour on the
morrow, but on the morrow bursts the avenging Persian, and
that long train of workers are still for ever.   But their unfin-
ished handicraft remains for the astonishment of our later centuries.   A perfect statue only awaits one final blow to detach
it from its parent rock—there runs the track of the wheels
which had come to transport it to either EDFOU or LUXOR ;
there may be seen the very marks of the tools which lay by its
side all night, and were never used on the next fatal morning.

Henceforth Egyptian art is transferred to the tombs and
palaces of the kings of Persia.   It is cheering to feel, that
as our knowledge of the significance of these treasures advances, they confirm the assertions of Holy Writ.   Among
the mural sculptures at KARNAK, one of the captives, with a
Jewish physiognomy, bears the title which we can now read
—YOUDAH MALEK, meaning a king of Judah.   THE ROSETTA
STONE in our National Museum, which is the basis of modern
Egyptology, was sculptured as late as B.C. 195, and contains
a decree of PTOLEMY EPIPHANES, to whom DANIEL is supposed
to refer.   The primæval antiquity of THE ZODIAC on the
majestic portico at DENDERA, has now been disproved.   "The
Greek Inscription on the pronaos refers to TIBERIUS and
HADRIAN."   The hieroglyphic legends on the oldest portion
of its walls belong to the last CLEOPATRA, while the Zodiac
was constructed between A.D. 12 and 132.   While we willingly allow the connection between Assyria and Egypt as early

as the thirteenth century before Christ, and admit the occurrence of its name on the Nimroud obelisk in the British
Museum,[1] and on the sculptures of Behistun and Nakhshi-
Rustam,[2] yet we contend against that assumption of a false
antiquity, which is assumed for the purpose of throwing
discredit upon the prophetic portions of our Sacred Oracles.

What, then, is the result of our rapid sketch of these remains of the dynasties of former eras? A complete overthrow of the baseless fabrications of German Neology. Till
the arrow-headed character was deciphered, the history of
NINEVEH was almost a blank to the world. As Assyria and
Babylon now breathe and live in resuscitated glory, so all
that DANIEL wrote is confirmed and amplified by the marbles
and tombs which have travelled to this Island of the West.
Hence this Captive of Judah really lived while the Head of
Gold was towering majestically upon the allegorical image.
Neither poet nor impostor of the reign of ANTIOCHUS could
have fancied or forged characters and events which accord
so exactly with the excavations of a LAYARD, or the de-
cipherings of a RAWLINSON. Sceptical infidelity must now
hide its head for ever, and speculations of the school of
Arnold must shrink into their original insignificance.

POSITIVE EVIDENCE.

The positive evidence of additional facts may also be adduced. This Book was translated by The Seventy many
years before the death of ANTIOCHUS, and the translation was
well known to JEROME, although it has not come down to
our age. Bishop CHANDLER has pointed out fifteen places
in which JEROME refers to it;[3] and Bishop HALIFAX has collected many conclusive arguments on these and kindred
topics.[4] The words of JOSEPHUS are explicit enough as to
the received opinion in his day, "you will find the Book of
DANIEL in our Sacred Writings."[5] MAIMONIDES, indeed, has
attempted to detract from its high reputation, but has been

[1] Kenrick's Ancient Egypt under the Pharaohs, vol. i. p. 44.
[2] Major Rawlinson's " Commentary," &c. p. 47.
[3] Vindication of the Def., chap. i. § 3.
[4] Warburtonian Lectures. Sermon II.   [5] Antiq., Book x. ch. x. 4.

sufficiently refuted by ABARBANEL and the son of JARCHI.[1]
The arrangement of the Jews, which places this Book among
the Hagiographa, and not among the Prophets, seems also
to be intended to depreciate its Canonical value ; but while
the earlier Talmudists place it with the Psalms and the
Proverbs, the later ones range it with Zechariah and Haggai.[2]
When Aquila and Theodotion translated their Versions, he
was admitted to the Prophetic rank : and although we cannot absolutely determine the point from the MS. of the Septuagint in the Chigian Library at Rome, yet the probability
is highly in its favour. ORIGEN places DANIEL among the
Prophets and before EZEKIEL, following the example of JOSE-
PHUS in his first book against Apion.

JEWISH TESTIMONIES.—SINAITIC INSCRIPTIONS.

Instead of following the beaten track of reference to JEWISH
COMMENTS and RABBINICAL TRADITIONS, which CALVIN always
quoted and refuted, we shall here introduce a collateral
branch of singular and valuable evidence. As the surface
of the Theological world is much agitated by doubts of historic facts, originating alike with Rationalists and Romanists,
it is desirable to fortify our evidence from existing inscriptions of correlative value with those of Nineveh. That far-
famed seceder to Rome, Dr. Newman, speaks of some "Scripture Narratives which are quite as difficult to the reason as
any miracles recorded in the History of the Saints ;" and he
then instances that " of the Israelites' flight from Egypt, and
entrance into the Promised Land."[3] Anxious as the votary
of either Superstition or of Reason may be to suggest doubts
as to the recorded facts, THE ROCKS OF SINAI are now vocal
with the voices of the moving Tribes ! Valley after valley
has been found in which these SINAITIC INSCRIPTIONS abound.
" Their numbers may be computed by thousands, their extent by miles, and their positions above the valleys being as

[1] Mor. Nevoch. p. ii. ch. 45.
[2] See the Bava-bathra and the Megilla c. ii. Prideaux Connex., p. 1, 65,
§ 2. Kennicott's Dis. Gen., p. 14, and Disser. Prelim. to Wintle's Translation, p x. &c.
[3] See his " Discourses addressed to Mixed Congregations." Edit. 2d.

often measurable by fathoms as by feet."[1] These hitherto
unreadable remnants of a former age have now been read,
and they become fresh confirmations of the truthfulness of
the Mosaic Narrative. It is enough for our present purpose
to refer to the conclusive labours of the Rev. CHARLES FORSTER,
who has compared the characters used with those of THE
ROSETTA STONE, with the Arrow-headed Character, and with
the Alphabets of Etruria, Palmyra, and Persepolis ; and has
been enabled to read what neither BEER could decipher nor
POCOCKE explain.[2] By him they are shewn to record the
bitterness of the Waters at Marah—the Flight of Pharaoh
on horseback—the Miracle of the feathered fowls, the Murmuring at Meribah—and the Uplifting of the hands of Moses
at the battle of Rephidim. Thus the "Written Valley," and
the "Written Mountain," have rendered their testimony in
favour of Revelation. "No difficulties of situation, no rug-
gedness of material, no remoteness of locality, has been any
security against the gravers of the one phalanx of mysterious
scribes. The granite rocks of the almost inaccessible Mount
Serbal, from its base to its summit, repeat the characters and
inscriptions of the Sandstones of the Mokateh." Countless
multitudes are supposed to be yet undiscovered. And what
people but the Israelites could have engraven them? Professor BEER allows them to be all of the same age—the soil
affords no sustenance for hordes of men, and never did provide for the existence of a settled population. This wilderness may be periodically travelled through, but never has
been permanently settled by mankind. The very execution
of such works requires the use of ladders and platforms,
ropes, baskets, and tools, and all the usual instruments of a
long established population. But no people could have executed all this unproductive labour without a ready supply of
water and food. If, then, a single generation carved and
graved these countless Inscriptions, how can we account for
the fact, except by the Mosaic narrative? Whence came

[1] Forster's "*One Primæval Language*," p. 33, where Lord Lindsay's
letters are quoted.
[2] Details are given at length in the interesting work quoted above. Professor Beer in his "Century of Sinaitic Inscriptions" utterly failed to unravel them. *Leipsic*, 1840.

the bodily aliments, by which so many workmen were enabled to carry out their hazardous employments for so long and continuous a period? Grant that ISRAEL coming out of Egypt performed them, and the difficulty is solved—adopt any other possibility, and the problem becomes perfectly insoluble! We forbear to enter further into this important discussion; it is enough to have awakened this train of thought, in accordance with our previous reasonings.[1]

THE CONTENTS OF THE BOOK OF DANIEL.

The CONTENTS of this Book admits of an easy and natural division. The first part has been called "The Historical," and the second "The Prophetical" portions. Each contains six chapters, and the Comments on each, with the Editor's Dissertations, will respectively occupy a Volume. THE HISTORICAL PORTION contains Predictions; but they were not uttered by DANIEL himself, and seem to spring naturally out of the events of the times. It is not without its difficulties. The learned have differed respecting the existence of a second NEBUCHADNEZZAR, the person and character of CYRUS, and the reign of DARIUS the Mede. Strenuous efforts have been made to shew that one NEBUCHADNEZZAR plundered the Temple, and another was afflicted by madness: that the Koresh of the last verse of the sixth chapter is not CYRUS THE GREAT, but an obscure Satrap of an earlier age. A noble Duke, whose scriptural researches confer higher honour on his name than the coronet he wears, has proposed an elaborate theory for the better explanation of "The Times of DANIEL,"[2] and the hypothesis has met with an equally learned reply by the author of "The Two later Visions of DANIEL."[3] A detail of the arguments on both sides will be found in the DISSERTATIONS previously referred to. The discrepancies between HERODOTUS and XENOPHON, which Archbishop SECKER tried in vain to reconcile, must be again discussed; the criti-

---

[1] Before Professor Beer's attempt to explain them, Montfauçon had drawn the attention of the literary world to their value. See his *Coll. Nov. Patr.*, t. ii. p. 206, where the narrative of Cosmas, the Indian traveller, is found in the original Greek.

[2] The Duke of Manchester.   [3] The Rev. T. R. Birks.

cal value of PTOLEMY'S Astronomical Canon ascertained, and many subordinate and collateral events examined.   CALVIN makes no pretensions to minute Historical Criticism: he adopts the received opinions of his day, and if he sometimes errs, he does so in ignorance of other sources of knowledge which have since been opened to the world.   But his diligence and his judgment have preserved him from errors of any ultimate importance; and it must be always remembered that the Antiquarian Researches of later times have thrown a flood of light upon these distant Eras.   Baseless conjecture has, indeed, done much to pervert and mystify the plainest truths; but the materials themselves are of a most varied and intricate character; and the satisfactory adjustment of these historical difficulties requires the highest powers of discrimination, as well as the most comprehensive grasp of all the conflicting evidence by which a doubtful event is embarrassed.

THE SEVENTY WEEKS.

In attempting to appreciate CALVIN'S COMMENTS on the Historical Portion of this Book, and of the celebrated period of "THE SEVENTY WEEKS," it will be necessary to advert to some abstruse points of Chronology.   We would willingly avoid any tedious discussion of dates and figures, but the interest of many important questions now frequently turns upon such arithmetical proofs.   A strong assertion of the Chevalier BUNSEN must justify us in the course which we are about to pursue.   " All the results," says he, " of Jewish or Christian Research are based upon the Writings of the Old Testament and their Interpretation, and upon the connection between the Chronological data they supply and divine Revelation.   There are points, therefore, relative to which it is of vital importance, both to the sound thinker and the sound critic, to arrive at a clear understanding before embarking upon his inquiry. . . . The question is, Whether the external History related in the Sacred Books be externally complete, and capable of chronological arrangement?"[1]

[1] Bunsen's Egypt's Place in Universal History, vol. i. p. 162.

The reply should be given "with a deep feeling of the respect due to the general chronological statements of Scripture, which have been considered during so many centuries as forming the groundwork of religious faith, and are even at the present moment intimately connected with the Christian Faith." Let but these principles of the learned Egyptologist guide us in our decisions, and we may hope for the blessing of Heaven in disentangling many of the Historical intricacies which will soon come under our notice.

THE PRÆTERIST, ANTI-PAPAL, AND FUTURIST VIEWS.

In attempting to determine the intrinsic value of these LECTURES, it becomes necessary to compare CALVIN'S Prophetic Interpretations with those of the Divines who preceded and have followed him. The scheme proposed for interpreting these VISIONS may be classed generally under this threefold division, viz., the PRÆTERIST, the ANTI-PAPAL, and the FUTURIST VIEWS. The first view is that usually adopted, with some slight modifications, by the Primitive Church and the Earlier Reformers. The second, sometimes called the "Protestant" System, supposes the Papal power to be prominently foretold by both DANIEL and ST. JOHN; while the Third System defers the accomplishment of many of these Prophecies to times yet future. If these three Systems be borne distinctly in mind, it will become easy to understand how the most popular modern explanations differ from those of the earlier period of the Reformation. The Primitive Church has, with few exceptions, agreed in considering The Head of Gold to mean, either the Babylonian Empire or the person of Nebuchadnezzar; the Silver denoting the Medo-Persian; the Brass the Greek; and the Iron the Roman; while the mixture of the Clay denotes the intermingling of Conquered Nations with the power of Heathen Rome. In interpreting the Four Beasts, the Lion denotes the Babylonian Empire; the Eagle Wings relate to Nebuchadnezzar's ambition; the Bear to the Medo-Persians; the Leopard to the Macedonians; and the Fourth Beast to the Romans. The Ten Horns were differently explained ; some referring them to Ten individual Kings, and others to Ten Divisions of the Empire ; some supposing them to commence with the Roman sway in the East, others not till the Fourth or Fifth Centuries after Christ.

CALVIN differs slightly from the earlier, and most materially from the later Commentators. Supposing the Fourth Beast to typify the Roman Empire, " The Ten Kings," he says, " were not persons succeeding each other in dominion, but rather the complex Form of the Government instead of a unity under one head." The number " ten " is, he thinks, indefinite, for " many," and the Sway of a Senate instead of a Monarchy is the true fulfilment of the Prophecy. The rise of one King and his oppressing three, refers to the two Cæsars, JULIUS and OCTAVIUS, with LEPIDUS and ANTONY. How unconscious was CALVIN that succeeding Protestant Writers would determine The " Little Horn " to be the POPE, and the Three Kings, the Exarchate of Ravenna, the Kingdom of Lombardy, and the State of Rome. Here the multitude of modern commentators differ most materially from the author of these LECTURES. The " Time, Times, and Half a Time " of this chapter, CALVIN refers to the persecution of the Christian Church under NERO, and similar tyrannical Emperors of Rome, and gives not the slightest countenance to any allusion in these words to a specified number of years. " Time and Times " are with him a long undefined period ; and " Half a Time " is added in the spirit of the promise to shorten the time for the Elects' sake. Those modern Writers, who think the Year-Day theory essential to the full exposition of the Visions of DANIEL, will be disappointed by the opinion of our Reformer. He takes no notice of either the 1260 years of the Papacy, or the 1290 years for the reign of Antichrist. Again, there are Writers who deny the Fourth Beast to refer to ROME at all. ROSENMULLER and TODD are instances ; and each of these has his own way of interpreting the concluding portion of this chapter. The former asserts it to be fulfilled in the Greek Empire in Asia after ALEXANDER's death, and the latter supposes it to be yet future. According to Dr. TODD and the Futurists, it has yet to be developed. Its fulfilment shall be the precursor of

THE FINAL ANTICHRIST, whom the Lord shall destroy with
the brightness of his PERSONAL ADVENT.   This Antichrist
shall tyrannize in the world for the "Time, Times, and
Half a Time," that is, for the definite space of three years
and a half, till the Ancient of Days shall proclaim THE FINAL
CLOSE OF THE GENTILE DISPENSATION.

The three views, then, of the Interpretation of these Prophecies are thus clearly distinguished.   The *Prœterist* view
treats them as fulfilled in past historical events, taking place
under the several Empires of Babylon, Persia, Greece, and
Heathen Rome.   The modern *Anti-Papal* view treats "The
Little Horn" as the Pope, and the days as years ; and this
stretches the predictions over the Twelve Centuries of Euro-
pean struggle between the Ecclesiastical and the Civil
Powers.   The *Futurist* is dissatisfied with the Year-Day
theory : he cannot agree with the past fulfilment of these
glowing images of future blessedness.   Hence, instead of
either ANTIOCHUS, MAHOMET, NERO, or THE POPE, he sees a
future Antichrist in the Eleventh Horn of the seventh
chapter, in The Little Horn of the eighth chapter, and in
The Wilful King of the eleventh chapter.   He rejects entirely the Year-Day explanation, and every assertion which
is based upon it ; he takes the days literally as days, and
supposes them yet unfulfilled.   The "Toes" of the image,
and the "Horns" of the beasts, are not to him Kingdoms or
Successions of Rulers of any kind, but single individual persons.   The phrase, THE POPE, as equivalent to a "Horn,"
is to him a fallacy : as it does not mean one person, like an
ALEXANDER or a SELEUCUS, or a single despotic Antichrist—
but a long succession of Rulers, one after another.[1]   FABER,
for example, interprets "the Scriptures of Truth," chap. xi.,
by extending it throughout all history, till the end of the
Gentile Dispensation.   Dr. TODD refers it solely to its close,
and contends very strongly against the usual explanation of
the Fourth verse.   ELLIOTT, again, (Horæ Apoc., vol. iii.,) ex-
pounds this chapter to the 35th verse with great propriety

---

[1] A list of the chief "Futurist" writers and of their sentiments will be
found in Birks' "First Elements of Sacred Prophecy," where the Year-
Day theory is ably advocated, and much useful information condensed.

and clearness, but passes at once from the Ptolemidæ and Seleucidæ to the Pope, as signified by " The Wilful King." The Days then become Years, and the various phases of the Papacy through many centuries are supposed to be predicted here, and fulfilled by the decrees of JUSTINIAN, persecutions of the Waldenses, French Revolutions, and catastrophes and convulsions yet to come. Our American brethren have adopted similar theories. Professor BUSH in his " Hierophant," has inserted an able exposition of the " Little Horn," as unquestionably the Ecclesiastical Power of the " Papacy,"[1] and introduced the GOTHS and CHARLEMAGNE as fulfilling their own portions of this interesting Vision. Professor STUART, however, of Andover, and some of his followers, have returned to the simplicity of the Earlier Expositors.[2]

CALVIN'S PROPHETIC SCHEME.

CALVIN, then, was on the whole, a Præterist. He saw in the history of the world before the times of the Messiah the fulfilment of the Visions of this Book. They extended from NEBUCHADNEZZAR to NERO. " The Saints of the Most High " were to him either the Hebrew or the Christian Church under heathen persecutors. He had a glimpse indeed of the times of the Messiah, and expressed his views in general language ; but he rejected the idea of any series of fulfilments through a succession of either Popes or Sultans. He saw in these four-footed beings, neither MAHOMET, nor JUSTINIAN, nor the Ottoman Empire, nor the Albigensian Martyrs. Heathen Rome, and its Senate, and its early Cæsars, were to him what Papal Rome, and its Priesthood, and its Gregories, have been to later Expositors.

Our SECOND VOLUME, which contains THE PROPHETICAL PORTION of the Book, will be illustrated by many *Dissertations*, which will condense the sentiments of later Expositors. Ample scope will then be given to important details. Extracts will be made from the most approved Moderns, and

[1] P. 109.   New York, 1844.
[2] Hints on the Interpretation of Prophecy, 1842 ; and Folsom's Daniel. Boston, 1842.

copious references to the best sources of information. It
will be sufficient here to insert the reply of Professor BUSH
of New York to Professor STUART of Andover, as illustrating
the importance of the difference between those who adopt
the Year-Day theory and those who do not : " Denying *in
toto*, as I do, and disproving, as I think I have done, the
truth of your theory in regard to the literal import of *Day*,
I can of course see no evidence, and therefore feel no interest in your reasonings respecting the events which you consider as the fulfilment of those splendid Visions. If a *Day*
stands for a *Year*, and a *Beast* represents an *Empire*, then
we are imperatively remanded to a far different order of
occurrences in which to read the realization of the mystic
scenery from that which you have indicated. As the Spirit
of Prophecy has under his illimitable ken the most distant
future as well as the nearest present, I know nothing, in
reason or exegesis, that should prevent the affairs of the
Christian economy being represented by DANIEL as well as
by JOHN. As the Fourth Beast of DANIEL lives and acts
through the space of 1260 years, and as the Seven-headed
and Ten-horned Beast of JOHN prevails through the same
period, and puts forth substantially the same demonstrations,
I am driven to the conclusion that they adumbrate precisely
the same thing—that they are merely different aspects of
the same reality—and this, I have no question, is the *Roman
Empire*. This you deny ; but I submit that the denial can
be sustained only by shewing an adequate reason why the
Spirit of God should be debarred from giving such extension
to the Visions of the Old Testament Prophets. Until this
demand is satisfied, no progress can be made towards convincing the general mind of Christendom of the soundness
of your Expositions. The students of Revelation will still
reiterate the query, Why the oracles of DANIEL should be so
exclusively occupied with the historical fates of ANTIOCHUS
EPIPHANES ? . . . If I do not err in the auguries of the
times, a struggle is yet to ensue on the prophetic field between two conflicting parties, on whose banners shall be
respectively inscribed, *Antiochus and Antichrist.*"[1]

[1] Hierophant, May 1843, p. 273. New York.

OECOLAMPADIUS, ZUINGLE, AND BULLINGER.

This is precisely the point that these LECTURES will assist in determining, and the following sketches of the opinions of the immediate predecessors and successors of our Reformer, will be useful in guiding the judgment of the reader.

One of the most learned of the Commentators among the Early Reformers was OECOLAMPADIUS, the well-known companion of ZUINGLE. BULLINGER published his notes on the Prophets about fifty years before BEZA edited CALVIN's Lectures. His character for piety and profound erudition stood high among his contemporaries, and his elaborate expositions of the Prophets form a tangible proof of his industry, ingenuity, and Christian proficiency. Some account of the method in which he treats these interesting questions will here be appropriate. He divides the Book into the two natural divisions—the Historical and the Prophetical. His remarks on the former portion contain nothing which demands our notice at present; but his second division contains some valuable comments. He takes the Four Beasts of chapter vii. for the Babylonian, Persian, Grecian, and Roman Empires, dwells on the cruelties of SYLLA and MARIUS, TIBERIUS and NERO; and accuses ABEN-EZRA and the Jews of denying this Fourth Beast to mean Heathen Rome, lest they should be compelled to embrace JESUS as their Messiah. He is not satisfied with JEROME's opinion, that the Ten Horns mean Ten Kings, who should divide among them the territories of the Roman power. He takes the numbers " ten" and " seven" for complete and perfect numbers, quoting from the parable, " The kingdom of heaven is like *ten* virgins." He quotes and approves of HIPPOLYTUS, who asserts " the Little Horn" to mean the Antichrist, to whom St. PAUL alludes in the Second Epistle to the Thessalonians. APOLLINARIUS and other Ecclesiastical Writers judge rightly in adopting this interpretation, while POLYCHRONIUS is deceived by PORPHYRY in referring it to ANTIOCHUS. But who is this Antichrist? Is he supposed to rule after the destruction of Heathen or of Papal Rome? OECOLAMPADIUS furnishes us

with many opinions—some supposing MAHOMET, others TRA-
JAN, and others the PAPAL SEE. He quotes the correspond-
ing passage in the APOCALYPSE, and implies that the successors of MAHOMET and the occupiers of the Chair of ST. PETER
are equally intended. By thus introducing the modern history of Europe and of Asia, he leans rather to the second
of those divisions into which Commentators on DANIEL have
been divided. On this testing question of "the Time, Times,
and Half a Time," he assumes it to mean three years and a
half : he has no limit of any extension of the time through
1260 years ; adding, "there is no reason why we should be
religiously bound to that number, or follow puerile and uncertain triflings." He will not allow Antichrist to be only
a single person, and thus throws an air of indefiniteness over
the whole subject.

Consistently with these principles, he interprets " The
Wilful King" of chapter xi. by both MAHOMET and the PA-
PACY ; and explains how this twofold power should be destroyed in the Holy Land. The repetition in the numbers
in chapter xii. is treated very concisely. Literal days are
said to be intended, and the possibility of ascertaining certainty is doubted. " If any one has detected any certainty
in these obscure dates, I do not envy him : the exposition
already offered satisfies me ; for it is not in our power to
know the precise divisions of the time (*articulos temporum*)."
Throughout the whole Comment of ŒCOLAMPADIUS, there is a
tone of piety, and a proficiency in correct interpretation
which we seek for in vain in some disciples of the Early
Reformers. He was evidently a spiritually-minded man, and
was always preaching Christ in his Comments on the Old
Testament. In this respect he equals, and if possible surpasses the more elaborate CALVIN. The extreme spirituality
of this eminent Reformer entitles him, in these days, to
more notice than he receives. His constant efforts to
honour Christ as his Redeemer, and the practical and persevering manner in which he preaches the gospel of his
Redeemer, in his *Old* Testament Exposition, should render his
writings familiar to every sincere and simple-minded Christian. And we are not surprised when we hear competent

judges of the difference between CALVIN and himself prefer
the tone of his remarks to that of his more vigorous ally.

GROTIUS.

The Commentary of GROTIUS is also worthy of comparison
with that of CALVIN. He is very precise and minute in
shewing how the history of the East has borne out the
truthfulness of the predictions ; and is, perhaps, more accurate in details than his predecessor : he differs, indeed, in a
few points of importance, which will be separately noticed,
but, on the whole, his remarks are correct and judicious.
The Ten Kings of the seventh chapter he considers to be Syrian Monarchs, and enumerates them as Seleuci, Antiochi,
and Ptolemæi. POLANUS and JUNIUS, two Commentators
who are constantly quoted by POOLE in his Synopsis, treat
the passage in a similar way. The king to arise after
them is still confined to the Jewish era, and " the Time,
Times," &c., are supposed to be literally three years and a
half. The 36th verse of chapter xi. GROTIUS interprets of
ANTIOCHUS EPIPHANES, and is supported by JUNIUS, POLA-
NUS, MALDONATUS, WILLET, and BROUGHTON. The "Days" of
the twelfth chapter are taken literally by all the Commentators quoted by POOLE from CALVIN to MEDE, and all suppose the period intended to be during the reign of the successors of ALEXANDER. MEDE was the well-known reviver
of the Year-Day theory. Before his time it was a vague
assertion : he first gave it shape, and form, and plausible
consistency, and since his day it has been adopted by many
intelligent Critics, among whom are Sir ISAAC NEWTON,
BISHOP NEWTON, FABER, FRERE, KEITH, and BIRKS.

MALDONATUS.

The Commentary of MALDONATUS, the Jesuit, demands
more extended notice, as he lived about the times of our
author, and calls him *Patriarcha Hereticorum*, and looks
upon the subject from exactly the opposite point of view.
His exposition of JEREMIAH, BARUCH, EZEKIEL, and DANIEL,

was published at Moguntiæ, (Mentz,) 1611. In his *prooe-mium* he sketches the life of DANIEL, and defends his Book against PORPHYRY, the Manichæans, and the Anabaptists. He quotes the mention made of DANIEL by EZEKIEL, and lays it down as a rule, that our ignorance of the author of a book does not impeach its Canonical Authority ; and in the spirit of his Religious Society, lays special stress upon the judgment and decision of "the Church." He next argues in favour of the Apocryphal Books attributed to this Prophet, and then prefers the authority of his Church to the testimony of JEROME. He defends the canonicity of the stories of Susannah and the Idol Bel, and comments on them in two additional chapters, and places "The Song of the Three Children" between the 23d and 24th verses of chapter iii., translating from Theodotion's version. There is nothing worthy of special notice in his remarks on the first six chapters; but the next six treat of the reigns of Christ and of Antichrist. In accordance with this view, he decides upon the Fourth Beast of the seventh chapter as the Roman Empire, after rejecting the opinion of ABEN-EZRA in favour of the Turks, and that of PORPHYRY, who thought it to be the successors of ALEXANDER. Respecting the "Little Horn," his wrath is stirred up, for "the heretical Lutherans and Calvinists, and other monstrous sects," had dared to pronounce it to be the Roman Pontiff. "But this interpretation even their master, CALVIN, has shewn to be absurd."[1] He combats the notion that by one term all the Roman Pontiffs are intended ; and then triumphantly asks, Where are the "Three" whom this single one was to pluck up ? He further inquires, Whether all were past in his own day, or all future ? He determines that it is all yet to be fulfilled, and thus becomes an adherent to the cause of the Futurists. As neither the Ten Horns nor the Eleventh have yet come into existence, it is natural to conclude the Eleventh to be that Antichrist whom JEROME represents not as a Demon, but a man in whom "a whole Satan shall corporally dwell." He shall reign, he thinks, three years and a half—a distinct and fixed period —objecting to what he calls "figura Calvini," viz., that an

---

[1] Comment., p. 673, chap. vii. 8.

uncertain period is intended by so clear an expression. The
various opinions of his predecessors on the 36th verse of
chapter xi. move rather his derision than his wrath. Their
notions about CONSTANTINE, and MAHOMET, and the ROMAN
PONTIFFS, do not need his serious refutation. Almost all
Catholics, he adds, both ancient and modern, refer it to the
Antichrist. He also accuses the greater part of " the New
Heretics" of stating the Michael of the 12th chapter to be
Messiah himself; and treats the " days" of the close of this
chapter as partly fulfilled under the Jewish and partly
under the Christian dispensations. His inconsistency in
this interpretation is more apparent than in the preceding
ones; while his work on the whole is worthy of perusal, as
he quotes with judgment the opinions of learned Jews and
of the earlier Commentators of the Christian Church.

Within the first century after the Reformation, the views
of Divines respecting these Prophecies were far more
in accordance with the ancient Greek and Latin Fathers
than those prevalent in the present day. The student who
would know how MELANCTHON, OSIANDER, and BULLINGER
treated the subject in reply to BELLARMINE, FERERIUS, and
other Romish Divines, may profitably consult WILLET'S Hexapla in Danielem, published at Cambridge in 1610, and
dedicated to King James I. The arguments of the ancients
in reply to " wicked PORPHIRIE" are collected and reviewed,
the opinions of various Jewish writers are stated and confuted, and no valuable remark of any preceding Commentator is overlooked. For instance, the Fourth Beast of the
seventh chapter is explained according to the Jews, as the
Turkish, and to JEROME, of the Roman empire: but he decides it to be the kingdom of Syria, under the sway of
Seleucus and his posterity. The " Little Horne" is said to be
ANTIOCHUS; and CALVIN'S view, connecting it with AUGUS-
TUS and the following Emperors, is thus treated :—" But
though these things may, by way of analogie, be thus applied,
yet, historically, as hath been shewed at large, this prophecy
was fulfilled before the coming of the Messiah into the world."
BULLINGER refers it to the Pope, and others to the Turks;
and " These applications, by way of analogie, we mislike

not." The "Times" are supposed, by the majority of these
writers quoted, to be single years, and the whole period
three years and a half. His laborious industry respecting
the "Seventy Weeks" is most instructive; and he deserves
the greatest possible credit for the patience with which he
has examined all authorities, and the acuteness with which
he has discussed the most opposite opinions. He is careful
in remarking the various readings of the text, and the different renderings of all preceding versions. The eleventh
chapter he treats as all fulfilled in the history of Syria and
Palestine before the birth of Christ. He discusses with
much ability the question, whether Antichrist is a single
person, or a succession of Rulers, as Caliphs or Popes,
and presents us with the decisions of the leading Fathers,
Romanists, and Reformers on the "notes and markes wherein Antiochus and Antichrist agree." All who would see
BELLARMINE fully confuted, and the enormities of this chapter brought home to the several occupants of the See of
Rome, will peruse WILLET with eagerness and profit. He
will also find CALVIN's Interpretations clearly stated and
fairly compared with those of the most celebrated Reformers
and their most acute antagonists. The days of the twelfth
chapter are taken literally, and no hint is given of any elaborate theory of a dozen centuries, extending through the
modern history of Europe. To all who love to trace the
progress of opinion, respecting the intercourse between men
and angels, "the Auncient of Daies," the Opening of the
Books, Michael the Prince, and the application of these Prophecies to the Turks, the Papacy, and the times of a yet
future Antichrist, will find in the "Hexapla" a storehouse of
valuable material, where he may exercise, with all freedom,
the liberty of choice. It proposes and answers 593 questions, and discusses 134 controversies, the greater part of
the latter division being directed against the doctrines and
practices of the Church of Rome.

JOSEPH MEDE.

A formidable opposition to the principles propounded in
these LECTURES is found in the writings of JOSEPH MEDE.

That learned and ingenious author is usually held as the ablest and earliest expositor of the Year-Day theory. It is neither necessary nor possible for us here either to confirm or confute all his hypotheses ; we can only refer to his " *Revelatio Antichristi, sive de Numeris Danielis,* MCCXC. MCCCXXXV." (Works, p. 717.) The first part is occupied by refuting BROUGHTON and JUNIUS, who assert those mystic days to have been literally fulfilled during the Wars of AN-TIOCHUS. The prediction, he thinks, fulfilled in the twelfth century of our era, when the persecutions of the Papal See, against the Heretics of those days, are said to verify the words of the Prophet. Dr. TODD has thought this treatise worthy of a detailed refutation, and to all who are interested in determining whether Antichrist is a Succession of Rulers or a single person, his learned remarks are worthy of attentive perusal. In pursuance of his own ideas respecting a personal future Antichrist, he is led to dispute the division of ALEXANDER's empire into four parts, and to quote at full length various authorities, especially VENEMA, who endeavoured to shew the number of divisions to be ten, and that the portion of chap. viii. usually interpreted of the Roman was really fulfilled by the Grecian Empire in the East.[1]

CALVIN then, we find, agrees entirely with VENEMA, and by anticipation confutes the arguments of Dr. TODD. He thinks it surprising, that men versed in Scripture can thus substitute darkness for light. He is supported by MELANC-THON and MICHAELIS, HENGSTENBERG and ROSENMULLER, as well as by THEODORET and most of the Greek Expositors. He treats those more leniently who modestly and considerately suppose the times of ANTIOCHUS to be figurative of those of Antichrist. At this "figura Calvini" MALDONATUS sneers; and yet if we determine that CALVIN's solution is right, it is the very principle by which the perusal of Holy Scripture becomes profitable to us. " I desire," says he, " to treat the Sacred Oracles reverently ; but I require something certain." " If any one wishes to adapt this passage to present use, he

[1] See Herm. Venem. Dis. ad Vat. Dan. Emblem., Dis. v. § 3-12, pp. 347-364, 4to. Leovard, 1745, as quoted at length in Todd's Discourses on Antichrist, pp. 504-515.

may refer it to Antichrist," on the principle, "that whatever happened to the Ancient Church, occurred for our instruction." Hence he allows of a double sense, and raises a question which has been ably contended for and against by many subsequent Divines. It is too important to be passed over, and will demand our notice in our Second Volume.

The followers of MEDE have met with a formidable antagonist, and the adherents of CALVIN a staunch supporter in the late Regius Professor of Hebrew in the University of Cambridge. Dr. LEE, in his pamphlet on the Visions of DANIEL and St. JOHN,[1] has stated his reasons for adhering to the Older Interpreters, thus adopting the principle of the Præterists, and entirely discarding the slightest reference to the Pope and the Papacy. His conclusions may be exhibited in a few words. Respecting Nebuchadnezzar's Image, "the feet must of necessity symbolize *Heathen* Rome in its last times."[2] "Papal Rome cannot, therefore, possibly be any prolongation of DANIEL's Fourth Empire." "These Kings," represented by the *Toes*, "may, therefore, be supposed in a mystical sense to be, as the digits ten, a round number, and signifying a whole series."[3] "The Little Horn" is said to be Heathen Rome—its persecuting Emperors from NERO to CONSTANTINE fulfilling the Prophetic conditions. The phrase "a Time, Times, and a Half," is said to refer to the "latter half (mystically speaking) of the Seventieth Week of our Prophet."[4] "DANIEL's Week of seven days—equivalent here to EZEKIEL's period of seven years—is, we find, divided into two parts mystically considered halves, or of three days and a half."[5] . . . "That the Roman Power took away the Daily Sacrifice, and cast down the place of its Sanctuary, it is impossible to doubt. TITUS, during the reign of his father VESPASIAN, desolated Jerusalem by destroying both the City and the Sanctuary." Thus in his general principles of Exposition, this celebrated Hebraist pronounces his verdict in favour of CALVIN and his interpretation.

No notice is taken in these LECTURES of the Deutero-

[1] Seeleys, London, 1851. [2] Sect. i. p. 1. [3] Ibid., p. 2.
[4] P. 16. [5] Introd., p. xliii.

Canonical additions to this Prophet. In the versions of the SEPTUAGINT, and that of THEODOTION, there are some additions to this Book which are not found in the Hebrew Canon. JEROME translated these from the version of THEODOTION, and ably replies to the objection of PORPHYRY, by denying the canonicity of the following treatises, viz., The Prayer of Azarias, the Song of The Three Children, the History of Susanna, and The Story of Bel and the Dragon. EUSEBIUS also denies the identity between the Prophet and the Son of Abdias, the priest who ate of the table of the King of Babylon. DE WETTE, in his *Lehrbuch*, has discussed the criticism of these treatises with great ability. As early as the second century, the Septuagint Version of Daniel was superseded by that of Theodotion ; and the former was lost till it was discovered and published at Rome in 1772. The views of DE WETTE, and of " ALBER OF PESTH, who contends against JAHN for the historic truth of these variations," will be found in the Addenda to DANIEL in Kitto's Cyclopædia. The Commentators of the Romish Church feel bound in honour to defend these additional portions. Their best arguments will be found in a praiseworthy attempt of J. G. KERKHERDERE, Historian to his Catholic Majesty Charles III., to explain some difficulties in this Prophet.[1] He considers the number of DANIEL's Treatises to be a dozen. He places the history of his own Youth first, that of Susanna second, the Story of Bel and the Dragon third, and Nebuchadnezzar's Dream fourth ; and then with great precision and clearness, enters upon those historical questions which need both acuteness and research in their treatment.[2] BELLARMINE also dwells on the testimony of the Greek Fathers, but meets with an able opponent in WILLET, the laborious author of the *Hexapla in Danielem.*[3]

It must not be forgotten that portions of this Book, like that of EZRA, are written in Chaldee. From the fourth verse of chap. ii. to the end of chap. vii., the language is Chaldee.

---

[1] See his " Prodromus Danielicus," p. 19. Lovanii, 1711.
[2] See the Appendix where the opinions of various writers are collected— especially pp. 331-336.
[3] See the Sixfold Commentarie, p. 10. Edit. 1610.

ROSENMULLER assigns as a reason for this, the desire of the author to represent NEBUCHADNEZZAR and the Magi as speaking in the language of their country. However valid this reason may be for the earlier chapters, it is not equally so for the sixth and seventh, since the Medes and Persians probably used the Persian tongue. ABARBENEL, in the preface to his *Commentarium*, supposes that Chaldee was no longer in use after the taking of the city ; and that DANIEL, through ignorance of Persian, returned to the use of Hebrew. C. B. MICHAELIS, however, demurs to this, and suggests that the use of either tongue was arbitrary, just as modern scholars use either Latin or their own vernacular tongue according to their convenience and taste. The occurrence of this older form of the Aramaic idiom has been seized upon by the opponents of the authenticity of this Book, while its use has been ably explained and vindicated by HENGSTENBERG.[1]

THE RELIGIOUS, SOCIAL, AND POLITICAL VALUE OF CALVIN'S METHOD OF EXPOSITION.

In concluding our INTRODUCTORY REMARKS it will be useful to offer a few suggestions on the Religious, Social, and Political value of CALVIN'S METHOD of EXPOSITION throughout these LECTURES. Such suggestions are the more appropriate in these days when views directly adverse to our Reformer's are extensively popular through the ingenious theories of FABER, ELLIOTT, and CUMMING. Those who have imbibed their views will pronounce these Volumes profitless and barren. " What can it benefit us," they will ask, " in the present day, to know how many Kings reigned from CYRUS to XERXES ; the changes in the Empire of ALEXANDER ; the troops which fought at Raphia ; the marriage of BERENICE, and the results of the invasion of Greece by ANTIOCHUS ?"[2] . . . " Why not suffer these antiquated facts

---

[1] *Authentie des Daniel*, p. 310—on the other side, see *Theologische Studien*, 1830, p. 290, *et seq.* ; as quoted in Kitto's Biblic. Cyc., Art. Chald. Lang.

[2] Birks, *ibid.* chap. xxi. Though the views of this writer, expressed from chap. xii. to xx. are diametrically opposed to those of Calvin, yet the remarks of chap. xxi. are so *excellent*, that we shall avail ourselves of a few appropriate sentences.

of history to sleep quietly in the dust, and bend our strength to the controversies and practical movements of the present hour ?" May we not reply, that he is best able to understand and unfold the religious phases of the age in which he lives, who is most familiar with the events and opinions of all preceding times. No man can permanently impress his own age with the precepts of spiritual wisdom, who knows nothing but what his own eyes have seen, and his own hands have handled. The ever varied messages of the Holy Spirit have always combined historical reality with the deepest spiritual significance. The details of Profane History and its comparison with the Sacred Text will never, by itself, enable us to reap the full harvest of solid improvement from the perusal of these Sacred Oracles. We must dive deeper than the surface. We must look at them in the light of one majestic and solemn truth. They are all " the foreseen counsels and works of the living God ; the vast scheme of Providence which he has ordained for his own glory, and steps in the fulfilment of his everlasting counsel."

We are fully aware, that many will pronounce these Volumes deficient in spiritual life, and in Protestant zeal. But the Christian who dares not dogmatize beyond the direct teachings of the Spirit of God, will apply them indirectly to the events of the present era, on the intelligible principles of SACRED ANALOGY. They thus become a portion of that Divine Lesson which fulfilled Prophecy is ever reading to the Church of God. They display His ceaseless dominion over the wills of Sovereigns and over the destinies of Nations. When abstract truths are felt to be powerless in breaking the spell of worldliness, and in piercing within the charmed circle of social strife and political party, these embodied proofs of an ever-watchful Deity may awe men into submission to his sovereign will. The hollow maxims of earthly policy will never be superseded till men reverence the GOD OF DANIEL, and, like the heavenly Elders, cast all their crowns of intellect and renown before His throne. From the days of NEBUCHADNEZZAR and of CYRUS, we see in every change the foot-prints of a guiding Deity. " The reigns of CAMBYSES, SMERDIS, and DARIUS ; the arma-

ment of XERXES, with its countless myriads; the marches,
and counter-marches, and conflicts, the subtle plots and
shifting alliances of contending kings, long before they
occurred, were noted down in 'the Scriptures of Truth'—
the Secret Volume of the Divine counsels. All of them, before they rose into birth, were revealed by the Son of God
to his holy Prophets; and they remain till the end of time
an imperishable monument of His Providence and foreknowledge. All was foreseen by His wisdom and ordained by
his Sovereign power. The passing generations of mankind,
while they see this blue arch of Providence above them, and
around them, sure and steadfast, age after age, like Him who
has ordained it, must feel a deep and quiet reverence take
possession of their soul." The minuteness of detail in the
visions concerning ALEXANDER and PTOLEMY SOTER, and the
repulse of ANTIOCHUS, convey the same instructive lesson.
" Every royal marriage, like that of BERENICE or CLEOPATRA,
with all its secret issues of peace or war, of discord or
union; the levying of every army, the capture of every fortress, the length of every reign, the issue of every battle, the
lies of deceitful ambition, the treachery of councillors, the
complex web of policy, woven out of ten thousand human
wiles, and each of them again the product of ten thousand
various influences of good and evil, all are pourtrayed with un-
erring accuracy in ' the Scriptures of Truth.' " . . . . " The
pride of ANTIOCHUS the Great, his successful ambition and
military triumphs, his schemes of politic affinity, nay, even his
prudent regard for the house of God, cannot avert the sentence
written against him, for his fraud and violence in the Word of
Truth. In the height of seeming power, his own reproach is
turned against him, and he tumbles and falls, and is not found."

If, then, we conclude with CALVIN, that the persecution
of the Little Horn and the idolatries of the Wilful King are
past, on what principle are we to derive instruction from
their perusal? By the inductions of a Divine analogy, by
the assertion that " *all which has passed is in some sense ty-
pical of all that is to come.*" " The Saints of the Most High"
are always the special objects of Jehovah's regard; they
ever meet with an oppressor as fierce as ANTIOCHUS, and as

hateful as " the Man of Sin ;" but still, whatever their sufferings under a GUISE or an ALVA, they shall ultimately "take
the Kingdom," and possess it for ever.   Strongholds of Mahuzzim there always will be, under either the successors of
MEDICI or the descendants of MAHOMET. The evidence of
GIBBON, which has been used so freely by many modern
theorists, is equally valuable on the hypothesis, that similar
relations between the Church and the world occur over and
over again in the course of successive ages. A parallel may
often be drawn by an ingenious mind between the persecutions of Heathen and of Papal Rome, and the temptation is
always great to refer the fulfilment of Prophecy exclusively
to that system of things with which we are immediately
and personally concerned. Military ambition, subtle policy,
the arts of Statesmen, the voice of excited multitudes,
the passions of every hour, the delusions of every age—all
must pass in silent review under the eye of heaven. They
are repeated with every successive generation under an infinite variety of outward form, but with a perfect identity in
spirit and in feeling. It may be safely asserted, that every
social and political change from the times of NEBUCHADNEZZAR
to those of CONSTANTINE, have had their historic parallel from
the days of CHARLEMAGNE to those of NAPOLEON.   Hence,
Predictions which originally related to the Empires of the
East, may be naturally transferred to the transactions of
Western Christendom. At the same time, there never may
have been the slightest intention in the mind of the writer
to apply them in this double sense. We cannot venture to
discuss all the arguments either for or against the double
sense of Prophecy. CALVIN, at least, opposed it strongly, and
whenever he swerved from the literal version, he substituted
the principle of accommodation, according to the educated
taste of an experienced Expounder of Holy Writ. It will,
perhaps, be our truest wisdom to listen to the judicious advice of Bishop HORSLEY :—" Every single text of prophecy
is to be considered as a portion of an entire system, and to
be understood in that sense which may best connect it with
the whole. The sense of Prophecy, in general, is to be sought
in the events which have actually taken place. . . . To

qualify the Christian to make a judicious application of these
rules, no skill is requisite in verbal criticism—no proficiency
in the subtleties of the logician's art—no acquisition of re-
condite learning.   That degree of understanding with which
serious minds are ordinarily blessed—those general views of
the schemes of Providence, and that general acquaintance
with the Prophetic language which no Christian can be
wanting in . . . these qualifications will enable the pious,
though unlearned Christian, to succeed in the application of
the Apostle's rules." (2 Pet. i. 20, 21.)[1] While this sentiment is cheering to the humble-minded believer, another
principle laid down by the same author must never be
omitted.   The meaning of a prediction "never can be
discovered without a general knowledge of the principal
events to which it alludes."   Let CALVIN, then, be judged by
this simple test—and before we venture to condemn him,
let us be equally patient, and equally careful to gather all
the information within our reach.

CONTEMPORARY EVENTS IN FRANCE.

The period when our Reformer addressed these LECTURES
TO ALL THE PIOUS WORSHIPPERS OF GOD IN FRANCE, is now
worthy of our attention.   CALVIN writes from GENEVA at the
close of the month of August A.D. 1561, immediately preceding that Colloquy at POISSY, to which reference was made
in the preface to EZEKIEL.[2]   His Letter depicts so faithfully
the state of persecution in which the Christians of France
were placed, and compares it so efficiently with the condition
of DANIEL and the pious worshippers of God under NEBU-
CHADNEZZAR, that the more we know of the times in which
CALVIN wrote, the more complete the parallel appears.   An
animated sketch of this eventful era has lately been published by the Queen's Professor of Modern History in the
University of Cambridge; and as the views of the Editor
accord with those of the Professor "On the Reformation and
the Wars of Religion" in France, we shall abridge and condense his narrative, as the best suited to our purpose.

[1] See his four Sermons on this passage.   [2] Calvin on Ezekiel, vol. i. p. xxix.

THE GENERAL SYNOD OF PROTESTANTS AT PARIS.

When CALVIN addressed his followers in France, as desirous of the firm establishment of Christ's kingdom in their native land, he was at his College in Geneva ; but his labours and his Writings were all-powerful in influence with the Reformed in France. Their numbers were large throughout the cities and villages of the Empire. LEFEVRE and FAREL were as father and son in ceaseless efforts to make known to these Gentiles " the unsearchable riches of Christ." Their evangelical preaching was signally blessed. BRICONNET, the Bishop of Meaux, aided them in translating the Evangelists and in heralding the word of God, and so rapidly and widely had their gospel been received, that " a Heretic of Meaux" became the popular title for an opponent of the Papacy. Notwithstanding the hideous spectacle and the odious MASSACRE of the 29th of January 1535, when Francis I. celebrated the Fête of Paris by the Martyrdom of the Saints of God, the Reformers were so numerous throughout the realm, that a serious conflict was approaching between themselves and their foes. On the 25th of May 1559, a GENERAL SYNOD OF ALL PROTESTANT CONGREGATIONS was solemnly convened and held at Paris—the ecclesiastical system of their Patriarch at Geneva was adopted, and his "*Institution Chrétienne*" became the source and basis of their Confession of Faith. Paris was but the energizing centre of an organized Church throughout the Sixteen Provinces of the Realm, while Synods, and Consistories, and Conferences formed a kind of Spiritual Republic, spreading like network over the land. But the hand and the eye of the Persecutor was upon them. Rome had its despotic tyrants both in Court and Camp. In the very midst of the Parliament at Paris, a confessor of the true faith appeared—but his courage was extinguished by his condemnation. DUBOURG, a magistrate of eminent learning and illustrious family, in the presence of the King, in his place in Parliament, invoked a National Council for the Reform of Religion, and denounced the persecution of Heretics as a crime against Him whose holy name they were accustomed to adore with their dying breath.

He expiated his audacity by his death, and before the grave
had been opened for him it had closed upon the Royal Tyrant, HENRY II., who bequeathed his crown to a second
FRANCIS in his sixteenth year. And who knows not the
crafty, treacherous, and intriguing wickedness of the Queen-
mother, CATHERINE OF MEDICI ? Who knows not the ambi-
tious worldliness of the two sons of CLAUDE OF LORRAINE—
Francis, the DUKE OF GUISE—the savage butcher of the HU-
GUENOTS of Champagne, and Charles, the CARDINAL LOR-
RAINE, the subtle agent of Rome's most hateful policy ? These
artful brothers worked their way to supreme influence in the
national councils. Having married their niece, MARY QUEEN
OF SCOTS, to their youthful Sovereign, they employed their
vast influence for the wholesale martyrdom of the defenceless
flock of Christ. In every Parliament of the kingdom they
established Chambers for trying and burning all persons
charged with heresy, which obtained the unenviable notori-
ety of " chambres ardentes." " But deep," says the eloquent
Lecturer, " called unto deep." The alarmed and exasperated HUGUENOTS, confident in their strength and deriving
courage from despair, rose in many parts of France to repel,
or at least to punish their antagonists. In the midst of
the anarchy of the times, a voice was raised in calm and
earnest remonstrance, urging toleration and peace. In August 1560, the renowned Chancellor L'HÔPITAL appeared before the King and an assembly of notables at Fontainebleau.
He presents a Petition from the whole Reformed Church of
the realm, and requests the royal permission for the free
performance of public worship. " Your Petition," says the
King, "is without a signature !" " True, sire," replies Co-
LIGNY, " but if you will allow us to meet for the purpose, I
will obtain 50,000 signatures in one day in Normandy
alone !" His zeal might occasion a slight exaggeration—
but the phrase presents us with data for conjecturing the
number of " the pious " whom our Reformer addressed about
a year afterwards. As soon as opportunity was given for
listening to the glad tidings of salvation, large accessions
were made to the hosts of the believers. FAREL, though
advanced in years, preached the truth to large and enthusi-

astic assemblages. In the neighbourhood of Paris, the followers of BEZA were numerous, and his admirers reckoned them at 40,000. L'HÔPITAL presented to the Queen-mother a list of 2150 Reformed Congregations, each under the ministry of a separate pastor, and he reckoned the number of the HUGUENOTS as one-third of that of the Romanists!

EDICT OF POISSY.

At the very moment when CALVIN was penning in his study the Letter which is prefixed to these LECTURES ON DANIEL, the Edict of July 1561 was issued. It bears the impress of the restored influence of the House of LORRAINE, which ever proved an implacable foe to the Gospel of Christ as preached by THE CALVINISTS. That Edict forbad their public assemblies, and yet tolerated their private and social worship. It protected them from injury on account of their opinions, and provided for a National Council which should, if possible, settle differences which were in their nature irreconcilable. This important enactment was issued in the Assembly at Poissy, held a few weeks after the date of the Letter which follows this Preface, and which has been alluded to in the Preface to EZEKIEL. CALVIN was absent, because the French Court refused to give those securities for his safety which the Republic of Geneva required. But he was ably represented by BEZA, and a dozen ministers, and twenty-two lay deputies of the Churches. The dramatic taste of the French mind was gratified by the scene, for the tournaments of belted knights had now given way to those of theological disputants. In the Refectory of the great Convent the boy King was seated on a temporary throne. The members of his family, the officers and ladies of his Court, were stationed on one side, six Cardinals, with an array of mitred Bishops, were assembled on the other. The rustic garb of BEZA and his associates, as they were introduced to their Sovereign by the Chancellor, contrasted strongly with the gorgeous apparel and the showy splendour of the Court and its attendants. The political CARDINAL OF LOR-

RAINE and the subtle General of the Jesuits, IAGO LASQUEZ, conducted the dispute against BEZA. The Doctors of the Sorbonne watched the sport with official keenness, while CATHERINE listened to the debate with secret contempt, having long ago determined to root out every Heretic as soon as she could throw the mantle of policy over her cruelty.

PARALLEL BETWEEN THE PROTESTANTS IN FRANCE AND THE JEWS IN BABYLON.

The matured Christian is now enabled to see at a glance, that such Conferences are, of necessity, worthless as to any progress of vital religion in the soul. The narrative, however, may enable the reader to enter a little into the state of the Christians in France when CALVIN indited his Prefatory Letter, and may justify the comparison which he makes between their lot, under the tyranny of such merciless rulers, and that of DANIEL under the sway of the imperious NEBUCHADNEZZAR, and at the tender mercy of his colleagues under DARIUS. The parallel is as complete as it could possibly be between the temporal position of the pious in FRANCE, and that of the devout Jews in BABYLON—and the graphic description of the Royal Professor of Modern History fully justifies the pastoral anxiety of the austere Theologian of Geneva.

EDITOR'S APOLOGIA

The CONTENTS of these Volumes are as follow :—

Before concluding these Prefatory Observations, THE EDITOR would briefly refer to the fundamental rules of THE CALVIN TRANSLATION SOCIETY, which very wisely exclude all expressions of private opinion. He hopes that no remarks in this PREFACE will be deemed inconsistent with so judicious a regulation. The clear illustration and the comprehensive defence of our Venerable Reformer seem to demand the candid statement of some views which are adverse to the popular current ; but this necessity need not induce him to step beyond the limits of his province. It has been his desire conscientiously to vindicate his Author's Interpretations wherever he is able to do so, and as fearlessly to point out wherever CALVIN is allowed to be in error; but in both cases, the EDITOR has scrupulously avoided taking any one-sided view of a great argument. He has attempted to exercise the utmost impartiality in quoting from a great variety of Standard Works which contain the most opposite conclusions; and yet, in accordance with the first principles of these Translations, he has at the same time carefully abstained from pressing any sentiments of his own on the attention of the intelligent reader.

T. M.

SHERIFF-HUTTON VICARAGE,
May 1852.

DEDICATORY EPISTLE

JOHN CALVIN

TO ALL THE PIOUS WORSHIPPERS OF GOD WHO DESIRE THE KINGDOM OF
CHRIST TO BE RIGHTLY CONSTITUTED IN FRANCE.

HEALTH.

ALTHOUGH I have been absent these six-and-twenty years, with little regret, from that native land which I own in common with yourselves, and whose agreeable climate attracts many foreigners from the most distant quarters of the world; yet it would be in no degree pleasing or desirable to me to dwell in a region from which the Truth of God, pure Religion, and the doctrine of eternal salvation are banished, and the very kingdom of Christ laid prostrate! Hence, I have no desire to return to it; yet it would be neither in accordance with human nor Divine obligation to forget the people from which I am sprung, and to put away all regard for their welfare. I think I have given some strong proofs, how seriously and ardently I desire to benefit my fellow-countrymen, to whom perhaps my absence has been useful, in enabling them to reap the greater profit from my studies. And the contemplation of this advantage has not only deprived my banishment of its sting, but has rendered it even pleasant and joyful.

Since, therefore, throughout the whole of this period I have publicly endeavoured to benefit THE INHABITANTS OF FRANCE, and have never ceased privately to rouse the torpid, to stimulate the sluggish, to animate the trembling, and to encourage the doubtful and the wavering to perseverance, I must now strive to the utmost that my duty towards them may not fail at a period so urgent and so pressing. A most excellent opportunity has been providentially afforded to me; for in publishing the LECTURES which contain my INTERPRETATION OF THE PROPHECIES OF DANIEL, I have the very best occasion of shewing you, beloved brethren, in this mirror, how God proves the faith of his people in these days by various trials; and how with wonderful wisdom he has taken care to strengthen their minds by ancient examples, that they should never be weakened by the concussion of the severest storms and tempests; or at least, if they should totter at all, that they should never finally fall away. For although the servants of God are required to run in a course impeded by many obstacles, yet whoever diligently reads this Book will find in it whatever is needed by a voluntary and active runner to guide him from the starting-post to the goal; while good and strenuous wrestlers will experimentally acknowledge that they have been sufficiently prepared for the contest.

First of all, a very mournful and yet profitable history will be recorded for us, in the exile of DANIEL and his companions while the kingdom and priesthood were still standing, as if God, through ignominy and shame, would devote the choicest flower of his elect people to extreme calamity. For what, at first sight, is more unbecoming, than that youths endued with almost angelic virtues should be the slaves and captives of a proud conqueror, when the most wicked and abandoned despisers of God remained at home in perfect safety? Was this the reward of a pious and innocent life, that, while the impious were sweetly flattering themselves through their escape from punishment, the saints should pay the penalty which they had deserved? Here, then, we observe, as in a living picture, that when God spares and even indulges the wicked for a time, he proves his servants like gold and silver; so that we ought not to consider it a grievance to be thrown into the furnace of trial, while profane men enjoy the calmness of repose.

Secondly, we have here an example of most manly prudence and of singular consistency, united with a magnanimity truly heroic. When pious youths of a tender age are tempted by the enticements of a Court, they not only overcome the temptations presented to them by their temperance, but perceive themselves cunningly enticed to depart by degrees from the sincere worship of God; and then, when they have extricated themselves from the snares of the devil, they boldly and freely despise all poison-stained honour, at the imminent risk of instant death. A more cruel and formidable contest will follow when the companions of DANIEL, as a memorable example of incredible constancy, are never turned aside by atrocious threats to pollute themselves by adoring the Image, and are at length prepared to vindicate the pure worship of God, not only with their blood, but in defiance of a horrible torture set before their eyes. Thus the goodness of God shines forth at the close of this tragedy, and tends in no slight degree to arm us with invincible confidence.

A similar contest and victory of DANIEL himself will be added ; when he preferred to be cast among savage lions, to desisting from the open profession of his faith three times a-day ; lest by perfidious dissembling he should prostitute the Sacred Name of God to the jests of the impious. Thus he was wonderfully drawn out of the pit which was all but his grave, and triumphed over Satan and his faction. Here philosophers do not come before us skilfully disputing about the virtues peacefully in the shade ; but the indefatigable constancy of holy men in the pursuit of piety, invites us with a loud voice to imitate them. Therefore, unless we are altogether unteachable, we ought to learn from these masters, if Satan lays the snares of flattery for us, to be prudent and cautious that we are not entangled in them ; and if he attacks us violently, to oppose all his assaults by a fearless contempt of death and of all evils. Should any one object, that the examples of either kind of deliverance which we have mentioned are rare, I confess indeed that God does not always stretch forth his hand from heaven in the same way to preserve his people ; but it ought to satisfy us that he has promised that he will be a faithful guardian of our life, as often as we are harassed by any trouble. We cannot be exposed to the power of the impious without his restraining their furious and turbulent plots against us, according to his pleasure. And we must not look at the results alone ; but observe how courageously holy men devoted themselves to death for the vindication of God's glory ; and although they were snatched away from it, yet their willing alacrity in offering themselves as victims is in no degree less deserving of praise.

It is also worth while to consider how variously the Prophet was tossed about and agitated during the Seventy years which he spent in exile. No King treated him so humanely as NEBUCHADNEZZAR, and yet he found him act like a wild beast. The cruelty of others was greater, until after the sudden death of BELSHAZZAR and the taking of the City, he was delivered up to its new masters, THE MEDES AND PERSIANS. Their hostile irruption struck terror into the minds of all, and there is no doubt that the Prophet partook of the general feeling. Although he was kindly received by DARIUS, so that his slavery was rendered tolerable, yet the envy of the nobles and their wicked conspiracy against him subjected him to the greatest dangers. But he was more anxious for the common safety of the Church than for his own personal security. He evidently suffered the greatest grief, and was distracted with the utmost anxiety, when the position of affairs discovered no limit to so severe and miserable an oppression of the people.   He acquiesced indeed, in the Prophecy of JEREMIAH ; still it was a proof of his incomparable forbearance that his hope, so long suspended, did not languish ; nay, that when tossed hither and thither amidst tempestuous waves, it was not entirely drowned.

I come now to THE PROPHECIES themselves.   The former part were uttered against THE BABYLONIANS ; partly, because God wished to adorn his servants with sure testimonies, which might compel that most proud and victorious Nation to revere him ; and partly, because His Name ought to be held in reverence with the profane.   Thus he would exercise the prophetic gift among his own people more freely, through being endued with authority. After his name had become celebrated among THE CHALDEANS, God entrusted him with Prophecies of greater moment, which were peculiar to his elect people.   Moreover, God so accommodated them to the use of his Ancient people, and they so soothed their sorrows by suitable remedies, and sustained their vacillating minds till THE ADVENT OF CHRIST—that they have no less value in our time ; for whatever was predicted concerning the changing and vanishing splendour of these Monarchies, and the perpetual existence of Christ's Kingdom, is *in these days* no less useful to be known than formerly.   For God shews how all earthly power which is not founded on Christ must fall ; and he threatens speedy destruction to all Kingdoms which obscure Christ's glory by extending themselves too much.   And those Kings whose sway is most extended shall feel by sorrowful experience how horrible a judgment will fall upon them, unless they willingly submit themselves to the sway of Christ !   And what is less tolerable than to deprive Him of his right by whose protection their dignity remains safe ? And we see how few of their number admit THE SON OF GOD ; nay, how they turn every stone and try every possible scheme to prevent his entrance into their territories !   Many of their Councillors studiously use their utmost endeavours and influence to close every avenue against him.   For while they put forward the name of Christianity, and boast themselves to be the best defenders of the Catholic Faith, their frivolous vanity is easily refuted, if men hold the true and genuine definition of the Kingdom of Christ. For his throne or sceptre is nothing else but the doctrine of the Gospel.   Nor does his Majesty shine elsewhere, nor his Empire

otherwise exist, than when all, from the highest to the lowest, hear
His voice with the calm docility of sheep, and follow wherever he
calls them. These Kings not only completely reject this doctrine,
which contains the substance of True Religion, and the lawful
Worship of God, in which the eternal salvation of men and their
true happiness consists; but they drive it far away from them by
threats and terrors, by the sword and flame, nor do they omit any
violence in their efforts to exterminate it. How great, how prodigious this blindness, when they cannot bear that those whom the
only-begotten Son of God invites mercifully to himself should embrace him! But many in their own pride, forsooth, think themselves reduced to the common level, if they lower their ensigns of
royalty to the Supreme King: others are unwilling to bridle their
lusts, and since hypocrisy seizes on all their senses, they seek darkness, and dread to be dragged into light. No plague is worse than
this fear, like Herod's! as if he who offers a celestial empire to the
least and most despised of the people, would snatch away the kingdoms of the earth from its monarchs. In addition to this, when
each regards the opinion of others, this mutual league retains them
all bound in a distinctive bond under the yoke of impiety. For if
they would seriously apply their minds to inquire what is true and
right; nay, if they would only open their eyes, they could not fail
to discover it.

Since it has often been found, by experience, that when Christ
goes forth with his Gospel serious commotions arise, thus Kings
have a plausible pretext for rejecting the heavenly doctrine by consulting for the public safety. I confess, indeed, that all change
which occasions disturbance ought to be esteemed odious; but the
injustice to God is great, unless this also is attributed to his *power*,
that whatever tumults arise he allays them, and thus the kingdom
of his Son is established! Although the heavens should mingle
with the earth, the worship of God is so precious, that not even the
least diminution of it can be compensated at any price. But those
who pretend that the Gospel is the source of disturbances, accuse
it falsely and unjustly. (Hag. ii. 7.) It is indeed true, that God
thunders therein with the vehemence of His voice, which shakes
heaven and earth; but while the Prophet gains attention to its
preaching by this testimony, such concussion is to be wished for and
expected. And, surely, if God's glory did not shine forth in its
own degree, until all flesh was humbled, it would be necessary that
man's pride should be humbled by the bold and strong hand of

God; since that pride raises itself against him, and never yields of its own accord.   But if the earth trembled at the promulgation of the Law, (Exod. xix. 18,) it is not surprising that the force and efficacy of the Gospel should appear more resplendent.   Wherefore, it becomes us to embrace that consoling doctrine which raises the dead from the grave, and opens heaven, and implants unaccustomed vigour in those whom the earth is unworthy to sustain, as if all the elements were subservient to our salvation.

But, lo! storms and tempests now flow from another fountain! Because the Rulers and Governors of the world do not willingly submit to the yoke of Christ, now even the rude multitude reject what is salutary before they even taste it.   Some delight themselves in filth, like pigs, and others excited by fury rejoice in slaughter. The devil instigates by especial fury those whom he has enslaved to himself to tumults of all sorts.   Hence the clash of trumpets; hence conflicts and battles.   Meanwhile, THE ROMAN PRIEST—a Heliogabalus—with his red and sanguinary cohorts and horned beasts,[1] rages with a hasty rush against Christ, and fetches from every side his allies from the filth of his foul Clergy,[2] all of whom sup the food on which they subsist from the same pot, though it be not equally dainty.   Many hungry fellows also run up to offer their assistance.   Most of the Judges are accustomed to gratify their appetites at these sumptuous banquets, and to fight for the kitchen and the kettle! and besides this, the haunts of the Monks,[3] and the dens of the Sorbonne,[4] send forth their gluttons who add fuel to the flame.   I omit the clandestine arts and wicked conspiracies of which my best witnesses are these notorious enemies to piety!   I mention no one by name: it is enough to point with the finger to those who are too well known to you.   In this confused assault of wild beasts, it is not surprising if those who depend only on the complicated events of things hesitate through perplexity, while they unjustly and unfairly throw the blame of their distrust upon the Sacred Gospel of Christ.   Let us suppose that all the infernal regions with their furies should offer us battle, will God sit at ease in heaven, and desert and betray his own cause? and when he has entered into the conflict, will either the crafty, cunning, or the impetuous rush of men deprive Him of his victory?

THE POPE, they say, will draw with him a large faction—it is the just reward of unbelief to tremble at the sound of a falling leaf!

---

[1] The Cardinals and Bishops.   [2] The Romish priesthood.
[3] The monasteries.   [4] The Sorbonne was a Popish seminary

(Lev. xxvi. 36.) Why, O ye counsellors, have ye so little fore-sight? Christ will take care that no novelty shall disturb you. In a short time ye will feel how far more satisfactory it is to have God propitious, to despise terrors as of no moment, and to rest in His protection, than to harass Him by open warfare, through fear of the wrath of the evil and the hypocritical. In truth, after all these discussions, the superstition which has hitherto reigned is with the defenders of the Pope, nothing else but well-placed evil,[1] and they think it cannot be removed, because the attempt would occasion irreparable damage. But those who regard the glory of God, and are endued with sincere piety, ought to have far higher objects in view, and so to submit themselves to the will of God as to approve of all the events of his providence. If he had not promised us anything, there might be just cause for fear and constant vacilla-tion; but since he has so often declared, that his help shall never be wanting in upholding the kingdom of his Christ, the reliance on this promise is the one sole basis of right action.

Hence it is your duty, dearest brethren, as far as lies in your power, and your calling demands it, to use your hearty endeavours, that true religion may recover its perfect state. It is not necessary for me to relate how strenuously I have hitherto endeavoured to cut off all occasion for tumult; yea, I call you all with the angels to witness before the Supreme Judge of all men, that it is no fault of mine if the kingdom of Christ does not progress quietly without any injury. And I think it is owing to my carefulness that private persons have not transgressed beyond their bounds. Now, although God by his wonderful skill has carried forward the restoration of his Church further than I had dared to hope for, yet it is well to remember what Christ taught his disciples, namely, that they should possess their souls in patience. (Luke xxi. 19.)

This is one object of the Vision which DANIEL has explained. The Stone by which those kingdoms were destroyed, which had made war on God, was not formed by the hand of man: and al-though it was rude and unpolished, yet it increased to a great mountain. I thought that ye required reminding of this, that ye may remain calm amidst the threatening thunders, while the empty clouds vanish away through being dispersed by heavenly agency.

---

[1] Latine, "*malum bene positum:*" the French translation takes the phrase as a proverb—"*comme dit le proverb, un mal qui est bien en repos.*" Anglice, "well-poised."

It does not escape me, while I pass by the numberless fires of thirty years, that ye have endured very great indignities during the last six months.   How often in many places an irruption was made against you by a ferocious populace, and how often ye were attacked at one time by stones, and at another by swords!   How your enemies plotted against you, and repressed your peaceful assemblies by sudden and unlooked for violence!   How some were slain in their dwellings, and others by the wayside, while the bodies of your dead were dragged about as a laughing-stock, your women ravished, and many of your party wounded, and even the pregnant female with her offspring pierced through, and their homes ransacked and made desolate.   But, although more atrocious things should be yet at hand, that ye may be approved as Christ's disciples, and be wisely instructed in his school, you must use every effort, that no madness of the impious who act thus intemperately, should deprive you of that moderation by which alone they have thus far been conquered and broken down.   And if the length of your affliction should cause you weariness, bear in mind that celebrated prophecy in which the Church's condition is depicted to the life.   God therein shews his Prophet what contests and anxieties, troubles and difficulties, awaited the Jews from the close of their exile, and from their joyful return to their country, until the advent of Christ.

The similarity of the times adapts these predictions to ourselves, and fits them for our own use.   DANIEL congratulated the wretched Church which had so long been submerged in a deluge of evils, when he collected from the computation of the years, that the day of deliverance predicted by Jeremiah was at hand. (Jer. xxv. 12, and xxix. 10.)   But he receives for an answer, that the lot of the people from the time of their permission to return would be more bitter, so that they would scarcely breathe again under a continual series of oppressive evils.   With the bitterest grief, and with many sorrows, the people had dragged on in hope for seventy years, but now God increases the period sevenfold, and inwardly inflicts a deadly wound on their heart.   He not only pronounces that the people, after their return home, should collect their strength and build their city and temple, and then suffer new anxieties, but he predicts fresh troubles amidst the very commencement of their joy, whilst they had scarcely tasted the sweetness of grace.   Then with regard to the calamities which shortly followed, the multiform catalogue here presented affrights us even who have only heard of them : then how bitter and how distressing were they to that rude nation !   To see the temple profaned by the audacity of a sacrilegious tyrant, its sacred rites shamefully mingled with foul pollutions, all the books of the law cast into the fire, and the whole of the ceremonies abolished,—how horrible the spectacle! Since all who professed to persist boldly and constantly in the worship of God were seized and subjected to the same burning, how could the tender and weak behold this without the greatest consternation! Yet this was the tyrant's plan, that the cruelty might excite the less earnest to deny their faith. Under the Maccabees, some relaxation seems to have taken place, but yet such as is soon deformed by the most cruel slaughters, and was never without its share of lamentation and wo. For since the enemy far excelled them in forces and in every equipment for war, nothing was left for those who had taken up arms for the defence of the Church but to hide themselves in the dens of wild beasts, or to wander through the woods in the greatest distress, and in utter destitution. Another source of temptation was added, since impious and abandoned men, in the boasting of a fallacious zeal, as DANIEL says, joined the party of Judas and his brethren, by which artifice of Satan infamy became attached to the band which Judas had collected, as if it had been a band of robbers. (Chap. xi. 34.)

But nothing was a source of greater sorrow to the righteous, than to find the priests themselves betraying the temple and worship of God, by wicked compacts according to the prompting of their interested ambition. For not only was that sacred dignity both bought and sold, but it was purchased by mutual murders and parricides. Hence it happened, that men of all ranks grew more and more profane, and corruptions multiplied everywhere with impunity, although circumcision and the sacrifices still remained in use, so that the expectation of the kingdom of God, when Christ appeared, was a strange and unheard of marvel. Very few, indeed, are entitled to even this praise. If then, in that unworthy deformity of the Church, if in the midst of its many dispersions and its dreadful terrors, of the devastation of the lands, the destruction of the dwellings, and the consequent dangers to life itself, this prophecy of DANIEL sustained the spirit of the pious, when the religious ceremonies were involved in obscure shadows, and doctrine was almost extinct, when the priests were most degenerate, and all sacred ordinances abolished,—how ashamed should we be of our cowardice, if the clearness of the Gospel, in which God shews to us his paternal face, does not raise us above all obstacles, and prop us up with unwearied constancy?

There is no doubt that the servants of God accommodated to

their own times the predictions of this Prophet concerning the exile
at Babylon, and thus lightened the pressure of present calamities.
Thus, also, we ought to have our eyes fixed on the miseries of the
Fathers, that we may not object to be joined with the body of that
Church to which it was said, " O, thou little flock, borne down by
the tempest and deprived of comfort, behold, I take thee up."
(Isaiah liv. 11.) And, again, after she has complained that her
back had been torn by the ungodly, like a field cut up by the
course of the furrows, yet she boasts immediately afterwards, that
their cords were cut away by a just God, so that they did not
prevail against her. (Psalm cxxix. 1-4.) The Prophet, then, not
only animates us to hope and patience, by the example of those
times, but adds an exhortation dictated by the Spirit, which extends to the whole reign of Christ, and is applicable to us. Wherefore it is no hardship to us to be comprehended in the number
of those whom he announces shall be proved and purified by
fire, since the inestimable happiness and glory which springs
from this process more than compensates for all its crosses and
distresses. And although these things are insipid to the majority,
lest their sloth and stupidity should render us too sluggish, we
should fix deeply in our hearts the denunciation of the Prophets,
namely, that the ungodly will act impiously, since they understand
nothing; while the sons of God will be endued with wisdom to
hold on the course of their divine calling. It is worth while, then,
to perceive the origin of that gross blindness which is commonly
observed, so that the heavenly doctrine may make us wise.
Hence, it too often happens that the multitude revile Christ and
his Gospel; they indulge themselves without either care, or fear,
or any perception of their dangers, and they are not aroused by
God's wrath to an ardent and serious desire for that redemption
which alone snatches us from the abyss of eternal destruction.
In the meantime they are caught or rather fascinated by luxuries,
pleasures, and other enticements, and pay no regard to the prospect of a happy eternity. Although there are many sects who
contemptuously despise the teaching of the Gospel, some are remarkable for pride, others for imbecility, some for want of sobriety
of mind, and others for a sleepy torpidity, yet we shall find that
contempt flows from profane security, since no one descends into
himself to shake off his own miseries, by finding a remedy for them.
Yet, when God's curse rests upon us, and his just vengeance urges
us, it is the height of madness to cast aside all anxiety, and to
please ourselves as if we need fear nothing. Yet it is a very com-

mon fault for those who are guilty of a thousand sins, and deserve a thousand eternal deaths, to discharge with levity a few frivolous ceremonies towards God, and then give themselves up to sloth and lethargy. Moreover, Paul denounces the savour of the Gospel (1 Cor. ii. 16) to be deadly towards all whose minds are fascinated by Satan ; so that to taste of its life-giving savour, it is necessary for us to stand at God's tribunal, and there also to cite our own consciences when wounded with serious terror.

Thus, we esteem, according to its proper worth and value, that reconciliation which Christ procured for us by his precious blood. Thus, the angel, that he might acquire reverence and respect for Christ's authority, brings a message concerning eternal justice which he sealed by the sacrifice of his death, and expresses the mode and plan by which iniquity was abolished and expiated. Thus, while the world revels in its lusts, let the knowledge of the condemnation which we have deserved inspire us with fear, and humble us before God : and while the profane involve themselves in the whirl of earthly gratifications, let us eagerly embrace this incomparable treasure, in which solid blessedness is laid up. Let our enemies jeer as they please, every man ought to take care to have God propitious to him, and it is clear that the very foundation of the faith is overthrown by those who think he is to be doubtfully invoked. Let them deride our faith with as much petulance as they please, but let us be sure of this, that no one obtains this privilege except by God's good gift, for men can only call God " Father" by relying on the advocacy of Christ, through a free and peaceful confidence. But the pursuit of piety will never flourish in us as it ought, until we learn to raise our minds upwards, since they are too inclined to grovel upon earth, and we should exercise them in continual meditation upon the heavenly life. And in this respect, the surprising vanity of the human race manifests itself, since though all speak eloquently, like philosophers, on the shortness of life, yet no one aspires to that perpetual existence. So that when Paul commends the faith and charity of the Colossians, he very truly says, that they were animated by a hope laid up in the heavens. (Col. i. 5.) And when discussing elsewhere the results of the grace which is open to us in Christ, he says—we must be so built up therein, that all impiety and worldly desires must be mortified, and we must live soberly, justly, and piously in this world, and wait for the blessed hope, and glorious advent of the great God and our Saviour Jesus Christ. (Tit. ii. 12, 13.)

Let, then, this expectation free us from all hinderances, and draw us towards itself, and though the world is steeped in more than epicurean pollution, lest the contagion should reach us, we ought to strive the more earnestly until we arrive at the goal. Although it is truly a matter of grief, that so great a multitude should wilfully perish, and rush devotedly on their own destruction, yet their foolish fury need not disturb us; for another admonition of DANIEL should succour us, namely, that certain salvation is laid up for all who have been found written in the book. But although our election is hidden in God's secret counsel, which is the prime cause of our salvation, yet, since the adoption of all who are inserted into the body of Christ, by faith in the gospel, is by no means doubtful, be ye content with this testimony, and persevere in the course which ye have happily begun. But if ye must contend still longer, (and I announce, that contests more severe than ye contemplate yet remain for you,) by whatsoever attack the madness of the impious bursts forth, as if it stirred up the regions below, remember that your course has been defined by a heavenly Master of the contest, whose laws ye must obey the more cheerfully, since he will supply you with strength unto the end.

Since, then, it is not lawful for me to desert the station to which God has appointed me, I have DEDICATED to you this my labour, as a pledge of my desire to help you, until at the completion of my pilgrimage our heavenly Father, of his immeasurable pity, shall gather me together with you, to his eternal inheritance.

May the LORD govern you by His Spirit, may He defend my most beloved brethren by His own protection, against all the plots of their enemies, and sustain them by his invisible power.

JOHN CALVIN.

GENEVA, *August* 19, 1561.

THE PRAYER

WHICH JOHN CALVIN WAS ACCUSTOMED TO USE AT THE
COMMENCEMENT OF HIS LECTURES.

GRANT unto us, O LORD, to be occupied in the mysteries
of thy Heavenly wisdom, with true progress in piety,
to thy glory and our own edification.—AMEN.

** This prayer is not inserted in the Geneva edition of 1617, but is
found in that of 1571. The FRENCH TRANSLATION renders it as follows :—
" May the Lord grant us grace so to treat the secrets of His celestial
wisdom, that we may truly profit in the fear of His holy name, to His
glory and to our edification. Amen."

COMMENTARIES

ON

THE PROPHET DANIEL

JOHN CALVIN'S PREFACE

TO HIS LECTURES ON DANIEL.

𝔏ecture 𝔉irst.

THE BOOK OF THE PROPHET DANIEL follows these Remarks, and its utility will be better understood as we proceed; since it cannot be conveniently explained all at once. I will, however, just present the Reader with a foretaste to prepare his mind, and render him attentive. But before I do so, I must make a brief SUMMARY OF THE BOOK. We may divide the Book into two parts, and this partition will materially help us. For DANIEL relates how he acquired influence over the unbelieving. It was necessary for him to be elevated to the prophetic office in some singular and unusual manner. The condition of the Jews, as is well known, was so confused, that it was difficult for any one to determine whether any Prophet existed. At first JEREMIAH was alive, and after him EZEKIEL. After their return, the Jews had their own Prophets: but Jeremiah and Ezekiel had almost fulfilled their office, when DANIEL succeeded them. Others too, as we have already seen, as HAGGAI, MALACHI, and ZECHARIAH, were created Prophets for the purpose of exhorting the people, and hence their duties were partially restricted. But DANIEL would scarcely have been considered a Prophet, had not God, as we have said, appointed him in a remarkable way. We shall perceive at the close of the sixth chapter, that he was divinely endued with remarkable signs, so that the Jews might surely ascertain that he had the gift of prophecy, unless they were basely ungrateful to God. His name was known and respected by the inhabitants of Babylon. If the Jews had despised what even the profane Gentiles admired, was not this purposely to suffocate and trample on the grace of God? DANIEL, then, had sure and striking marks by which he could be recognised as God's Prophet, and his calling be rendered unquestionable.

A Second Part is afterwards added, in which God predicts by his agency the events which were to occur to his elect people. The Visions, then, from the seventh chapter to the end of the Book, relate peculiarly to the Church of God. There God predicts what should happen hereafter. And that admonition is the more necessary, since the trial was severe, when the Jews had to bear an exile of seventy years; but after their return to their country, instead of seventy years, God protracted their full deliverance till seventy weeks of years. So the delay was increased sevenfold. Their spirits might be broken a thousand times, or even utterly fail; for the Prophets speak so magnificently about their redemption, that the Jews expected their state to be especially happy and prosperous, as soon as they were snatched from the Babylonish Captivity. But since they were oppressed with so many afflictions, and that, too, not for a short period, but for more than four hundred years, their redemption might seem illusory since they were but seventy years in exile. There is no doubt, then, that Satan seduced the minds of many to revolt, as if God were mocking them by bringing them out of Chaldea back again to their own country. For these reasons God shews his servant in a Vision what numerous and severe afflictions awaited his elect people. Besides, DANIEL so prophesies that he describes almost historically events previously hidden. And this was necessary, since in such turbulent convulsions the people would never have tasted that these had been divinely revealed to DANIEL, unless the heavenly testimony had been

proved by the event. This holy man ought so to speak and
to prophesy concerning futurity, as if he were relating what.
had already happened. But we shall see all these things in
their own order.

I return, then, to what I commenced with, that we may
see in few words how useful this Book is to the Church of
Christ. First of all, the matter itself shews how DANIEL
did not speak from his own discretion, but whatever he
uttered was dictated by the Holy Spirit: for whence could
he conceive the things which we shall afterwards behold, if
he were only endued with human prudence ? for instance,
that other Monarchies should arise to blot out that Babylonian Empire which then had the greatest authority in all
the world ? Then, again, how could he divine concerning
Alexander the Great and his Successors ? for long before
Alexander was born, DANIEL predicted what he should accomplish. Then he shews that his kingdom should not last,
since it is directly divided into four horns. Other events
also clearly demonstrate that he spoke by the dictation of
the Holy Spirit. But our confidence in this is strengthened
by other narratives, where he represents the various miseries
to which the Church should be subject between two most
cruel enemies, the kings of Syria and Egypt. He first recites their treaties, and then their hostile incursions on both
sides, and afterwards so many changes, as if he pointed at
the things themselves with his finger ; and he so follows
through their whole progress, that God appears to speak by
his mouth. This, then, is a great step, and we shall not repent of taking it, when we acknowledge DANIEL to have been
only the organ of the Holy Spirit, and never to have brought
anything forward by his own private inclination. The authority, too, which he obtained, and which inspired the Jews
with perfect confidence in his teaching, extends to us also.
Shameful, indeed, and base would be our ingratitude, if we
did not embrace him as God's Prophet, whom the Chaldeans
were compelled to honour—a people whom we know to have
been superstitious and full of pride. These two nations, the
Egyptians and Chaldeans, placed themselves before all others;
for the Chaldeans thought wisdom's only dwelling-place

was with themselves: hence they would never have been inclined to receive DANIEL, unless the reality had compelled them, and the confession of his being a true prophet of God had been extorted from them.

Since DANIEL's authority is thus established, we must now say a few words about the subjects which he treats. Respecting THE INTERPRETATION OF THE DREAMS, the first of those of Nebuchadnezzar embraces a matter of great importance, as we shall see, namely, how all the splendour and power of the world vanish away, Christ's kingdom alone remaining stable, and that nothing else is self-enduring. In the Second Dream of Nebuchadnezzar, DANIEL's admirable constancy is displayed. Very invidious, indeed, was the office of throwing down the mightiest Monarch of the whole world as he did: "Thou exceptest thyself from the number of men, and art worshipped like a god; thou shalt hereafter become a beast!" No man of these days would dare thus to address Monarchs; nay, who dares to admonish them even mildly, if they have sinned at all? When, therefore, DANIEL intrepidly predicted to King Nebuchadnezzar the disgrace which awaited him, he thus gave a rare and memorable proof of his constancy. And in this way, again, his calling was sealed, since this fortitude sprang from God's Spirit.

But the Second Part is peculiarly worthy of notice, since we there perceive how God cares for his Church. God's providence is, indeed, extended to the whole world. For if a sparrow does not fall to the ground without his permission, he, doubtless, is mindful of the human race! (Matt. x., and Luke xii.) Nothing, therefore, happens to us by chance, but God in this Book affords us light, while we know his Church to be so governed by him, as to be the object of his peculiar care. If matters ever were so disturbed in the world, that one could suppose God to be asleep in heaven, and to be forgetful of the human race, surely such were the changes of those times, nay, so multiform, so extensive, and so various were they, that even the most daring must be confounded, since there was no end to the wars Egypt prevailed at one time, while at another there were commotions in Syria. Seeing, then, all things turned up-side down, what judgment could be passed, except that God neglected the world, and the Jews were miserably deceived in their hope? They thought that as God had been their deliverer, so would he have been the perpetual guardian of their safety. Although all nations were then subject in common to various slaughters, yet if the Syrians were victorious over the Egyptians, they abused their power against the Jews, and Jerusalem lay exposed as their prey, and the reward of their victory: if, again, the opposite side were the conquerors, they revenged the injury, or sought compensation against the Jews. Thus on every side those miserable people were fleeced, and their condition was much worse after their return to their country, than if they had always been exiles or strangers in other regions. When, therefore, they were admonished concerning the future, this was the best prop on which they could repose. But the use of the same doctrine is at this day applicable to us. We perceive, as in a glass or picture, how God was anxious about his Church, even when he seemed to cast away all regard for it: hence when the Jews were exposed to the injuries of their enemies, it was but the accomplishment of his designs.

From the Second Part we recognise their wonderful preservation, and that too, by a greater and more surprising exercise of God's power, than if they had lived in peace, and no one had molested them. We learn this from the seventh to the ninth chapters. Now, when DANIEL numbers the years till THE ADVENT of CHRIST, how clear and distinct is the testimony which we may oppose against Satan, and all the taunts of the impious! and how certain it is that the Book of DANIEL was familiarly used by men before this event. But when he enumerates THE SEVENTY WEEKS, and says, that Christ should then come, all profane men may come, and boast, and swell with increased swaggering, yet they shall fall down convicted, since Christ is that true Redeemer whom God had promised from the beginning of the world. For He was unwilling to make him known without the most certain demonstration, such as all the mathematicians can never equal. First of all, it is worthy of observation, that DANIEL afterwards discoursed on the various calamities of the Church, and prophesied the time at which God pleased to shew his only-begotten Son to the world. His dissertation on the office of Christ is one of the principal supports of our faith. For he not only describes his Advent, but announces the abolition of the shadows of the Law, since the Messiah would bring with him its complete fulfilment. And when he predicts the Death of Christ, he shews for what purpose he should undergo death, namely, to abolish Sin by his sacrifice, and to bring in Eternal Righteousness. Lastly, this also must be noticed,—as he had instructed the people to bear their cross, so also he warns them that the Church's state would not be tranquil even when the Messiah came. The sons of God should be militant until the end, and not hope for any fruit of their victory until the dead should rise again, and Christ himself should collect us into his own Celestial Kingdom. Now, we comprehend in few words, or rather only taste how useful and fruitful this Book is to us.

I now come to the words themselves: I wished, as I said, just to catch a foretaste of a few things, and the reading of the Book will shew us better what advantage we may derive from each of its chapters.

CHAPTER FIRST.

1. In the third year of the reign of Jehoiakim king of Judah came Nebuchadnezzar king of Babylon unto Jerusalem, and besieged it.

2. And the Lord gave Jehoiakim king of Judah into his hand, with part of the vessels of the house of God, which he carried into the land of Shinar, to the house of his god; and he brought the vessels into the treasure-house of his God.

1. Anno tertio regni Jehoiakim regis Jehudah venit Nebuchadnezzar rex Jerosolyma Babylonis, et obsedit eam.

2. Et tradidit Deus in manum regis Jehoiakim Regem Jehuda, et partem vasorum domus Dei, et traduxit ea[1] in terram Sinear in domum dei sui[2] quod vasa posuerit in domo thesauri dei sui.

These are not two different things, but the Prophet ex-

---

[1] Or *eos*. Either may be read; for the Hebrews do not use the neuter gender; yet I had rather use the neuter gender, on account of what follows. —*Calvin*.

[2] This would not suit either the king or the captives; hence the Prophet seems to speak of "vessels;" and a repetition of the same sentence afterwards follows.—*Calvin*.

plains and confirms the same sentiments by a change of phrase, and says that the vessels which Nebuchadnezzar had brought into the land of Sinaar were laid up in the house of the treasury. The Hebrews, as we know, generally use the word "house" for any place, as they call the temple God's "house." Of the land of Sinaar, it must be remarked, that it was a plain adjacent to Babylon ; and the famous temple of Belus, to which the Prophet very probably refers, was erected there.

Here Daniel marks the time in which he was led into captivity together with his companions, namely, in the third year of Jehoiakim. A difficult question arises here, since Nebuchadnezzar began to reign in the fourth year of Jehoiakim. How then could he have besieged Jerusalem in the third year, and then led away the people captives according to his pleasure? Some interpreters solve this difficulty by what appears to me a frivolous conjecture, that the four years ought to refer to the beginning of his reign, and so the time may be brought within the third year. But in the second chapter we shall see Daniel brought before the king in the second year of his reign. They explain this difficulty also by another solution. They say —the years are not reckoned from the beginning of the reign, and,—this was the second year from the Conquest of the Jews and the taking of Jerusalem ; but this is too harsh and forced. The most probable conjecture seems to me, that the Prophet is speaking of the first King Nebuchadnezzar, or at least uses the reign of the second, while his father was yet alive. We know there were two kings of the same name, father and son ; and as the son did many noble and illustrious actions, he acquired the surname of Great. Whatever, therefore, we shall afterwards meet with concerning Nebuchadnezzar, cannot be understood except of the second, who is the son. But Josephus says the son was sent by his father against the Egyptians and the Jews : and this was the cause of the war, since the Egyptians often urged the Jews to a change of affairs, and enticed them to throw off the yoke. Nebuchadnezzar the younger was carrying on the war in Egypt at the death of his father, and speedily returned home, lest any one should supersede him. When, however, he found all things as he wished, Josephus thinks he put off that expedition, and went to Jerusalem. There is nothing strange, nay, it is very customary to call him King who shares the command with his father. Thus, therefore, I interpret it: In the third year of the reign of Jehoiakim, Nebuchadnezzar came, under the command and direction of his father, or if any one prefers it, the father himself came. For there is nothing out of place, whether we refer it to the father or to the son. *Nebuchadnezzar*, then, *king of Babylon, came to Jerusalem*, that is, by the hand of his son besieged Jerusalem. But if a different explanation is preferred, since he was there himself and carried on the war in person, that view may be taken: still, the events happened in the third year of Jehoiakim's reign. Interpreters make many mistakes in this matter. Josephus, indeed, says this was done in the eighth year, but he had never read the Book of Daniel.[1] He was an unlearned man, and by no means familiar with the Scriptures; nay, I think he had never read three verses of Daniel. It was a dreadful judgment of God for a priest to be so ignorant a man as Josephus. But in another passage on which I have commented, he seems to have followed Metasthenes and others whom he cites, when speaking of the destruction of that monarchy. And this seems to suit well enough, since in the third year of the reign of Jehoiakim the city was once taken, and some of the nobles of the royal race were led away in triumph, among whom were Daniel and his companions. When Jehoiakim afterwards rebelled, his treatment was far more severe, as Jeremiah had predicted. But while Jehoiakim possessed the kingdom by permission of King Nebuchadnezzar, Daniel was already a captive, so that Jeremiah's prediction was fulfilled—the condition of the figs prematurely ripe was improved; for those who were

---

[1] Calvin's expression is *tam brutus homo* in Latin, and *si stupide et brutal* in French; but he is evidently too severe on so valuable an annalist, who, in so many passages, confirms and elucidates the scriptural narrative. Besides, Calvin seems to have overlooked the passage in his Antiq., lib. xi. cap. 8, § 5, where this Book is mentioned, and its contents alluded to at length.

led into exile last thought themselves better off than the rest. But the Prophet deprives them of their vain boast, and shews the former captives to have been better treated than the remnant of the people who as yet remained safe at home. (Jer. xxiv. 2, 8.) I assume, then, that Daniel was among the first fruits of the captivity ; and this is an instance of God's judgments being so incomprehensible by us. For had there been any integrity in the whole people, surely Daniel was a remarkable example of it : for EZEKIEL includes him among the three just men by whom most probably God would be appeased. (Chap. xiv. 14.) Such, then, was the excellence of Daniel's virtues, that he was like a celestial angel among mortals ; and yet he was led into exile, and lived as the slave of the king of Babylon. Others, again, who had provoked God's wrath in so many ways, remained quiet in their nests : the Lord did not deprive them of their country and of that inheritance which was a sign and pledge of their adoption.[1]

Should any wish here to determine why DANIEL was among the first to be led into captivity, will he not betray his folly ? Hence, let us learn to admire God's judgments, which surpass all our perceptions ; and let us also remember the words of Christ, "If these things are done in the green tree, what will be done in the dry ?" (Luke xxiii. 31.) As I have already said, there was an angelic holiness in Daniel, although so ignominiously exiled and brought up among the king's eunuchs. When this happened to so holy a man, who from his childhood was entirely devoted to piety, how great is God's indulgence in sparing us ? What have we deserved ? Which of us will dare to compare himself with Daniel ? Nay, we are unworthy, according to the ancient proverb, to loosen the tie of his shoes. Without the slightest doubt Daniel, through the circumstances of the time,

[1] Much light has been thrown upon the chronology of these times since the age of Calvin : later Commentators have dated from the third year of Jehoiakim's restoration to his kingdom after his rebellion. See 2 Kings xxiv. 2, 3. The subject is discussed with clearness by Bleek in his Theolog. Zeitschrist. Pt. iii. p. 280, &c. ; and R. Sal. Jarchi on this passage may be consulted, p. 735, edit. Gothæ, 1713. See DISSERTATION I. at the end of this Volume.

wished to manifest the singular and extraordinary gift of God, since this trial did not oppress his mind and could not turn him aside from the right course of piety.   When, therefore, Daniel saw himself put forward as an example of integrity, he did not desist from the pure worship of God.   As to his assertion that Jehoiakim was delivered into the hand of King Nebuchadnezzar by God's command, this form of speech takes away any stumblingblock which might occur to the minds of the pious.   Had Nebuchadnezzar been altogether superior, God himself might seem to have ceased to exist, and so his glory would have been depressed. But Daniel clearly asserts that King Nebuchadnezzar did not possess Jerusalem, and was not the conqueror of the nation by his own valour, or counsel, or fortune, or good luck, but because God wished to humble his people.   Therefore, Daniel here sets before us the providence and judgments of God, that we may not think Jerusalem to have been taken in violation of God's promise to Abraham and his posterity. He also speaks by name of the vessels of the temple. Now, this might seem altogether out of place, and would shock the minds of the faithful.   For what does it mean ? That God's temple was spoiled by a wicked and impious man.   Had not God borne witness that his rest was there ? This shall be my rest for ever : here will I dwell because I have chosen it.   (Ps. cxxxii. 14.)   If any place in the world were impregnable, here truly honour ought to remain entire and untainted in the temple of God.   When, therefore, it was robbed and its sacred vessels profaned, and when an impious king had also transferred to the temple of his own god what had been dedicated to the living God, would not, as I have said, such a trial as this cast down the minds of the holy ?   No one was surely so stout-hearted whom that unexpected trial would not oppress.   Where is God, if he does not defend his own temple ?   Although he does not dwell in this world, and is not enclosed in walls of either wood or stone, yet he chose this dwelling-place for himself, (Ps. lxxx. 1, and xcix. 1, and Isa. xxxvii. 16,) and often by means of his Prophets asserted his seat to be between the Cherubim.   What then is the meaning of this? As I have already said, Daniel recalls us to the judgment of God, and by a single word assures us that we ought not to be surprised at God inflicting such severe punishments upon impious and wicked apostates. For under the name of God, there is a silent antithesis; as the Lord did not deliver Jehoiakim into the hand of the Babylonians without just reason: *God*, therefore, exposed him as a prey that he might punish him for the revolt of his impious people. It now follows:—

3. And the king spake unto Ashpenaz, the master of his eunuchs, that he should bring *certain* of the children of Israel, and of the king's seed, and of the princes.	3. Et mandavit[1] Rex Aspenazo[2] principi eunuchorum, ut educeret e filiis Israel et ex semine regio, et ex principibus.[3]

Here Daniel pursues his narrative, and shews the manner in which he was led away together with his companions. The king had demanded young men to be brought, not from the ordinary multitude, but from the principal nobility, who stood before him, that is, ministered to him. Hence, we ascertain why Daniel and his companions were chosen, because they were noble young men and of the royal seed, or at least of parents who surpassed others in rank. The king did this purposely to shew himself a conqueror; he may also have taken this plan designedly, to retain hostages in his power; for he hoped, as we shall see, that those who were nourished in his palace would be degenerate and hostile to the Jews, and he thought their assistance would prove useful to himself. He also hoped, since they were born of a noble stock, that the Jews would be the more peaceable, and thus avoid all danger to those wretched exiles who were relations of the kings and the nobles. With regard to the words, he calls this *Aspenaz* the prince of eunuchs, under which name he means the boys who were nourished in the king's palace to become a seminary of nobles; for it is scarcely possible that this Aspenaz was set over other leaders. But we gather from this place, that the boys

[1] Or, declared.—*Calvin.*
[2] Or, said to Aspenaz, as those who retain the Hebrew phrase translate it.—*Calvin.*
[3] Or, elders.—*Calvin.*

whom the king held in honour and regard were under his custody. The Hebrews call eunuchs סריסים, *serisim*, a name which belongs to certain prefects; for Potiphar is called by this name though he had a wife. So this name is everywhere used in Scripture for the satraps of a king; (Gen. xxxvii. 36; xl. 2, 7;) but since satraps also were chosen from noble boys, they were probably called eunuchs, though they were not made so, yet Josephus ignorantly declares these Jewish children to have been made eunuchs. But when eunuchs existed among the luxuries of Oriental kings, as I have already said, those youths were commonly called by this name whom the king brought up as a kind of school of nobles, whom he might afterwards place over various provinces.

The king, therefore, commanded some of the children of Israel of the royal seed and of the nobles to be brought to him. So the sentence ought to be resolved; he did not command any of the common people to be brought to him, but some of the royal race, the more plainly to shew himself their conqueror by doing all things according to his will. He means those "elders" who yet were in chief authority under the king of Judah. And Daniel also was of that tribe, as we shall afterwards see. The word פרתמים, *pharthmim,* "princes," is thought to be derived from *Perah,* which is the Euphrates, and the interpreters understand prefects, to whom the provinces on the banks of the Euphrates were committed; but this does not suit the present passage where Jews are treated of. We now see the general signification of this name, and that all the elders ought to be comprehended under it.[1]—The rest to-morrow.

---

[1] This word has caused great difference of opinion among commentators. Theodotion does not attempt to explain it. Symmachus takes it for the Parthians. Jerome interprets it by *tyranni,* and Saadias by their offspring. Aben-Ezra considers it a foreign word; and R. Salom. Jarchi calls it Persian, and translates it "leaders." Hottinger and Aug. Pfeiffer both treat it as Persian, but derive it from different roots. "Nobles" or "elders" seems its best English equivalent.

PRAYER.

Grant, Almighty God, since thou settest before us so clear a mirror of thy wonderful providence and of thy judgments on thine ancient people, that we may also be surely persuaded of our being under thy hand and protection:—Grant, that relying on thee, we may hope for thy guardianship, whatever may happen, since thou never losest sight of our safety, so that we may invoke thee with a secure and tranquil mind. May we so fearlessly wait for all dangers amidst all the changes of this world, that we may stand upon the foundation of thy word which never can fail; and leaning on thy promises may we repose on Christ, to whom thou hast committed us, and whom thou hast made the shepherd of all thy flock. Grant that he may be so careful of us as to lead us through this course of warfare, however troublesome and turbulent it may prove, until we arrive at that heavenly rest which he has purchased for us by his own blood.—Amen.

Lecture Second.

4. Children in whom *was* no blemish, but well-favoured, and skilful in all wisdom, and cunning in knowledge, and understanding science, and such as *had* ability in them to stand in the king's palace, and whom they might teach the learning and the tongue of the Chaldeans.

4. Pueros, quibus nulla esset macula[1] et pulchros aspectu,[2] et intelligentes in omni prudentia,[3] et intelligentes scientiam, et diserte exprimentes cognitionem, et in quibus vigor, ut starent in palatio regis, et ad docendum ipsos literaturam et linguam Chaldæorum.

In yesterday's Lecture we saw how the prefect or master of the eunuchs was commanded to bring up some noble youths, the offspring of the king and the elders; and Daniel now describes their qualities, according to Nebuchadnezzar's order. They were *youths*, not so young as seven or eight years, but growing up, *in whom there was no spot;* that is, in whom there was no defect or unsoundness of body. They were also of *beautiful aspect*, meaning of ingenuous and open countenance: he adds also, *skilled in all prudence, and understanding knowledge;* and then, *expressing their thoughts.* I think those interpreters right who take this participle

[1] For I omit the Hebraism which has already been explained.—*Calvin.*
[2] Or countenance.—*Calvin.* [3] That is, skilled in all wisdom.—*Calvin.*

actively, otherwise the repetition would be cold and value-less. Their eloquence seems to me pointed out here ; because there are some who inwardly understand subjects presented to them, but cannot express to others what they retain in their minds ; for all have not the same dexterity in expressing exactly what they think. Daniel, therefore, notices both qualifications here—the acquisition of know-ledge, and the power of communicating it.

And in whom was vigour : for חכ, *cach*, usually signifies fortitude, as in Isaiah. (Chap. xl. 9.) Those who fear God shall change their fortitude, or renew their vigour. Then in Psalm xxii., (ver. 15,) "my strength or vigour has failed." He adds, the fortitude or vigour of intelligence, knowledge, and eloquence ; or a healthy habit of body, which is the same thing.[1] *That they might stand in the king's palace, and be taught literature,* (I cannot translate the particle ספר, *sepher*, otherwise : verbally it is a " letter," but it means learning or discipline,) *and the language of the Chaldees.* We now see how the king regarded not only their rank, when he ordered the most excellent of the royal and noble children to be brought to him ; but he exercised his choice that those who were to be his servants should be clever ; they were of high birth, as the phrase is ; so they ought to prevail in eloquence and give hopeful promise of general excellence in both body and mind. Without doubt he wished them to be held in great estimation, that he might win over other Jews also. Thus, if they afterwards obtained authority, should circumstances allow of it, they might become rulers in Judea, bearing sway over their own people, and yet remain attached to the Babylonian empire. This was the king's design ; it affords no reason why we should praise his liberality, since it is sufficiently apparent that he consulted nothing but his own advantage.

Meanwhile, we observe, that learning and the liberal arts were not then so despised as they are in this age, and

---

[1] It can scarcely be correct to confound bodily with mental endowments. *Wintle* explains the three clauses very appositely, referring the first to " excellent natural abilities," the second to " the greatest improvement from cultivation," and the last to " the communication of our perceptions in the happiest manner to others."

in those immediately preceding it. So strongly has barbarism prevailed in the world, that it is almost disgraceful for nobles to be reckoned among the men of education and of letters ! The chief boast of the nobility was to be destitute of scholarship—nay, they gloried in the assertion, that they were " no scholars," in the language of the day ; and if any of their rank were versed in literature, they acquired their attainments for no other purpose than to be made bishops and abbots : still, as I have said, they generally despised all literature. We perceive the age in which Daniel lived was not so barbarous, for the king wished to have these boys whom he caused to be so instructed, among his own princes, as we have said, to promote his own advantage ; still we must remark upon the habit of that age. As to his requiring so much knowledge and skill, it may seem out of place, and more than their tender age admitted, that they should be so accomplished in prudence, knowledge, and experience. But we know that kings require nothing in moderation : when they order anything to be prepared, they often ascend beyond the clouds. So Nebuchadnezzar speaks here ; and Daniel, who relates his commands, does so in a royal manner. Since the king commanded all the most accomplished to be brought before him, if they really manifested any remarkable qualities, we need not be surprised at their knowledge, skill, and prudence. The king simply wished those boys and youths to be brought to him who were ingenious and dexterous, and adapted to learn with rapidity ; and then those who were naturally eloquent and of a healthy constitution of body. For it follows directly, *that they might learn* or be taught *the literature and language of the Chaldees.* We perceive that King Nebuchadnezzar did not demand teachers, but boys of high birth, and good talents, and of promising abilities ; he wished them to be liberally instructed in the doctrine of the Chaldees : he was unwilling to have youths of merely polished and cultivated minds without natural abilities. His desire to have them acquainted with the language of Chaldea arose from his wish to separate them by degrees from their own nation, to induce them to forget their Jewish birth, and to acquire the Chaldean manners, since language is a singular bond of communication. Respecting their learning, we may ask, whether Daniel and his companions were permitted to learn arts full of imposition, which we know to be the nature of the Chaldean learning. For they professed to know every one's fate, as in these days there are many impostors in the world, who are called fortune-tellers. They abused an honourable name when they called themselves mathematicians, as if there were no scientific learning separate from those arts and diabolic illusions. And as to the use of the word, the Cæsars, in their laws, unite Chaldeans and mathematicians, treating them as synonymous. But the explanation is easy,—the Chaldeans not only pursued that astrology which is called " Judicial," but were also skilled in the true and genuine knowledge of the stars. The ancients say, that the course of the stars was observed by the Chaldeans, as there was no region of the world so full of them, and none possessed so extensive an horizon on all sides. As the Chaldeans enjoyed this advantage of having the heavens so fully exposed to the contemplation of man, this may have led to their study, and have conduced to the more earnest pursuit of astrology. But as the minds of men are inclined to vain and foolish curiosity, they were not content with legitimate science, but fell into foolish and perverse imaginations. For what fortune-tellers predict of any one's destiny is merely foolish fanaticism. Daniel, therefore, might have learned these arts ; that is, astrology and other liberal sciences, just as Moses is said to have been instructed in all the sciences of Egypt. We know how the Egyptians were infected with similar corruptions ; but it is said both of Moses and of our Prophet, that they were imbued with a knowledge of the stars and of the other liberal sciences. Although it is uncertain whether the king commanded them to proceed far in these studies, yet we must hold that Daniel abstained, as we shall see directly, from the royal food and drink, and was not drawn aside nor involved in these Satanic impostures. Whatever the king's commandment was, I suppose Daniel to have been content with the pure and genuine knowledge of natural things. As far as the king is concerned, as we have already said, he consulted simply his own interests ; wishing Daniel and his companions to pass over into a foreign tribe, and to be drawn away from their own people, as if they had been natives of Chaldea. It now follows :—

5. And the king appointed them a daily provision of the king's meat, and of the wine which he drank : so nourishing them three years, that at the end thereof they might stand before the king.

5. Et constituit illis rex demensum diei in die suo[1] ex frusto[2] cibi regis, et ex vino potus ejus. Et ut educarentur annis tribus : et a fine illorum[3] starent coram rege.

In this verse, Daniel shews that the king had ordered some youths to be brought to him from Judea, and to be so nourished as to be intoxicated with delicacies, and thus rendered forgetful of their own nation. For we know that wherever there is any cunning in the world, it reigns especially in kings' palaces ! So Nebuchadnezzar, when he perceived he was dealing with an obstinate people, (and we know the Jews to have been of a hard and unsubdued spirit,) wished to acquire servants spontaneously obedient, and thus endeavoured to soften them with luxuries. This was the reason why he provided for them *an allotment of his own meat and drink ;* as at present it is the greatest honour at princes' tables to be served with a *bon-bouche,* as they say. Nebuchadnezzar wished this Daniel and his companions, though but captives and exiles, to be brought up not only splendidly but royally, as if of the royal race. Through his right of conquest he had drawn them away violently from their country, as we said yesterday. Hence he does not act thus from any feeling of liberality, and his feeding those miserable exiles from his own table should not be esteemed a virtuous action ; but, as we have said, he cleverly reconciles the minds of the boys to be reckoned Chaldeans rather than Jews, and thus to deny their own race. This, then, was the king's intention ; but we shall see how God governed

---

[1] דבר, *deber,* " the matter," for each day.—*Calvin.* " The allotment for each day."—*Wintle.* It means " daily bread," as in our Lord's Prayer, and occurs often in Exodus.

[2] Verbally, it here signifies a portion.—*Calvin.*

[3] Some translate it " a part," meaning " some part of them," but there is no doubt that the Prophet means a space of time, as we shall soon see. —*Calvin.*

Daniel and his companions by His Spirit, and how they became aware of these snares of the devil, and abstained from the royal diet, lest they should become polluted by it. This point will hereafter be treated in its place—we are now only commenting on the craftiness of the king. He commanded a daily portion of diet to be distributed to them, not that the spirit of parsimony dictated this daily portion, but the king wished their food should be exactly the same as his own and that of the chiefs.

He adds, *that they should be educated for three years;* meaning, until they were thoroughly skilled in both the language and knowledge of the Chaldeans. Three years were sufficient for both these objects, since he had selected youths of sufficient talent to learn with ease both languages and sciences. As they were endued with such capacity, it is not surprising that the space of three years had been prescribed by the king. At length, he says, *at the end of them,* meaning of the three years. We have shewn how this ought not to be referred to the boys, as if the king afterwards selected some of them, for we shall see in its own place that a distinct time was fixed beforehand; hence no long refutation is needed. It is certain, then, that the Prophet speaks of the close of the three years. It had been said just before, *that they might stand in the palace;* but this ought also to be understood of the time of which mention has been made. They did not stand before the king immediately, but were reserved for this purpose. Since the king commanded them to be brought up for the purpose of using their services afterwards. Daniel twice repeats — they were splendidly educated—seeing the king wished them to become his servants at table and in other duties.

6. Now among these were, of the children of Judah, Daniel, Hananiah, Mishael, and Azariah;

7. Unto whom the prince of the eunuchs gave names: for he gave unto Daniel *the name* of Belteshazzar; and to Hananiah, of Shadrach; and to Mishael, of Meshach; and to Azariah, of Abednego.

6. Et fuit in illis ex filiis Jehudah Daniel, Hananiah, Misael, et Azariah.

7. Et imposuit illis princeps eunuchorum[1] nomina: imposuit inquam, Danieli Balthsazar, et Hananiæ Sadrak, et Misæl Mesack, et Azariæ Abednego.

[1] That is, the master of the eunuchs.—*Calvin.*

The Prophet now comes to what properly belongs to his purpose. He did not propose to write a full narrative, but he touched shortly on what was necessary, to inform us how God prepared him for the subsequent discharge of the prophetic office. After he had stated their selection from the royal and noble seed, as excelling in talent, dexterity, and eloquence, as well as in vigour of body, he now adds, that he and his companions were among them. He leaves out the rest, because he had nothing to record of them worthy of mention ; and, as I have said, the narrative hitherto is only subsidiary. The Prophet's object, then, must be noticed, since he was exiled, and educated royally and sumptuously in the palace of King Nebuchadnezzar, that he might afterwards be one of the prefects, and his companions be elevated to the same rank. He does not say that he was of the royal house, but only of the tribe of Judah ; but he was probably born of a noble rather than of a plebeian family, since kings more commonly selected their prefects from their own relations than from others. Moreover, since the kingdom of Israel was cut off, perhaps through a feeling of modesty, Daniel did not record his family, nor openly assert his origin from a noble and celebrated stock. He was content with a single word,— he and his companions were of the tribe of Judah, and brought up among the children of the nobility. He says —*their names were changed ;* so that by all means the king might blot out of their hearts the remembrance of their own race, and they might forget their own origin. As far as interpretations are concerned, I think I have said enough to satisfy you, as I am not willingly curious in names where there is any obscurity, and especially in these Chaldee words. As to the Hebrew names, we know Daniel's name to mean the judge, or judgment of God. Therefore, whether by the secret instinct of God, his parents had imposed this name, or whether by common custom, Daniel was called by this name, as God's judge. So also of the rest ; for Hananiah has a fixed meaning, namely, one who has obtained mercy from God ; so Misael means required or demanded by God ; and so Azariah, the help of God, or one

whom God helps. But all these things have already been
better explained to you, so I have only just touched on these
points, as the change has no adequate reason for it. It is
enough for us that the names were changed to abolish the
remembrance of the kingdom of Judah from their hearts.
Some Hebrews also assert these to have been the names of
wise men. Whether it was so or not, it was the king's plan
to draw away those boys that they should have nothing in
common with the elect people, but degenerate to the manners of the Chaldeans. Daniel could not help the prince or
master of the eunuchs changing his name, for it was not in
his power to hinder it ; the same must be said of his companions. But they had enough to retain the remembrance
of their race, which Satan, by this artifice, wished utterly to
blot out. And yet this was a great trial, because they suffered
from their badge of slavery. Since their names were changed,
either the king or his prefect Aspenaz wished to force them
under the yoke, as if he would put before their eyes the
judgment of their own slavery as often as they heard their
names. We see, then, the intention of the change of name,
namely, to cause these miserable exiles to feel themselves
in captivity, and cut off from the race of Israel ; and by
this mark or symbol they were reduced to slavery, to the
king of Babylon and his palace. This was, indeed, a hard
trial, but it mattered not to the servants of God to be
contemptuously treated before men, so long as they were not
infected with any corruption ; hence we conclude them to
have been divinely governed, as they stood pure and spotless.
For Daniel afterwards says—

8. But Daniel purposed in his heart that he would not defile himself with the portion of the king's meat, nor with the wine which he drank : therefore he requested of the prince of the eunuchs that he might not defile himself.	8. Et posuit Daniel super cor suum,[1] ne pollueretur in portione cibi regis, et in vino potuum ejus : et quæsivit a magistro[2] Eunuchorum, ne pollueretur.

Here Daniel shews his endurance of what he could neither
cast off nor escape ; but meanwhile he took care that he did

[1] Or in his heart : that is, determined or decreed with himself.—
Calvin.
[2] That is, asked the master.—*Calvin.*

not depart from the fear of God, nor become a stranger to his race, but he always retains the remembrance of his origin, and remains a pure, and unspotted, and sincere worshipper of God.   He says, therefore,—*he determined in his heart not to pollute himself with the king's food and drink, and that he asked the prefect,* under whose charge he was, that he should not be driven to this necessity.   It may be asked here, what there was of such importance in the diet to cause Daniel to avoid it ?   This seems to be a kind of superstition, or at least Daniel may have been too morose in rejecting the king's diet.   We know that to the pure all things are pure, and this rule applies to all ages.   We read nothing of this kind concerning Joseph, and very likely Daniel used all food promiscuously, since he was treated by the king with great honour.   This, then, was not perpetual with Daniel ; for he might seem an inconsiderate zealot, or this might be ascribed, as we have said, to too much moroseness.   If Daniel only for a time rejected the royal food, it was a mark of levity and inconsistency afterwards to allow himself that liberty from which he had for the time abstained.   But if he did this with judgment and reason, why did he not persist in his purpose ?   I answer, —Daniel abstained at first from the luxuries of the court to escape being tampered with.   It was lawful for him and his companions to feed on any kind of diet, but he perceived the king's intention.   We know how far enticements prevail to deceive us ; especially when we are treated daintily ; and experience shews us how difficult it is to be moderate when all is affluence around us, for luxury follows immediately on plenty.   Such conduct is, indeed, too common, and the virtue of abstinence is rarely exercised when there is an abundance of provisions.

But this is not the whole reason which weighed with Daniel.   Sobriety and abstinence are not simply praised here, since many twist this passage to the praise of fasting, and say Daniel's chief virtue consisted in preferring pulse to the delicacies of a palace.   For Daniel not only wished to guard himself against the delicacies of the table, since he perceived a positive danger of being eaten up by such enticements; hence he simply determined in his heart not to taste the diet of the court, desiring by his very food perpetually to recall the remembrance of his country. He wished so to live in Chaldea, as to consider himself an exile and a captive, sprung from the sacred family of Abraham. We see, then, the intention of Daniel. He desired to refrain from too great an abundance and delicacy of diet, simply to escape those snares of Satan, by which he saw himself surrounded. He was, doubtless, conscious of his own infirmity, and this also is to be reckoned to his praise, since through distrust of himself he desired to escape from all allurements and temptations. As far as concerned the king's intention, this was really a snare of the devil, as I have said: Daniel rejected it, and there is no doubt that God enlightened his mind by his Spirit as soon as he prayed to him. Hence, he was unwilling to cast himself into the snares of the devil, while he voluntarily abstained from the royal diet. This is the full meaning of the passage.

It may also be asked, Why does Daniel claim this praise as his own, which was shared equally with his companions? for he was not the only one who rejected the royal diet. It is necessary to take notice, how from his childhood he was governed by the Spirit of God, that the confidence and influence of his teaching might be the greater; hence he speaks peculiarly of himself, not for the sake of boasting, but to obtain confidence in his teaching, and to shew himself to have been for a long period formed and polished by God for the prophetic office. We must also remember that he was the adviser of his companions; for this course might never have come into their minds, and they might have been corrupted, unless they had been admonished by Daniel. God, therefore, wished Daniel to be a leader and master to his companions, to induce them to adopt the same abstinence. Hence also we gather, that as each of us is endued more fruitfully with the grace of the Spirit, so should we feel bound to instruct others. It will not be sufficient for any one to restrain himself and thus to discharge his own duty, under the teaching of God's Spirit, unless he also extend his hand to others, and endeavour to unite in an alliance of piety, and of the fear and worship of God.   Such an example is here proposed to us in Daniel, who not only rejected the delicacies of the palace, by which he might be intoxicated and even poisoned ; but he also advised and persuaded his companions to adopt the same course.   This is the reason why he calls tasting the king's food pollution or abomination, though, as I have said, there was nothing abominable in it of itself.   Daniel was at liberty to eat and drink at the royal table, but the abomination arose from the consequences.   Before the time of these four persons living in Chaldea, they doubtless partook of ordinary food after the usual manner, and were permitted to eat whatever was offered to them. They did not ask for pulse when at an inn, or on their journey ; but they began to desire it when the king wished to infect them with his delicacies, and to induce them if possible to prefer that condition to returning to their own friends.   When they perceived the object of his snares, then it became both a pollution and abomination to feed on those dainties, and to eat at the king's table.   Thus we may ascertain the reason why Daniel thought himself polluted if he fared sumptuously and partook of the royal diet ; he was conscious, as we have already observed, of his own infirmities, and wished to take timely precautions, lest he should be enticed by such snares, and fall away from piety and the worship of God, and degenerate into the manners of the Chaldeans, as if he were one of their nation, and of their native princes.   I must leave the rest till to-morrow.

PRAYER.

Grant, Almighty God, as long as our pilgrimage in this world continues, that we may feed on such diet for the necessities of the flesh as may never corrupt us ; and may we never be led aside from sobriety, but may we learn to use our abundance by preferring abstinence in the midst of plenty : Grant also, that we may patiently endure want and famine, and eat and drink with such liberty as always to set before us the glory of thy Name. Lastly, may our very frugality lead us to aspire after that fulness by which we shall be completely refreshed, when the glory of thy countenance shall appear to us in heaven, through Jesus Christ our Lord.—Amen.

Lecture Third.

9. Now God had brought Daniel into favour and tender love with the prince of the eunuchs.

9. Dederat autem Deus Danielem[1] in clementiam et miserationes coram prefecto eunuchorum.

DANIEL, yesterday, related what he had asked from the master to whose care he had been committed : he now inserts this sentence, to shew this demand to be quite unobjectionable, since the prefect of the eunuchs treated him kindly. The crime would have been fatal had Daniel been brought into the king's presence. Although very probably he did not use the word "pollution," and openly and directly call the royal diet a "defilement," yet it may be easily conjectured from these words which he now records, that he asked the prefect to be permitted to eat pulse, because he did not think himself permitted to partake of the royal diet. We yesterday gave the reason ; but the king of Babylon would immediately have been angry, had he known this. What ! he would say, I honour those captives, when I might abuse them as slaves ; nay, I nourish them delicately like my own children, and yet they reject my food, as if I were polluted. This, therefore, is the reason why Daniel here relates his being in favour with that prefect. For, as we shall see in the next verse, the prefect simply denied his request. Where was then any favour shewn ? But though he was not willing to acquiesce in the prayers of Daniel, he shewed a singular kindness in not taking him before the king, since courtiers are ready for any accusation for the sake of obtaining favour. Then, very probably, the prefect would know that this had been granted to Daniel by his servant. If then there was any connivance on the part of the prefect, this is the favour and pity of which Daniel now speaks. His intention, then, is by no means doubtful, since he did not hesitate to adopt a different course of life, in order to remain pure and spotless, and uncontaminated with the delicacies of the palace of Babylon. He expresses how he escaped the danger, because the prefect treated

[1] Had put Daniel.—*Calvin.*

him kindly, when he might have instantly caused his death. But we must notice the form of speech here used ;—*God placed him in favour and pity before that prefect.* He might have used the usual phrase, merely saying he was favourably treated ; but, as he found a barbarian so humane and merciful, he ascribes this benefit to God.   This phrase, as we have expounded it, is customary with the Hebrews ; as when it is said, (Ps. cvi. 46,) God gave the Jews favour in the sight of the heathen who had led them captive ; meaning, he took care that their conquerors should not rage so cruelly against them as they had done at first.   For we know how the Jews were often treated harshly, roughly, and contemptuously.   Since this inhumanity was here mitigated, the Prophet attributes it to God, who prepared mercies for his people.   The result is this,—Daniel obtained favour with the prefect, since God bent the heart of a man, otherwise unsoftened, to clemency and humanity.   His object in this narrative is to urge us to greater earnestness in duty, if we have to undergo any difficulties when God calls us.

It often happens that we cannot discharge everything which God requires and exacts without imminent danger to our lives.   Sloth and softness naturally creep over us, and induce us to reject the cross.   Daniel, therefore, gives us courage to obey God and his commands, and here states his favour with the prefect, since God granted his servant favour while faithfully performing his duty.   Hence let us learn to cast our care upon God when worldly terror oppresses us, or when men forbid us with threats to obey God's commands.   Here let us acknowledge the power of God's hand to turn the hearts of those who rage against us, and to free us from all danger.   This, then, is the reason why Daniel says the prefect was kind to him.   Meanwhile, we gather the general doctrine from this passage, that men's hearts are divinely governed, while it shews us how God softens their iron hardness, and turns the wolf into the lamb.   For when he brought his people out of Egypt, he gave them favour with the Egyptians, so that they carried with them their most precious vessels.   It is clear enough that the Egyptians were hostile towards the Israelites.   Why then did they so freely offer them the most valuable of their household goods? Only because the Lord inspired their hearts with new affections. So, again, the Lord can exasperate our friends, and cause them afterwards to rise up in hostility against us. Let us perceive, then, that on both sides the will is in God's power, either to bend the hearts of men to humanity, or to harden those which were naturally tender. It is true, indeed, that every one has a peculiar disposition from his birth: some are ferocious, warlike, and sanguinary; others are mild, humane, and tractable. This variety springs from God's secret ordination; but God not only forms every one's disposition at his birth, but every day and every moment, if it seems good to him, changes every one's affections. He also blinds men's minds, and rouses them again from their stupor. For we sometimes see the rudest men endued with much acuteness, and shew a singular contrivance in action, and others who excel in foresight, are at fault when they have need of judgment and discretion. We must consider the minds and hearts of men to be so governed by God's secret instinct, that he changes their affections just as he pleases. Hence there is no reason why we should so greatly fear our enemies, although they vomit forth their rage with open mouth, and are overflowing with cruelty; for they can be turned aside by the Lord. And thus let us learn from the example of Daniel to go on fearlessly in our course, and not to turn aside, even if the whole world should oppose us; since God can easily and readily remove all impediments: and we shall find those who were formerly most cruel, become humane when the Lord wishes to spare us. We now understand the sense of the words of this verse, as well as the Prophet's intention. It follows:

10. And the prince of the eunuchs said unto Daniel, I fear my Lord the king, who hath appointed your meat and your drink: for why should he see your faces worse liking than the

10. Et dixit præfectus eunuchorum Danieli, Timeo ego Dominum meum regem qui, constituit[1] cibum vestrum, et potus vestros: quare videbit facies vestras tristes,[2] præ

[1] For מנה, *minneh*, which is "to relate," means to "ordain," "appoint." —*Calvin.*

[2] Or emaciated, or austere, or sullen: for, it is derived from the word זעף, *zegneph*, which signifies "to be angry," and hence, by a change of object, faces are called emaciated, austere, or sullen.—*Calvin.*

| children which *are* of your sort? then shall ye make *me* endanger my head to the king. | pueris, qui sunt vobis similes,[1] et obnoxium[2] reddetis caput meum regi. |

Daniel suffers a repulse from the prefect ; and truly, as I have lately remarked, his humanity is not praised through his listening to Daniel's wish and prayer; but through his burying in silence whatever might have brought him into difficulties. And his friendship appears in this ; for although he denies his request, yet he does so mildly and civilly, as if he had said he would willingly grant it unless he had feared the king's anger. This, therefore, is the meaning,—the prefect, though he did not dare to comply with Daniel's request, yet treated both him and his companions kindly by not endangering their lives. He says,—*he was afraid of the king who had ordered the food.* He is not to be blamed as if he feared man more than the living God, for he could not have any knowledge of God. Although he may have been persuaded that Daniel made his request in the earnest pursuit of piety, yet he did not think himself authorized to comply ; for he thought the Jews had their peculiar method of worship, but meanwhile he clung entirely to the religion of Babylon. Just as many profane persons now think us quite right in casting away superstitions, but yet they slumber in this error,—it is lawful for themselves to live in the ancient manner, since they were so brought up and instructed by their forefathers. Hence they use rites which they allow to be disapproved by us. So also this prefect might feel rightly concerning Daniel and his associates ; at the same time he was not so touched by them as to desire to learn the difference between the two religions. Therefore he simply excuses himself, as not being at liberty to grant Daniel's request, since this would endanger his own head with the king. It now follows :—

| 11. Then said Daniel to Melzar, whom the prince of the eunuchs had | 11. Et dixit Daniel ad Meltsar, quem constituerat præfectus eu- |

[1] Others translate " equals," " those who are like you :" this may be the sense, because they are now like you, but will afterwards become fat and stout while you are lean. This change will endanger me.—*Calvin.*

[2] For כוב, *chob*, in Hebrew is " debtor:" whence this word is derived, signifying to " render subject."—*Calvin.*

set over Daniel, Hananiah, Mishael, and Azariah,

12. Prove thy servants, I beseech thee, ten days ; and let them give us pulse to eat, and water to drink.

13. Then let our countenances be looked upon before thee, and the countenance of the children that eat of the portion of the king's meat ; and as thou seest, deal with thy servants.

nuchorum super Danielem, Hananiah, Misael, et Azariah,

12. Proba[1] servos tuos diebus decem, et apponantur nobis de leguminibus,[2] et comedemus,[3] et aquæ, quas bibamus.

13. Et inspiciantur coram facie tua vultus nostri, et vultus puerorum, qui vescuntur portione[4] cibi regis : et quemadmodum videris fac cum servis tuis.

Since Daniel understood from the answer of the prefect that he could not obtain his wish, he now addresses his servant. For the prefect had many servants under him, according to the custom of important stewardships. Most probably the steward's duty was similar to that of the Chief Steward of the Household,[5] as it exists at this time in France. Daniel and his companions were under the care of one of these servants ; Daniel descends to this remedy and obtains his wish, though, as we shall see, not without some artifice. And here Daniel's singular constancy is observable, who after trying the matter once in vain, did not cease to pursue the same object. It is a clear and serious proof of our faith, when we are not fatigued when anything adverse occurs, and never consider the way closed against us. Then if we do not retrace our steps, but try all ways, we truly shew the root of piety fixed in our hearts. It might have seemed excusable in Daniel, after he had met with his first repulse ; for who would not have said he had discharged his duty, and that an obstacle had prevailed over him ! But since he did not prevail with the chief prefect, he goes to his servant. Thus voluntarily to incur risk was the result of no common prudence. For this servant could not make the same objection, as we have just heard the prefect did. Without doubt he had heard of Daniel's request, and of his repulse and denial ; hence Daniel is beforehand with him, and shews how the servant may comply without the slightest danger ; as if he had said,—We, indeed, did not obtain our wish from

---

[1] Or try.—*Calvin.*

[2] Which we may eat.—*Calvin.*

[5] Du grand Escuyer.—*Fr. Trans.*

[3] Simply pulse.—*Calvin.*

[4] A piece, as we said.—*Calvin.*

the prefect because he was afraid of his life, but I have now thought of a new scheme by which you may both gratify us and yet not become chargeable with any crime, as the whole matter will be unknown. *Try thy servants,* therefore, *for ten days,* and prove them ; *let nothing but pulse be given us to eat and water to drink.* If after that time our faces are fresh and plump, no suspicion will attach to thee, and no one will be persuaded that we are not treated delicately according to the king's commandment. Since, then, this proof will be sufficiently safe for thee, and cautious enough for us both, there is no reason why you should reject our prayers. Besides, without the slightest doubt, when Daniel brought this forward, he was directed by God's Spirit to this act of prudence, and was also impelled to make this request. By the singular gift of the Holy Spirit Daniel invented this method of bending the mind of the servant under whose care he was placed. We must hold, then, that this was not spoken rashly or of his own will, but by the instinct of the Holy Spirit. It would not have been duty but rashness, if Daniel had been the author of this plan, and had not been assured by the Lord of its prosperous issue. Without doubt he had some secret revelation on the subject ; and if the servant allowed him and his associates to feed on pulse, it was a happy answer to his prayers. Hence, I say, he would not have spoken thus, except under the guidance and command of the Spirit. And this is worthy of notice, since we often permit ourselves to do many things which turn out badly, because we are carried away by the mere feelings of the flesh, and do not consider what is pleasing to God. It is not surprising, then, when men indulge in various expectations, if they feel themselves deceived at last, since every one occasionally imposes upon himself by foolish hopes, and thus frustrates his designs. Indeed, it is not our province to promise ourselves any success. Hence let us notice how Daniel had not undertaken or approached the present business with any foolish zeal ; and did not speak without due consideration, but was assured of the event by the Spirit of God.

But he says, *let pulse be put before us to eat, and water to drink.* We see, then, that the four youths did not abstain from the royal food for fear of pollution ; for there was no law to prevent any one drinking wine, except the Nazarites, (Numb. vi. 2,) and they might eat of any kind of flesh, of which there was abundance at the royal table. Whence then sprang this scrupulousness ? because, as we said yesterday, Daniel was unwilling to accustom himself to the delicacies of the palace, which would cause him to become degenerate. He wished, therefore, to nourish his body not only frugally, but abstemiously, and not to indulge in these tastes ; for although he was raised to the highest honours, he was always the same as if still among the most wretched captives. There is no occasion for seeking other reasons for this abstinence of Daniel's. For he might have fed on ordinary bread and other less delicate food ; but he was content with pulse, and was continually lamenting and nourishing in his mind the remembrance of his country, of which he would have been directly forgetful if he had been plunged into those luxuries of the palace. It follows :

14. So he consented to them in this matter, and proved them ten days.	14. Et audivit eos in hoc verbo, et probavit eos decem diebus.
15. And at the end of ten days their countenances appeared fairer and fatter in flesh than all the children which did eat the portion of the king's meat.	15. Et a fine decem dierum visus est vultus eorum pulcher,[1] et *ipsi* pinguiores carne præ omnibus pueris,[2] qui comedebant portiones cibi regii.

Now this surprising event took place,—Daniel contracted neither leanness nor debility from that mean food, but his face was as shining as if he had continued to feed most delicately ; hence we gather as I have already said, that he was divinely impelled to persist firmly in his own design, and not to pollute himself with the royal diet. God, therefore, testified by the result that he had advised Daniel and his companions in this their prayer and proposal. It is clear enough that there is no necessary virtue in bread to nourish us ; for we are nourished by God's secret blessing, as Moses says, Man lives not by bread alone, (Deut. viii. 3,) implying that the bread itself does not impart

---

[1] Or plump.—*Calvin.*   [2] Namely, the rest.—*Calvin.*

strength to men, for the bread has no life in it; how then can it afford us life? As bread possesses no virtue by itself, we are nourished by the word of God; and because God has determined that our life shall be sustained by nourishment, he has breathed its virtue into the bread— but, meanwhile, we ought to consider our life sustained neither by bread nor any other food, but by the secret blessing of God. For Moses does not speak here of either doctrine or spiritual life, but says our bodily life is cherished by God's favour, who has endued bread and other food with their peculiar properties. This, at least, is certain, —whatever food we feed on, we are nourished and sustained by God's gratuitous power. But the example which Daniel here mentions was singular. Hence God, as I have said, shews, by the event, how Daniel could not remain pure and spotless with his companions, otherwise than by being content with pulse and water. We must observe, for our improvement, in the first place,—we should be very careful not to become slaves of the palate, and thus be drawn off from our duty and from obedience and the fear of God, when we ought to live sparingly and be free from all luxuries. We see at this day how many feel it a very great cross if they cannot indulge at the tables of the rich, which are filled with abundance and variety of food. Others are so hardened in the enjoyment of luxuries, that they cannot be content with moderation; hence they are always wallowing in their own filth, being quite unable to renounce the delights of the palate. But Daniel sufficiently shews us, when God not only reduces us to want, but when, if necessary, all indulgences must be spontaneously rejected. Daniel indeed, as we saw yesterday, does not attach any virtue to abstinence from one kind of food or another; and all we have hitherto learnt has no other object than to teach him to guard against imminent danger, to avoid passing over to the morals of a strange nation, and so to conduct himself at Babylon as not to forget himself as a son of Abraham. But still it was necessary to renounce the luxuries of the court. Although delicate viands were provided, he rejected them of his own accord; since, as we have seen, it would be deadly pollution,

not in itself but in its consequences. Thus Moses, when he
fled from Egypt, passed into a new life far different from his
former one; for he had lived luxuriously and honourably in
the king's palace, as if he had been the king's grandson.
But he lived sparingly in the Desert afterwards, and obtained
his support by very toilsome labour. He preferred, says the
Apostle, the cross of Christ to the riches of Egypt. (Heb.
xi. 26.) How so? Because he could not be esteemed an
Egyptian and retain the favour which had been promised to
the sons of Abraham. It was a kind of self-denial always to
remain in the king's palace.

We may take this test as a true proof of our frugality
and temperance, if we are able to satisfy the appetite when
God compels us to endure poverty and want ; nay, if we can
spurn the delicacies which are at hand but tend to our
destruction. For it would be very frivolous to subsist entirely on pulse and water ; as greater intemperance sometimes
displays itself in pulse than in the best and most dainty
dishes. If any one in weak health desires pulse and other
such food which is injurious, he will surely be condemned
for intemperance. But if he feeds on nourishing diet, as they
say, and thus sustains himself, frugality will have its praise.
If any one through desire of water, and being too voracious,
rejects wine, this as we well know would not be praiseworthy.
Hence we ought not to subsist on this kind of food to discover the greatness of Daniel's virtue. But we ought always
to direct our minds to the object of his design, namely, what
he wished and what was in his power—so to live under the
sway of the king of Babylon, that his whole condition should
be distinct from that of the nation at large, and never to
forget himself as an Israelite—and unless there had been
this great difference, Daniel would have been unable to
sharpen himself and to shake off his torpor, or to rouse himself from it. Daniel necessarily kept before his mind some
manifest and remarkable difference which separated him
from the Chaldeans ; he desired pulse and water, through
the injurious effects of good living.

Lastly, this passage teaches us, although we should meet
with nothing but the roots and leaves of trees, and even if

the earth herself should deny us the least blade of grass, yet God by his blessing can make us healthy and active no less than those who abound in every comfort. God's liberality, however, is never to be despised when he nourishes us with bread and wine and other diet ; for Paul enumerates, among things worthy of praise, his knowing how to bear both abundance and penury. (Phil. iv. 12.) When, therefore, God bountifully offers us both meat and drink, we may soberly and frugally drink wine and eat savoury food ; but when he takes away from us bread and water, so that we suffer from famine, we shall find his blessing sufficient for us instead of all nutriment. For we see that Daniel and his companions were ruddy and plump, and even remarkably robust by feeding on nothing but pulse. How could this occur, unless the Lord, who nourished his people in the Desert on manna alone, when other diet was deficient, even at this day turns our food into manna, which would otherwise be injurious to us. (Exod. xvi. 4.) For if any one asks the medical profession, whether pulse and other leguminous plants are wholesome ? they will tell us they are very injurious, since they know them to be so. But at the same time, when we have no choice of viands and cannot obtain what would conduce most to our health, if we are content with herbs and roots, the Lord, as I have said, can nourish us no less than if he put before us a table well supplied with every dainty. Temperance does not exist in the food itself, but in the palate—since we are equally intemperate if pleasure entices us to gratify the appetite on inferior food—so, again, we may remain perfectly temperate though feeding on the best diet. We must form the same opinion of the properties of various viands, which do not support us by their own inherent qualities, but by God's blessing, as he sees fit. We sometimes see the children of the rich very emaciated, although they may receive the greatest attention. We see also the children of the country people most beautiful in form, ruddy in countenance, and healthy in condition ; and yet they feed on any kind of food, and sometimes upon what is injurious. But although they are deprived of tasty sauces, yet God gives them his blessing, and their unripe fruit, pork, lard, and even herbs, which seem most unwholesome, become more nourishing than if the people abounded in every delicacy. This, therefore, must be remarked in the words of Daniel. It follows:

16. Thus Melzar took away the portion of their meat, and the wine that they should drink, and gave them pulse.	16. Et factum est, ut Melsar tolleret sibi portionem cibi illorum et vinum potionum eorum,[1] et daret illis legumina.

After Melsar saw it possible to gratify Daniel and his companions without danger and promote his own profit, he was humane and easily dealt with, and had no need of long disputation. For an intervening obstacle often deters us from the pursuit of gain, and we forbear to seek what we very much crave when it requires oppressive labour; but when our profit is at hand, and we are freed from all danger, then every one naturally pursues it. We see, then, what Daniel means in this verse, namely, when Melsar saw the usefulness of this plan, and the possibility of his gaining by the diet assigned by the king to the four youths, then he gave them pulse. But we must notice also Daniel's intention. He wishes to shew that we ought not to ascribe it to the kindness of man, that he and his companions could preserve themselves pure and unspotted. Why so? Because he never could have obtained anything from this man Melsar, until he perceived it could be granted safely. Since, therefore, Melsar consulted his own advantage and his private interest, and wished to escape all risks and hazards, we easily gather that the benefit is not to be ascribed entirely to him. Daniel and his companions obtained their wish, but God's providence rendered this man tractable, and governed the whole event. Meanwhile, God openly shews how all the praise was due to himself, purposely to exercise the gratitude of Daniel and his associates.

[1] That is wine, which the king had appointed them to drink.—*Calvin.*

PRAYER.

Grant, Almighty God, since we are now encompassed by so many enemies, and the devil does not cease to harass us with fresh snares, so that the whole world is hostile to us, that we may perceive even the devil himself to be restrained by thy bridle. Grant, also, that all the impious may be subjected to thee, that thou mayest lead them whithersoever thou wishest. Do thou direct their hearts, and may we be experimentally taught how safe and secure we are under the protection of thy hand. And may we proceed, according to thy promise, in the course of our calling, until at length we arrive at that blessed rest which is laid up for us in heaven, by Christ our Lord. — Amen.

Lecture Fourth.

17. As for these four children, God gave them knowledge and skill in all learning and wisdom: and Daniel had understanding in all visions and dreams.

17. Et pueris illis quatuor, dedit, *inquam*, illis Deus cognitionem et scientiam in omni literatura et sapientia: et Daniel intellexit in omni visione et somniis.

THE Prophet here shews what we have already touched upon, how his authority was acquired for exercising the prophetic office with greater advantage. He ought to be distinguished by fixed marks, that the Jews first, and foreigners afterwards, might acknowledge him to be endued with the prophetic spirit. But a portion of this favour was shared with his three companions; yet he excelled them all, because God fitted him specially for his office. Here the end is to be noticed, because it would be incorrect to say that their reward was bestowed by God, because they lived both frugally and heavenly, and spontaneously abstained from the delicacies of the palace; for God had quite a different intention. For he wished, as I have already said, to extol Daniel, to enable him to shew with advantage that Israel's God is the only God; and as he wished his companions to excel hereafter in political government, he presented them also with some portion of his Spirit. But it is worth while to set Daniel before our eyes; because, as I have said, before God appointed him his Prophet, he wished to adorn

him with his own *insignia*, to procure confidence in his
teaching.   He says, therefore, *to those four boys*, or youths,
knowledge and science were given in all literature and wisdom.
Daniel was endued with a very singular gift—he was to
be an interpreter of dreams, and an explainer of visions.
Since Daniel here speaks of literature, without doubt he
simply means the liberal arts, and does not comprehend
the magical arts which flourished then and afterwards in
Chaldea. We know that nothing was sincere among unbelievers ; and, on the other hand, I have previously admonished
you, that Daniel was not imbued with the superstitions
in those days highly esteemed in that nation.   Through dis-
content with genuine science, they corrupted the study of
the stars ; but Daniel and his associates were so brought up
among the Chaldeans, that they were not tinctured with
those mixtures and corruptions which ought always to be
separated from true science.   It would be absurd, then, to
attribute to God the approval of magical arts, which it is
well known were severely prohibited and condemned by the
law itself. (Deut. xviii. 10.)   Although God abominates
those magical superstitions as the works of the devil, this
does not prevent Daniel and his companions from being
divinely adorned with this gift, and being very well versed in
all the literature of the Chaldees.   Hence this ought to be
restricted to true and natural science.   As it respects Daniel,
he says, he *understood even visions and dreams :* and we
know how by these two methods the Prophets were instructed in the will of God.   (Num. xii. 6.)   For while God
there blames Aaron and Miriam, he affirms this to be his
usual method ; as often as he wishes to manifest his designs
to the Prophets, he addresses them by visions and dreams.
But Moses is treated out of the common order of men,
because he is addressed face to face, and mouth to mouth.
God, therefore, whenever he wished to make use of his Prophets, by either visions or dreams, made known to them what
he wished to be proclaimed to the people.   When, therefore, it is here said,—*Daniel understood dreams and visions*, it has the sense of being endued with the prophetic
spirit.   While his companions were superior masters and

teachers in all kinds of literature, he alone was a Prophet of God.

We now understand the object of this distinction, when an acquaintance with visions and dreams was ascribed peculiarly to Daniel. And here our previous assertion is fully confirmed, namely, that Daniel was adorned with the fullest proofs of his mission, to enable him afterwards to undertake the prophetic office with greater confidence, and acquire greater attention to his teaching. God could, indeed, prepare him in a single moment, and by striking terror and reverence into the minds of all, induce them to embrace his teaching; but he wished to raise his servant by degrees, and to bring him forth at the fitting time, and not too suddenly : so that all might know by marks impressed for many years how to distinguish him from the common order of men. It afterwards follows :

18. Now, at the end of the days that the king had said he should bring them in, then the prince of the eunuchs brought them in before Nebuchadnezzar.

18. Et a fine dierum, quibus edixerat Rex ut producerentur, introduxit eos princeps[1] eunuchorum coram Nebuchadnezzar.

19. And the king communed with them ; and among them all was found none like Daniel, Hananiah, Mishael, and Azariah : therefore stood they before the king.

19. Et loquutus est cum illis rex : et non inventus est ex omnibus sicut Daniel, Hananiah, Misael, et Azariah, et steterunt coram rege.

20. And in all matters of wisdom *and* understanding, that the king enquired of them, he found them ten times better than all the magicians *and* astrologers that *were* in all his realm.

20. Et in omni verbo, sapientia et intelligentia, quod sciscitatus est ab eis rex, invenit eos decuplo supra omnes genethliacos et astrologos[2] qui erant in toto regno ejus.

Now, Daniel relates how he and his companions were brought forward at a fixed time, since three years was appointed by the king for their instruction in all the science of the Chaldees : and on that account the prefect of the eunuchs produces them. He shews how he and his companions were approved by the king, and were preferred to all the rest. By these words he confirms my remark, that the Lord through a long interval had adorned them with much favour, by rendering them conspicuous throughout the royal

[1] Or, prefect.—*Calvin.*
[2] That is, superior to all the soothsayers and astrologers.—*Calvin.*

palace, while the king himself acknowledged something uncommon in them.   He, as well as the courtiers, ought all
to entertain such an opinion concerning these four youths,
as should express his sincere reverence for them.   Then
God wished to illustrate his own glory, since without doubt
the king was compelled to wonder how they could surpass all the Chaldeans.   This monarch had spared no expense on his own people, and had not neglected to instruct
them ; but when he saw foreigners and captives so superior,
a spirit of rivalry would naturally spring up within him.
But, as I have already said, God wished to extol himself in
the person of his servants, so that the king might be compelled to acknowledge something divine in these young men.
Whence, then, was this superiority? for the Chaldeans boasted
of their wisdom from their birth, and esteemed other nations
as barbarians.   The Jews, they would argue, are eminent
beyond all others ; verily the God whom they worship distributes at his will talent and perception, since no one is
naturally gifted unless he receives this grace from heaven.
God, therefore, must necessarily be glorified, because Daniel
and his comrades very far surpassed the Chaldeans.   Thus
God usually causes his enemies to gaze with wonder on his
power, even when they most completely shun the light.   For
what did King Nebuchadnezzar propose, but to extinguish
the very remembrance of God?   For he wished to have
about him Jews of noble family, who should oppose the very
religion in which they were born.   But God frustrated this
plan of the tyrant's, and took care to make his own name
more illustrious.   It now follows:

21. And Daniel continued *even*   21. Et fuit Daniel usque ad an-
unto the first year of king Cyrus.   num primum Cyri regis.

Expositors are puzzled with this verse, because, as we
shall afterwards see, the Vision occurred to Daniel in the
third year of Cyrus's reign.   Some explain the word היה,
haiah, by to be " broken ;" but this is by no means in accordance with the history.   Their opinion is right who say
that Daniel continued to the first year of the reign of Cyrus
in the discharge of the prophetic office, although expositors
do not openly say so ; but I state openly what they say ob-

scurely. For since he afterwards set out into Media, they say this change is denoted here. But we may understand the words better in the sense of Daniel's flourishing among the Chaldeans and Assyrians, and being acknowledged as a celebrated Prophet; because he is known to have interpreted King Belshazzar's vision, on the very night on which he was slain. The word here is simple and complete —*he was*—but it depends on the succeeding ones, since he always obtained the confidence and authority of a Prophet with the kings of Babylon. This, then, is the true sense.[1]

CHAPTER SECOND.

In this second chapter we are informed how God brought Daniel into a theatre, to exhibit that prophetic office to which he had been destined. God had already engraven, as we have said, distinct marks by which Daniel might be acknowledged as a Prophet, but he wished really to prove the effect of the grace which he had conferred upon Daniel. First of all, a simple history is narrated, then Daniel proceeds to the interpretation of a dream. This is the heading of the chapter.

1. And in the second year of the reign of Nebuchadnezzar, Nebuchadnezzar dreamed dreams, wherewith his spirit was troubled, and his sleep brake from him.

1. Anno autem secundo regni Nebuchadnezzar somniavit Nebuchadnezzar somnia : et contritus fuit spiritus ejus, et somnus ejus interruptus est ei.[2]

Daniel here says,—King Nebuchadnezzar dreamt in the second year of his reign. This seems contrary to the opinion expressed in the first chapter. For if Nebuchadnezzar besieged Jerusalem in the first year of his reign, how could Daniel be already reckoned among the wise men and astrologers, while he was as yet but a disciple? Thus it is easily gathered from the context that he and his companions were already brought forward to minister before the king. At the first glance these things are not in accordance, because in the first year of Nebuchadnezzar's reign Daniel and his companions were delivered into training; and

[1] See the DISSERTATIONS at the end of this Volume.
[2] As they translate, or " departed from him," or was upon him.—*Calvin.*

in the second he was in danger of death through being in the number of the Magi. Some, as we have mentioned elsewhere, count the second year from the capture and destruction of the city, for they say Nebuchadnezzar was called king from the time at which he obtained the monarchy in peace. Before he had cut off the City and Temple with the Nation, his Monarchy could not be treated as united ; hence they refer this to the capture of the city, as I have said. But I rather incline to another conjecture as more probable —that of his reigning with his father, and I have shewn that when he besieged Jerusalem in the time of Jehoiachim, he was sent by his father ; he next returned to Chaldea from the Egyptian expedition, through his wish to repress revolts, if any one should dare to rebel. In this, therefore, there is nothing out of place. Nebuchadnezzar reigned before the death of his father, because he had already been united with him in the supreme power ; then he reigned alone, and the present narrative happened in the second year of his reign. In this explanation there is nothing forced, and as the history agrees with it, I adopt it as the best.

He says—*he dreamt dreams,* and yet only one Dream is narrated ; but since many things were involved in this dream, the use of the plural number is not surprising. It is now added, *his spirit was contrite,* to shew us how uncommon the dream really was. For Nebuchadnezzar did not then begin to dream, and was not formerly so frightened every night as to send for all the Magi. Hence, in this dream there was something extraordinary, which Daniel wished to express in these words. The clause at the end of the verse which they usually translate *his sleep was interrupted,* does not seem to have this sense ; another explanation which our brother D. Antonius gave you[1] suits it better ; namely,—his sleep was upon him, meaning he began to sleep again. The genuine and simple sense of the words seems to me—*his spirit was confused,* that is, very great terror had seized on his mind. He knew, indeed, the dream to be sent from heaven ; next, being astonished, he slept

---

[1] This clause "which our brother D. Antonius gave you," is omitted in the French editions of 1562 and 1569.

again, and became like a dead man, and when he considered the interpretation of the dream, he became stupified and returned to sleep and forgot the vision, as we shall afterwards see.   It follows—

2. Then the king commanded to call the magicians, and the astrologers, and the sorcerers, and the Chaldeans, for to shew the king his dreams. So they came and stood before the king.	2. Et edixit rex ut vocarentur[1] astrologi, et conjectores, et divini, et Chaldei, annuntiarent regi somnia sua:[2] et venerunt et steterunt in conspectu regis.

This verse more clearly proves what I have already said—that the dream caused the king to feel God to be its author.   Though this was not his first dream, yet the terror which God impressed on his mind, compelled him to summon all the Magi, since he could not rest even by returning to sleep.   He felt as it were a sting in his mind, since God did not suffer him to rest, but wished him to be troubled until he received an interpretation of the dream.   Even profane writers very correctly consider dreams connected with divine agency.   They express various opinions, because they could not know anything with perfect certainty; yet the persuasion was fixed in their minds relative to some divine agency in dreams.   It would be foolish and puerile to extend this to all dreams; as we see some persons never passing by a single one without a conjecture, and thus making themselves ridiculous.   We know dreams to arise from different causes; as, for instance, from our daily thoughts.   If I have meditated on anything during the daytime, something occurs to me at night in a dream; because the mind is not completely buried in slumber, but retains some seed of intelligence, although it be suffocated.   Experience also sufficiently teaches us how our daily thoughts recur during sleep, and hence the various affections of the mind and body produce many dreams.   If any one retires to bed in sorrow from either the death of a friend, or any loss, or through suffering any injury or adversity, his dreams will partake of the previous preparation of his mind.   The body itself causes dreams, as we see in the case of those

[1] I hardly know by what equivalent expressions to render these Hebrew words.   I will speak, therefore, of the thing itself.—*Calvin.*
[2] That is, to expound his dreams to the king.—*Calvin.*

who suffer from fever; when thirst prevails they imagine fountains, burnings, and similar fancies. We perceive also how intemperance disturbs men in their sleep; for drunken men start and dream in their sleep, as if in a state of phrensy. As there are many natural causes for dreams, it would be quite out of character to be seeking for divine agency or fixed reason in them all; and on the other hand, it is sufficiently evident that some dreams are under divine regulation. I omit events which have been related in ancient histories; but surely the dream of Calphurnia, the wife of Julius Cæsar, could not be fictitious; because, before he was slain it was commonly reported, " Cæsar has been killed," just as she dreamt it. The same may be said of the physician of Augustus, who had ordered him to leave his tent the day of the battle of Pharsalia, and yet there was no reason why the physician should order him to be carried out of the tent on a litter, unless he had dreamt it to be necessary. What was the nature of that necessity? why, such as could not be conjectured by human skill, for the camp of Augustus was taken at that very moment. I doubt not there are many fabulous accounts, but here I may choose what I shall believe, and I do not yet touch on dreams which are mentioned in God's word, for I am merely speaking of what profane men were compelled to think on this subject. Although Aristotle freely rejected all sense of divination, through being prejudiced in the matter, and desiring to reduce the nature of Deity within the scope of human ingenuity, and to comprehend all things by his acuteness; yet he expresses this confession, that all dreams do not happen rashly, but that μαντίκη, that is " divination," is the source of some of them. He disputes, indeed, whether they belong to the intellectual or sensitive portion of the mind, and concludes they belong to the latter, as far as it is imaginative. Afterwards, when inquiring whether they are causes or anything of that kind, he is disposed to view them only as symptoms or accidents fortuitously contingent. Meanwhile, he will not admit dreams to be sent from heaven; and adds as his reason, that many stupid men dream, and manifest the same reason in them as the wisest. He notices next the brute creation, some of which, as elephants, dream. As the brutes dream, and wise men more seldom than the rudest idiots, Aristotle does not think it probable that dreams are divinely inspired. He denies, therefore, that they are sent from God, or divine, but asserts that they spring from the *Daimones ;*[1] that is, he fancies them to be something between the natures of the Deity and the Daimones. We know the sense in which philosophers use that word, which, in Scripture, has usually a bad sense. He says that dreams were occasioned by those aërial inspirations, but are not from God ; because, he says, man's nature is not divine, but inferior ; and yet more than earthly, since it is angelic. Cicero discourses on this subject at great length, in his first book on Divination ; although he refutes in the second all he had said, while he was a disciple of the Academy.[2] For among other arguments in proof of the existence of deities, he adds dreams ;—if there is any divination in dreams, it follows that there is a Deity in heaven, for the mind of man cannot conceive of any dream without divine inspiration. Cicero's reasoning is valid ; if there is divination in dreams, then is there also a Deity. The distinction made by Macrobius is worthy of notice ; although he ignorantly confounds species and genera, through being a person of imperfect judgment, who strung together in rhapsodies whatever he read, without either discrimination or arrangement. This, then, should remain fixed,—the opinion concerning the existence of some kind of divine agency in dreams was not rashly implanted in the hearts of all men. Hence that expression of Homer's, a dream is from Jupiter.[3] He does not mean this generally and promiscuously of all dreams ; but he takes notice of it, when bringing the characters of his heroes before us, since they were divinely admonished in their sleep.

I now come to NEBUCHADNEZZAR's DREAM. In this, two points are worthy of remark : First, all remembrance of its

---

[1] Calvin uses the Greek words διόπεμπτα, θεῖα, and δαιμόνια. The Greek *Daimones* corresponded with our idea of angels, and were said to be the origin of human souls. See most interesting passages in the Dialogues of Plato, also the DISSERTATION on this verse at the close of the Volume.

[2] De Divin., lib. i. § 21-23 ; and lib. ii. § 58, *et seq.*

[3] Iliad, book i. v. 63.

subject was entirely obliterated; and secondly, no interpretation was found for it. Sometimes the remembrance of
a dream was not lost while its interpretation was unknown.
But here Nebuchadnezzar was not only perplexed at the
interpretation of the dream, but even the vision itself had
vanished, and thus his perplexity and anxiety was doubled.
As to the next point, there is no novelty in Daniel making
known the interpretation; for it sometimes, but rarely,
happens that a person dreams without a figure or enigma,
and with great plainness, without any need of conjurors—a
name given to interpreters of dreams. This indeed happens but seldom, since the usual plan of dreams is for God
to speak by them allegorically and obscurely. And this
occurs in the case of the profane as well as of the servants
of God. When Joseph dreamt that he was adored by the
sun and moon, (Gen. xxxvii. 9,) he was ignorant of its
meaning; when he dreamt of his sheaf being adored by his
brothers' sheaves, he understood not its meaning, but related
it simply to his brothers. Hence God often speaks in enigmas by dreams, until the interpretation is added. And such
was Nebuchadnezzar's dream.

We perceive, then, that God reveals his will even to unbelievers, but not clearly; because seeing they do not see,
just as if they were gazing at a closed book or sealed letter; as Isaiah says,—God speaks to unbelievers in broken
accents and with a stammering tongue. (Is. xxviii. 11,
and xxix. 11.) God's will was so revealed to Nebuchadnezzar that he still remained perplexed and lay completely
astonished. His dream would have been of no use to him,
unless, as we shall see, Daniel had been presented to him
as its interpreter. For God not only wished to hold the
king in suspense, but he thus blotted out the remembrance of the dream from his mind, to increase the power
of his sting. As mankind are accustomed to neglect the
dreams which they do not remember, God inwardly fastened
such a sting in the mind of this unbeliever, as I have
already said, that he could not rest, but was always wakeful
in the midst of his dreaming, because God was drawing him
to himself by secret chains. This is the true reason why God

denied him the immediate explanation of his dream, and blotted out the remembrance of it from his mind, until he should receive both from Daniel. We will leave the rest till to-morrow.

PRAYER.

Grant, Almighty God, since every perfect gift comes from thee, and since some excel others in intelligence and talents, yet as no one has anything of his own, but as thou deignest to distribute to man a measure of thy gracious liberality,—Grant that whatever intelligence thou dost confer upon us, we may apply it to the glory of thy name. Grant also, that we may acknowledge in humility and modesty what thou hast committed to our care to be thine own; and may we study to be restrained by sobriety, to desire nothing superfluous, never to corrupt true and genuine knowledge, and to remain in that simplicity to which thou callest us. Finally, may we not rest in these earthly things, but learn rather to raise our minds to true wisdom, to acknowledge thee to be the true God, and to devote ourselves to the obedience of thy righteousness; and may it be our sole object to devote and consecrate ourselves entirely to the glory of thy name throughout our lives, through Jesus Christ our Lord.—Amen.

Lecture Fifth.

WE yesterday saw the Magi sent for by the king's edict, not only in order to explain his dream to him, but also to narrate the dream itself which had slipt from his memory. But since four kinds of Magi are used here, or at least three, and their description is added in the fourth place, I shall briefly touch upon what seems to me their meaning. הרטמים, *Hartummim*, is usually explained by " soothsayers," and afterwards אשפים, *Assaphim*, they think, means " physicians." I am unwilling to contend against the first interpretation ; but I see no reason for the second. They interpret it as "physicians," because they judge of men's health by feeling the pulse, but having no better reason than this, I adopt the opinion that it refers to astrologers. In the third place, מכשפים, *Mecasphim*, is used, meaning "sorcerers," though some change the signifi-

cation, and say it means "star-gazers," who indicate future
events and predict unknown ones from the position of
the stars. I have nothing to bring forward more probable
than this, except the uncertainty of what the Hebrews meant
by the word : for since the matter itself is so buried in oblivion, who can distinguish between words which belong to
the profession of an unknown art ? כשדים, *Casdim*, is
doubtless put for a race, for it is the name of a nation, yet
on account of its excellence, the Magi appropriated it to
themselves, as if the nobility and excellence of the whole
nation was in their power ; and this name is known to be in
common use in Greece and Italy. All who professed their
ability to predict future or hidden events from the stars or
other conjectures, were called Chaldees. With respect to
the three other words, I do not doubt their honourable
meaning, and for this reason they called themselves Mathematicians, as if there were no science in the world except
with them. Besides, although their principles were good,
they were certainly stuffed with many superstitions, for they
were soothsayers and diviners, and we know them to have
given especial attention to augury. Although they were
highly esteemed by their fellow-countrymen, yet they are
condemned by God's law, for all their pretence to science was
complete imposture. They are generally called Magi, and
also Chaldeans, as shortly afterwards, when Daniel will repeat what they have spoken before the king, he will not
enumerate those three species, but will simply call them
Chaldees. It is surprising that Daniel and his companions
were not called among them, for he ought to have been
called among the first, since the king, as we have said, found
these four to be ten times better than all the Magi and
Diviners throughout his kingdom ! Since their dexterity
was not unknown to the king, why does he pass them
completely by, while the other Magi are at hand and are
called in to a case so arduous ? Very probably the king
omitted them because he trusted more in the natives ; or
suspected the captives, and was unwilling to entrust them
with his secrets, as he had not yet sufficiently tried their
fidelity and constancy. This might have been the reason,

but it is better for us to consider the intention of the Almighty, for I have no doubt that this forgetfulness on the part of the king occurred by God's providence, as he was unwilling from the first to mingle his servant Daniel and the rest with the Magi and Soothsayers. This accounts for Daniel not being sent for with the rest ; whence, as we shall see, his divination would afterwards become more illustrious. It now follows :

3. And the king said unto them, I have dreamed a dream, and my spirit was troubled to know the dream.	3. Et dixit illis rex, Somnium somniavi, et contritus est spiritus meus, ad sciendum[1] somnium.

I will add the next verse :

4. Then spake the Chaldeans to the king in Syriack, O king, live for ever : tell thy servants the dream, and we will shew the interpretation.	4. Et dixerunt Chaldæi regi Syriace, Rex in eternum vive : dic somnium servis tuis, et expositionem indicabimus.

Daniel relates first the great confidence of the Chaldeans, since they dared to promise the interpretation of a dream as yet unknown to them. *The king says he was troubled through desire to understand the dream ;* by which he signifies that a kind of riddle was divinely set before him. He confesses his ignorance, while the importance of the object may be gathered from his words. Since, then, the king testifies his desire to inquire concerning a matter obscure and profound, and exceeding his comprehension, and since he clearly expresses himself to be contrite in spirit, some kind of fear and anxiety ought to have touched these Chaldeans ; yet they securely promise to offer the very best interpretation of the dream as soon as they understood it. When they say, *O king, live for ever,* it is not a simple and unmeaning prayer, but they rather order the king to be cheerful and in good spirits, as they are able to remove all care and anxiety from his mind, because the explanation of the dream was at hand. We know how liberal in words those impostors always were ; according to the language of an ancient poet, they enriched the ears and emptied the purses of others. And truly those who curiously court the breeze with their ears deserve to feed upon it, and to be taken in by such deceits. And all ages have proved that nothing

---

[1] For understanding.—*Calvin.*

exceeds the confidence of astrologers, who are not content with true science, but divine every one's life and death, and conjecture all events, and profess to know everything.

We must hold generally that the art of conjecturing from dreams is rash and foolish ; there is, indeed, a certain fixed interpretation of dreams, as we said yesterday, yet as we shall afterwards see, this ought not to be ascribed to a sure science, but to God's singular gift. As, therefore, a prophet will not gather what he has to say from fixed reasonings, but will explain God's oracles, so also he who will interpret dreams correctly, will not follow certain distinct rules ; but if God has explained the meaning of the dream, he will then undertake the office of interpreting it according to his endowment with this gift. Properly speaking, these two things are opposite to each other and do not mutually agree, general and perpetual science, and special revelation. Since God claims this power of opening by means of a dream, what he has engraven on the minds of men, hence art and science cannot obtain it, but a revelation from the spirit must be waited for. When the Chaldeans thus boldly promise to become good interpreters of the dream, they not only betray their rashness, but become mere impostors, who pretend to be proficients in a science of which they know nothing, as if they could predict by their conjectures the meaning of the king's dream. It now follows :

5. The king answered and said to the Chaldeans, The thing is gone from me: if ye will not make known unto me the dream, with the interpretation thereof, ye shall be cut in pieces, and your houses shall be made a dunghill.

5. Respondit rex et dixit Chaldæis, Sermo a me exiit,[1] si non indicaveritis mihi somnium et interpretationem ejus, frusta efficiemini,[2] et domus vestræ ponentur sterquilinium.[3]

Here the king requires from the Chaldeans more than they professed to afford him ; for although their boasting, as we have said, was foolish in promising to interpret any dream, yet they never claimed the power of narrating to any one his dreams. The king, therefore, seems to me to act unjustly

---

[1] Or, has departed.—*Calvin.*

[2] Some translate הרמין, *hedmin,* by " blood ;" but the received meaning is better, and since there is little difference in the matter itself, I shall not trouble you concerning it.—*Calvin.*

[3] That is, shall be made a dunghill.—*Calvin.*

in not regarding what they had hitherto professed, and the limits of their art and science, if indeed they had any science! When he says—the matter or speech had departed from him, the words admit of a twofold sense, for מִלְּתָה, *millethah*, may be taken for an "edict," as we shall afterwards see; and so it might be read, *has flowed away;* but since the same form of expression will be shortly repeated when it seems to be used of the dream, (ver. 8,) this explanation is suitable enough, as the king says his dream had vanished: so I leave the point undecided.   It is worth while noticing again what we said yesterday, that terror was so fastened upon the king as to deprive him of rest, and yet he was not so instructed that the least taste of the revelation remained; just as if an ox, stunned by a severe blow, should toss himself about, and roll over and over.   Such is the madness of this wretched king, because God harasses him with dreadful torments; all the while the remembrance of the dream is altogether obliterated from his mind.   Hence he confesses—*his dream had escaped him;* and although the Magi had prescribed the limits of their science, yet through their boasting themselves to be interpreters of the gods, he did not hesitate to exact of them what they had never professed.   This is the just reward of arrogance, when men puffed up with a perverse confidence assume before others more than they ought, and forgetful of all modesty wish to be esteemed angelic spirits.   Without the slightest doubt God wished to make a laughingstock of this foolish boasting which was conspicuous among the Chaldees, when the king sharply demanded of them to relate his dream, as well as to offer an exposition of it.

He afterwards adds threats, clearly tyrannical; *unless they expound the dream, their life is in danger.*   No common punishment is threatened, but he says they should become "pieces"—if we take the meaning of the word to signify "pieces."   If we think it means "blood," the sense will be the same.   This wrath of the king is clearly furious, nay, Nebuchadnezzar in this respect surpassed all the cruelty of wild beasts.   What fault could be imputed to the Chaldeans if they did not know the king's dream?—surely, they had

never professed this, as we shall afterwards see ; and no king
had ever demanded what was beyond the faculty of man.
We perceive how the king manifested a brutal rage when
he denounced death and every cruel torture on the Magi and
sorcerers.   Tyrants, indeed, often give the reins to their
lust, and think all things lawful to themselves ; whence, also,
these words of the tragedian, Whatever he wishes is lawful.   And Sophocles says, with evident truth, that any one
entering a tyrant's threshold must cast away his liberty ;
but if we were to collect all examples, we should scarcely
find one like this.   It follows, then, that the king's mind was
impelled by diabolic fury, urging him to punish the Chaldees who, with respect to him, were innocent enough.   We
know them to have been impostors, and the world to have
been deluded by their impositions, which rendered them deserving of death, since by the precepts of the law it was a
capital crime for any one to pretend to the power of prophecy
by magic arts.   (Lev. xx. 6.)   But, as far as concerned the
king, they could not be charged with any crime.   Why, then,
did he threaten them with death ? because the Lord wished
to shew the miracle which we shall afterwards see.   For if
the king had suffered the Chaldeans to depart, he could have
buried directly that anxiety which tortured and excruciated
his mind.   The subject, too, had been less noticed by the
people ; hence God tortured the king's mind, till he rushed
headlong in his fury, as we have said.   Thus, this atrocious and cruel denunciation ought to have aroused all
men ; for there is no doubt that the greatest and the least
trembled together when they heard of such vehemence in
the monarch's wrath.   This, therefore, is the complete sense,
and we must mark the object of God's providence in thus
allowing the king's anger to burn without restraint.[1]   It
follows :

[1] Calvin is correct in preferring the sense of " pieces " to that of " blood ;"
for הדם, *hedem*, is a Chaldee word, and the ן is the Chaldee plural ending ;
his criticism, too, on מלה, *meleh*, is also correct ; for it is the Chaldee
equivalent for דבר, *deber*, a " word " or thing, and justly rendered " edict."
As great light has been thrown upon the meaning and derivation of single
words since Calvin's time, we may often find that modern knowledge has
rendered his derivations untenable ; still the soundness of his judgment is

6. But if ye shew the dream, and the interpretation thereof, ye shall receive of me gifts and rewards, and great honour: therefore shew me the dream, and the interpretation thereof.

6. Et si somnium, et interpretationem ejus indicaveritis, donum, et munus, et honorem, vel *pretium*, magnum accipietis a facie mea:[1] propterea somnium, et interpretationem ejus indicate mihi.

Here the king, on the other hand, desires to entice them by the hope of gain, to apply themselves to narrate his dream. He had already attempted to strike them with horror, that even if they are unwilling he may wrest the narration of the dream from them, as well as its interpretation. Meanwhile, if they could be induced by flattery, he tries this argument upon them ; for he promises *a gift, and reward, and honour*, that is, he promises a large remuneration if they narrated his dream, and were faithful interpreters. Hence we gather, what all history declares, that the Magi made a gain of their predictions and guesses. The wise men of the Indies, being frugal and austere in their manner of living, were not wholly devoted to gain ; for they are known to have lived without any need of either money, or furniture, or anything else. They were content with roots, and had no need of clothing, slept upon the ground, and were thus free from avarice. But the Chaldeans, we know, ran hither and thither to obtain money from the simple and credulous. Hence the king here speaks according to custom when he promises a large reward. We must remark here, how the Chaldeans scattered their prophecies for the sake of gain ; and when knowledge is rendered saleable, it is sure to be adulterated with many faults. As when Paul speaks of corruptors of the Gospel, he says,—they trafficked in it, (2 Cor. ii. 17,) because when a profit is made, as we have previously said, even honourable teachers must necessarily degenerate and pervert all sincerity by their lying. For where avarice reigns, there is flattery, servile obsequiousness, and cunning of all kinds, while truth is utterly extinguished. Whence it

worthy of notice. It may be added, too, that the perplexity is increased when Chaldee forms are used, although there is a uniform change of single letters observable in the two languages. Thus שׁ, *sh*, becomes ת, *th*, as in verses 7 and 14; the Hebrew ז, *z*, becomes ד, *d*, in ver. 26; so the צ, *tz*, becomes ע, *gn ;* the final ה, *h*, is turned into א, *a*, and the final ם, *m*, into ן, *n*.

[1] That is, by me.—*Calvin.*

is not surprising if the Chaldeans were so inclined to deceit, as it became natural to them through the pursuit of gain and the lust for wealth. Some honest teachers may receive support from the public treasury ; but, as we have said, when any one is drawn aside by lucre, he must necessarily pervert and deprave all purity of doctrine. And from this passage we gather, further, the anxiety of the king, as he had no wish to spare expense, if by this means he could elicit the interpretation of his dream from the Chaldeans; all the while he is furiously angry with them, because he does not obtain what the offered reward ought to procure. It now follows :

7. They answered again, and said, Let the king tell his servants the dream, and we will shew the interpretation of it.

8. The king answered and said, I know of certainty that ye would gain the time, because ye see the thing is gone from me.

7. Responderunt secundo, et dixerunt, Rex somnium exponat[1] servis suis, et interpretationem indicabimus.

8. Respondit rex et dixit, Vere[2] novi ego[3] quod tempus redimitis, quia scitis quod exierit sermo a me.[4]

We may add the following verse ;

9. But if ye will not make known unto me the dream, *there is but* one decree for you; for ye have prepared lying and corrupt words to speak before me, till the time be changed : therefore tell me the dream, and I shall know that ye can shew me the interpretation thereof.

9. Propterea si somnium non indicaveritis mihi, una hæc sententia *est;* et sermonem mendacem[5] et corruptum præparastis ad dicendum coram me, donec tempus mutetur;[6] propterea somnium narrate mihi, et cognoscam quod interpretationem ejus mihi indicetis.[7]

Here the excuse of the Magi is narrated. They state the truth that their art only enabled them to discover the interpretation of a dream ; but the king wished to know the dream itself. Whence he appears again to have been seized with prodigious fury and became quite implacable. Kings sometimes grow warm, but are appeased by a single admonition, and hence this sentiment is very true,—anger is assuaged by mild language. But since the fair re-

---

[1] Narrate.—*Calvin.*   [2] In truth.—*Calvin.*
[3] Now I know.—*Calvin.*
[4] That is, that the dream has fallen out of my mind, or the sentence has gone out of my lips.—*Calvin.*
[5] Or, fallacious.—*Calvin.*   [6] That is, pass by.—*Calvin.*
[7] That is, ye may be able to explain to me.—*Calvin.*

ply of the Magi did not mitigate the king's wrath, he was quite hurried away by diabolical vehemence. And all this, as I have said, was governed by God's secret counsel, that Daniel's explanation might be more noticed. They next ask the king—*to relate his dream*, and then they promise as before to interpret it directly. And even this was too great a boast, as we have said, and they ought to have corrected their own conceit and foolish boasting when in such a difficulty. But since they persist in that foolish and fallacious self-conceit, it shews us how they were blinded by the devil, just as those who have become entangled by superstitious deceptions confidently defend their own madness. Such an example we have in the Magi, who always claimed the power of interpreting dreams.

The king's exception now follows :—*I know*, says he, *that ye would gain time, since you are aware that the matter has gone from me*, or the word has been pronounced, if we adopt the former sense. The king here accuses them of more disgraceful cunning, since the Magi have nothing to offer, and so desire to escape as soon as they know that the king has lost all remembrance of his dream. It is just as if he had said—You promised me to be sure interpreters of my dream, but this is false ; for if I could narrate the dream, it would be easy to prove your arrogance, since ye cannot explain that enigma ; but as ye know I have forgotten my dream, for that reason ye ask me to relate it ; but *this is only to gain time*, says he ; thus ye manage to conceal your ignorance and retain your credit for knowledge. But if my dream still remained in my memory I should soon detect your ignorance, for ye cannot perform your boasting. We see, therefore, how the king here loads the Magi with a new crime, because they were impostors who deluded the people with false boastings ; and hence he shews them worthy of death, unless they relate his dream. The argument indeed is utterly vicious ; but it is not surprising when tyrants appear in the true colours of their cruelty. Meanwhile we must remember what I have said,—the Magi deserved this reproof, for they were puffed up with vanity and made false promises, through conjecturing the future from dreams, auguries, and the like. But in the king's case, nothing was more unjust than to invent such a crime against the Magi, since if they deceived others it arose from being self-deceived. They were blinded and fascinated by the foolish persuasion of their own wisdom, and had no intention of deceiving the king; for they thought something might immediately occur which would free his mind from all anxiety. But the king always pursued the blindest impulse of his rage. Meanwhile we must notice the origin of this feeling,—he was divinely tormented, and could not rest a single moment till he obtained an explanation of his dream. He next adds, *If ye do not explain my dream, this sentence alone remains for you,* says he; that is, it is already decreed concerning you all, I shall not inquire particularly which of you is in fault and which wishes to deceive me; but I will utterly cut off all the tribe of the Magi, and no one shall escape punishment, unless ye explain to me both the dream and its interpretation.

He adds again, *Ye have prepared a fallacious and corrupt speech to relate here before me,* as your excuse. Again, the king charges them with fraud and malice, of which they were not guilty; as if he had said, they purposely sought specious pretences for practising deceit. But he says, *a lying speech,* or fallacious *and corrupt;* that is, yours is a stale excuse, as we commonly say, and I loathe it. If there were any colourable pretext I might admit what ye say, but I see in your words nothing but fallacies, and those too which savour of corruption. Now, therefore, we observe the king not only angry because the Magi cannot relate his dream, but charging it against them, as a greater crime, that they brought a stale excuse and wished purposely to deceive him. He next adds, *tell me the dream and then I shall know it;* or then I shall know that ye can faithfully interpret its meaning. Here the king takes up another argument to convict the Magi of cunning. Ye boast, indeed, that you have no difficulty in interpreting the dream. How can ye be confident of this, for the dream itself is still unknown to you? If I had told it you, ye might then say whether ye could explain it or not; but when I now ask you about the

dream of which both you and I are ignorant, ye say, when I
have related the dream, the rest is in your power ; I therefore shall prove you to be good and true interpreters of
dreams if ye can tell me mine, since the one thing depends
on the other, and ye are too rash in presuming upon what
is not yet discovered. Since, therefore, ye burst forth so
hastily, and wish to persuade me that ye are sure of the
interpretation, you are evidently quite deceived in this
respect ; and your rashness and fraud are herein detected,
because ye are clearly deceiving me. This is the substance
—the rest to-morrow.

PRAYER.

Grant, Almighty God, since during our pilgrimage in this world
we have daily need of the teaching and government of thy Spirit,
that with true modesty we may depend on thy word and secret inspiration, and not take too much on ourselves,—Grant, also, that
we may be conscious of our ignorance, blindness, and stupidity,
and always flee to thee, and never permit ourselves to be drawn
aside in any way by the cunning of Satan and of the ungodly.
May we remain so fixed in thy truth as never to turn aside from
it, whilst thou dost direct us through the whole course of our
vocation, and then may we arrive at that heavenly glory which
has been obtained for us through the blood of thine only begotten Son.—Amen.

Lecture Sixth.

10. The Chaldeans answered before the king, and said, There is
not a man upon the earth that can
shew the king's matter: therefore
there is no king, lord, nor ruler, *that*
asked such things at any magician,
or astrologer, or Chaldean.

10. Responderunt Chaldæi coram
rege, et dixerunt, Non est homo super
terram qui sermonem[1] regis posset
explicare ; propterea nullus rex,
princeps, vel prefectus rem consimi-
lem exquisivit ab ullo mago, et as-
trologo, et Chaldæo.

THE Chaldeans again excuse themselves for not relating
the king's dream. They say, in reality, this is not their
peculiar art or science ; and they know of no example handed
down of wise men being asked in this way, and required to
answer as well *de facto* as *de jure,* as the phrase is. They

---

[1] Or, the matter.— *Calvin.*

boasted themselves to be interpreters of dreams, but their conjectures could not be extended to discover the dreams themselves, but only their interpretation. This was a just excuse, yet the king does not admit it, but is impelled by his own wrath and by the divine instinct to shew the Magi, and sorcerers, and astrologers, to be mere impostors and deceivers of the people. And we must observe the end in view, because God wished to extol his servant Daniel, and to separate him from the common herd. They add, that no kings had ever dealt thus with Magi and wise men. It afterwards follows :—

11. And *it is* a rare thing that the king requireth ; and there is none other that can shew it before the king, except the gods, whose dwelling is not with flesh.

11. Et sermo de quo rex inquirit pretiosus est ;[1] et nullus est qui possit exponere coram rege, nisi dii, quorum habitatio cum carne non est ipsis.[2]

They add, that the object of the king's inquiry surpassed the power of human ingenuity. There is no doubt that they were slow to confess this, because, as we said before, they had acquired the fame of such great wisdom, that the common people thought nothing unknown to them or concealed from them. And most willingly would they have escaped the dire necessity of confessing their ignorance in this respect, but in their extremity they were compelled to resort to this subterfuge. There may be a question why they thought the matter about which the king inquired was precious ; for as they were ignorant of the king's dream, how could they ascertain its value ? But it is not surprising that men, under the influence of extreme anxiety and fear, should utter anything without judgment. They say, therefore,— *this matter is precious ;* thus they mingle flattery with their excuses to mitigate the king's anger, hoping to escape the unjust death which was at hand. *The matter of which the king inquires is precious ;* and yet it would probably be said, since the matter was uncommon, that the dream was divinely sent to the king, and was afterwards suddenly buried in oblivion. There certainly was some mystery here, and

[1] Or, rare.—*Calvin.*
[2] Many words are superfluous, through the nature of the language.—*Calvin.*

hence the Chaldeans very reasonably considered the whole subject to surpass in magnitude the common measure of human ability ; therefore they add,—*there cannot be any other interpreters than gods or angels.* Some refer this to angels, but we know the Magi to have worshipped a multitude of gods. Hence it is more simple to explain this of the crowd of deities which they imagined. They had, indeed, lesser gods ; for among all nations a persuasion has existed concerning a supreme God who reigns alone. Afterwards they imagined inferior deities, and each fabricated a god for himself according to his taste. Hence they are called "gods," according to common opinion and usage, although they ought rather to be denoted genii or demons of the air. For we know that all unbelievers were imbued with this opinion concerning the existence of intermediate deities. The Apostles contended strongly against this ancient error, and we know the books of Plato[1] to be full of the doctrine that demons or genii act as mediators between man and the Heavenly Deity.

We may, then, suitably understand these words that the Chaldeans thought angels the only interpreters ; not because they imagined angels as the Scriptures speak of them clearly and sincerely, but the Platonic doctrine flourished among them, and also the superstition about the genii who dwell in heaven, and hold familiar intercourse with the supreme God. Since men are clothed in flesh, they cannot so raise themselves towards heaven as to perceive all secrets. Whence it follows, that the king acted unjustly in requiring them to discharge a duty either angelic or divine. This excuse was indeed probable, but the king's ears were deaf because he was carried away by his passions, and God also spurred him on by furies, which allowed him no rest. Hence this savage conduct which Daniel records.

12. For this cause the king was angry and very furious, and commanded to destroy all the wise *men* of Babylon.

12. Propterea rex in ira et indignatione magna edixit ut interficerent omnes sapientes Babylonis.

[1] A most interesting and singular allegory on this subject occurs in Plato's *Phœdrus*, edit. Bekker, § 51 ; edit. Priestley, (Lond., 1826,) p.71, *et seq.;* see also *Cic. Tusc. Quœst.* i. 16 ; *Aristot. Metaph.* i. 5 ; and *De anima,* i. 2 ; *Diog. Laert.*, viii 83.

The former denunciation was horrible, but now Nebuchadnezzar proceeds beyond it; for he not merely threatens the
Chaldeans with death, but commands it to be inflicted.   Such
an example is scarcely to be found in history ; but the cause
of his wrath must be noticed, since God wished his servant
Daniel to be brought forward and to be observed by all men.
This was the preparation by which it became generally evident that the wise men of Babylon were proved vain,
through promising more than they could perform ; even
if they had been endowed with the greatest wisdom, they
would still have been destitute of that gift of revelation
which was conferred upon Daniel.   Hence it happened that
the king denounced death against them all by his edict ; for
he might then perhaps acknowledge what he had never
perceived before, namely, that their boasting was nothing
but vanity, and their arts full of superstitions.   For when
superstition fails of success, madness immediately succeeds, and when those who are thought and spoken of as
remarkably devout, perceive their fictitious worship to be of
no avail, then they burst forth into the madness which
I have mentioned, and curse their idols, and detest what
they had hitherto followed.   So it occurred here, when
Nebuchadnezzar suspected imposture in so serious a matter, and no previous suspicion of it had entered his mind ;
but now, when he sees through the deception, in so perplexing a case, and in such great anxiety, when left destitute of the advice of those from whom he hoped all things,
then he is a hundredfold more infuriated than if he had
been previously in a state of perfect calmness.   It afterwards follows :—

13. And the decree went forth that the wise *men* should be slain; and they sought Daniel and his fellows to be slain.

13. Et edictum exiit et sapientes interficiebantur: et quærebant Daniel et socios ejus ad interficiendum.

14. Then Daniel answered with council and wisdom to Arioch the captain of the king's guard, which was gone forth to slay the wise *men* of Babylon:

14. Et tunc Daniel sciscitatus est *de* consilio et edicto ab Arioch principe satellitum regis, qui exierat ad interficiendum sapientes Babylonis.

15. He answered and said to Arioch the king's captain, Why *is*

15. Respondit et dixit ipsi Arioch præfecto [1] regis, Ad quid edic

[1] It is the same noun which was lately used.—*Calvin.*

the decree *so* hasty from the king? tum festinat è conspectu regis? Then Arioch made the thing known Tunc rem[1] patefecit Arioch ipsi to Daniel. Danieli.

It appears from these words that some of the wise men had been slain, for Daniel at first is not required for slaughter; but when the Magi and Chaldeans were promiscuously dragged out for punishment, Daniel and his companions were in the same danger. And this is clearly expressed thus— *when the edict had gone forth,* that is, was published, according to the Latin phrase, *and the wise men were slain,* then Daniel was also sought for; because the king would never suffer his decree to be despised after it had once been published; for if he had publicly commanded this to be done, and no execution had been added, would not this have been ridiculous? Hence, very probably, the slaughter of the Magi and Chaldeans was extensive. Although the king had no lawful reason for his conduct, yet they deserved their punishment; for, as we said yesterday, they deserved to be exterminated from the world, and the pest must be removed if it could possibly be accomplished. If Nebuchadnezzar had been like David, or Hezekiah, or Josiah, he might most justly have destroyed them all, and have purged the land from such defilements; but as he was only carried away by the fervour of his wrath, he was himself in fault. Meanwhile, God justly punishes the Chaldeans, and this admonition ought to profit the whole people. They were hardened in their error, and were doubtless rendered more excuseless by being blinded against such a judgment of God. Because Daniel was condemned to death, though he had not been called by the king, the injustice of the edicts of those kings who do not inquire into the causes of which they are judges, becomes more manifest.

Nebuchadnezzar had often heard of Daniel, and had been compelled to admire the dexterity of his genius, and the singular gift of his wisdom. How comes it, then, that he passed him by when he had need of his singular skill? Although the king anxiously inquires concerning the dream, yet we observe he does not act seriously; since it would

---

[1] Or, discourse.—*Calvin.*

doubtless have come into his mind, "Behold, thou hadst formerly beheld in the captives of Judah the incredible gift of celestial wisdom——then, in the first place, send for them!" Here the king's sloth is detected because he did not send for Daniel among the rest. We have stated this to be governed by the secret providence of God, who was unwilling that his servant should mix with those ministers of Satan, whose whole knowledge consisted in juggling and errors. We now see how the king had neglected the gift of God, and had stifled the light offered to him; but Daniel is next dragged to death. Therefore, I said, that tyrants are, for this reason, very unjust, and exercise a cruel violence because they will not undertake the labour and trouble of inquiry. Meanwhile we see that God wonderfully snatches his own people from the jaws of death, as it happened in Daniel's case; for we may be surprised at Arioch sparing his life when he slew the others who were natives. How can we account for Daniel meeting with more humanity than the Chaldeans, though he was a foreigner and a captive? Because his life was in the hand and keeping of God, who restrained both the mind and the hand of the prefect from being immediately savage with him. But it is said——Daniel *inquired concerning the counsel and the edict.* Some translate *prudently* and *cunningly:* and עטא, *gneta,* signifies "prudence," just as טעם, *tegnem,* metaphorically is received for "intelligence" when it signifies taste.[1] But we shall afterwards find this latter word used for an edict, and because this sense appears to suit better, I therefore adopt it, as Daniel had inquired of the prefect the meaning of the edict and the king's design. Arioch also is called the Prince of Satellites. Some translate it of executioners, and others of cooks, for טבח, *tebech,* signifies "to slay," but the noun deduced from this means a cook. Thus Potiphar is called, to whom Joseph was sold. (Gen. xxxix. 1.) It seems to me a kind of absurdity to call him the prince of gaolers; and if we say the prefect of cooks, it is equally unsuitable to his office of being sent to slay the Chaldeans. I therefore

[1] So translated in Auth. Vers., Exod. xvi. 31; Num. xi. 8; Job vi. 6; and Jer. xlviii. 11.

prefer interpreting it more mildly, supposing him to be the prefect of the guards ; for, as I have said, Potiphar is called רב טבחים, *reb tebechim,* and here the pronunciation only is changed.   It follows:

Daniel also had said, Whither does the edict hasten from before the king ? It seems by these words, that Daniel obliquely blames the king's anger and ingratitude, because he did not inquire with sufficient diligence before he rushed forward to that cruel punishment. Then he seems to mark his ingratitude, since he is now undeservedly doomed to death without being sent for, though the king might have known what was in him. As he refers to haste, I do not doubt his expostulating with the king, since he was neither called for nor listened to, and yet was to be slain with the rest, as if he were guilty of the same fault as the Chaldeans. The conclusion is,—there was no reason for such haste, since the king would probably find what he desired, if he inquired more diligently. It is afterwards added, *Arioch explained the matter to Daniel.* Whence it appears that Daniel was formerly ignorant of the whole matter ; and hence we may conjecture the amount of the terror which seized upon the pious man. For he had known nothing about it, and was led to punishment suddenly and unexpectedly, as if he had been guilty. Hence, it was necessary for him to be divinely strengthened, that he might with composure seek the proper time from both the prefect and the king, for relating the dream and adding its interpretation. Daniel's power of acting so composedly, arose from God's singular gift, since terror would otherwise have seized on his mind ; for we are aware that in sudden events, we become deprived of all plan, and lose our presence of mind. Since nothing of this kind was perceived in Daniel, it becomes clear that his mind was governed by God's Spirit. It is afterwards added—

16. Then Daniel went in, and desired of the king that he would give him time, and that he would shew the king the interpretation.

16. Et Daniel ingressus est, et postulavit a rege, ut tempus daret sibi, et expositionem[1] afferret regi.

This verse contains nothing new, unless we must notice what is not expressed, namely, that the prefect was not en-

[1] Interpretation.—*Calvin.*

tirely without fear in giving Daniel an introduction to the king. For he knew the king to be very angry, and himself under serious displeasure, for not immediately executing the edict. But, as we have already said, God had taken Daniel into his confidence, and so bends and tames the mind of the prefect, that he no longer hesitates to introduce Daniel to the king. Another point is also gathered from the context, namely, Daniel's obtaining his request ; for it is said, *he returned home*, doubtless, because he obtained a single day from the king with the view of satisfying his demands on the next day. And yet it is surprising that this favour was granted, since the king wished the dream narrated to him immediately. Although Daniel does not here relate the reasons which he used with the king, yet most probably he confessed what we shall afterwards observe in its own place, namely, that he was not endued with sufficient intelligence to expound the dream, but hoping in God's kindness, he would return next day with a new revelation. Otherwise the king would never have permitted this, if Daniel had petitioned doubtfully ; or if he had not borne witness to his hopes of some secret revelation from God, he would have been rejected immediately, and would have provoked still further the anger of the king. The Hebrews very commonly mention afterwards, in the context, whatever they omit in its proper place. So when he modestly confesses his inability to satisfy the king, till he has received from the Lord a faithful message, the king grants him the required time, as we shall see more clearly afterwards. It follows—

17. Then Daniel went to his house, and made the thing known to Hananiah, Mishael, and Azariah, his companions :

18. That they would desire mercies of the God of heaven concerning this secret; that Daniel and his fellows should not perish with the rest of the wise *men* of Babylon.

17. Tunc Daniel in domum venit,[1] et Hananiæ, et Misaeli, et Azariæ sociis suis sermonem[2] patefecit.

18. Et misericordias ad petendum[3] a facie Dei cœlorum super arcano hoc, ut ne interficerentur Daniel et socii ejuscum residuo sapientum Babylonis.[4]

[1] Departed.—*Calvin.*
[2] Or, the matter.—*Calvin.*
[3] Verbally, to implore mercy.—*Calvin.*
[4] That is, with the rest of the wise men of Babylon.—*Calvin.*

We observe with what object and with what confidence Daniel demanded an extension of time. His object was to implore God's grace. Confidence was also added, since he perceived a double punishment awaiting him, if he disappointed the king; if he had returned the next day without a reply, the king would not have been content with an easy death, but would have raged with cruelty against Daniel, in consequence of his deception. Without the slightest doubt, Daniel expected what he obtained—namely, that the king's dream would be revealed to him. He therefore urges his companions to implore unitedly mercy from God. Daniel had already obtained the singular gift of being an interpreter of dreams, and as we have seen, he alone was a Prophet of God. God was accustomed to manifest his intentions to his Prophets by dreams or visions, (Numb. xii. 6,) and Daniel had obtained both. Since Misael, Hananiah, and Azariah were united with him in prayer, we gather that they were not induced by ambition, to desire anything for themselves; for if they had been rivals of Daniel, they could not have prayed in concord with him. They did not pray about their own private concerns, but only for the interpretation of the dream being made known to Daniel. We observe, too, how sincerely they agree in their prayers, how all pride and ambition is laid aside, and without any desire for their own advantage. Besides, it is worthy of notice why they are said *to have desired mercy from God.* Although they do not here come into God's presence as criminals, yet they hoped their request would be graciously granted, and hence the word "mercy" is used. Whenever we fly to God to bring assistance to our necessities, our eyes and all our senses ought always to be turned towards his mercy, for his mere good-will reconciles him to us. When it is said, at the close of the verse,—*they should not perish with the rest of the wise men of Babylon,* some explain this, as if they had been anxious about the life of the Magi, and wished to snatch them also from death. But although they wished all persons to be safe, clearly enough they here separate themselves from the Magi and Chaldeans; their conduct was far different. It now follows—

19. Then was the secret revealed unto Daniel in a night vision. Then Daniel blessed the God of heaven.

19. Tunc Danieli in visione noctis arcanum patefactum est : tunc Daniel benedixit Deum cœli.

Here it may be gathered, that Daniel did not vacillate nor pray with his companions through any doubt upon his mind. For that sentence of James ought to come into our memory, namely, Those who hesitate, and tremble, and pray to God with diffidence, are unworthy of being heard. Let not such a one, says James, think he shall obtain anything from the Lord, if he is driven about variously like the waves of the sea. (Chap. i. 6.) As God, therefore, shewed himself propitious to the prayers of Daniel, we conclude him to have prayed with true faith, and to be clearly persuaded that his life was in God's hands ; hence, also, he felt that God did not vainly harass the mind of King Nebuchadnezzar, but was preparing some signal and remarkable judgment for him. Because Daniel was imbued with this firm persuasion, he exercises a sure confidence, and prays to God as if he had already obtained his request. On the other hand, we perceive that God never closes his ears when rightly and cordially invoked, as also it is said in the Psalms, (cxlv. 18,) He is near to all who pray to him in truth ; for there cannot be truth when faith is wanting ; but as Daniel brought faith and sincerity to his prayers, he was listened to, and the secret concerning the dream was made known to him in a vision by night. I cannot now proceed any further.

PRAYER.

Grant, Almighty God, since we are in danger every day and every moment, not merely from the cruelty of a single tyrant, but from the devil, who excites the whole world against us, arming the princes of this world, and impelling them to destroy us,—Grant, I pray thee, that we may feel and demonstrate, by experience, that our life is in thy hand, and that under thy faithful guardianship thou wilt not suffer one hair of our heads to fall. Do thou also so defend us, that the impious themselves may acknowledge that we do not boast this day in vain in thy name, nor invoke thee without success. And when we have experienced thy paternal anxiety, through the whole course of our life, may we arrive at that blessed immortality which thou hast promised us, and which is laid up for us in heaven, through Jesus Christ our Lord.—Amen.

Lecture Seventh.

20. Daniel answered and said, Blessed be the name of God for ever and ever: for wisdom and might are his.	20. Loquutus est[1] Daniel et dixit, Sit nomen Dei benedicitum a seculo et in seculum: ejus est sapientia, et robur ipsius.[2]

DANIEL here pursues his narrative, and thanks God after King Nebuchadnezzar's dream had been made known to him, while he relates the sense of the words which he had used. *May God's name be blessed,* says he, *from age to age.* We ought daily to wish for this; for when we pray that God's name may be hallowed, continuance is denoted under this form of prayer. But Daniel here breaks forth into the praises of God with greater vehemence, because he acknowledges his singular benefit in being snatched away from death, together with his companions, beyond his expectation. Whenever God confers any remarkable blessing on his servants, they are the more stirred up to praise him, as David says, (Psalm xl. 3,) Thou hast put a new song into my mouth. And Isaiah also uses this form of speech twice, (chap. xlii. 10,) as if God had given him material for a new and unusual song, in dealing so wonderfully with his Church. So also, there is no doubt that Daniel here wished to praise God in a remarkable manner, since he had received a rare proof of his favour in being delivered from instant death. Afterwards he adds, *whose* (or *since his*) *is the wisdom and the strength;* for the relative is here taken for the causal particle, and the sentence ought to be so expressed; the additional particles may avail to strengthen the expression, and be taken exclusively, as if he had said,—to God alone ought the praise of wisdom and virtue to be ascribed. Without him, indeed, both are sought in vain; but these graces do not seem to suit the present purpose; for Daniel ought rather to celebrate God's praises, through this vision being opened, and this was enough to content him. But he may here speak of God's glory as well from his power as his

[1] Verbally, answered.—*Calvin.*
[2] These particles are superfluous: there is nothing obscure in the sense.—*Calvin.*

wisdom ; as, where Scripture wishes to distinguish the true God from all fictions, it takes these two principles—first, God governs all things by his own hand, and retains them under his sway ; and secondly, nothing is hid from him —and these points cannot be separated when his majesty is to be proved. We see mankind fabricating deities for themselves, and thus multiplying gods, and distributing to each his own office ; because they cannot rest in simple unity, when God is treated of. Some fancy God retains but half his attributes ; as for instance, the praters about bare foreknowledge. They admit nothing to be hidden to God, and his knowledge of all things ; and this they prove by the prophecies which occur in the Scriptures. What they say is true ; but they very much lessen the glory of God ; nay, they tear it to pieces by likening him to Apollo, whose office it formerly was, in the opinion of the heathen, to predict future events. When they sought predictions of future events, they endued Apollo with the virtue of making known to them future occurrences. Many at the present time think God able to foresee all things, but suppose him either to dissemble or purposely withdraw from the government of the world.

Lastly, Their notion of God's foreknowledge is but a cold and idle speculation. Hence I said, they rob God of half his glory, and, as far as they can, tear him to pieces. But Scripture, when it wishes to assert what is peculiar to God, joins these two things inseparably ; first, God foresees all things, since nothing is hidden from his eyes ; and next, he appoints future events, and governs the world by his will, allowing nothing to happen by chance or without his direction. Daniel here assumes this principle, or rather unites the two, by asserting Israel's God alone to deserve the name, since both wisdom and strength are in his power. We must remember how God is defrauded of his just praise, when we do not connect these two attributes together—his universal foresight and his government of the world allowing nothing to happen without his permission. But as it would be too cold to assert that to God alone belongs wisdom and strength, unless his wisdom was conspicuous, and his strength openly acknowledged, hence it follows immediately afterwards—

21. And he changeth the times and the seasons: he removeth kings, and setteth up kings: he giveth wisdom unto the wise, and knowledge to them that know understanding.	21. Et ipse[1] mutat tempora, et articulos temporum : constituit reges et admovet reges: dat sapientiam sapientibus, et scientiam iis qui scientiam cognoscunt.[2]

Daniel explains, in these words, what might have been obscure ; for he teaches God to be the true fountain of wisdom and virtue, while he does not confine them to himself alone, but diffuses them through heaven and earth.   And we must mark this diligently ; for when Paul affirms God alone to be wise, this praise does not seem magnificent enough, (Rom. xvi. 27 ;) but when we think of God's wisdom, and set before our eyes all around and about us, then we feel more strongly the import of Paul's words, that God only is wise. God, therefore, as I have already stated, does not keep his wisdom confined to himself, but makes it flow throughout the whole world.   The full sense of the verse is,—whatever wisdom and power exists in the world, is a testimony to the Almighty's.   This is man's ingratitude ; whenever they find anything worthy of praise in themselves or others, they claim it directly as their own, and thus God's glory is diminished by the depravity of those who obtain their blessings from him.   We are here taught not to detract anything from God's wisdom and power, since wherever these qualities are conspicuous in the world, they ought rather to reflect his glory.   We now perceive the Prophet's meaning—God places before our eyes, as in a glass, the proofs of his wisdom and power, when the affairs of the world roll on, and mankind become powerful through wisdom, and some are raised on high, and others fall to the ground.   Experience teaches us these events do not proceed from human skill, or through the equable course of nature, while the loftiest kings are cast down and others elevated to the highest posts of honour.   Daniel, therefore, admonishes us not to seek in heaven alone for God's wisdom and power, since it is apparent to us on earth, and proofs of it are daily presented

[1] Or, it is he who.—*Calvin.*
[2] That is, to those who are skilled in science.—*Calvin.*

to our observation. We now see how these two verses are mutually united. He had stated wisdom to belong exclusively to God; he now shews that it is not hidden within him, but is made manifest to us; and we may perceive by familiar experience, how all wisdom flows from him as its exclusive fountain. We ought to feel the same concurring power also.

It is he, then, *who changes times and portions of time.* We know it to be ascribed to fortune when the world passes through such uncertain changes that everything is daily changing. Hence the profane consider all things to be acted on by blind impulse, and others affirm the human race to be a kind of sport to God, since men are tossed about like balls. But, as I have already said, it is not surprising to find men of a perverse and corrupt disposition thus perverting the object of all God's works. For our own practical improvement we should consider what the Prophet is here teaching, how revolutions, as they are called, are testimonies of God's power, and point out with the finger to the truth that the affairs of men are ruled by the Most High. For we must of necessity adopt one or the other of these views, either that nature rules over human events, or else fortune turns about in every direction, things which ought to have an even course. As far as nature is concerned, its course would be even, unless God by his singular counsel, as we have seen, thus changes the course of the times. Yet those philosophers who assign the supreme authority to nature are much sounder than others who place fortune in the highest rank. For if we admit for a moment this latter opinion that fortune directs human affairs by a kind of blind impulse, whence comes this fortune? If you ask them for a definition, what answer will they make? They will surely be compelled to confess this, the word "fortune" explains nothing. But neither God nor nature will have any place in this vain and changeable government of the world, where all things throw themselves into distinct forms without the least order or connection. And if this be granted, truly the doctrine of Epicurus will be received, because if God resigns the supreme government of the world, so that all things are rashly mingled together, he is no longer God. But in this variety he rather displays his hand in claiming for himself the empire over the world. In so many changes, then, which meet us on every side, and by which the whole face of things is renewed, we must remember that the Providence of God shines forth ; and things do not flow on in an even course, because then the peculiar property of God might with some shew of reason be ascribed to nature. God, I say, so changes empires, and times, and seasons, that we should learn to look up to him. If the sun always rose and set at the same period, or at least certain symmetrical changes took place yearly, without any casual change ; if the days of winter were not short, and those of summer not long, we might then discover the same order of nature, and in this way God would be rejected from his own dominion. But when the days of winter not only differ in length from those of summer, but even spring does not always retain the same temperature, but is sometimes stormy and snowy, and at others warm and genial ; and since summers are so various, no year being just like the former one ; since the air is changed every hour, and the heavens put on new appearances—when we discern all these things, God rouses us up, that we may not grow torpid in our own grossness, and erect nature into a deity, and deprive him of his lawful honour, and transfer to our own fancy what he claims for himself alone. If then, in these ordinary events, we are compelled to acknowledge God's Providence, if any change of greater moment arises, as when God transfers empires from one hand to another, and all but transforms the whole world, ought we not then to be the more affected, unless we are utterly stupid ? Daniel, therefore, very reasonably corrects the perverse opinion which commonly seizes upon the senses of all, that the world either rolls on by chance, or that nature is the supreme deity, when he asserts—God changes times and seasons.

It is evident from the context, that he is here properly speaking of empires, since *he appoints and removes kings.* We feel great difficulty in believing kings placed upon their thrones by a divine power, and afterwards deposed again, since we naturally fancy that they acquire their power by their own talents, or by hereditary right, or by fortuitous accident. Meanwhile all thought of God is excluded, when the industry, or valour, or success, or any other quality of man is extolled! Hence it is said in the Psalms, neither from the east nor the west, but God alone is the judge. (Psalm lxxv. 6, 7.) The Prophet there derides the discourses of those who call themselves wise, and who gather up reasons from all sides to shew how power is assigned to man, by either his own counsel and valour, or by good fortune or other human and inferior instruments. Look round, says he, wherever you please, from the rising to the setting of the sun, and you will find no reason why one man becomes lord of his fellow-creatures rather than another. God alone is the judge; that is, the government must remain entirely with the one God. So also in this passage, the Lord is said to appoint kings, and to raise them from the rest of mankind as he pleases. As this argument is a most important one, it might be treated more copiously; but since the same opportunity will occur in other passages, I comment but shortly on the contents of this verse; for we shall often have to treat of the state of kingdoms and of their ruin and changes. I am therefore unwilling to add anything more at present, as it is sufficient to explain Daniel's intention thus briefly.

He afterwards adds,—*he gives wisdom to the wise, and knowledge to those who are endued with it.* In this second clause, the Prophet confirms what we have already said, that God's wisdom is not shrouded in darkness, but is manifested to us, as he daily gives us sure and remarkable proofs of this. Meanwhile he here corrects the ingratitude of men who assume to themselves the praise of their own excellencies which spring from God, and thus become almost sacrilegious. Daniel, therefore, asserts that men have no wisdom but what springs from God. Men are, indeed, clever and intelligent, but the question arises, whether it springs from themselves? He also shews us how mankind are to be blamed in claiming anything as their own, since they have really nothing belonging to them, however they may be wrapt in admiration of themselves. Who then will boast

of becoming wise by his own innate strength? Has he
originated the intellect with which he is endowed? Because God is the sole author of wisdom and knowledge, the
gifts by which he has adorned men ought not to obscure his
glory, but rather to illustrate it.   He afterwards adds—

22. He revealeth the deep and secret things : he knoweth what *is* in the dark- ness, and the light dwelleth with him.	22. Ipse patefecit profunda et abscondita : cognoscit quod in te- nebris,[1] et lux cum eo habitat.[2]

He pursues the same sentiment, and confirms it,—that all
mortals receive from God's Spirit whatever intelligence and
light they enjoy; but he proceeds a step further in this
verse than in the last.   He had said generally, that men receive wisdom and understanding by God's good will; but
here he speaks specially; for when a man's understanding
is rare and unusual, there God's gift shines forth more
clearly; as if he had said—God not only distributes to every
one according to the measure of his own liberality, whatever
acuteness and ingenuity they possess, but he adorns some
with such intelligence that they appear as his interpreters.
He speaks, therefore, here, specially of the gift of prophecy;
as if he had said, God's goodness is conspicuous, not only in
the ordinary prudence of mankind, for no one is so made as
to be unable to discover between justice and injustice, and
to form some plan for regulating his life; but in Prophets
there is something extraordinary, which renders God's wisdom more surprising.   Whence, then, do Prophets obtain the
power of prophesying concerning hidden events, and pene-
trating above the heavens, and surpassing all bounds?   Is
this common to all men?   Surely this far exceeds the ordinary ability of man, while the Prophet here teaches that
God's beneficence and power deserve more praise, *because
he reveals hidden and secret things ;* and in this sense he
adds—*light dwells with God ;* as if he had said,—God
differs very much from us, since we are involved in many
clouds and mists; but to God all things are clear; he has
no occasion to hesitate, or inquire, and has no need to be
hindered through ignorance.   Now, we fully understand the
Prophet's meaning.

[1] Lies hid.—*Calvin.*   [2] Or, in his power.   *Calvin.*

Let us learn from this passage to attribute to God that praise which the greater part of the world claims to itself with sacrilegious audacity, though God shews it to belong to himself. Whatever understanding or judgment we may possess, we should remember that it was first received from God. Hence, also, if we have but a small portion of common sense, we are still equally indebted to God, for we should be like stocks or stones unless by his secret instinct he endued us with understanding. But if any one excels others, and obtains the admiration of all men, he ought still modestly to submit himself to God, and acknowledge himself the more bound to him, because he has received more than others. For who knows himself fully but God ? The more, therefore, he excels in understanding, the more he will lay aside all claims of his own, and extol the beneficence of God. Thirdly, let us learn that the understanding of spiritual things is a rare and singular gift of the Holy Spirit, in which God's power shines forth conspicuously. Let us guard against that diabolical pride by which we see almost the whole world to be swollen and intoxicated. And in this respect we should chiefly glorify God, as he has not only adorned us with ordinary foresight, enabling us to discern between good and evil, but raised us above the ordinary level of human nature, and so enlightened us that we can understand things far exceeding our capacities. When Daniel pronounces *light to be with God,* we must supply a tacit antithesis ; since he indicates, as I have already said, that men are surrounded by thick darkness, and grope about in obscurity. The habitation of men is here obliquely contrasted with the sanctuary of God ; as if the Prophet had said, there is no pure and perfect light but in God alone. Hence, when we remain in our natural state, we must necessarily wander in darkness, or at least be obscured by many clouds. These words naturally lead us not to rest satisfied in our own position, but to seek from God that light in which he only dwells. Meanwhile, we should remember how God dwells in light unapproachable, (1 Tim. vi. 16,) unless he deigns to stretch forth his hand to us. Hence, if we desire to become partakers of this divine light, let us be on our guard against audacity, and mind-

ful of our ignorance ; let us seek God's illumination. Thus
his light will not be inaccessible to us, when, by his Spirit,
he shall conduct us beyond the skies. He afterwards
adds—

23. I thank thee, and praise thee, O thou God of my fathers, who hast given me wisdom and might, and hast made known unto me now what we desired of thee : for thou hast *now* made known unto us the king's matter.

23. Tibi confiteor, Deus patrum meorum et laudo ego,[1] qui dedisti mihi sapientiam et robur, et nunc notificasti mihi quæ postulavimus abs te ; qui negotium[2] regis patefecisti nobis.

Daniel turns his discourse to God. *I confess to thee*, says
he, *O God of my fathers, and praise thee.* Here he more
openly distinguishes the God of the Israelites from all the
fictions of the nations. Nor does he use this epithet in
vain, when he praises the God of his fathers ; for he wishes
to reduce to nothing all the fabrications of the Gentiles concerning a multitude of deities. Daniel rejects this as a
vain and foolish thing, and shews how the God of Israel
alone is worthy of praise. But he does not found the glory
of God on the authority of their fathers, as the Papists,
when they wish to ascribe the supreme power to either
George, or Catharine, or any others, count up the number of
ages during which the error has prevailed. Thus they wish
whatever the consent of mankind has approved to be received
as oracular. But if religion depended on the common consent
of mankind, where would be its stability ? We know nothing
vainer than the minds of men. If man is weighed, says the
Prophet, with vanity in a balance, vanity itself will prepon-
derate. (Psalm lxii. 9.) Nothing, therefore, is more foolish than this principle of this king,—what has prevailed by
the consent of many ages must be religiously true. But here
Daniel partially commends the God of their fathers, as their
fathers were the sons of God. For that sacred adoption
prevailed among the Jews, by which God chose Abraham
and his whole family for himself. Daniel, therefore, here
does not extol the persons of men, as if they either could or
ought to add anything they pleased to God ; but this is the
reason why he says, *the God of Israel is the God of their fathers*, since he was of that race which the Almighty had

---

[1] And I also praise thee.—*Calvin.*	[2] Or, question.—*Calvin.*

adopted. On the whole, he so opposes the God of Israel to all the idols of the Gentiles, that the mark of separation is in the covenant itself, and in the celestial doctrine by which he revealed himself to the sacred fathers. For while the Gentiles have no certain vision, and follow only their own dreams, Daniel here deservedly sets forth *the God of their fathers.*

He afterwards adds, *because thou hast given me wisdom and strength.* As far as relates to wisdom, the reason is clear enough why Daniel thanks God, since he had obtained, as he soon afterwards says, the revelation of the dream. He had also formerly been endued with the prophetic spirit and with visions, as he related in the first chapter, (ver. 17.) We may here inquire what he means by *strength ?* He was not remarkable for his honour among men, nor was he ever a commander in military affairs, and he had no superior gift of magnificent power to cause him to return thanks to God. But Daniel regards this as the principal point, that the God of Israel was then acknowledged as the true and only God ; because, whatever wisdom and virtue exists in the world, it flows from him as its only source. For this reason he speaks of himself as well as of all others, as if he had said —If I have any strength or understanding, I ascribe it all to thee ; it is thine entirely. And, truly, though Daniel was neither a king nor a prefect, yet that unconquered greatness of mind which we have seen was not to be esteemed as without value. Hence he very properly acknowledges something of this kind to have been conferred upon him by heaven. Lastly, his intention is to debase himself and to attribute to God his own; but he speaks concisely, as we have said, since under the phrases " power" and " wisdom" he had previously embraced the proof of his divinity. He afterwards adds, *Thou hast revealed to me what we demanded of thee; thou hast made known to us the king's inquiry.* There seems here a slight discrepancy, as he praises God for granting him a revelation of the dream, and then unites others to himself. Yet the revelation was not common to them, but peculiar to himself. The solution is easy ; for he first expresses that this was given to himself specially, that he might know the king's dream and understand its interpretation. When he has confessed this, he extends the benefit to his companions, and deservedly so ; because though they did not yet understand what God had conferred upon Daniel, yet he had obtained this in their favour,—they were all snatched from death, and all their prayers attended to. And this availed very much for the confirmation of their faith, as it assured them they had not prayed in vain. For we said that there was no ambition in their prayers, as if any one desired any peculiar gift by which he might acquire honour and estimation for himself in the world. Nothing of the kind. It was enough for them to shew forth God's name among unbelievers ; because by his kindness, they had been delivered from death. Hence Daniel very properly says, the king's dream was made known to him with its interpretation ; and this he will afterwards transfer to his companions.

PRAYER.

Grant, Almighty God, since we have so many testimonies to thy glory daily before our eyes, though we seem so blind as to shut out all the light by our ingratitude ; grant, I pray, that we may at length learn to open our eyes ; yea, do thou open them by thy Spirit. May we reflect on the number, magnitude, and importance of thy benefits towards us ; and while thou dost set before us the proof of thy eternal divinity, grant that we may become proficient in this school of piety. May we learn to ascribe to thee the praise of all virtues, till nothing remains but to extol thee alone. And the more thou deignest to declare thyself liberal towards us, may we the more ardently desire to worship thee. May we devote ourselves to thee without reserving the slightest self-praise, but caring for this only, that thy glory may remain and shine forth throughout all the world, through Christ our Lord.—Amen.

Lecture Eighth.

24. Therefore Daniel went in unto Arioch, whom the king had ordained to destroy the wise *men* of Babylon :	24. Itaque ingressus est Daniel ad Arioch, quem prefecerat rex ad perdendum[1] sapientes Baby-

[1] To slay.—*Calvin.*

he went and said thus unto him, Destroy not the wise *men* of Babylon: bring me in before the king, and I will shew unto the king the interpretation.

lonis: venit ergo, et sic loquutus est ei, Sapientes Babylonis ne perdas: introduc me ad regem et interpretationem regi indicabo.

BEFORE Daniel sent his message to the king, as we saw yesterday, he discharged the duty of piety as he ought, for he testified his gratitude to God for revealing the secret. But he now says, *that he came to Arioch, who had been sent by the king to slay the Magi, and asked him not to kill them, for he had a revelation ;* of which we shall afterwards treat. Here we must notice that some of the Magi were slain, as I have said. For after Arioch had received the king's mandate, he would never have dared to delay it even a few days; but a delay occurred after Daniel had requested a short space of time to be afforded him. Then Arioch relaxed from the severity of the king's order against the Magi ; and now Daniel asks him to spare the remainder. He seems, indeed, to have done this with little judgment, because we ought to desire the utter abolition of magical arts, for we saw before that they were diabolical sorceries. It may be answered thus,—although Daniel, saw many faults and corruptions in the Magi and their art, or science, or false pretensions to knowledge, yet, since the principles were true, he was unwilling to allow what had proceeded from God to be blotted out. But it seems to me that Daniel's object was somewhat different, for although the Magi might have been utterly destroyed without the slightest difficulty, yet he looks rather to the cause, and therefore wished the persons to be spared. It will often happen that wicked men are called in question as well as those who have deserved a tenfold death; but if they are not punished for any just reason, we ought to spare their persons, not through their worthiness, but through our own habitual sense of equity and rectitude. It is therefore probable that Daniel, when he saw the king's command concerning the slaughter of the Magi to be so tyrannical, went out to meet him, lest they should all be slain with savage and cruel violence, without the slightest reason. I therefore think that Daniel spared the Magi, but not through any personal regard ; he wished them to be safe, but for another purpose, namely, to await their punishment from God. Their iniquity was not yet ripe for destruction through the indignation of the king. It is not surprising, then, that Daniel wished, as far as possible, to hinder this cruelty. It afterwards follows,—

25. Then Arioch brought in Daniel before the king in haste, and said thus unto him, I have found a man of the captives of Judah that will make known unto the king the interpretation.

25. Tunc Arioch cum festinatione introduxit Danielem ad regem, et sic locutus est ei, Inveni virum ex filiis captivitatis Jehudah, qui interpretationem regi notam faciet.

It may here be a question, in what sense Arioch speaks of bringing Daniel before the king, as if it were something new. For Daniel had already requested from the king time for prayer, as we have seen. Why then does Arioch now boast of *having found a man of the captives of Judah,* as if he were speaking of an obscure and unknown person? But very probably Daniel requested the time for prayer from Arioch, since we learn from history how difficult it was to approach those kings ; for they thought it a profanation of their majesty to be polite and humane. The conjecture, therefore, is probable, that Arioch was the channel through whom the king granted the time to Daniel ; or, we may suppose the words of Arioch are not simply related, but that Daniel shews the great boasting of courtiers, who always praise their own good offices, and adorn them with the splendour of words. Hence Arioch reminds the king how he had met with Daniel, and had at length obtained what the king very urgently desired. I do not therefore dwell longer on this, since either Arioch then explained more clearly to the king that Daniel could interpret his dream ; or he joined what had formerly been done ; or else Daniel had obtained this before ; or he had begged of the king that some time should be given to Daniel. He puts *sons of transmigration, or captivity,* a usual scriptural phrase for captives, although this noun is collective. It now follows,—

26. The king answered and said to Daniel, whose name *was* Belteshazzar, Art thou able to make known unto me the dream which I

26. Respondit rex, et dixit Danieli cujus nomen *erat* Baltesazzar, Estne tibi facultas ad notificandum[1]   mihi   somnium

[1] To declare.—*Calvin.*

have seen, and the interpretation   quod vidi, et interpretationem
thereof?   ejus?

The king uses these words through his despair of an
interpretation, since he perceived all the Magi in this
respect without judgment and understanding; for he was
at first persuaded that the Magi alone were the possessors of
wisdom. Since he had asked them in vain, the error with
which he was imbued, as I have said, prevented him from
hoping for anything better elsewhere. Through surprise,
then, he here inquires, as if the thing were impossible,
Have you that power? There is no doubt that God drew
this interrogation from the proud king to render his grace in
Daniel more illustrious. The less hope there was in the
king himself, the more there was in the revelation of both
dignity and reverence, as we shall afterwards see; for the
king was astonished, and fell prostrate through stupor upon
the earth before a captive! This is the reason why Daniel
relates the use of this interrogation by the king. It now
follows,—

27. Daniel answered in the presence. of the king, and said, The secret which the king hath demanded cannot the wise *men*, the astrologers, the magicians, the soothsayers, shew unto the king;

27. Respondit Daniel regi, et dixit, Arcanum quod rex postulat sapientes, magi, astrologi, genethliasi non possunt indicare regi.

28. But there is a God in heaven that revealeth secrets, and maketh known to the king Nebuchadnezzar what shall be in the latter days. Thy dream, and the visions of thy head upon thy bed, are these.

28. Sed est Deus in cœlis, qui revelat arcana; et indicavit regi Nebuchadnezzar quid futurum sit in fine[1] dierum: somnium tuum, et visio capitis tui super lectum tuum, hæc est.

First, with respect to these names we need not trouble
ourselves much, since even the Jews themselves are compelled to guess at them. They are very bold in their defini-
tions and rash in their affirmations, and yet they cannot
clearly distinguish how one kind of wise man differed from
the others; hence it is sufficient for us to hold that the
discourse now concerns those then esteemed " wise men,"
under the various designations of Magi, Soothsayers, and
Astrologers. Now, as to Daniel's answer. He says it was
not surprising that the king did not find what he hoped for
among the Magi, since God had breathed into him this dream

---

[1] In the extremity.—*Calvin*.

beyond the comprehension of human intellect. I know not whether those interpreters are right who think magical arts here simply condemned ; for I rather think a comparison is instituted between the king's dream and the substance of the science of the Magi. I always exclude superstitions by which they vitiated true and genuine science. But as far as the principles are concerned, we cannot precisely condemn astronomy and whatever belongs to the consideration of the order of nature. This appears to me the whole intention,—the king's dream was not subjected to human knowledge, for mortals have no such natural skill as to be able to comprehend the meaning of the dream, and God manifests those secrets which need the peculiar revelation of the Spirit. When Daniel says the Magi, Astrologers, and the rest cannot explain to the king his dream, and are not suitable interpreters of it, the true reason is, because the dream was not natural and had nothing in common with human conjectures, but was the peculiar revelation of the Spirit. As when Paul disputes concerning the Gospel, he collects into order every kind of intelligence among men, because those who are endued with any remarkable acuteness or ability think they can accomplish anything. But the doctrine of the Gospel is a heavenly mystery (1 Cor. ii. 14) which cannot be comprehended by the most learned and talented among men. The real sense of Daniel's words is this,—the Magi, Astrologers, and Soothsayers had no power of expounding the king's dream, since it was neither natural nor human.

This is clearly evident from the context, because he adds, *there is a God in heaven who reveals secrets.* For I take ברם, *berem,* here for the adversative particle. He opposes therefore the revelation of God to the conjectures and interpretations of the Magi, since all human sciences are included, so to speak, within their own bounds and bolts. Daniel, therefore, says that the matter requires the singular gift of the Holy Spirit. The same God also who revealed the king's dream to Daniel, distributes to each of us ability and skill according to his own pleasure. Whence does it arise that some are remarkable for quickness and others for stupidity

and sloth ?—that some become proficients in human arts and
learning, and others remain utterly ignorant, unless God
shews, by this variety, how by his power and will the minds
of men become enlightened or remain blunt and stupid ?
As the Almighty is the supreme origin of all intelligence
in the world, what Daniel here says is not generally true ;
and this contrast, unless we come to particulars, is either
cold or superfluous. We understand, therefore, why he said
in the former verse that the Magi and Astrologers could not
explain the king's dream, since the Almighty had raised
King Nebuchadnezzar above the common level for the purpose of explaining futurity to him through his dream.

There is then *a God in heaven who reveals secrets ; he
shews to king Nebuchadnezzar what will come to pass.* He
confirms what I have said, that the king was utterly unable
to comprehend the meaning of his own dream. It often
happens that men's minds move hither and thither, and thus
make clever guesses ; but Daniel excludes all human *media*,
and speaks of the dream as proceeding directly from God.
He adds, *what shall happen at the end* or extremity *of the
days.* We may inquire what he means by the word " extremity."   Interpreters think this ought to be referred to
the advent of Christ ; but they do not explain why this
word signifies Christ's advent.   There is no obscurity in the
phrase ; " the end of the days" signifies the advent of Christ,
because it was a kind of renewal to the world.   Most truly,
indeed, the world is still in the same state of agitation
as it was when Christ was manifest in the flesh ; but, as we
shall afterwards see, Christ came for the very purpose of
renovating the world, and since his Gospel is a kind of perfection of all things, we are said to be "in the last days."
Daniel compares the whole period preceding Christ's advent
with this extremity of the days.   God therefore wished to
shew the king of Babylon what should occur after one
monarchy had destroyed another, and also that there should
be an end of those changes whenever Christ's kingdom
should arrive.   At present I touch but briefly on this point,
since more must be said upon it by and bye.

This, says he, *is the dream and vision of thy head upon thy couch.* It may seem absurd for Daniel here to profess to explain to the king the nature of his dream and its interpretation, and yet to put in something else. But, as he will add nothing out of place, we ought not to question the propriety of his saying, this was the king's vision and his dream ; for his object was to rouse the king the more urgently to attend to both the dream and its interpretation. Here we must take notice how the Prophet persists in this, with the view of persuading the king that God was the author of the dream about which he inquired of Daniel ; for the words would be entirely thrown away unless men were thoroughly persuaded that the explanation given proceeded from God. For many in the present day will hear willingly enough what may be said about the Gospel, but they are not inwardly touched by it, and then all they hear vanishes away and immediately escapes them. Hence reverence is the principle of true and solid understanding. Thus Daniel does not abruptly bring forward either the explanation or the narration of the dream, but prepares the proud king to listen, by shewing him that he neither dreamt at random nor in accordance with his own thoughts, but was divinely instructed and admonished concerning hidden events. It now follows,—

29. (As for thee, O king, thy thoughts came *into thy mind* upon thy bed what should come to pass hereafter ; and he that revealeth secrets maketh known to thee what shall come to pass.

29. Tibi, rex, cogitationes tuæ super lectum tuum ascenderunt, quid futurum esset posthac ; et qui revelat arcana exposuit tibi quid futurum esset.

He again confirms what I have just touched upon, for he wished to impress this upon the king's mind—that God was the author of the dream, to induce the king to prepare for its interpretation with becoming sobriety, modesty, and docility. For unless he had been seriously affected, he would have despised Daniel's interpretation ; just as we see men fail to profit through their own pride or carelessness even when God addresses them familiarly. Hence we must observe this order, and be fully prepared to listen to God, and learn to put a bridle upon ourselves on hearing his sacred name, never rejecting whatever he proposes to us, but treating it with proper gravity. This is the true reason why Daniel repeats again that King Nebuchadnezzar

was divinely instructed in future events. He says, in the
first clause, *The king's thoughts ascended,*—the phrase is
Hebrew and Chaldee. Thoughts are said to ascend when
they are revolved in the brain or head, as we formerly saw—
this vision was in thy head ; since the seat of the reasoning
faculty is in the head. Daniel therefore aserts the king to
be anxious about futurity, as the greatest monarchs think
of what shall happen after their death, and every one
dreams about enjoying the empire of the whole world. So
King Nebuchadnezzar was very probably indulging these
thoughts. But it follows immediately, that his thoughts
could not profit him unless God unveiled the future, because
it was his peculiar office, says the Prophet, *to reveal secrets.*
Here we see clearly how vainly men disturb themselves
when they turn over and over again subjects which surpass
their abilities. King Nebuchadnezzar might have fatigued
himself for a long time without profit if he had not been instructed by the oracle. Hence there is weight in these
words—*He who reveals secrets has explained to the king what
shall happen ;* that is, thou canst not understand the dream
by thine own thoughts, but God has deemed thee worthy of
this peculiar favour when he wished to make thee conscious
of mysteries which had been otherwise altogether hidden
from thee, for thou couldst never have penetrated to such a
depth.

He afterwards adds—

30. But as for me, this secret is not revealed to me for *any* wisdom that I have more than any living, but for *their* sakes that shall make known the inter- pretation to the king, and that thou mightest know the thoughts of thy heart.)	30. Et ego,[1] non in sapientia quæ sit in me præ cunctis vi- ventibus, arcanum hoc pate- factum *est* mihi ;[2] sed ut inter- pretationem regi exponerem, et cogitationes cordis tui cog- nosceres.

Here Daniel meets an objection which Nebuchadnezzar
might make,—If God alone can reveal secrets, how, I pray
thee, canst thou, a mere mortal, do it ? Daniel anticipates
this, and transfers the whole glory to God, and ingenuously

---

[1] That is, to me.—*Calvin.*
[2] The repetition is superfluous, but it does not obscure the sense.—
Calvin.

confesses that he has no interpretation of his own to offer, but represents himself as led forward by God's hand to be its interpreter; and as having nothing by his own natural talents, but acting as God pleased to appoint him his servant for this office, and as using his assistance. *This secret,* then, says he, *has been made known to me.* By these words he sufficiently declares, how his undertaking to interpret the dream was God's peculiar gift. But he more clearly expresses this gift to be supernatural, as it is called, by saying, *not in the wisdom which belongs to me.* For if Daniel had surpassed the whole world in intelligence, yet he could never divine what the king of Babylon had dreamt! He excelled, indeed, in superior abilities and learning, and was endowed, as we have said, with remarkable gifts; yet he could never have obtained this power which he acquired from God through prayer, (I repeat it again,) through his own study or industry, or any human exertions.

We observe how Daniel here carefully excludes, not only what men foolishly claim as their own, but also what God naturally confers; since we know the profane to be endowed with singular talents, and other eminent faculties; and these are called natural, since God desires his gracious gifts to shine forth in the human race by such examples as these. But while Daniel acknowledges himself endowed with no common powers, through the good pleasure and discipline of God, though he confesses this, I say, yet he places this revelation on a higher footing. We observe also how the gifts of the Spirit mutually differ, because Daniel acted in a kind of twofold capacity with regard to the endowments with which it pleased God to adorn him. First of all, he made rapid progress in all sciences, and flourished much in intellectual quickness, and we have already clearly shewn this to be owing to the mere liberality of God. This liberality puts all things in their proper order, while it shews God's singular favour in the explanation of the dream.

This secret, then, *was not made known to me on account of any wisdom in me beyond the rest of mankind.* Daniel does not affirm himself to be superior to all men in wisdom, as some falsely twist these words, but he leaves this in doubt by saying, This ought not to be ascribed to wisdom, for if I were the acutest of all men, all my shrewdness would avail me nothing ; and, again, if I were the rudest idiot, still it is God who uses me as his servant in interpreting the dream to you. You must not, therefore, expect anything human from me, but you must receive what I say to you, because I am the instrument of God's Spirit, just as if I had come down from heaven. This is the simple sense of the words. Hence we may learn to ascribe the praise to God alone, to whom it is due ; for it is his peculiar office to illuminate our minds, so that we may comprehend heavenly mysteries. For although we are naturally endued with the greatest acuteness, which is also his gift, yet we may call it a limited endowment, as it does not reach to the heavens. Let us learn, then, to leave his own to God, as we are admonished by this expression of Daniel.

He afterwards adds, *But that I may make known to the king the interpretation, and thou mayest know the thoughts of thy heart.* Daniel uses the plural number, but indefinitely ; as if he had said, God has left thee indeed hitherto in suspense ; but yet he did not inspire thee with this dream in vain. These things, therefore, are mutually united, namely, —God has revealed to thee this secret, and has appointed me his interpreter. Thus we perceive Daniel's meaning. For Nebuchadnezzar might object, Why does God torment me thus ? What is the meaning of my perplexity ;—first I dream, and then my dream escapes me, and its interpretation is unknown to me ? Lest, therefore, Nebuchadnezzar should thus argue with God, Daniel here anticipates him, and shews how neither the dream nor the vision occurred in vain ; but God now grants what was there wanting, namely, the return of the dream to Nebuchadnezzar's memory, and at the same time his acknowledgment of its purport, and the reason of its being sent to him.

PRAYER.

Grant, Almighty God, since thou desirest us to differ from the brutes, and hence didst impress our minds with the light of intellect,—Grant, I pray thee, that we may learn to acknowledge and to magnify this singular favour, and may we exercise ourselves in the knowledge of those things which induce us to reverence thy sovereignty.   Besides this, may we distinguish between that common sense which thou hast bestowed upon us, and the illumination of thy Spirit, and the gift of faith, that thou alone mayest be glorified by our being grafted by faith into the body of thine only-begotten Son.   We entreat also from thee further progress and increase of the same faith, until at length thou bring us to the full manifestation of light.   Then, being like thee, we shall behold thy glory face to face, and enjoy the same in Christ our Lord.—Amen.

Lecture Ninth.

31. Thou, O king, sawest, and behold a great image. This great image, whose brightness *was* excellent, stood before thee, and the form thereof *was* terrible.

32. This image's head *was* of fine gold, his breast and his arms of silver, his belly and his thighs of brass,

33. His legs of iron, his feet part of iron and part of clay.

34. Thou sawest till that a stone was cut out without hands, which smote the image upon his feet *that were* of iron and clay, and brake them to pieces.

35. Then was the iron, the clay, the brass, the silver, and the gold, broken to pieces together, and became like the chaff of the summer thrashing-floors; and the wind carried them away, that no place was

31. Tu rex videbas, et ecce imago una grandis, imago illa magna, et splendor ejus[1] pretiosus[2] stabat coram te, et species ejus terribilis.

32. Hujus imaginis caput ex auro bono,[3] pectus ejus et brachia ejus ex argento, venter ejus et femora ejus ex ære, *œs*.

33. Crura ejus ex ferro,[4] pedes ejus partim ex ferro, et partim testa.

34. Videbas, quousque excisus fuit lapis, qui non ex manibus,[5] et percussit imaginem ad pedes qui erant ex ferro et testa, et contrivit eos.

35. Tunc contrita sunt simul ferrum, testa, æs, argentum, et aurum: et fuerunt quasi quisquiliæ[6] ex area æstivali : et abstulit ea ventus, et non inventus est locus eorum; et lapis qui percusserat imaginem,

---

[1] Or, appearance, in common language—its splendour, therefore.—*Calvin.*

[2] Or, excellent.—*Calvin.*

[3] Pure gold.—*Calvin.*

[4] Iron.—*Calvin.*

[5] Which was cut out without human hands.—*Calvin.*

[6] Or, chaff.—*Calvin.*

found for them: and the stone that smote the image became a great mountain, and filled the whole earth.

fuit in montem magnum, et implevit totam terram.

ALTHOUGH Daniel here records the dream, and does not touch on its interpretation, yet we must not proceed farther without discoursing on the matter itself. When the interpretation is afterwards added, we shall confirm what we have previously said, and amplify as the context may guide us. Here Daniel records how Nebuchadnezzar saw an image consisting of gold, silver, brass, and iron, but its feet were mixed, partly of iron and partly of clay. We have already treated of the name of the "Vision," but I briefly repeat again, —king Nebuchadnezzar did not see this image here mentioned, with his natural eyes, but it was a specimen of the revelation which he knew with certainty to have been divinely offered to him. Otherwise, he might have thrown off all care, and acted as he pleased ; but God held him down in complete torment, until Daniel came as its interpreter.

Nebuchadnezzar then saw an image. All writers endowed with a sound judgment and candidly desirous of explaining the Prophet's meaning, understand this, without controversy, of the Four Monarchies, following each other in succession. The Jews, when pressed by this interpretation, confuse the Turkish with the Roman empire, but their ignorance and unfairness is easily proved. For when they wish to escape the confession of Christ having been exhibited to the world, they seek stale calumnies which do not require refutation ; but still something must afterwards be said in its proper place. My assertion is perfectly correct, that interpreters of moderate judgment and candour, all explain the passage of the Babylonian, Persian, Macedonian, and Roman monarchies : and Daniel himself afterwards shews this sufficiently by his own words. A question, however, arises, why God represented these four monarchies under this image ? for it does not seem to correspond throughout, as the Romans had nothing in common with the Assyrians. History has fully informed us how the Medes and Persians succeeded the Chaldeans ; how Babylon was besieged by the enemy ; and how Cyrus, after obtaining the victory,

CHAP. II. 31-35.   COMMENTARIES ON DANIEL.   163

transferred the empire to the Medes and Persians. It may, perhaps, seem absurd that one image only should be proposed. But it is probable—nay, it may be shewn—that God does not here regard any agreement between these four monarchies, for there was none at all, but the state of the world at large. God therefore wished, under this figure, to represent the future condition of the world till the advent of Christ. This is the reason why God joined these four empires together, although actually different ; since the second sprang from the destruction of the first, and the third from that of the second. This is one point, and we may now inquire, secondly, why Daniel calls the kingdom of Babylon by the honourable term *golden.* For we know the extent of its tyranny and the character of the Assyrians, and their union with the Chaldeans. We are also aware of the destruction of Nineveh, and how the Chaldeans made Babylon their capital city, to preserve the seat of empire among themselves. If we consider the origin of that monarchy, we shall surely find the Assyrians like savage beasts, full of avarice, cruelty, and rapacity, and the Chaldeans superior to all these vices. Why, then, is that empire called *the head* —and why a *golden head ?*

As to the name, " head," since that monarchy arose first, there is nothing surprising in Daniel's assigning the highest place to it. And as to his passing by Nineveh, this is not surprising, because that city had been already cut off, and he is now treating of future events. The Chaldean empire, then, was first in the order of time, and is called " golden " by comparison ; because the world grows worse as it becomes older ; for the Persians and Medes who seized upon the whole East under the auspices of Cyrus, were worse than the Assyrians and Chaldeans. So profane poets invented fables about *The Four Ages,* the Golden, Silver, Brazen, and Iron. They do not mention the clay, but without doubt they received this tradition from Daniel. If any one object, that Cyrus excelled in the noblest qualities, and was of a heroic disposition, and celebrated by historians for his prudence and perseverance, and other endowments, I reply, we must not look here at the character of any one man, but at the continued state of the Persian empire. This is sufficiently probable on comparing the empire of the Medes and Persians with that of the Babylonians, which is called "silver;" since their morals were deteriorated, as we have already said. Experience also demonstrates how the world always degenerates, and inclines by degrees to vices and corruptions.

Then as to the Macedonian empire, it ought not to seem absurd to find it compared to brass, since we know the cruelty of Alexander's disposition. It is frivolous to notice that politeness which has gained him favour with historians; since, if we reflect upon his natural character, he surely breathed cruelty from his very boyhood. Do we not discern in him, when quite a boy, envy and emulation? When he saw his father victorious in war, and subduing by industry or depraved arts the cities of Greece, he wept with envy, because his father left him nothing to conquer. As he manifested such pride when a boy, we conclude him to have been more cruel than humane. And with what purpose and intention did he undertake the expedition by which he became king of kings, unless through being discontented not only with his own power, but with the possession of the whole world? We know also how he wept when he heard from that imaginative philosophy, that there were more worlds than this. "What," said he, "I do not possess even one world!" Since, then, one world did not suffice for a man who was small of stature, he must indeed put off all humanity, as he really appeared to do. He never spared the blood of any one; and wherever he burst forth, like a devouring tempest, he destroyed everything. Besides, what is here said of that monarchy ought not to be restricted to the person of Alexander, who was its chief and author, but is extended to all his successors. We know that they committed horrible cruelties, for before his empire was divided into four parts, constituting the kingdoms of Asia, Syria, Egypt, and Macedonia, how much blood was shed! God took away from Alexander all his offspring. He might have lived at home and begotten children, and thus his memory would have been noble and celebrated among all posterity; but God exterminated all his family from the world. His mother perished by the sword at the age of eighty years ; also his wife and sons, as well as a brother of unsound mind. Finally, it was a horrible proof of God's anger against Alexander's offspring, for the purpose of impressing all ages with a sense of his displeasure at such cruelty.   If then we extend the Macedonian empire to the period when Perseus was conquered, and Cleopatra and Ptolemy slain in Egypt, and Syria, Asia, and Egypt reduced under the sway of Rome— if we comprehend the whole of this period, we shall not wonder at the prophet Daniel calling the monarchy "brazen."

When he speaks of THE ROMAN EMPIRE as " iron," we must always remember the reason I have noticed, which has reference to the world in general, and to the depraved nature of mankind ; whence their vices and immoralities always increase till they arrive at a fearful height.   If we consider how the Romans conducted themselves, and how cruelly they tyrannized over others, the reason why their dominion is called " iron " by Daniel will immediately appear. Although they appear to have possessed some skill in political affairs, we are acquainted with their ambition, avarice, and cruelty.   Scarcely any nation can be found which suffered like the Romans under those three diseases, and since they were so subject to these, as well as to others, it is not surprising that the Prophet detracts from their fame and prefers the Macedonians, Persians, Medes, and even Assyrians and Chaldeans to them.

When he says, *the feet of the image were partly of iron and partly of clay*, this ought to be referred to the ruin which occurred, when God dispersed and cut in pieces, so to speak, that monarchy.   The Chaldean power fell first ; then the Macedonians, after subduing the East, became the sole monarchs to whom the Medes and Persians were subservient. The same event happened to the Macedonians, who were at length subdued by the Romans ; and all their kings who succeeded Alexander were cut off.   But there was another reason why God wished to overthrow the Roman monarchy. For it fell by itself according to the prediction of this prophecy.   Since, then, without any external force it fell to pieces by itself, it easily appears that it was broken up by

Christ, according to this dream of King Nebuchadnezzar. It is positively certain, that nothing was ever stable from the beginning of the world, and the assertion of Paul was always true—the fashion of this world passeth away.   (1 Cor. vii. 31.) By the word "fashion" he means whatever is splendent in the world is also shadowy and evanescent : he adds, also, that all which our eyes gaze upon must vanish away.   But, as I have said, the reason was different when God wished to destroy the empire of the Chaldees, the Persians, and the Macedonians; because this was more clearly shewn in the case of the Romans, how Christ by his advent took away whatever was splendid, and magnificent, and admirable in the world.   This, therefore, is the reason why God assigns specially to the Romans *feet of clay.*   Thus much, then, with respect to the four empires.

In the third place, it may be doubted why *Christ* is said *to have broken this image from the mountain.*   For if Christ is the eternal wisdom of God (Prov. viii. 15) by whom kings reign, this seems scarcely to accord with it ; for how, by his advent, should he break up the political order which we know God approves of, and has appointed and established by his power ?   I answer,—earthly empires are swallowed and broken up by Christ accidentally, as they say.   (Ps. ii. 9.) For if kings exercise their office honestly, clearly enough Christ's kingdom is not contrary to their power.   Whence, then, does it happen that Christ strikes kings with an iron sceptre, and breaks, and ruins, and reduces them to nothing? Just because their pride is untameable, and they raise their heads to heaven, and wish, if possible, to draw down God from his throne.   Hence they necessarily feel Christ's hand opposed to them, because they cannot and will not subject themselves to God.

But another question may be raised :—When Christ was made manifest, those monarchies had fallen long previously; for the Chaldean, the Persian, and that of the successors of Alexander, had passed away.   The solution is at hand, if we understand what I have previously mentioned—that under one image the whole state of the world is here depicted for us.   Although all events did not occur at the same moment, yet we shall find the Prophet's language essentially true, that Christ should destroy all monarchies. For when the seat of the empire of the East was changed, and Nineveh destroyed, and the Chaldeans had fixed the seat of empire among themselves, this happened by God's just judgment, and Christ was already reigning as the king of the world. That monarchy was really broken up by his power, and the same may be said of the Persian empire. For when they degenerated from a life of austerity and sobriety into one of foul and infamous luxury ; when they raged so cruelly against all mankind, and became so exceedingly rapacious, their empire necessarily passed away from them, and Alexander executed the judgment of God. The same occurred to Alexander and his successors. Hence the Prophet means, that before Christ appeared, he already possessed supreme power, both in heaven and earth, and thus broke up and annihilated the pride and violence of all men.

But Daniel says—the image perished when the Roman empire was broken up, and yet we observe in the East and the neighbouring regions the greatest monarchs still reigning with very formidable prowess. I reply, we must remember what we said yesterday—the dream was presented to King Nebuchadnezzar, that he might understand all future events to the renovation of the world. Hence God was not willing to instruct the king of Babylon further than to inform him of the four future monarchies which should possess the whole globe, and should obscure by their splendour all the powers of the world, and draw all eyes and all attention to itself ; and afterwards Christ should come and overthrow those monarchies. God, therefore, wished to inform King Nebuchadnezzar of these events ; and here we must notice the intention of the Holy Spirit. No mention is made of other kingdoms, because they had not yet emerged into importance sufficient to be compared to these four monarchies. While the Assyrians and Chaldeans reigned, there was no rivalry with their neighbours, for the whole of the East obeyed them. It was incredible that Cyrus, springing from a barbarous region, could so easily draw to himself such resources, and seize upon so many provinces in so short a time !

For he was like a whirlwind which destroyed the whole East. The same may be said of the third monarchy ; for if the successors of Alexander had been mutually united, there was then no empire in the world which could have increased their power. The Romans were fully occupied in struggling with their neighbours, and were not yet at rest on their own soil ; and afterwards, when Italy, Greece, Asia, and Egypt were obedient to them, no other empire rivalled their fame ; for all the power and glory of the world was at that period absorbed by their arms.

We now understand why Daniel mentioned those four kingdoms, and why he places their close at the advent of Christ. When I speak of Daniel, this ought to be understood of the dream ; for without doubt God wished to encourage the Jews not to despair, when first the brightness of the Chaldean monarchy, then that of the Persian, next the Macedonian, and lastly, the Romans overwhelmed the world. For what could they have determined by themselves at the time when Nebuchadnezzar dreamt about the four empires ? The kingdom of Israel was then utterly destroyed, the ten tribes were exiles, the kingdom of Judah was reduced to desolation. Although the city Jerusalem was yet standing, still where was the kingdom ? It was full of ignominy and disgrace ; nay, the posterity of David then reigned precariously in the tribe of Judah, and even there over but a part of it ; and afterwards, although their return was permitted, yet we know how miserably they were afflicted. And when Alexander, like a tempest, devastated the East, they suffered, as we know, the greatest distress; they were frequently ravaged by his successors ; their city was reduced almost to solitude, and the temple profaned ; and when their condition was at the best, they were still tributary, as we shall afterwards see. It was certainly necessary for their minds to be supported in so great and such confused perturbation. This, therefore, was the reason why God sent the dream about those monarchies to the king of Babylon. If Daniel had dreamt, the faithful would not have had so remarkable a subject-matter for the confirmation of their faith ; but when the king's dream is spread abroad through almost

the whole East, and when its interpretation is equally celebrated, the Jews might recover their spirits and revive their
hopes at their own time, since they understood from the first
that these four monarchies should not exist by any mere
changes of fortune; for the same God who had foretold to
King Nebuchadnezzar future events, determined also what
he should do, and what he wished to take place.

The Jews knew that the Chaldeans were reigning only
by the decree of heaven; and that another more destructive empire should afterwards arise; thirdly, that they
must undergo a servitude under the Macedonians; lastly,
that the Romans should be the conquerors and masters
of the world—and all this by the decree of heaven.   When
they reflected on these things, and finally heard of the
Redeemer, as, according to promise, a perpetual King, and
all the monarchies, then so refulgent, as without any stability—all this would prove no common source of strength.
Now, therefore, we understand with what intention God
wished what had hitherto been hidden, to be everywhere
promulgated; the Jews, too, would hand down to their sons
and grandsons what they had heard from Daniel, and afterwards this prophecy would be extant, and become an admiration to them throughout all ages.

When we come to the words, he says, *one image was great
and large, its splendour was precious, and its form terrible.*
By this phrase, God wished to meet a doubt which might
creep into the minds of the Jews, on perceiving each of
those empires prosperous in its turn.   When the Jews, captive and forlorn, saw the Chaldeans formidable throughout
the whole world, and, consequently, highly esteemed and
all but adored by the rest of mankind, what could they
think of it?   Why, they would have no hope of return, because God had raised their enemies to such great power
that their avarice and cruelty were like a deep whirlpool.
The Jews might thus conclude themselves to be drowned in
a very deep abyss, whence they could not hope to escape.
But when the empire was transferred to the Medes and
Persians, although they were allowed the liberty of returning, still we know how small a number used this indulgence,

and the rest were ungrateful. Whether or not this was so, few of the Jews returned to their country; and these had to make war upon their neighbours, and were subject to continual molestation. As far as common sense would guide them, it was easier for them not to stir a step from Chaldea, Assyria, and the other parts of the East, since their neighbours in their own country were all so hostile to them. As long as they were tributary and esteemed almost as serfs and slaves, and while their condition was so humiliating, the same temptation remained. For, if they were God's people, why did he not care for them so far as to relieve them from that cruel tyranny? Why did he not restore them to calmness, and render them free from such various inconveniences, and from so many injuries? When the Macedonian empire succeeded, they were more miserable than before; they were daily exposed as a prey, and every species of cruelty was practised towards them. Then, with regard to the Romans, we know how proudly they domineered over them. Although Pompey, at his first assault, did not spoil the temple, yet at length he became bolder, and Crassus shortly afterwards destroyed everything, till the most horrible and prodigious slaughter followed. As the Jews must suffer these things, this consolation must necessarily be offered to them—the Redeemer shall at length arrive, who shall break up all these empires.

As to Christ being called *the stone cut out without human hands*, and being pointed out by other phrases, I cannot explain them now.

PRAYER.

Grant, Almighty God, since we so travel through this world that our attention is easily arrested, and our judgment darkened, when we behold the power of the impious refulgent and terrible to ourselves and others: Grant, I say, that we may raise our eyes upwards, and consider how much power thou hast conferred upon thine only-begotten Son. Grant, also, that he may rule and govern us by the might of his Spirit, protect us by his faithfulness and guardianship, and compel the whole world to promote our salvation; thus may we rest calmly under his protection, and fight with that boldness and patience which he both commands and commends, until at length we enjoy the fruit of the victory which thou hast promised, and which thou wilt provide for us in thy heavenly kingdom.— Amen.

Lecture Tenth.

WE have already explained God's intention in offering to King Nebuchadnezzar the dream concerning the four monarchies, and the kingdom of Christ which should put an end to them.   We have shewn it to have been not for the king's sake so much as for the consolation and support of the remnant of the faithful in those very severe troubles which awaited them, and were close at hand.   For when redemption had been promised to them, and the Prophets had extolled that remarkable beneficence of God in magnificent terms, their confidence might fail them amidst those revolutions which afterwards followed.   For God wished to sustain their spirits, so that amidst such agitations and tumults they might remain constant, and patiently and quietly wait for the promised Redeemer.   Meanwhile God wished to render all the Chaldeans without excuse, because this dream of the king's was everywhere celebrated, and yet none of them profited by it, as far as Christ's eternal reign is concerned. But this was the principal point in the dream, as we shall afterwards see.   But God wished, in the first place, to consult the interests of his elect, lest they should despond among those so-called revolutions, which might seem contrary to those numerous prophecies, by which not merely simple liberty was promised, but perpetual and continued happiness under God's hand.   We now understand the end which God intended by this dream.   We must now treat its explanation.   We have already touched upon some points, but Daniel himself shall lead the way along which we are to proceed.   First of all he says—

36. This *is* the dream; and we will tell the interpretation thereof before the king.

37. Thòu, O king, *art* a king of kings: for the God of heaven hath given thee a

36. Hoc est somnium: et interpretationem ejus dicemus coram rege.

37. Tu rex, rex regum *es*, cui Deus cœlorum regnum, po-

kingdom, power, and strength, and glory.

38. And wheresoever the children of men dwell, the beasts of the field, and the fowls of the heaven, hath he given into thine hand, and hath made thee ruler over them all. Thou *art* this head of gold.

tentiam et robur dedit,[1] et gloriam tibi.[2]

38. Et ubicunque habitant filii hominum, bestia agri, et volucris cœlorum,[3] dedit in manum tuam, et præfecit te omnibus :[4] tu ipse caput *es* aureum.

Daniel here declares " the golden head of the image" to be the Babylonian kingdom. We know that the Assyrians were subdued before the monarchy was transferred to Babylon ; but since they did not prevail sufficiently to be considered as supreme rulers in that eastern territory, the Babylonian empire is here mentioned first. It is also worth while to remark, that God was unwilling to refer here to what had already occurred, but he rather proposed that the people should in future depend on this prophecy and rest upon it. Here it would have been superfluous to say anything about the Assyrians, since that empire had already passed away. But the Chaldeans were still to reign for some time —say seventy or at least sixty years. Hence God wished to hold the minds of his own servants in suspense till the end of that monarchy, and then to arouse them by fresh hopes, until the second monarchy should pass away, so that afterwards they might rest in patience under the third and fourth monarchies, and might perceive at length the time of Christ's advent to be at hand. This is the reason why Daniel places the Chaldean monarchy here in the first rank and order. And in this matter there is no difficulty, because he states King Nebuchadnezzar to be the golden head of the image. We may gather the reason of his being called *the golden head* from the context, namely, because its integrity was then greater than under the empire of the Medes and Persians. It is very true that the Chaldeans were the most cruel robbers, and we know how Babylon was then detested by all the pious and sincere worshippers of God. Still, since things usually become worse by process of time, the state of the world was as yet tolerable under that sovereignty.

[1] Some translate the nouns by adjectives or epithets—a strong and powerful kingdom.— *Calvin.*

[2] The word לְךְ, *lek*, " to thee," is redundant.— *Calvin.*

[3] That is, " birds ;" there is a change of number.— *Calvin.*

[4] Verbally, has made thee ruler over them all.— *Calvin.*

This is the reason why Nebuchadnezzar is called " the head of gold ;" but this ought not to be referred to him personally, but rather extended to his whole kingdom, and all his successors, among whom Belshazzar was the most hateful despiser of God ; and by comprehension he is said to form part of this head of gold.   But Daniel shews that he did not flatter the king, since he assigns this reason for Nebuchadnezzar being the golden head—God had set him up above all the earth.   But this seems to be common to all kings, since none of them reign without God's permission—a sentiment which is partially true, but the Prophet implies that Nebuchadnezzar was raised up in an especial manner, because he excelled all other sovereigns.   It now follows—

| 39. And after thee shall arise another kingdom inferior to thee, and another third kingdom of brass, which shall bear rule over all the earth. | 39. Et post te exsurget regnum aliud inferius te,[1] et regnum tertium aliud quod *erit* æneum : et dominabitur in tota terra. |

In this verse Daniel embraces the Second and Third Monarchies.   He says the second should be inferior to the Chaldean in neither power nor wealth ; for the Chaldean empire, although it spread so far and so wide, was added to that of the Medes and Persians.   Cyrus subdued the Medes first ; and although he made his father-in-law, Cyaxares, his ally in the sovereignty, yet he had expelled his maternal grandfather, and thus obtained peaceable possession of the kingdom throughout all Media.   Then he afterwards conquered the Chaldeans and Assyrians, as well as the Lydians and the rest of the nations of Asia Minor.   We see then that his kingdom is not called inferior through having less splendour or opulence in human estimation, but because the general condition of the world was worse under the second monarchy, as men's vices and corruptions increase more and more. Cyrus was, it is true, a prudent prince, but yet sanguinary. Ambition and avarice carried him fiercely onwards, and he wandered in every direction, like a wild beast, forgetful of all humanity.   And if we scan his disposition accurately, we shall discover it to be, as Isaiah says, very greedy of human blood. (Chap. xiii. 18.)   And here we may remark, that

[1] That is, to thine.—*Calvin.*

he does not treat only of the persons of kings, but of their counsellors and of the whole people.   Hence Daniel deservedly pronounces the second state of the kingdom inferior to the first; not because Nebuchadnezzar excelled in dignity, or wealth, or power, but because the world had not degenerated so much as it afterwards did.   For the more these monarchies extend themselves, the more licentiousness increases in the world, according to the teaching of experience.   Whence the folly and madness of those who desire to have kings very powerful is apparent, just as if any one should desire a river to be most rapid, as Isaiah says when combating this folly.   (Chap. viii. 7.)   For the swifter, the deeper, and the wider a river flows on, the greater the destruction of its overflow to the whole neighbourhood.   Hence the insanity of those who desire the greatest monarchies, because some things will by positive necessity occur out of lawful order, when one man occupies so broad a space; and this did occur under the sway of the Medes and Persians.

The description of the Third Monarchy now follows.   It is called *brazen*, not so much from its hardness as from its being worse than the second.   The Prophet teaches how the difference between the second and third monarchies is similar to that between silver and brass.   The rabbis confound the two monarchies, through their desire to comprehend under the second what they call the kingdom of the Greeks; but they display the grossest ignorance and dishonesty.   For they do not err through simple ignorance, but they purposely desire to overthrow what Scripture here states clearly concerning the advent of Christ.   Hence they are not ashamed to mingle and confuse history, and to pronounce carelessly on subjects unknown to them—unknown, I say, not because they escape men moderately versed in history, but through their being brutal themselves, and discerning nothing. For instead of Alexander the son of Philip, they put Alexander the son of Mammea, who possessed the Roman empire, when half its provinces had been already separated from it. He was a spiritless boy, and was slain in his tent with the greatest ignominy by his own soldiers; besides that, he never really governed, but lived as a minor under the sway of his mother.   And yet the Jews are not ashamed to distort and twist what relates to the king of Macedon to this Alexander the son of Mammea.   But their wickedness and ignorance is easily refuted by the context, as we shall afterwards see. Here Daniel states shortly that there shall be a third monarchy: he does not describe its character, nor explain it fully; but we shall see in another place the meaning of his prophecy.   He now interprets the dream of the king of Babylon, as the vision of the four empires had been offered to him.   But the angel afterwards confirms the same to him by a vision, and very clearly, too, as will be seen in its own place.   Without doubt this narrative of the brazen image relates to the Macedonian kingdom.   How, then, is all doubt removed?   By the description of the fourth empire, which is much fuller, and clearly indicates what we shall soon see, that the Roman empire was like the feet, partly of clay and partly of iron.   He says, therefore,—

40. And the fourth kingdom shall be strong as iron: forasmuch as iron breaketh in pieces and subdueth all *things;* and as iron that breaketh all these, shall it break in pieces and bruise.

41. And whereas thou sawest the feet and toes, part of potter's clay, and part of iron, the kingdom shall be divided; but there shall be in it of the strength of the iron, forasmuch as thou sawest the iron mixed with miry clay.

42. And *as* the toes of the feet *were* part of iron, and part of clay; *so* the kingdom shall be partly strong, and partly broken.

43. And whereas thou sawest iron mixed with miry clay, they shall mingle themselves with the seed of men: but they shall not cleave one to another, even as iron is not mixed with clay.

40. Et regnum quartum erit robustum instar ferri: quia sicuti ferrum conterit et comminuit omnia, et sicuti ferrum contundit omnia hæc, conteret et contundet.

41. Quod autem vidisti pedes et digitos partim ex luto fictili,[1] et partim ex ferro: regnum divisum erit: et de fortitudine ferri erit in eo, propterea vidisti ferrum mixtum cum testa luti.[2]

42. Et digiti pedum[3] partim ex ferro, et partim ex terra,[4] ex parte regnum *illud* erit robustum, et ex parte erit fragile.

43. Quòd vidisti ferrum commixtum testæ luteæ,[5] commiscebunt se inter se in semine hominis, et non cohærebunt alius cum alio, sicuti ferrum non miscetur cum testa.

Here the Fourth Empire is described, which agrees only

---

[1] Or, potter's clay.—*Calvin.*   [2] Or, moist clay.—*Calvin.*
[3] Or, if we repeat the verb, it is the accusative case.—*Calvin.*
[4] Or, of the clay which he mentioned.—*Calvin.*
[5] For vessels.—*Calvin.*

with the Roman, for we know that the four successors of
Alexander were at length subdued. Philip was the first
king of Macedon, and Antiochus the second; but yet Philip
lost nothing from his own kingdom; he only yielded it to
the free cities of Greece. It was, therefore, hitherto entire,
except as it paid tribute to the Romans for some years on
account of the expenses of the war. Antiochus, also, when
compelled to adopt the conditions imposed by the conqueror,
was driven beyond Mount Taurus; but Macedonia was reduced to a province when Perseus was overcome and captured. The kings of Syria and Asia suffered in the same
way; and, lastly, Egypt was seized upon by Augustus. For
their posterity had reigned up to that period, and Cleopatra
was the last of that race, as is sufficiently known. When,
therefore, the three monarchies were absorbed by the Romans, the language of the Prophet suits them well enough;
for, as the sword diminishes, and destroys, and ruins all
things, thus those three monarchies were bruised and broken
up by the Roman empire. There is nothing surprising in
his here enumerating that popular form of government among
"monarchies," since we know how few were rulers among
this people, and how customary it was to call every kind of
government among them an empire, and the people themselves the rulers of the whole world! But the Prophet
compares them to "iron," not only on account of its hardness, although this reason is clearly expressed, but also
through another kind of similitude,—they were worse than
all others, and surpassed in cruelty and barbarity both the
Macedonians and the Medo-Persians. Although they boast
much in their own prowess, yet if any one exercises a sound
judgment upon their actions, he will discover their tyranny
to be far more cruel than all the rest; although they
boast in their senators being as great as ordinary kings,
yet we shall find them no better than robbers and tyrants,
for scarcely one in a hundred of them shewed a grain of
equity, either when sent into any province or when discharging any magistracy; and with regard to the body of
the empire itself, it was all horrible pollution. This, then, is
the reason why the Prophet says that monarchy was partly

composed of iron, and partly of potter's clay, since we know how they suffered under intestine disorders. The Prophet requires no other interpretation here, because, he says, this mixture of iron and clay, which unites so badly, is a sign of disunion, through their never mingling together.

The kingdom, therefore, *shall be divided*, and he adds yet another mixture, — *they shall mingle themselves with the seed of men*, that is, they shall be neighbours to others, and that mutual interchange which ought to promote true friendship, shall become utterly profitless. The opinion of those who introduce the alliance of Pompey and Cæsar is farfetched, for the Prophet is speaking of a continued government. If stability is sought for in any kind of government, it surely ought to shine forth in a republic, or at least in an oligarchy in preference to a despotism ; because, when all are slaves, the king cannot so confidently trust his subjects, through their constant fear for themselves. But when all unite in the government, and the very lowest receive some mutual advantage from their commonwealth, then, as I have said, superior stability ought to be conspicuous. But Daniel pronounces, that even if the superior power should reside in the senate and the people—for there is dignity in the senate, and majesty in the people—yet that empire should fall. Besides, although they should be mutually united in neighbourhood and kindred, yet this would not prevent them from contending with each other with savage enmity, even to the destruction of their empire. Here then the Prophet furnishes us with a vivid picture of the Roman empire, by saying *that it was like iron,* and also *mingled with clay,* or mud, as they destroyed themselves by intestine discord after arriving at the highest pitch of fortune. Thus far concerning the four monarchies.

We may now inquire why Daniel said, *The stone which was to be cut out of the mountain should destroy all these empires ;* since it does not appear, at first sight, to suit the kingdom of Christ. The Babylonian monarchy had been previously abolished—the Medes and Persians had been utterly prostrated by Alexander—and after Alexander's conquests, had been divided into four kingdoms ; the Romans subdued all those lands ; and then it is objected that the Prophet's language is absurd, *a stone shall come out of a mountain which shall break up all empires.* The solution, as I have said above, is at hand. Daniel does not here state that the events shall happen together, but simply wishes to teach how the empires of the world shall fail, and one kingdom shall be eternal. He does not regard, therefore, when or why the empires of the Chaldees and of the Persians fell, but he compares the kingdom of Christ with all those monarchies which have been mentioned. And we must always remember what I have touched upon, that the Prophet speaks for the captive people, and accommodates his style to the faithful, to whom he wished to stretch forth the hand, and to strengthen them in those most serious concussions which were at hand. And hence, when he speaks of all lands and nations, if any one objects—there were then other empires in the world, the answer is easy, the Prophet is not here describing what should happen through all the ages of the world, but only what the Jews should see. For the Romans were the lords of many regions before they passed over into Greece ; we know they had two provinces in Spain, and after the close of the second Punic war were masters of that upper sea, and held undisputed possession of all the islands, as well as of Cisalpine Gaul and other regions. No notice is taken of this empire, till it was made known to the Jews, as they might have given themselves up to utter despair, when they could not perceive an end to those storms which almost ruined the world ; and, meanwhile, they were the most miserable of all men, because the various and continual calamities of the world never ceased. We must remember this view of things, as otherwise the whole prophecy would be cold and profitless to us. I now return to the kingdom of Christ.

THE KINGDOM OF CHRIST is said *to break up all the empires of the world,* not directly, but only accidentally, as the phrase is. For Daniel here assumes a principle, sufficiently understood by the Jews ; namely, those monarchies were opposed to Christ's kingdom. For the Chaldees had overthrown God's temple, and had endeavoured as far as possible to extinguish the whole of his worship, and to exterminate piety from the world. As far as concerns the Medes and Persians, although by their kindness a permission to return was granted to the people, yet very soon afterwards the kings of the Medes and Persians raged against that most miserable people, until the greater part of them preferred remaining in exile to returning home. At length came the Macedonian fury ; and although the Jews were spared for a short period, we know how impetuously the kings of Syria and Egypt overran Judea, how cruelly they treated the wretched people by rapine and plunder, and the shedding of innocent blood. Again, the extreme barbarity of Antiochus in ordering all the Prophetic Books to be burned, and in all but exterminating the religion itself (1 Macc. i. 59) is well ascertained.

No wonder, then, that Daniel here opposes the reign of Christ to such monarchies ! Next, as to the Romans, we know how thoroughly and proudly they despised the name of " Christian !" nay, they endeavoured by all means to root out from the world the Gospel and the doctrine of salvation, as an abominable thing. With all this we are familiar. Hence, to inform the faithful of their future condition until Christ's advent, Daniel shews how all the empires of the world should be adverse to God, and all its most powerful kings and sovereigns should be his very worst and most cruel enemies, and should use every means in their power to extinguish true piety. Thus he exhorts them to bear their cross, and never to yield to those wretched and sorrowful spectacles, but to proceed steadily in the course of their calling, until the promised Redeemer should appear. We stated this to be " accidental," since all the kingdoms of this world are clearly founded on the power and beneficence of Christ ; but a memorable proof of God's anger ought to exist against them all, because they raised themselves against the Son of God, the Supreme King, with such extreme fury and hostility.

Now, Christ is compared *to a stone cut out of a mountain.* Some restrict this, unnecessarily, to the generation of Christ, because he was born of a virgin, out of the usual course of nature. Hence he says, as we have seen, *that it was cut out of a mountain without the hand of man ;* that is, he was divinely sent, and his empire was separated from all earthly ones, since it was divine and heavenly. Now, therefore, we understand the reason of this simile.

With respect to the word " stone," Christ is not here called a *stone* in the sense of the word in Ps. cxviii. 22, and Is. viii. 14, and Zechariah ix. 15, and elsewhere. For there the name of a stone is applied to Christ, because his Church is founded on it. The perpetuity of his kingdom is denoted there as well as here; but, as I have already said, these phrases ought to be distinguished. It must now be added, —Christ is called a stone cut out without human hands, because he was from the beginning almost without form and comeliness, as far as human appearance goes. There is also a silent contrast between its magnitude, which the Prophet will soon mention, and this commencement. *The stone cut out of the mountain shall descend, and it shall become a great mountain, and shall fill the whole earth.* We see how the Prophet here predicts the beginning of Christ's Kingdom, as contemptible and abject before the world. It was not conspicuous for excellence, as it is said in Isaiah, A branch is sprung from the root of Jesse. (xi. 1.) When the posterity of David were deprived of all dignity, the royal name was utterly buried, and the diadem trodden under foot, as it is said in Ezekiel. (xvii. 19.) Hence, Christ first appeared cast down and lowly ; but the branch increased wonderfully and beyond all expectation and calculation, unto an immense size, till it filled the whole earth. We now perceive how appositely Daniel speaks of Christ's kingdom : but we must treat the rest to-morrow.

PRAYER.

Grant, Almighty God, that we may remember ourselves to be pilgrims in the world, and that no splendour of wealth, or power, or worldly wisdom may blind our eyes, but may we always direct our eyes and all our senses towards the kingdom of thy Son. May we always fix them there, and may nothing hinder us from hastening on in the course of our calling, until at length we pass over the course and reach the goal which thou hast set before us, and to which thou dost this day invite us by the heralding of thy gospel. Do thou at length gather us unto that happy eternity which has been obtained for us through the blood of the same, thy Son. May we never be separated from him, but, being sustained by his power, may we at last be raised by him to the highest heavens.—Amen.

Lecture Eleventh.

WE must now explain more clearly what we yesterday stated concerning the eternal kingdom of Christ. In relating the dream, the Prophet said—*The stone cut out of the mountain without hands is the fifth kingdom,* by which the four kingdoms were to be broken up and destroyed, according to the vision shewn to King Nebuchadnezzar. We must now see whether or not this is the kingdom of Christ. The Prophet's words are these :

44. And in the days of these kings shall the God of heaven set up a kingdom, which shall never be destroyed : and the kingdom shall not be left to other people, *but* it shall break in pieces and consume all these kingdoms, and it shall stand for ever.

45. Forasmuch as thou sawest that the stone was cut out of the mountain without hands, and that it brake in pieces the iron, the brass, the clay, the silver, and the gold ; the great God hath made known to the king what shall come to pass hereafter : and the dream *is* certain, and the interpretation thereof sure.

44. Et in diebus illis regum illorum suscitabit Deus cœlorum regnum, quod in seculum non dissipabitur,[1] et regnum *hoc* populo alieno non derelinquetur : confringet et conteret omnia illa regna, et ipsum stabit perpetuo.

45. Propterea vidisti, nempe e monte excisum lapidem et absque manu, qui confregit[2] ferrum, æs, testam, argentum et aurum : Deus magnus patefecit regi quid futurum esset postero tempore : et verum est somnium, et fidelis interpretatio ejus.

The Jews agree with us in thinking this passage cannot be otherwise understood than of the perpetual reign of Christ, and willingly and eagerly ascribe to the glory of their own nation whatever is written everywhere throughout the Scriptures ; nay, they often cry down many testimonies of Scripture for the purpose of boasting in their own privileges. They do not therefore deny the dream to have been

[1] Or, shall not be destroyed.—*Calvin.*
[2] Verbally, " and broke," but the copula ought to be rendered as the relative.—*Calvin.*

sent to King Nebuchadnezzar concerning Christ's kingdom ;
but they differ from us, in expecting a Christ of their own.
Hence they are compelled in many ways to corrupt this
prophecy ; because, if they grant that the fourth empire or
monarchy was accomplished in the Romans, they must necessarily acquiesce in the Gospel, which testifies of the arrival
of that Messiah who was promised in the Law.   For Daniel
here openly affirms that Messiah's kingdom should arrive at
the close of the fourth monarchy.   Hence they fly to the
miserable refuge that by the fourth monarchy should be
understood the Turkish empire, which they call that of the
Ishmaelites ; and thus they confound the Roman with the
Macedonian empire.   But what pretence have they for
making only one empire out of two such different ones ?
They say the Romans sprang from the Greeks ; and if we
grant this, whence did the Greeks spring ?   Did they not
arise from the Caspian Mountains and Higher Asia ?   The
Romans referred their origin to Troy, and at the time when
the prophecy ought to be fulfilled, this had become utterly
obscure—but what is this to the purpose when they had no
reputation for a thousand years afterwards ?   But the Turks
a long time afterwards, namely 600 years, suddenly burst
forth like a deluge.   In such a variety of circumstances,
and at such a distance of time, how can they form one
single kingdom ?   Then they shew no difference between
themselves and the rest of the nations.   For they recall us
to the beginning of the world, and in this way make one
kingdom out of two, and this mixture is altogether without
reason, or any pretension to it.   There is no doubt then,
that Daniel intended the Romans by the fourth empire,
since we yesterday saw, how in a manner contrary to nature,
that empire ultimately perished by intestine discord.   No
single monarch reigned there, but only a democracy.   All
thought themselves to be equally kings, for they were all
related.   This union ought to have been the firmest bond of
perpetuity.   But Daniel here witnesses beforehand, how,
even if they were intimately related, that kingdom would
not be social, but would perish by its own dissensions.
Finally, it is now sufficiently apparent that the Prophet's

words cannot be otherwise explained than of the Roman empire, nor can they be drawn aside, except by violence, to the Turkish empire.

I shall now relate what our brother Anthony has suggested to me, from a certain Rabbi Barbinel,[1] who seems to excel others in acuteness. He endeavours to shew by six principal arguments, that the fifth kingdom cannot relate to our Christ—Jesus, the son of Mary. He *first* assumes this principle, since the four kingdoms were earthly, the fifth cannot be compared with them, except its nature is the same. The comparison would be, he says, both inappropriate and absurd. As if Scripture does not always compare the celestial kingdom of God with those of earth! for it is neither necessary nor important for all points of a comparison to be precisely similar. Although God shewed to the king of Babylon the four earthly monarchies, it does not follow that the nature of the fifth was the same, since it might be very different. Nay, if we weigh all things rightly, it is necessary to mark some difference between those four and this last one. The reasoning, therefore, of that rabbi is frivolous, when he infers that Christ's kingdom ought to be visible, since it could not otherwise correspond with the other kingdoms. The *second* reason, by which he opposes us, is this,—if religion makes the difference between kingdoms, it follows that the Babylonian, and Persian, and Macedonian are all the same ; for we know that all those nations worshipped idols, and were devoted to superstition ! The answer to so weak an argument is easy enough, namely, these four kingdoms did not differ simply in religion, but God deprived the Babylonians of their power, and transfer-

---

[1] The Rabbi Barbinel, to whose opinion Calvin's attention was drawn, was the celebrated Jewish statesman and commentator, Isaac Abarbanel. He claimed descent from the family of King David, being born in Lisbon 1437, and died at Venice 1508. From Dr. M'Caul's preface to Tegg's *Prideaux*, (1845,) we learn that his " Commentary to Daniel" was entitled *Mayene ha-yeshuah*, and published after his death in 1551, 4to, and also at Amsterdam, 1647. The younger Buxtorf translated it into Latin, and it was refuted at length by Carpzov, Hulsius, and Varenius. Several of his works are still unprinted. He was a strong opponent of the Christian interpretation of Daniel, and an equally determined combatant of the rationalistic views of Moses the Egyptian, the son of Maimon.

red the monarchy to the Medes and Persians ; and by the same providence of God the Macedonians succeeded them ; and then, when all these kingdoms were abolished, the Romans possessed the sway over the whole East. We have already explained the Prophet's meaning. He wished simply to teach the Jews this,—they were not to despair through beholding the various agitations of the world, and its surprising and dreadful confusion ; although those ages were subject to many changes, the promised king should at length arrive. Hence the Prophet wished to exhort the Jews to patience, and to hold them in suspense by the expectation of the Messiah. He does not distinguish these four monarchies through diversity of religion, but because God was turning the world round like a wheel while one nation was expelling another, so that the Jews might apply all their minds and attention to that hope of redemption which had been promised through Messiah's advent.

The *third* argument which that rabbi brings forward may be refuted without the slightest trouble. He gathers from the words of the Prophet that the kingdom of our Christ, the son of Mary, cannot be the kingdom of which Daniel speaks, since it is here clearly expressed that there should be no passing away or change of this kingdom : *it shall not pass on to another* or a strange *people.* But the Turks, says he, occupy a large portion of the world, and religion among Christians is divided, and many reject the doctrine of the Gospel. It follows, then, that Jesus, the son of Mary, is not that king of whom Daniel prophesied—that is, about whom the dream which Daniel explained occurred to the king of Babylon. But he trifles very foolishly, because he assumes what we shall ever deny—that Christ's kingdom is visible. For however the sons of God are dispersed, without any reputation among men, it is quite clear that Christ's kingdom remains safe and sure, since in its own nature it is not outward but invisible. Christ did not utter these words in vain, " My kingdom is not of this world." (John xviii. 36.) By this expression he wished to remove his kingdom from the ordinary forms of government. Although, therefore, the Turks have spread far and wide, and the world is filled with impious despisers of God, and the Jews yet occupy a part of it, still Christ's kingdom exists and has not been transferred to any others.   Hence this reasoning is not only weak but puerile.

A *fourth* argument follows:—It seems very absurd that Christ, who was born under Octavius or Augustus Cæsar, should be the king of whom Daniel prophesied.   For, says he, the beginning of the fourth and fifth monarchy was the same, which is absurd ; for the fourth monarchy ought to endure for some time, and then the fifth should succeed it.   But here he not only betrays his ignorance, but his utter stupidity, since God so blinded the whole people that they were like restive dogs.   I have had much conversation with many Jews : I have never seen either a drop of piety or a grain of truth or ingenuousness—nay, I have never found common sense in any Jew.   But this fellow, who seems so sharp and ingenious, displays his own impudence to his great disgrace.   For he thought the Roman monarchy began with Julius Cæsar! as if the Macedonian empire was not abolished when the Romans took possession of Macedon and reduced it to a province, when also Antiochus was reduced into order by them—nay, when the third monarchy, namely, the Macedonian, began to decline, then the fourth, which is the Roman, succeeded it.   Reason itself dictates to us to reckon in this way, since unless we confess the fourth monarchy to have succeeded directly on the passing away of the third, how could the rest follow on ? We must observe, also, that the Prophet does not look to the Cæsars when he treats of these monarchies ; nay, as we saw concerning the mingling of races, this cannot in any way suit the Cæsars ; for we shewed yesterday how those who restrict this passage to Pompey and Cæsar are only trifling, and are utterly without judgment in this respect.   For the Prophet speaks generally and continuously of a popular state, since they were all mutually related, and yet the empire was not stable, through their consuming themselves internally by intestine warfare.   Since this is the case, we conclude this rabbi to be very foolish and palpably absurd in asserting the Christ not to be the son of Mary who was born under Augustus, although I do not argue for the kingdom of Christ commencing at his nativity.

His *fifth* argument is this :—Constantine and other Cæsars professed the faith of Christ.   If we receive, says he, Jesus the son of Mary as the fifth king, how will this suit ? as the Roman Empire was still in existence under this king. For where the religion of Christ flourishes, where he is worshipped and acknowledged as the only King, that kingdom ought not to be separated from his.   When therefore Christ, under Constantine and his successors, obtained both glory and power among the Romans, his monarchy cannot be separated from theirs.   But the solution of this is easy, as the Prophet here puts an end to the Roman Empire when it began to be torn in pieces.   As to the time when Christ's reign began, I have just said it ought not to be referred to the time of his birth, but to the preaching of the Gospel. From the time when the Gospel began to be promulgated, we know the Roman monarchy to have been dissipated and at length to vanish away.   Hence the empire did not endure through Constantine or other emperors, since their state was different ; and we know that neither Constantine nor the other Cæsars were Romans.   From the time of Trojan the empire began to be transferred to strangers, and foreigners reigned at Rome.   We also know by what monsters God destroyed the ancient glory[1] of the Roman people !—for nothing could be more abandoned or disgraceful than the conduct of many of the emperors.   If any one will but run through their histories, he will discover immediately that no other people ever had such monsters for rulers as the Romans under Heliogabalus and others like him,—I omit Nero and Caligula, and speak only of foreigners.   The Roman Empire was therefore abolished after the Gospel began to be promulgated and Christ became generally known throughout the world.   Thus we observe the same ignorance in this argument of the rabbi as in the others.

The *last* assertion is,—The Roman empire as yet partially survives, hence what is here said of the fifth monarchy can-

[1] This word is omitted in the edition published at Geneva A.D. 1667, but is correctly inserted in that of Bart. Vincentius, A.D. 1571.—*Tr.*

not belong to the son of Mary ; it is necessary for the fourth empire to be at an end, if the fifth king began to reign when Christ rose from the dead and was preached in the world. I reply, as I have said already, the Roman empire ceased, and was abolished when God transferred their whole power with shame and reproach to foreigners, who were not only barbarians, but horrible monsters ! It would have been better for the Romans to suffer the utter blotting out of their name, rather than submit to such disgrace. We perceive how this sixth and last reason vanishes away. I wished to collect them together, to shew you how foolishly those Jewish reasoners make war with God, and furiously oppose the clear light of the Gospel.

I now return to Daniel's words. He says, *A kingdom shall come and destroy all other kingdoms.* I explained yesterday the sense in which Christ broke up those ancient monarchies, which had come to an end long before his advent.   For Daniel does not wish to state precisely what Christ would do at any one moment, but what should happen from the time of the captivity till his appearance. If we attend to this intention, all difficulty will be removed from the passage. The conclusion, therefore, is this ; the Jews should behold the most powerful empires, which should strike them with terror, and utterly astonish them, yet they should prove neither stable nor firm, through being opposed to the kingdom of the Son of God. But Isaiah denounces curses upon all the kingdoms which do not obey the Church of God. (Chap. lx. 12.) As all those monarchs erected their crests against the Son of God and true piety, with diabolical audacity, they must be utterly swept away, and God's curse, as announced by the Prophet, must become conspicuous upon them. Thus Christ rooted up all the empires of the world. The Turkish empire, indeed, at this day, excels in wealth and power, and the multitude of nations under its sway ; but it was not God's purpose to explain future events after the appearance of Christ. He only wished the Jews to be admonished, and prevented from sinking under the weight of their burden, since they would be in imminent danger through the rise of so many fresh tyrannies in the world, and the absence of all repose. God wished, therefore, to brace their minds by fortitude. One reason was this—to cause them to dwell upon the promised redemption, and to experience how evanescent and uncertain are all the empires of the world which are not founded in God, and not united to the kingdom of Christ. *God, therefore, will set up the kingdoms of the heavens, which shall never be dissipated.* It is here worth while to notice the sense in which Daniel uses the term "perpetuity." It ought not to be restricted to the person of Christ, but belongs to all the pious and the whole body of the Church. Christ is indeed eternal in himself, but he also communicates his eternity to us, because he preserves the Church in the world, and invites us by the hope of a better life than this, and begets us again by his Spirit to an incorruptible life. The perpetuity, then, of Christ's reign, is twofold, without considering his person. *First,* in the whole body of believers; for though the Church is often dispersed and hidden from men's eyes, yet it never entirely perishes; but God preserves it by his incomprehensible virtue, so that it shall survive till the end of the world. Then there is a *second* perpetuity in each believer, since each is born of incorruptible seed, and renewed by the Spirit of God. The sons of Adam are now not mortal only, but bear within them heavenly life; since the Spirit within them is life, as St. Paul says, in the Epistle to the Romans. (Chap. viii. 10.) We hold, therefore, that whenever Scripture affirms Christ's reign to be eternal, this is extended to the whole body of the Church, and need not be confined to his person. We see, then, how the kingdom from which the doctrine of the Gospel began to be promulgated, was eternal; for although the Church was in a certain sense buried, yet God gave life to his elect, even in the sepulchre. Whence, then, did it happen that the sons of the Church were buried, and a new people and a new creation required, as in Ps. cii. 18? Hence it easily appears that God is served by a remnant, although they are not evident to human observation.

He adds, *This kingdom shall not pass away to another people.* By this phrase the Prophet means that this sovereignty cannot be transferred, as in the other instances. Darius was conquered by Alexander, and his posterity was extinguished, till at length God destroyed that ill-fated Macedonian race, until no one survived who boasted himself to be sprung from that family. With respect to the Romans, although they continued to exist, yet they were so disgracefully subjected to the tyranny of strangers and barbarians, as to be completely covered with shame and utterly disgraced. Then, as to the reign of Christ, he cannot be deprived of the empire conferred upon him, nor can we who are his members lose the kingdom of which he has made us partakers. Christ, therefore, both in himself and his members, reigns without any danger of change, because he always remains safe and secure in his own person. As to ourselves, since we are preserved by his grace, and he has received us under his own care and protection, we are beyond the reach of danger ; and, as I have already said, our safety is ensured, for we cannot be deprived of the inheritance awaiting us in heaven. We, therefore, who are kept by his power through faith, as Peter says, may be secure and calm, (1 Pet. i. 5,) because whatever Satan devises, and however the world attempts various plans for our destruction, we shall still remain safe in Christ. We thus see how the Prophet's words ought to be understood, when he says that this fifth empire is not to be transferred and alienated to another people. The last clause of the sentence, which is this, *it shall bruise and break all other kingdoms, and shall stand perpetually itself,* does not require any long exposition. We have explained the manner in which Christ's kingdom should destroy all the earthly kingdoms of which Daniel had previously spoken ; since whatever is adverse to the only-begotten Son of God, must necessarily perish and utterly vanish away. A Prophet exhorts all the kings of the earth to kiss the Son. (Ps. ii. 12.) Since neither the Babylonians, nor Persians, nor Macedonians, nor Romans, submitted themselves to Christ, nay, even used their utmost efforts to oppose him, they were the enemies of piety, and ought to be extinguished by Christ's kingdom ; because, although the Persian empire was not in existence when Christ appeared in the world, yet its remembrance was

cursed before God. For Daniel does not here touch only
on those things which were visible to men, but raises our
minds higher, assuring us most clearly that no true support on which we can rest can be found except in Christ
alone. Hence he pronounces, that without Christ all the
splendour, and power, opulence, and might of the world, is
vain, and unstable, and worthless. He confirms the same
sentiment in the following verse, where God shewed the king
of Babylon what should happen in the last times, when he
pointed out *a stone cut out of the mountain without hands.*
We stated Christ to be cut out of the mountain without
hands, because he was divinely sent, so that men cannot
claim anything for themselves in this respect, since God,
when treating of the redemption of his own people, speaks
thus, by Isaiah,—Since God saw no help in the world, he
relied upon his own arm and his own power. (lxiii. v. 5.)
As, therefore, Christ was sent only by his heavenly Father,
he is said to be *cut out without hands.*

Meanwhile, we must consider what I have added in the
second place, that the humble and abject origin of Christ is
denoted, since it was like a rough and unpolished stone.
With regard to the word "mountain," I have no doubt
Daniel here wished to shew Christ's reign to be sublime, and
above the whole world. Hence the figure of the mountain
means, in my opinion, —Christ should not spring out of
the earth, but should come in the glory of his heavenly
Father, as it is said in the Prophet : And thou, Bethlehem
Ephratah, art the least among the divisions of Judah; yet out
of thee shall a leader in Israel arise for me, and his reign
shall be from the days of eternity. (Micah v. 2.) Daniel,
then, here condescends to those gross imaginations to which
our minds are subjected. Because, at the beginning, Christ's
dignity did not appear so great as we discern it in the kings
of the world, and to this day it seems to some obscured by
the shame of the cross, many, alas! despise him, and do
not acknowledge any dignity in him. Daniel, therefore,
now raises aloft our eyes and senses, when he says *this stone
should be cut out of the mountain.* Meanwhile, if any one
prefers taking the mountain for the elect people, I will not

object to it, but this seems to me not in accordance with the genuine sense of the Prophet.   At length he adds, *And the dream is true, and its interpretation trustworthy.*   Here Daniel securely and intrepidly asserts, that he does not bring forward doubtful conjectures, but explains faithfully to King Nebuchadnezzar what he has received from the Lord. Here he claims for himself the Prophetic authority, to induce the king of Babylon to acknowledge him a sure and faithful interpreter of God.   We see how the prophets always spoke with this confidence, otherwise all their teaching would be useless.   If our faith depended on man's wisdom, or on anything of the kind, it would indeed be variable. Hence it is necessary to determine this foundation of truth, —Whatever the Prophets set before us proceeds from God ; and the reason why they so constantly insist on this is, lest their doctrine should be supposed to be fabricated by men.   Thus also in this place, Daniel first says, *the dream is true ;* as if he said, the dream is not a common one, as the poets fable concerning a gate of horn ; the dream is not confused, as men imagine when scarcely sane, or stuffed with meat and drink, or through bodily constitution, either melancholy or choleric.   He states, therefore, the king of Babylon's dream to have been a true oracle ; and adds, *its interpretation is certain.*   Where, as in the next clause, the Prophet again urges his own authority, lest Nebuchadnezzar should doubt his divine instructions to explain the truth of his dream.   It now follows,—

46. Then the king Nebuchadnezzar fell upon his face, and worshipped Daniel, and commanded that they should offer an oblation and sweet odours unto him.	46. Tunc rex Nebuchadnezer cecidit in faciem suam, et Danielem adoravit: et oblationem, et suffitum odoriferum,[1] jussit illi sacrificari.

When the king of Babylon *fell upon his face*, it is partly to be considered as worthy of praise and partly of blame. It was a sign of both piety and modesty, when he prostrated himself before God and his Prophet.   We know the fierceness and pride of kings ; nay, we see them act like madmen, because they do not reckon themselves among mortals, and become blinded with the splendour of their

[1] That is, a sweet-smelling fragrance.—*Calvin.*

greatness. Nebuchadnezzar was really a very powerful monarch, and it was difficult for him so to regulate his mind as
to attribute the glory to God. Thus the dream which Daniel
explained could not be pleasing to him. He saw his monarchy cursed before God, and about to perish in ignominy:
others, too, which should succeed it were ordained in heaven;
and though he might receive some comfort from the destruction of the other kingdoms, yet it was very harsh to delicate ears, to hear that a kingdom, which appeared most
flourishing, and which all men thought would be perpetual,
was of but short duration and sure to perish. As, therefore,
the king so prostrated himself before Daniel, it is, as I have
said, a sign of piety in thus reverencing God, and in embracing the prophecy, which would otherwise be bitter and
distasteful.   It was also a sign of modesty, because he
humbled himself so before God's Prophet   Thus far the
king of Babylon is worthy of praise, and we will discuss to-
morrow the deficiency in his reverence.

PRAYER.

Grant, Almighty God, since thou hast shewn us by so many, such
clear and such solid testimonies, that we can hope for no other
Redeemer than him whom thou hast set forth : and as thou hast
sanctioned his divine and eternal power by so many miracles,
and hast sealed it by both the preaching of the Gospel and the
seal of thy Spirit in our hearts, and dost confirm the same by
daily experience,—Grant that we may remain firm and stable
in him.   May we never decline from him : may our faith never
waver, but withstand all the temptations of Satan : and may we
so persevere in the course of thy holy calling, that we may be
gathered at length unto that eternal blessedness and perpetual
rest which has been obtained for us by the blood of the same,
thy Son.—Amen.

Lecture Twelfth.

WE said yesterday that King Nebuchadnezzar was worthy
of praise, because he prostrated himself before Daniel after
he had heard the narration of his dream and the interpre-

tation which was added.   For he gave them some testimony
of piety, since in the person of Daniel he adored the true
God, as we shall mention hereafter.   Hence he shewed
himself teachable, since the prophecy might exasperate his
mind ; because tyrants can scarcely ever bear anything to
detract from their power.   But he cannot be entirely excused.   Although he confesses the God of Israel to be the
only God, yet he transfers a part of his worship to a mortal
man.   Those who excuse this do not sufficiently remember
how profane men mingle heavenly and earthly things; though
they occasionally have right dispositions, yet they relax immediately to their own superstitions.   Without doubt the
confession which we shall meet with directly was confined
to this single occasion.   Nebuchadnezzar was not really and
completely converted to true piety, so as to repent of his
errors, but he partially recognised the supreme power to be
with the God of Israel.   This reverence, however, did not
correct all his idolatries, but by a sudden impulse, as I have
said, he confessed Daniel to be a servant of the true God.
At the same time he did not depart from the errors to which
he had been accustomed, and he afterwards returned to
greater hardness, as we shall find in the next chapter.   So
also we see Pharaoh giving glory to God, but only for a moment, (Exod. ix. 27, and x. 16 ;) meanwhile he continued
determinately proud and cruel, and never put off his original
disposition.   Our opinion of the king of Babylon ought to
be of the same kind, though different in degree.   King
Nebuchadnezzar's obstinacy was not equal to the pride of
Pharaoh.   Each, indeed, shewed some sign of reverence, but
neither was truly and heartily submissive to the God of
Israel.   Hence he bows before Daniel, not thinking him a
God, but mingling and confounding, as profane men do,
black and white ; and we know that from the beginning
even the dullest men had some perception of the only God.
For no one ever denied the existence of a Supreme Deity,
but men afterwards fabricated for themselves a multitude
of gods, and transferred a part of the divine worship to
mortals.   As King Nebuchadnezzar was involved in these
errors, we are not surprised at his adoring Daniel, and at the

same time confessing there is but one God! And at this
day we see how all in the papacy confess this truth, and yet
they tear up the name of God, not in word, but in reality;
for they so divide the worship of God, that each has part of
the spoil and the plunder. Daniel relates what experience
even now teaches us. This adoration was, it is true, commonly received among the Chaldeans, since the Orientals
were always extravagant in their ceremonies, and we know
their kings to have been adored as gods. But since the word
for sacrificing is here used, and the word מנחה, *mencheh*,
for "offering" also occurs, it is quite clear that Daniel was
worshipped without consideration, as if he had been a demi-
god dropped down from heaven. Hence we must conclude
that King Nebuchadnezzar did wrong in offering this honour
to Daniel.

There ought to be moderation in our respect for God's
Prophets, as we should not extol them beyond their deserts;
we know the condition on which the Lord calls us forth—
that he alone may be exalted, while all his teachers, and
prophets, and servants, should remain in their own position.
A question arises concerning the Prophet himself,—Why did
he allow himself to be worshipped? For if Nebuchadnezzar
sinned, as we have said, the Prophet had no excuse for allowing it. Some commentators labour anxiously to excuse
him; but if he passed this by in silence, we must be compelled to confess him in some degree corrupted by the
allurements of the court, since it is difficult to be familiar
there without immediately being subject to its contagion.
The defence of any man, however perfect, ought never to
interfere with this fixed principle—nothing must be subtracted from the honour of God, and—it is a mark of
perverseness whenever and howsoever the worship which
is peculiar to God is transferred to creatures. Perhaps
Daniel decidedly refused this, and so restrained the folly of
the king of Babylon; but I leave the point in doubt, as
nothing is said about it. Although it is scarcely probable
that he took no notice at the time, when he saw the honour
of God partly transferred to himself; for this would have
been to make himself a partaker of sacrilege and impiety.

A holy Prophet could scarcely fall into this snare. We know many things are omitted in the narrative, and Daniel does not record what was done, but what the king ordered. He prostrated himself on his face; but perhaps Daniel shewed this to be unlawful. When he ordered sacrifice to be offered, Daniel might have rejected it as a great sin. For Peter properly corrected the error of Cornelius, which was more tolerable, since he wished to adore Peter after the common fashion. If, therefore, the Apostle did not endure this, but boldly rebuked the deed, (Acts x. 26,) what must be said about the Prophet? But, as I have said, I dare not assert anything on either side, unless what conjecture renders probable, that God's servant rejected this preposterous honour. If, indeed, he allowed it, he had no excuse for his sin; but still, as we have said, it is very difficult for those who desire to retain their purity to have much intercourse with courts, without contracting some spots of corruption. We see this even in the person of Joseph. Although he was completely dedicated to God, yet in his language, as shewn by his swearing, he was tainted by the Egyptian custom. (Gen. xlii. 15.) And since this was sinful in him, the same may be said of Daniel. Let us go on :—

47. The king answered unto Daniel, and said, Of a truth *it is*, that your God *is* a God of gods, and a Lord of kings, and a revealer of secrets, seeing thou couldest reveal this secret.

47. Respondit rex Danieli, et dixit, Ex vero Deus vester ipse *est* Deus deorum, et dominus regum, et revelator arcanorum, quod potueris revelare arcanum hoc.

This confession is quite pious and holy, and is fraught with rectitude and sincerity; it may even be taken as a proof of true conversion and repentance. But, as I have lately reminded you, profane men are sometimes seized with an admiration of God; and then they profess largely and copiously whatever may be expected from God's true worshippers. Still this is but momentary, for all the while they remain wrapt up in their own superstitions. God, therefore, extorts this language from them, when they speak so piously; but they inwardly retain their faults, and afterwards easily fall back to their accustomed habits—as a memorable example will shortly prove to us. Whatever sense be adopted, God wished his glory to be proclaimed by the mouth of the profane king, and desired him to be the herald of his own power and influence. But this was peculiarly profitable to those Jews who still remained firm in their allegiance ; for the greater part had revolted—notoriously enough, and had degenerated with great facility from the pure worship of God. When led into captivity, they became idolaters and apostates, and denied the living God ; but a small number of the pious remained ; God wished to promote their benefit, and to strengthen their minds when he drew this confession from the king of Babylon. But another object was gained, since the king as well as all the Chaldeans and Assyrians were rendered more excuseless. For if the God of Israel was truly God, why did Bel in the meantime retain his rank ? *He is the God of gods*—then it must be added at once, he is the enemy of false gods. We observe how Nebuchadnezzar here mingles light with darkness, and black with white, while he confesses the God of Israel to be supreme among gods, and yet continues to worship other deities. For if the God of Israel obtains his right, all idols vanish away. Hence, Nebuchadnezzar contends with himself in this language. But, as I have said, he is seized by a violent impulse, and is not quite in his senses when he so freely declares the power of the only God.

As far then as words go, he says, *truly your God is himself a God of gods*. The particle *truly* is by no means superfluous here ; it is strongly affirmative. For if any one had inquired of him whether Bel and other idols were to be worshipped as gods, he might answer, " yes ;" but doubtfully, and according to pre-conceived opinion, since all superstitious worshippers are perplexed, and if ever they defend their superstitions, they do so with the rashness which the devil suggests, but not according to their judgment. In truth, their minds are not composed when they dare to assert their own superstitions to be pious and holy. But Nebuchadnezzar seems here formally to renounce his own errors ; as if he had said—Hitherto I acknowledged other gods, but I now change my opinion ; I have discovered your God to be the chief of all gods. And, truly, if he really spoke his own mind, he might perceive he was doing injus-

tice to his own idols, if there was any divinity in them ;
Israel's God was confessedly held in utter hatred and abomination by the profane nations. By extolling him above all
gods, he degrades Bel and the whole crew of false gods
which the Babylonians worshipped. But, as we have said,
he was swayed by impulse and spoke without thinking. He
was in a kind of enthusiasm, since God astonished him, and
then drew him on to wonder at and to declare his own power.
He calls him *Lord of kings,* by which eulogium he claims
for him the supreme dominion over the world ; he means to
assert that Israel's God not only excels all others, but holds
the reins of government over the world. For if he is the
Lord of kings, all people are under his hand and dominion !
and the multitude of mankind cannot be drawn away from
his empire, if he rules their very monarchs. We understand,
therefore, the meaning of these words, namely, whatever
deity is worshipped is inferior to the God of Israel, because
he is high above all gods ; then his providence rules over
the world, while he is Lord of all peoples and kings, and
governs all things by his will.

He adds, *he is a revealer of secrets.* This is our proof
of Divinity, as we have said elsewhere. For Isaiah, when
wishing to prove the existence of only one God, takes these
two principles, viz., Nothing happens without his permission ;
and his foreseeing all things. (Chap. xlviii. 3-5.) These
two principles have been inseparably united. Although
Nebuchadnezzar did not understand what was the true peculiarity of Divinity, yet he is here impelled by the secret instinct of God's Spirit clearly to set forth God's power and
wisdom. Hence he confesses the God of Israel to excel all
gods, since he obtains power in the whole world, and nothing
whatever is concealed from him. He adds the reason—
Daniel could reveal that secret. This reason does not seem
a very good one ; for he infers the world to be governed by
one God, because Daniel made this secret known. But
then " this has no reference to his power." The answer to
this remark is easy ; we shewed elsewhere how we ought not
to imagine a god like Apollo who can only predict future
events. And, truly, it is far too insipid to attribute to God

simple prescience, as if the events of the world had any other
dependence than upon his power; for God is said to have a
previous knowledge of future events, because he determined
what he wished to have done.   Hence Nebuchadnezzar
concluded the dominion of the whole world to be in God's
hands, because he could predict futurity ; for unless he had
the full power over the future, he could not predict anything
with certainty.   As, therefore, he really predicts future
events, this clearly determines all things to be ordained by
him, and disproves the existence of chance, while he fulfils
whatever he has decreed.

Let us learn from this passage, how insufficient it is to
celebrate God's wisdom and power with noisy declamation,
unless we at the same time reject all superstitions from
our minds, and so cling to the only God as to bid all others
heartily farewell.   No fuller verbal confession can be required than is here set before us ; and yet we observe how
Nebuchadnezzar was always involved in Satan's impostures,
because he wished to retain his false gods, and thought it
sufficient to yield the first place to the God of Israel.   Let us
learn again, to do our best in purging the mind from all
superstitions, that the only God may pervade all our senses.
Meanwhile, we must observe how severe and dreadful a
judgment awaits Papists, and all like them, who at least
ought to be imbued with the rudiments of piety, while they
confess the existence of but one supreme God, and yet
mingle together a great multitude of deities, and dishonour
both his power and wisdom, and at the same time observe
what is here said by a profane king.   For the Papists not
only divide God's power, by distributing it in parts to each
of their saints ; but also when they speak of God himself,
they fancy him as knowing all things beforehand, and yet
leaving all things contingent on man's free will ; first creating all things, and then leaving every event in suspense.
Hence heaven and earth, as they bear either men's merits
or crimes, at one time become useful, and at another adverse
to mankind.   Truly enough, neither rain, nor heat, nor
cloudy nor serene weather, nor anything else happens without God's permission ; and whatever is adverse is a sign of

his curse; whatever is prosperous and desirable is the sign of his favour. This, indeed, is true, but when the Papists lay their foundation in the will of man, we see how they deprive God of his rights. Let us learn, then, from this passage, not to attribute to God less than was conceded by this profane king.

| 48. Then the king made Daniel a great man, and gave him many great gifts, and made him ruler over the whole province of Babylon, and chief of the governors over all the wise *men* of Babylon. | 48. Tunc rex Danielem magnificavit, et munera præclara, et magna dedit ei,[1] et constituit eum super totam povinciam Babylonis, et magistrum procerum super omnes sapientes Babylonis. |

Here also another point is added, namely, how King Nebuchadnezzar raised God's Prophet and adorned him with the highest honours. We have spoken of that preposterous worship which he himself displayed and commanded others to offer. As far as concerns gifts and the discharge of public duties, we can neither condemn Nebuchadnezzar for honouring God's servant, nor yet Daniel for suffering himself to be thus exalted. All God's servants ought to take care not to make a gain of their office, and we know how very pestilent the disease is when prophets and teachers are addicted to gain, or easily receive the gifts offered them. For where there is no contempt of money, many vices necessarily spring up, since all avaricious and covetous men adulterate God's word and make a traffic of it. (2 Cor. ii. 17.) Hence all prophets and ministers of God ought to watch against being covetous of gifts. But as far as Daniel is concerned, he might receive what the king offered him just as Joseph could lawfully undertake the government of the whole of Egypt. (Gen. xli. 40.) There is no doubt that Daniel had other views than his private and personal advantage. We must not believe him covetous of gain while he bore his exile so patiently, and, besides this, when at the hazard of his life he had preferred abstinence from the royal food to alienating himself from the people of God. As he manifestly preferred the shame of the cross by which God's people were then oppressed, to opulence, luxury, and honour, who will think him blinded by avarice through receiving gifts?

[1] Or, gave him many gifts, as some translate.—*Calvin.*

But since he saw the sons of God miserably and cruelly oppressed by the Chaldeans, he wished as far as he could to succour them in their miseries. As he well knew this would afford some consolation and support to his race, he allowed himself to be made prefect of a province. And the same reason influenced him to seek some place of authority for his companions, as follows,—

49. Then Daniel requested of the king, and he set Shadrach, Meshach, and Abed-nego, over the affairs of the province of Babylon : but Daniel *sat* in the gate of the king.

49. Et Daniel petiit a rege ; et constituit super opus[1] provinciæ Babylonis Sidrach, Mesach, et Abednego : Daniel autem *erat* in porta regis.

Some ambition may be noticed here in the Prophet, since he procures honours for his own companions. For when the king spontaneously offers him a command, he is obliged to accept it ; he need not offend the mind of the proud king. There was a necessity for this, because he himself seeks from the king prefectships for others. What shall we say was the origin of this conduct ? As I have already hinted, Daniel may be here suspected of ambition, for it might be charged against him as a crime that he made a gain of the doctrine which he had been divinely taught. But he rather regarded his people, and wished to bring some comfort to them when oppressed. For the Chaldeans treated their slaves tyrannically, and we are aware how the Jews were utterly hated by the whole world. When therefore Daniel, through the feeling of pity, seeks some consolation from the people of God, there is no reason for accusing him of any fault, because he was not drawn aside by private advantage, and did not desire honours for either himself or his companions ; but he was intent on that object to enable his companions to succour the Jews in their troubles. Hence the authority which he obtains for them has no other object than to cause the Jews to be treated a little more humanely, as their condition would not be so harsh and bitter while they have prefects of their own people who should study to treat them as brethren. We now see how Daniel may be rightly acquitted of this charge without any difficulty or argument ; for the

[1] Or, administration.—*Calvin.*

matter itself is sufficiently clear, and we may readily collect that Daniel was both pious and humane, and free from all charge of sin.   From the words—*was in the king's gate*, we ought not to understand his being a gate-keeper.   Some suppose this phrase to be used, because they were accustomed to exercise justice there; but they transfer to the Chaldeans what Scripture teaches us of the Jews.   I take it more simply.   Daniel was chief over the king's court, since he held the supreme command there ; and that sense is more genuine.   Besides, we are fully aware of the custom of the Chaldeans and Assyrians to make the approach to the king difficult.   Daniel is therefore said *to be at the gate*, to prevent any entrance into the king's palace, unless by his permission.   It now follows,—

CHAPTER THIRD.

1. Nebuchadnezzar the king made an image of gold, whose height *was* threescore cubits, *and* the breadth thereof six cubits: he set it up in the plain of Dura, in the province of Babylon.

1. Nebuchadnezer rex fecit imaginem ex auro, altitudo ejus cubitorum sexaginta, latitudo cubitorum sex: erexit eam in planitie Dura,[1] in provincia Babylonis.

Very probably this statue was not erected by King Nebuchadnezzar within a short period, as the Prophet does not notice how many years had passed away ; for it is not probable that it was erected within a short time after he had confessed the God of Israel to be the Supreme Deity. Yet as the Prophet is silent, we need not discuss the matter. Some of the rabbis think this statue to have been erected as an expiation ; as if Nebuchadnezzar wished to avert the effect of his dream by this charm, as they say.   But their guess is most frivolous.   We may inquire, however, whether Nebuchadnezzar deified himself or really erected this statue to Bel the principal deity of the Chaldeans, or invented some new-fangled divinity ?   Many incline to the opinion that he wished to include himself in the number of the deities, but

---

[1] Some make this word a noun appellative, and translate it, " habitable land," but the following translation is more correct :—He placed an image on the plains of Dura.—*Calvin.*

this is not certain—at least I do not think so. Nebuchadnezzar seems to me rather to have consecrated this statue to some of the deities ; but, as superstition is always joined with ambition and pride, very likely Nebuchadnezzar was also induced by vain glory and luxury to erect this statue. As often as the superstitious incur expense in building temples and in fabricating idols, if any one asks them their object, they immediately reply—they do it in honour of God ! At the same time they are all promoting their own fame and reputation. All the superstitious reckon God's worship valueless, and rather wish to acquire for themselves favour and estimation among men. I readily admit this to have been Nebuchadnezzar's intention, and indeed I am nearly certain of it. But at the same time some pretence to piety was joined with it ; for he pretended that he wished to worship God. Hence, also, what I formerly mentioned appears more clear, namely,—King Nebuchadnezzar was not truly and heartily converted, but rather remained fixed in his own errors, when he was attributing glory to the God of Israel. As I have already said, that confession of his was limited, and he now betrays what he nourished in his heart ; for when he erected the statue he did not return to his own natural disposition, but rather his impiety, which was hidden for a time, was then detected. For that remarkable confession could not be received as a proof of change of mind. All therefore would have said he was a new man, if God had not wished it to be made plain that he was held bound and tied by the chains of Satan, and was still a slave to his own errors. God wished then to present this example to manifest Nebuchadnezzar to be always impious, although through compulsion he gave some glory to the God of Israel.

PRAYER.

Grant, Almighty God, since our minds have so many hidden recesses that nothing is more difficult than thoroughly to purge them from all fiction and lying,—Grant, I say, that we may honestly examine ourselves. Do thou also shine upon us with the light of thy Holy Spirit ; may we truly acknowledge our hidden faults and put them far away from us, that thou mayest be our only God, and our true piety may obtain the palm of thine approbation.   May we offer thee pure and spotless worship, and meanwhile may we conduct ourselves in the world with a pure conscience ; and may each of us be so occupied in our duties as to consult our brother's advantage as well as our own, and at length be made partakers of that true glory which thou hast prepared for us in heaven through Christ our Lord.—Amen.

Lecture Thirteenth.

WE began in the last Lecture to treat of THE GOLDEN STATUE which Nebuchadnezzar erected, and placed in the plain or open country of Dura. We stated this statue to have been erected for a religious reason, when the ambition of that king or tyrant was at its full sway, which we may always observe in the superstitious.   For although they always put forward the name of God, and persuade themselves that they are worshipping God, yet pride always impels them to desire the approbation of the world.   Such was the desire of King Nebuchadnezzar in erecting this statue, as its very magnitude displays.   For the Prophet says, *the height of the statue was sixty cubits, and its breadth six cubits.* Such a mass must have cost much expense, for the image was made of gold.   Probably this gold was acquired by much rapine and plunder ; but whether it was so or not, we may here view, as I have said, the profane king so worshipping God as to propagate the remembrance of his own name to posterity. The region in which he placed the image seems to imply this.   Without doubt the Prophet here points out some celebrated place which men were accustomed to frequent for the sake of merchandise and other necessities.   But as far as the king's special intention is concerned, we stated their conjecture to be out of place who think the statue to have been erected for the sake of expiating his dream.   It is more probable, since the Jews were dispersed throughout Assyria and Chaldea, that this image was erected, lest those foreigners who were exiles from their country should introduce any novelty.   This conjecture carries some weight with it ; for Nebuchadnezzar knew the Jews to be so attached to the God of their fathers as to be averse to all the superstitions of the Gentiles. He feared, therefore, lest they should seduce others to their own opinions, and he wished to counteract this by erecting a new statue, and commanding all his subjects to bow down to it. Meanwhile, we see how quickly the acknowledgment of Israel's God, whose glory and power he had so lately celebrated, had vanished from his mind! Now this trophy is erected to reproach him, as if he had been vanquished as well as the idols of the heathen. But, we have said elsewhere, Nebuchadnezzar never seriously acknowledged the God of Israel, but by a sudden impulse was compelled to confess him to be the Supreme and only God, though he was all the while drowned in his own superstitions. Hence his confession was rather the result of astonishment, and did not proceed from true change of heart. Let us now come to the remainder :

2. Then Nebuchadnezzar the king sent to gather together the princes, the governors, and the captains, the judges, the treasurers, the counsellors, the sheriffs, and all the rulers of the provinces, to come to the dedication of the image which Nebuchadnezzar the king had set up.

2. Tunc Nebuchadnezer rex misit ad congregandum satrapas, duces, et quæstores, primates, *vel proceres,* judices, magistratus, optimates, et omnes præfectos provinciarum, ut venirent ad dedicationem imaginis, quam erexerat Nebuchadnezer rex.

I do not know the derivation of the word "Satrap;" but manifestly all these are names of magistracies, and I allow myself to translate the words freely, since they are not Hebrew, and the Jews are equally ignorant of their origin. Some of them, indeed, appear too subtle ; but they assert nothing but what is frivolous and foolish. We must be content with the simple expression—*he sent to collect the satraps.*

3. Then the princes, the governors, and captains, the judges, the treasurers, the counsellors, the sheriffs, and all the rulers of the provinces, were gathered together unto the dedication of the image that Nebuchadnezzar the king had set up; and they stood before the image that Nebuchadnezzar had set up.

3. Tunc congregati sunt satrapæ, duces, proceres, quæstores, magistratus, judices, optimates, et omnes præfecti provinciarum ad dedicationem imaginis, quam erexerat Nebuchadnezer rex : et steterunt coram imagine quam erexerat Nebuchadnezer.

Let us add the context, as the subject is continued :

4. Then an herald cried aloud, To you it is commanded, O people, nations, and languages,

4. Et præco clamabat in fortitudine:[1] Vobis edicitur, populi, gentes, et linguæ,[2]

5. *That* at what time ye hear the sound of the cornet, flute, harp, sackbut, psaltery, dulcimer, and all kinds of music, ye fall down and worship the golden image that Nebuchadnezzar the king hath set up.

5. Simulac audieritis vocem cornu, *vel, tubæ,* fistulæ, citharæ, sambucæ, psalterii, symphoniæ, et omnia instrumenta musices: ut procidatis, et adoretis imaginem auream, quam erexit Nebuchadnezer rex.

I do not know of what kind these musical instruments were.

6. And whoso falleth not down and worshippeth, shall the same hour be cast into the midst of a burning fiery furnace.

6. Et quisquis non prociderit[3] et adoraverit, eadem hora,[4] projicietur in medium fornacem ignis ardentis, *vel, ardentem.*

7. Therefore at that time, when all the people heard the sound of the cornet, flute, harp, sackbut, psaltery, and all kinds of music, all the people, the nations, and the languages, fell down *and* worshipped the golden image that Nebuchadnezzar the king had set up.

7. Itaque simulatque, *eadem hora atque,* audierint omnes populi vocem cornu, fistulæ, citharæ, sambucæ, psalterii, et omnium instrumentorum musices, prociderunt omnes populi, gentes et linguæ adorantes imaginem auream, quam erexerat Nebuchadnezer rex.

We see how Nebuchadnezzar wished to establish among all the nations under his sway a religion in which there should be no mixture of foreign novelty. He feared dissension as a cause of disunion in his empire. Hence we may suppose the king to have consulted his own private ease and advantage, as princes are accustomed to consult their own wishes rather than God's requirements in promulgating edicts concerning the worship of God. And from the beginning, this boldness and rashness have increased in the world, since those who have had supreme power have always dared to fabricate deities, and have proceeded beyond this even to ordering the gods which they have invented to be worshipped. The different kinds of gods are well known as divided into three—the PHILOSOPHICAL, the POLITICAL, and the POETICAL. They called those gods "PHILOSOPHICAL" which natural reason prompts men to worship. Truly, indeed, philosophers are often foolish when they dispute about the essence

---

[1] Or, in the midst of the multitude; for היל, *hil,* may be explained both ways.— *Calvin.*

[2] That is, nations of all languages.—*Calvin.*

[3] That is, shall not bend the knee.—*Calvin.*

[4] That is, instantly.—*Calvin.*

or worship of God; but since they follow their own fancies they are necessarily erroneous. For God cannot be apprehended by human senses, but must be made manifest to us by his own word; and as he descends to us, so we also in turn are raised to heaven. (1 Cor. ii. 14.) But yet philosophers in their disputes have some pretexts, so as not to seem utterly insane and irrational. But the poets have fabled whatever pleases them, and thus have filled the world with the grossest and at the same time the foulest errors. As all theatres resounded with their vain imaginations, the minds of the vulgar have been imbued with the same delusions; for we know human dispositions are ever prone to vanity. But when the devil adds fire to the fuel, we then see how furiously both learned and unlearned are carried away. So it happened when they persuaded themselves of the truth of what they saw represented in their theatres. Thus, that religion which was founded on the authority of the Magi was considered certain by the heathen, as they called those gods " POLITICAL " which were received by the common consent of all. Those also who were considered prudent said it was by no means useful to object to what the philosophers taught concerning the nature of the gods, since this would tear asunder all public rites, and whatever was fixed without doubt in men's minds. For both the Greeks and Latins, as well as other barbarous nations, worshipped certain gods as the mere offspring of opinion, and these they confessed to have once been mortal. But philosophers at least retained this principle—the gods are eternal; and if the philosophers had been listened to, the authority of the Magi would have fallen away. Hence the most worldly-wise were not ashamed, as I have mentioned, to urge the expulsion of philosophy from sacred things.

With regard to the POETS, the most politic were compelled to succumb to the petulance of the common people, and yet they taught at the same time what the poets feigned and fabled concerning the nature of the gods was pernicious. This, then, was the almost universal rule throughout the world as to the worship of God, and the very foundation of piety—namely, no deities are to be worshipped except those which have been handed down from our forefathers. And this is the tendency of the oracle of Apollo which Xenophon[1] in the character of Socrates so greatly praises, namely, every city ought to worship the gods of its own country ! For when Apollo was consulted concerning the best religion, with the view of cherishing the errors by which all nations were intoxicated, he commanded them not to change anything in their public devotions, and pronounced that religion the best for every city and people which had been received from the furthest antiquity. This was a wonderful imposture of the devil, as he was unwilling to stir up men's minds to reflect upon what was really right, but he retained them in that old lethargy—" Aha ! the authority of your ancestors is sufficient for you !" The greatest wisdom among the profane was, as I have said, to cause consent to be taken for reason. Meanwhile, those who were supreme either in empire, or influence, or dignity, assumed to themselves the right of fashioning new deities ; for we see how many dedicated temples to fictitious deities, because they were commanded by authority. Hence it is by no means surprising for Nebuchadnezzar to take this license of setting up a new deity. Perhaps he dedicated this statue to Bel, who is considered as the Jupiter of the Chaldeans ; but yet he wished to introduce a new religion by means of which his memory might be celebrated by posterity. Virgil[2] derides this folly when he says:

And he increases the number of deities by altars. For he means, however men may erect numerous altars on earth, they cannot increase the number of the gods in heaven. Thus, therefore, Nebuchadnezzar increased the number of the deities by a single altar, that is, introduced a new rite to make the statue a monument to himself, and his own name famous as long as that religion flourished. Here we perceive how grossly he abused his power ; for he did not consult his own Magi as he might have done, nor even reflect within himself whether that religion was lawful or not ; but

---

[1] Xenophon in Comment., et Cicero de Legibus, lib. ii. § 8.

[2] Æneid, lib. vii. 211, " . . . et numerum Divorum altaribus addit." Heyne reads " addit;" Calvin, " auget."

through being blinded by pride, he wished to fetter the minds of all, and to compel them to adopt what he desired. Hence we gather how vain profane men are when they pretend to worship God, while at the same time they wish to be superior to God himself. For they do not admit any pure thought, or even apply themselves to the knowledge of God, but they make their will law, just as it pleases them. They do not adore God, but rather their own fiction. Such was the pride of King Nebuchadnezzar, as appears from his own edict :

King Nebuchadnezzar sent to collect all the satraps, generals, and prefects, to come to the dedication of the image, which King Nebuchadnezzar had erected. The name of the king is always added, except in one place, as though the royal power raised mortals to such a height that they could fabricate deities by their own right ! We observe how the king of Babylon claimed the right of causing the statue to be worshipped as a god, while it was not set up by any private or ordinary person but by the king himself. While the royal power is rendered conspicuous in the world, kings do not acknowledge it to be their duty to restrain themselves within the bounds of law, so long as they remain obedient to God. And at this day we see with what arrogance all earthly monarchs conduct themselves. For they never inquire what is agreeable to the word of God, and in accordance with sincere piety ; but they defend the errors received from their forefathers, by the interposition of the royal name, and think their own previous decision to be sufficient, and object to the worship of any god, except by their permission and decree. With respect to the dedication, we know it to have been customary among the heathens to consecrate their pictures and statues before they adored them. And to this day the same error is maintained in the Papacy. For as long as images remain with the statuary or the painter, they are not venerated ; but as soon as an image is dedicated by any private ceremony, (which the Papists call a " devotion,") or by any public and solemn rite, the tree, the wood, the stone, and the colours become a god ! The Papists also have fixed ceremonies among their exorcisms in consecrating statues and pictures. Nebuchadnezzar, therefore, when he wished his image to be esteemed in the place of God, consecrated it by a solemn rite, and as we have said, this usage was customary among the heathen. He does not here mention the common people, for all could not assemble in one place; but the prefects and elders were ordered to come, and they would bring numerous attendants with them: then they bring forward the king's edict, and each takes care to erect some monument in his own province, whence it may spread the appearance of all their subjects worshipping as a god the statue which the king had erected.

It now follows—*All the satraps, prefects, generals, elders, treasurers, and magistrates came and stood before the image which King Nebuchadnezzar had set up.* It is not surprising that the prefects obeyed the king's edict, since they had no religion but what they had received from their fathers. But obedience to the king weighed with them more then reverence for antiquity; as in these times, if any king either invents a new superstition, or departs from the papacy, or wishes to restore God's pure worship, a sudden change is directly perceived in all prefects, and in all countries, and senators. Why so? Because they neither fear God nor sincerely reverence him, but depend on the king's will and flatter him like slaves, and thus they all approve, and if need be applaud, whatever pleases the king. It is not surprising then if the Chaldean elders, who knew nothing experimentally of the true God or of true piety, are so prone to worship this statue. Hence also, we collect the great instability of the profane, who have never been taught true religion in the school of God. For they will bend every moment to any breezes, just as leaves are moved by the wind blowing among trees; and because they have never taken root in God's truth, they are necessarily changeable, and are borne hither and thither with every blast. But a king's edict is not simply a wind, but a violent tempest, and no one can oppose their decrees with impunity; consequently those who are not solidly based upon God's word, do not act from true piety, but are borne away by the strength of the storm.

It is afterwards added—*A herald cried out lustily,* or among the multitude. This latter explanation does not suit so well—the herald crying amidst the multitude—since there were a great concourse of nations, and the kingdom of Babylon comprehended many provinces : *The herald, therefore, cried with a loud voice, An edict is gone forth for you, O nations, peoples, and tongues.* This would strike them with terror, since the king made no exception to his command for every province to worship his idol ; for each person would observe the rest, and when every one sees the whole multitude obedient, no one would dare to refuse ; hence all liberty is at an end. It now follows,—*When ye hear the sound of the trumpet,* or horn, *harp, pipe, psaltery, sackbut,* &c., *ye must fall down and adore the image. But whoever did not fall down before it, should be cast the same hour into a burning fiery furnace.* This would excite the greater terror, since King Nebuchadnezzar sanctioned this impious worship with a punishment so severe ; for he was not content with a usual kind of death, but commanded every one who did not worship the statue to be cast into the fire. Now, this denunciation of punishment sufficiently demonstrates how the king suspected some of rebellion. There would have been no dispute if Jews had not been mixed with Chaldeans and Assyrians, for they always worshipped the same gods, and it was a prevailing custom with them to worship those deities whom their kings approved. Hence it appears that the statue was purposely erected to give the king an opportunity of accurately ascertaining whether the Jews, as yet unaccustomed to Gentile superstitions, were obedient to his command. He wished to cause the sons of Abraham to lay aside sincere piety, and to submit to his corruptions, by following the example of others, and framing their conduct according to the king's will and the practice of the people among whom they dwelt. But we shall treat this hereafter.

Respecting the required adoration, nothing but outward observance was needed. King Nebuchadnezzar did not exact a verbal profession of belief in this deity, that is, in the divinity of the statue which he commanded to be worshipped ;

it was quite sufficient to offer to it merely outward worship. We here see how idolatry is deservedly condemned in those who pretend to worship idols, even if they mentally refrain and only act through fear and the compulsion of regal authority. That excuse is altogether frivolous. We see, then, how this king or tyrant, though he fabricated this image by the cunning of the devil, exacted nothing else than the bending the knees of all the people and nations before the statue. And truly he had in this way alienated the Jews from the worship of the one true God, if this had been extorted from them. For God wishes first of all for inward worship, and afterwards for outward profession. The principal altar for the worship of God ought to be situated in our minds, for God is worshipped spiritually by faith, prayer, and other acts of piety. (John iv. 24.) It is also necessary to add outward profession, not only that we may exercise ourselves in God's worship, but offer ourselves wholly to him, and bend before him both bodily and mentally, and devote ourselves entirely to him, as Paul teaches. (1 Cor. vii. 34; 1 Thess. v. 23.) Thus far, then, concerning both the adoration and the penalty.

It follows again,—*As soon as the burst of the trumpets was heard and the sound of so many instruments, all nations, peoples, and tongues fell down and adored the image which King Nebuchadnezzar had set up.* Here I may repeat what I said before—all men were very obedient to the injunctions of their monarchs; whatever they ordered was obeyed, so long as it did not cause complete ruin; and they often bore the heaviest burdens with the view of perfect conformity. But we must remark how our propensities have always a vicious tendency. If King Nebuchadnezzar had commanded the God of Israel to be worshipped, and all temples to be overthrown, and all altars throughout his empire to be thrown down, very great tumults would doubtless have arisen; for the devil so fascinates men's minds that they remain pertinaciously fixed in the errors which they have imbibed. Hence the Chaldeans, Assyrians, and others would never have been induced to obey without the greatest difficulty. But now, on the appearance of the signal, they directly fall

down and adore the golden statue. Hence we may learn to
reflect upon our own character, as in a mirror, with the view
of submitting ourselves to God's Word, and of being immovable in the right faith, and of standing unconquered in our
consistency, whatever kings may command. Although a
hundred deaths may threaten us, they must not weaken our
faith, for unless God restrain us by his curb, we should instantly start aside to every species of vanity; and especially
if a king introduces corruptions among us, we are immediately carried away by them, and, as we said, are far too
prone to vicious and perverse modes of worship. The Prophet repeats again the king's name to shew us how little the
multitude thought of pleasing God; never considering whether the worship was sacred and sound, but simply content
with the king's nod. The Prophet deservedly condemns
this easy indifference.

We should learn also from this passage, not to be induced
by the will of any man to embrace any kind of religion, but
diligently to inquire what worship God approves, and so to
use our judgment as not rashly to involve ourselves in any
superstitions. Respecting the use of musical instruments,
I confess it to be customary in the Church even by God's
command; but the intention of the Jews and of the Chaldeans was different. For when the Jews used trumpets and
harps and other instruments in celebrating God's praises,
they ought not to have obtruded this custom on God as if it
was the proof of piety; but it ought to have another object,
since God wished to use all means of stirring men up from
their sluggishness, for we know how cold we grow in the
pursuits of piety, unless we are aroused. God, therefore,
used these stimulants to cause the Jews to worship him with
greater fervour. But the Chaldeans thought to satisfy their
god by heaping together many musical instruments. For,
like other persons, they supposed God like themselves, for
whatever delights us, we think must also please the Deity.
Hence the immense heap of ceremonies in the Papacy, since
our eyes delight in such splendours; hence we think this to
be required of us by God, as if he delighted in what pleases
us. This is, indeed, a gross error. There is no doubt that

the harp, trumpet, and other musical instruments with which Nebuchadnezzar worshipped his idol, formed a part of his errors, and so also did the gold. God, indeed, wished his sanctuary to manifest some splendour; not that gold, silver, and precious stones please him by themselves, but he wished to commend his glory to his people, since under this figure they might understand why everything precious should be offered to God, as it is sacred to him. The Jews, indeed, had many ceremonies, and much of what is called magnificent splendour in the worship of God, and still the principle of spiritual worship yet remained among them. The profane, while they invented gross deities which they reverenced according to their pleasure, thought it a proof of perfect sanctity, if they sang beautifully, if they used plenty of gold and silver, and if they employed showy utensils in these sacrifices. I must leave the rest for to-morrow.

PRAYER.

Grant, Almighty God, since we always wander miserably in our thoughts, and in our attempts to worship thee we only profane the true and pure reverence of thy Divinity, and are easily drawn aside to depraved superstition,—Grant that we may remain in pure obedience to thy word, and never bend aside from it in any way. Instruct us by the unconquered fortitude of thy Spirit. May we never yield to any terrors or threats of man, but persevere in reverencing thy name even to the end. However the world may rage after its own diabolic errors, may we never turn out of the right path, but continue in the right course in which thou invitest us, until, after finishing our race, we arrive at that happy rest which is laid up for us in heaven, through Christ our Lord.—Amen.

Lecture Fourteenth.

8. Wherefore at that time certain Chaldeans came near, and accused the Jews.

8. Itaque statim,[1] appropinquarunt viri Chaldæi, et vociferati sunt accusationem contra Iudæos.[2]

[1] The same hour.—*Calvin.*
[2] That is, accused them clamorously and with tumult. Others translate, "brought forward an accusation." For אכל, *akel*, signifies to "devour," and they say that it is used metaphorically for "to accuse" when

9. They spake, and said to the king Nebuchadnezzar, O king, live for ever.	9. Loquuti sunt, et dixerunt Nebuchadnezer regi, Rex, in æternum vive.
10. Thou, O king, hast made a decree, that every man that shall hear the sound of the cornet, flute, harp, sackbut, psaltery, and dulcimer, and all kinds of music, shall fall down and worship the golden image :	10. Tu, rex, posuisti edictum, ut omnis homo cum audiret vocem cornu, *vel, tubœ,* fistulæ, citharæ, sambucæ, psalterii, et symphoniæ, et omnium instrumentorum musices, procideret, et adoraret imaginem auream.
11. And whoso falleth not down and worshippeth, *that* he should be cast into the midst of a burning fiery furnace.	11. Et qui non prociderit, et adoraverit, projiciatur in medium, *vel, intra,* fornacem ignis ardentis.
12. There are certain Jews, whom thou hast set over the affairs of the province of Babylon, Shadrach, Meshach, and Abed-nego : these men, O king, have not regarded thee ; they serve not thy gods, nor worship the golden image which thou hast set up.	12. Sunt viri Iudæi, quos ipsos posuisti, *id est, præfecisti,* super administrationem, *vel, opus,* provinciæ Babylonis, Sadrach, Mesach, et Abednego, viri isti non posuerunt ad te, rex, cogitationem,[1] deum tuum[2] non colunt, et imaginem auream quam tu erexisti non adorant.

Although their intention is not here expressed who accused Shadrach, Meshach, and Abed-nego, yet we gather from this event that the thing was most probably done on purpose when the king set up the golden image. We see how they were observed, and, as we said yesterday, Nebuchadnezzar seems to have followed the common practice of kings. For although they proudly despise God, yet they arm themselves with religion to strengthen their power, and pretend to encourage the worship of God for the single purpose of retaining the people in obedience. When, therefore, the Jews were mingled with Chaldeans and Assyrians, the king expected to meet with many differences of opinion, and so he placed the statue in a celebrated place by way of trial and experiment, whether the Jews would adopt the Babylonian rites. Meanwhile this passage teaches us how the king was probably instigated by his counsellors, as they were indignant at strangers being made prefects of the province of Babylon while they were slaves ; for they had become exiles by the right of warfare. Since then the Chal-

joined to this noun. But since it also signifies " to cry out," this sense is suitable, as the accusers were clamorous.—*Calvin.*

[1] Others translate, " reason."—*Calvin.*

[2] Or, " thy gods," but there is not much difference.—*Calvin.*

deans were indignant, they were impelled by envy to suggest this advice to the king.   For how did they so suddenly discover that the Jews paid no reverence to the statue, and especially Shadrach, Meshach, and Abed-nego?   Truly, the thing speaks for itself.   These men watched to see what the Jews would do; and hence we readily ascertain how they, from the beginning, laid the snare by advising the king to fabricate the statue.   And when they tumultuously accuse the Jews, we perceive how they were filled with envy and hatred.   It may be said, they were inflamed with jealousy, since superstitious men wish to impose the same law upon all, and then their passion is increased by cruelty.   But simple rivalry, as we may perceive, corrupted the Chaldeans, and caused them clamorously to accuse the Jews.

It is uncertain whether they spoke of the whole nation generally, namely, of all the exiles, or pointed out those three persons only.   The accusation was probably restricted to Shadrach, Meshach, and Abed-nego.   If these three could be broken down, the victory over the rest was easy.   But few could be found in the whole people hardy enough to resist.   We may well believe these clamourers wished to attack those whom they knew to be spirited and consistent beyond all others, and also to degrade them from those honours which they could not bear them to enjoy.   It may be asked, then, why did they spare Daniel, since he would never consent to dissemble by worshipping the statue which the king commanded to be set up?   They must have let Daniel alone for the time, since they knew him to be in favour with the king; but they brought the charge against these three, because they could be oppressed with far less trouble.   I think them to have been induced by this cunning in not naming Daniel with the other three, lest his favour should mitigate the king's wrath.   The form of accusation is added—*O king, live for ever!*   It was the common salutation.   *Thou, O king!*—this is emphatic, as if they had said, "Thou hast uttered this edict from thy royal authority, *whoever hears the sound of the trumpet,* or horn, *harp, pipe, psaltery, and other musical instruments, shall fall down before the golden statue; whoever should refuse to*

*do this should be cast into the burning fiery furnace. But
here are some Jews whom thou hast set over the administration
of the province of Babylon.* They add this through hatred,
and through reproving the ingratitude of men admitted to
such high honour and yet despising the king's authority, and
inducing others to follow the same example of disrespect.
We see then how this was said to magnify their crime. *The
king has set them over the province of Babylon, and yet these
men do not adore the golden image nor worship thy gods.*
Here is the crime. We see how the Chaldeans, throughout
the whole speech, condemn Shadrach, Meshach, and Abed-
nego of this single crime—a refusal to obey the king's edict.
They enter into no dispute about their own religion, for it
would not have suited their purpose to allow any question to
be raised as to the claim their own deities had to supreme
adoration. They omit, therefore, everything which they
perceive would not suit them, and seize upon this weapon—
the king is treated with contempt, because Shadrach, Meshach, and Abed-nego do not worship the image as the king's
edict ordered them to do.

Here, again, we see how the superstitious do not apply their
minds to the real inquiry how they should piously and properly worship God ; but they neglect this duty and follow
their own audacity and lust. Since therefore the Holy
Spirit sets before us such rashness, as in a mirror, let us learn
that God cannot approve of our worship unless it be offered
up with truth. Here human authority is utterly unavailing,
because unless we are sure that our religion is pleasing to
God, whatever man can do for us will only add to our weakness. While we observe those holy men charged with the
crime of ingratitude and rebellion, we in these times ought
not to be grieved by it. Those who calumniate us reproach
us with despising the edicts of kings who wish to bind us
by their errors ; but, as we shall see by and bye, our defence
is obvious and easy. Meanwhile we ought to undergo this
infamy before the world, as if we were disobedient and unmanageable ; and with respect to ingratitude, even if a
thousand wicked men should load us with reproaches, we
must bear their calumnies for the time patiently, until the

Lord shall shine upon us as the assertor of our innocence.
It now follows,—

13. Then Nebuchadnezzar, in *his* rage and fury, commanded to bring Shadrach, Meshach, and Abed-nego. Then they brought these men before the king.

14. Nebuchadnezzar spake, and said unto them, *Is it* true, O Shadrach, Meshach, and Abed-nego, do not ye serve my gods, nor worship the golden image which I have set up?

15. Now, if ye be ready, that at what time ye hear the sound of the cornet, flute, harp, sackbut, psaltery, and dulcimer, and all kinds of music, ye fall down and worship the image which I have made, *well :* but if ye worship not, ye shall be cast the same hour into the midst of a burning fiery furnace ; and who *is* that God that shall deliver you out of my hands?

13. Tunc Nebuchadnezer cum iracundia et excandescentia,[1] jussit adduci Sadrach, Mesach, et Abednego : viri autem illi adduxerunt coram rege.[2]

14. Loquutus est Nebuchadnezer, et dixit illis, Verumne, Sadrach, Mesach, et Abednego, deos meos non colitis,[3] et imaginem auream quam statui,[4] non adoratis?

15. Nunc ecce parati eritis,[5] simulac audiveritis vocem cornu, *vel, tubœ,* fistulæ, citharæ, sambucæ, psalterii, symphoniæ, et omnium instrumentorum musices, ut procidatis, et adoretis imaginem quam feci. Quoad si non adoraveritis, eadem hora projiciemini in medium fornacis ignis ardentis ; et quis ille Deus qui eruat vos e manu mea?

This narrative clearly assures us, how kings consult only their own grandeur by a show of piety, when they claim the place of their deities. For it seems very wonderful for King Nebuchadnezzar to insult all the gods, as if there was no power in heaven unless what he approved of. *What god,* says he, *can pluck you out of my hand ?* Why then did he worship any deity? Simply to retain the people by a curb, and thus to strengthen his own power, without the slightest affection of piety abiding within his mind. At the beginning Daniel relates how the king was inflamed with wrath. For nothing is more troublesome to kings than to see their authority despised ; they wish every one to be obedient to themselves, even when their commands are most unjust. After the king is cool again, he asks Shadrach, Meshach, and Abed-nego, whether they were prepared to worship his god and his golden image? Since he addresses them doubtfully, and gives them a free choice, his words imply moderation. He seems to free them from all blame, if they will

---

[1] Some translate, fury.—*Calvin.*
[2] We must understand, them.—*Calvin.*
[3] Or rather, my god.— *Calvin.*   [4] Or, I have erected.—*Calvin.*
[5] Some read it interrogatively, Are ye prepared?—*Calvin.*

only bow themselves down hereafter. He now adds directly, *if ye are not prepared, behold I will throw you into a furnace of burning fire;* and at length breaks forth into that sacrilegious and dreadful blasphemy—There is no god who can deliver the saints alive out of his hand !

We see, then, in the person of Nebuchadnezzar, how kings swell with pride, while they pretend some zeal for piety; since in reality no reverence for God influences them, while they expect all men to obey every command. And thus, as I have said, they rather substitute themselves for God, than desire to worship him and promote his glory. This is the meaning of the words, *the statue which I have created, and which I have made;* as if he had said, You are not allowed to deliberate about worshipping this image or not; my orders ought to be sufficient for you. I have erected it purposely and designedly; it was your duty simply to obey me. We see then how he claims the supreme power, by fashioning a god. Nebuchadnezzar is not now treating matters of state policy; he wishes the statue to be adored as a deity, because he had decreed it, and had promulgated his edict. And we must always remember what I have touched upon, namely, this example of pride is set before us, to shew us not to attach ourselves to any religion with rashness, but to listen to God and depend on his authority and commands, since if we listen to man, our errors would be endless. Although kings are so proud and ferocious, yet we must be guided by this rule—Nothing pleases God but what he has commanded in his word; and the principle of true piety is the obedience which we ought to render to him alone. With respect to blasphemy, it clearly demonstrates my previous assertion, however kings put forward some desire for piety, yet they despise every deity, and think of nothing but extolling their own magnificence. ` Hence, they traffic in the name of God to attract greater reverence towards themselves; but at the same time, if they choose to change their deities a hundred times a-day, no sense of religion will hinder them. Religion, then, is to the kings of the earth nothing but a pretext; but they have neither reverence nor fear of God in their minds, as the language of this profane king proves. *What*

God? says he, clearly there is no God.   If any one reply—
he speaks comparatively, since he here defends the glory of
his own god whom he worshipped, still he utters this blasphemy against all gods, and is impelled by intolerable arrogance and diabolical fury.   We are now coming to the principal point where Daniel relates the constancy with which
Shadrach, Meshach, and Abed-nego were endued.

16. Shadrach, Meshach, and Abed-nego, answered and said to the king; O Nebuchadnezzar, we *are* not careful to answer thee in this matter.	16. Responderunt Sadrach, Mesach, et Abednego, et dixerunt regi; Nebuchadnezer, non sumus soliciti super hoc sermone,[1] quid respondeamus tibi.[2]
17. If it be *so,* our God, whom we serve, is able to deliver us from the burning fiery furnace; and he will deliver *us* out of thine hand, O king.	17. Ecce est Deus noster, quem nos colimus, potens, *id est, potest,* liberare nos e fornace ignis ardentis, et e manu tua, rex eruet.
18. But if not, be it known unto thee, O king, that we will not serve thy gods, nor worship the golden image which thou hast set up.	18. Et si non, notum sit tibi, O rex, quod deos tuos nos non colimus, et imaginem auream quam erexisti, non adorabimus.

In this history it is necessary to observe with what unbroken spirit these three holy men persisted in the fear of
God, though they knew they were in danger of instant death.
When, therefore, this kind of death was placed straight before
their eyes, they did not turn aside from the straightforward
course, but treated God's glory of greater value than their
own life, nay, than a hundred lives, if they had so many to
pour forth, and opportunity had been given them.   Daniel
does not relate all their words, but only their import, in
which the unconquered virtue of that Holy Spirit, by which
they had been instructed, is sufficiently evident; for that
denunciation was certainly dreadful, when the king said, *If
ye are not prepared to fall down at the sound of the trumpet
before the image, it is all over with you, and ye shall be directly
cast into a furnace of fire.*   When the king had so fulmi-
nated, they might have winced, as men usually do, since life
is naturally dear to us, and a dread of death seizes upon our
senses.   But Daniel relates all these circumstances, to assure
us of the great fortitude of God's servants when they are led
by his Spirit, and yield to no threats, and succumb to no

[1] Or, business.—*Calvin.*

[2] Others translate, we ought not to answer thee about this business; and they think ל, the letter L, to be superfluous, as it often is.—*Calvin.*

terrors. They answer the king, We do not need any long deliberation. For when they say they care not, they mean by this word, the matter is settled; just as that sentence of Cyprian is related by Augustine,[1] when courtiers persuaded him to preserve his life, for it was with great reluctance that the emperor devoted him to death, when flatterers on all sides urged him to redeem his life by the denial of piety, he answered, There can be no deliberation in a matter so sacred! Thus those holy men say, *We do not care*, we do not enter into the consideration of what is expedient or useful, no such thing! for we ought to settle it with ourselves never to be induced by any reason to withdraw from the sincere worship of God.

If you please to read—*we ought not to answer you*, the sense will be the same. They imply that the fear of death was set before them in vain, because they had determined and resolved in their inmost souls, not to depart a single inch from the true and lawful worship of God. Besides they here give a double reason for rejecting the king's proposal. They say God has sufficient power and strength to liberate them; and then, even if they must die, their life is not of so much value as to deny God for the sake of preserving it. Hence they declare themselves prepared to die, if the king persists in urging his wish for the adoration of the image. This passage is therefore worthy of the greatest attention. First of all, we must observe the answer—for when men entice us to deny the true God we must close our ears, and refuse all deliberation; for we have already committed an atrocious insult against God, when we even question the propriety of swerving from the purity of his worship through any impulse or any reason whatever. And I heartily wish every one would observe this! How excellent and striking is the glory of God, and how everything ought to yield to it, whenever there is danger of its being either diminished or obscured. But at this day, this fallacy deceives the multitude, since they think it lawful to debate whether it is allowable to swerve from the true worship of God for a time,

---

[1] Cyprian was martyred under the edict of Valerian, A.D. 257.—See Euseb. Eccl. Hist., lib. vii. chap. 10.

whenever any utility presents itself on the opposite side. Just as in our days, we see how hypocrites, of whom the world is full, have pretences by which they cloak their delinquencies, when they either worship idols with the impious, or deny at one time openly, and at another obliquely, true piety. " Oh ! what can happen ?—such a one will say—of what value is consistency ? I see some evident advantage if I can only dissemble a little, and not betray what I am. Ingenuousness is injurious not only to me privately, but to all around me !" If a king has none around him who endeavour to appease his wrath, the wicked would give way to their passions, and by their greater license would drive him to the extremity of cruelty. It is, therefore, better to have some mediators on the watch to observe whether the wicked are planning anything. Thus, if they cannot openly, they may covertly avert danger from the heads of the pious. By such reasoning as this, they think they can satisfy God. As if Shadrach, Meshach, and Abed-nego, had not the same excuse ; as if the following thought would not occur to them —" Behold ! we are armed with some power in favour of our brethren ; now what barbarity, what cruelty will be exercised against them, if the enemies of the religion which they profess succeed us ? For as far as they can, they will overthrow and blot out our race and the very remembrance of piety. Is it not better for us to yield for a time to the tyranny and violent edict of the king than to leave our places empty ?— which the furious will by and bye occupy, who will utterly destroy our wretched race which is now dreadfully oppressed." Shadrach, Meshach, and Abed-nego might, I say, collect all these pretences and excuses to palliate their perfidy if they had bent the knee before the golden image for the sake of avoiding danger ; but they did not act thus. Hence, as I have already said, God retains his rights entire when his worship is upheld without the slightest doubt, and we are thoroughly persuaded that nothing is of such importance as to render it lawful and right to swerve from that profession which his word both demands and exacts.

On the whole, that security which ought to confirm the pious in the worship of God is opposed here to all those tortuous and mistaken counsels which some men adopt, and thus, for the sake of living, lose life itself, according to the sentiment of even a profane poet. For of what use is life except to serve God's glory? but we lose that object in life for the sake of the life itself—that is, by desiring to live entirely to the world, we lose the very purpose of living! Thus, then, Daniel opposes the simplicity which ought to mark the sons of God to all those excuses which dissemblers invent with the view of hiding their wickedness by a covering. *We are not anxious*, say they, and why not? Because we have already determined God's glory to be of more consequence than a thousand lives, and the gratification of a thousand senses. Hence, when this magnanimity flourishes, all hesitation will vanish, and those who are called upon to incur danger through their testimony for the truth need never trouble themselves; for, as I before said, their ears are closed to all the enticements of Satan.

And when they add—*God is sufficiently powerful to preserve us; and if not, we are prepared for death*, they point out to us what ought to raise our minds above all trials, namely, the preciousness of our life in God's sight, since he can liberate us if he pleases. Since, therefore, we have sufficient protection in God, let us not think any method of preserving our life better than to throw ourselves entirely on his protection, and to cast all our cares upon him. And as to the second clause, we must remark this, even if the Lord should wish to magnify his own glory by our death, we ought to offer up this as a lawful sacrifice; and sincere piety does not flourish in our hearts unless our minds are always prepared to make this sacrifice. Thus I wished to remark these things shortly now, and with God's permission, I will explain them fully to-morrow.

PRAYER.

Grant, Almighty God, since we see the impious carried away by their impure desires with so strong an impulse; and while they are so puffed up with arrogance, may we learn true humility, and so subject ourselves to thee that we may always depend upon thy word and always attend to thy instructions. When we have learned what worship pleases thee, may we constantly persist unto the end, and never be moved by any threats, or dangers, or violence, from our position, nor drawn aside from our course; but by persevering obedience to thy word, may we shew our alacrity and obedience, until thou dost acknowledge us as thy sons, and we are gathered to that eternal inheritance which thou hast prepared for all members of Christ thy Son.—Amen.

Lecture Fifteenth.

WE said yesterday that the constancy of Shadrach, Meshach, and Abed-nego, was based upon these two reasons :— Their certain persuasion that God was the guardian of their life, and would free them from present death by his power if it were useful. And also their determination to die boldly and fearlessly, if God wished such a sacrifice to be offered. What Daniel relates of these three men belongs to us all. Hence we may gather this general instruction. When our danger for the truth's sake is imminent, we should learn to place our life in God's hand, and then bravely and fearlessly devote ourselves to death. As to the *first* point, experience teaches us how very many turn aside from God and the profession of faith, since they do not feel confidence in God's power to liberate them. It may be said with truth of us all —God takes care of us, since our life is placed in his hand and will; but scarcely one in a hundred holds this deeply and surely fixed in his heart, since every one takes his own way of preserving his life, as if there were no virtue in God. Hence he has made some proficiency in God's word who has learnt to place his life in God's care, and to consider it safe under his protection. For if he has made progress thus far, he may be in danger a hundred times, yet he will never hesitate to follow wherever he is called. This one feeling frees him from all fear and trembling, since God can extricate his servants from a thousand deaths, as it is said in the Psalm, (lxviii. 20,) The issues of death are in his power. For death seems to consume all things; but God snatches from that whirlpool whom he pleases. So this persuasion ought to inspire us with firm and unassailable constancy, since it is necessary for those who so repose the whole care

of their life and safety upon God, to be thoroughly conscious
and undoubtedly sure that God will defend a good cause.
And this is also expressed by these words of Shadrach, Meshach, and Abed-nego: *Behold our God whom we worship.*
When they bring forward God's worship, they bear testimony
to the sureness of their support, when they undertake nothing
rashly, but are worshippers of the true God, and labour for
the defence of piety.   For this is the difference between
martyrs and malefactors, who are often compelled to suffer
the penalty of their madness for attempting to overthrow all
things.   We see, indeed, the majority tossed about by their
own intemperance.   If they happen to suffer punishment,
they are not to be reckoned among God's martyrs ; for, as
Augustine says, the martyr is made by his cause, and not
by his punishment.   Hence the weight of these words, when
these three men attest their worship of God, since in this
way they boast in their power of enduring any urgent danger
not rashly, but only as supported by the sure worship of God.
I now come to the *second* point.

*If God be unwilling to deliver us from death, be it known
to thee, O king, we will not worship thy gods.*   I said first
of all, we should be constantly prepared to undergo every
conflict, to commit our life to his charge, to submit to his
will and hand, and to the protection of his custody.   But
the desire of this earthly and fading life ought not to retain
its hold upon us, and to hinder us from the free and candid
confession of the truth.   For God's glory ought to be more
precious to us than a hundred lives.   Hence we cannot be
witnesses for God without we lay aside all desire of this
life, and at least prefer God's glory to it.   Meanwhile, we
must remark the impossibility of doing this, without the
hope of a better life drawing us towards itself.   For where
there is no promise of any eternal inheritance implanted in
our hearts, we shall never be torn away from this world.   We
are naturally desirous of existence, and that feeling cannot
be eradicated, unless faith overcome it ; as Paul says, Not
that we wished to be unclothed, but clothed upon.   (2 Cor.
v. 4.)   Paul confesses that men cannot be naturally induced
to wish for departure from the world, unless, as we have

said, through the power of faith.   But when we understand our inheritance to be in heaven, while we are strangers upon earth, then we put off that clinging to the life of this world to which we are too much devoted.

These then are the two points which prepare the sons of God for martyrdom, and remove hesitation as to their offering their life in sacrifice to God.   *First,* if they are persuaded that God is the protector of their life and will certainly liberate them should it be expedient ; and *secondly,* when they live above the world and aspire to the hope of eternal life in heaven, while prepared to renounce the world.   This magnanimity is to be remarked in their language, when they say, *Be it known to thee, O king, that we do not worship thy gods nor adore the statue which thou hast set up.*   Here they obliquely accuse the king of arrogating too much to himself, and of wishing religion to stand or fall by his own will.   *Thou hast erected the statue,* but thy authority is of no moment to us, since we know it to be a fictitious deity whose image thou wishest us to worship.   The God whom we worship has revealed himself to us ; we know him to be the maker of heaven and earth, to have redeemed our fathers from Egypt, and to intend our chastisement by driving us into exile. Since, therefore, we have a firm foundation for our faith, hence we reckon thy gods and thy sway valueless.   It follows :

19. Then was Nebuchadnezzar full of fury, and the form of his visage was changed against Shadrach, Meshach, and Abed-nego : *therefore* he spake, and commanded that they should heat the furnace one seven times more than it was wont to be heated.	19. Tunc Nebuchadnezer repletus fuit iracundia, et forma faciei ejus mutata fuit[1] erga Sadrach, Mesach, et Abednego : loquutus est, jussit, *vel, edixit,* accendi fornacem uno septies, *hoc est, septuplo,* magis quam solebat accendi.
20. And he commanded the most mighty men that *were* in his army to bind Shadrach, Meshach, and	20. Et viris præstantibus robore, *vel, robustis virtute,* qui erant in ejus satellitio[2] mandavit ut vincirent

[1] צלם, *tzelem,* is here taken in a different sense from its previous one, for Daniel sometimes uses it for " image," but here for the " figure " or " countenance " of the king, which was changed.—*Calvin.*

[2] חיל, *hil,* is here used for " attendants," or " servants," properly it means " army," but as the king is not at war, it doubtless means " attendants ;" he chose, therefore, the strongest of his attendants.—*Calvin.*

Abed-nego, *and* to cast *them* into the burning fiery furnace.

Sadrach, Mesach, et Abednego, ut projicerent *illos* in fornacem ignis ardentis.

Here, at first sight, God seems to desert his servants, since he does not openly succour them. The king orders them to be thrown into a furnace of fire : no help from heaven appears for them. This was a living and remarkably efficacious proof of their faithfulness. But they were prepared, as we have seen, to endure everything. These bold answers were not prompted simply by their trust in God's immediate help, but by a determination to die ; since a better life occupied their thoughts, they willingly sacrificed the present life. Hence they were not frightened at this terrible order of the king's, but followed on their course, fearlessly submitting to death for the worship of God. No third way was opened for them, when a choice was granted either to submit to death, or apostatize from the true God. By this example we are taught to meditate on our immortal life in times of ease, so that if God pleases, we may not hesitate to expose our souls by the confession of the true faith. For we are so timorous when we are attacked by calamity, we are seized with fear and torpor, and then when we are not pressed by any urgency we feign for ourselves a false security. When we are allowed to be at ease, we ought to apply our minds to meditation upon a future life, so that this world may become cheap to us, and we may be prepared when necessary to pour forth our blood in testimony to the truth. And this narrative is not set before us simply to lead us to admire and celebrate the courage of these three holy ones, but their constancy is proposed to us as an example for imitation.

With reference to King Nebuchadnezzar, Daniel here shews, as in a glass, the pride and haughtiness of kings when they find their decrees disobeyed. Surely a mind of iron ought to grow soft by the answer which we have just narrated, on hearing Shadrach, Meshach, and Abed-nego committing their lives to God ; but when it heard how they could not be drawn aside from their faithfulness by the fear of death, its anger was only increased. In considering this fury, we ought to take into account the power of Satan in seizing and occupying the minds of men. For there is no moderation in them, even if they shew some great and remarkable hope of virtues,—for, as we have seen, Nebuchadnezzar was endued with many virtues; but as Satan harassed him, we discern nothing but cruelty and barbarity. Meanwhile, let us remember how pleasing our constancy is to God, though it may not produce any immediate fruit before the world. For many indulge in pleasure through thinking they would be rash in devoting themselves to death, without any apparent utility. And on this pretext, they excuse themselves from not contending more boldly for the glory of God, by supposing they would lose their labour, and their death would be fruitless. But we hear what Christ pronounces, namely, this sacrifice is pleasing to God, when we die for the testimony of the heavenly doctrine, although the generation before which we bear witness to God's name is adulterous and perverse, nay, even hardened by our constancy. (Matt. v. 11, and x. 32, and Mark viii. 38.)

And such an example is here set before us in these three holy men; because, although Nebuchadnezzar was more inflamed by the freedom of their confession, yet that liberty pleased God, and they did not repent of it, though they did not discern the fruit of their constancy which they wished. The Prophet also expresses this circumstance to demonstrate the king's fury, since *he ordered the furnace to be heated seven times hotter than before;* and then, *he chose from his own servants the strongest of all to bind these holy men, and cast them into the furnace of fire.*

But from the result it is very evident, that this did not occur without God's secret impulse; for the devil will sometimes throw discredit on a miracle, unless all doubt is removed. Since therefore the king ordered the furnace to be heated sevenfold more than before, next when he chose the strongest attendants, and commanded them to follow him, God thus removed all doubts, by liberating his servants, because light emerges more clearly from the darkness, when Satan endeavours to shut it out. Thus God is accustomed to frustrate the impious; and the more impious they are in opposing his glory, the more he makes his honour and doctrine conspicuous. In like manner, Daniel here paints, as in a picture, how King Nebuchadnezzar passed nothing by, when he wished to strike terror into the minds of all the Jews by this cruel punishment. And yet he obtained nothing else by his plans than a clearer illustration of God's power and grace towards his servants. It now follows :—

21. Then these men were bound in their coats, their hosen, and their hats, and their *other* garments, and were cast into the midst of the burning fiery furnace

22. Therefore because the king's commandment was urgent, and the furnace exceeding hot, the flame of the fire slew those men that took up Shadrach, Meshach, and Abednego.

23. And these three men, Shadrach, Meshach, and Abed-nego, fell down bound into the midst of the burning fiery furnace.

21. Tunc viri illi vincti sunt, *vel, ligati*, in suis chlamydibus,[1] et cum tiaris suis :[2] in vestitu suo : et projecti sunt in fornacem ignis ardentis.

22. Propterea quod urgebat, *vel, festinabat, ad verbum*, præceptum regis, et fornacem vehementer jusserat accendi, viros illos qui extulerant Sadrach, Mesach, et Abednego occidit favilla, *alii vertunt flammam*, ignis.

23. Et viri illi tres Sadrach, Mesach, et Abednego ceciderant in medium fornacis ignis,[3] ardentis vincti.

Here Daniel relates the miracle by which God liberated his servants. It has two parts: first, these three holy men walked untouched in the midst of the flame ; and the fires consumed those attendants who cast them into the furnace. The Prophet diligently enumerates whatever tends to prove the power of God. He says, *since the king's command was urgent*, that is, since the king ordered in such anger the furnace to be heated, the flames devour the men who executed his orders. For in Job, (xviii. 5,) שׁביב, *shebib*, means " spark," or the extremity of a flame. The sense of the Prophet is by no means obscure, since the extremity of the flame consumed those strong attendants by playing round them, while Shadrach, Meshach, and Abed-nego walked through the fuel in

[1] Some translate sandals, or, shoes, others hose ; but the majority take the second noun for hose; but we need not trouble ourselves too much about the words, if we only understand the thing itself.—*Calvin.*

[2] We know that the Orientals then wore turbans as they do now, for they wrap up the head ; and though we do not see many of them, yet we know the Turkish dress; then the general name is added.—*Calvin.* See also the note on this passage in Wintle's translation, which is full of good explanatory notes.

[3] That is, within the furnace of fire.—*Calvin.*

the fire and flame.   They were not in the extremity of the flame; for it is as if the Prophet had said,—the king's slaves were consumed by the very smoke, and the fire was without the slightest effect on the servants of God.   Hence he says, *these three fell down in the furnace of fire.*   By saying *they fell*, it means they could not take care of themselves or attempt to escape; for he adds, *they were bound.*   This might at first naturally suffocate them, till they were immediately consumed; but they remained untouched, and then walked about the furnace loose.   We hereby see how conspicuous was God's power, and how no falsehood of Satan's could obscure it.   And next, when the very points of the flame, or the fiery sparks, devour the servants, here again the deed is proved to be of God.   Meanwhile, the result of the history is the preservation of these three holy men, so surprisingly beyond their expectation.

This example is set before us, to show us how nothing can be safer than to make God the guardian and protector of our life.   For we ought not to expect to be preserved from every danger because we see those holy men delivered; for we ought to hope for liberation from death, if it be useful, and yet we ought not to hesitate to meet it without fear, if God so please it.   But we should gather from our present narrative the sufficiency of God's protection, if he wishes to prolong our lives, since we know our life to be precious to him; and it is entirely in his power, either to snatch us from danger, or to withdraw us to a better existence, according to his pleasure.   We have an example of this in the case of Peter; for he was on one day led forth from prison, and the next day put to death.   Even then God shewed his care of his servant's life, though Peter at length suffered death.   How so?   Because he had finished his course.   Hence, as often as God pleases, he will exert his power to preserve us; if he leads us onwards to death, we must be assured it is best for us to die, and injurious to us to enjoy life any longer.   This is the substance of the instruction which we may receive from this narrative.   It now follows :—

24. Then Nebuchadnezzar the

24. Tunc Nebuchadnezer rex con-

king was astonied, and rose up in haste, *and* spake, and said unto his counsellors, Did not we cast three men bound into the midst of the fire? They answered and said unto the king, True, O king.

25. He answered and said, Lo, I see four men loose, walking in the midst of the fire, and they have no hurt; and the form of the fourth is like the Son of God.

tremuit,[1] et surrexit in festinatione, *celeriter :* loquutus est, et dixit consiliariis suis:[2] An non viros tres projecimus in fornacem ligatos? *vinctos ?* Responderunt, et dixerunt regi, Vere, rex.

25. Respondit, et dixit, Atqui ego video viros quatuor solutos, ambulantes in igne, et nulla noxa in ipsis est: et facies quarti similis est filio Dei.

Here Daniel relates how God's power was manifest to the profane—to both the king and his courtiers, who had conspired for the death of these holy men. He says, then, *the king trembled* at that miracle; since God often compels the impious to acknowledge his power, and when they stupify themselves, and harden all their senses, they are compelled to feel God's power whether they will or not. Daniel shews how this happened to King Nebuchadnezzar. *He trembled,* says he, *and rose up quickly, and said to his companions, Did we not cast three men bound into the fire ?* When they say, *It is so,* Nebuchadnezzar was doubtless impelled by a Divine impulse, and a secret instinct, to inquire of his companions to extract this confession from them. For Nebuchadnezzar might easily approach the furnace, but God wished to extract this confession from his enemies, that both they and the king might allow the rescue of Shadrach, Meshach, and Abed-nego, to have proceeded from no earthly medium, but from the admirable and extraordinary power of God. We may here remark, how the impious are witnesses to God's power, not willingly, but because God placed this question in the king's mouth, and also in his not permitting them to escape or turn aside from the confession of the truth. But Nebuchadnezzar says, *four men walked in the fire, and the face of the fourth is like the son of a god.* No doubt God here sent one of his angels, to support by his presence the minds of his saints, lest they should faint. It was indeed a formidable spectacle to see the furnace so hot, and to be cast

---

[1] Or, was terrified.—*Calvin.*

[2] Some translate, to his companions; and the word may be derived from either *consilium* or *consuetudo:* hence it might mean companions who were around the king; but soon afterwards it means counsellors, and there is no need of variety.—*Calvin.*

into it.   By this consolation God wished to allay their anxiety, and to soften their grief, by adding an angel as their companion.   We know how many angels have been sent to one man, as we read of Elisha. (2 Kings vi. 15.)   And there is this general rule—He has given his angels charge over thee, to guard thee in all thy ways ; and also, The camps of angels are about those who fear God.   (Ps. xci. 11, and xxxiv. 7.) This, indeed, is especially fulfilled in Christ ; but it is extended to the whole body, and to each member of the Church, for God has his own hosts at hand to serve him.   But we read again how an angel was often sent to a whole nation. God indeed does not need his angels, while he uses their assistance in condescension to our infirmities.   And when we do not regard his power as highly as we ought, he interposes his angels to remove our doubts, as we have formerly said. A single angel was sent to these three men ; Nebuchadnezzar calls him a son of God ; not because he thought him to be Christ, but according to the common opinion among all people, that angels are sons of God, since a certain divinity is resplendent in them ; and hence they call angels generally sons of God.   According to this usual custom, Nebuchadnezzar says, *the fourth man is like a son of a god.*   For he could not recognise the only-begotten Son of God, since, as we have already seen, he was blinded by so many depraved errors.   And if any one should say it was enthusiasm, this would be forced and frigid.   This simplicity, then, will be sufficient for us, since Nebuchadnezzar spoke in the usual manner, as one of the angels was sent to those three men— since, as I have said, it was then customary to call angels sons of God.   Scripture thus speaks, (Ps. lxxxix. 6, and elsewhere,) but God never suffered truth to become so buried in the world as not to leave some seed of sound doctrine, at least as a testimony to the profane, and to render them more inexcusable—as we shall treat more at length in the next lecture.[1]

[1] See DISSERTATION XIII. at the end of this volume.

PRAYER.

Grant, Almighty God, since our life is only for a moment, nay, is only vanity and smoke, that we may learn to cast all our care upon thee, and so to depend upon thee, as not to doubt thee as our deliverer from all urgent perils, whenever it shall be to our advantage. Grant us also to learn to neglect and despise our lives, especially for the testimony of thy glory; and may we be prepared to depart as soon as thou callest us from this world. May the hope of eternal life be so fixed in our hearts, that we may willingly leave this world and aspire with all our mind towards that blessed eternity which thou hast testified to be laid up for us in heaven, through the gospel, and which thine only-begotten Son has procured for us through his blood.—Amen.

Lecture Sixteenth.

26. Then Nebuchadnezzar came near to the mouth of the burning fiery furnace, *and* spake, and said, Shadrach, Meshach, and Abed-nego, ye servants of the most high God, come forth, and come *hither.* Then Shadrach, Meshach, and Abed-nego came forth of the midst of the fire.

26. Tunc accessit Nebuchadnezer ad ostium fornacis ignis ardentis: loquutus est et dixit, Sadrach, Mesach, et Abednego servi Dei excelsi, egredimini, et venite. Tunc egressi sunt Sadrach, Mesach, et Abednego e medio ignis.

HERE a sudden change is described in the mood of this cruel and proud king. We have already seen how confidently he exacted worship from the servants of God, and when he saw them disobedient to his command, how mightily he raged against them. Now Daniel shews in how short a time this pride was subdued and this cruelty appeased; but we must remark that the king was not so changed as entirely to put off his disposition and manners. For when he was touched with this present miracle, he gave God the glory, but only for a moment; and still he did not return to wisdom. We cannot take too diligent notice of examples of this kind, as many estimate the characters of others from a single action. But the worst despisers of God can submit to him for a short time, not merely by feigning to do so before men, but in real seriousness, since God compels them by his power, but meanwhile they retain their pride and

ferocity within their breasts. Of this kind, then, was the
conversion of King Nebuchadnezzar. For when astonished
by the miracle, he could no longer resist the Almighty, he
was still inconsistent, as we shall afterwards see. We may
also notice how the impious, who are unregenerate by God's
Spirit, are often impelled to worship God ; but this is only
temporary, and this equable tenor never remains through
their whole life. But when God renews his own, he undertakes to govern them even to the end ; he animates them
to perseverance, and confirms them by his Spirit.

We must here remark how God's glory is illustrated by
this temporary and vanishing conversion of the reprobate ;
because, whether they will or not, yet they yield to God
for a time, and thus the greatness of his power is acknowledged. God, therefore, turns an event which does not profit
the reprobate to his own glory, and at the same time
punishes them more severely. For Nebuchadnezzar's conduct was less excusable after his once acknowledging the
God of Israel to be the supreme and only God, and then re-
lapsing into his former superstitions. He says, therefore,—
*He approached the door of the furnace, and spoke thus,—
Shadrach, Meshach, and Abed-nego, servants of the most high
God, come forth and come hither.* A short time before, he
wished his own statue to be worshipped, and his own name
to be esteemed the only one in heaven and earth, since this
was pleasing to him. We then saw how he claimed the
right of subjecting the religion and worship of God to his
own will and lust ; but now, as if he were a new man, he
calls Shadrach, Meshach, and Abed-nego, servants of the
most high God ! What place, then, was left to him and to
all the Chaldeans ? How could they now worship those fictitious gods and idols which they had fabricated ? But
God extracted these words from the proud and cruel king,
as when criminals are compelled, by tortures, to say what
they would otherwise refuse. Thus Nebuchadnezzar confessed God to be *the most high God of Israel,* as if he had
been tortured, but not of his own accord, or in a composed
state of mind. He does not pretend this before men, as I
have said ; but his mind was neither pure nor perfect, since

it was in a ferment with this temporary commotion. And this must also be added—the instinct was rather violent than voluntary.

Daniel afterwards relates—*His companions came forth from the midst of the fire.* By these words he again confirms the miracle ; for God could extinguish the fire of the furnace, but he wished it to burn in the sight of all, to render the power of this deliverance the more conspicuous. Meanwhile we must notice *the three men walking in the furnace*, until the king commanded them to come forth, because God had issued no command. They saw themselves perfectly safe and sound in the midst of the furnace ; they were content with God's present benefit, but still they had no free departure, until fetched by the king's voice. As when Noah, in the ark, saw safety prepared for him in that tomb, yet he did not try anything until commanded to come forth. (Gen. viii. 16.) So also Daniel asserts that his companions did not come forth from the furnace till the king commanded them. Then at length they understood how what they had heard from the king was pleasing to God ; not because he was a Prophet or teacher, but because they were cast into the furnace by his command. So also when he recalls them, they know the end of their cross to be arrived, and thus they pass from death unto life. It follows—

27. And the princes, governors, and captains, and the king's counsellors, being gathered together, saw these men, upon whose bodies the fire had no power, nor was an hair of their head singed, neither were their coats changed, nor the smell of fire had passed on them.

27. Et congregati sunt satrapæ, duces, præfecti, et consiliarii regis[1] ad conspiciendos viros illos, quod non dominatus esset ignis corporibus eorum, et pilus capitis eorum non adustus esset, et vestibus eorum non esset mutatus, et odor ignis non pervasisset, *vel, non penetrasset*, ad eos.[2]

Daniel relates how the satraps were gathered together with the leaders, prefects, and councillors of the king. The gathering was simply a collection of numbers, and if they deliberated about anything of importance, they all agreed. And this confirms the miracle, since if they had been stupi-

[1] Some translate the last " prefects," but badly : it properly signifies either counsellors or familiar friends, as appears from many passages.— *Calvin.*

[2] Or, " to them," for the relative may apply either to their persons or their clothing, and it is of little consequence to which. —*Calvin.*

fied, how could the great power of God be proposed to the eyes of the blind ?　Although they were so astonished, they were not altogether foolish.　And Daniel implies this by saying, *they were assembled together.* After they had discussed the matter, he says, they came to behold that specimen of the incredible power of God.　Then he enumerates many reasons, which clearly shew these three men not to have been preserved by any other means than God's singular good will. He says, *The fire had no power over their bodies :* then, *a hair of their head was not burnt :* thirdly, *their garments were unchanged :* lastly, *the smell of fire had not penetrated to themselves or their garments.* He expresses more by the word *smell* than if he had simply said,—the fire had not penetrated.　For fire must naturally consume and burn up whatever is submitted to it ; but when not even the smell of fire has passed over any substance, the miracle is more conspicuous.　Now, we understand the Prophet's intention. On the whole, he shews how the benefit of freedom was no small one, since *Shadrach, Meshach, and Abed-nego came safe out of the furnace.* Besides, these satraps, prefects, and governors, were witnesses of the power of God.　Their testimony would be the more valuable, as all the Jews were spectators of this grace of God, which even they scarcely believed.　But since these men were clearly and professedly enemies to true piety, they would willingly have concealed the miracle, had it been in their power.　But God draws them against their wills, and compels them to be eye-witnesses, and they are thus obliged to confess what cannot be in the slightest degree doubtful.　It follows—

28. *Then* Nebuchadnezzar spake, and said, Blessed *be* the God of Shadrach, Meshach, and Abed-nego, who hath sent his angel, and delivered his servants that trusted in him, and have changed the king's word, and yielded their bodies, that they might not serve nor worship any god except their own God.

28. Loquutus est Nebuchadnezer, et dixit, Benedictus Deus ipsorum, nempe Sadrach, Mesach, et Abednego, qui misit angelum suum, et eripuit, *servavit,* servos suos, qui confisi sunt in ipso, et verbum regis mutarunt,[1] et tradiderunt corpora sua, ne colerent, vel adorarent omnem deum,[2] præter Deum suum.

[1] Transgressed, that is, deprived the king's edict of its confidence and authority.—*Calvin.*
[2] That is, adore any other god.—*Calvin.*

This, indeed, is no common confession, but the event proved how suddenly King Nebuchadnezzar was acted on by impulse, without having the living root of the fear of God in his heart. And I repeat this again, to shew that repentance does not consist in one or two works, but in perseverance, as Paul says,—"If ye live in the Spirit, walk also in the Spirit." (Gal. v. 25.) Here he requires constancy in the faithful, by which they may shew themselves to be truly born again of God's Spirit. Nebuchadnezzar celebrated the God of Israel as if inspired by an enthusiasm, but at the same time he mingled his idols with the true God, so that there was no sincerity in him. So when the impious feel God's power, they do not dare to proceed with obstinacy against him, but wish to appease him by a false repentance, without putting off their natural disposition. Thus we readily conclude Nebuchadnezzar to be always the same, although God extracted from him this confession,—*Blessed*, says he, *be the God of Shadrach, Meshach, and Abed-nego!* Why does he not rather speak of him as his own God? This may be excused, had he really devoted himself to the God of Israel, and abjured his former superstitions. As he does not act thus, his confession is worthless; not because he wished to obtain men's favour or good opinion by what he said, but he deceived himself after the manner of hypocrites. He pronounces the God of Shadrach, Meshach, and Abed-nego to be blessed: if he really felt this, he must at the same time curse his idols, for the glory of the one true God cannot be extolled without all idols being reduced to nothing. For how can God's praise exist without his being solely conspicuous? If any other deity is opposed to him, his majesty is already buried in complete obscurity. Hence we may collect that Nebuchadnezzar was not touched with true repentance when he blessed the God of Israel. He adds, *Who sent his angel, and delivered his servants.* Here Daniel shews more clearly the absence of conversion in Nebuchadnezzar, and his failure to embrace the God of Israel, and worship him with sound and complete surrender of his affections. Why so? Because piety is always founded upon the knowledge of the true God, and this requires instruction. Nebuchadnezzar knew the God of Israel to be majestic from the display of his power, for he had such a spectacle presented to him as he could not despise, if he wished.   Here he confesses that Israel's God was mighty, since he was taught it by a miracle; but this, as I have reminded you, is not sufficient for solid piety, unless instruction is added, and occupies the first place.   I allow, indeed, that miracles prepare men to believe, but if miracles only occurred without the knowledge of God being added from his Word, faith will vanish away—as the example sufficiently remarkable here sets before us.   We term the faith of Nebuchadnezzar to be but momentary, because, while his senses were fixed upon the miracle, he was content with the spectacle without inquiring into the character of the God of Israel, and the bearing of his law.   He was not anxious about a Mediator; hence he neglected the chief point of piety, and rashly seized upon one part of it only. We clearly observe this in many profane men, for God often humbles them, to induce them suppliantly to fly to him for safety; but meanwhile they remain perplexed by their own senses; they do not deny their own superstitions, nor regard the true worship of God.   To prove our obedience to God, we must uphold this principle—nothing pleases him which does not spring from faith.   (Rom. xiv. 23.)   But faith cannot be acquired by any miracle, or any perception of the Divine power; it requires instruction also.   The miracles avail only to the preparation for piety or for its confirmation; they cannot by themselves bring men to worship the true God.   This is surprising indeed, when a profane king says *the angel was sent by God.*

It is sufficiently evident from heathen writings that something was always known about angels.   This was, as it were, a kind of anticipation and previous persuasion, since all people are persuaded that angels exist, so that they had some idea of angels, although but a partial one.   For, when a short time ago Daniel said the fourth appearance in the furnace was called by the king of Babylon "a son of a god," then, as I have explained it, Nebuchadnezzar professed some belief in angels.   He now says more expressly, *God sent his angel.*   As angels afford supplies to the elect and the faith-

ful, I treat the subject here but shortly, since I am not in
the habit of dwelling upon ordinary passages. It is enough
for the present passage to shew how the impious, who have
learnt nothing from either God himself or from piety at large,
were yet imbued with these principles, since God is accustomed to use the assistance of angels to preserve his people.
For this reason Nebuchadnezzar now says, *the angel was sent
by God to deliver his servants.* He next adds, *who trusted in
him ;* and this is worthy of notice, since it is added as a reason why these three men were so wonderfully preserved,
through reposing all their hopes on God. Although Nebuchadnezzar was very like a log or a stone with relation to the
doctrine of faith, yet God wished by means of this stone and
log to instruct us, to inspire us with shame, and to reprove
us of incredulity, since we are unable to conform our lives to
his will, and to approach all dangers boldly, whenever it
becomes necessary. For if we are thoroughly persuaded that
God is the guardian of our life, surely no threats, nor terrors,
nor death itself, should hinder us from persevering in our
duty. But distrust is the cause of slothfulness, and whenever we deflect from a straightforward course, we deprive
God of his honour, by becoming backsliders, while some want
of faith betrays itself and is palpably apparent. Hence let us
learn, if we wish our life to be protected by God's hand, to
commit ourselves entirely to him, since he will never disappoint us when we confide in him. We saw how doubtful
about the event Shadrach, Meshach, and Abed-nego were ;
but their doubt did not diminish their hope and confidence.
They were placed in this alternative—either God will take
us from the furnace, or, if we must die, he will preserve us
for some better state, and gather us into his kingdom.
Although they dared not persuade themselves that he would
notice them, yet they reposed their lives in the hand and
care of God. Hence they are deservedly complimented by
Nebuchadnezzar, when he said,—*They trusted in their God,*
and afterwards, *they changed the king's edict,* that is, reduced
it to nothing, and abrogated it, because they were endued with
greater power. For whoever rests in God, easily despises
all mankind, and whatever is lofty and magnificent in the

world. And this context is worthy of observation, since faith ought to be put as a foundation, and then fortitude and constancy must be added, with which Shadrach, Meshach, and Abed-nego were endowed ; because any one who reposes upon God can never be moved aside from the discharge of his duty ; and however numerous the impediments which may occur, he will be borne aloft on the wings of his confidence. He who knows God to be on his side, will be superior to the whole world, and will neither wonder at the sceptre and diadems of kings, nor dread their power, but rather surpass all the majesty of the earth which may oppose him, and never to turn aside from this course.

He afterwards adds, *they delivered up their bodies instead of worshipping or adoring any god except their own God.* That very thing which the king is compelled to praise in these three men, at this day many who boast themselves to be Christians wish to escape. For they fancy their faith to be buried in their hearts, and bring forth no fruit of their profession. There is no doubt God wished these things to be related by his Prophet, to shew the detestable cunning of those who wish to defraud God of his lawful honour, and at the same time shelter themselves from his gaze, lest he should notice their insult. Such as these are unworthy of being convinced by the word of God, but Nebuchadnezzar is here appointed their master, censor, and judge. And we must diligently remark this,—Nebuchadnezzar praises these three, because they refused to worship any other god except their own. Why then did he mingle together a great multitude of deities ? For he did not depart from his own errors and give himself up entirely to the God of Israel, and embrace his worship in its purity. Why then does he praise in others what he does not imitate ? But this is far too common ; for we see virtue praised and yet frozen to death, as in this instance, for many are willing to offer him lip-service. (Juvenal, Sat. i.) Although Nebuchadnezzar seemed here to speak seriously, yet he did not consider himself ; but he took away all pretext for excuse, since he could not afterwards pretend ignorance and error, after asserting with his own mouth that no other god ought to be worshipped. Hence he may cause those who now wish to be called Christians to be ashamed, unless they depart far away from all superstitions, and consecrate themselves entirely to God, and retain his worship in its sincerity. We must remember then how King Nebuchadnezzar does not simply praise the constancy of these three men, because he does not acknowledge any god, for he does reckon the God of Israel to be a true deity. Hence it follows, that all others were fictitious and utterly vain. But he spoke to no purpose, because God did not thereby touch his heart, as he usually works in his elect when he regenerates them. It follows,—

29. Therefore I make a decree, That every people, nation, and language, which speak anything amiss against the God of Shadrach, Meshach, and Abed-nego, shall be cut in pieces, and their houses shall be made a dunghill; because there is no other God that can deliver after this sort.

29. Et a me positum est, *hoc est, ponitur*, edictum,[1] ut omnis populus, natio,[2] et lingua quæ protulerit *aliquid* transversum,[3] contra Deum ipsorum, nempe Sadrach, Mesach, et Abednego, in frusta fiet, et domus ejus *in* latrinam, *vel, in sterquilinium*, redigetur: quia non est Deus alius qui possit servare hoc modo.

Here Nebuchadnezzar is urged further forward—for we must use this phrase—since he does not take up the worship of one God from his heart, and bid his errors finally farewell. Hence it is as if God was thrusting him violently forward, while he promulgates this edict. The edict is by itself pious and praiseworthy ; but, as we have already said, Nebuchadnezzar is borne along by a blind and turbulent impulse, because piety had no root in his heart. Though he is always intent on this miracle, his faith is only momentary, and his fear of God but partial. Why then is Nebuchadnezzar now seen as the patron of God's glory ? Because he was frightened by the miracle, and thus being acted on by impulse alone, he could not be soundly restrained by the fear of God alone. And finally, this desire which he expresses is nothing but an evanescent movement. It is useful to remark this, since we see many borne along by impetuous zeal and rage to vindicate God's glory ; but they lack tact and judgment, so that

[1] Or, decree,—we have already explained this word.—*Calvin.*

[2] Some translate, family.—*Calvin.*

[3] שלח, *sheleh*, signifies to err; hence the noun is derived, which many translate error, and others rashness; but it means a perverse speech—whoever, therefore, utters a perverse speech.—*Calvin.*

they deserve no praise. And many wander still further—as we see in the Papacy—when many edicts of kings and princes fly about ; and if any one should ask them why they are so eager as not to spare even human blood, they put forth indeed a zeal for God, but it is mere madness without a spark of true knowledge. We must hold, therefore, that no law can be passed nor any edict promulgated concerning religion and the worship of God, unless a real knowledge of God shines forth. Nebuchadnezzar indeed had a reason for this edict, but, as I have already said, there was a special motive for his conduct. Some, indeed, now wish to be thought Christian princes, and yet are only inflamed by a hypocritical zeal, and so they pour forth innocent blood like cruel beasts. And why so ? Because they make no distinction between the true God and idols. But I shall discuss this point at greater length to-morrow, and so pass over casually what I shall treat at length, when the fit opportunity arrives.

Every people, therefore, and nation, and language, which shall have offered a perverse speech against their God. Nebuchadnezzar again extolled the God of Israel, but how was he taught the majesty of God ? By this one proof of his power, for he neglected the chief point—the ascertaining from the law and the prophets the nature of God and the power of his will. Thus we see, on one side, how God's glory is asserted here, and yet the principal point in his worship, and in true piety, is neglected and omitted. No light punishment is added— *he must be cut in pieces, next, his house must be turned into a dunghill, since he has spoken reproachfully of the God of Israel.* Hence we gather how this severity is not to be utterly condemned, when God's worship is defended by severe punishments ; yet a correct sentence ought to be passed in each case. But I put this off also till to-morrow. It is now added, *because there is no other God who can deliver after this manner ;* and this confirms what I have formerly touched upon, namely, King Nebuchadnezzar does not regard the law in his edict, nor yet the other requisites of piety ; but he is only impelled and moved by the miracle, so as not to bear or desire anything to be said opprobriously against the God of Israel. Hence the edict is deserving of blame in this point, since he does not inquire what God's nature is, with the view of obtaining a sufficient reason for issuing it. It is added at length,—

30. Then the king promoted Shadrach, Meshach, and Abed-nego, in the province of Babylon.	30. Tunc rex prosperare fecit,[1] Sadrach, Mesach, et Abednego, in provincia Babylonis.

This seems to be of slight consequence; but yet it was not added in vain. We are to understand that the miracle was confirmed throughout the whole province and region, because all the Chaldeans knew those three men were cast into the furnace, and then afterwards shared in the imperial sway and were restored to their former honours. In consequence of this event, God's power could not be unknown. It was just as if God had sent forth three heralds through the whole region, who everywhere proclaimed how they were wonderfully delivered from death by God's special interposition. Whence, also, it would be understood how worthless were all the deities then worshipped in Chaldea, and how that great deity whose statue Nebuchadnezzar had set up had been despised, and how the true God proved his consistency in snatching his servants from death.

PRAYER.

Grant, Almighty God, since thou hast instructed us by the doctrine of thy law and Gospel, and dost daily deign to make known thy will to us with familiarity, that we may remain fixed in the true obedience of this teaching, in which thy perfect justice is manifested; and may we never be moved away from thy worship. May we be prepared, whatever happens, rather to undergo a hundred deaths than to turn aside from the profession of true piety, in which we know our safety to be laid up. And may we so glorify thy name as to be partakers of that glory which has been acquired for us through the blood of thine only-begotten Son.— Amen.

[1] Verbally, for צלח, *tzelech*, signifies " to prosper ;" hence the word is deduced, which signifies " to rest in a state of prosperity;" that is, he caused those three men to become prosperous.—*Calvin*.

Lecture Seventeenth.

CHAPTER FOURTH.

1. Nebuchadnezzar the king, unto all people, nations, and languages, that dwell in all the earth; Peace be multiplied unto you.

2. I thought it good to shew the signs and wonders that the high God hath wrought toward me.

3. How great *are* his signs! and how mighty *are* his wonders! his kingdom *is* an everlasting kingdom, and his dominion *is* from generation to generation.

1. Nebuchadnezer rex omnibus populis, nationibus, et linguis; quæ habitant in tota terra, pax vobiscum multiplicetur.

2. Signa et mirabilia quæ fecit mecum Deus excelsus pulchrum coram me enarrare.

3. Signa ejus quam magna *sunt!* et mirabilia ejus quam fortia! regnum ejus regnum seculare,[1] et dominatio ejus cum ætate, et ætate.

SOME join these verses to the end of the third chapter, but there is no reason for this; and it will clearly appear from the context that the edict is here set forth in the king's name, and other events are inserted. Daniel, therefore, here speaks in the person of the king; he afterwards narrates what happened to the king, and then returns to his own person. Those who separate these three verses from the context of the fourth chapter, do not seem to have sufficiently considered the intention and words of the Prophet. This passage may seem harsh and rough, when Daniel introduces the king of Babylon as speaking—then speaks in his own name—and afterwards returns to the person of the king. But since this variety does not render the sense either doubtful or obscure, there is no reason why it should trouble us. We now see how all the sentences which we shall explain in their places are mutually united.

The contents of this chapter are as follow : Nebuchadnezzar was sufficiently instructed in the worship of the God of Israel as one God, and was compelled at the time to confess this; yet he did not depart from his own superstitions; his conceptions of the true God were but momentary, and hence he suffered the punishment due to such great ingratitude. But God intended him to become more and more blinded, as he is accustomed to treat the reprobate

---

[1] That is, perpetual.—*Calvin.*

and even his elect at times.   When men add sin to sin, God
loosens his reins and allows them to destroy themselves.
Afterwards he either extends his hand towards them, or
withdraws them by his hidden virtue, or reduces them to
order by his rod, and completely humbles them.   He treated
the king of Babylon in this way.   We shall afterwards discuss the dream ; but we must here briefly notice the king's
admonition, that he might feel himself without excuse when
he was so utterly broken down.   God indeed might justly
punish him as soon as he saw he was not truly converted ;
but before he inflicted the final chastisement—as we shall
see in its place—he wished to admonish him, if there were
any hope of his repentance.   Although he seemed to receive
with the greatest modesty what God had manifested by his
dream through Daniel's interpretation of it, yet he professed
with his mouth what he did not really possess.   And he
shews this sufficiently, because, when he ought to be afraid
and cautious, he does not lay aside his pride, but glories in
himself as a king of kings, and in Babylon as the queen of
the whole world ! Since, then, he spoke so confidently after
being admonished by the Prophet, we perceive how little he
had profited by his dream.   But God wished in this way to
render him more inexcusable, and although he did not bring
forth fruit immediately, yet a long time afterwards, when
God touched his mind, he very properly recognised this
punishment to have been divinely inflicted.   Hence this
dream was a kind of entrance and preparation for repentance, and as seed seems to lie putrid in the earth before it
brings forth its fruit, and God sometimes works by gentle
processes, and provides for the teaching, which seemed for a
long time useless, becoming both efficacious and fruitful.

I now come to the words themselves ; the preface to the
edict is, *Nebuchadnezzar the king to all peoples, nations, and
languages, which dwell in the whole earth,* namely, under his
sway.   He does not mean this to be extended to Scythia, or
Gaul, or other distant regions ; but since his empire extended
far and wide, he spoke boastingly.   Thus we see the Romans,
whose sway did not reach near so far, called Rome itself the
seat of the empire of the whole world !   Here Nebuchad-

nezzar now predicts the magnificence and mightiness of his
own monarchy.   Hence he sends his edict *to all peoples, and
nations, and languages, which dwell on the earth.*   He afterwards adds, *it seemed to me good to relate the signs and wonders which the mighty God hath wrought with me.*   No doubt
he feels himself to have paid the penalty of his ingratitude,
since he had so punctiliously ascribed the glory to one true
God, and yet had relapsed into his own superstitions, and had
never really said farewell to them.   We see how often King
Nebuchadnezzar was chastised before he profited by the rod
of the Almighty.   Hence we need not be suprised if God
often strikes us with his hand, since the result of experience
proves us to be dull, and, to speak truly, utterly slothful.
When God, therefore, wishes to lead us to repentance, he is
compelled to repeat his blows continually, either because
we are not moved when he chastises us with his hand, or we
seem roused for the time, and then we return again to our
former torpor.   He is therefore compelled to redouble his
blows.   And we perceive this in the narrative before us, as
in a glass.   But the singular benefit of God was this, Nebuchadnezzar, after God had often chastised him, yielded at
length.   It is unknown whether or not this confession proceeded from true and genuine repentance : I must leave it
in doubt.   Yet without the slightest doubt Daniel recited
this edict, to shew the king so subdued at length, as to confess the God of Israel to be the only God, and to bear witness to this among all people under his sway.

Meanwhile we must remark, how this edict of the king of
Babylon receives the testimony of the Spirit ; for Daniel has
no other object or purpose in relating the edict, than to shew
the fruit of conversion in King Nebuchadnezzar.   Hence,
without doubt, King Nebuchadnezzar bore witness to his
repentance when he celebrated the God of Israel among all
people, and when he proclaimed a punishment to all who
spoke reproachfully against God.   Hence this passage is
often cited by Augustine against the Donatists.[1]   For they
wished to grant an act of impunity to themselves, when they
disturbed the Church with rashness and corrupted pure doc-

[1] Ep. clxvi. ad Donat. et alibi.

trine, and even permitted themselves to attack it like robbers. For some were then discovered to have been slain by them, and others mutilated in their limbs. Since, then, they allowed themselves to act so licentiously and still desired to commit crimes with impunity, yet they held this principle as of first importance. No punishment ought to be inflicted on those who differ from others in religious doctrine; as we see in these days, how some contend far too eagerly about this subject. What they desire is clear enough. If any one carefully observes them, he will find them impious despisers of God; they wish to render everything uncertain in religion, and as far as they can they strive to tear away all the principles of piety. With the view then of vomiting forth their poison, they strive eagerly for freedom from punishment, and deny the right of inflicting punishment on heretics and blasphemers.

Such is that dog Castalio[1] and his companions, and all like him, such also were the Donatists; and hence, as I have mentioned, Augustine cites this testimony in many places, and shews how ashamed Christian princes ought to be of their slothfulness, if they are indulgent to heretics and blasphemers, and do not vindicate God's glory by lawful punishments, since King Nebuchadnezzar who was never truly converted, yet promulgated this decree by a kind of secret instinct. At all events, it ought to be sufficient for men of moderate and quiet tastes to know how King Nebuchadnezzar's edict was praised by the approval of the Holy Spirit. If this be so, it follows that kings are bound to defend the worship of God, and to execute vengeance upon those who profanely despise it, and on those who endeavour to reduce it to nothing, or to adulterate the true doctrine by their errors, and so dissipate the unity of the faith and disturb the Church's peace. This is clear enough from the Prophet's context; for Nebuchadnezzar says at first, *it pleases me to relate the signs and wonders which God has*

---

[1] Sebastian Castalio is here referred to. He was an opponent of Calvin, and banished from Geneva by his influence. Being a man of extensive learning he was appointed Greek professor at Basil. See Mosheim, cent. xvi. sec. iii. pt. 2, and the authorities there quoted.

prepared for me. He had already explained how wonderfully God had treated him ; but this had passed away. Now God seizes him a second and even a third time, and then he confesses it to be his boast to explain the wonderful signs of God. He afterwards breaks forth into the exclamation, *How mighty are his signs ! How remarkable his miracles ! His kingdom is a kingdom of an age, and his dominion is from age to age.* Without doubt Nebuchadnezzar wished to excite his subjects to the attentive perusal of this edict, and to the acknowledgment of its value, and thus to subject themselves to the true and only God. He calls him *The High God,* meaning, doubtless, the God of Israel ; meanwhile, we do not know whether he cast away his superstitions. I however incline to the opposite conjecture, since he did not put off his errors, but was compelled to give glory to the Most High God. He so acknowledged the God of Israel as to join inferior deities with him as allies and companions, just as all unbelievers, while admitting one supreme deity, imagine a multitude of others. So also Nebuchadnezzar confessed Israel's God to be Most High ; yet he did not correct the idolatry which still flourished under his sway ; nay, he mingled and confused the false gods with the God of Israel. Thus he did not leave behind his own corruptions. He celebrates indeed with magnificence the glory of the supreme God, but this is not sufficient without abolishing all superstitions, and promoting that religion alone which is prescribed by the word of God, and causing his pure and perfect worship to flourish.

In fine, this preface might seem a proof of an important conversion ; but we shall directly see how far Nebuchadnezzar was from being entirely purged of his errors. It ought, indeed, to affect us exceedingly to behold the king wrapt up in so many errors, and yet seized with admiration of the Divine virtue, since he cannot express his thoughts, but exclaims,—*His signs how mighty ! his wonders how powerful !* He added, *His kingdom is a perpetual kingdom, and his dominion is from age to age.* Here he confesses God's power not to be dependent upon man's will, since he had just before said, the statue which he had erected was to be worshipped, because he had chosen so to decree it. Now, however, he remits much of this pride by confessing God's kingdom to be a perpetual one. The narrative now follows. Thus far we have merely a preface, because the edict was diffused among his subjects to render them attentive to the most important subjects.

4. I Nebuchadnezzar was at rest in mine house, and flourishing in my palace:	4. Ego Nebuchadnezer quietus, *aut, felix*, eram domi meæ, et florens, *aut, viridis*, in palatio meo.
5. I saw a dream which made me afraid, and the thoughts upon my bed, and the visions of my head, troubled me.	5. Somnium vidi, et exterruit me,[1] et cogitationes super cubile meum et visiones capitis mei conturbaverunt me.
6. Therefore made I a decree to bring in all the wise *men* of Babylon before me, that they might make known unto me the interpretation of the dream.	6. Et a me positum fuit decretum, ut adducerentur, *hoc est, accerserentur*, coram me omnes sapientes Babylonis, qui interpretationem somnii patefacerent mihi.

Nebuchadnezzar here explains how he acknowledged the Supreme God. He does not relate the proofs which he had previously received; but since his pride was subdued in this last dream, he makes a passing allusion to it. Meanwhile, as he doubtless recalled his former dreams to mind, and condemned himself for his ingratitude, in burying in oblivion this great power of God, and in wiping away the remembrance of those benefits by which God had adorned him. Here, however, he speaks only of his last dream, which we shall see in its own place. But before he comes as far as the dream, he says, *he was at rest.* שלה, *seleh*, signifies "rest" and "happiness;" and since prosperity renders men secure, it is metaphorically used for "security." David, when he pronounces the same sentence upon himself, uses the same words, (Ps. xxx. 6,) "I said in my prosperity," or rest ; שלוה, *selueh*, which some translate "abundance;" but it rather signifies a quiet or prosperous state. Nebuchadnezzar, therefore, here marks the circumstance of time ; hence we may know him to have been divinely seized, because prosperous fortune had rendered him stupid and drunken. There is nothing surprising in this, for the old and common proverb is, "fulness is the parent of ferocity,"

---

[1] Or, I was terrified. The copula may be resolved into the relative pronoun, "I saw a dream which frightened or terrified me."—*Calvin.*

as we see horses when too much fed, prance about and throw their riders. Thus also it happens with men. For if God treats them rather indulgently and liberally, they become fierce and insolent towards all men, and strike off God's yoke, and forget themselves to be but men. And when this happened to David, what shall happen to the profane and to others who are still too much devoted to the world? For David confesses himself to have been so deceived by his quiet and felicity, as to determine within himself that he had nothing else to fear,—"I said in my happiness," or my quiet, "I shall not be removed;" and he afterwards adds, "O Lord, thou didst chastise me, and I was laid low." (Ps. xxxviii. 7.) Since, therefore, David promised himself perpetual quiet in the world, because God spared him for a time, how ought our tranquillity to be suspected lest we should grow torpid on our lees? Nebuchadnezzar, then, does not recite this in vain—*I was quiet at home, I flourished in my palace*, since this was the cause of his confidence and pride, and of his carelessly despising God. He afterwards adds, he *saw a dream and was disturbed.* He, doubtless, wished here to distinguish his dreams from common ones, which often arise from either a disturbance of the brain, or our daily thoughts, or other causes, as we have elsewhere seen. It is not necessary to repeat what we have already treated more copiously. It is sufficient to state, briefly, how this dream, in which God previously informed him of the future punishment at hand, is separated from others which are either troubled, or fluctuating, or without reason. He says, therefore, *he saw a dream, and was disturbed,* while he was awake. He adds, *his thoughts were upon his bed;* and then, *he was disturbed by visions of the head.* These expressions only look towards that heavenly oracle, or vision, or dream, of which we shall afterwards speak more fully. It follows, *he put forth a decree to summon all the wise men of Babylon to explain,* or make manifest, *the interpretation of the dream.* Doubtless the king often dreamt, and did not always call together the Magi and soothsayers, and astrologers, and others who were skilled in the science of divination, or at least professed to be so. He did not consult them on all his dreams; but because God had inscribed in his heart a distinct mark by which he had denoted this dream, hence the king could not rest till he heard its interpretation. As we previously saw the authority of the first dream about the Four Monarchies and the Eternal Kingdom of Christ confirmed, so the king perceived this one to have proceeded from heaven. There is another difference between this dream and the one formerly explained. For God blotted out the remembrance of the dream about the Four Monarchies from King Nebuchadnezzar, so that it became necessary for Daniel to bring his dream before the king, and at the same time to add the interpretation. Daniel was then more obscure, for although he proved himself to have excelled all the Chaldeans, yet King Nebuchadnezzar would have wondered at him less if he had only been an interpreter of a dream. God wished, therefore, to acquire greater reverence for his Prophet and his doctrine, when he enjoined upon him two duties; first, the divination of the dream itself, and then the explanation of its sense and purpose. In this second dream Daniel is only an interpreter. God had already sufficiently proved him to be endued with a heavenly spirit, when Nebuchadnezzar not only called him among the rest of the Magi, but separated him from them all. He afterwards says:

7. Then came in the magicians, the astrologers, the Chaldeans, and the soothsayers: and I told the dream before them; but they did not make known unto me the interpretation thereof.

7. Tunc ingressi sunt magi, astrologi, Chaldæi, *hoc est, sapientes,* et physici, *vel, mathematici,* et somnium, *inquit,* exposui ego coram ipsis, et interpretationem ejus non patefecerunt mihi.

With respect to the words used above, we have formerly freed ourselves from all trouble, because we cannot accurately define what science each professed. Clearly enough they covered their shamelessness by honourable titles, although they gave themselves up to every possible imposture. They called themselves by the usual name of learned men, when they were really unacquainted with any art or science, and deluded mankind by miserable predictions; hence, by these words, Daniel comprehended all the Magi, soothsayers, astrologers, and augurs, who professed the art of divination.   Here Nebuchadnezzar confesses that he sent for these men in vain.   Hence it follows, this whole science was a fallacy, or, at least, Daniel's exposition of the dream was not by human skill, but by revelation from heaven.   I embrace this opinion, since Nebuchadnezzar wished clearly to express that Daniel's power of interpreting his dream did not spring from man, but was a singular gift of the Spirit. He had considered it a settled point that, if any knowledge or skill in divination existed, it must belong to the Magi, soothsayers, augurs, and other Chaldeans who boasted in the possession of perfect wisdom.   This, therefore, was without controversy—that the astrologers and the rest were most powerful in divination, and as far as human faculties would allow, nothing escaped them.   Hence it follows, on the other hand, that Daniel was divinely instructed, since if he had been only an astrologer or magician, he must, like others, have required a long apprenticeship to this science.   Nebuchadnezzar, therefore, wishes here to extol Daniel beyond all the Magi, as if he had said—He is a heavenly Prophet! And this, also, will appear better from what is added, as follows:

8. But at the last Daniel came in before me, (whose name *was* Belteshazzar, according to the name of my god, and in whom *is* the spirit of the holy gods,) and before him I told the dream, *saying,*

9. O Belteshazzar, master of the magicians, because I know that the spirit of the holy gods *is* in thee, and no secret troubleth thee, tell me the visions of my dream that I have seen, and the interpretation thereof.

8. Quousque tandem coram me introductus est Daniel cujus nomen Beltsazar secundum nomen dei mei, et in quo spiritus deorum sanctorum: et somnium coram ipso narravi.

9. Beltsazar princeps, *vel, magister,* magorum, quia ego novi quod spiritus deorum sanctorum in te *sit,* et nullum arcanum te anxium reddit,[1] visiones somnii mei quod vidi, et interpretationem ejus expone.

Here the king of Babylon addresses Daniel kindly, since he saw himself deserted by his own teachers.   And hence we gather that no one comes to the true God, unless impelled by necessity.   Daniel was not either unknown or far off; for we saw him to have been in the palace.   Since then the king had Daniel with him from the first, why did he pass him over?   Why did he call the other Magi from all quarters by

[1] Some translate, "may be troublesome to thee," but I shall treat this word by and bye.—*Calvin.*

his edict ?   Hence, as I have said, it clearly appears he would never have given glory to God, unless when compelled by extreme necessity.   Hence he never willingly submitted to the God of Israel ; and his affections were clearly but momentary, whenever they manifested any sign of piety. Because he besought Daniel so imploringly, we see his disposition to have been servile ; just as all proud men swell out when they do not need any one's help, and become overbearing in their insolence ; but when they are reduced to extremity, they would rather lick the dust than not obtain the favour which they need.   Such was the king's disposition, since he willingly despised Daniel, and purposely preferred the Magi.   But as soon as he saw himself left in difficulties, and unable to find any remedy except in Daniel, this was his last refuge ; and he now seems to forget his own loftiness while speaking softly to God's holy Prophet.   But I shall proceed with the rest to-morrow.

PRAYER.

Grant, Almighty God, since thou here proposest a remarkable example before our eyes, that we may learn thy power to be so great as not to be sufficiently celebrated by any human praises : and since we hear how its herald was a profane king, nay, even a cruel and proud one, and thou hast afterwards deigned to manifest thyself to us familiarly in Christ,—Grant, that in the spirit of humility we may desire to glorify thee, and to cleave entirely to thee.   May we declare thee to be ours, not only in mouth and tongue, but also in works; not only as our true and only God, but our Father, since thou hast adopted us in thine only-begotten Son, until at length we enjoy that eternal inheritance which is laid up for us in heaven by the same Christ our Lord.—Amen.

Lecture Eighteenth.

9. *O Belteshazzar, master of the Magi, since I know that the spirit of the holy gods is in thee, and no secret can escape thee*—or overcome thee, as I shall soon explain the word—*relate the visions of my sleep which I saw, and their interpretation.*   We yesterday shewed King Nebuchadnezzar to be a suppliant to Daniel, when reduced to extremity.   He

did not seek him at first, but consulted his Magicians, and he is now compelled to venerate the person whom he had despised. He calls him *Belteshazzar*, and doubtless the name severely wounded the Prophet's mind ; for another name had been imposed upon him by his parents from his earliest infancy; whence he could recognise himself as a Jew, and could draw his origin from a holy and elect nation. For his change of name was doubtless made by the tyrant's cunning, as we have previously said, as to cause him to forget his own family. King Nebuchadnezzar wished, by changing his name, to render this holy servant of God degenerate. Hence, as often as he was called by this name, he was clearly offended in no slight degree. But this evil could not be remedied, since he was a captive, and knew he had to deal with a people victorious, proud, and cruel. Thus, in the last verse, Nebuchadnezzar had used this name according to the name of his god. Since then Daniel had a name of his own, which his parents had given him by God's appointment, Nebuchadnezzar wished to blot out that sacred name, and so called him as a mark of respect Belteshazzar, which we may believe to have been deduced from the name of an idol. Hence this doubled the Prophet's grief, when he was stained with that base spot in bearing an idol's mark on his name ; but it was his duty to endure this scourge of God among his other trials. Thus God exercised his servant in every way by enduring a cross.

He now calls him *Prince of the Magi*, and this doubtless wounded the holy Prophet's feelings. He wished nothing better than separation from the Magi, who deceived the world by their impostures and soothsaying. For although they were skilled in the science of astrology, and knew some principles worthy of praise, yet we are sure they corrupted all the sciences. Hence Daniel did not willingly hear himself included among them; but he could not free himself from this infamy. Thus we see his patience to have been divinely proved in various ways. Now, Nebuchadnezzar adds, *because I know the spirit of the holy gods to be in thee*. Many understand this of angels; and this interpretation is not objectionable, as I have hinted elsewhere. For the existence of a supreme God was known to all the nations, but they fancied angels to be inferior deities. Whatever be the true meaning, Nebuchadnezzar here betrays his own ignorance, since he had made no real progress in the knowledge of the true God; because he was entangled in his former errors, and retained many gods, as from the beginning he had been imbued with that superstition. This passage might have been translated in the singular number, as some do, but it would be too forced, and the reason for such a translation is too weak; for they think Nebuchadnezzar to have been truly converted; but the vanity of this is proved by the whole context; and being occupied by this opinion, they wish to relieve him from all fault. But since it is clear that in this edict of Nebuchadnezzar many proofs of his old ignorance are comprehended, there is no reason why we should depart from the simple sense of the words. Hence he attributes a divine spirit to Daniel, but meanwhile imagines many gods. Since, therefore, *the spirit of the holy gods is in thee,* he says, *and no secret overcomes thee.* Some translate אנס, *anes,* to be troublesome; it properly signifies to compel, or to force; for those who translate "there is no secret which can surpass thee," depart from the correct sense. Others translate it, " to be troublesome." This would be a more tolerable translation, but they would do better by translating, " no secret renders thee anxious or perplexed." If the rules of grammar would allow the א, *aleph,* to be a servile letter, the sense would be more suitable. For נסה, *neseh,* signifies to try, or prove, and also to elevate. We may translate it, " No secret is loftier than thy understanding;" or, " No secret proves thee;" if he had said,—Daniel was endued with a divine spirit ;—he does not examine any proposition, and has no need to make an experiment in any science, since his answer is easy and at hand. But it is necessary to remember what I said,—No secret renders thee anxious, or confounds thee. Nebuchadnezzar knew this. Then why did he not directly call him to himself in his perplexity? As Daniel could free him from all perplexity, the king's ingratitude is proved, because he admitted the Magi to his counsels, and neglected Daniel. We see then how he always endeavoured to avoid God, till he was drawn along by a violent hand, and thereby displayed the absence of conversion. For repentance is voluntary, and those only are said to repent who willingly return by a change of mind to the God from whom they had revolted; and this cannot be done without faith and the love of God. He then asks him *to relate his dream and its interpretation.* But the dream was not unknown, and he relates it to Daniel. There is, therefore, something superfluous in these words, but no doubt about the sense—as Nebuchadnezzar only asks for the explanation of his dream. It follows :—

10. Thus *were* the visions of mine head in my bed: I saw, and behold a tree in the midst of the earth, and the height thereof *was* great.

11. The tree grew, and was strong, and the height thereof reached unto heaven, and the sight thereof to the end of all the earth :

12. The leaves thereof *were* fair, and the fruit thereof much, and in *it was* meat for all : the beasts of the field had shadow under it, and the fowls of the heaven dwelt in the boughs thereof, and all flesh was fed of it.

10. Visiones autem capitis mei super cubile meum, Videbam, et ecce arborem in medio terræ, et altitudo ejus magna.

11. Crevit, *multiplicata est,* arbor, et invaluit, et altitudo ejus pertigit, *hoc est, ut altitudo ejus pertingeret,* ad cœlos, et conspectus ejus' ad extremum totius, *vel, universæ,* terræ.

12. Ramus ejus pulcher, et fructus ejus copiosus,[1] et esca omnibus in ea: sub ea umbrabat[2] bestia agri : et in ramis ejus habitabant[3] aves cœlorum, et ex ea alebatur omnis caro.

The following verses ought to be joined on :—

13. I saw in the visions of my head upon my bed, and, behold, a watcher and an holy one came down from heaven :

14. He cried aloud, and said thus, Hew down the tree, and cut off his branches, shake off his leaves, and scatter his fruit : let the beasts get away from under it, and the fowls from his branches :

15. Nevertheless, leave the stump of his roots in the earth, even with

13. Videbam *etiam* in visionibus capitis mei super cubile meum, et ecce vigil et sanctus descendit e cœlis.

14. Clamavit in fortitudine, *hoc est, fortiter,* et ita loquutus est, Succidite arborem, et diripite folia ejus,[4] excutite ramos ejus, et dispergite fructus ejus : fugiat bestia ex umbra ejus, *de subtus, ad verbum,* et aves ex frondibus ejus, *vel ex ramis ejus.*

15. Tandem imum radicum ejus in terra relinquite, et in vinculo ferri,

---

[1] שַׂגִּיא, *segia,* signifies large, or much.—*Calvin.*

[2] Verbally, took shelter.—*Calvin.*　　　[3] Or, nestled.—*Calvin.*

[4] It is better not to repeat boughs twice, as some do. I confess the word עֲנַף, *gnef,* here used, means leaf as well as bough, but עֲנָף, *gnefa,* means bough ; hence the repetition is not superfluous—seize or cut off its leaves.—*Calvin.*

a band of iron and brass, in the tender grass of the field ; and let it be wet with the dew of heaven, and *let* his portion *be* with the beasts in the grass of the earth :

16. Let his heart be changed from man's, and let a beast's heart be given unto him; and let seven times pass over him.

hoc est, ferreo, et æneo, in herba agri, et pluvia cœlorum irrigetur, et cum bestia sit portio ejus in herba terræ.

16. Cor ejus ab humano, *simpliciter, ab homine,* mutent,[1] et cor bestiæ detur ei : et septem tempora transeant super eam.

Here Nebuchadnezzar relates his dream, of which the interpretation will follow in its place. Yet because this narrative is cold and useless unless we should say something of the subject itself, it is necessary to make some remarks—the rest shall be deferred. First of all, under the figure of a tree Nebuchadnezzar himself is intended, not because it fully represents the king's office, but because God appointed the existence of governments in the world for this purpose—to be like trees on whose fruits all men feed, and under whose shadow they rest. Hence this ordinance of God flourishes, because tyrants, however they are removed from the exercise of just and moderate dominion, whether they wish it or not, are compelled to be like trees ; since it is better to live under the most cruel tyrant than without any government at all. Let us suppose all to be on one equal level, what would such anarchy bring forth ? No one would wish to yield to others ; every one would try the extent of his powers, and thus all would end in prey and plunder, and in the mere license of fraud and murder, and all the passions of mankind would have full and unbridled sway. Hence I have said, tyranny is better than anarchy, and more easily borne, because where there is no supreme governor there is none to preside and keep the rest in check. Wherefore they philosophize too minutely who think this to be a description of a king endued with superior virtues; for there was no such superiority in justice and equity in King Nebuchadnezzar. God principally wished to shew, by this figure, with what intention and with what political order he desires the world to be governed ; and why he sets over it kings and monarchies and other magistrates. Then he desired to shew, *secondly,* although tyrants and other princes forget their

---

[1] That is, shall be changed, as elsewhere appears.—*Calvin.*

duty, it is still divinely enjoined upon them, and yet God's grace always shines forth in all governments. Tyrants endeavour to extinguish the whole light of equity and justice, and to mingle all things ; but the Lord meanwhile restrains them in a secret and wonderful manner, and thus they are compelled to act usefully to the human race, whether they will or not. This then is the meaning of the figure or image of the tree.

It is now added, *the birds of heaven dwelt amidst the branches, and the beasts lived by its sustenance*—which ought to be referred to mankind. For although even the beasts of the field profit by political order, yet we know society to have been ordained by God for the benefit of men. There is no doubt at all of the whole discourse being metaphorical, —nay, properly speaking, it is an allegory, since an allegory is only a continued metaphor. If Daniel had only represented the king under the figure of a tree, it would have been a metaphor ; but when he pursues his own train of thought in a continuous tenor, his discourse becomes allegorical. He says, therefore, *the beasts of the field dwelt under the tree*, because we are sheltered by the protection of magistrates ; and no heat of the sun so parches and burns up miserable men as living deprived of that shade under which God wished them to repose. *The birds of heaven also nestled in its boughs and leaves.* Some distinguish, with too much subtlety, between birds and beasts. It is sufficient for us to observe the Prophet noticing how men of every rank feel no small utility in the protection of princes ; for if they were deprived of it, it were better for them to live like wild beasts than mutually to confide in each other. Such protection is needful, if we reflect upon the great pride natural to all, and the blindness of our self-love, and the furiousness of our lusts. As this is the case, God shews, in this dream, how all orders among us need the protection of magistrates ; while *pasture* and *food* and *shelter* signify the various forms of usefulness which political order provides for us. For some might object—they have no need of government either for one reason or another; for if we discharge properly all the duties of life, we shall always find God's blessing sufficient for us.

It is now added, *its height was great ;* then, *it grew till it reached even to heaven, and its aspect extended itself to the furthest bounds of the land.* This is restricted to the Babylonian monarchy, for there were then other empires in the world, but they were either powerless or but slightly important. The Chaldeans, also, were then so powerful that no prince could approach to such majesty and power. Since, therefore, King Nebuchadnezzar was so pre-eminent, the loftiness of the tree here described is not surprising, though it reached to heaven ; while the altitude rendered it visible throughout the whole land. Some of the rabbis place Babylon in the middle of the earth, because it was under the same line or parallel with Jerusalem—which is very foolish. Those also who place Jerusalem in the centre of the earth are equally childish; although Jerome, Origen, and other ancient authors, treat Jerusalem as in the centre of the world. In this conjecture of theirs they deserve the laughter of the Cynic who, when asked to point out the middle of the earth, touched the ground with his staff immediately under his feet ! Then when the questioner objected to this determination of the centre of the earth, he said, " Then do you measure the earth !" As far as concerns Jerusalem, their conjectures are not worth mentioning. That proud Barbinel [Abarbanel] wished to seem a philosopher, but nothing is more insipid than the Jews when they depart from their own rules of grammar ; and the Lord so blinded them and delivered them up to a reprobate sense, when he wished them to be spectacles of horrible blindness and prodigious stupidity,—and in a small and minute matter that silly fellow shews his absurdity.

He now says, *Its boughs were beautiful, and its fruit copious.* This must be referred to the common opinion of the vulgar ; for we know men's eyes to be dazzled by the splendour of princes. For if any one excels others in power, all men adore him and are seized with admiration, and are incapable of judging correctly. When the majesty of a general or a king comes before them, they are all astonished and perceive nothing, and they do not think it lawful for them to inquire strictly into the conduct of princes. Since, then, the power and wealth of King Nebuchadnezzar were so great,

CHAP. IV. 10-16.   COMMENTARIES ON DANIEL.   259

no wonder the Prophet says, *His branches were beautiful, and their fruit copious.* But meanwhile we must remember what I lately said, namely, God's blessing shines forth in princes, even if they materially neglect their duty, because God does not suffer all his grace in them to be extinguished; and hence they are compelled to bring forth some fruit. It is much better, therefore, to preserve the existence of some kind of dominion than to have all men's condition equal, when each attracts the eyes of his neighbours. And this is the meaning of what I have said—*there was food and provision for all,* as I have lately explained it.

The *second* part of the dream follows here. Hitherto Nebuchadnezzar has described the beauty and excellency of his state under the figure of a lofty tree which afforded shade to the beasts and on whose fruit they fed, and next as giving nests to the birds of heaven under its boughs. The cutting down of the tree now follows. *I saw,* says he, *in the visions of my head upon my couch, and, behold, a watcher and a holy one came down from heaven.* No doubt we ought to understand an angel by a watcher. He is called "a holy one," which is only another form of expression for an angel; and they are worthy of this name, because they are perpetually watchful in the performance of God's commands. They are not subject to slumber, they are not nourished by either food or drink, but live a spiritual life; hence they have no use for sleep, which is the result of drink and food. Lastly, as angels have no bodies, their very spiritual nature makes them watchful. But this phrase not only expresses their nature but also their duty ; because God has them at hand to fulfil his bidding, and destines them to the performance of his commands, hence they are called "watchers." (Psalm ciii. 20.) In this Psalm angels are said to do his bidding, because, by an agility incomprehensible to us, they run about hither and thither, and fly directly from heaven to earth, from one end of the world to another—from the rising even to the setting sun. Since, therefore, angels can so easily and promptly fulfil God's orders, they are deservedly called "watchers." They are called "holy ones," because they are not infected by human infirmities. But we are filled with many sins, not merely because we are earthly, but since we have contracted pollution from our first parents, which vitiates alike the whole body and mind. By this expression, then, Nebuchadnezzar desired to distinguish between angels and mortals. For although God here sanctifies his elect, yet as long as they dwell in the prison of the body they never arrive at the holiness of angels. Here then we mark the difference between angels and men. Nebuchadnezzar could not understand this by himself, but he was taught of God to perceive the destruction of the tree to arise not from man but from the Almighty.

He afterwards adds—*the angel cried with a loud voice, cut down the tree, strip off the leaves, cut off its boughs, scatter its fruits,* (or throw them away,) *and let the beasts flee from its shadow, and the birds of heaven dwell no longer under its branches.* By this figure God meant to express that King Nebuchadnezzar should be for a time like a beast. This ought not to seem absurd, although it is but rough to speak of a tree being deprived of a human heart, since men know trees to have no other life than that usually called vegetable. The dignity or excellence of the tree cannot be lessened by its being without a human heart, for it never had one originally. But though this is rather a rough mode of expression, yet it contains in it nothing absurd, although Daniel bends a little aside from the strictness of the allegory ; nay, Nebuchadnezzar himself had an allegorical dream, and yet God mingled something with it by which he might comprehend the meaning veiled under the image of a tree. The angel, then, orders the tree to be deprived of its human heart, and its bough and fruit to be torn down and cast away, after it had been cut down ; next he orders the heart of a beast to be given to it, and thus its portion might be with the wild animals of the woods. But as this must be repeated elsewhere, I now pass it by rather hastily. The general meaning is this ; King Nebuchadnezzar was to be deprived for a time not only of his empire but even of his human sense, and to be in no way different from the beasts, since he was unworthy of holding even the lowest place among mankind. Although he seemed to surpass the human race in his elevation, yet he must be cast down and thrown below even the lowest mortals !

The reason for this punishment follows, when it is added, *seven times shall pass over him ;* and then, *do not cut off its lowest root, but let the rain of heaven water it ;* and next, *his portion shall be with the wild beasts.* Although the chastisement is hard and horrible, when Nebuchadnezzar is expelled from the society of men, and rendered like wild beasts ; but it is something in his favour when God does not tear him up by the roots, but allows the root to remain, for the tree to spring up again and flourish, and be planted again in its own place, and recover new vigour through its roots. Here Daniel reviews the punishment inflicted on King Nebuchadnezzar, in which God afforded a specimen of his clemency, in sparing him and not utterly cutting him down, but in allowing his root to remain. Some here discourse about the mitigation of penalties when God sees those repent whom he has chastised with rods ; but I do not think it applicable here. There was no true conversion in King Nebuchadnezzar, as we said before, and shall see again more clearly. God did not wish to press him too hard, and this we must attribute to his clemency ; because when he seems to set no bounds to his punishment of men's sins, yet in all temporal punishments he allows men to taste his pity ; so that even the reprobate remain without excuse. The assertion of some— that punishments are not remitted without the fault being excused, is false ; as we see in the example of Ahab. For God remitted the fault to the impious king, but because he seemed to shew some signs of repentance, God abstained from greater punishment. (1 Kings xxi. 29.) So also we may see the same in the case of Nebuchadnezzar. God was unwilling utterly to root him out—for the metaphor of the tree shews this—but he desired *seven times to pass over him.* Some understand seven weeks, others seven years ; but we shall treat this point more copiously by and bye. Lastly, we must notice this ; in the midst of the time during which God's wrath seemed to rage against this wretched king, his benefits were also mingled with it. We learn this from the words, *his portion shall be with the beasts of the field ;* that is, he shall feed upon some food by which life shall be preserved; and then, *it shall be watered* or irrigated *with the rain of heaven.* For God signifies—though he wished to punish King Nebuchadnezzar, and to render him a remarkable example of his wrath—his knowledge of what he could bear; hence, he so tempers his punishment as to leave hope remaining for the future. Thus he took his food even with the beasts of the earth, but he is not deprived of the irrigation of the dew of heaven.

PRAYER.

Grant, Almighty God, since we see it so difficult for us to bear prosperity without injury to the mind, that we may remember ourselves to be mortal—may our frailty be ever present to our eyes, and render us humble, and lead us to ascribe the glory to thee. Being advised by thee, may we learn to walk with anxiety and fear, to submit ourselves to thee, and to conduct ourselves modestly towards our brethren. May none of us despise or insult his brother, but may we all strive to discharge our duties with moderation, until at length thou gatherest us into that glory which has been obtained for us by the blood of thine only-begotten Son.—Amen.

Lecture Nineteenth.

17. This matter *is* by the decree of the watchers, and the demand by the word of the holy ones; to the intent that the living may know that the most High ruleth in the kingdom of men, and giveth it to whomsoever he will, and setteth up over it the basest of men.

17. In decreto vigilum verbum,[1] et in sermone sanctorum postulatio, ut cognoscant viventes, quod dominator *sit* excelsus in regno hominum: et cui voluerit tradet illud, et humilem,[2] hominum[3] eriget super ipsum.

In this verse God confirms what he had shewn to the king of Babylon by means of a dream. He says, then, the king was instructed in a certain thing; since it had been so determined before God and his angels. The full meaning is this,—Nebuchadnezzar must know it to be impossible to escape the punishment whose image he had seen in the dream. There is, however, some ambiguity in the words,

---

[1] Or, edict, for it may be conveniently translated so.—*Calvin.*
[2] Or, abject.—*Calvin.*   [3] Or, among men.—*Calvin.*

since interpreters find great difficulties with the second clause; for they say the angels ask the question, to afford proof to the king of Babylon, and that all men may acknowledge the supreme power of the one God. But this seems to me too forced. As far as the word פִּתְגָּמָא, *pethegma*, is concerned, it signifies "word" in Chaldee; but here I think it properly used for "edict," as in the first chapter of Esther, (ver. 20;) and this is a very suitable sense, as the edict was promulgated in the decree so that the "word" or vision might not prove vain and inefficient; since God wished to point out to the king what was already fixed and determined in heaven. We now understand the Prophet's intention. But a new question still remains, because it seems absurd to attribute power and authority to those angels, lest in this way they seem to be equal to God. We know God to be judge alone, and hence it is his proper office to determine what pleases him; and if this is transferred to angels, it seems as if it lessened his supreme authority, because it is not becoming to make them companions of his Majesty. But we know it to be no new thing in Scripture for God to join angels with himself, not as equals but as attendants, and to attribute to them so much honour as to deign to call them into counsel. Hence angels are often called God's counsellors. As in this place they are said to decree together with God; and not by their own will or pleasure, as they say, but because they subscribe to God's judgment. Meanwhile, we must remark the double character assigned to them. In the first clause, Daniel makes them subscribe to the decree, and afterwards uses the word *demand*. And this suits the sense well enough; because the angels urge God by their prayers to humble all mortals and to exalt himself alone. Thus, whatever obscures his glory may be reduced into order. It is right for angels constantly to desire this, since we know them to desire nothing in comparison with the adoration of God by themselves in alliance with all mankind. But when they see God's authority diminished by man's pride and audacity, the object of their demand is that God would reduce under his yoke the proud who erect their crests against him.

We now see why Daniel says, *this was declared in the decree of the watchers, and was demanded in their speech;* as if he should say, "thou hast all angels opposed to thee; for by one consent and with one mouth they accuse thee before God, for as far as possible thou obscurest his glory; and God, assenting to their prayers, has determined to cast thee away, and to render thee an object of contempt and reproach before the whole world; and this decree has been signed by all the angels, as if it were common between him and them. For by their subscription and agreement he might prevail in confirming the confidence of the profane king. Without doubt God, after his usual manner, accommodated the vision to the understanding of a man who never was taught in his law, but only imbued with a confused notion of his divinity, so that he could not distinguish between God and angels. Meanwhile, this sentiment is true—the edict was promulgated at the united consent and demand of the whole celestial host; for angels bear with the greatest reluctance whatever detracts from God's glory, and all the folly of mankind when they wish to draw and attract to themselves the peculiar attributes of the only God. This seems to be the genuine sense. The following sentence flows very suitably, —*mortals must know God to be a ruler in the kingdoms of men.* For Daniel marks the end of the demand, since angels desire God's rights to remain entire, and to be quite unaffected by the ingratitude of mankind. But men cannot ascribe even the slightest merit to themselves without detracting from God's praise; hence angels continually seek from God the casting down of all the proud, and that he will not permit himself to be defrauded of his proper rights, but maintain in all its integrity his own sovereign powers. This also must be diligently observed—*mortals should notice how the Lord reigns in the kingdoms of men.* For even the worst of men confess the mighty power of God; they dare not draw him down from his heavenly throne by their blasphemies, but they imagine themselves able to obtain and defend their worldly kingdoms, by either their exertions or their wealth, or by some other means. Unbelievers, therefore, willingly shut up God in heaven, just as Epicurus fancied

him to be enjoying his own delights at his ease.   Hence
Daniel shews God to be deprived of his rights, *unless he is
recognised as a ruler in the kingdoms of men,* that is, on
earth to humble all whom he pleases.   So also it is said in
the Psalms, (lxxv. 7,) Power springs not from either the
east or the west, but from heaven ; and elsewhere, God
raises the poor out of the mire, (Ps. cxiii. 6.)   Then in the
sacred Canticle of the Virgin, he casts down the proud from
their seat, and exalts the abject and the humble. (Luke i. 52.)
All indeed confess this, but scarcely one in a hundred feels
in his mind the dominion of God over the earth, and that no
man can raise himself, or remain in any post of honour, since
this is the peculiar gift of God.   Because men are persuaded
of this with difficulty, Daniel eloquently expresses it, *the
Lord shall be lofty in the kingdoms of men ;* that is, shall not
only exercise his power in heaven, but also govern the human
race, and assign to every one his own grade and position.
He will give it to whom he wills.   He speaks of different empires in the singular number ; just as if God had said, some
are raised up by God's will, and others are cast down ; and
the whole happens according to God's pleasure.   The meaning is this—every one has his own condition divinely assigned
to him ; and thus a man's ambition, or skill, or prudence, or
wealth, or the help of others, do not profit men in aspiring
to any altitude, unless God raises them by his stretched
out hand.   Paul also teaches the same thing in other words ;
there is no power but from God, (Rom. xiii. 1,) and after
wards Daniel often repeats the same sentiment.

He adds, *he raises up the humble man above himself.*   In
a change so remarkable as this, God's power shines forth
better while he raises from the dust those who were formerly
obscure and contemptible, and even sets them above kings.
When this happens, profane men say, God is playing with
them, and rolls men about like balls in his hand, which are
first tossed upwards and then thrown down upon the ground.
But they do not consider the reason why God by open
proofs wishes to shew how we are under his absolute power,
on which our condition entirely depends ; when we do not
comprehend this of our own accord, examples are necessarily

set before us by which we are compelled to perceive what almost all are willingly ignorant of. We now understand the whole intention of the Prophet. Angels seek from God by continual prayers to declare his own power to mortals, and thus to lay prostrate the proud who think to excel by their own power and industry, or else by chance, or by the help of men. To induce God to punish men for their sacrilegious deeds, the angels desire him to prostrate them, and thus to shew himself to be not only the king and ruler of heaven, but also of earth. Now, this not only happens in the case of a single king, but we know history to be full of such proofs. Whence, then, or from what order have kings often been created? And when there was no greater pride in the world than in the Roman empire, we see what happened. For God brought forward certain monsters which caused the greatest astonishment among the Greeks and all the Orientals, the Spaniards, Italians, and Gauls; for nothing was more monstrous than some of the emperors. Then their origin was most base and shameful, and God could not shew more clearly how empires were not transferred by the will of man, nor even acquired by valour, counsel, and powerful troops, but remained under his own hand to bestow upon whomsoever he pleased. Let us go on:

18. This dream I king Nebuchadnezzar have seen. Now thou, O Belteshazzar, declare the interpretation thereof, forasmuch as all the wise *men* of my kingdom are not able to make known unto me the interpretation: but thou *art* able; for the spirit of the holy gods *is* in thee.

18. Hoc somnium vidi ego Rex Nebuchadnezer: et tu Beltsazar, interpretationem enarra,[1] quoniam cuncti sapientes regni mei non potuerunt interpretationem patefacere mihi: tu vero potes: quia spiritus deorum sanctorum in te.

Here Nebuchadnezzar repeats what he had formerly said about seeking an interpretation for his dream. He understood the figure which was shewn to him, but he could not understand God's intentions nor even determine its relation to himself. On this point he implores Daniel's confidence; he affirms his vision in a dream to induce Daniel to pay great attention to its interpretation. Then he adds, with the same purpose, *All the wise men of his kingdom could not*

[1] Verbally, say.—*Calvin.*

explain the dream; where he confesses all the astrologers, and diviners, and others of this kind to be utterly vain and fallacious, since they professed to know everything.   For some were augurs, some conjecturers, some interpreters of dreams, and others astrologers, who not only discoursed on the course, distances, and orders of the stars, and the peculiarities of each, but wished to predict futurity from the course of the stars.   Since, therefore, they boasted so magnificently in their superior knowledge of all events, Nebuchadnezzar confesses them to have been impostors.   But he ascribes this power in reality to Daniel, because he was endued by the divine Spirit.   Hence he excludes all the wise men of Babylon from so great a gift through his having proved them destitute of God's Spirit.   He does not assert this in so many words, but this meaning is easily elicited from his expressions implying all the variety of the Chaldean wise men.   Then in the second clause he exempts Daniel from their number, and states the reason to be his excelling in the divine Spirit. Nebuchadnezzar, therefore, here asserts what is peculiar to God, and acknowledges Daniel to be his Prophet and minister.   When he calls angels *holy deities*, we have mentioned this already as an expression which ought not to seem surprising in a heathen, uninstructed in the true doctrine of piety, and only just initiated in its elements.   But we know this common opinion respecting angels being mingled together with the one God.   Hence Nebuchadnezzar speaks in the ordinary and received language when he says, the spirit of the holy gods dwells in Daniel.   It now follows :

19. Then Daniel (whose name *was* Belteshazzar) was astonied for one hour, and his thoughts troubled him.   The king spake, and said, Belteshazzar, let not the dream, or the interpretation thereof, trouble thee.   Belteshazzar answered and said, My lord, the dream *be* to them that hate thee, and the interpretation thereof to thine enemies.

19. Tunc Daniel, cui nomen Beltsazar, obstupefactus fuit circiter horam unam : et cogitationes ejus turbabant eum.   Respondit rex et dixit, Beltsazar, somnium et interpretatio *ejus* ne conturbet te, *terreat.*   Respondit Beltsazar et dixit, Domine mi, somnium *sit* inimicis tuis, et interpretatio ejus hostibus tuis.

Here Daniel relates how he was in some sense astonished. And I refer this to the sorrow which the holy Prophet had endured from that horrible punishment which God had shewn under a figure ; nor ought it to seem surprising for Daniel to be grievously afflicted on account of the calamity of the king of Babylon ; for although he was a cruel tyrant, and had harassed and all but destroyed God's Church, yet since he was under his sway, he was bound to pray for him. But God had clearly taught the Jews this, by means of Jeremiah, Pray ye for the prosperous state of Babylon, because your peace shall be in it. (Jer. xxix. 7.) At the close of seventy years it was lawful for the pious worshippers of God to beg him to free them ; but until the time predicted by the Prophet had elapsed, it was not lawful either to indulge in hatred against the king, or to invoke God's wrath upon him. They knew him to be the executor of God's just vengeance, and also to be their sovereign and lawful ruler. Since then Daniel was treated kindly by the king when by the rights of warfare he was dragged into exile, he ought to be faithful to his own king, although he exercised tyranny against the people of God. This was the reason why he suffered so much sorrow from that sad oracle. Others think he was in an ecstasy ; but this seems to suit better because he does not simply speak of being astonished, but even disturbed and terrified in his thoughts. Meanwhile, we must remark, how variously the Prophets were affected when God uses them in denouncing his approaching judgments. Whenever God appointed his Prophets the heralds of severe calamities, they were affected in two ways ; on the one side, they condoled with those miserable men whose destruction they saw at hand, and still they boldly announced what had been divinely commanded ; and thus their sorrow never hindered them from discharging their duty freely and consistently. In Daniel's case we see both these feelings. The sympathy, then, was right in his condoling with his king and being silent for about an hour. And when the king commands him to be of good courage and not to be disturbed, we have here depicted the security of those who do not apprehend the wrath of God. The Prophet is terrified, and yet he is free from all evil ; for God does not threaten him, nay, the very punishment which he sees prepared for the king, afforded the hope of future deliverance. Why then is he frightened? because the faithful, though God spares them and shews himself merciful and propitious, cannot view his judgments without fear, for they acknowledge themselves subject to similar penalties, if God did not treat them with indulgence. Besides this, they never put off human affections, and so pity takes possession of them, when they see the ungodly punished or even subject to impending wrath. For these two reasons they suffer sorrow and pain. But the impious, even when God openly addresses and threatens them, are not moved, but remain stupid, or openly deride his power and treat his threats as fabulous, till they feel them seriously. Such is the example which the Prophet sets before us in the king of Babylon.

Belteshazzar, he says, *let not thy thoughts disturb thee ; let not the dream and its interpretation frighten thee!* Yet Daniel was afraid for his sake. But, as I have already said, while the faithful are afraid though they feel God to be propitious, yet the impious sleep in their security, and are unmoved and unterrified by any threats. Daniel adds the cause of his grief,—*O my lord*, he says, *may the dream be for thine enemies, and its interpretation to thy foes!* Here Daniel explains why he was so astonished — because he wished so horrible a punishment to be turned away from the person of the king ; for although he might deservedly have detested him, yet he reverenced the power divinely assigned to him. Let us learn, therefore, from the Prophet's example, to pray for blessings on our enemies who desire to destroy us, and especially to pray for tyrants if it please God to subject us to their lust ; for although they are unworthy of any of the feelings of humanity, yet we must modestly bear their yoke, because they could not be our governors without God's permission ; and not only for wrath, as Paul admonishes us, but for conscience' sake, (Rom. xiii. 5,) otherwise we should not only rebel against them, but against God himself. But, on the other hand, Daniel shews the impossibility of his being changed or softened by any sentiment of pity, and thus turned from his intended course :

20. The tree that thou sawest, which grew, and was strong, whose

20. Arbor quam vidisti, quæ magna erat et robusta, et cujus magnitudo

height reached unto the heaven, and
the sight thereof to all the earth:

21. Whose leaves *were* fair, and
the fruit thereof much, and in it *was*
meat for all; under which the beasts
of the field dwelt, and upon whose
branches the fowls of the heaven had
their habitation:

22. It *is* thou, O king, that art
grown and become strong: for thy
greatness is grown, and reacheth
unto heaven, and thy dominion to
the end of the earth.

pertingebat ad cœlos, et aspectus
ejus ad totam terram.

21. Et folium ejus pulchrum
erat,[1] et fructus ejus copiosus: et in
qua,[2] cibus cunctis: sub qua habitabant bestiæ agri, et in cujus ramis
quiescebant aves cœli.

22. Tu *es* ipse rex, qui multipli-
catus es et roboratus,[3] ita ut magnitudo tua multiplicata fuerit, et per-
tigerit ad cœlos, et potestas tua ad
fines terræ.

Here we see what I have touched upon, namely, how
Daniel acted respectfully to the king, and thus was mindful
of his prophetic duty, while he punctually discharged the
commands of God. We must notice this distinction, for
nothing is more difficult for ministers of the Word than to
maintain this middle course. Some are always fulminating
through a pretence of zeal, and forget themselves to be but
men : they shew no sign of benevolence, but indulge in mere
bitterness. Hence they have no authority, and all their
admonitions are hateful. Next, they explain God's Word
with pride and boasting, when they frighten sinners without
either humanity, or pain, or sympathy. Others, again, who
are wicked and perfidious flatterers, gloss over the grossest
iniquities ; they object to both Prophets and Apostles,
esteeming the fervour of their zeal to have driven away all
human affections ! Thus they delude miserable men, and
destroy them by their flattery. But our Prophet, as all the
rest, here shews how God's servants ought to take a middle
course. Thus Jeremiah, when prophesying adversity, feels
sorrow and bitterness of spirit, and yet does not turn aside
from unsparing reproof of the severest threats, as both sprang
from God. (Jer. ix. 1.) The rest of the prophets also act
in the same manner. Here Daniel, on the one hand, pities
the king, and on the other, through knowing himself to be
the herald of God's anger, he is not frightened by any danger while setting before the king the punishment which he
had despised. Hence we gather why he was not astonished.

[1] That is, whose leaves were beautiful.—*Calvin.*
[2] Verbally, " in it."—*Calvin.*
[3] That is, who hast become great and strong.—*Calvin.*

He felt no fear of the tyrant, although many do not dare to discharge their duty when an odious message is entrusted to them, which stimulates the impious and the unbelievers to madness. Daniel, however, was not astonished with any fear of this kind; he only wished God to act mercifully towards his king. For he says here, *Thou art king thyself.* He does not speak with any doubt or hesitation, neither does he use obscurity nor a number of excuses, but plainly announces king Nebuchadnezzar to be intended by the tree which he saw. Hence *the tree which thou sawest is large and strong, under the shade of which the beasts of the field were dwelling, and in the boughs of which the birds of the air were making their nests: thou,* says he, *art the king.* Why so? *Thou hast become great and strong; thy magnitude has extended to the heavens, and thy power to the ends of the earth.* Now, what follows?

23. And whereas the king saw a watcher and an holy one coming down from heaven, and saying, Hew the tree down, and destroy it; yet leave the stump of the roots thereof in the earth, even with a band of iron and brass, in the tender grass of the field; and let it be wet with the dew of heaven, and *let* his portion *be* with the beasts of the field, till seven times pass over him;

24. This *is* the interpretation, O king, and this *is* the decree of the most High, which is come upon my lord the king.

23. Et quod vidit rex, vigilem, et sanctum descendere è cœlis, qui dixit:[1] Succidite arborem, et dispergite eam: tantummodo imum radicum ejus in terra relinquite: et *sit* in vinculo ferri et æris in herba agri, et rore cœlorum proluatur, et cum bestiis agri portio ejus, donec septem tempora transeant super eam.

24. Hæc interpretatio, rex, et decretum excelsi est, quod spectat ad dominum meum regem.

Daniel follows up what he had begun with perseverance, shewing judgment to be overhanging the king of Babylon. He calls him lord, indeed, with cordiality; meanwhile he was the ambassador of the Supreme King, he did not hesitate to elevate his discourse above the king's command—as all the prophets do who rise up against mountains and hills, as Jeremiah does in chap. i. 10. Thus this sentence is worthy of notice,—"I have appointed thee over kingdoms and peoples, to pluck them up and to plant them, to build and to destroy." God, therefore, wishes to assert so great a reverence for his Word, because there is nothing in the

[1] Verbally, "and he said," for the copula ought to be resolved into the relative pronoun.—*Calvin.*

world so magnificent or splendid which does not yield to it. Daniel, then, as far as concerns human events and political order, confesses the king to be his master; but meanwhile he goes on with the embassy entrusted to him. *The king then*, says he, *saw a watcher descend from heaven*. He always speaks of an angel.[1] We have stated why Scripture calls angels "watchers," since they are at hand to perform God's commands; and we know God executes his decrees by their agency: I said angels always discharge this duty, and keep watch over the faithful. But the name "watcher" is a general one, and implies the promptness with which angels are endued, to enable them to discharge with the utmost celerity whatever God enjoins upon them. *Thou hast seen, then, one descend from heaven, who said, Cut down the tree, and scatter it abroad*. He repeats what he had said before, namely, the time of his punishment was defined here, because God would destroy the king of Babylon and all remembrance of him. An exception is then added,— *Until seven times pass over*. I have said nothing of those times, but their opinion is probable who take it for an indefinite number, meaning, until a long time shall pass away. Others think months denoted; others, years; but I willingly incline to this interpretation, since God wishes for no short time to punish King Nebuchadnezzar. It may not seem customary, indeed, but as he wished to put forth an example for all ages, he desired to prolong his punishment. This, therefore, seems the meaning of the seven years; for we know the number seven years to signify a long time in Scripture, since it denotes perfection.

PRAYER.

Grant, Almighty God, since thou settest before us our sins, and at the same time announcest thyself as our judge, that we may not abuse thy forbearance and lay up for ourselves a treasure of greater wrath through our sloth and torpor. Grant, also, that we may fear thee reverently, and be anxiously cautious ourselves: may we be frightened by thy threats, and enticed by thy sweetness, and be willing and submissive to thee: may we never desire more than to consecrate ourselves entirely to obey thee, and to glorify thy name through Jesus Christ our Lord.— Amen.

[1] See DISSERTATION XIV. at the end of this Vol.

Lecture Twentieth.

25. That they shall drive thee from men, and thy dwelling shall be with the beasts of the field, and they shall make thee to eat grass as oxen, and they shall wet thee with the dew of heaven, and seven times shall pass over thee, till thou know that the most High ruleth in the kingdom of men, and giveth it to whomsoever he will.

25. Et te expellent ab hominibus, et cum bestiis agrestibus erit habitatio tua: et herba sicut boves te pascent, et rore cœlorum te irrigabunt: et septem tempora transibunt super te, donec cognoscas, quod dominator *sit* excelsus in regno hominum, et cui voluerit det illud.

DANIEL proceeds with the explanation of the king's dream, to whom the last verse which I explained yesterday applies. This ought to be expressed, because this message was sorrowful and bitter for the king. We know how indignantly kings are usually compelled not only to submit to orders, but even to be cited before God's tribunal, where they must be overwhelmed in shame and disgrace. For we know how prosperity intoxicates the plebeian race. What, then, can happen to kings except forgetfulness of the condition of our nature when they attempt to free themselves from all inconvenience and trouble? For they do not consider themselves subject to the common necessities of mankind. As, therefore, Nebuchadnezzar could scarcely bear this message, here the Prophet admonishes him in a few words concerning the cutting down of the tree as the figure of that ruin which hung over him. He now follows this up at length, when he says, *They shall cast thee out from among men, and thy habitation shall be with the beasts of the field.* When Daniel had previously discoursed upon the Four Monarchies, there is no doubt about the king's mind being at first exasperated ; but this was far more severe, and in the king's opinion far less tolerable, as he is compared to wild beasts, and cut off from the number of mankind, and then he was driven into the fields and woods to feed with the wild beasts. If Daniel had only said the king was to be despoiled of his royal dignity, he would have been greatly offended by that disgrace, but when he was subject to such extreme shame, he was, doubtless, inwardly maddened by it. But God still restrained his fury lest he should desire to be revenged upon the supposed injury which he suffered. For we shall afterwards see from the context that he did not grow wise again. Since, therefore, he always cherished the same pride, there is no doubt of his cruelty, for these two vices were united ; but the Lord restrained his madness, and spared his holy Prophet. Meanwhile, the constancy of God's servant is worthy of observation, as he does not obliquely hint at what should happen to the king, but relates clearly and at length how base and disgraceful a condition remained for him. *They shall cast thee out,* says he, *from among men.* If he had said, thou shalt be as it were one of the common herd, and shalt not differ from the very dregs of the people, this would have been very severe. But when the king is ejected from the society of mankind, so that not a single corner remains, and he is not allowed to spend his life among ox-herds and swine-herds, every one may judge for himself how odious this would be ; nor does Daniel here hesitate to pronounce such a judgment.

The following clause has the same or at least similar weight,—*Thy dwelling,* says he, *shall be with the beasts of the field, and its herb shall feed thee.* The plural number is used indefinitely in the original ; and hence it may be properly translated, "Thou shalt feed on grass ; thou shalt be watered by the dew of heaven ; thy dwelling shall be with wild beasts." I do not wish to philosophize with subtlety, as some do, who understand angels. I confess this to be true ; but the Prophet simply teaches punishment to be at hand for the king of Babylon, while he should be reduced to extreme ignominy, and differ in nothing from the brutes. This liberty, therefore, as I have said, is worthy of notice, to shew us how God's servants, who have to discharge the duty of teaching, cannot faithfully act their part unless they shut their eyes and despise all worldly grandeur. Hence, by the example of the king, let us learn our duty, and not be stubborn and perverse when God threatens us. Although, as we have said, Nebuchadnezzar did not grow wise, as the context will shew us, yet we shall see how he bore the terrible judgment denounced against him. If, therefore, we, who are but as refuse compared to him, cannot bear God's threats when they are set before us, he will be our witness and judge, who, though possessed of such mighty power, dared nothing against the Prophet. Now, at the end of the verse, the sentence formerly explained is repeated,—*Until thou dost acknowledge,* says he, *how great a Lord there is in the kingdom of men, who delivers it to whomsoever he will.* This passage teaches us again how difficult it is for us to attribute supreme power to God. In our language, indeed, we are great heralds of God's glory, but still every one restricts his power, either by usurping something to himself, or by transferring it to some one else. Especially when God raises us to any degree of dignity, we forget ourselves to be men, and snatch away God's honour from him, and desire to substitute ourselves for him. This disease is cured with difficulty, and the punishment which God inflicted on the king of Babylon is an example to us. A slight chastisement would have been sufficient unless this madness had been deeply seated in his bowels and marrow, since men claim to themselves the peculiar property of God. Hence they have need of a violent medicine to learn modesty and humility. In these days, monarchs, in their titles, always put forward themselves as kings, generals, and counts, by the grace of God; but how many falsely pretend to apply God's name to themselves, for the purpose of securing the supreme power! For what is the meaning of that title of kings and princes— 'by the grace of God?" except to avoid the acknowledgment of a superior. Meanwhile, they willingly trample upon that God with whose shield they protect themselves,—so far are they from seriously thinking themselves to reign by his permission! It is mere pretence, therefore, to boast that they reign through God's favour. Since this is so, we may easily judge how proudly profane kings despise God, even though they make no fallacious use of his name, as those triflers who openly fawn upon him, and thus profane the name of his grace! It now follows:

26. And whereas they commanded to leave the stump of the tree roots; thy kingdom shall be sure unto thee, after that thou shalt have known that the heavens do rule.	26. Et quod dixerunt de relinquenda radice stirpium arboris, regnum tuum tibi stabit, ex quo cognoveris quod potestas *sit* cœlorum.[1]

[1] Or, that there is dominion in the heavens.—*Calvin.*

Here Daniel closes the interpretation of the dream, and shews how God did not treat King Nebuchadnezzar so severely by not giving way to clemency. He mitigates, indeed, the extreme rigour of the punishment, to induce Nebuchadnezzar to call upon God and repent, through indulging the hope of pardon, as a clearer exhortation will afterwards follow. But Daniel now prepares him for penitence, by saying *His kingdom should stand.* For God might cast him out from intercourse with mankind, and thus he would always remain among wild beasts. He might instantly remove him from the world; but this is a mark of his clemency, since he wished to restore him, not to a merely moderate station, but to his former dignity, as if it had never been trenched upon. We see, therefore, how useful the dream was to King Nebuchadnezzar, so long as he did not despise the Prophet's holy admonition, through ingratitude towards God; because Daniel not only predicted the slaughter which was at hand, but brought at the same time a message of reconciliation. God, therefore, had instructed the king to some purpose, unless he had been unteachable and perverse, like the majority of mankind. Besides, we may gather from this the general doctrine of our being invited to repentance when God puts an end to his chastisements; since he sets before us a taste of his clemency to induce in us the hope of his being entreated, if we only fly to him heartily and sincerely. We must notice also what Daniel adds in the second part of the verse, *from which thou mayest know that there is power in heaven:* for under these words the promise of spiritual grace is included. Since God will not only punish the king of Babylon, to humble him, but will work in him and change his mind, as he afterwards fulfilled, though at a long interval.

From which thou shalt know, then, says he, *that power is in heaven.* I have stated the grace of the Spirit to be here promised, as we know how badly men profit, even if God repeats his stripes an hundredfold. Such is the hardness and obstinacy of our hearts—for we rather grow more and more obdurate, while God calls us to repentance. And, doubtless, Nebuchadnezzar had been like Pharaoh, unless

God had humbled him, not only with outward penalties, but had added also the inward instinct of his Spirit, to allow himself to be instructed, and to submit himself to the judgment and power of heaven. Daniel means this when he says, *Wherefore thou shalt know;* for Nebuchadnezzar would never have acquired this knowledge of his own accord, unless he had been touched by the secret movement of the Spirit. He adds, *That there is power in heaven;* meaning, God governs the world and exercises supreme power; for he here contrasts heaven with earth, meaning all mankind. For if kings see all things tranquil around them, and if no one causes them terror, they think themselves beyond all chance of danger, as they say; and through being desirous of certainty in their station, they look round on all sides, but never raise their eyes upwards to heaven, as if God did not concern himself to behold the kingdoms of the earth, and to set up whom he would, and to prostrate all the proud. The princes of this world never consider their power to be from heaven, as if this were entirely out of God's hands; but, as I have said, they look right and left, before and behind. This is the reason why Daniel said, Power is from heaven. There is a contrast then between God and all mankind, as if he had said, Thou shalt know God reigns—as we have formerly seen. It follows:

27. Wherefore, O king, let my counsel be acceptable unto thee, and break off thy sins by righteousness, and thine iniquities by shewing mercy to the poor; if it may be a lengthening of thy tranquillity.	27. Propterea, rex, consilium meum placeat apud te,[1] et peccata tua[2] justitia redimas,[3] et iniquitatem tuam in misericordia erga pauperes: ecce erit prolongatio paci tuæ.[4]

Since interpreters do not agree about the sense of these words, and as the doctrine to be derived from them depends partly upon that, we must remark, in the *first* place, that מלכי, *meleki,* means " my counsel." Some translate it " my

[1] שפר, *shepher,* signifies to be beautiful; but it is metaphorically transferred to approbation or complacency, as the phrase is, "therefore my counsel shall please thee."—*Calvin.*

[2] Or, " that" for ו, *vau,* may be used in this way.—*Calvin.*

[3] So it is usually translated: we shall discuss the word by and bye.— *Calvin.*

[4] The Greeks translate—if by chance—or a medicine for their error.— *Calvin.*

king," and both words are derived from the same root מלך,
melek, signifying " to reign ;" but it also signifies " counsel."
There is no doubt that this passage ought to be explained
thus :—*May my counsel therefore please thee, and mayest thou
redeem thy sins.* The word פרוק, *peruk*, is here translated
" to redeem ;" it often signifies " to break off," or " separate,"
or " abolish." In this passage it may conveniently be translated, " separate or break off thy sins" by pity and humanity ;
as if he had said, Thus thou shalt make an end of sin, and
enter upon a new course, and thus thy cruelty may be
changed into clemency, and thy tyrannical violence into pity.
But this is not of much consequence. The verb often signifies to free and to preserve ; the context does not admit the
sense of preserving, and it would be harsh to say, Free thy
sins by thy righteousness. Hence I readily embrace the
sense of Daniel exhorting the king of Babylon to a change
of life, so as to break off his sins in which he had too long
indulged. With respect to the clause at the end of the verse,
behold there shall be a cure for thine error, as I have mentioned, the Greeks translate, " if by chance there should be
a cure ;" but the other sense seems to suit better ; as if he
had said, " this is the proper and genuine medicine," some
translate, " a promulgation," since ארך, *arek,* signifies " to
produce ;" and at the same time they change the signification of the other noun, for they say, " there shall be a prolongation to thy peace or quiet." That sense would be
tolerable, but the other suits better with the grammatical
construction ; besides, the more received sense is, *this medicine may be suitable to the error.* A different sense may be
elicited without changing the words at all ; *there shall be a
medicine for thine errors ;* meaning, thou mayest learn to
cure thine errors. For length of indulgence increases the
evil, as we have sufficiently noticed. Hence this last part of
the verse may be taken, and thus Daniel may proceed with
his exhortation ; as if he had said,—it is time to cease from
thine errors, for hitherto thou hast deprived thyself of all
thy senses by giving unbridled license to thy lusts. If, therefore, there is any moderation in thine ignorance, thou mayest
open thine eyes and understand at length how to repent.

I now return to the substance of the teaching. *May my counsel please thee!* says he. Here Daniel treats the profane king more indulgently than if he had addressed his own nation ; for he used the prophetic office. But because he knew the king did not hold the first rudiments of piety, he here undertakes only the office of a counsellor, since he was not an ordinary teacher. As to Nebuchadnezzar sending for him, this was not a daily thing, nor did he do this, because he wished to submit to his doctrine. Daniel therefore remembers the kind of person with whom he was treating, when he tempers his words and says, *may my counsel be acceptable to thee!* He afterwards explains his counsel in a few words,—*Break away,* says he, *thy sins*—or cast them away—*by righteousness, and thy iniquities by pity to the poor.* There is no doubt that Daniel wished to exhort the king to repentance ; but he touched on only one kind, which we know was very customary with the Prophets. For when they recall the people to obedience by repentance, they do not always explain it fully, nor define it generally, but touch upon it by a figure of speech, and treat only of the outward duties of penitence. Daniel now follows this custom. If inquiry is made concerning the nature of repentance, it is the conversion of man towards God, from whom he had been alienated. Is this conversion then only in the hands, and feet, and tongue ? Does it not rather begin in the mind and the heart, and then pass on to outward works ? Hence true penitence has its source in the mind of men, so that he who wished to be wise must set aside his own prudence, and put away his foolish confidence in his own reason. Then he must subdue his own depraved affections and submit them to God, and thus his outward life will follow the inward spirit. Besides this, works are the only testimonies to real repentance ; for it is a thing too excellent to allow its root to appear to human observation. By our fruits therefore we must testify our repentance. But because the duties of the second table, in some sense, open the mind of man ; hence the Prophets in requiring repentance, only set before us the duties of charity, as Daniel says. *Redeem,* therefore, *thy sins,* says he, or break away, or cast them away—but how ? namely, by righteousness. Without doubt the word "justice" means here the same as "grace" or "pity." But those who here transfer "grace" to "faith," twist the Prophet's words too violently; for we know of nothing more frequent among the Hebrews than to repeat one and the same thing under two forms of speech. As, therefore, Daniel here uses sins and iniquities in the same sense, we conclude justice and pity ought not to be separated, while the second word expresses more fully the sense of justice. For when men see their life must be changed, they feign for themselves many acts of obedience which scarcely deserve the name. They have no regard for what pleases God, nor for what he commands in his word; but just as they approve of one part or another, they thrust themselves rashly upon God, as we see in the Papacy. For what is a holy and religious life with them? To run about here and there; to undertake pilgrimages imposed by vows; to set up a statue; to found masses, as they call it; to fast on certain days; and to lay stress on trifles about which God has never said a single word. As, therefore, men err so grossly in the knowledge of true righteousness, the Prophet here adds the word "pity" by way of explanation; as if he had said, Do not think to appease God by outward pomps, which delight mankind because they are carnal and devoted to earthly things, and fashion for themselves a depraved idea of God according to their own imagination; let not then this vanity deceive you; but learn how true justice consists in pity towards the poor. In this second clause, then, only a part of the idea is expressed, since true justice is not restricted simply to the meaning of the word, but embraces all the duties of charity. Hence we ought to deal faithfully with mankind, and not to deceive either rich or poor, nor to oppress any one, but to render every one his own. But this manner of speaking ought to be familiar to us, if we are but moderately versed in the prophetic writings.

The meaning of the phrase is this:—Daniel wished to shew the king of Babylon the duty of living justly, and cultivating faith and integrity before men, without forgetting the former table of the law. For the worship of God is more precious than all the righteousness which men cultivate

among themselves. But true justice is known by its outward
proofs, as I have said. But he treats here the second table
rather than the first: for, while hypocrites pretend to worship God by many ceremonies, they allow themselves to
commit all kinds of cruelty, rapine, and fraud, without obeying any law of correct living with their neighbours. Because
hypocrites cover their malice by this frivolous pretence,
God sets before them a true test to recall them to the
duties of charity. This, then, is the meaning of the verse
from which we have elicited a double sense. If we retain
the future time, *behold, there shall be a medicine!* it will be
a confirmation of the former doctrine; as if he had said,
We must not travel the long and oblique circuits—there is
this single remedy: or, if we are better pleased with the
word of exhortation, the context will be suitable; may there
be a medicine for thine errors! Mayest thou not indulge
thyself hereafter as thou hast hitherto done, but thou must
open thine eyes and perceive how miserably and wickedly
thou hast lived, and so desire to heal thine errors. As the
Papists have abused this passage, to shew God to be appeased by satisfactions, it is too frivolous and ridiculous to
refute their doctrine; for when they speak of satisfactions,
they mean works of supererogation. If any one could fulfil
God's law completely, yet he could not satisfy for his sins.
The Papists are compelled to confess this; what then remains?—The offering to God more than he demands, which
they call works not required! But Daniel does not here
exact of King Nebuchadnezzar any work of supererogation;
he exacts justice, and afterwards shews how a man's life
cannot be justly spent unless humanity prevails and flourishes
among men, and especially when we are merciful to the poor.
Truly there is no supererogation here!   To what end then
serves the law?   Surely this has no reference to satisfactions,
according to the ridiculous and foolish notions of the Papists!
But if we grant them this point, still it does not follow that
their sins are redeemed before God, as if works compensated
either their fault or penalty, as they assert; for they confess
their fault not to be redeemed by satisfactions—this is one
point gained—and then as to the penalty, they say it is re-

deemed; but we must see whether this agrees with the Prophet's intention.

I will not contend about a word; I will allow it to mean " to redeem"—Thou mayest redeem thy sins; but we must ascertain, whether this redemption is in the judgment of God or of man ?   Clearly enough, Daniel here regards the conduct of Nebuchadnezzar as unjust and inhuman, in harassing his subjects, and in proudly despising the poor and miserable. Since, therefore, he had so given himself up to all iniquity, Daniel shews the remedy; and if this remedy is treated as a redemption or liberation, there is nothing absurd in saying, we redeem our sins before men while we satisfy them.   I redeem my sins before my neighbour, if after I have injured him, I desire to become reconciled to him, I acknowledge my sins and seek for pardon.   If, therefore, I have injured his fortunes, I restore what I have unjustly taken, and thus redeem my transgression.   But this does assist us in expiating sin before God, as if the beneficence which I put in practice was any kind of expiation.   We see, therefore, the Papists to be foolish and silly when they wrest the Prophet's words to themselves.   We may now inquire in the last place, to what purpose Daniel exhorted King Nebuchadnezzar to break away from or redeem his sins?   Now this was either a matter of no consequence—which would be absurd—or it was a heavenly decree, as the king's dream was a promulgation of the edict, as we have formerly seen.   But this was determined before God, and could not be changed in any way; it was therefore superfluous to wish to redeem sins. If we follow a different explanation, no difficulty will remain; but even if we allow the Prophet to be here discoursing of the redemption of sins, yet the exhortation is not without its use.

In whatever way Nebuchadnezzar ought to prepare to bear God's chastisement, yet this would prove most useful to him, to acknowledge God to be merciful.   And yet the time might be contracted, during which his obstinate wickedness should extend; not as if God changed his decree, but because he always warns by threatening, for the purpose of treating men more kindly, and tempering vigour with his wrath, as is evident from many other examples.   This would not have been without its use to a teachable disposition, nor yet without fruit, when Daniel exhorted King Nebuchadnezzar to redeem his sins, because he might obtain some pardon, even if he had paid the penalty, since not even a single day had been allowed out of the seven years.   Yet this was a great progress, if the king had at last humbled himself before God, so as to be in a fit state for receiving the pardon which had been promised.   For as a certain time had been fixed beforehand, or at least shewn by the Prophet, hence it would have profited the king, if through wishing to appease his judge he had prepared his mind for obtaining pardon.   This doctrine was therefore in every way useful, because the same reason avails with us.   We ought always to be prepared to suffer God's chastisements ; yet it is no slight or common alleviation of our sufferings, when we so submit ourselves to God, as to be persuaded of his desire to be propitious to us, when he sees us dissatisfied with ourselves, and heartily detesting our transgressions.

PRAYER.

Grant, Almighty God, that we may learn to bear patiently all adverse misfortunes, and know that thou exercisest towards us the duties of a judge, as often as we are afflicted in this world.   Thus may we prevent thy wrath, and so condemn ourselves with true humility, that trusting in thy pity we may always flee to thee, relying upon the mediation of thy only-begotten Son, which thou hast provided for us.   Grant, also, that we may beg pardon of thee, and resolve upon a true repentance, not with vain and useless fictions, but by true and serious proofs, cultivating true charity and faith among ourselves, and testifying in this way our fear of thy name, that thou mayest be truly glorified in us by the same our Lord.—Amen.

Lecture Twenty-first.

28. All this came upon the king Nebuchadnezzar.

29. At the end of twelve months

28. Hoc totum impletum fuit, *vel*, *incidit*, super Nebuchadnezer regem

29. In fine mensium duodecim,[1]

[1] That is, after twelve months.—*Calvin.*

he walked in the palace of the kingdom of Babylon.

30. The king spake, and said, Is
not this great Babylon, that I have
built for the house of the kingdom,
by the might of my power, and for
the honour of my majesty ?

31. While the word *was* in the
king's mouth, there fell a voice from
heaven, *saying*, O king Nebuchadnezzar, to thee it is spoken ; The
kingdom is departed from thee :

32. And they shall drive thee from
men, and thy dwelling *shall be* with
the beasts of the field : they shall
make thee to eat grass as oxen, and
seven times shall pass over thee, until thou know that the most High
ruleth in the kingdom of men, and
giveth it to whomsoever he will.

in palatio regni, quod est in Baby-
lone, deambulabat.

30. Loquutus est rex et dixit, An
non hæc est Babylon magna, quam
ego ædificavi in domum regni,[1] in
robore fortitudinis meæ, et in pretium, *vel, excellentiam,* decoris mei ?

31. Adhuc sermo *erat* in ore regis,[2]
vox e cœlis cecidit, Tibi dicunt, rex
Nebuchadnezer, regnum *tuum* mi-
gravit, *vel, discessit,* abs te.

32. Et ex hominibus te ejicient,
et cum bestia agri habitatio tua :
herbam sicuti boves gustare te faci-
ent :[3] et septem tempora transibunt
super te, donec cognoscas quod dominator *sit* excelsus in regno hominum, et cui voluerit det illud.

After Nebuchadnezzar has related Daniel to be a herald
of God's approaching judgment, he now shews how God
executed the judgment which the Prophet had announced.
But he speaks in the third person, according to what we
know to be a common practice with both the Hebrews and
Chaldees.   Thus Daniel does not relate the exact words of
the king, but only their substance.   Hence he first introduces the king as the speaker, and then he speaks himself
in his own person.   There is no reason why this variety should
occasion us any trouble, since it does not obscure the sense.
In the first verse, Nebuchadnezzar shews the dream which
Daniel had explained not to have been in vain.   Thus the
miracle shews itself to be from heaven, by its effects ; because dreams vanish away, as we know well enough.   But
since God fulfilled, at his own time, what he had shewn to
the king of Babylon by his dream, it is clear there was
nothing alarming in the dream, but a sure revelation of the
future punishment which fell upon the king.   Its moderation is also expressed.   Daniel says, when a year had passed
away, and the king was walking in his own palace, and
boasting in his greatness, at that moment a voice came down
from heaven, and repeated what he had already heard in

---

[1] That is, that it may be a royal seat.—*Calvin.*
[2] That is, when the speech was in the king's mouth.—*Calvin.*
[3] Or, the grass shall feed thee as it does oxen.— *Calvin.*

the dream. He afterwards relates how he had been expelled from human society, and dwelt for a long time among the brutes, so as to differ from them in nothing. As to the use of words, since מַהֲלַךְ, *mehelek*, occurs here, some think that he walked upon the roof of his palace, whence he could behold all parts of the city. The inhabitants of the east are well known to use the roofs of their houses in this way; but I do not interpret the phrase with such subtlety, since the Prophet seems to wish nothing else than to shew how the king enjoyed his own ease, luxury, and magnificence. There is nothing obscure in the rest of the language.

I now approach the matter before us. Some think Nebuchadnezzar to have been touched with penitence when instructed by God's anger, and thus the time of his punishment was put off. This does not seem to me probable, and I rather incline to a different opinion, as God withdrew his hand till the end of the year, and thus the king's pride was the less excusable. The Prophet's voice ought to have frightened him, just as if God had thundered and lightened from heaven. He now appears to have been always like himself. I indeed do not deny that he might be frightened by the first message, but I leave it doubtful. Whichever way it is, I do not think God spared him for a time, because he gave some signs of repentance. I confess he sometimes indulges the reprobate, if he sees them humbled. An example of this, sufficiently remarkable, is displayed in King Ahab. (1 Kings xxi. 29.) He did not cordially repent, but God wished to shew how much he was pleased with his penitence, by pardoning a king impious and obstinate in his wickedness. The same might be said of Nebuchadnezzar, if Scripture had said so; but as far as we can gather from these words of the Prophet, Nebuchadnezzar became prouder and prouder, until his sloth arrived at its height. The king continued to grow proud after God had threatened him so, and this was quite intolerable. Hence his remarkable stupidity, since he would have been equally careless had he lived an hundred years after he heard that threat! Finally, I think although Nebuchadnezzar perceived some dreadful and horrible punishment to be at hand, yet, while frightened for the

time, he did not lay aside his pride and haughtiness of mind.
Meanwhile, he might think this prediction to be in vain ; and
what he had heard probably escaped from his mind for a
long time, because he thought he had escaped ; just as the
impious usually abuse God's forbearance, and thus heap up
for themselves a treasure of severer vengeance, as Paul says.
(Rom. ii. 5.) Hence he derided this prophecy, and hardened
himself more and more.   Whatever sense we attach to it,
nothing else can be collected from the Prophet's context,
than the neglect of the Prophet's warning, and the oracle
rendered nugatory by which Nebuchadnezzar had been called
to repentance.   If he had possessed the smallest particle of
soundness of mind, he ought to flee to the pity of God, and
to consider the ways in which he had provoked his anger,
and also to devote himself entirely to the duties of charity.
As he had exercised a severe tyranny towards all men, so he
ought to study benevolence ; yet when the Prophet exhorted
him, he did not act thus, but uttered vain boastings, which
shew his mind to have been swollen with pride and contempt
for God.   As to the space of time here denoted, it shews how
God suspended his judgments, if perchance those who are
utterly deplorable should be reclaimed ; but the reprobate
abuse God's humanity and indulgence, as they make this an
occasion of hardening their minds, while they suppose God
to cease from his office of judge, through his putting it off
for a time.   *At the end,* then, *of twelve months, the king was
walking in his palace ; he spoke, and said.*   This doubling of
the phrase shews us how the king uttered the feelings of
premeditated pride.   The Prophet might have said more
simply, The king says,—but he says, *he spoke, and said.*   I
know how customary it is with both the Hebrews and Chaldees to unite these words together ; but I think the repetition emphatic in this place, since the king then uttered what
he had long ago conceived and concealed in his mind ; *Is not
this great Babylon, which I have built for a royal palace, and
that too in the mightiness of my valour ; as I have built it in
the splendour of my excellency ?*   In these words we do not
see any open blasphemy which could be very offensive to
God, but we must consider the king by this language to

claim to himself supreme power, as if he were God ! We may gather this from the verse, " Is not this great Babylon ?" says he. He boasts in the magnitude of his city, as if he wished to raise it giant-like to heaven ; *which I*, says he— using the pronoun with great emphasis—*which I have built, and that too in the greatness of my valour.* We see that by claiming all things as his own, he robs God of all honour.

Before I proceed further, we must see why he asserts Babylon to have been founded by himself. All historians agree in the account of the city being built by Semiramis. A long time after this event, Nebuchadnezzar proclaims his own praises in building the city. The solution is easy enough. We know how earthly kings desire, by all means in their power, to bury the glory of others, with the view of exalting themselves and acquiring a perpetual reputation. Especially when they change anything in their edifices, whether palaces or cities, they wish to seem the first founders, and so to extinguish the memory of those by whom the foundations were really laid. We must believe, then, Babylon to have been adorned by King Nebuchadnezzar, and so he transfers to himself the entire glory, while the greater part ought to be attributed to Semiramis or Ninus. Hence this is the way in which tyrants speak, as all usurpers and tyrants do, when they draw towards themselves the praises which belong to others. *I*, therefore, says he, *have built it, by the strength of my hand.* Now it is easy to see what had displeased God in this boasting of the king of Babylon, namely, his sacrilegious audacity in asserting the city to have been built by his own mightiness. But God shews this praise to be peculiar to himself and deservedly due to him. Unless God builds the city, the watchman watches but in vain. (Psalm cxxvii. 1.) Although men labour earnestly in founding cities, yet they never profit unless God himself preside over the work. As Nebuchadnezzar here extols himself and opposes the strength of his fortitude to God and his grace, this boasting was by no means to be endured. Hence it happened that God was so very angry with him. And thus we perceive how this example proves to us what Scripture always inculcates,—God's resistance of the proud, his humbling

their superciliousness, and his detestation of their arrogance.
(Psalm xviii. 27.)   Thus God everywhere announces himself
as the enemy of the proud, and he confirms it by the present
example, as if he set before us in a mirror the reflection of
his own judgment.   (James iv. 6; 1 Peter v. 5.)   This is
one point.   The reason also must be noticed why God declares war on all the proud, because we cannot set ourselves
up even a little, without declaring war on God; for power
and energy spring from him.   Our life is in his hands; we
are nothing and can do nothing except through him.   Whatever, then, any one assumes to himself he detracts from God.
No wonder then if God testifies his dislike of the haughty
superciliousness of men, since they purposely weary him
when they usurp anything as their own.   Cities, indeed, are
truly built by the industry of men, and kings are worthy of
praise who either build cities or adorn them, so long as they
allow God's praise to be inviolate.   But when men exalt
themselves and wish to render their own fortitude conspicuous, they bury as far as they can the blessing of God.   Hence
it is necessary for their impious rashness to be judged by
God, as we have already said.   The king also confesses his
vanity when he says, *I have built it for a royal palace, and
for the excellency of my splendour.*   By these words he does
not dissemble how completely he looked at his own glory in
all those buildings by which he hoped to hand down his
name to posterity.   Hence, on the whole, he wishes to be
celebrated in the world, both during his life and after his
death, so that God may be nothing in comparison with himself, as I have already shewn how all the proud strive to
substitute themselves in the place of God.

It now follows,—*While the speech was in the mouth of the
king, a voice descended from heaven—They say unto thee, O
King Nebuchadnezzar, thy kingdom has departed from thee!*
God does not now admonish the king of Babylon by either
the mouth of a Prophet or a dream by night; but he sends
forth his own voice from heaven; and as if he had not tamed
down the pride by which the king was puffed up, a voice
is now heard from heaven which inspires greater terror than
either the Prophet's oracle or interpretation.   Thus God is

in the habit of dealing with the hardened and impenitent, since he causes his own prophets to denounce the penalty which hangs over them. Besides, when he sees them untouched or unaffected, he doubles the terror, until the final execution follows, as in the case of this tyrant. *The word was in the king's mouth when the voice was heard.* We see how God restrains in a moment the madness of those who raise themselves extravagantly. But it is not surprising that the voice was so suddenly heard, because time for repentance was allowed to King Nebuchadnezzar. In the form of speech, *they say to thee,* it is not necessary to inquire anxiously to whom these words apply. Some restrict them to angels ; but I do not agree to this ; it seems rather to be used in the customary way, *they say*—meaning " it is said," as if sanctioned by common consent. Hence *they say to thee, O King Nebuchadnezzar ;* God does not simply call him by his name, but uses the word king—not for the sake of honour, but of ridicule, and to strike away from the king all the allurements by which he deceived himself. Thou indeed art intoxicated by thy present splendour, for while all adore thee, thou art forgetful of thy frailty ; but this royal majesty and power will not hinder God from laying thee prostrate ; for since thou wilt not humble thyself, thy kingdom shall be taken from thee ! This indeed appeared incredible, since Nebuchadnezzar had the tranquil possession of the kingdom in his hand ; no one dared to shew himself his enemy ; he had subdued all his neighbours ; his monarchy was terrible to all nations ; hence God pronounces, *The kingdom has passed away from thee !* And this shews the certainty of the oracle ; and thus Nebuchadnezzar may know the time to be fulfilled, and the punishment to be no longer delayed, because he had trifled with God's indulgence.

It follows,—*They shall expel thee from among men, and thy habitation shall be with the beasts of the field*—or of the country,—*they shall make thee eat grass like oxen !* Some think Nebuchadnezzar to have been changed into a beast ; but this is too harsh and absurd. We need not fancy any change of nature ; but he was cut off from all intercourse with men, and with the exception of a human form, he did

not differ from the brutes,—nay, such was his deformity in
his exile that, as we shall afterwards see, he became a horrid
spectacle ;—all the hairs of his body stood up and grew like
eagles' feathers ; his claws were like those of birds.   In
these points he was like the beasts, in others like the rest of
mankind. It is uncertain whether God struck this king with
madness, causing him to escape and lie hid for a length of
time, or whether he was cast forth by a tumult and conspiracy of nobles, or even the consent of the whole people.   All
this is doubtful, since the history of those times is unknown
to us.   Whether, then, Nebuchadnezzar was snatched away
by madness, and while he continued a maniac was separated
from the society of men, or was cast forth as many tyrants
have been, his dwelling with beasts for a time, becomes a
memorable example to us. He was probably rendered stupid,
by God's leaving him a human form while he deprived him of
reason, as the context will make evident to us.   *They shall
cast thee out from human society ; thy dwelling shall be with
wild beasts ; they shall make thee eat grass like an ox !* that
is, when deprived of all delight, nay, of the commonest and
plainest food, thou wilt find no other sustenance than that
of oxen. Thou shalt eat the grass like an animal, *and seven
times shall pass over thee.*   Of the " seven times" we have
spoken before.   Some restrict this to days, but this is contrary not only to every reason, but to every pretext.   Nor do
I explain it of months ; the space of time would have been
much too short.   Hence the opinion of those who extend it
to seven years is more probable.   If Nebuchadnezzar had
been cast out by a tumult, he would not have been so quickly
recalled : then, since God wished to make an example of him
for all generations, I suppose him to have been driven out
from common society for a length of time.   For if the penalty
had been for seven months only, we see how coolly God's
judgments would be received in the world.   Hence, with the
view of engraving this penalty more deeply in the hearts of
all, he wished to protract it longer—I will not say to seven
years, since I have previously expounded the certain number
as put for an uncertain one, implying a long space of time.
  Seven years, then, *shall pass away,* says he, *until thou shalt*

know that there is a lofty ruler in the kingdoms of men. This is the end of the punishment, as we have previously said, for I need not repeat my former remarks. But we must remember this—God mitigates the bitterness of the penalty by making it temporary. Then he proposed this end to induce Nebuchadnezzar to repent, as he required many blows for this purpose, according to the old proverb about the fool who can never be recalled to a sound mind without suffering calamity. Thus King Nebuchadnezzar ought to be beaten with stripes, to render him submissive to God, as he never profited by any holy admonition or any heavenly oracle. God does not treat all in this way. Hence we have here a special example of his clemency, which provides for the punishment inflicted on King Nebuchadnezzar, being both useful and profitable. For the reprobate are more and more hardened against God, and are ever stirred up and excited to madness. It was an act, then, of special grace, when Nebuchadnezzar was chastised for the time by the hand of God, to cause his repentance and his owning God's entire sway over the whole world.

He says, *that God may be Lord in the kingdom of men;* because nothing is more difficult than to persuade tyrants to submit to the power of God. On the one side they confess themselves to reign by his grace; but at the same time, they suppose their own sway to be obtained by either valour or good fortune, and to be retained by their own guards, counsels, and wealth. Hence, as far as they can, they shut God out from the government of the world, while they are puffed up with a false conceit of themselves, as if all things were maintained in their present state by their valour or advice. This, then, was an ordinary effect when Nebuchadnezzar began to feel *God to be the ruler in the kingdom of men,* since kings wish to place him somewhere between themselves and the multitude. They confess the people to be subject to God's power, but think themselves exempt from the common order of events, and in possession of a privilege in favour of their lusts, relieving them from the hand and empire of God. Hence, as I have said, it was no common thing for Nebuchadnezzar to acknowledge *God to reign in the earth;* for tyrants usually enclose God in heaven, and think him content with his own happiness, and careless about mingling in the concerns of men.   Hence *thou mayest know him to be the ruler.*   He afterwards adds the kind of dominion, *because God raises up whomsoever he pleases, and casts down others :* God is not only supreme in the sense of sustaining all things by his universal providence, but because no one without his will obtains empire at all. He binds some with a belt, and looseth the bonds of others, as it is said in the book of Job. (Chap. xii. 18.) We ought not, therefore, to imagine God's power to be at rest, but we should join it with present action, as the phrase is. Whether tyrants obtain power, or sovereigns are pious and just, all are governed by God's secret counsel, since otherwise there could be no king of the world.   It follows :

33. The same hour was the thing fulfilled upon Nebuchadnezzar; and he was driven from men, and did eat grass as oxen, and his body was wet with the dew of heaven, till his hairs were grown like eagles' *feathers,* and his nails like birds' *claws.*	33. In illa hora sermo completus fuit super Nebuchadnezer, et ab hominibus ejectus est, et herbam tanquam boves comedit, et rore cœlorum corpus ejus irrigatum fuit, donec pilus ejus quasi aquilæ crevit, et ungues ejus quasi avium.

The Prophet concludes what he had said : As soon as the voice had come down from heaven, Nebuchadnezzar was cast out from mankind !   Some occasion of expelling him might have preceded this ; but since the divination is uncertain, I had rather leave undetermined what the Holy Spirit has not revealed.   I only wished to touch upon this point shortly, when he boasted in the foundation of Babylon by the fortitude of his own energy ; since his own nobles must have become disgusted when they saw him carried away with such great pride ; or he might have spoken in this way when he thought snares were prepared for him, or when he felt some crowds moved against him.   Whatever be the meaning, God sent forth his voice, and the same moment he expelled King Nebuchadnezzar from the company of mankind.   Hence, *in the same hour,* says he, *the speech was fulfilled.*   If a long period had interposed, it might have been ascribed to either fortune or other inferior means, as a reason ; but when such is the connection between the language and its effect, the judgment is too clear to be obscured by the malignity of mankind. He says, therefore, *He was cast forth and fed with herbs,* differing in nothing from oxen: *his body was soaked in rain,* since he lay out in the open air. We are ourselves often subject to the drenching shower, and in the fields are sure to meet with it, and travellers often reach their inn wet through. But the Prophet speaks of the continuance of God's judgment, since he had no roof to shelter him, and always lay out in the fields. Hence he says, *he was moistened by the dew of heaven until,* says he, *his nails became claws, and his hair like the wings of eagles.* This passage confirms what has been said concerning the explanation of the seven times as a long period, for his hair could not have grown so in seven months, nor could such great deformity arise. Hence this change, thus described by the Prophet, sufficiently shews King Nebuchadnezzar to have suffered his punishment for a length of time, for he could not be so quickly humbled, because pride is not easily tamed in a man of moderate station, how much less then in so great a monarch! It afterwards follows:

34. And at the end of the days I Nebuchadnezzar lifted up mine eyes unto heaven, and mine understanding returned unto me, and I blessed the most High, and I praised and honoured him that liveth for ever, whose dominion *is* an everlasting dominion, and his kingdom *is* from generation to generation.	34. Et a fine dierum,[1] ego Nebuchadnezer oculos meos in cœlum extuli, et intellectus meus ad me rediit, et excelsum benedixi, et viventem *in* secula laudavi et glorificavi, quia potestas ejus potestas seculi,[2] et regnum ejus cum ætate et ætate.[3]

The Prophet again introduces King Nebuchadnezzar as the speaker. He says, then, *After that time had elapsed, he raised his eyes to heaven.* Without doubt, he means those seven years. As to his then beginning to raise his eyes to heaven, this shews how long it takes to cure pride, the disease under which he laboured. For when any vital part of the body is corrupt and decaying, its cure is difficult and tedious; so also when pride exists in men's hearts, and gains an entrance within the marrow, and infects the inmost soul,

[1] That is, when the time was passed over.—*Calvin.*
[2] That is, eternal.—*Calvin.*
[3] That is, of perpetual duration.—*Calvin.*

it is not easily plucked out; and this is worthy of notice.
Then we are taught how God by his word so operated upon
King Nebuchadnezzar, as not immediately and openly to
withdraw the effect of his grace. Nebuchadnezzar profited
by being treated disgracefully during those seven years or
times, and by being driven from the society of mankind;
but he could not perceive this at once till God opened his
eyes. So, therefore, God often chastises us, and invites us
by degrees, and prepares us for repentance, but his grace
is not immediately acknowledged. But lest I should be too
prolix, I will leave the rest till to-morrow.

PRAYER.

Grant, Almighty God, (since we are nothing in ourselves, and yet
we cease not to please ourselves, and so are blinded by our vain
confidence, and then we vainly boast in our virtues, which are
worthless,) that we may learn to put off these perverse affections.
May we so submit to thee as to depend upon thy mere favour:
may we know ourselves, to stand and be sustained by thy strength
alone: may we learn so to glorify thy name that we may not
only obey thy word with true and pure humility, but also earnestly implore thy assistance, and distrusting ourselves, may rely
upon thy favour as our only support, until at length thou gatherest us into thy heavenly kingdom, where we may enjoy that
blessed eternity which has been obtained for us by thine only-
begotten Son.—Amen.

Lecture Twenty=second.

I shall now continue the comments which were interrupted yesterday. From Nebuchadnezzar saying, *he raised
his eyes to heaven, and his intellect returned to him*, we
understand him to have been for the time deprived of his
mind. He is much astonished, in my opinion, by feeling his
own evils, but meanwhile he bites the bit and is like a
madman. Some think him to have been a complete maniac;
I do not contend about this; it is enough for me to know
he was deprived of his senses and was altogether like the
brutes. But it is probable there was no intelligence remain-

ing, to cause him to feel torture at his slaughter. Meanwhile, he did not raise his eyes to heaven until God drew him to himself. God's chastisements do not profit us unless they work inwardly by his Spirit, as we said yesterday. The phrase only means, he began to think God to be a just judge. For while at the time he felt the sting of his own disgrace, yet as it is said elsewhere, he did not regard the hand of the striker. (Is. ix. 13.) He began, therefore, to acknowledge God to be the avenger of pride, after the aforesaid time had elapsed. For those who cast their eyes down to the earth raise their eyes to heaven. As Nebuchadnezzar ought to awake from his stupor and rise up towards God, of whom he had been formerly forgetful, so he ought to prostrate himself to the earth, as he had already received the reward of his haughtiness. He had dared to raise his head above the lot of man, when he assumed to himself what was peculiar to God. He does not raise his eyes to heaven by any vain confidence, as he had formerly been intoxicated by the splendour of his monarchy; but he looked up to God, while mentally cast down and prostrate.

He afterwards adds, *and I blessed him on high, and praised and glorified him living for ever.* This change shews the punishment to have been chiefly and purposely inflicted on King Nebuchadnezzar, since he spoiled God of his just honour. He here describes the fruit of his repentance. If this feeling flowed from repentance, and Nebuchadnezzar really blessed God, it follows that he was formerly sacrilegious, as he had deprived God of lawful honour and wished to raise himself into his place, as we have already said. Hence, also, we must learn what the true praise of God really is; namely, when reduced to nothing, we acknowledge and determine all things to be according to his will; for, as we shall afterwards see, he is the Governor of heaven and earth, and we should esteem his will as the source of law and reason, and the final appeal of justice. For we may sometimes celebrate the praises of God with ostentation, but it will then be mere pretence; for no one can sincerely and heartily praise him, without ascribing to him all the properties which we shall afterwards see. First of all, Nebuchadnezzar says, *Because his power is eternal, and his kingdom from age to age.* In the first place, he here confesses God to be an eternal king ; which is a great step. For human frailty is opposed to this perpetuity ; because the greatest monarchs, who excel in power, have nothing firm ; they are not only subject to chance and change, as profane men express it— or rather depend upon the will of God—but they utterly fade away through their vanity. We see the whole world fluctuating like the waves of the sea. If there be any tranquillity, in one direction or another, yet every moment something new and sudden may happen, quite unexpectedly. As a tempest arises directly in a calm and serene sky, so also we see it occur in human affairs. Since it is so, no condition upon earth is firm, and monarchs especially disturb themselves by their own turbulent agitations. This is, therefore, the perpetuity which is here predicted by King Nebuchadnezzar ; because God as an absolute sovereign rules his own empire for himself, and is thus beyond all danger of change. This is the first point. It now follows :

35. And all the inhabitants of the earth *are* reputed as nothing : and he doeth according to his will in the army of heaven, and *among* the inhabitants of the earth ; and none can stay his hand, or say unto him, What doest thou ?	35. Et omnes habitatores terræ quasi nihil reputantur, et secundum voluntatem suam facit in exercitu cœlorum, et *in* habitatoribus terræ ; et non est qui prohibeat manum ejus,[1] et dicat ei, Quid fecisti ?[2]

Now the opposite clause is added to complete the contrast, because though it follows that nothing is firm or solid in mankind, yet this principle flourishes, namely, God is eternal ; yet few reason thus, because in words all allow God to be firm and everlasting, yet they do not descend into themselves and seriously weigh their own frailty. Thus, being unmindful of their own lot, they rage against God himself. The explanation then which occurs here is required ; for after Nebuchadnezzar praises God, because his power is eternal, he adds by way of contrast, *all the dwellers on the earth are considered as nothing.* Some take כלה, *keleh,* for a single word, meaning "anything complete," for

[1] Or, who can abolish ; for מחא, *mecha,* signifies either to blot out or to prohibit.—*Calvin.*

[2] Or, why hast thou done so ?—*Calvin.*

כלה, *keleh*, is to " finish," or "complete ;" it also signifies to
"consume" sometimes, whence they think the noun to be
derived, because men are limited within their own standard,
but God is immense.   This is harsh ; the more received
opinion is, that ה, *he*, is put for א, *a*, here ; and thus Nebuchadnezzar says, men are esteemed as of no value before God.
Already, then, we see how suitably these two clauses agree
together ; for God is an eternal king, and men are as nothing
in comparison with him.   For if anything is attributed to
men as springing from themselves, it so far detracts from the
supreme power and empire of God.   It follows, then, that
God does not entirely receive his rights, until all mortals are
reduced to nothing.   For although men make themselves of
very great importance, yet Nebuchadnezzar here pronounces
himself by the Spirit's instinct, to be of no value before God ;
for otherwise they would not attempt to raise themselves,
unless they were utterly blind in the midst of their darkness.   But when they are dragged into the light they feel
their own nothingness and utter vanity.   For whatever we
are, this depends on God's grace, which sustains us every
moment, and supplies us with new vigour.   Hence it is our
duty to depend upon God only ; because as soon as he withdraws his hand and the virtue of his Spirit, we vanish away.
In God we are anything he pleases, in ourselves we are
nothing.

It now follows : *God does according to his pleasure in the
army of the heavens, and among the dwellers upon earth.*
This may seem absurd, since God is said to act according to
his will, as if there were no moderation, or equity, or rule
of justice, with him.   But we must bear in mind, what we
read elsewhere concerning men being ruled by laws, since
their will is perverse, and they are borne along in any direction by their unruly lust ; but God is a law to himself, because
his will is the most perfect justice.   As often, then, as Scripture sets before us the power of God, and commands us to be
content with it, it does not attribute a tyrannical empire to
God, according to the calumnies of the impious.   But because we do not cease to cavil against God, and oppose our
reason to his secret counsels, and thus strive with him, as

if he did not act justly and fairly when he does anything which we disapprove; hence God pronounces all things to be done according to his own will, so that the Holy Spirit may restrain this audacity. We should remember then, when mention is made of God, how impossible it is for anything either perverse or unjust to belong to him; his will cannot be turned aside by any affection, for it is the perfection of justice. Since this is so, we should remember how extremely unbridled and perverse our rashness is, while we dare object to anything which God does; whence the necessity of this teaching which puts the bridle of modesty upon us is proved, since God does all things according to his will, as it is said in Psalm cxv. 3, Our God in heaven does what he wishes. From this sentence we gather that nothing happens by chance, but every event in the world depends on God's secret providence. We ought not to admit any distinction between God's permission and his wish. For we see the Holy Spirit—the best master of language—here clearly expresses two things; *first*, what God does; and *next*, what he does by his own will. But *permission*, according to those vain speculators, differs from *will;* as if God unwillingly granted what he did not wish to happen! Now, there is nothing more ridiculous than to ascribe this weakness to God. Hence the efficacy of action is added; *God does what he wishes*, says Nebuchadnezzar. He does not speak in a carnal but in a spiritual sense, or instinct, as we have said; since the Prophet must be attended to just as if he had been sent from heaven. Now, therefore, we understand how this world is administered by God's secret providence, and that nothing happens but what he has commanded and decreed; while he ought with justice to be esteemed the Author of all things.

Some object here to the apparent absurdity of saying God is the author of sin, if nothing is done without his will; nay, if he himself works it! This calumny is easily answered, as the method of God's action differs materially from that of men. For when any man sins, God works in his own manner, which is very different indeed from that of man, since he exercises his own judgment, and thus is said to blind and to harden.　As God therefore commands both the reprobate and the evil one, he permits them to indulge in all kinds of licentiousness, and in doing so, executes his own judgments.　But he who sins is deservedly guilty, and cannot implicate God as a companion of his wickedness. And why so?　Because God has nothing in common with him in reference to sinfulness.　Hence we see how these things which we may deem contrary to one another, are mutually accordant, since God by his own will governs all events in the world, and yet is not the author of sin.　And why so?　Because he treats Satan and all the wicked with the strict justice of a judge.　We do not always see the process, but we must hold this principle with firmness—supreme power is in God's hands; hence we must not cavil at his judgments, however inexplicable they may appear to us. Wherefore this phrase follows, *There is no one who can hinder his hand, or can say unto him, Why dost thou act thus?* When Nebuchadnezzar says, God's hand cannot be hindered, he uses this method of deriding human folly which does not hesitate to rebel against God.　Already they raise their finger to prevent, if possible, the power of his hand; and even when convicted of weakness, they proceed in their own fury.　Nebuchadnezzar, then, deservedly displays their ridiculous madness in conducting themselves so intemperately in wishing to restrain the Almighty, and to confine him within their bounds, and to fabricate chains for the purpose of restricting him.　When mankind thus burst forth into sacrilegious fury, they deserve to be laughed at, and this is here the force of Daniel's words.

He afterwards adds, *No one can say, Why dost thou act thus?*　We know how they gave way to the language of extreme petulance; since scarcely one man in a hundred restrains himself with such sobriety as to attribute the glory to God, and to confess himself just in his works.　But Nebuchadnezzar does not here consider what men are accustomed to do, but what they ought to do.　He says therefore, and with strict justice, God cannot be corrected; since however the reprobate chatter, their folly is self-evident, for it has neither reason nor the pretence of reason to support it.

The whole sense is—God's will is our law, against which we strive in vain ; and then, if he permits us sufficient license, and our infirmity breaks forth against him, and we contend with him, all our efforts will be futile. God himself will be justified in his judgments, and thus every human countenance must submit to him. (Ps. li. 6.) This is the general rule.

We must now notice the addition, *God's will must be done as well in the army of heaven as among the inhabitants of earth.* By "the army of heaven" I do not understand, as in other places, the sun, moon, and stars, but angels and even demons, who may be called heavenly without absurdity, if we consider their origin, and their being "princes of the air." Hence Daniel means to imply angels, demons, and men, to be equally governed by God's will ; and although the impious rush on intemperately, yet they are restrained by a secret bridle, and are prevented from executing whatever their lusts dictate. God therefore is said *to do in the army of the heavens and also among men whatsoever he wishes ;* because he has the elect angels always obedient to him, and the devils are compelled to obey his command, although they strive in the contrary direction. We know how strongly the demons resist God, but yet they are compelled to obey him, not willingly, but by compulsion. But God acts among angels and demons just as among the inhabitants of the earth. He governs others by his Spirit, namely, his elect, who are afterwards regenerated by his Spirit, and they are so treated by him that his justice may truly shine forth in all their actions. He also acts upon the reprobate, but in another manner ; for he draws them headlong by means of the devil ; he impels them with his secret virtue ; he strikes them by a spirit of dizziness; he blinds them and casts upon them a reprobate spirit, and hardens their hearts to contumacy. Behold how God does all things according to his own will among men and angels ! There is also another mode of action, as far as concerns our outward condition ; for God raises one aloft and depresses another. (Ps. cxiii. 7.) Thus we see the rich made poor, and others raised from the dunghill, and placed in the highest stations of honour. The

profane call this the sport of fortune !   But the moderation
of God's providence is most just, although incomprehensible.
Thus God acts according to his will among men and angels;
but that interior action must be put in the first place, as we
have said.   It now follows :

36. At the same time my reason returned unto me; and, for the glory of my kingdom, mine honour and brightness returned unto me : and my counsellors and my lords sought unto me; and I was established in my kingdom; and excellent majesty was added unto me.

36. Et in tempore illo[1] intellectus meus rediit ad me, et ad excellentiam regni mei,[2] decor meus et dignitas mea reversa est ad me : et me consiliarii mei et proceres mei requisierunt : et in regno meo confirmatus sum, et dignitas mea amplior aucta[3] fuit mihi.

Here Nebuchadnezzar explains at length what he had
previously touched upon but shortly; for he had recovered
his soundness of mind, and thus commends God's mercy in
being content with a moderate and temporary chastisement;
and then he stretched forth his hand, and out of a beast
formed a man again !   He was not changed into a brute,
as we have said, but he was treated with such ignominy, and
made like wild beasts, and pastured with them.   This deformity, then, was so dreadful, that his restoration might be
called a kind of new creation.   Hence with very good
reason Nebuchadnezzar celebrates this grace of God.   *At
that time*, therefore, *my intellect returned to me;* he had
said this once before, but since understanding and reason
are inestimable blessings of God, Nebuchadnezzar inculcates
this truth, and confesses himself to have experienced God's
singular grace, because he had returned to a sound mind.
And at the same time he adds, *he had returned to the
honour and glory of his kingdom; because he had been consulted again by his counsellors and elders.*   How this was
accomplished is unknown, since the memory of those times
is buried, unless the princes of his kingdom were inclined to
clemency—which is very probable—and desired among them
the king who had been cast out.   We do not say this was
done by them on purpose, because God made use of them,

---

[1] Although זמנא, *zemena*, properly is a time fixed before hand and determined.—*Calvin.*

[2] Namely, " I returned;" for the phrase is elliptical.—*Calvin.*

[3] Was added.—*Calvin.*

and they were ignorantly carrying out his purposes. They had heard the voice from heaven, *O King Nebuchadnezzar, to thee it is said, thy kingdom is departed from thee !* This indeed would be universally known and understood among all men ; but we know how easily oblivion creeps over men when God speaks. These princes, then, were unaware of their doing God's work when they demanded their king. In this way he returned to the dignity of his kingdom ; and even additional dignity was next conferred upon him. At length it follows :

37. Now I Nebuchadnezzar praise, and extol, and honour the King of heaven, all whose works *are* truth, and his ways judgment : and those that walk in pride he is able to abase.	37. Nunc ego Nebuchadnezer laudo, et extollo, et glorifico Regem cœlorum : quia omnia opera ejus veritas, et viæ ejus judicium : et eos qui ambulant in superbia potest humiliare.[1]

At the close of the edict, Nebuchadnezzar joins the ingenuous confession of his faults with the praises of God ! What he says of the proud, he doubtless applies properly to himself ; as if he had said, God wished to constitute me a remarkable monument of his method of humbling the proud for the instruction of all mankind. For I was inflated with pride, and God corrected this by so remarkable a punishment, that my example ought to profit the world at large. Hence I said, King Nebuchadnezzar does not simply return thanks to God, but at the same time confesses his fault, for though subdued with deserved harshness, yet his haughtiness could not be arrested by any lighter remedy. First of all he says, *I praise, extol, and glorify the king of heaven !* This heaping together of words doubtless proceeded from vehement affection. At the same time a contrast must be understood, on the principle formerly mentioned ; since God is never rightly praised unless the ignominy of men is detected ; he is not properly extolled, unless their loftiness is cast down ; he is never glorified unless men are buried in shame and lie prostrate in the dust. Hence, while Nebuchadnezzar here praises, extols, and glorifies God, he also confesses himself and all mortals to be nothing—as he did before—to deserve no praise but rather the utmost ignominy.

[1] That is, for humbling the proud.—*Calvin.*

He adds, *since all his works are truth.* Here קְשׁוֹט, *kesot*, is taken for " rectitude or integrity." For דִּינִי־אֱמֶת, *dini-ameth*, mean true judgments, but refer here to equity. *God's works are* therefore *all truth*, that is, all integrity, as if he had said, none of God's works deserve blame. Then the explanation follows, *All his ways are judgments.* We see here the praise of God's perfect justice ; this ought to be referred to Nebuchadnezzar personally, as if he had said, God does not deal with me too strictly ; I have no reason for expostulating with him, or for murmuring as if he were too severe with me. I confess, therefore, that I deserve whatever punishment I sustain. And why so ? *All his ways are justice ;* meaning the highest rectitude. Then, *All his works are truth ;* that is, nothing contrary to equity is found there, nothing crooked, but everywhere the highest justice will shine forth. We see then how Nebuchadnezzar by this language condemns himself out of his own mouth by declaring God's justice to be in all his works. This general form of expression does not prevent Nebuchadnezzar from openly and freely confessing himself a criminal before God's tribunal ; but it acquires greater force by his example, which admonishes us by the general confession of God's justice, rectitude, and truthfulness in whatever he does. And this is worthy of notice, since many find no difficulty in celebrating God's justice and rectitude when they are treated just as they like ; but if God begins to treat them with severity, they then vomit forth their poison, and begin to quarrel with God, and to accuse him of injustice and cruelty. Since therefore Nebuchadnezzar here confesses God to be just and true in all his works, without any exception, notwithstanding his own severe chastisements, this confession is not feigned ; for he necessarily utters what he says from the lowest depths of his heart, through his having experienced the rigour of the divine judgment.

He now adds at last, *He can humble those who walk in pride.* Here Nebuchadnezzar more openly displays his own disgrace, for he is not ashamed to confess his fault before the whole world, because his punishment was known to every one. As God then wished his folly to be universally detested, by making so horrible an example of him by his punishment, so Nebuchadnezzar now brings his own case forward, and bears witness to the justice of the penalty, in consequence of his extreme pride. Here then we see God's power joined with his justice, as we have previously mentioned. He does not attribute to God a tyranny free from all law ; for as soon as Nebuchadnezzar had confessed all God's ways to be just, he condemns himself of pride directly afterwards. Hence he does not hesitate to expose his disgrace before mankind, that God may be glorified. And this is the true method of praising God, not only by confessing ourselves to be as nothing, but also by looking back upon our failings. We ought not only to acknowledge ourselves inwardly guilty before him, but also openly to testify the same before all mankind whenever it is necessary. And when he uses the word " humility," this may be referred to outward dejection ; for Nebuchadnezzar was humbled when God cast him out into the woods to pass his life in company with the wild beasts. But he was also humbled for another reason, as if he had been a son of God. Since this humbling is twofold, Nebuchadnezzar wishes here to express the former kind, because God prostrates and throws down the proud. This is one kind of humiliation ; but it becomes profitless unless God afterwards governs us by a spirit of submission. Hence Nebuchadnezzar does not here embrace the grace of God, which was worthy of no common praise and exaltation ; and in this edict he does not describe what is required of a pious man long trained in God's school ; yet he shews how he had profited under God's rod, by attributing to him the height of power. Besides this, he adds the praise of justice and rectitude, while he confesses himself guilty, and bears witness to the justice of the punishment which had been divinely inflicted on him.

PRAYER.

Grant, Almighty God, since the disease of pride remains fixed in us all through our original corruption in our father Adam,—Grant, I say, that we may learn to mortify our spirits, and to be displeased with our conduct, as we ought ; may we feel ourselves to be deprived of all wisdom and rectitude without thee alone. May we fly to thy pity, and confess ourselves utterly subject to eternal death; may we rely on thy goodness which thou hast deigned to offer us through thy Gospel; may we trust in that Mediator whom thou hast given us; may we never hesitate to fly to thee, to call upon thee as our Father, and having been renewed by thy Spirit, may we walk in true humility and modesty, till at length thou shalt raise us to that heavenly kingdom which has been obtained for us by the blood of thine only-begotten Son.—Amen.

Lecture Twenty-third.

CHAPTER FIFTH.

1. Belshazzar the king made a great feast to a thousand of his lords, and drank wine before the thousand.	1. Beltsazar rex fecit convivium magnum proceribus suis mille, et coram mille vinum bibit.

DANIEL here refers to the history of what happened at the taking of Babylon; but meanwhile he leaves those judgments of God to the consideration of his readers, which the Prophets had predicted before the people had become exiles. He does not use the prophetic style, as we shall afterwards see, but is content with simple narrative; while the practice of history may be learnt from the following expressions. It is our duty now to consider how this history tends towards building us up in the faith and fear of God. First of all we notice the time at which Belshazzar celebrated this banquet. Seventy years had passed away from the time when Daniel had been led into exile with his companions. For although Nebuchadnezzar will soon be called the father of Belshazzar, yet it is clear enough that Evil-Merodach lived between them; for he reigned twenty-three years. Some reckon two kings before Belshazzar; for they place Regassar after Labassardach; and these two will occupy eight years. Metasthenes has stated it so, and he has many followers. But Nebuchadnezzar the Great, who took Daniel captive, and was the son of the first king of that name, evidently reigned forty-five years. Some transfer two years to the reign of his father; at any rate, he held the regal power for forty-five years; and if the twenty-three years of Evil-Merodach are added, they will make sixty-eight years—in which Belshazzar had reigned eight years. We see, then, how seventy-two years had passed away from the period of Daniel being first led captive. Metasthenes reckons thirty years for the reign of Evil-Merodach ; and then, if we add eight years, this makes more than eighty years—which appears probable enough, although Metasthenes seems to be in error in supposing different kings instead of only different names.[1]   For Herodotus does not call Belshazzar, of whom we are now speaking, a king, but calls his father Labynetus, and gives him the same name.[2] Metasthenes makes some mistakes in names, but I readily embrace his computation of time, when he asserts Evil-Merodach to have reigned thirty years. For when we treat of the seventy years which Jeremiah had formerly pointed out, we ought not to begin with Daniel's exile, nor yet with the destruction of the city, but with the slaughter which occurred between the first victory of king Nebuchadnezzar, and the burning and ruin of the temple and city. For when the report concerning the death of his father was first spread abroad, as we have elsewhere said, he returned to his own country, lest any disturbance should occur through his absence. Hence we shall find the seventy years during which God wished the people's captivity to last, will require a longer period for the reign of Evil-Merodach than twenty-three years ; although there is not any important difference, for soon after Nebuchadnezzar returned, he carried off the king, leaving the city untouched. Although the temple was then standing, yet God had inflicted the severest punishment upon the people, which was like a final slaughter, or at least nearly equal to it. However this was, we see that Belshazzar was celebrating this banquet just as the time of the deliverance drew nigh.

Here we must consider the Providence of God, in arranging the times of events, so that the impious, when the time of their destruction is come, cast themselves headlong of their own accord. This occurred to this wicked king. Wonderful

---

[1] See the DISSERTATIONS at the end of this volume, in which these historical points are treated at length.

[2] Herod., lib. i. sect. 188.   Comp. *Cyropœd.*, lib. iv. and vii.

indeed was the stupidity which prepared a splendid banquet filled with delicacies, while the city was besieged. For Cyrus had begun to besiege the city for a long time with a large army. The wretched king was already half a captive; and yet, as if in spite of God, he provided a rich banquet, and invited a thousand guests. Hence we may conjecture the extent of the noise and of the expense in that banquet. For if any one wishes to entertain only ten or twenty guests, it will occasion him much trouble, if he wishes to treat them splendidly. But when it was a royal entertainment, where there were a thousand nobles with the king's wife and concubines, and so great a multitude assembled together, it became necessary to obtain from many quarters what was required for such a festival; and this may seem incredible! But Xenophon though he related many fables and preserved neither the gravity nor the fidelity of a historian, because he desired to celebrate the praises of Cyrus like a rhetorician; although he trifles in many things, yet here had no reason or occasion for deception. He says a treasure was laid up, so that the Babylonians could endure a siege of even ten or more years. And Babylon was deservedly compared to a kingdom; for its magnitude was so large as to surpass belief. It must really have been very populous, but since they drew their provisions from the whole of Asia, it is not surprising that the Babylonians had food in store, sufficient to allow them to close their gates, and to sustain them for a long period. But in this banquet it was most singular that the king, who ought to have been on guard, or at least have sent forth his guards to prevent the city from being taken, was as intent upon his delicacies as if he had been in perfect peace, and exposed to no danger from any outward enemy. He had a contest with a strong man, if any man ever was so. Cyrus was endued with singular prudence, and in swiftness of action by far excelled all others. Since, then, the king was so keenly opposed, it is surprising to find him so careless as to celebrate a banquet. Xenophon, indeed, states the day to have been a festival. The assertion of those Jews who think the Chaldeans had just obtained a victory over the Persians, is but trifling. For Xenophon—who may be

trusted whenever he does not falsify history in favour of
Cyrus, because he is then a very grave historian, and entirely worthy of credit; but when he desires to praise Cyrus,
he has no moderation—is here historically correct, when he
says the Babylonians were holding a usual annual festival.
He tells us also how Babylon was taken, viz., by Gobryas and
Gadatas his generals. For Belshazzar had castrated one of
these to his shame, and had slain the son of the other in
the lifetime of his father. Since then the latter burnt with
the desire of avenging his son's death, and the former his
own disgrace, they conspired against him. Hence Cyrus
turned the many channels of the Euphrates, and thus Babylon
was suddenly taken. The city we must remember was twice
taken, otherwise there would not have been any confidence
in prophecy; because when the Prophets threaten God's
vengeance upon the Babylonians, they say their enemies
should be most fierce, not seeking gold or silver, but desiring
human blood; and then they narrate every kind of atrocious
deed which is customary in war. (Jer. l. 42.) But nothing
of this kind happened when Babylon was taken by Cyrus;
but when the Babylonians freed themselves from the Persian
sway by casting off their yoke, Darius recovered the city by
the assistance of Zopyrus, who mutilated his person, and
pretended to have suffered such cruelty from the king as to
induce him to betray the city. But then we collect how
hardly the Babylonians were afflicted, when 3000 nobles
were crucified! And what usually happens when 3000
nobles are put to death, and all suspended on a gallows—
nay, even crucified? Thus it easily appears, how severely
the Babylonians were punished at the time, although they
were then subject to a foreign power, and treated shamefully
by the Persians, and reduced to the condition of slaves. For
they were forbidden the use of arms, and were taught from
the first to become the slaves of Cyrus, and dare not wear a
sword. We ought to touch upon these things shortly to
assure us of the government of human events by the judgment of God, when he casts headlong the reprobate when
their punishment is at hand. We have an illustrious example of this in King Belshazzar.

The time of the deliverance predicted by Jeremiah was at hand—the seventy years were finished—Babylon was besieged. (Jer. xxv. 11.) The Jews might now raise up their heads and hope for the best, because the arrival of Cyrus approached, contrary to the opinion of them all; for he had suddenly rushed down from the mountains of Persia when that was a barbarous nation. Since, therefore, the sudden coming of Cyrus was like a whirlwind, this change might possibly give some hope to the Jews; but after a length of time, so to speak, had elapsed in the siege of the city, this might cast down their spirits. While king Belshazzar was banqueting with his nobles, Cyrus seems able to thrust him out in the midst of his merriment and hilarity. Meanwhile the Lord did not sit at rest in heaven; for he blinds the mind of the impious king, so that he should willingly incur punishments, yet no one drew him on, for he incurred it himself. And whence could this arise, unless God had given him up to his enemy? It was according to that decree of which Jeremiah was the herald. Hence, although Daniel narrates the history, it is our duty, as I have said, to treat of things far more important; for God who had promised his people deliverance, was now stretching forth his hand in secret, and fulfilling the predictions of his Prophets. (Jer. xxv. 26.)

It now follows—*King Belshazzar was drinking wine before a thousand.* Some of the Rabbis say, "he strove with his thousand nobles, and contended with them all in drinking to excess;" but this seems grossly ridiculous. When he says, *he drank wine before a thousand,* he alludes to the custom of the nation, for the kings of the Chaldeans very rarely invited guests to their table; they usually dined alone, as the kings of Europe now do; for they think it adds to their dignity to enjoy a solitary meal. The pride of the kings of Chaldea was of this kind. When, therefore, it is said, *Belshazzar drank wine before a thousand,* something extraordinary is intended, since he was celebrating this annual banquet contrary to his ordinary custom, and he deigned to treat his nobles with such honour as to receive them as his guests. Some, indeed, conjecture that he drank wine openly, as he was accustomed to become intoxicated when there were no witnesses present; but there is no force in this comment: the word *before* means in the presence or society of others. Let us go on:

2. Belshazzar, whiles he tasted the wine, commanded to bring the golden and silver vessels which his father Nebuchadnezzar had taken out of the temple which *was* in Jerusalem; that the king and his princes, his wives and his concubines, might drink therein.

2. Beltsazar præcepit[1] in gustu, *vel, sapore,* vini, ut afferrent vasa auri et argenti,[2] quæ asportaverat, *vel, extulerat,* Nebuchadnezer pater ejus ex templo quod *est* in Jerusalem, ut biberent in illis rex, et proceres ejus, uxores et concubinæ.[3]

Here king Belshazzar courts his own punishment, because he furiously stirred up God's wrath against himself, as if he was dissatisfied with its delay while God put off his judgment for so long a period. This is according to what I have said. When the destruction of a house is at hand, the impious remove the posts and gates, as Solomon says. (Prov. xvii. 19.) God therefore, when he wishes to execute his judgments, impels the reprobate by a secret instinct to rush forward of their own accord, and to hasten their own destruction. Belshazzar did this. His carelessness was the sign of his stupidity, and also of God's wrath, when in the midst of his own pride and crimes he could delight in revelling. Thus his blindness more clearly points out God's vengeance, since he was not content with his own intemperance and excesses, but must openly declare war against God. *He ordered,* therefore, says he, *the gold and silver vessels to be brought to him which he had taken away from Nebuchadnezzar.* These vessels appear to have been laid up in the treasury; hence Nebuchadnezzar had never abused these vessels in his lifetime; we do not read that Evil-Merodach did anything of this kind, and Belshazzar now wishes purposely to inflict this insult on God. There is no doubt he brought forth those vessels by way of ridicule, for the purpose of triumphing over the true God, as we shall afterwards see.

[1] Verbally it means said, but here it signifies commanded.—*Calvin.*

[2] Made of gold and silver.—*Calvin.*

[3] Some translate his wife, since there was one principal wife, who alone was the king's companion, and she received the name of Queen, as we shall afterwards see.—*Calvin.*

We have already explained the sense in which the Prophet calls Nebuchadnezzar the father of Belshazzar, since it is usual in all languages to speak of ancestors as fathers; for Belshazzar was of the offspring of Nebuchadnezzar, and being really his grandson, he is naturally called his son; and this will occur again.   There are some who think Evil-Merodach was stricken with that grievous affliction mentioned in the last chapter: possibly his name was Nebuchadnezzar, but there is no reason for adopting their opinion;[1] it is frivolous to fly directly to this conjecture when the name of the father occurs.   The Prophet says *Belshazzar committed this under the influence of wine.*   Since טעם, *tegnem*, signifies "to taste," no doubt he here speaks of tasting; and since this may be metaphorically transferred to the understanding, some explain it to mean being impelled by wine, and thus his drunkenness took the place of reason and judgment. Nights and love and wine, says Ovid, have no moderation in them.[2]   This explanation I think too forced; it seems simply to mean, when Belshazzar grew warm with wine, he commanded the vessels to be brought to him; and this is the more usual view.   When, therefore, the savour of the wine prevailed,—that is, when it seized upon the king's senses, *then he ordered the vessels to be brought.*   It is worth while to notice this, to induce us to be cautious concerning intemperance in drinking, because nothing is more common than the undertaking many things far too rashly when our senses are under the influence of wine.   Hence we must use wine soberly, that it may invigorate not only the body but the mind and the senses, and may never weaken, or enervate, or stupify our bodily or mental powers.   And this is, alas! too common, since the vulgar proverb is well known—pride springs from drunkenness.   For this reason the poets supposed Bacchus to have horns, since intemperate men are

---

[1] This is the view of the Duke of Manchester; it is ably supported in his learned volume on "The Times of Daniel."   As we have had occasion to review the general argument elsewhere, we merely allude to it here.— See DISSERTATIONS.

[2] Ars. Amor., Eleg. vi.   The French translation is worthy of notice,—
"La nuiet, l'amour, le boire sans mesure,
N' induit a rien sinon a toute ordure."—*Ed.*

always puffed up, and the most wretched fancy themselves kings. What then must happen to monarchs, when in their forgetfulness they dream themselves kings of kings, and even deities ? The Prophet wishes to mark this fault when he says, *Belshazzar, under the influence of wine, ordered vessels to be brought to him.* It now follows,—

3. Then they brought the golden vessels that were taken out of the temple of the house of God which *was* at Jerusalem ; and the king and his princes, his wives and his concubines, drank in them.	3. Tunc attulerunt vasa aurea quæ extulerant ex templo domus Dei quæ erat in Jerusalem : et biberunt in illis rex, et proceres ejus, et uxor,[1] et concubinæ ipsius.

The Prophet uses the word "golden," probably, because the most precious vessels were brought ; silver might also have been added, but the more splendid ones are noticed. He does not say that Nebuchadnezzar carried them off, but implies it to be the common act of all the Babylonians. They obtained the victory under the direction of this king, hence he used the spoils ; and since they were all engaged in the victory, the Prophet speaks of them all. In using the phrase, "the temple," he expresses more than before, by saying, not from Jerusalem only but from the temple of God's house.

4. They drank wine, and praised the gods of gold, and of silver, of brass, of iron, of wood, and of stone.	4. Biberunt vinum, et laudarunt deos aureos, et argenteos, æreos, ferreos, ligneos, et lapideos.

Here the Prophet shews more distinctly and clearly how the king insulted the true and only God, by ordering his vessels to be brought to him. For when they had been brought forth, *they praised,* says he, *all their gods of gold and silver ;* meaning in defiance of the true God they celebrated the praises of their false deities, and thanked them, as we find in Habakkuk. (Ch. i. 16.) Although there is no doubt they sacrificed heartily the produce of their industry, as the Prophet there expresses it, yet they exalted their own gods, and thus obliterated the glory of the true God. And this is the reason why the Prophet now takes pains to state those vessels to have been brought *from the temple of God's house.* For he here strengthens the impiety of the king and his

---

[1] Or, " wives," in the plural number.—*Calvin.*

nobles for erecting their horns against the God of Israel. There is then a great contrast between God who commanded his temple to be built at Jerusalem, and sacrifices to be offered to him and false gods.   And this was the head and front of Belshazzar's offending, because he thus purposely rose up against God, and not only tyrannically and miserably oppressed the Jews, but triumphed over their God—the Creator of heaven and earth.   This madness accelerated his ultimate destruction, and it occurred for the purpose of hastening the time of their deliverance.   Hence I have represented him to have been drawn by God's great instinct to such madness that vengeance might be ripened.

They drank, says he, *wine, and praised their gods.*   The Prophet does not ascribe the praise of their gods to drunkenness, but he obliquely shews their petulance to have been increased by drink.   For if each had been sober at home, he would not have thus rashly risen up against God ; but when impiety exists in the heart, intemperance becomes an additional stimulus.   The Prophet seems to me to mean this, when he repeats, *they were drinking ;* for he had said, *the king and his nobles, his wife, and concubines, were drinking.* He now inculcates the same thing in similar words, but adds, *they drank wine,*—meaning their madness was the more inflamed by the excitement of the wine.   *Then they praised the gods of silver,* &c.   The Prophet here reproachfully mentions *gods of gold, silver, brass, wood, and stone,* since we know God to have nothing in common with either gold or silver.   His true image cannot be expressed in corruptible materials ; and this is the reason why the Prophet calls all the gods which the Babylonians worshipped, *golden, silver, brazen, wooden, and stone.*   Clearly enough the heathen never were so foolish as to suppose the essence of Deity to reside in gold, or silver, or stone ; they only called them images of their deities ; but because in their opinion the power and majesty of the deity was included within the material substance, the Prophet is right in so completely condemning their criminality, because we hear how carefully idolaters invent every kind of subtlety.   In the present times, the Papacy is a glaring proof how men cling to gross superstitions when they desire to excuse their errors; hence the Prophet does not here admit those vain pretences by which the Babylonians and other heathens disguise their baseness, but he says, *their gods were of silver and gold.* And why so? for although they orally confessed that gods reign in heaven, (so great was the multitude and crowd of their deities that the supreme God was quite shrouded in darkness,) although therefore the Babylonians confessed their gods to have dwelt in heaven, yet they fled to statues and pictures. Hence the Prophet deservedly chides them *for adoring gods of gold and silver.* As to his saying, *then the vessels were brought,* it shews how the slaves of tyrants obey them in the worst actions, because no delay intervened in bringing the vessels from the treasury. Daniel therefore signifies how all the king's servants were obedient to his nod, and desirous of pleasing a person brutish and drunken; at the same time he shews the shortness of that intemperate intoxication; for he says,—

5. In the same hour came forth fingers of a man's hand, and wrote over against the candlestick upon the plaster of the wall of the king's palace; and the king saw the part of the hand that wrote.	5. In illa hora egressi sunt digiti manus hominis, et scribebant e regione lucernæ[1] super calcem parietis[2] palatii regis, et rex cernebat palmam[3] manus scribentis.

Here Daniel begins his narration of the change which took place, for at that instant the king acknowledged something sorrowful and disturbing to be at hand. Yet, as he did not at once understand what it was, God gave him a sign as an omen of calamity, according to the language of the profane. In this way God sent him warning when he saw the king and his nobles raging with mad licentiousness. *There appeared,* then, *the hand of a man,* says the Prophet, using this expression from its similitude and form. We are sure it was not a man's hand; it had the appearance of one, and hence was called so. Scripture often uses this method of expression, especially when treating external symbols.

[1] Or, "candlestick;" some explain it, "window."—*Calvin.*
[2] Some consider it the surface, others the roof, which is probable.—*Calvin.*
[3] Others translate it "finger."—*Calvin.*

This is, then, a sacramental form of speech,[1] if I may use the expression. God, indeed, wrote the inscription by his own power, but he shews King Belshazzar the figure as if a man had written it on the wall ; hence *the fingers of a hand were put forth.* This expression conduces in no slight degree to the reality of the miracle ; for if Belshazzar had seen this on the wall from the very first, he might have supposed some artifice had placed the hand there ; but when the wall was previously bare, and then the hand suddenly appeared, we may readily understand the hand to have been a sign from heaven, through which God wished to shew something important to the king. *The fingers of a hand,* then, *were put forth, and wrote from the midst of the candlestick,* or lamp. Clearly, then, this was a feast by night, and Babylon was taken in the midst of the night. No wonder their banquets were protracted to a great length, for intemperance has no bounds. When men are accustomed to spend the day in luxury, I confess indeed they do not usually continue their banquets till midnight; but when they celebrate any splendid and remarkable feast, they do not find the daylight sufficient for their festivites and the grosser indulgences of the table.

Hence *the hand appeared from the candlesticks* to render it the more conspicuous. That hand, says the Prophet, wrote on the surface of the palace wall. If any one had announced to the king this appearance of a human hand, he might have doubted it ; but he says the king was an eye-witness, for God wished to terrify him, as we shall afterwards see, and hence he set before him this spectacle. *The king,* then, *perceived it ;* perhaps his nobles did not ; and we shall afterwards see how the terror operated upon the king alone, unless, indeed, some others trembled with him. When, therefore, they saw his countenance changed and exhibiting proofs of terror, they began to fear, although they were all desirous of affording him some consolation. Hence God wished to summon this impious king to His tribunal when the hand of a man appeared before him in the act of writing. We shall see what it wrote in its proper place.

[1] This phrase is worthy of notice. The Latin is " *sacramentalis locutio ;*" the French, " *est aussi sacramentale.*" See our *Ezekiel,* vol. ii., p. 312 and note, where the Sabbath is termed *a Sacrament.*

PRAYER.

Grant, Almighty God, since we are so prone to forgetfulness and
to our own indulgence in the desires and pleasures of the flesh,—
Grant, I say, to each of us to be recalled to the contemplation
of thy judgments; and may we be anxious to walk as in thy
sight.   May we be afraid of thy just vengeance, be careful not
to provoke it by our petulance and other vices; but may we
submit ourselves to thee, be held up, and propped up by thy
hands, and proceed in the sacred course of thy calling, until at
length thou shalt raise us to thy heavenly kingdom, which has
been acquired for us by the blood of thine only-begotten Son.—
Amen.

Lecture Twenty-fourth.

6. Then the king's countenance was changed, and his thoughts troubled him, so that the joints of his loins were loosed, and his knees smote one against another.	6. Tunc Regis vultus[1] mutatus est: et cogitationes ejus terruerunt eum, et ligamina lumborum ejus solvebantur,[2] et poplites ejus invicem collisi sunt.

HERE Daniel shews how the king's mind was struck with
fear, lest any one should think his fright without foundation.
But he expresses, by many circumstances, how disturbed the
king was, and thus the sufficiency of the reason would easily
appear.   It was needful for him to be so struck, that all
might understand how God was seated on his throne, and
summoned him as a criminal.   We mentioned before how
Daniel impresses us with the pride of this king, and his
careless security is a clear proof of it.   When the daily siege
of the city ought to have rendered him anxious, he was celebrating his usual banquets, as if in profound peace.   Whence
he appears to be corrupted by a kind of spiritual drunkenness, so as not to feel his own calamities.   This, then, is the
reason why God roused him up and awakened him from his
lethargy, because no ordinary means were effectual in re-
calling him to soundness of mind.   The fear which he experienced might seem a convenient preparation for penitence.

[1] " The form or figure," verbally.—*Calvin.*
[2] " His hip-joints," for the Hebrews and Chaldees use roundabout expressions.—*Calvin.*

But we see the same thing in this case as we do in that of Esau ; for he was not only touched with contrition when he saw himself cut off, but he uttered a loud and piercing lamentation when seeking his father's "blessing," and yet he was too late. (Gen. xxvii. 34.) A similar occurrence is related here of King Belshazzar, but we must remark upon everything in order. Daniel says, *The king's countenance was changed ;* then, *the joints of his limbs were loosened, and he was disturbed,* or frightened, *in his thoughts ;* and lastly, he adds, *his knees smote together.* The word properly signifies, to strike one against another. By these signs the Prophet shews how King Belshazzar was frightened by the vision already mentioned. Without doubt, as I have just said, God inspired him with this terror, for we know even when God has openly ascended to his own tribunal, how stupid the reprobate remain, and how immovable ! But God wished to affect the mind of this impious king, and to render his ignorance without excuse.

Here we may remark, generally, in how many ways God touches men's hearts—not those of the reprobate only, but also of his elect, for we see even the best men slow and slothful when God summons them to his judgment-seat. It becomes necessary to chastise them with rods, otherwise they never approach God of their own accord. He might, indeed, move their minds without violence ; but he wishes to set before us, as in a glass, our slowness and slothfulness, since we do not obey his word with natural willingness. Hence he tames his children with cords when they will not profit by his word. With regard to the reprobate, he often chides their obstinacy, because, before he undertakes the office of judge, he kindly entices them ; when they do not profit by this, he threatens ; and when his threats are useless and devoid of efficacy, he then calls them to his tribunal. Respecting the fate of the King of Babylon, God had suffered Daniel to be silent, for his ingratitude and pride had closed the door, so as to prevent Daniel from undertaking the office of a teacher as he was prepared to do ; hence the King of Babylon continued without one. But God suddenly appeared as a judge, by the writing of which we have shortly spoken, and of which we shall say more in the proper place. Whatever its meaning may be, we see King Belshazzar not only admonished by an outward sign of his approaching death, but inwardly stirred up to acknowledge himself to be dealing with God. For the reprobate often enjoy their own pleasures, as I have said, although God shews himself to be their judge. But he treats King Belshazzar differently: he desires to inspire him with terror, to render him more attentive to the perusal of the writing. This time was, as I have said, a preparation for repentance; but he failed in the midst of his course, as we see too many do who tremble at the voice of God and at the signs of his vengeance, as soon as he admonishes them; but these feelings are but evanescent; thus proving how little they have learnt of the necessary lesson.

The example of Esau is similar to this, since he despised God's grace when he heard himself deprived of the inheritance divinely promised him. (Gen. xxv. 33.) He treated the blessing as a fable till he found it a serious matter; he then began to lament, but all in vain. Such also was the fright of King Belshazzar, as we shall soon perceive. Even when Daniel explained the writing to him, he was by no means moved by it, but adorned Daniel with royal tokens of regard. Yet the object and use of this was totally different, for when the nobles were moved, and the reality became manifest, God in this way demonstrated his glory: and Darius, who took the city, with his son-in-law Cyrus, understood how his own valour and perseverance were not the sole cause of his victory, and how the satraps, Gobryas and Gadata, would not have assisted him so materially unless the whole affair had been under God's auspices. Thus God shewed himself as in a glass to be the avenger of his people, as he had promised seventy years previously. It now follows:—

7. The king cried aloud to bring in the astrologers, the Chaldeans, and the soothsayers. *And* the king spake, and said to the wise *men* of Babylon, Whosoever shall read this writing, and shew me the interpretation thereof, shall be clothed with

7. Clamavit rex fortiter, ut introducerentur magi, Chaldæi, et astrologi,[1] et loquutus est rex, et dixit sapientibus Babylonis, Quisquis legerit scripturam hanc, et interpretationem ejus indicaverit mihi, purpura vestietur, et torques ex

[1] We have previously explained these words.—*Calvin.*

scarlet, and *have* a chain of gold about his neck, and shall be the third ruler in the kingdom.

auro, *hoc est, aureus*, super collum ejus, et tertius in regno dominabitur.

The Prophet narrates how King Belshazzar sought a remedy for his anxiety; hence we gather how his mind was so immediately wounded, and how he felt he could not escape God's hand, otherwise he would not have called the wise men so suddenly in the midst of the banquet.   Again, when the Prophet says, *He cried out loudly,* he was clearly so astonished as to forget his being king, for to cry out at table was not consistent with his dignity.   But God expelled all pride from him, by compelling him to burst forth into a cry, like a man completely beside himself.   We must now consider the remedy to which he resorted : he ordered the *Chaldeans, and magi, and astrologers to be called.*   We learn from this how exceedingly prone men are to vanity, lying, and falsehood.   Daniel ought to have been first, even among the Chaldeans, for that was an answer worthy of remembrance which he had given to the grandfather of this king, when he predicted his becoming like the beasts of the forest. Since this prophecy was verified by the event, his authority ought to have flourished even to a thousand years.   He was daily in the king's sight, and yet he was neglected, while the king sent for all the Chaldeans, and astrologers, and diviners, and magi.   Truly enough, these men were then in so great repute that they deservedly obscured the fame of Daniel, for they were indignant at a captive being preferred to native teachers, when they knew their own glory amongst all peoples depended upon the persuasion of their being the only wise men.   As, therefore, they wished to retain their good opinion, as being God's counsellors, no wonder they despised this stranger.   But this feeling cannot avail for a moment before God: for what can be urged in defence of the king's impiety ?   His grandfather was a memorable instance of God's vengeance, when rejected from the company of men, and compelled to dwell among the wildest beasts of the forest.   This, truly, could not appear a matter of chance. God, then, had first admonished him by a dream, and next sent his own Prophet as the interpreter of the oracle and the

vision.   As I have said, the fame of this event ought to
have been perpetual among the Chaldeans, yet the grandson
of King Nebuchadnezzar had forgotten his example, insulted
the God of Israel, profaned the vessels of the temple, and
triumphed with his idols!   When God sets before him the
sign of his judgment, he calls together the magi and the
Chaldeans, and passes by Daniel.   And what possible excuse can he have for this?   We have seen, as I have said,
how very prone men are to be deluded by Satan's impostures, and the well-known proverb becomes true,—The world
loves to be deceived!

This, also, is worthy of notice, because in the present day,
and in troublous times, many protect themselves behind the
shield of their ignorance.   But the explanation is at hand—
they are willingly blind; they shut their eyes amidst the
clearest light; for if God considered King Belshazzar without excuse when the Prophet was once presented to him,
what excuse can the blind of these days allege?   Oh! if I
could determine what God's will is for me, I would submit
myself instantly to it, because God daily and openly calls to
us and invites us, and shews us the way; but none answer
him, none follow him, or at least how very few!   Hence we
must diligently consider the example of the King of Babylon
when we see him full of anxiety, and yet not seeking God
as he ought.   And why so?   He wanders about in great
hesitation; he sees himself constrained, and yet he cannot
fly from the judgment of God, but seeks consolation in magi,
Chaldeans, and other impostors; for, as we have seen, they
had been once or twice proved so, and this ought to have
been sufficiently celebrated and notorious to all men.   We
see, then, how blind King Belshazzar was, since he closed
his eyes to the light offered him.   So in the present day
almost all the world continues in blindness; it is not allowed
to wander in darkness, but when light shines upon it, it
closes its eyes, rejects God's grace, and purposely desires to
cast itself headlong.   This conduct is far too common.

Now the Prophet says,—*The king promised the wise men a
present of a chain of gold to whoever read the writing;* and
besides this, *raiment of purple, and the third rank in the*

kingdom! This shews him not to have been sincerely touched by the fear of God. And this repugnance is worthy of observation in the wicked, who dread God's judgments, and yet the pride of their hearts is not corrected and subdued, as we saw in the case of this king. For *his knees smote one against the other, and the joints of his loins were loosened :* he trembles throughout his entire frame, and becomes half dead with fear, because God's terror seizes on all his senses. Meanwhile, we see a hidden pride lurking in his mind, which breaks forth in the promise, *whoever shall interpret the writing, shall be the third in rank in the kingdom!* God had already deprived him of his royal dignity; yet he still wishes to raise others on high in defiance of God ! What, then, is the meaning of this ? We see how often the wicked are terrified, and how deeply they cherish a hidden contumacy, so that God never subdues them. They shew, indeed, many signs of repentance; but if any one carefully weighs all their words and deeds, he will find the Prophet's narration concerning King Belshazzar completely verified, because they rage against God, and are never teachable or obedient, but utterly stupified. We saw this partly in a former verse, and shall see it again more clearly at the end of the chapter. As to the latter clause of the verse, *he shall rule as third in the kingdom,* it is uncertain whether he promises the third portion or the third rank; for many think the queen, of whom mention will soon be made, was the wife of King Nebuchadnezzar, and grandmother of King Belshazzar. It follows :—

8. Then came in all the king's wise *men :* but they could not read the writing, nor make known to the king the interpretation thereof.

9. Then was king Belshazzar greatly troubled, and his countenance was changed in him, and his lords were astonied.

8. Tunc ingressi sunt omnes sapientes regis, et non potuerunt scripturam legere, et interpretationem ejus patefacere regi.

9. Tunc rex Beltsazar multum territus fuit, et vultus ejus mutatus fuit super eum, *in eo :* et principes ejus *fuerunt* obstupefacti.[1]

Here Daniel relates how deceived the king was in his opinion, in hoping for any interpretation of the writing from either the magi or the astrologers, the Chaldeans or the

[1] Or, anxious.—*Calvin.*

soothsayers; for none of them could read it.   Hence he
pays here the punishment of his ingratitude in passing over
God's Prophet, while he knew he had predicted truth to his
grandfather just as it had happened, as well as Daniel's
general excellence in wisdom.   Hence the proofs of his
calling were sufficiently numerous and trustworthy.   Since,
then, he had so despised God's unparalleled benefit, he is
destitute of counsel, and sees himself call in vain upon all
the Chaldeans and astrologers.   For Daniel says, *There was
no one who could read the writing or reveal its interpretation
to the king.*   Because this seems absurd, many Rabbis have
hazarded various conjectures.   Some think the letters were
transposed; others guess that they were changed into their
counterparts and equivalents; and others think the characters were changed.   But we have elsewhere shewn how
bold the Jews are in their conjectures, whenever they have
no certain guide.   We do not require their guesses, because,
very probably, the writing was visible to the king and concealed from all the Chaldeans, or else they were so blind that
they could see nothing; just as God denounced against the
Jews a stupor of this kind.   We see what he pronounces, by
Isaiah, (xxix. 11,) " Your law shall be like a sealed book :
If it shall be said to any one, ' Read it,' he shall say, ' The
book is sealed, I cannot :' or the book may be opened and
ye shall all become blind : even those who seem to be
sharper than all others, shall say they are ignorant and
unlettered men."   Whatever God threatened against the
Jews we know was fulfilled, and is fulfilled to this day, since
a veil is put before their eyes, as Paul says.   (2 Cor. iii. 14.)
Hence they were blind in the midst of the brightest light.
What wonder then if the same thing happened to the Chaldeans, so that they could not read the writing ?   There is
no necessity to conjecture any transposition of letters, or
any inversion of their order, or any change of one into
another; for the word תקל, *tekel*, went first, and afterwards
מנא, מנא, *Mena, Mena.*   These guesses then are frivolous ;
and thus much is certain, God wished the king to be made
aware of his approaching destruction ; next, his soul was
moved, not with repentance, but only enough to render his

sloth without excuse; and hence, whether willingly or not, he was compelled to send for some remedy, since he knew himself to be dealing with God.

Now, with regard to the writing itself, God could not be a free agent unless he possessed the power of addressing one man at one time, and a number of men at another. He wished King Belshazzar to be conscious of this writing, while the magi were all as unable to read it as if they were blind. And then, with reference to the interpretation, their perplexity need not surprise us. For God spoke enigmatically, when he said MENE, MENE, and then TEKEL, that is *weighed*, and PERES, *divided*. If the magi could have read these words a hundred times over, they could never either conjecture or comprehend their true meaning. The prophecy was allegorical, until an interpreter was divinely ordained for it. So far as the mere letters are concerned, there is no reason why we should be surprised at the eyes of the magi being blinded, since God pleased it to be so, and wished to cite the king to his tribunal, as we have already said. The Prophet says, *The king was frightened, his countenance was changed, and the princes also were disturbed.* The publicity of the event ought to have increased the sense of God's judgment, for, as we shall afterwards see, King Belshazzar himself was slain that very night. Cyrus entered while the Babylonians were feasting, and enjoying their luxuries in security. So remarkable an example of God's juctice might have been instantly buried in that drunken revel, had it not been rendered conspicuous to many bystanders. Hence Daniel repeats, *The king was disturbed,* after he saw no prospect of either aid or advice from his magi and astrologers. He says also, *his princes were astonished,* because not only the king ought to be troubled but the whole Court, and the report ought to flow forth not only through the city, but to foreign nations, since there is no doubt that Cyrus was afterwards informed of this prophecy; for he would not have courted Daniel so much, nor honoured him so remarkably, unless this occurrence had been made known to him. It afterwards follows:

10. *Now* the queen, by reason of the words of the king and his lords, came into the banquet-house; *and* the queen spake, and said, O king, live for ever: let not thy thoughts trouble thee, nor let thy countenance be changed:

11. There is a man in thy kingdom in whom *is* the spirit of the holy gods; and in the days of thy father, light and understanding, and wisdom, like the wisdom of the gods, was found in him; whom the king Nebuchadnezzar thy father, the king, I *say*, thy father, made master of the magicians, astrologers, Chaldeans, *and* soothsayers.

10. Regina propter verba regis et procerum in domum symposii,[1] ingressa est, loquuta est et dixit, Rex, in æternum vive: ne terreant te cogitationes tuæ, et vultus tuus ne mutetur.

11. Est vir in regno tuo, in quo spiritus *est* deorum sanctorum: et in diebus patris tui intelligentia,[2] et scientia, et sapientia quasi sapientia deorum reperta est in eo: et Rex Nebuchadnezer pater tuus magistrum magorum,[3] astrologorum, Chaldæorum, aruspicum constituit ipsum, pater tuus rex, *inquam*.

Here Daniel relates the occasion of his being brought before the king, as the reader and interpreter of the writing. The queen, he says, did this. It is doubtful whether it was the wife of King Belshazzar, or his grandmother. She was probably an old woman, as she refers to events in the time of King Nebuchadnezzar. This conjecture has no sufficient foundation, and hence it is better to suspend our judgment than to assert anything rashly; unless, as we before saw, his wife was at table with him. As far as we can gather the words of the Prophet with certainty, we must diligently notice them, and thus convict the king of ingratitude, because he did not admit Daniel among the magi, Chaldeans, and astrologers. The holy man had no wish to be reckoned in that company; he would have deserved to lose God's prophetic spirit had he thus mingled with impostors; and he is clearly to be distinguished from them. King Nebuchadnezzar had set him over all the magi; he had no wish to exercise this honour, unless, as I have just said, he would deprive himself of the singular gift of prophecy; for we must always take care how far we can go. We know how very prone we are to be enticed by the blandishments of the world, especially when ambition blinds us and disturbs all our senses. No plague is worse than this, because when any

---

[1] It must be translated in this way, because the noun is derived from שתה, *shetheh*, to drink.—*Calvin.*

[2] Verbally, "light," used metaphorically.—*Calvin.*

[3] I do not stop to explain these words.—*Calvin.*

one sees a prospect of the acquisition of either profit or honour, he does not regard either what he ought to do or what God permits, but is hurried on by a blind fury. This would have happened to Daniel, unless he had been restrained by a sense of true piety, and hence he repudiated the honour offered him by King Nebuchadnezzar. He never wished to be reckoned among soothsayers, and astrologers, and impostors of this kind, who deluded that nation with prodigies. Here the queen enters and mentions Daniel; but this does not render the king without excuse; for, as we have already said, Daniel had acquired a name of renown among men of all ages, and God wished to signalize him by a distinct mark, to fix the minds of all upon him, as if he were an angel from heaven. As King Belshazzar was ignorant of the existence of such a Prophet in his kingdom, this was the result of his gross and brutish indifference. God, therefore, wished King Belshazzar to be reproved by a woman, who said, *Let not thy thoughts disturb thee !* She calms him quietly, because she saw how frightened he was; but, meanwhile, she shews him the grossness of his error in wandering about in uncertainty, when the way was plain before him. God had put his torch in the Prophet's hand for the very purpose of lighting the king, unless he wilfully desired to wander in darkness, as all the wicked do. Hence, we may learn from the example of this king, the common fault of our nature; for no one runs out of the right way, unless he indulges in his own ignorance, and desires all light to be extinct within him. As to the language of the queen, *The spirit of the holy gods is in Daniel !* we have elsewhere explained its meaning. It is not surprising that the profane use this language, since they cannot discern between the one God and angels. Hence they promiscuously call anything divine and celestial, *a god.* Thus also the queen calls angels, *holy gods,* and places the true God among them. But it is our privilege to acknowledge the true God as shining forth alone, and the angels as all taking their own ranks without any excellence in heaven or earth to obscure the glory of the only God. The writing has this tendency—the exaltation of God in the highest degree, and

the magnifying of his excellency and his majestic supremacy.
We here see how needful it is for us to be instructed in the
essential unity of God, since from the very beginning of the
world men have always been persuaded of the existence of
some Supreme Deity ; but after they became vain in their
imaginations, this idea entirely escaped them, and they
mingled God and angels in complete confusion. Whenever
we perceive this, let us feel our need of Scripture as a guide
and instructor which shines on our path, urging us to think
of God as inviting us to himself and willingly revealing
himself to us.

PRAYER.

Grant, Almighty God, since thou dost constantly address us by thy
Prophets, and permittest us not to wander in the darkness of error,
—Grant us, I say, to be attentive to thy voice, and make us docile
and tractable towards thee ; especially when thou settest before
us a Master in whom are included all treasures of wisdom and
knowledge. Grant us further, I pray thee, to be subject to
thine only-begotten Son, to hold on in the right course of our
holy calling, and to be always pressing onwards to that goal to
which thou callest us, until we are successful in all our contests
with this world, and at length arrive at that blessed rest which
thou hast obtained for us through the blood of the same thy
Son.—Amen.

Lecture Twenty-fifth.

WE began yesterday to explain the passage where
Daniel relates how the queen advised King Belshazzar to
send for the Prophet. We shewed how the king was here
convicted of ingratitude, in suffering such a Prophet of God
to be in obscurity so long, because that memorable prophecy,
already treated, ought to have been well known and in
everybody's mouth, as conferring a permanent authority on
the holy man. Now, when Daniel says, *the queen entered the
banqueting-room;* very probably she was not the king's wife,
but his grandmother. I have expressed my intention of not
contending the point, since in doubtful cases every one ought

to enjoy his own unbiassed judgment. But it is incongruous to say, The king was feasting with his wife and concubines, and then to add, "the queen entered the banqueting-room." Hence we suppose her to be called Queen, through the honour, rank, and respect which she still enjoyed, without any power. The testimony of Herodotus confirms this view, for he praises the queen of King Nebuchadnezzar for her singular prudence, calling him Labynetus and her Nitocris.[1] It is far more probable that this matron was absent from a banquet unsuitable to her age and gravity, since she would scarcely be feasting with those who were thus devoting themselves to luxury. When she enters the room, she reminds the king of Daniel, and she now gives the reason why he surpasses all the magi and soothsayers, the diviners and the Chaldees.

12. Forasmuch as an excellent spirit, and knowledge, and understanding, interpreting of dreams, and shewing of hard sentences, and dissolving of doubts, were found in the same Daniel, whom the king named Belteshazzar: now let Daniel be called, and he will shew the interpretation.

12. Propterea quod spiritus excellens, et intelligentia, et cognitio, interpretatio somniorum, et arcanorum revelatio, et solutio nodorum[2] inventa est in eo, *nempe* Daniel, cui rex imposuerit nomen Beltsazar: et nunc Daniel vocetur, et interpretationem patefaciat.

The queen here assigns the reason why Daniel had obtained the honour of being esteemed the prince and master of all the wise men; because she said, *An excellent spirit was found in him, as he interpreted dreams, revealed secrets, and solved difficulties.* The three gifts in which Daniel excelled are here enumerated, and this proves him to have surpassed the other magi, since none of them could be compared with him. The magi boasted in their ability to interpret dreams, to solve all difficulties, and explain enigmas; but this boast of theirs was twice shewn to be vanity and folly. The queen therefore deservedly claims these three qualities for Daniel, while shewing his superiority to all others. Hence she reasons with authority when she says, A name was imposed upon him by the king. We have already spoken of this

[1] Herod., lib. i. c. 185 and 188.

[2] That is, he resolved difficulties by prudence and knowledge, as I said previously. I read it all in one context, though verbs and nouns are intermingled, for I wish to make it simple, and to avoid ambiguity.—*Calvin.*

name, Belteshazzar; but the queen now refers to this name,
to inform the king in what great esteem and honour he was
held by his grandfather. The name of his father is here
expressed, since Belshazzar might despise all strangers; yet
reason would dictate the propriety of deferring to the judgment of his grandfather, whom every one knew to be a most
remarkable character, whom God humbled for a time, as we
saw, and as Daniel will now allude to it. Let us proceed,—

13 Then was Daniel brought in before the king. *And* the king spake, and said unto Daniel, *Art* thou that Daniel, which *art* of the children of the captivity of Judah, whom the king my father brought out of Jewry?

14. I have even heard of thee, that the spirit of the gods *is* in thee, and *that* light, and understanding, and excellent wisdom, is found in thee.

15. And now the wise *men*, the astrologers, have been brought in before me, that they should read this writing, and make known unto me the interpretation thereof: but they could not shew the interpretation of the thing:

16. And I have heard of thee, that thou canst make interpretations, and dissolve doubts: now, if thou canst read the writing, and make known to me the interpretation thereof, thou shalt be clothed with scarlet, and *have* a chain of gold about thy neck, and shalt be the third ruler in the kingdom.

13. Tunc Daniel adductus est coram rege: loquutus est rex, et dixit Danieli, Tu *ne es*[1] ille Daniel, qui, ex filiis captivitatis Jehudah, quem abduxit rex pater meus e Jehudah.

14. Et audivi de te, quod spiritus deorum in te, et intelligentia, et cognitio, et sapientia excellens, inventa sit in te.

15. Et nunc producti sunt coram me sapientes, arioli,[2] qui scripturam hanc legerent, et interpretationem ejus patefacerent mihi: et non potuerunt interpretationem sermonis indicare.

16. Et ego audivi de te, quod possis nodos solvere, et arcana explicare: nunc si poteris scripturam legere et interpretationem ejus patefacere mihi, purpura vestieris, et torques ex auro super collum tuum, et tertius in regno dominaberis.

Here the king does not acknowledge his own folly, but
without any modesty he interrogates Daniel, and that, too,
as a captive,—*Art thou that Daniel, of the captives of Judah,
whom my father led away?* He seems to speak contemptuously here, to keep Daniel in servile obedience; although we
may read this sentence as if Belshazzar inquired, *Are you
that Daniel? In truth, I have heard of thee!* He had heard
before, and had said nothing; but now, when extreme necessity urges him, he pays the greatest respect to Daniel. *I have
heard*, therefore, *that the spirit of the gods is in thee, since thou*

---

[1] If we read it interrogatively; or, " Thou art Daniel ?"—*Calvin.*
[2] Or, conjurors. I do not dwell on this as I said before.—*Calvin.*

canst unravel intricacies and reveal secrets. With regard to
the spirit of the gods, we have already mentioned how King
Belshazzar, by the common custom of all nations, promiscuously mingled angels with God ; because those miserable
ones could not extol God as they ought, and treat angels as
entirely under his feet. But this sentence shews men never
were so brutal as not to ascribe all excellence to God, as we
see in profane writers; whatever promotes human advantage,
and is remarkable for superiority and dignity, they treat as
benefits derived from the gods. Thus the Chaldeans called
the gift of intelligence a spirit of the gods, being a rare and
singular power of penetration ; since men acknowledge they
do not acquire and attain to the prophetic office by their
own industry, but it is a heavenly gift. Hence men are
compelled by God to assign to him his due praise; but because the true God was unknown to them, they speak im-
plicitly, and, as I have said, they called angels gods, since in
the darkness of their ignorance they could not discern which
was the true God. Whatever be the meaning, Belshazzar
here shews in what estimation he holds Daniel, saying, he
depends on the reports received from others, and thus dis-
playing his own slothfulness. He ought to have known the
Prophet by personal experience ; but from his being content
with simple rumour, he proudly neglected the teacher offered
to him, and neither reflected upon nor wished to confess his
own disgrace. But thus God often extracts a confession
from the impious, by which they condemn themselves, even
if they wish exceedingly to escape censure.

The following phrase has the same meaning :—*All the
wise men were brought before me, and the soothsayers or
diviners, to read this writing to me, and to reveal its interpretation; and they could not do it,* said he ; for God punished him by shewing how profitless were all the Chaldeans
and soothsayers, in whom he trusted at the moment of his
extremity. While he was thus disappointed in his hopes,
he acknowledges himself to have been deceived ; and when
he preferred the magi and soothsayers, he thought himself
fortified by their counsel, as long as they were on his side.
Meanwhile his rejection of the holy Prophet was deservedly

intolerable to God. Belshazzar confesses this without intending to do so ; hence I said his confession was not
ingenuous or voluntary, but violently extorted by the secret
instinct of God. He also promises Daniel what he had previously promised the magi,—*Thou shalt be clothed in purple
if thou canst read this writing, and wear a golden chain round
thy neck, and thou shalt reign as the third person in the kingdom.* But the end of his reign was now close at hand, and yet
in security he offers this dignity to Daniel. This shews how
rapidly the terror which God had occasioned him had vanished away. He is agitated by the greatest uneasiness, just
like madmen, for they having no certainty exult amidst
their terror, and wish to leap or fly towards heaven itself.
Thus also this tyrant though he trembles at God's judgment,
yet retains a hidden obstinacy in his heart, and imagines
his kingdom will permanently continue, while he promises
wealth and honours to others. It now follows,—

17. Then Daniel answered and said before the king, Let thy gifts be to thyself, and give thy rewards to another; yet I will read the writing unto the king, and make known to him the interpretation.	17. Tunc respondit Daniel, et dixit coram rege, Dona tua tibi sint,[1] et munera tua alteri da : tamen scripturam legam regi, et interpretationem *ejus* patefaciam ei.

First of all, Daniel here rejects the proffered gifts. We
do not read of his doing so before ; he rather seemed to delight in the honours conferred by King Nebuchadnezzar. We
may inquire into the reason for this difference. It is not
probable that the intention, feeling, or sentiments of the
Prophet were different. What then could be his intention
in allowing himself to be previously ennobled by Nebuchadnezzar, and by now rejecting the offered dignity ? Another
question also arises. At the end of this chapter we shall
see how he was clothed in purple, and a herald promulgated
an edict, by which he became third in the kingdom. The
Prophet seems either to have forgotten himself in receiving
the purple which he had so magnanimously rejected, or we
may ask the reason why he says so, when he did not refuse
to be adorned in the royal apparel. With respect to the first
question, I have no doubt of his desire to treat the impious

---

[1] That is, may they remain with thee.—*Calvin.*

and desperate Belshazzar with greater asperity, because in the case of King Nebuchadnezzar there still remained some feelings of honour, and hence he hoped well of him and treated him more mildly. But with regard to King Belshazzar, it was necessary to treat him more harshly, because he had now arrived at his last extremity. This, I have no doubt, was the cause of the difference, since the Prophet proceeded straight forward in his course, but his duty demanded of him to distinguish between different persons, and as there was greater pertinacity and obstinacy in King Belshazzar, he shews how much less he deferred to him than to his grandfather. Besides, the time of his subjection was soon to be finished, and with this end in view he had formerly honoured the Chaldean empire.

As to the contrast apparent between his reply and his actions, which we shall hereafter see, this ought not to seem absurd, if the Prophet had from the beginning borne his testimony against the king's gifts, and that he utterly rejected them. Yet he does not strive very vehemently, lest he should be thought to be acting cunningly, for the purpose of escaping danger. In each case he wished to display unconquered greatness of mind; at the beginning he asserted the king's gifts to be valueless to him, for he knew the end of the kingdom to be at hand, and afterwards he received the purple with other apparel. If he had entirely refused them, it would have been treated as a fault and as a sign of timidity, and would have incurred the suspicion of treason. The Prophet therefore shews how magnificently he despised all the dignities offered him by King Belshazzar, who was already half dead. At the same time he shews himself intrepid against all dangers; for the king's death was at hand and the city was taken in a few hours—nay, in the very same hour! Daniel therefore did not reject this purple, shewing his resolution not to avoid death if necessary. He would have been safer in his obscurity, had he dwelt among the citizens at large, instead of in the palace; and if he had resided among the captives, he might have been free from all danger. As he did not hesitate to receive the purple, he displays his perfect freedom from all fear. Meanwhile he, doubtless, wished to lay prostrate the king's foolish arrogance, by which he was puffed up, when he says, *Let thy gifts remain with thee, and give thy presents to another !* I care not for them.   Because he so nobly despises the king's liberality, there is no doubt of his desire to correct the pride by which he was puffed up, or at least to wound and arouse his mind to feel God's judgment, of which Daniel will soon become both the herald and the witness.   It now follows,—

18. O thou king, the most high God gave Nebuchadnezzar thy father a kingdom, and majesty, and glory, and honour:	18. O rex,[1] Deus excelsus imperium, et magnitudinem, et præstantiam, et splendorem dedit Nebuchadnezer patri tuo.
19. And for the majesty that he gave him, all people, nations, and languages, trembled and feared before him: whom he would he slew, and whom he would he kept alive, and whom he would he set up, and whom he would he put down.	19. Et ob magnitudinem quam dederat ei, omnes populi, gentes et linguæ tremuerunt, et formidarunt a conspectu ejus: quem volebat, occidebat:[2] et quem volebat *percutere,* percutiebat: et quem volebat *attollere,* attollebat: et quem volebat *dejicere,* dejiciebat.
20. But when his heart was lifted up, and his mind hardened in pride, he was deposed from his kingly throne, and they took his glory from him.	20. Quando autem elevatum fuit cor ejus, et spiritus ejus roboratus est[3] ad superbiam, dejectus fuit e solio regni, et gloriam abstulerunt ab eo.

Before Daniel recites the writing, and adds its interpretation, he explains to King Belshazzar the origin of this prodigy.   He did not begin the reading at once, as he might conveniently have done, saying *Mene, Mene !* as we shall see at the end of the chapter, since the king could not have profited by his abrupt speech.   But here Daniel shews it to be by no means surprising, if God put forth his hand and shewed the figure of a hand describing the king's destruction, since the king had too obstinately provoked his anger. We see then why Daniel begins by this narrative, since King Nebuchadnezzar was a most powerful monarch, subduing the whole world to himself and causing all men to tremble at his word, and was afterwards hurled from the throne of his kingdom.   Hence it more clearly appears that Belshazzar did not live in ignorance, for he had so signal

---

[1] Verbally, " Thou, O king," as he addresses him.—*Calvin.*
[2] That is, " whom he wished to slay was slain."—*Calvin.*
[3] Or, " he was hardened."—*Calvin.*

and remarkable an example that he ought to have conducted himself with moderation.   Since then that domestic admonition did not profit him, Daniel shews the time to be ripe for the denunciation of God's wrath by a formidable and portentous sign.   This is the sense of the passage.   Passing on to the words themselves, he first says, *To King Nebuchadnezzar God gave an empire, and magnificence, and loftiness, and splendour ;* as if he had said, he was magnificently adorned, as the greatest monarch in the world.   We have stated elsewhere, and Daniel repeats it often, that empires are bestowed on men by divine power and not by chance, as Paul announces, There is no power but of God.   (Rom. xiii. 1.) God wishes his power to be specially visible in kingdoms. Although, therefore, he takes care of the whole world, and, in the government of the human family even the most miserable things are regulated by his hand, yet his singular providence shines forth in the empire of the world.   But since we have often discussed this point at length, and shall have many opportunities of recurring to it, it is now sufficient just briefly to notice the principle of the exaltation of earthly kings by the hand of God, and not by the chances of fortune.

When Daniel confirms this doctrine, he adds, *On account of the magnificence which God conferred upon him, all mortals trembled at the sight of him !*   By these words he shews how God's glory is inscribed on kings, although he allows them to reign supreme.   This indeed cannot be pointed out with the finger, but the fact is sufficiently clear ; kings are divinely armed with authority, and thus retain under their hand and sway a great multitude of subjects.   Every one desires the chief power over his fellow-creatures.   Whence happens it, since ambition is natural to all men, that many thousands are subject to one, and suffer themselves to be ruled over and endure many oppressions ?   How could this be, unless God entrusted the sword of power to those whom he wishes to excel ?   This reason, then, must be diligently noticed, when the Prophet says, *All men trembled at the sight of King Nebuchadnezzar,* because God conferred upon him that majesty, and wished him to excel all the monarchs of the world.   God has many reasons, and often hidden ones, why he raises one man and humbles another ; yet this point ought to be uncontroverted by us. No kings can possess any authority unless God extends his hand to them and props them up. When he wishes to remove them from power, they fall of their own accord ; not because there is any chance in the changes of the world, but because God, as it is said in the Book of Job, (xii. 18,) deprives those of the sword whom he had formerly entrusted with it.

It now follows, *Whom he wished to slay he slew, and whom he wished to strike he struck.* Some think the abuse of kingly power is here described ; but I had rather take it simply, for Nebuchadnezzar being able to cast down some, and to raise others at his will, since it was in his power to give life to some and to slay others. I, therefore, do not refer these words to tyrannical lust, as if Nebuchadnezzar had put many innocent persons to death, and poured forth human blood without any reason ; or as if he had despoiled many of their fortunes, and enriched others and adorned them with honour and wealth. I do not take it so. I think it refers to his arbitrary power over life and death, and over the rise of some and the ruin of others. On the whole, Daniel seems to me to describe the greatness of that royal power which they may freely exercise over their subjects, not through its being lawful, but through the tacit consent of all men. Whatsoever pleases the king, all are compelled to approve of it, or at least no one dares to murmur at it. Since, therefore, the regal license is so great, Daniel here shews how King Nebuchadnezzar was not carried away by his own plans, or purposes, or good fortune, but was entrusted with supreme power and rendered formidable to all men, because God had designed him for his own glory. Meanwhile, kings usually despise what they are permitted to enjoy, and what God allows them. For powerful as they are, they must hereafter render an account to the Supreme King. We are not to gather from this, that kings are appointed by God without any law, or any self-restraint ; but the Prophet, as I have said, speaks of the royal power in itself. Since kings, therefore, have power over their subjects for life and death, he says, the life of all men was in the hand of King Nebuchadnezzar.   He now adds, *When his heart was exalted, then he was cast down* (or ejected) *from the throne of his kingdom, and they deprived him of his majesty.*   He follows up his own narrative.   He wishes to shew King Belshazzar how God bears with the insolence of those who forget him, when they have obtained the summit of power.   Desiring to make this known, he says, King Nebuchadnezzar, thy grandfather, was a mighty monarch.   He did not obtain this mightiness by himself, nor could he have retained it, except he had been supported by God's hand. Now his change of circumstances was a remarkable proof that the pride of those who are ungrateful to God can never be endured unto the end, as they never acknowledge their sway to proceed from his benevolence.   *When*, therefore, says he, *his heart was raised up and his spirit strengthened in pride*, a sudden change occurred.   Hence you and all his posterity ought to be taught, lest pride still further deceive you, and ye profit not by the example of your father; as we shall afterwards relate.   Hence this writing has been set before thee, for the purpose of making known the destruction of thy life and kingdom.

PRAYER.

Grant, Almighty God, since our own station in life has been assigned to us, that we may be content with our lot, and when thou dost humble us, may we willingly be subject to thee, and suffer ourselves to be ruled by thee, and not desire any exaltation, which may lead us down to destruction.   Grant us also, to conduct ourselves so modestly in our various callings, that thou mayest always shine forth in us.   May nothing else be set before us than to assist our brethren to whom we are attached, as in thy sight; and thus glorify thy name among all men, through Jesus Christ our Lord.— Amen.

Lecture Twenty=sixth.

In the sentence which we began to explain yesterday, the clause must be noticed where Daniel says, *The heart of King*

Nebuchadnezzar was strengthened by pride, signifying that he was not suddenly elated by folly, as vain men often swell with pride without a cause ; nor does any interior affection of the mind precede; but he wishes to express in addition, the length of time during which this pride had been conceived ; as if he had said, he was not seized by any sudden vanity, but his pride was studied, and obstinacy and obduracy were added to it. The change of number which afterwards occurs from singular to plural, some refer to the angels, as if they deprived him by God's command; but I rather think these words are taken indefinitely, implying merely his being deprived of his glory, as we have formerly observed similar forms of speech. It now follows—

21. And he was driven from the sons of men ; and his heart was made like the beasts, and his dwelling *was* with the wild asses : they fed him with grass like oxen, and his body was wet with the dew of heaven ; till he knew that the most high God ruled in the kingdom of men, and *that* he appointeth over it whomsoever he will.	21. Et a filiis hominum exterminatus fuit : et cor ejus cum bestiis positum est : et cum onagris habitatio ejus : herba sicut tauros cibaverunt eum : et rore cœli corpus ejus irrigatum fuit, donec cognosceret quod dominetur Deus excelsus in regno hominum, et quem velit imponat in illo.

First, with respect to the text ; verbally, it is " he put," and thus some translate, " he placed his own heart among the brutes," which makes a tolerable sense ; but others rather refer this to God, who placed his heart among beasts, and we know how often the noun substantive is defective in Hebrew and Chaldee ; hence we may translate it verbally, Nebuchadnezzar himself placed his own heart, that is, assimilated his own senses to the brutes, so as to differ in no respect from them. It may also mean, God placed his heart among the brutes, that is, infatuated him so, as to render him like them. Others take the word שְׁוִי, *shevi,* absolutely ; but it ought rather to be explained actively. Again, some translate the next clause, " Made him taste the grass, like a brute ;" and others, that the grass supported him. The number is changed, but there is no doubt about the sense ; for if we read, " The herb of the field supported him," the expression will be indefinite, similar to many others previously noticed ; but if any one prefers using the plural number, the sense will be equally suitable; for " the herbs of the field gave him nourishment."

This verse does not need any long explanation, since Daniel only repeats what he had formerly written : His grandfather, Nebuchadnezzar, although not changed into a wild beast, was driven from the common society of men, and his whole body was deformed, whilst he abhorred the habits of men and preferred to dwell with the brutes. This was a horrible prodigy, especially in so great a monarch ; and it was an example worthy of being handed down by posterity even to a thousand generations, had the monarchy endured so long. But his grandson quickly forgot this event, and thus he is deservedly convicted of the basest slothfulness. This is the reason why Daniel repeats the history again, *He was driven*, says he, *from the children of men ; his heart was placed among the beasts*, meaning he was deprived of reason and judgment. We know this to be the principal difference between men and brutes—men understand and reason, but brutes are carried away by their senses. God, therefore, set forth a memorable example in despoiling this king of his reason and intelligence. *His dwelling*, says he, *was with the wild asses ;* formerly he had dwelt in a palace, conspicuous throughout the world at large, from whom all the people of the East sought their laws. Since he was habitually worshipped as a god, this was a horrible judgment, since he afterwards dwelt among wild beasts, and *like a bull received his sustenance from the grass of the field*, when he had previously revelled in every delicacy, and was accustomed to luxurious habits, and to the whole wealth of a kingdom ; especially, when we know how luxuriously the Orientals indulged themselves. Babylon was the mother of all indulgences, and when the king's condition was thus changed, no one could be ignorant of its cause—not mere chance or accident, but the rare and singular judgment of God !

He afterwards adds what he had formerly said, *His body was moistened by the dews of heaven, until he acknowledged God to reign supreme in the kingdom of men.* Here again the end of the punishment is expressed—that Nebuchadnezzar might feel himself to have been created king by divine power, and to shew how earthly kings could not stand unless God propped them up by his hand and influence. They think themselves placed beyond the changes of fortune, and although they verbally boast of reigning by the grace of God, yet they despise every deity and transfer the glory of the divinity to themselves! We gather from these words that this is the folly of all kings. For if Nebuchadnezzar had been persuaded of God's appointment of kings, of their dependence upon his will, and of their fall or stability according to his decree, he had not needed this punishment, as these words clearly imply. He excluded God, then, from the government of the world; but this is common with all earthly kings, as I have lately stated. All indeed will profess something, but the Holy Spirit does not regard those false protestations, as they are called. Hence in the character of King Nebuchadnezzar we have set before us, as in a glass, the drunken confidence of all kings, in supposing themselves to stand by their own power, and to free themselves from the authority of God, as if he were not seated as a judge in heaven. Nebuchadnezzar, therefore, ought to be humbled, until he acknowledged God's reign upon earth, since the common opinion fixed him up in heaven, as if contented with his own ease, and careless of the affairs of the human race. At length it is added, *and whom he wills, he exalts*, or sets up. What has been said obscurely is better expressed, since Nebuchadnezzar acknowledged, by being severely punished and subdued, the reign of God on the earth. For when earthly kings see themselves surrounded by guards, powerful in riches, and able to collect mighty armies by their nod; when they see they inspire universal terror, they think God deprived of his rights, and are unable to conceive any change; as it is said in the Psalms of all the proud, (Ps. x. 4,) and as Isaiah says to the same purport, Even should a blast pass by, or a deluge overwhelm the whole earth, yet evil shall not touch us. (Is. xxviii. 15.) As if they had said, although God should thunder from heaven, yet we shall be safe from all disaster and disturbance. Kings persuade themselves of this. Hence they begin to acknowledge God as king of the earth, when they feel themselves in his hand and at his disposal, to cast down those whom he has raised up, and to exalt the lowly and abject, as we have already seen. This clause of the verse, then, is an explanation of the former sentence. It now follows :

22. And thou his son, O Belshaz-zar, hast not humbled thine heart, though thou knewest all this.

22. Et tu filius ejus Beltsazar, non humiliasti cor tuum: qua prop-ter[1] totum hoc cognoveras.

Daniel here shews why he related what we have hitherto heard concerning King Nebuchadnezzar's punishment ; for Belshazzar ought to have been so affected by that domestic example, as to submit himself to God. We may believe, in-deed, that his father Evil-Merodach had forgotten his pun-ishments, since he would not have conducted himself so petulantly against God, nor trampled on true and sincere piety ; for God spared the wretched tyrant who restrained himself within the bounds of moderation. But as to his grandfather Belshazzar, he was altogether intolerable ; hence God stretched forth his hand. The Prophet now teaches this. *Thou art his son*, says he. This circumstance urges upon him with greater force the duty of not seeking an example in foreign nations, since he acknowledged himself to have sufficient at home of what was both necessary and useful. He enlarges upon his crime in another way, by say-ing, *Yet thou didst know this*. Men are accustomed to shield themselves under their ignorance with the view of extenuat-ing the guilt of their crimes, but those who sin knowingly and wilfully are without the slightest excuse. The Prophet therefore convinces the king of manifest obstinacy ; as if he had said, You have provoked God's anger on purpose ; since he ought to have been aware of the horrible judgment await-ing all the proud, when he had such a remarkable and sin-gular proof of it in his grandfather, which he ought to have kept constantly before his eyes. It follows,—

23. But hast lifted up thyself against the Lord of heaven ; and they have brought the vessels of his

23. Et contra Dominum cœli te extulisti, et vasa domus ejus,[2] pro-tulerunt in conspectum tuum : et tu,

[1] Verbally—but it means, " since."—*Calvin.*
[2] That is, of his temple.—*Calvin.*

house before thee, and thou and thy lords, thy wives and thy concubines, have drunk wine in them; and thou hast praised the gods of silver, and gold, of brass, iron, wood, and stone, which see not, nor hear, nor know: and the God in whose hand thy breath *is*, and whose *are* all thy ways, hast thou not glorified.

et proceres tui, uxores tuæ,[1] et concubinæ tuæ vinum bibistis in illis: et deos argenti, *hoc est, argenteos,* et aureos, æneos, ferreos, ligneos, et lapideos, qui non vident, et non audiunt, et non intelligunt, laudasti: et Deum, cui *est* in manu ejus anima tua,[2] et cujus[3] omnia tua, non honorasti.

The Prophet continues his own sentence, and confirms what I have said, namely, King Belshazzar was intractable and wilfully blind to God's judgment. *For thou hast raised thyself,* says he, *against the Lord of heaven.* If he had raised himself thus insolently against men, his sin would be worthy of punishment; but when he had provoked God on purpose, this arrogance neither could nor ought to be borne. Again, therefore, the Prophet increases the guilt of the king's pride by saying, *he raised himself against the King of heaven.* He also expresses the manner of his doing so, *by commanding the vessels of the temple to be brought to sight ; he drank from them !* This profanation was an indecent sacrilege, but Belshazzar was not content with that indignity ; he used these vessels for luxury and foul debauchery, abusing them in the company of concubines and abandoned women ; and added a yet greater reproach against God, *in praising his gods of silver and gold, brass and iron, wood and stone, which cannot feel.* This had not been said previously; but since Daniel here sustains the character of a teacher, he does not relate the events so shortly as at first. When he said at the beginning of this chapter, Belshazzar celebrated that impure banquet, he spoke historically ; but he now executes, as I have said, the office of a teacher. *Thou,* says he, *hast praised the gods made of corruptible material, who neither see, nor hear, nor understand ; but thou hast defrauded the living God of his honour, in whose hand is thy life,* on which thou dependest, and whence all in which thou boastest proceeds. Because thou hast so despised the living God, who had been so gracious unto thee, this ingratitude was both base and shameful. We see, therefore, how severely the Prophet

---

[1] Or, thy wife.—*Calvin.*
[2] That is, in whose hand is thy life.—*Calvin.*
[3] In whose power are all things.—*Calvin.*

reproves the impious tyrant of sacrilege, and mad rashness, and foul ingratitude towards God.   I pass over these things lightly, since they have been treated elsewhere.   It now follows,—

| 24. Then was the part of the hand sent from him; and this writing was written. | 24. Tunc a conspectu ejus missa est particula manus,[1] et scriptura hæc notata *fuit*. |

Some stress must be laid upon the adverb באדין, *badin*, " at that time," because God's wrath, or at least its denunciation, was now ripe.   Daniel, therefore, shews how very patiently God had borne with King Belshazzar in not instantly taking up arms and inflicting punishment ; but he now begins to come forth as a judge, and to ascend his judgment seat ; for the haughtiness was now desperate, and the impiety no longer tolerable.   We observe with what emphasis the word *then* is used ; as if he had said, Thou canst not complain of the swiftness of the penalty, as if God had exacted it before the time.   Thou canst not here complain of God's swiftness in punishing thee; for think and consider in how many ways, and for how long a time, thou hast provoked his anger.   And with regard to thy last crime, thou certainly hadst arrived at the height of impiety, when that hand appeared to thee.   God, therefore, now drags thee to punishment in proper time, since he has hitherto borne with thee and thy sins.   After this forbearance, what remains to prevent his destroying thee, because thou hast so proudly insulted him, and art utterly hardened, without the slightest hope of amendment.

He says also, *from himself ;* for Belshazzar need not inquire whence the hand proceeded, it came *from the presence of God ;* that is, This hand is a witness to the wrath of heaven ; do not consider it as a spectre which will vanish away, but see in this appearance a proof of God's displeasure at thy wickedness ; and because thou hast arrived at thy last extremity, thy punishment is also ready for thee.   *And this writing,* says he, *has been marked ;* as if he had said, The eyes of King Belshazzar were not deceived, since this

---

[1] Some translate, " the palm," but they understand a hand separate from the body—that portion of a hand, that is, a hand as if cut off from the body, was sent from God's presence, says he.—*Calvin.*

was really God's hand, being sent from his sight as a certain
testimony of his wrath. He afterwards adds,—

25. And this *is* the writing that was written, MENE, MENE, TEKEL, UPHARSIN.	25. Et hæc *est* scriptura quæ notata *est*,[1] MENE, MENE, numeratum est, numeratum est, TEKEL, appensum est,[2] UPHARSIN, et dividentes.
26. This *is* the interpretation of the thing : MENE ; God hath numbered thy kingdom, and finished it.	26. Hæc interpretatio est sermonis : MENE, numeravit Deus regnum tuum et complevit.[3]
27. TEKEL ; Thou art weighed in the balances, and art found wanting.	27. TEKEL, appende, *vel, appensum est*, appensus es in trutina,[4] et inventus es deficiens.
28. PERES ; Thy kingdom is divided, and given to the Medes and Persians.	28. Peres *pro upharsin*, divisum est regnum tuum, et datum Medis et Persis.

Daniel here explains these four verses which were written
upon the wall. The king could not read them, either through
stupor, or because God blunted all his senses, and blinded
his eyes, as was formerly said. The same thing must be
said of the magi and the soothsayers, for they could have
read, had they not been rendered blind. First of all, Daniel
recites the four words, MENE, MENE, TEKEL, UPHARSIN, and
then adds their interpretation. He repeats the word MENE
twice. Some conjecture this to apply to the numbering of
the years of the king's life, and also to the time of his
reign ; but the guess seems to be without any foundation.
I think the word is used twice for the sake of confirmation ;
as if the Prophet meant the number to be completed, since
men usually allow calculations to be liable to error. To impress upon Belshazzar that his life and kingdom were at
stake, God affirms the number to be complete, meaning, not
a moment of time can be added to the boundary already determined. So also Daniel himself interprets it : *God,* says
he, *has numbered thy kingdom ;* implying, God has appointed
and prescribed a fixed end to thy kingdom ; hence it must
necessarily come to an end, since its period is fulfilled.

Although God here addresses but one king by the writing
set before his eyes, we may still gather this general instruc-

---

[1] Or, engraved.—*Calvin.*
[2] Some translate, number, number, weigh.—*Calvin.*
[3] Or, finished.—*Calvin.*   [4] Or, in a balance.—*Calvin.*

tion—God has prescribed a certain time for all kingdoms. (Job xiv. 5.) The Scripture bears the same witness concerning the life of each of us. If God has prescribed to each of us the length of his life, surely this applies more forcibly to public empires, of so much greater importance. Hence we may know how not only kings live and die according to God's pleasure, but even empires are changed, as we have formerly said. He fixes alike their origin and their destiny. Hence we may seek consolation, when we see tyrants rushing on so impetuously, and indulging their lust and cruelty without moderation. When, therefore, they rush on, as if they would mingle heaven and earth, let us remember this instruction, Their years are numbered ! God knows how long they are to rage ; He is not deceived ; He knows whether it is useful to the Church and his elect, for tyrants to prevail for a time. By and bye he will surely restrain them, but since he determined the number of their days from the beginning, the time of his vengeance is not yet quite at hand, while he allows them a little longer to abuse without restraint the power and the sway which he had divinely granted them.

The exposition of the word TEKEL, *to weigh,* now follows :— *Since thou hast been weighed in the balance,* or scale, *and found wanting.* Here Daniel shews God so moderating his judgments, as if he was carrying a balance in his hand. The emblem is taken from the custom of mankind ; for men know the use of the balance for accurate measurement. So also God is said to treat all things by weight and measure, since he does nothing with confusion, but uses moderation ; and, according to ordinary language, nothing is more or less than it should be. (Wisdom xi. 21.) For this reason, Daniel says God *weighed Belshazzar in a balance,* since he did not make haste to inflict punishment, but exacted it with justice according to his own uniform rule of government. *Since he was found deficient,* that is, was found light and without weight. As if he had said, Thou thinkest thy dignity must be spared, since all men revere thee ; thou thinkest thyself worthy of honour ; thou art deceived says he, for God judges otherwise ; God does not use a common scale, but holds his own, *and there thou art found deficient;* that is, thou art found a man of no consequence, in any way. From these words there is no doubt that the tyrant was greatly exasperated, but as his last end was approaching, he ought to hear the voice of the herald. And God, without doubt, restrained his fierceness, that he should not rise up against Daniel.

The word פְרֵס, PHERES, is added, for the word PHERSIN, meaning *his kingdom was divided* among the Medes and Persians. I have no doubt that by this word God signified the dispersion of the Monarchy which was at hand. When, therefore, he says UPHARSIN, *and they shall divide,* it signifies the instability of the Monarchy, since he wished to destroy or utterly abolish it. But the Prophet alludes very appositely to the division made between the Medes and Persians; and thus his disgrace was increased by the Babylonians being compelled to serve many masters. This is indeed a grave and serious disgrace, when a people has obtained a wide and extensive empire, to be afterwards conquered and subjected to the yoke of a single master; but when it suffers under two masters, then the indignity is greatly increased. So Daniel here shews how God's wrath was complicated in the destruction of the monarch of Babylon, since it added to the severity of their punishment, to be subdued by both Medes and Persians. The city, indeed, was truly taken by the valour and industry of Cyrus; but since Cyrus admitted his father-in-law to the great honour of allowing him to partake of the royal authority, hence the Medes and Persians are said to have divided the kingdom, although there was properly no division of the kingdom. Cyrus afterwards engaged in other expeditions, as he was led away by his insatiable avarice and ambition. But Darius, as we shall afterwards see, died at the age of sixty years, dwelt quietly at home, and it is very well known that he was a Mede; and if we may believe the majority of historians, his sister, the mother of Cyrus, had been banished to Persia, in consequence of the oracle concerning the fortune and greatness of Cyrus. Since his grandfather had exposed him, he afterwards avenged the injury, yet not so cruelly as to take his life, for he desired him to retain some dignity, and hence appointed

him a satrap.   But his son afterwards reigned over the
Medes, with the full permission of Cyrus, who next married
his daughter ; and thus, on account of this relationship, and
through the influence of this new alliance, he wished to have
him as a partner in the empire.   In this sense, then, Daniel
narrates the division of the Monarchy to be at hand, since
the Medes and the Persians should divide it among them.
It follows,—

29. Then commanded Belshazzar, and they clothed Daniel with scarlet, and *put* a chain of gold about his neck, and made a proclamation concerning him, that he should be the third ruler in the kingdom.	29. Tunc jussit Beltsazar, et vestierunt Danielem purpura, et torques aureus super collum ejus :[1] et clamabant coram ipso quod dominaretur tertius in regno.

This order of the king may excite surprise, since he had
been so sharply reproved by the Prophet.   He next seemed
to have lost all spirit, for he had grown pale a hundred times,
and would have devoted the holy Prophet of God to a thousand deaths !   How happens it, then, that he ordered him to
be adorned with royal apparel, and next to be proclaimed
by his own herald the third person in the kingdom ?   Some
think this was done because the laws of kings were sacred
among the Babylonians ; nay, their very words were held as
binding, and whatever they proclaimed, they desired it to
be esteemed firm and inviolable.   They suppose King Belshazzar to have acted thus through ambition, that he might
keep his promises.   My opinion is, that he was at first utterly
astonished, and through listening to the Prophet he became
like a stock or a stone !   I think he did so to consult his
own ease and safety ; otherwise he would have been contemptible to his nobles.   To shew himself unmoved, he commands Daniel to be clothed in these robes, as if his threat
had been perfectly harmless.   He did not despise what the
Prophet had said, but he wished to persuade his nobles and
all his guests of his perfect indifference to God's threats, as
if he did not utter them for the purpose of executing them,
but only of terrifying them all.   Thus kings, when greatly
terrified, are always exceedingly careful not to shew any sign
of their timidity, since they think their authority would

[1] Was placed.—*Calvin.*

become materially weakened. To continue, therefore, his reverence among his subjects, he is desirous of appearing exceedingly careless and undisturbed; and I do not hesitate to pronounce this to have been the tyrant's intention in ordering Daniel to be clad in purple and in royal magnificence.

PRAYER.

Grant, Almighty God, that as thou didst once send forth a proof of thy wrath against all the proud, so it may be useful to us in these days. May we be admonished by the punishment inflicted on this man, and thus learn to conduct ourselves with moderation and humility. May we not desire any greatness which can be displeasing to thee; and may we so remain in our station of life as to serve thee, and to extol and glorify thy sacred name, without being even separated from thee. Grant us also so to bear thy yoke in this world, and to suffer ourselves to be ruled by thee, that we may at length arrive at that happy rest and portion in thy heavenly kingdom, which thou hast prepared and procured for us, through the blood of thine only-begotten Son.—Amen.

Lecture Twenty=seventh.

30. In that night was Belshazzar the king of the Chaldeans slain.

31. And Darius the Median took the kingdom, *being* about threescore and two years old.

30. In illa nocte occisus *fuit* Beltsazar rex Chaldæorum.

31. Et Darius Medus accepit regnum, cum natus *esset* annos sexaginta et duos.

HERE Daniel shortly relates how his prophecy was fulfilled that very night. As we have before explained it, a customary feast-day had occurred which the Babylonians celebrated annually, and on this occasion the city was betrayed by two satraps, whom Xenophon calls Gobryas and Gadatas. On this passage the Rabbis display both their impudence and ignorance; as, according to their usual habit, they babble with audacity about what they do not understand. They say the king was stabbed, because one of his guards heard the Prophet's voice, and wished to execute that heavenly judgment; as if the sentence of God depended upon the will of a single heathen! We must pass by these puerile trifles and cling to the truth of history; for Belshazzar was

seized in his own banqueting-room, when he was grossly
intoxicated, with his nobles and concubines.   Meanwhile,
we must observe God's wonderful kindness towards the Prophet.   He was not in the slightest danger, as the rest were.
He was clad in purple, and scarcely an hour had passed when
the Medes and Persians entered the city.   He could scarcely
have escaped in the tumult, unless God had covered him
with the shadow of his hand.   We see, then, how God takes
care of his own, and snatches us from the greatest dangers,
as if he were bringing us from the tomb.   There is no doubt
that the holy Prophet was much agitated amidst the tumult,
for he was not without sensibility.[1]   But he ought to be thus
exercised to cause him to acknowledge God as the faithful
guardian of his life, and to apply himself more diligently to
his worship, since he saw nothing preferable to casting all
his cares upon him!

Daniel adds, *the kingdom was transferred to the king of
the Medes*, whom he calls Darius, but Xenophon terms him
Cyaxares.   It is clear enough that Babylon was taken by
the skill and under the auspices of Cyrus; since he was a
persevering warrior possessed of great authority, though he
is not mentioned here.   But since Xenophon relates that
Cyaxares, here called Darius, was Cyrus's father-in-law, and
thus held in the highest honour and estimation, it is not surprising to find Daniel bringing that king before us.   Cyrus
was content with his own power and with the praise and
fame of his victory, and readily conceded this title to his
father-in-law, whom he perceived to be now growing aged
and infirm.   It is uncertain whether he was the son of Astyages, and thus the uncle of Cyrus.   Many historians concur
in stating that Astyages was the grandfather of Cyrus who
married his daughter to Cambyses; because the astrologers
had informed him how an offspring should be born of her
who should possess the sovereignty over all Asia!   Many
add the story of his ordering the infant Cyrus to be slain,
but since these matters are uncertain, I leave them undecided.   I rather think Darius was the uncle of Cyrus, and

---

[1] The Latin is "stipes:" the French, "une souche de bois;" literally, a
log or block of wood.—*Ed.*

also his father-in-law; though, if we believe Xenophon, he was unmarried at the capture of Babylon; for his uncle, and perhaps his father-in-law, had sent him to bring supplies when he was inferior in numbers to the Babylonians and Assyrians. However this may be, the Prophet's narrative suits the circumstances well enough, for Darius, as king of the Medes, obtained the royal authority. Cyrus was, indeed, higher than he in both rank and majesty, but he granted him the title of King of Babylon, and under this name he reigned over the Chaldeans. It now follows,—

CHAPTER SIXTH.

1. It pleased Darius to set over the kingdom an hundred and twenty princes, which should be over the whole kingdom;

2. And over these three presidents, of whom Daniel *was* first; that the princes might give accounts unto them, and the king should have no damage.

1. Placuit coram Dario, et præfecit super regnum præsides provinciarum centum et viginti, qui essent in toto regno.

2. Et super illos *essent, atque ut essent super eos,* satrapæ tres, quorum Daniel unus *esset:* et ut præsides provinciarum illis redderent rationem: et rex non pateretur damnum.

As to the translation, some translate the last clause of the second verse, "That the king should not have any trouble;" but since פזק, *nezek*, signifies "to suffer loss," I willingly adopt this sense; because the king did not escape trouble, through a desire for ease, as he might have done, being an old man, but he willingly managed his own affairs, and committed the care of them to three men, lest anything should be lost through passing through too many hands. For experience shews us how confusion is caused by a multitude. If there had been only there an hundred and twenty governors of provinces, many inconveniences must have happened, and much loss would have occurred; hence the king placed three prefects over these hundred and twenty.

Here again we may perceive how God cared for his Prophet, not so much for any private reason or through private respect, as by his aid the wretched captives and exiles should be benefited. God wished to stretch forth his hand to the Jews by means of Daniel. And we may deservedly call him

God's hand in sustaining the Jews. The Persians, being
barbarians, were not naturally more merciful than others;
hence God interposed his servant Daniel to succour them.
We must notice, in the context of this history, how Daniel
alone was chosen by Darius one of these three superior officers. He was the third in rank under king Belshazzar, although for a moment, yet it might occasion envy under the
new king that so great an honour was conferred upon him.
Very probably Darius was informed of the previous predictions of Daniel ; how the hand appeared upon the wall, how
he interpreted the writing, and became a heaven-sent messenger to denounce destruction on king Belshazzar. For
unless this rumour had reached Darius, Daniel would never
have obtained so much authority under him. His own army
abounded in numbers, and we know how every conqueror is
surrounded in war by many dependents, all of whom wish
to share in the spoil. Darius, therefore, would never have
noticed a stranger and a captive, and admitted him to such
great honour and power, unless he had understood him to be
a known Prophet of God, and also a herald in denouncing
destruction against the Babylonish monarchy. Thus we
gather how providential it was for him to be among the first
satraps, and even third in the kingdom, as this brought him
more quickly under the notice of Darius. For if Daniel had
been cast down by king Belshazzar he would have remained
at home in concealment ; but when he appeared clothed in
royal apparel, the king inquired who he was ? He heard
the means of his arriving at so high an honour ; hence he
acknowledged him as God's Prophet, and appointed him one
of the three prefects. Here also God's providence is again
set before us, not only in preserving his servant in safety,
but in providing for the safety of the whole Church, lest the
Jews should be still more oppressed by the change of masters.
But a temptation is afterwards inflicted, by which the holy
Prophet and the whole people were severely tried ; for the
Prophet says :

3. Then this Daniel was preferred   3. Tunc Daniel ipse fuit superior,[1]

[1] The word נְצַח, netzech, means to surpass; hence he was superior or
more excellent.—Calvin.

above the presidents and princes, because an excellent spirit *was* in him; and the king thought to set him over the whole realm.

4. Then the presidents and princes sought to find occasion against Daniel concerning the kingdom; but they could find none occasion nor fault; forasmuch as he *was* faithful, neither was there any error or fault found in him.

5. Then said these men, We shall not find any occasion against this Daniel, except we find *it* against him concerning the law of his God.

supra satrapas et præsides provinciarum : propterea quod spiritus amplior, *vel, præstantior,* in ipso *erat :* et rex cogitabat eum erigere super totum regnum.

4. Tunc satrapæ, et præsides provinciarum quæsierunt occasionem invenire contra Danielem a parte regni,[1] et omnem occasionem,[2] et nullum crimen potuerunt invenire : quia verax[3] ipse : et nulla culpa, et nullum crimen,[4] inveniebatur in ipso.

5. Tunc viri illi dixerunt, non inveniemus in hoc Daniele ullam occasionem, nisi inveniamus in ipso ob legem Dei sui.

The Prophet now relates, as I have said, the origin of a temptation which might naturally cast down the spirits of the elect people as well as his own. For although Daniel alone was cast into the lion's-den, as we shall afterwards see, yet, unless he had been liberated, the condition of the people would have been more grievous and severe. For we know the wicked petulantly insult the wretched and the innocent, when they see them suffering any adversity. If Daniel had been torn by the lions, all men would have risen up in a body against the Jews. God, therefore, here exercised the faith and patience of his servant, and also proved all the Jews by the same test, since they saw themselves liable to the most extreme sufferings in the person of a single individual, unless God had speedily afforded the assistance which he rendered. Daniel, first of all, says, *he excelled all others, since a more excellent or superior spirit was in him.* It does not always happen that those who are remarkable for prudence or other endowments obtain greater authority and rank. In the palaces of kings we often see men of brutal dispositions holding high rank, and we need not go back to history for this. In these days kings are often gross and infatuated, and more like horses and asses than men ! Hence audacity and recklessness obtain the highest honours of the palace. When Daniel says *he excelled,* he brings to our notice

[1] That is, in his administration.—*Calvin.*
[2] That is, no occasion.—*Calvin.*
[3] Since he was faithful and thoroughly trusty.—*Calvin.*
[4] He repeats the noun for " crime" twice, שׁחיתה, *shechitheh.*—*Calvin.*

God's two-fold benefit: *first*, a greater portion of his Spirit was bestowed upon him; and *secondly*, Darius acknowledged this, and raised him to honour when he saw him endued with no ordinary industry and wisdom. We now understand the Prophet's teaching here, as first divinely adorned with prudence and other endowments; and then, Darius was a competent judge of this, in estimating his prudence and other virtues, and holding them in great repute. Since, therefore, *a noble spirit was in him*, hence *he overcame all others*, says he; therefore *the king determined to set him above the whole kingdom*, that is, to place him first among the three satraps. Although it was a singular privilege with which God once blessed his people and his Prophet, yet we ought to weep over the heartlessness of kings in these days, who proudly despise God's gifts in all good men who surpass the multitude in usefulness; and at the same time enjoy the society of the ignorant like themselves, while they are slaves to avarice and rapine, and manifest the greatest cruelty and licentiousness. Since, then, we see how very unworthy kings usually are of their empire and their power, we must weep over the state of the world, because it reflects like a glass the wrath of heaven, and kings are thus destitute of counsel. At the last day, King Darius alone will be sufficient to condemn them, for he had discretion enough not to hesitate to set a captive and a foreigner over all his satraps; for this was a royal, nay, a heroic virtue in Darius to prefer this man to all his own friends. But now kings think of nothing else than preferring their own panders, buffoons, and flatterers; while they praise none but men of low character, whom God has branded with ignominy. Although they are unworthy of being reckoned among mankind, yet they esteem themselves the masters of their sovereigns, and treat the kings of these days as their slaves. This happens through their mere slothfulness, and their discarding every possible anxiety. Hence they are compelled to deliver up their command to others, and retain nothing but the title. This, as I said, is a sure proof of the wrath of heaven, since the world is at this day unworthy of the government which God exercises over it by his hand.

With respect to the envy felt by the nobles, we see this vice rampant in all ages, since the aspirants to any greatness can never bear the presence of virtue. For, being guilty of evil themselves, they are necessarily bitter against the virtue of others. Nor ought it to seem surprising that the Persians who sustained the greatest labours, and passed through numerous changes of fortune, should be unable to bear with an obscure and unknown person, not only associated with them, but appointed as their superior. Their envy, then, seems to have had some pretext, either real or imaginary. But it will always be deserving of condemnation, when we find men selfishly pursuing their own advantage without any regard for the public good. Whoever aspires to power and self-advancement, without regarding the welfare of others, must necessarily be avaricious and rapacious, cruel and perfidious, as well as forgetful of his duties. Since, then, the nobles of the realm envied Daniel, they betrayed their malice, for they had no regard for the public good, but desired to seize upon all things for their own interests. In this example we observe the natural consequence of envy. And we should diligently notice this, since nothing is more tempting than gliding down from one vice to a worse. The envious man loses all sense of justice while attempting every scheme for injuring his adversary. These nobles report Daniel to have been preferred to themselves unworthily. If they had been content with this abuse, it would have been, as I said, a vice and a sign of a perverse nature. But they go far beyond this, for they seek for an occasion of crime in Daniel. We see, then, how envy excites them to the commission of crime. Thus all the envious are perpetually on the watch, while they become spies of the fortunes of those whom they envy, to oppress them by every possible means. This is one point; but when they find no crime, they trample upon justice, without modesty and without humanity, and with cruelty and perfidy lay themselves out to crush an adversary. Daniel relates this of his rivals. He says, *They immediately sought occasion against him, and did not find it.* Then he adds how unjustly and perfidiously they sought occasion against him. There is no doubt they knew Daniel to be a pious man and approved by God; hence, when they plot against his holy Prophet, they purposely wage war with God himself, while they are blinded with the perverse passion of envy. Whence, then, does it spring? Surely from ambition. Thus we see how pestilential a plague ambition is, from which envy springs up, and afterwards perfidy and cruelty!

Besides this, Daniel admonishes us by his own example to study to strive after integrity, and thus to deprive the malevolent and the wicked of all occasion against us, which they seek. We shall find no better defence against the envious and the slanderous than to conduct ourselves righteously and innocently. Whatever snares they may lay for us, they will never succeed, for our innocence will repel their malice like a shield. Meanwhile we see how Daniel escaped utter ruin, since they sought a pretext against him in something else, namely, his worship of God. Hence let us learn how we ought to esteem piety and an earnest desire for it of more value than life itself. Daniel was faithful and upright in his administration: he discharged his duty so as to close the mouth of his enemies and detractors. Thus, as I have said, integrity is the best of all protectors. Again, Daniel was in danger because he would not leave off the sincere worship of God and its outward profession. Hence we must bravely undergo all dangers whenever the worship of God is at stake. This temporary life ought not to be more precious to us than that most sacred of all things—the preservation of God's honour unstained. We therefore see how we, by these means, are urged to the cultivation of integrity, since we cannot be more secure than when fortified by a good conscience, as Peter in his first epistle exhorts us to the same purpose, (iii. 16.) Now, whatever we may fear, and whatever events await us, even if we become subject to a hundred deaths, we ought never to decline from the pure worship of God, since Daniel did not hesitate to submit to death and enter the lion's den, because he openly professed the worship of Israel's God. As these nobles entered into this barbarous and cruel counsel for oppressing Daniel under the pretence of religion, here, again, we gather the blind-

ness and rashness of mankind when ambition and envy
seize upon their minds. For it is a matter of no moment
with them to come into collision with the Almighty,[1] for they
do not approach Daniel as a fellow-creature, but they leap
into an insane and sacrilegious contest when they wish to
extinguish the worship of God and give way to their own
indulgence. Thus, as I have said, we are admonished by
this example how ambition is to be guarded against and
avoided, and also the envy which arises from it. The nature
of this charge—the worship of God—afterwards follows :—

6. Then these presidents and princes assembled together to the king, and said thus unto him, King Darius, live for ever.

7. All the presidents of the kingdom, the governors, and the princes, the counsellors, and the captains, have consulted together to establish a royal statute, and to make a firm decree, that whosoever shall ask a petition of any god or man for thirty days, save of thee, O king, he shall be cast into the den of lions.

6. Tunc satrapæ et provinciarum præsides illi sociati sunt[2] apud regem,[3] et sic locuti sunt ei: Dari rex, in æternum vive.

7. Consilium ceperunt omnes satrapæ regni, proceres et præsides provinciarum, consiliarii, et duces, ut statuatur statutum regis,[4] et sanciatur edictum, ut quisquis petierit petitionem ab ullo deo et homine usque ad dies triginta hos, præterquam a te, rex, projiciatur in speluncam leonum.

The nobles of the kingdom purposely endeavoured to ruin
the holy Prophet, either by casting him into the lion's den
to perish, or else by causing him to desist from the outward
profession of worshipping God. They knew him to be so
really in earnest that he would not redeem his life by so
great an act of impiety, and hence they thought him doomed
to death. We perceive in them great cunning; but God met
them on the other hand and aided his servant, as we shall see.
Meanwhile their malice was the more detestable, since they
desired to destroy Daniel by this very pretence. Although
they did not worship Israel's God, they knew the Prophet's
mind to be pious and straightforward, and then they experienced the power of that God who was unknown to them.

[1] The French editions of 1562 and 1569, a Geneva, translate the idiomatic phrase, susque deque illis est, by ce leur est tout un ; "it is all one to them."—Ed.

[2] For רְגַשׁ, reges, properly signifies to "join and associate with."—Calvin.

[3] That is, they made a conspiracy, and approached the king.—Calvin.

[4] That is, royal, or from the king.—Calvin.

They did not condemn Daniel, nor blame the religion which he practised ; for, as I have said, their hatred of this man urged them to such cruelty that they rushed against the Almighty.   They could not disguise from themselves the duty of worshipping God : they worshipped and adored unknown deities, and did not dare to condemn the worship of Israel's God.   We see how the devil fascinated them when they dared to impute this as a crime to the holy Prophet ; while we are ignorant of the manner in which their opinion was changed.

Some suppose this was done because Darius could not bear with composure the glory of his son-in-law.   For since he was an old man, and his relative in the flower of his age, he thought himself despised.   Others think Darius to have been touched by secret emulation, and that he allowed his nobles to approach him for the purpose of deceiving the miserable and doting old man, and thus to throw dust in his eyes.   But this conjecture does not seem to me sufficiently valid.   Nor need I give myself much trouble in this matter, because it might happen that at the beginning of a new reign they wished to congratulate the king, and they fixed upon something new and unaccustomed, as we see often done by flatterers of royalty.   Hence the old man might be deceived in this matter, since the monarchy was newly established.   The king had hitherto ruled over none but Medes ; now Chaldeans, Assyrians, and many other nations were added to his sway.   Such an addition might intoxicate him with vain-glory, and his nobles might think this a plausible reason for offering to him divine honours.   This single reason seems to me sufficient ; I do not inquire further, but embrace what is probable and obvious at first sight.   I defer the remainder till to-morrow.

PRAYER.

Grant, Almighty God, as thou didst govern thy servant Daniel when honours were flowing around on all sides, and he was raised to the highest dignity, and preserve him safe in his integrity and innocency amidst the universal licentiousness,—Grant, I pray thee, that we may learn to restrain ourselves within that

moderation to which thou restrictest us. May we be content
with our humble station and strive to prove ourselves innocent before thee and before those with whom we have to deal ;
so that thy name may be glorified in us, and we may proceed
under thy shelter against the malice of mankind. Whenever
Satan besieges us on every side, and the wicked lay snares for
us, and we are attacked by the fierceness of wild beasts, may we
remain safe under thy protection, and even if we have to undergo
a hundred deaths, may we learn to live and die to thee, and may
thy name be glorified in us, through Christ our Lord.—Amen.

Lecture Twenty-eighth.

WE said, yesterday, that the nobles who laid snares against
Daniel were inspired with great fury when they dared to dictate to the king the edict recorded by Daniel. It was an
intolerable sacrilege thus to deprive all the deities of their
honour ; yet he subscribed the edict, as we shall afterwards
see, and thus put to the test the obedience of his people
whom he had lately reduced under the yoke by the help of
his son-in-law. There is no doubt of his wish to subdue the
Chaldees, who up to that time had been masters ; and we
know how ferocity springs from the possession of authority.
Since then the Chaldees had formerly reigned so far and
wide, it was difficult to tame them and render them submissive, especially when they found themselves the slaves of
those who had previously been their rivals. We know how
many contests there were between them and the Medes ;
and although they were subdued in war, their spirits were
not yet in subjection ; hence Darius desired to prove their
obedience, and this reason induced him to give his consent.
He does not purposely provoke the anger of the gods ; but
through respect for the men, he forgets the deities, and substitutes himself in the place of the gods, as if it was in his
power to attract the authority of heaven to himself ! This,
as I have said, was a grievous sacrilege. If any one could
enter into the hearts of kings, he would find scarcely one in
a hundred who does not despise everything divine. Although they confess themselves to enjoy their thrones by
the grace of God, as we have previously remarked, yet they

wish to be adored in his stead. We now see how easily flatterers persuade kings to do whatever appears likely to extol
their magnificence. It follows :

8. Now, O king, establish the decree, and sign the writing, that it be
not changed, according to the law of
the Medes and Persians, which alter-
eth not.

9. Wherefore king Darius signed
the writing and the decree.

8. Nunc, rex, statue edictum, et
obsigna scripturam, quæ non ad mu-
tandum,[1] secundum legem Medorum
et Persarum, quæ non transit.

9. Itaque *ipse* rex Darius obsignavit scripturam et edictum.

Here, as I have said, it is sufficiently apparent how inclined to fallacies are the minds of kings when they think
they can benefit themselves and increase their own dignity.
For the king did not dispute long with his nobles but subscribed the edict ; for he thought it might prove useful to
himself and his successors, if he found the Chaldeans obedient to himself and rather prepared to deny the existence of
every god than to refuse whatever he commanded ! As to
the use of the word, some translate אסרא, *asra*, by " writing," deriving it from " *to cut in,*" as we know that all laws
were formerly graven on tablets of brass ; but I interpret it
more simply of their seeking from the king a signature of
the writing, that is, he was to sign the edict after it was
written. *Which cannot be changed,* they say—meaning, the
edict is unchangeable and inviolable, *according to the law of
the Medes and Persians, which does not pass away*—that is,
which does not vanish, as also Christ says, Heaven and earth
shall pass away, but my words shall not pass away, or shall
never become vain. (Matt. xxiv. 35 ; Mark xiii. 31.) As
to his joining the Medes with the Persians, this arises from
what we said before, since Cyrus and Darius reigned in common as colleagues. Greater dignity was granted to Darius,
while the power was in the hands of Cyrus ; besides, without
controversy, his sons were heirs of either kingdom and of
the Monarchy of the East, unless when they began to make
war on each other. When they say, the law of the Medes
and Persians *is immutable,* this is worthy of praise in laws,
and sanctions their authority ; thus they are strong and obtain their full effect. When laws are variable, many are

[1] That is, which is immutable.— *Calvin.*

necessarily injured, and no private interest is stable unless
the law be without variation ; besides, when there is a liberty
of changing laws, license succeeds in place of justice.   For
those who possess the supreme power, if corrupted by gifts,
promulgate first one edict and then another.   Thus justice
cannot flourish where change in the laws allows of so much
license.   But, at the same time, kings ought prudently to
consider lest they promulgate any edict or law without grave
and mature deliberation ; and secondly, kings ought to be
careful lest they be counteracted by cunning and artful plots,
to which they are often liable.   Hence, constancy is praiseworthy in kings and their edicts, if only they are preceded
by prudence and equity.   But we shall immediately see how
foolishly kings affect the fame of consistency, and how their
obstinacy utterly perverts justice.   But we shall see this directly in its own place.   It follows :

| 10. Now when Daniel knew that the writing was signed, he went into his house ; and, his windows being open in his chamber toward Jerusalem, he kneeled upon his knees three times a day, and prayed, and gave thanks before his God, as he did aforetime. | 10. Daniel autem ubi cognovit quod obsignata *esset* scriptura, venit, *vel, ingressus est,* in domum suam (fenestræ autem apertæ *erant* ei in cœnaculo suo versus Jerusalem) et temporibus tribus in die,[1] inclinabat se super genua sua,[2] et precabatur, et confitebatur coram Deo suo, quemadmodum fecerat a pristino illo tempore.[3] |

Daniel now relates how he was clothed in the boldness of
the Spirit of God to offer his life as a sacrifice to God, because he knew he had no hope of pardon left, if his violation
of the king's edict had been discovered ; he knew the king
himself to be completely in shackles even if he wished to
pardon him—as the event proved.   If death had been before
the Prophet's eyes, he preferred meeting it fearlessly rather
than ceasing from the duty of piety.   We must remark that
the internal worship of God is not treated here, but only the
external profession of it.   If Daniel had been forbidden to
pray, this fortitude with which he was endued might seem
necessary ; but many think he ran great risks without sufficient reason, since he increased the chance of death when

[1] That is, three times every day.—*Calvin.*

[2] The verb and the noun are from the same root ; " he bent upon his
knees or inclined himself."—*Calvin.*

[3] That is, as he was accustomed to do.—*Calvin.*

only outward profession was prohibited. But as Daniel here is not the herald of his own virtue, but the Spirit speaks through his mouth, we must suppose that this magnanimity in the holy Prophet was pleasing to God. And his liberation shewed how greatly his piety was approved, because he had rather lose his life than change any of his habits respecting the worship of God. We know the principal sacrifice which God requires, is to call upon his name. For we hereby testify him to be the author of all good things; next we shew forth a specimen of our faith; then we fly to him, and cast all our cares into his bosom, and offer him our prayers. Since, therefore, prayer constitutes the chief part of our adoration and worship of God, it was certainly a matter of no slight moment when the king forbade any one to pray to God; it was a gross and manifest denial of piety.

And here, again, we collect how blind was the king's pride when he could sign so impious and foul an edict! Then how mad were the nobles who, to ruin Daniel as far as they possibly could, endeavoured to abolish all piety, and draw down God from heaven! For what remains, when men think they can free themselves from the help of God, and pass him over with security? Unless he prop us up by his special aid, we know how entirely we should be reduced to nothing. Hence the king forbade any one to offer up any prayer during a whole month—that is, as I have said, he exacts from every one a denial of God! But Daniel could not obey the edict without committing an atrocious insult against God and declining from piety; because, as I have said, God exacts this as a principal sacrifice. Hence it is not surprising if Daniel cordially opposed the sacrilegious edict. Now, with respect to the profession of piety, it was necessary to testify before men his perseverance in the worship of God. For if he had altered his habits at all, it would have been a partial abjuration; he would not have said that he openly despised God to please Darius; but that very difference in his conduct would have been a proof of perfidious defection. We know that God requires not only faith in the heart and the inward affections, but also the witness and confession of our piety.

Daniel, therefore, was obliged to persevere in the holy practice to which he was accustomed, unless he wished to be the very foulest apostate ! He was in the habit of praying with his windows open : hence he continued in his usual course, lest any one should object that he gratified his earthly king for a moment by omitting the worship of God. I wish this doctrine was now engraven on the hearts of all men as it ought to be ; but this example of the Prophet is derided by many, not perhaps openly and glaringly, but still clearly enough, the Prophet seems to them too inconsiderate and simple, since he incurs great danger, rashly, and without any necessity. For they so separate faith from its outward confession as to suppose it can remain entire even if completely buried, and for the sake of avoiding the cross they depart a hundred times from its pure and sincere profession. We must maintain, therefore, not only the duty of offering to God the sacrifice of prayer in our hearts, but that our open profession is also required, and thus the reality of our worship of God may clearly appear.

I do not say that our hasty thoughts are to be instantly spread abroad, rendering us subject to death by the enemies of God and his gospel ; but I say these things ought to be united and never to be separated, namely, faith and its profession. For confession is of two kinds : first, the open and ingenuous testimony to our inward feelings ; and secondly, the necessary maintenance of the worship of God, lest we shew any sign of a perverse and perfidious hypocrisy, and thus reject the pursuit of piety. With regard to the first kind, it is neither always nor everywhere necessary to profess our faith ; but the second kind ought to be perpetually practised, for it can never be necessary for us to pretend either disaffection or apostasy. For although Daniel did not send for the Chaldeans by the sound of a trumpet whenever he wished to pray, yet he framed his prayers and his vows in his couch as usual, and did not pretend to be forgetful of piety when he saw his faith put to the test, and the experiments made whether or not he would persevere in his constancy. Hence he distinctly says, *he went home,* after being made acquainted with the signing of the decree. Had he been admitted to the council, he would doubtless have spoken out, but the rest of the nobles cunningly excluded him, lest he should interfere with them, and they thought the remedy would be too late, and utterly in vain as soon as he perceived the certainty of his own death. Hence, had he been admitted to the king's council, he would there have discharged his duty, and heartily interposed; but after the signing of the edict, and the loss of all opportunity for advising the king, he retired to his house.

We must here notice the impossibility of finding an excuse for the king's advisers, who purposely escape when they see that unanimity of opinion cannot be obtained, and think God will be satisfied in this way, if they only maintain perfect silence. But no excuse can be admitted for such weakness of mind. And, doubtless, Daniel is unable to defend them by his example, since, as we have already said, he was excluded by the cunning and malice of the nobles from taking his place among them as usual, and thus admonishing the king in time. He now says, *His windows were open towards Jerusalem.* The question arises, Whether it was necessary for Daniel thus to open his windows? For some one may object—he did this under a mistaken opinion; for if God fills heaven and earth, what signified his windows being open towards Jerusalem? There is no doubt that the Prophet used this device as a stimulus to his fervour in prayer. For when praying for the liberation of his people, he directed his eyes towards Jerusalem, and that sight became a stimulus to enflame his mind to greater devotion. Hence the opening of the Prophet's windows has no reference to God, as if he should be listened to more readily by having the open heaven between his dwelling and Judea; but he rather considered himself and his natural infirmity. Now, if the holy Prophet, so careful in his prayers, needed this help, we must see whether or not our sloth in these days has need of more stimulants! Let us learn, therefore, when we feel ourselves to be too sluggish and cold in prayer, to collect all the aids which can arouse our feelings and correct the torpor of which we are conscious. This, then, was the Prophet's intention *in opening his windows towards Jerusa-*

lem. Besides, he wished by this symbol to shew his domestics his perseverance, in the hope and expectation of the promised redemption. When, therefore, he prayed to God, he kept Jerusalem in sight, not that his eyes could penetrate to so distant a region, but he directed his gaze towards Jerusalem to shew himself a stranger among the Chaldeans, although he enjoyed great power among them, and was adorned with great authority, and excelled in superior dignity. Thus he wished all men to perceive how he longed for the promised inheritance, although for a time he was in exile. This was his second reason for opening his windows.

He says, *He prayed three times a-day.* This is worthy of observation, because, unless we fix certain hours in the day for prayer, it easily slips from our memory. Although, therefore, Daniel was constant in pouring forth prayers, yet he enjoined upon himself the customary rite of prostrating himself before God three times a-day. When we rise in the morning, unless we commence the day by praying to God, we shew a brutish stupidity, so also when we retire to rest, and when we take our food and at other times, as every one finds most advantageous to himself. For here God allows us liberty, but we ought all to feel our infirmities, and to apply the proper remedies. Therefore, for this reason, Daniel was in the habit of praying thrice. A proof of his fervour is also added, when he says, *He prostrated himself on his knees;* not that bending the knee is necessary in prayer, but while we need aids to devotion, as we have said, that posture is of importance. First of all, it reminds us of our inability to stand before God, unless with humility and reverence; then, our minds are better prepared for serious entreaty, and this symbol of worship is pleasing to God. Hence Daniel's expression is by no means superfluous: *He fell upon his knees whenever he wished to pray to God.* He now says, *he uttered prayers and confessions before God,* or he praised God, for we must diligently notice how many in their prayers mutter to God. For although they demand either one thing or another, yet they are carried along by an immoderate impulse, and, as I have said, they are violent in their requests unless God instantly grants their petitions.

This is the reason why Daniel joins praises or the giving of thanks with prayers; as, also, Paul exhorts us respecting both. Offer up, says he, your prayers to God, with thanksgiving, (Phil. iv. 6,) as if he had said, We cannot rightly offer vows and prayers to God unless when we bless his holy name, although he does not immediately grant our petitions. In Daniel's case we must remark another circumstance: he had been an exile for a long time, and tossed about in many troubles and changes; still he celebrates God's praises. Which of us is endued with such patience as to praise God, if afflicted with many trials through three or four years? Nay, scarcely a day passes without our passions growing warm and instigating us to rebel against God! Since Daniel, then, could persevere in praising God, when oppressed by so many sorrows, anxieties, and troubles—this was a remarkable proof of invincible patience. And, doubtless, he signifies a continuous act, by using the demonstrative pronoun דנה, deneh, which refers to his ordinary habit—as he had done before, and from former times. By noticing the time, he marks, as I have said before, a perseverance, since he was not only accustomed to pray once or twice, but by a regular constancy he exercised himself in this duty of piety every day. It afterwards follows:—

11. Then these men assembled, and found Daniel praying and making supplication before his God.

11. Tunc viri illi sociati sunt,[1] et invenerunt Danielem orantem et precantem coram Deo suo.

Here the nobles of Darius display their fraud when they observe Daniel, and unite in a conspiracy against him: for no other object but the death of Daniel could have induced them to dictate this edict. Hence they agree together, and find Daniel uttering prayers and supplications to his God. If Daniel had prayed with the slightest secrecy, he would not have been a victim to their snares; but he did not refuse the prospect of death. He knew the object of the edict, and expected the arrival of the nobles. We see, then, how willingly he submitted to instant death, and for no other purpose than to retain the pure worship of God, together with its outward profession. Go to, now, ye who desire to shield

[1] Or, "collected," as others translate.—Calvin.

your perfidy, pretending that you ought not to incur danger
rashly, and when the wicked surround you on all sides! You
become cautious lest you should rashly throw away your
lives! For Daniel, in their opinion, was to be blamed for
too great simplicity and folly, since he willingly and knowingly encountered certain danger. But we have already
said, he could not escape from their snare without indirectly
revolting from God, for he might have been immediately re-
proached—Why do you desist from your accustomed habit?
Why do you close your windows? Why do you not dare to
pray to your God? It appears, then, you regard the king
of more importance than the reverence and fear of God.
Because God's honour would have been thus sullied, Daniel,
as we have already seen, spontaneously offered himself
to death as a sacrifice. We are taught, also, by this example, how snares are prepared for the sons of God, however circumspectly they act, and however soberly they conduct themselves. But they ought to conduct themselves so
prudently as neither to be too cunning nor too anxious, that
is, they should not regard their own security so as in the
meantime to forget God's requirements, and the preciousness of his name, and the necessity of a confession of faith
in the proper place and time. It now follows:

12. Then they came near, and spake before the king concerning the king's decree; Hast thou not signed a decree, that every man that shall ask *a petition* of any god or man within thirty days, save of thee, O king, shall be cast into the den of lions? The king answered and said, The thing *is* true, according to the law of the Medes and Persians, which altereth not.	12. Tunc accesserunt et dixe-runt[1] coram rege super edicto regio, An non edictum obsignasti, ne quisquam homo peteret ab ullo deo vel homine, usque ad tri-ginta dies *hos*, præterquam abs te, rex,[2] projiceretur in speluncam leonum? Respondit rex et dixit, Firmus est sermo secundum legem Medorum et Persarum, quæ non transit.

Now the king's nobles approach the king as conquerors,
but they do so cunningly; for they do not openly say anything about Daniel, whom they knew to be a favourite with
the king; but they repeat their previous assertion concerning the impossibility of changing the edict, since the

[1] And they have said.—*Calvin.*
[2] It is preferable to translate it "that any man should ask from any
god or man, for thirty days, except of thee, O king."—*Calvin.*

law of the Medes and Persians is inviolable and cannot be rendered void.   Again, therefore, as far as they possibly can, they sanction that edict, lest the king should afterwards be free, or dare to retract what he had once commanded.   We must mark the cunning with which they indirectly circumvent the king, and entangle him, by preventing the change of a single word; *They come*, therefore, *and discourse concerning the royal edict.*   They do not mention the name of Daniel, but dwell upon the royal decree, so as to bind the king more firmly.   It follows—*The king answered, The discourse is true.*   We here see how kings desire praise for consistency, but they do not perceive the difference between consistency and obstinacy.   For kings ought to reflect upon their own decrees, to avoid the disgrace of retracting what they have hastily promulgated.   If anything has escaped them without consideration, both prudence and equity require them to correct their errors; but when they have trampled upon all regard for justice, they desire every inconsiderate command to be strictly obeyed!   This is the height of folly, and we ought not to sanction a perseverance in such obstinacy, as we have already said.   But the rest to-morrow.

PRAYER.

Grant, Almighty God, since thou hast reconciled us to thyself by the precious blood of thy Son, that we may not be our own, but devoted to thee in perfect obedience, and may consecrate ourselves entirely to thee : May we offer our bodies and souls in sacrifice, and be rather prepared to suffer a hundred deaths than to decline from thy true and sincere worship.   Grant us, especially, to exercise ourselves in prayer, to fly to thee every moment, and to commit ourselves to thy Fatherly care, that thy Spirit may govern us to the end.   Do thou defend and sustain us, until we are collected into that heavenly kingdom which thy only-begotten Son has prepared for us by his blood.— Amen.

Lecture Twenty=ninth.

WE began yesterday to explain Daniel's narrative of the calumny invented against him before King Darius. The nobles of the kingdom, as we have said, used cunning in their interview with the king; because if they had begun with Daniel, the king might have broken his word. But they dwell upon the royal decree; they shew the imminence of the danger, unless the authority of all the king's decrees was upheld. By this artifice we see how they obtained their object; for the king confirms their assertion respecting the wickedness of rendering abortive what had been promulgated in the king's name. For kings are pleased with their own greatness, and wish their own pleasure to be treated as an oracle. That edict was detestable and impious by which Darius forbade entreaties to be offered to any deity; yet he wished it to remain in force, lest his majesty should be despised by his subjects. Meanwhile, he does not perceive the consequences which must ensue. Hence we are taught by this example, that no virtue is so rare in kings as moderation, and yet none is more necessary; for the more they have in their power, the more it becomes them to be cautious lest they indulge their lusts, while they think it lawful to desire whatever pleases them. It now follows:

13. Then answered they, and said before the king, That Daniel, which *is* of the children of the captivity of Judah, regardeth not thee, O king, nor the decree that thou hast signed, but maketh his petition three times a-day.	13. Tunc loquuti sunt, et dixerunt coram rege: Daniel, qui *est* ex filiis captivitatis Jehudah, non posuit super te, rex, sensum,[1] neque ad edictum quod obsignasti: et vicibus tribus in die precatur petitionem suam.[2]

Now, when Daniel's calumniators see that King Darius had no wish to defend his cause, they open up more freely what they had previously conceded; for, as we have said, if they had openly accused Daniel, their accusation could have been instantly and completely refuted; but after this sentiment had been expressed to the king, their statement is final,

---

[1] Or, has not added his own sense, or given his mind to thee.—*Calvin.*

[2] That is, prays according to his custom, or as usual.—*Calvin.*

since by the laws of the Medes and Persians a king's decree ought to be self-acting ; hence, after this is accomplished, they then come to the person. *Daniel, say they, one of the captives of Judah, has not obeyed thy will, O king, nor the decree which thou hast signed.* By saying, " Daniel, one of the Jewish captives," they doubtless intended to magnify his crime and to render him odious. For if any Chaldean had dared to despise the king's edict, his rashness would not have been excused. But now when Daniel, who was lately a slave and a Chaldean captive, dares to despise the king's command, who reigned over Chaldea by the right of conquest, this seemed less tolerable still. The effect is the same as if they had said, "He was lately a captive among thy slaves ; thou art supreme lord, and his masters to whom he was subject are under thy yoke, because thou art their conqueror ; he is but a captive and a stranger, a mere slave, and yet he rebels against thee !" We see then how they desired to poison the king's mind against him by this allusion, *He is one of the captives !* The words are very harmless in themselves, but they endeavour to sting their monarch in every way, and to stir up his wrath against Daniel. *He does not direct his mind to thee, O king ;* that is, he does not reflect upon who you are, and thus he despises thy majesty and *the edict which thou hast signed.* This is another enlargement : *Daniel, therefore, did not direct his mind either to thee or to thy edict ;* and wilt thou bear this ? Next, they recite the deed itself—*he prays three times a-day.* This would have been the simple narrative, Daniel has not obeyed thy command in praying to his own God ; but, as I have said, they exaggerate his crime by accusing him of pride, contempt, and insolence. We see, therefore, by what artifices Daniel was oppressed by these malicious men. It now follows :

14. Then the king, when he heard *these* words, was sore displeased with himself, and set *his* heart on Daniel to deliver him ; and

14. Tunc rex, postquam sermonem audivit, valde tristatus est,[1] in se : et ad Danielem apposuit cor,[2] ad ipsum servandum : et usque ad

[1] Others translate " disturbed ;" others again, "was very much displeased" or grieved, for בְאֵשׁ, *bash*, signifies to grieve.—*Calvin.*

[2] There is a change in the letters here ; for בַל, *bel*, is put for לֵב, *leb ;* here it means, " he applied his heart."—*Calvin.*

he laboured till the going down of the sun to deliver him.

15. Then these men assembled unto the king, and said unto the king, Know, O king, that the law of the Medes and Persians is, That no decree nor statute which the king establisheth may be changed.

occasum solis fuit solicitus ad ipsum eruendum.[1]

15. Tunc conglobati sunt viri illi[2] ad regem, et dixerunt, Scias, rex, quod lex Medis et Persis *est*, ut omne edictum et statutum quod rex statuerit, non mutetur.

In the first place, Daniel recites that the king was disturbed, when he perceived the malice of his nobles which had formerly escaped him ; for their intention and their object had never occurred to him ; he perceives himself deceived and entrapped, and hence he is disturbed. Here again we are taught how cautiously kings ought to avoid depraved counsels, since they are besieged on every side by perfidious men, whose only object is to gain by their false representations, and to oppress their enemies, and those from whom they hope for booty or who may favour their evil courses. Because so many snares surround kings, they ought to be the more cautious in providing against cunning. They are too late in acknowledging themselves to have been overreached, when no remedy is left, partly through fear, and partly through wishing to consult their own credit ; and they prefer offending God to suffering any outward disrespect from men. Since, therefore, kings consider their own honour so sacred, they persevere in their evil undertakings, even when their conscience accuses them ; and even if justice itself were to appear visibly before them, yet this restraint would not be sufficient to withhold them, when ambition urges them in the opposite direction, and they are unwilling to lose the slightest portion of their reputation among men. The case of Darius supplies us with an example of this kind.

First of all, it is said, *He was sorrowful when he heard these words, and was anxious till the setting of the sun about the way of snatching Daniel from death.* He wished this to be done, if his own honour were sound and safe, and his nobles

[1] Or, to deliver him; that is, he desired to snatch him away.—*Calvin.*

[2] That is, conspired together, as if they approached the king in a body, to inspire the greater terror ; " they assembled themselves therefore."—*Calvin.*

were satisfied. But on the one side, he fears disunion if his nobles should conspire to produce disturbance ; and on the other side, he is moved by a foolish fear, because he does not wish to incur the charge of levity which awaited him, and hence he is vanquished and obeys the lusts of the wicked. Although, therefore, he laboured till the setting of the sun to free Daniel, yet that perverse shame prevailed of which I have spoken, and then the fear of dissension. For when we do not lean upon God's help, we are always compelled to vacillate, although anxious to be honestly affected. Thus Pilate wished to liberate Christ, but was terrified by the threats of the people, when they denounced against him the displeasure of Cæsar. (John xix. 12.) And no wonder, since faith is alone a certain and fixed prop on which we may lean while fearlessly discharging our duty, and thus overcome all fears. But when we want confidence, we are, as I have said, sure to be changeable. Hence Darius, through fear of a conspiracy of his nobles against himself, permitted Daniel to be an innocent sufferer from their cruelty. Then that false shame is added which I have mentioned, because he was unwilling to appear without consideration, by suddenly revoking his own edict, as it was a law with the Medes and Persians that whatever proceeded from kings was inviolable ! Daniel now states this. He says, *those men assembled together ;* when they saw the king hesitate and doubt, they became fierce and contentious with him. When it is said they meet together, this relates to their inspiring him with fear. They say, *Know, O king !* He knew it well enough, and they need not instruct him in any unknown matter, but they treat him in a threatening manner. "What ? dost thou not see how utterly the royal name will be hereafter deprived of its authority if he violates thine edict with impunity ? Will you thus permit yourself to become a laughingstock ? Finally, they intimate, that he would not be king unless he revenged the insult offered him by Daniel in neglecting his commandment. *Know,* therefore, O king, *that the Persians and Medes*—he was himself king of the Medes, but it is just as if they said, What kind of rumour will be spread through all thy subject provinces ; for thou knowest how far this pre-

vails among the Medes and Persians—the king must not
change his edict. If, therefore, thou shouldst set such an
example, will not all thy subjects instantly rise against thee?
and wilt thou not be contemptible to them?" We see, then,
how the satraps rage against their king, and frighten him
from any change of counsel. And they also join the edict
with the statute, which the king had resolved upon, with
the view of impressing upon him the necessity of not changing a single decree which he had often and repeatedly sanctioned. It follows:

16. Then the king commanded, and they brought Daniel, and cast *him* into the den of lions. *Now* the king spake, and said unto Daniel, Thy God, whom thou servest con- tinually, he will deliver thee.	16. Tunc rex loquutus est,[1] et adduxerunt Danielem, et projecerunt *eum* in foveam leonum. Respondit rex, et dixit Danieli, Deus tuus quem tu colis ipsum jugiter,[2] ipse liberabit te.[3]

The king, as we have said, frightened by the denunciation
of the nobles, condemns Daniel to death. And hence we
gather the reward which kings deserve in reference to their
pride, when they are compelled to submit with servility to
their flatterers. How was Darius deceived by the cunning
of his nobles! For he thought his authority would be
strengthened, by putting the obedience of all men to this
test of refusing all prayer to any god or man for a whole
month. He thought he should become superior to both gods
and men, if all his subjects really manifested obedience of
this kind. We now see how obstinately the nobles rise
against him, and denounce ultimate revolt, unless he obey
them. We see that when kings take too much upon themselves, how they are exposed to infamy, and become the
veriest slaves of their own servants! This is common enough
with earthly princes; those who possess their influence and
favour applaud them in all things and even adore them;
they offer every kind of flattery which can propitiate their
favour; but, meanwhile, what freedom do their idols enjoy?
They do not allow them any authority, nor any intercourse
with the best and most faithful friends, while they are

---

[1] That is, he decreed or commanded.—*Calvin.*

[2] The pronoun is superfluous.—*Calvin.*

[3] Or, if we receive it in the manner of a prayer—"may he deliver
thee"—*Calvin.*

watched by their own guards.   Lastly, if they are compared
with the wretches who are confined in the closest dungeon,
not one who is thrust down into the deepest pit, and watched
by three or four guards, is not freer than kings themselves!
But, as I have said, this is God's most just vengeance ; since,
when they cannot contain themselves in the ordinary rank
and station of men, but wish to penetrate the clouds and
become on a level with God, they necessarily become a
laughingstock.   Hence they become slaves of all their attendants, and dare not utter anything with freedom, and are
without friends, and are afraid to summon their subjects to
their presence, and to intrust either one or another with their
wishes.   Thus slaves rule the kingdoms of the world, because
kings assume superiority to mortals.   King Darius is an instance of this when he sent for Daniel, and commanded him
to be thrown into the den of lions ; his nobles force this from
him, and he unwillingly obeys them.   But we should notice
the reason.   He had lately forgotten his own mortality, he
had desired to deprive the Almighty of his sway, and as it
were to drag him down from heaven !   For if God remains
in heaven, men must pray to him ; but Darius forbade any
one from even daring to utter a prayer ; hence as far as he
could he deprived the Almighty of his power.   Now he is
compelled to obey his own subjects, although they exercise
an almost disgraceful tyranny over him.

Daniel now adds—*the king said this to him, Thy God, whom
thou servest,* or worshippest, *faithfully, he will deliver thee!*
This word may be read in the optative mood, as we have
said.   There is no doubt that Darius really wished this ;
but it may mean, Thy God whom thou worshippest will deliver thee—as if he had said, "Already I am not my own
master, I am here tossed about by the blast of a tempest ;
my nobles compel me to this deed against my will ; I, therefore, now resign thee and thy life to God, because it is not
in my power to deliver thee ;" as if this excuse lightened his
own crime by transferring to God the power of preserving
Daniel.   This reason causes some to praise the piety of King
Darius ; but as I confess his clemency and humanity to be
manifest in this speech, so it is clear that he had not a grain

of piety when he thus wished to adorn himself in the spoils of deity! For although the superstitious do not seriously fear God, yet they are restrained by some dread of him; but he here wished to reduce the whole divinity to nothing. What sort of piety was this? The clemency of Darius may therefore be praised, but his sacrilegious pride can by no means be excused. Then why did he act so humanely towards Daniel? Because he had found him a faithful servant, and the regard which rendered him merciful arose from this peculiarity. He would not have manifested the same disposition towards others. If a hundred or a thousand Jews had been dragged before his tribunal, he would carelessly have condemned them all because they had disobeyed the edict! Hence he was obstinately impious and cruel. He spared Daniel for his own private advantage, and thus embraced him with his favour; but in praising his humanity, we do not perceive any sign of piety in him. But he says, *the God whom thou worshippest, he will deliver thee*, because he had formerly known Daniel's prophecy concerning the destruction of the Chaldean monarchy; hence he is convinced, how Israel's God is conscious of all things, and rules everything by his will; yet, in the meantime, he neither worships him nor suffers others to do so; for as far as he could he had excluded God from his own rights. In thus attributing to God the power of delivering him, he does not act cordially; and hence his impiety is the more detestable, when he deprives God of his rights while he confesses him to be the true and only one endued with supreme power; and though he is but dust and ashes, yet he substitutes himself in his place! It now follows,—

17. And a stone was brought, and laid upon the mouth of the den; and the king sealed it with his own signet, and with the signet of his lords; that the purpose might not be changed concerning Daniel.

17. Ed adductus fuit lapis unus et positus super os speluncæ: et obsignavit eum rex annulo suo et annulo procerum suorum, ne mutaretur placitum in Daniele.[1]

[1] That is, "concerning Daniel." Those who render it "against," as if the king had purposely wished to oppose their violence, pervert the whole sense, since it was doubtless done at their instigation, lest the king should secretly provide for his liberation.—*Calvin*.

There is no doubt that God's counsel provided that the nobles should seal the stone with their own rings, and thus close the mouth of the cave, and render the miracle more illustrious. For when the king approached on the morrow, the rings were all entire, and the seals all unbroken. Thus the preservation of this servant of God was manifestly by the aid of heaven and not by the art of men. Hence we see how boldly the king's nobles had compelled him to perform their pleasure. For he might seem deprived of all royal power when he delivered up to them a subject dear and faithful to himself, and ordered him to be thrown into the lions' den. They are not content with this compliance of the king ; they extort another point from him—the closing up of the mouth of the cave ; and then they all seal the stone, lest any one should release Daniel. We see, then, when once liberty has been snatched away, all is over, especially when any one has become a slave by his own faults, and has attached himself to the counsels of the ungodly. For, at first, such slavery will not prevail as to induce a man to do everything which he is ordered, since he seems to be free ; but when he has given himself up to such slavery as I have described, he is compelled to transgress not once or twice, but constantly and without ceasing. For example, if any one swerves from his duty through either the fear of man or flattery, or any other depraved affection, he will grant various things, not only when asked, but when urgently compelled. But when he has once submitted to the loss of freedom, he will be compelled, as I have already said, to consent to the most shameful deeds at the nod of any one. If any teacher or pastor of the Church should turn from the right path through the influence of ambition, the author of his declension will come to him again and say, What ! do you dare to refuse me ? Did I not obtain from you, yesterday or the day before, whatever I wished ? Thus he will be compelled to transgress a second time in favour of the person to whom he has joined himself, and will also be forced to repeat the transgression continually. Thus princes also, who are not free agents through being under the tyranny of others, if they permit themselves to be overcome contrary to their conscience, lay aside all their authority, and are drawn aside in all directions by the will of their subjects. This example, then, is proposed to us in the case of King Darius, who after inflicting unjust punishment upon Daniel, adds this, *He must be enclosed in the cave,* and then, *the stone must be sealed,*—and for what object ?—*lest the doom should be changed ;* meaning, he did not dare to attempt anything in Daniel's favour. We see, then, how the king submitted to the greatest disgrace, because his nobles had no confidence in him ; they refused to trust him when he ordered Daniel to be thrown into the lions' den, but they exacted a guarantee against his liberation, and would not suffer him to attempt anything. We thus see how disgracefully they withdrew their confidence from their king ; next they use their authority against him, lest he should dare to remove the stone which had been sealed, unless he would incur the charge of falsehood by corrupting the public signatures, and of deception by falsifying the public documents. Hence this passage admonishes us against prostituting ourselves in slavery to the lust of men. Let every one serve his nearest neighbours as far as charity will allow and as custom demands. Meanwhile, no one ought to permit himself to be turned aside in different directions contrary to his conscience, because when he loses his free agency, he will be compelled to endure many affronts and to obey the foulest commands. This we see exemplified in the case of the panders to the avarice, or ambition, or cruelty of princes ; for when once they are under the power of such men, they are most miserable victims ; they cannot avoid the most extreme necessities, they become wretched slaves, and call down against themselves, a hundred times over, the anger of both God and man. It now follows,—

18. Then the king went to his palace, and passed the night fasting : neither were instruments of musick brought before him ; and his sleep went from him.

18. Tunc profectus est rex in palatium suum, et pernoctavit in jejunio, *jejunus,* et instrumenta musica[1] non fuerint allata coram ipso,[2] et somnus *etiam* discessit ab eo.

[1] Others translate "banquet" or "supper ;" but this does not agree, because he first said the king passed the night fasting, therefore a different interpretation is more suitable, namely, "musical instruments."—*Calvin.*

[2] And thus all joys and delights ceased.—*Calvin.*

Here Daniel relates the tardy repentance of the king, because although he was in the greatest grief, yet he did not correct his fault.   And this occurs to many who are not hardened by contempt of God and their own depravity; they are drawn aside by others, and are dissatisfied with their own vices, while they still indulge in them.   Would that the examples of this evil were rare in the world! but they occur everywhere before our eyes.   Darius therefore is here proposed to us as intermediate between the ungodly and the wicked—the righteous and the holy.   The wicked do not hesitate to stir up the Almighty against them, and after they have dismissed all fears and all shame, they revel in their own licentiousness.   Those who are ruled by the fear of God, although they sustain hard contests with the flesh, yet impose a check upon themselves, and bridle their perverse affections.   Others are between the two, as I have said, not yet obstinate in their malice, and not quite satisfied with their corruptions, and still they follow them as if bound to them by ropes.   Such was Darius; for he ought constantly to have repelled the calumny of his nobles; but when he saw himself so entangled by them, he ought to have opposed them manfully, and to have reproved them for so abusing their influence over him; yet he did not act thus, but rather bent before their fury.   Meanwhile he bewails in his palace, and abstains from all food and delicacies.   He thus shews his displeasure at the evil conduct at which he connived.   We see then how ineffectual it is for our own conscience to smite us when we sin, and to cause us sorrow for our faults; we must go beyond this, so that sorrow may lead us on to repentance, as also Paul teaches us.   (2 Cor. vii. 10.)   Darius, then, had reduced himself to difficulties; while he bewails his fault, he does not attempt to correct it.   This was, indeed, the beginning of repentance, but nothing more; and when he feels any compunction, this stirs him up and allows him neither peace nor comfort.   This lesson, then, we are to learn from Daniel's narrative of King Darius passing the whole of that night in wailing.   It follows afterwards,—

19. Then the king arose very early   19. Tunc rex in aurora,[1] surrexit

[1] That is, "in the morning."—*Calvin.*

in the morning, and went in haste unto the den of lions.	cum illucesceret, et in festinatione,[1] ad speluncam leonum venit.
20. And when he came to the den, he cried with a lamentable voice unto Daniel: *and* the king spake and said to Daniel, O Daniel, servant of the living God, is thy God, whom thou servest continually, able to deliver thee from the lions?	20. Et cum appropinquasset ad foveam, ad Danielem in voce tristi, *aut, lugubri,* clamavit, loquutus est rex, et dixit Danieli, Daniel serve Dei viventis, Deus tuus quem tu colis ipsum jugiter, an potuit ad servandum te a leonibus ?[2]

Here the king begins to act with a little more consistency, when he approaches the pit. He was formerly struck down by fear as to yield to his nobles, and to forget his royal dignity by delivering himself up to them as a captive. But now he neither dreads their envy nor the perverseness of their discourse. *He approaches the lions' den early in the morning,* says he,—that is, at dawn, before it was light, coming during the twilight, *and in haste.* Thus we see him suffering under the most bitter grief, which overcomes all his former fears ; for he might still have suffered from fear, through remembrance of that formidable denunciation,— Thou wilt no longer enjoy thy supreme command, unless thou dost vindicate thine edict from contempt ! But, as I have said, grief overcomes all fear. And yet we are unable to praise either his piety or his humanity ; because, though he approaches the cave and calls out, "Daniel!" with a lamentable voice, still he is not yet angry with his nobles till he sees the servant of God perfectly safe. Then his spirits revive, as we shall see ; but as yet he persists in his weakness, and is in a middle place between the perverse despisers and the hearty worshippers of God, who follow with an upright intention what they know to be just.

PRAYER.

Grant, Almighty Father, since thou shewest us, by the example of thy servant Daniel, how we ought to persevere with consistency in the sincere worship of thee, and thus proceed towards true greatness of mind, that we may truly devote ourselves to thee. May we not be turned aside in any direction through the lust of men, but may we persist in our holy calling, and so conquer all dangers, and arrive at length at the fruit of victory—that happy immortality which is laid up for us in heaven, through Christ our Lord.—Amen.

[1] That is, "hastily."—*Calvin.*   [2] That is, could he preserve thee?—*Calvin.*

Lecture Thirtieth.

WANT of time compelled me to break off our last Lecture at the point where Daniel relates how *the king approached the cave.*   Now he reports his words,—*O Daniel, servant of the living God ! thy God whom thou worshippest constantly, has he been able to deliver thee ?* says he.   Darius declares the God of Israel to be the living One.   But if there is a living God, he excludes all those imaginary deities whom men fancy for themselves by their own ingenuity.   For it is necessary that deity should be one, and this principle is acknowledged by even the profane.   However men may be deluded by their dreams, yet they all confess the impossibility of having more gods than one.   They distort, indeed, God's character, but they cannot deny his unity.   When Darius uttered this praise of the God of Israel, he confesses all other deities to be mere fictions ; but he shews how, as I have said, the profane hold the first principle, but afterwards allow it to escape entirely from their thoughts.   This passage does not prove, as some allege, the real conversion of King Darius, and his sincere adoption of true piety ; for he always worshipped his own idols, but thought it sufficient if he raised the God of Israel to the highest rank.   But, as we know, God cannot admit a companion, for he is jealous of his own glory.   (Isaiah xlii. 8.)   It was too cold, then, for Darius simply to acknowledge the God whom Daniel worshipped to be superior to all others ; because where God reigns, all idols must of necessity be reduced to nothing ; as also it is said in the Psalms, Let God reign, and let the gods of all nations fall before him.   Darius then proceeded so far as to devote himself to the true and only God, but was compelled to pay the greatest respect to Israel's God.   Meanwhile he always remained sunk in his own superstitions to which he had been accustomed.

He afterwards adds, *Thy God, whom thou worshippest continually, could he free thee from the lions ?*   He here speaks doubtfully, as unbelievers do, who seem to have some ground for hope, but no firm or sure persuasion in their own minds.

I suppose this invocation to be natural, since a certain secret instinct naturally impels men to fly to God; for although scarcely one in twenty leans upon God's word, yet all men call upon God occasionally. They wish to discover whether God desires to assist them and to aid them in their necessities; meanwhile, as I have said, there is no firm persuasion in their hearts, which was the state of the mind of King Darius: *Could God deliver thee?* says he; as if God's power could possibly be doubted! If he had said, Has God delivered thee? this would have been tolerable. For God was not bound by any law to be always snatching his people from death, since, we very well know, this rests entirely with his good pleasure. When, therefore, he permits his people to suffer under the lusts of the impious, his power is by no means diminished, since their liberation depends upon his mere will and pleasure. His power, therefore, ought by no means to be called in question. We observe, that Darius was never truly converted, and never distinctly acknowledged the true and only God, but was seized with a blind fear, which, whether he would or not, compelled him to attribute the supreme honour to Israel's God. And this was not an ingenuous confession, but was rather extorted from him. It now follows:—

21. Then said Daniel unto the king, O king, live for ever.

22. My God hath sent his angel, and hath shut the lions' mouths, that they have not hurt me: forasmuch as before him innocency was found in me; and also before thee, O king, have I done no hurt.

21. Tunc Daniel cum rege loquutus est, rex, in eternum vive.

22. Deus meus misit angelum suum, et conclusit os leonum, et non nocuerunt mihi: quoniam coram ipso innocentia,[1] inventa est in me: atque atiam coram te, rex, pravitatem non commisi.

Here Daniel answers the king moderately and softly, although he had been cast into the cave by his command. He might have deservedly been angry and expostulated with him, because he had been so impiously deserted by him, for King Darius had found him a faithful servant, and had used his services for his own advantage. When he saw himself oppressed by unjust calumnies, the king did not take his part so heartily as he ought; and at length, being overcome by the threats of his nobles, he ordered Daniel to be cast

[1] Or, integrity.—*Calvin.*

into the pit.   Daniel might, as I have said, have complained
of the king's cruelty and perfidy.   He does not do this, but
is silent concerning this injury, because his deliverance
would sufficiently magnify the glory of God.   The holy Prophet desired nothing else, except the king's welfare, which
he prays for.   Although he uses the ordinary phrase, yet he
speaks from his heart, when he says, *O king, live for ever!*
that is, may God protect thy life and bless thee perpetually.
Many salute their kings and even their friends in this way
through mere form; but there is no doubt that Daniel heartily
wished the king the enjoyment of long life and happiness.
He afterwards adds, *My God,* says he, *sent his angel, and
shut the lions' mouths!*   Thus we see that Daniel openly
assigns to angels the duty of rendering assistance, while the
whole power remains in the hands of God himself.   He says,
therefore, that he was freed by the hand and assistance of
an angel, but shews how the angel was the agent and not
the author of his safety.   *God,* therefore, says he, *sent his
angel.*   We have often seen how indistinctly the Chaldeans
spoke when mentioning the Deity; they called their deities
holy, but Daniel here ascribes the entire glory to God alone.
He does not bring forward a multitude of deities according
to the prevalent opinion among the profane.   He puts prominently forward the unity of God; and then he adds the
presence of angels as assisting God's servants, shewing how
they perform whatever is enjoined upon them.   Thus the
whole praise of their salvation remains with the one God,
since angels do not assist whomsoever they please, and are
not moved by their own will, but solely in obedience to God's
commands.

We must now notice what follows: *God had shut the lions'
mouths.*   For by these words the Prophet shews how lions
and the most cruel beasts are in the hands of God, and are
restrained by his secret curb, so that they can neither rage
nor commit any injury unless by God's permission.   We may
thus learn that savage beasts are only so far injurious to us
as God may permit them to humble our pride.   Meanwhile,
we may perceive that no beast is so cruel as to injure us by
either his claws or his teeth, unless God give him the reins.

And this instruction is worthy of especial notice, since we tremble at the least danger, even at the noise of a falling leaf. As we are necessarily exposed to many dangers on all sides, and surrounded by various forms of death, hence we should be harassed by wretched anxiety unless this principle supported us; not only is our life under God's protection, but nothing can injure us while he directs everything by his will and pleasure. And this principle ought to be extended to the devils themselves, and to impious and wicked men, for we know the devil to be always anxious to destroy us, like a roaring lion, for he prowls about seeking whom he may devour, as Peter says in his First Epistle, (v. 8.) For we see how all the impious plot for our destruction continually, and how madly they are inflamed against us. But God, who can close the lion's mouth, will also both restrain the devil and all the wicked from hurting any one without his permission. Experience also shews us how the devil and all the impious are controlled by him, for we should perish every moment unless he warded off by his opposing influence the numberless evils which ever hang over us. We ought to perceive how the singular protection of God preserves us in daily safety amidst the ferocity and madness of our foes. Daniel says he suffered no loss of any kind, *because before God his righteousness was found in him.* These words signify that his preservation arose from God wishing to vindicate his own glory and worship which he had commanded in his law. The Prophet does not here boast in his own righteousness, but rather shews how his deliverance arose from God's wishing to testify by a certain and clear proof his approval of that worship for which Daniel had contended even to death. We see, then, how Daniel refers all things to the approval of the worship of God. The conclusion is, he was the advocate of a pious and holy cause, and prepared to undergo death, not for any foolish imagination, nor by any rash impulse, nor any blind zeal, but because he was assured of his being a worshipper of the one God. His being the defender of the cause of piety and holiness was, as he asserts, the reason of his preservation. This is the correct conclusion.

Hence we readily gather the folly of the Papists who, from

this and similar passages, endeavour to establish the merit and righteousness of good works. Oh! Daniel was preserved because righteousness was found in him before God; hence God repays every man according to the merits of his works! But we must first consider Daniel's intention in the narrative before us; for, as I have said, he does not boast in his own merits, but wishes his preservation to be ascribed to the Deity as a testimony to his true and pure worship, so as to shame King Darius, and to shew all his superstitions to be impious, and especially to admonish him concerning that sacrilegious edict by which he arrogated to himself the supreme command, and, as far as he could, abolished the very existence of God. With the view, then, of admonishing Darius, the Prophet says his cause was just. And to render the solution of the difficulty more easy, we must remark the difference between eternal salvation and special deliverances. God frees us from eternal death, and adopts us into the hope of eternal life, not because he finds any righteousness in us but through his own gratuitous choice, and he perfects in us his own work without any respect to our works. With reference to our eternal salvation, our righteousness is by no means regarded, because whenever God examines us, he only finds materials for condemnation. But when we consider particular deliverances, he may then notice our righteousness, not as if it were naturally ours, but he stretches forth his hand to those whom he governs by his Spirit and urges to obey his call; and if they incur any danger in their efforts to obey his will, he delivers them. The meaning then is exactly the same as if any one should assert that God favours righteous causes, but it has nothing to do with merits. Hence the Papists trifle, like children, when they use this passage to elicit from it human merits; for Daniel wished to assert nothing but the pure worship of God, as if he had said, not only his reason proceeded from God, but there was another cause for his deliverance, namely, the wish of the Almighty to shew the world experimentally the justice of his cause.

He adds, *And even before thee,* O king, *I have committed nothing wrong.* It is clear that the Prophet had violated the king's edict. Why, then, does he not ingenuously confess this? Nay, why does he contend that he has not transgressed against the king? Because he conducted himself with fidelity in all his duties, he could free himself from every calumny by which he knew himself oppressed, as if he had despised the king's sovereignty. But Daniel was not so bound to the king of the Persians when he claimed for himself as a god what ought not to be offered to him. We know how earthly empires are constituted by God, only on the condition that he deprives himself of nothing, but shines forth alone, and all magistrates must be set in regular order, and every authority in existence must be subject to his glory. Since, therefore, Daniel could not obey the king's edict without denying God, as we have previously seen, he did not transgress against the king by constantly persevering in that exercise of piety to which he had been accustomed, and by calling on his God three times a-day. To make this the more evident, we must remember that passage of Peter, "Fear God, honour the king." (1 Pet. ii. 17.) The two commands are connected together, and cannot be separated from one another. The fear of God ought to precede, that kings may obtain their authority. For if any one begins his reverence of an earthly prince by rejecting that of God, he will act preposterously, since this is a complete perversion of the order of nature. Then let God be feared in the first place, and earthly princes will obtain their authority, if only God shines forth, as I have already said. Daniel, therefore, here defends himself with justice, since *he had not committed any crime against the king;* for he was compelled to obey the command of God, and he neglected what the king had ordered in opposition to it. For earthly princes lay aside all their power when they rise up against God, and are unworthy of being reckoned in the number of mankind. We ought rather utterly to defy than to obey them whenever they are so restive and wish to spoil God of his rights, and, as it were, to seize upon his throne and draw him down from heaven. Now, therefore, we understand the sense of this passage. It follows,—

23. Then was the king exceeding glad for him, and commanded that

23. Tunc rex valde exhilaratus in se, *vel, super eo,* Danielem jussit educi

they should take Daniel up out of the den. So Daniel was taken up out of the den, and no manner of hurt was found upon him, because he believed in his God.

ex spelunca: et eductus fuit Daniel ex spelunca: et nulla corruptio, *vel,* *læsio,* inventa fuit in eo: quia credidit, *vel, confisus est,* Deo suo.

Daniel confirms what he had formerly narrated concerning the feelings of King Darius. As he had departed in anxiety to his palace, had abstained from food and drink, and had laid aside all pleasures and delights, so also he rejoiced in hearing of the wonderful deliverance from death of God's holy servant. He afterwards adds, *And by the king's command Daniel was drawn out of the cave, and no corruption was found in him.* This cannot be ascribed to good fortune. Hence God made his power conspicuous in providing for Daniel's safety from the grasp of the lions. He would have been torn to pieces had not God closed their mouths; and this contributes in no slight degree to magnify the miracle, since no scratch or touch was found upon his body. As the lions then spared him, it arose from God's secret counsel; and he marked this more clearly, when his calumniators were thrown into the cave, and were immediately torn by the lions, as he will soon add. But we must notice the reason which is given: *He was preserved, since he trusted in his God!* It will often happen, that a person may have a good cause, and yet succeed badly and unhappily; because he adds to what is otherwise worthy of praise, too great a confidence in his own counsels, prudence, and industry. Hence it is not surprising if those who undertake good causes often fail of success, as we often see among the profane. For the history of all ages bears witness, to the perishing of those who cherish a just cause; but this arises through their perverse confidence, since they never contemplated the service of God, but rather considered their own praise and the applause of the world. Hence, as ambition seized them, they became pleased with their own plans. Thus arose that saying of Brutus, " Virtue is a frivolous thing!" because he thought himself unworthily treated in fighting for the liberty of Rome, while the gods were adverse instead of propitious. As if God ought to have conferred upon him that aid which he had never hoped and never sought. For we know the pride of that hero's disposition. I bring forward but one example; but if we diligently weigh the motives which impel the profane when they fight strenuously for good objects, we shall find ambition to be the prevailing motive. No wonder then if God deserted them in this particular, since they were unworthy of experiencing his help. For this reason Daniel states, that he was safely preserved, *because he trusted in his God.*

The Apostle refers to this in the eleventh chapter of the Epistle to the Hebrews, (verse 33,) where he says some were snatched away or preserved from the mouths of lions through faith. Hence he assigns the cause of Daniel's escaping in safety, and recalls us to faith. But we must here consider the meaning and force of the word "believing." For the Prophet does not simply speak of his deliverance as springing from believing Israel's God to be the true and only God, the Maker of heaven and earth, but from his committing his life to him, from his reposing on his grace, from his fixed determination that his end must be happy, if he worshipped him. Since, therefore, Daniel was certainly persuaded that his life was in God's hand, and that his hope in him was not in vain, he boldly incurred danger, and intrepidly suffered for the sincere worship of God ; hence he says, *he believed in God.* We see then that the word "belief" is not taken coldly, as the Papists dream, since their notion implies an unfolded or dead and shapeless faith, for they think faith nothing else but a confused apprehension of the Deity. Whenever men have any conception of God at all, the Papists think this to be faith ; but the Holy Spirit teaches us far otherwise. For we must consider the language of the Apostle,—We do not properly believe in God, unless we determine him to be a rewarder of all who diligently seek him. (Heb. xi. 6.) God is not sought by foolish arrogance, as if by our merits we could confer an obligation upon him ; but he is sought by faith, by humility, and by invocation. But when we are persuaded that God is the rewarder of all who seek him, and we know how he ought to be sought, this is true faith. So Daniel did not doubt that God would deliver him, because he did not distrust that teaching of piety which he had learnt from a boy, and through reliance on which he had always called upon God. This, therefore, was the cause of his deliverance. Meanwhile, it is clear that Daniel's trust in God did not spring from any previous instruction concerning the result; for he rather committed his life to God, since he was prepared for death. Therefore Daniel could not acknowledge this before he was cast into the cave, and exposed to the lions, being ignorant whether God would deliver him, as we previously saw in the case of his companions, "God, if he pleases, will deliver us; but if not, we are prepared to worship Him, and to disobey thy edict." If Daniel had been taught the issue beforehand, his constancy would not have deserved much praise; but since he was willing to meet death fearlessly for the worship of God, and could deny himself and renounce the world, this is a true and serious proof of his faith and constancy. *He believed therefore in God*, not because he hoped for such a miracle, but because he knew his own happiness to consist in persisting in the true worship of God. So Paul says, Christ is gain to me, both in life and in death. (Phil. i. 21.) Daniel therefore rested in the help of God, but he closed his eyes to the event, and was not remarkably anxious concerning his life, but since his mind was erected towards the hope of a better life, even if he had to die a hundred times, yet he never would have failed in his confidence, because our faith is extended beyond the boundaries of this frail and corruptible life, as all the pious know well enough. What I have already touched upon afterwards follows,—

24. And the king commanded, and they brought those men which had accused Daniel, and they cast *them* into the den of lions, them, their children, and their wives: and the lions had the mastery of them, and brake all their bones in pieces or ever they came at the bottom of the den.

24. Et jussit rex, et adduxerunt viros illos qui instruxerant[1] accusationem adversus eum, nempe Danielem; et in foveam, *speluncam*, leonum projecti sunt ipsi, liberi ipsorum, et uxores eorum, et nondum pervenerant ad fundum,[2] speluncæ, quando dominati sunt,[3] in eos leones, et omnia ossa eorum fregerunt.

By this circumstance God's virtue shone forth more clearly

---

[1] "Had enacted," "had cried out;" *qui avoyent dressè ceste calomnie.* —Calvin's own translation into French.

[2] Or, pavement.—*Calvin.*

[3] Or, prevailed.—*Calvin.*

in preserving Daniel, because those who had accused him were immediately destroyed by the lions. For if any one should say that the lions were satisfied, or there was any other reason why Daniel was not destroyed, why, when he was withdrawn, did such great madness immediately impel those beasts to tear and devour, not one man only, but a great multitude? Not one of the nobles was preserved; next their wives and children were added. Lions scarcely ever proceed to such a pitch of savageness, and yet they all perished to a man; then how did Daniel escape? We surely see how God by this comparison wished to bear witness to his own virtue, lest any one should object that Daniel was left by the lions because they were already gorged, and desired no other prey, for they would have been content with either three or four men; but they devoured men, women, and children. Hence the mouths of the lions were clearly restrained by the divine power, since Daniel was safe during a whole night, but they perished immediately, as soon as they were cast into the cave; because we again see how these beasts were impelled by sudden madness, so that they did not wait till their prey arrived at the bottom, but devoured them as they fell. We shall leave the rest till to-morrow.

PRAYER.

Grant, Almighty God, since we were created and placed in this world by thee, and are also nourished by thy bounty, for the very purpose of consecrating our life to thee,—Grant, I pray, that we may be prepared to live and die to thee. May we seek only to maintain the pure and sincere worship of thyself. May we so acquiesce in thy help as not to hesitate about breaking through all difficulties, and to offer ourselves to instant death, whenever thou requirest it. May we rely not only on thy promise, which remains for ever, but upon the many proofs which thou hast granted us of the present vitality of thy mighty power. Mayest thou be our deliverer in every sense, whether we live or die; and may we be blessed in persevering in our confidence in thy name, and thy true confession, until at length we are gathered into thy heavenly kingdom, which thou hast prepared for us by the blood of thine only-begotten Son.—Amen.

Lecture Thirty=first.

At the end of yesterday's Lecture, the enemies of Daniel who had malignantly, enviously, and cruelly slandered him, were cast into the lions' den, and were torn to pieces with their wives and children; and thus the miracle was more clearly conspicuous, as we have previously said. Here, again, we may learn how lions are governed by God's hand, and are restrained from shewing their ferocity everywhere and against every one, except when God permits them. As it is said in the ninety-first Psalm, Thou shalt walk upon the lion and the basilisk, and tread upon the lion and the dragon ; (verse 13.) So also, on the other hand, God denounces against the unbelievers by the Prophet Amos, (chap. v. 19,) The lions shall come to meet them, if they go forth from their houses. We see, then, how God restrains the cruelty of lions as often as he pleases, and how he excites them to madness when he wishes to punish mankind. With regard to their wives and children being also cast into the den, we need not dispute with any anxiety, whether or not this punishment was just. For it seems to be a sure rule of equity, that punishment should not pass on to the innocent, especially when it involves their life. In all ages, it has been the custom of well-ordered States, for many punishments to be inflicted on children as well as their parents, as in a public sale of goods, or any charge of violence or treason ; in criminal cases also, the infamy of parents extends to the children, (but this is far more severe, to slay children with their parents,) though they cannot possibly be guilty of the same crime. Yet, although this is not one of the customary cases, we must not hastily condemn it as unjust. We see how God orders whole families to be exterminated from the world as a mark of his hatred ; but, as a just Judge, he always is moderate in his severity. This example, then, cannot be precisely condemned, but we had better leave it in doubt. We are aware of the cruel and barbarous manner in which the kings of the East exercise their sway, or rather their tyranny, on their subjects. Hence there is no reason why any one should fatigue himself with the question, since King Darius was so much grieved at his being deceived. Hence he not only exacted punishment from these wicked slanderers for oppressing Daniel, but because he was himself affected by their injustice. He wished rather to avenge himself than Daniel ; he was not content with retaliation, but condemned their children also to destruction. It follows,—

25. Then king Darius wrote unto all people, nations, and languages, that dwell in all the earth; Peace be multiplied unto you.	25. Tunc Darius rex, scripsit omnibus populis, et gentibus, et linguis qui habitabant in tota terra, Pax vestra multiplicetur.
26. I make a decree, that in every dominion of my kingdom men tremble and fear before the God of Daniel; for he *is* the living God, and stedfast for ever, and his kingdom *that* which shall not be destroyed, and his dominion *shall be even* unto the end.	26. A me positum est decretum in omni dominatione,[1] regni mei, ut sint metuentes et paventes,[2] a conspectu Dei Danielis;[3] quia ipse *est* Deus vivus, et permanens in seculum : et regnum ejus non corrumpetur, et dominatio ejus[4] usque in finem.
27. He delivereth and rescueth, and he worketh signs and wonders in heaven and in earth, who hath delivered Daniel from the power of the lions.	27. Eripiens et liberans, et edens signa et miracula[5] in cœlo et in terra: qui eripuit Danielem e manu leonum.

Here Daniel adds the king's edict, which he wished to be promulgated. And by this edict he bore witness that he was so moved by the deliverance of Daniel, as to attribute the supreme glory to the God of Israel. Meanwhile, I do not think this a proof of the king's real piety, as some interpreters here extol King Darius without moderation, as if he had really repented and embraced the pure worship prescribed by the law of Moses. Nothing of this kind can be collected from the words of the edict—and this circumstance shews it—for his empire was never purged from its superstitions. King Darius still allowed his subjects to worship idols ; and he did not refrain from polluting himself with such defilements ; but he wished to place the God of Israel on the highest elevation, thus attempting to mingle fire and water ! We have previously discussed this point. For the

[1] Or, throughout the whole of the dominions.—*Calvin.*
[2] That is, that they should fear and be afraid.—*Calvin.*
[3] That is, before the God of Daniel.—*Calvin.*
[4] Or, power.—*Calvin.*
[5] " Wonders," as some translate it.—*Calvin.*

profane think they discharge their duty to the true God, if they do not openly despise him, but assign him some place or other ; and, especially, if they prefer him to all idols, they think they have satisfied God.   But this is all futile ; for unless they abolish all superstitions, God by no means obtains his right, since he allows of no equals.   Hence this passage by no means proves any true and serious piety in King Darius ; but it implies simply his being deeply moved by the miracle, and his celebrating through all the regions subject to him the name and glory of the God of Israel. Finally, as this was a special impulse on King Darius, so it did not proceed beyond a particular effect ; he acknowledged God's power and goodness on all sides ; but he seized upon that specimen which was placed directly before his eyes. Hence he did not continue to acknowledge the God of Israel by devoting himself to true and sincere piety ; but, as I have said, he wished him to be conspicuously superior to other gods, but not to be the only God.   But God rejects this modified worship ; and thus there is no reason for praising King Darius.   Meanwhile his example will condemn all those who profess themselves to be catholic or Christian kings, or defenders of the faith, since they not only bury true piety, but, as far as they possibly can, weaken the whole worship of God, and would willingly extinguish his name from the world, and thus tyrannize over the pious, and establish impious superstitions by their own cruelty.   Darius will be a fit judge for them, and the edict here recited by Daniel will be sufficient for the condemnation of them all.

He now says, *The edict was written for all people, nations, and tongues, who dwell in the whole earth.*   We see how Darius wished to make known God's power not only to the neighbouring people, but studied to promulgate it far and wide. He wrote not only for Asia and Chaldea, but also for the Medes and Persians.   He had never been the ruler of Persia, yet since his father-in-law had received him into alliance in the empire, his authority extended thither.   This is the sense of the phrase, *the whole earth.*   This does not refer to the whole habitable world, but to that monarchy which extended through almost the entire East, since the Medes and Persians then held the sway from the sea as far as Egypt. When we consider the magnitude of this empire, Daniel may well say, the edict was promulgated *through the whole earth. Peace be multiplied unto you !* We know how kings in this way soothe their subjects, and use soft persuasions for more easily accomplishing their wishes, and thus obtain the implicit obedience of their subjects. And it is gratuitous on their part to implore peace on their subjects. Meanwhile, as I have already said, they court their favour by these enticements, and thus prepare their subjects to submit to the yoke. By the term " peace," a state of prosperity is implied ; meaning, may you be prosperous and happy. He afterwards adds, *the decree is placed in their sight,* that is, they display their command before all their subjects. This, then, is the force of the phrase, *my edict has been placed ;* that is, if my authority and power prevail with you, you must thus far obey me ; *that all may fear,* or, that all may be afraid and *tremble before the God of Daniel !* By fear and terror he means simply reverence, but he speaks as the profane are accustomed to do, who abhor God's name. He seems desirous of expressing how conspicuous was the power of the God of Israel, which ought properly to impress every one, and induce all to worship with reverence, and fear, and trembling. And this method of speaking is derived from a correct principle ; since lawful worship is never offered to God but when we are humbled before him. Hence God often calls himself terrible, not because he wishes his worshippers to approach him with fear, but, as we have said, because the souls of men will never be drawn forth to reverence unless they seriously comprehend his power, and thus become afraid of his judgment. But if fear alone flourishes in men's minds, they cannot form themselves to piety, since we must consider that passage of the Psalm, " With thee is propitiation that thou mayest be feared." (Psalm cxxx. 4.) God, therefore, cannot be properly worshipped and feared, unless we are persuaded that he may be entreated ; nay, are quite sure that he is propitious to us. Yet it is necessary for fear and dread to precede the humiliation of the pride of the flesh.

This, then, is the meaning of the phrase, *that all should fear or be afraid of the God of Daniel.* The king calls him so, not because Daniel had fabricated a God for himself, but because he was his only worshipper.   We very properly speak of Jupiter as the god of the Greeks, since he was deified by their folly, and hence obtained a name and a celebrity throughout the rest of the world.   Meanwhile, Jupiter, and Minerva, and the crowd of false deities received their names from the same origin.   There is another reason why King Darius calls the God whom Daniel worshipped *Daniel's God,* as he is called the God of Abraham, not through deriving any precarious authority from Abraham, but through his manifesting himself to Abraham.   To explain this more clearly—Why is he called the God of Daniel rather than of the Babylonians ? because Daniel had learnt from the law of Moses the pure worship of God, and the covenant which he had made with Abraham and the holy fathers, and the adoption of Israel as his peculiar people.   He complied with the worship prescribed in the Law, and that worship depended on the covenant.   Hence this name is not given as if Daniel had been free to fashion or imagine any god for himself; but because he had worshipped that God who had revealed himself by his word.   Lastly, this phrase ought to be so understood as to induce all to fear that God who had made a covenant with Abraham and his posterity, and had chosen for himself a peculiar people.   He taught the method of true and lawful worship, and unfolded it in his law, so that Daniel worshipped him.   We now understand the meaning of the clause.   Thus we may learn to distinguish the true God from all the idols and fictions of men, if we desire to worship him acceptably.   For many think they worship God when they wander through whatever errors they please, and never remain attached to one true God.   But this is perverse, nay, it is nothing but a profanation of true piety to worship God so confusedly.   Hence, we must contemplate the distinction which I have pointed out, that our minds may be always included within the bounds of the word, and not wander from the true God, if indeed we desire to retain him and to follow the religion which pleases him.   We must continue, I say, within the limits of the word, and not turn away on either one side or the other; since numberless fallacies of the devil will meet us immediately, unless the word holds us in strict obedience. As far as concerns Darius, he acknowledged the one true God, but as we have already said, he did not reject that fictitious and perverse worship in which he was brought up;—such a mixture is intolerable before God!

He adds, *Because he is alive, and remains for ever !* This seems to reduce all false gods to nothing; but it has been previously said, and the circumstances prove it true, that when the profane turn their attention to the supreme God, they begin to wander directly. If they constantly acknowledged the true God, they would instantly exclude all fictitious ones; but they think it sufficient if God obtains the first rank; meanwhile they add minor deities, so that he lies hid in a crowd, although he enjoys a slight pre-eminence. Such, then, was the reasoning and the plan of Darius, because he held nothing clearly or sincerely concerning the essence of the one true God; but he thought the supreme power resident in the God of Israel, just as other nations worship their own deities! We see, then, that he did not depart from the superstitions which he had imbibed in his boyhood; and hence, we have no reason for praising his piety, unless in this particular case. But, meanwhile, God extorted a confession from him, in which he describes his nature to us. He calls him " the living God," not only because he has life in himself, but out of himself, and is also the origin and fountain of life. This epithet ought to be taken actively, for God not only lives but has life in himself; and he is also the source of life, since there is no life independent of him. He afterwards adds, *He remains for ever*, and thus distinguishes him from all creatures, in which there is no firmness nor stability. We know also how everything in heaven, as well as heaven itself, is subject to various changes. In this, therefore, God differs from everything created, since he is unchangeable and invariable. He adds, *His kingdom is not corrupted, and his dominion remains for ever.* Here he clearly expresses what he had formerly stated respecting the firmness of God's estate, since he not only remains essentially the same, but exercises his power throughout the whole world, and governs the world by his own virtue, and sustains all things. For if he had only said, " God remains for ever," we are so perverse and narrow-minded as to interpret it merely as follows :—God, indeed, is not changeable in his own essence, but our minds could not comprehend his power as universally diffused. This explanation, then, is worthy of notice, since Darius clearly expresses that God's kingdom is incorruptible and his dominion everlasting.

Secondly, he calls God his deliverer. Those who consider this edict as an illustrious example of piety, will say Darius spoke evangelically as a herald of the mercy of God. But, as we have previously said, Darius never generally embraced what Scripture teaches concerning God's cherishing his people with clemency, his helping them through his being merciful to them, and nourishing them with a father's kindness. King Darius knew nothing of this reason. Daniel's deliverance was well known ; this was a particular proof of God's favour. If Darius had only partially perceived God's lovingkindness towards his servants, then he would have acknowledged his readiness to preserve and deliver them. This would be too frigid unless the cause was added,—*God is a deliverer!* since he has deigned to choose his servants, and bears witness to his being their Father, and listens to their prayers, and pardons their transgressions. Unless, therefore, the hope of deliverance is founded on God's gratuitous adoption and pity, any acknowledgment of him will be but partial and inefficient. Darius, then, does not speak here as if truly and purely instructed in the mercy of God ; but he speaks of him only as the deliverer of his own people. He correctly asserts in general, " God is a deliverer," *since he snatched Daniel from the mouth of lions*, that is, from their power and fierceness. Darius, I say, reasons correctly, when he derives from one example the more extensive doctrine concerning the power of God to preserve and snatch away his people whenever he pleases ; meanwhile, he acknowledges God's visible power in a single act, but he does not understand the principal cause and fountain of God's affection to Daniel to be, his belonging to the sons of Abraham, and his paternal favour in preserving him. Hence this instruction should profit us and touch our minds effectually, since God is our deliverer; and, in the first place, we must confess ourselves to be admitted to favour on the condition of his pardoning us, and not treating us according to our deserts, but indulging us as sons through his amazing liberality. This then is the true sense.

He afterwards says, *he performs signs and wonders in heaven and earth !* This ought to be referred to power and dominion, as previously mentioned ; but Darius always considers the events before his eyes. He had seen Daniel dwelling safely with lions, and all the rest destroyed by them ; these were manifest proofs of God's power ; hence he properly asserts, *he performs signs and wonders.* But there is no doubt, that Darius was admonished by the other signs which had taken place before he possessed the monarchy ; he had doubtless heard what had happened to King Nebuchadnezzar, and then to King Belshazzar, whom Darius had slain when he seized his kingdom. He collects, therefore, more testimonies to God's power, for the purpose of illustrating his glory in the preservation of Daniel. In short, if Darius had renounced his superstitions, the confession of his piety would have been pure, and full, and ingenuous ; but because he did not forsake the worship of his false gods, and continued his attachment to their pollution, his piety cannot deserve our praise, and his true and serious conversion cannot be collected from his edict. This is the complete sense. It now follows :

28. So this Daniel prospered in the reign of Darius, and in the reign of Cyrus the Persian.

28. Daniel autem ipse prospere egit[1] in regno Darii et in regno Cyri Persæ.

The word צְלַח, *tzelech*, properly signifies to " pass over," and the signification is here metaphorical, in the sense of being prosperous. There is no doubt, however, of there being a silent contrast between the kingdom of the Persians and the Chaldean monarchy, that is, to speak more concisely

---

[1] Or, passed.—*Calvin.*

and clearly, between the twofold condition of Daniel. For, as we have said, he was for some time in obscurity under Nebuchadnezzar; when this monarchy was about to perish he became conspicuous ; and throughout the whole period of the reign of the Chaldeans he was obscure and contemptible. All indeed had heard of him as a remarkable and illustrious Prophet, but he was rejected from the palace. At one time he was seated at the king's gate, in great honour and respect, and then again he was cast out. During the continuance of the Chaldee monarchy, Daniel was not held in any esteem ; but under that of the Medes and Persians he prospered, and was uniformly treated with marked respect, for Cyrus and Darius were not so negligent as instantly to forget the wonderful works of God performed by his hand. Hence the word " passing through," pleases me, since, as I have said, it is a mark of the continual possession of honour ; for not only King Darius, but also Cyrus exalted him and raised him into the number of his nobles, when he heard of his favour. It is clear that he left Babylon and went elsewhere. Very probably he was not long among the Medes, for Darius or Cyaxares died without any heirs, and then his whole power passed to Cyrus alone, who was his nephew, through his sister, and his son-in-law being his daughter's husband. No doubt Daniel here commends God's favour and kindness towards himself, because this was not the usual solace of exile, to obtain the highest favour among foreign and barbarous nations, or attain the largest share of their honour and reverence. God, therefore, alleviated his sorrow by this consolation in his exile. Hence Daniel here not only regards himself in his private capacity, but also the object of his dignity. For God wished his name to be spread abroad and celebrated over all those regions through which Daniel was known, since no one could behold without remembering the power and glory of Israel's God. Daniel, therefore, wished to mark this. On the other hand also, no doubt, it was a matter of grief to him to be deprived of his country, not like the rest of mankind, but because the land of Canaan was the peculiar inheritance of God's people. When Daniel was snatched away and led off to a distance, as far as Media and Persia, without the slightest hope of return, there is no doubt that he suffered continual distress. Nor was the splendour of his station among the profane of such importance as to induce him to prefer it to that pledge of God's favour and paternal adoption in the land of Canaan. He had doubtless inscribed on his heart that passage of David's, I had rather be in the court of the Lord, than in the midst of the greatest riches of the ungodly : then, I had rather be a despised one in the house of God, than to dwell in the tents of the unrighteous." (Ps. lxxxiv. 10.) Thus Daniel had been taught. Ezekiel, too, properly includes him among the three most holy men who have lived since the beginning of the world. (xiv. 14.)[1] This was of the greatest moment ; for when he was a youth, or at least but middle aged, he was joined with Job and Noah, and was the third in rare and almost incredible sanctity ! Since this was his character, he was no doubt affected with the greatest sorrow when he perceived himself subject to perpetual exile, without the slightest hope of return, and of being able to worship God in his temple and to offer sacrifice with the rest. But lest he should be ungrateful to God, he desires to express his sense of the uncommon benevolence with which, though an exile and a stranger, and subject to reproach among other captives, he was treated and even honoured among the Medes and Persians. This, therefore, is the simple meaning of the passage. It is quite clear, as I have lately said, that Cyrus, after the death of Darius, succeeded to the whole monarchy ; and we shall afterwards see in its proper place how Daniel dwelt with Cyrus, who reigned almost thirty years longer. Thus, a long time intervened between his death and that of Darius. This, therefore, did not occur without the remarkable counsel of God, since the change in the kingdom did not influence the position of Daniel, as it usually does. For new empires we know to be like turning the world upside down. But Daniel always retained his rank, and thus God's goodness was displayed in him, and wherever he went he carried with him this testimony of God's favour. I shall not proceed further, as we shall discuss a new prophecy to-morrow.

[1] See DISSERTATION, No. xxv., at the close of this Volume.

PRAYER.

Grant, Almighty God, since by means of a man entangled in many
errors, thou wishest to testify to us the extent of thy power, that
we may not at this day grope about in darkness, while thou
offerest us light, through the Sun of righteousness, Jesus Christ,
thy Son.   Meanwhile, may we not be ashamed to profit by the
words of a heathen, who was not instructed in thy law, but who
celebrated thy name so magnificently when admonished by a
single miracle : hence may we learn by his example to acknowledge thee, not only the Supreme but the Only God.   As thou
hast bound us to thyself by entering into a covenant with us in
the blood of thine only-begotten Son, may we ever cleave to thee
with true faith; may we renounce all the clouds of error, and be
always intent upon that light to which thou invitest us, and towards which thou drawest us ; until we arrive at the sight of thy
glory and majesty, and being conformed to thee, may we at length
enjoy in reality that glory which we now but partially behold.—
Amen.

END OF VOLUME I

A COMMENTARY ON
DANIEL

VOLUME II

TABLE OF CONTENTS

Volume II

THE PRAYER

WHICH JOHN CALVIN WAS ACCUSTOMED TO USE AT THE
COMMENCEMENT OF HIS LECTURES.

GRANT unto us, O LORD, to be occupied in the mysteries
of thy Heavenly wisdom, with true progress in piety,
to thy glory and our own edification.—AMEN.

⁎ This prayer is not inserted in the Geneva edition of 1617, but is
found in that of 1571. The FRENCH TRANSLATION renders it as follows:—
" May the Lord grant us grace so to treat the secrets of His celestial
wisdom, that we may truly profit in the fear of His holy name, to His
glory and to our edification.—Amen."

COMMENTARIES

ON

THE PROPHET DANIEL

Lecture Thirty=Second.

CHAPTER SEVENTH.

1. In the first year of Belshazzar king of Babylon, Daniel had a dream, and visions of his head upon his bed: then he wrote the dream, *and* told the sum of the matters.	1. Anno primo Beltsazar Regis Babylonis, Daniel somnium vidit, et visiones capitis ejus in lecto ejus. Tunc somnium scripsit, summam sermonum exposuit.
2. Daniel spake, and said, I saw in my vision by night, and, behold, the four winds of the heaven strove upon the great sea.	2. Loquutus est Daniel, et exposuit: Vidi in visione mea per noctem, et ecce quatuor venti cœlorum pugnantes,[1] in mari magno.

HERE Daniel begins to offer instruction peculiar to the Church. For God had formerly appointed him an interpreter and instructor to profane kings. But he now appoints him a teacher to the Church, that he may exercise his office within it, and instruct the sons of God in the bosom of the Church. We must notice this first of all, because thus far his predictions extended beyond the limits of the household of faith, but here Daniel's duty is restricted to the Church. He says: *This vision was bestowed upon him in the first year of King Belshazzar*, before that change happened, which we have previously seen. First of all, we must try to understand the design of the Holy Spirit; that is, the end and use for which he opened up to Daniel the material of this chapter. All the prophets had held out to the elect people the hope of deliverance, after God had punished them for

---

[1] Some translate " rising out of."—*Calvin.*

their ingratitude and obstinacy. When we read what other prophets announce concerning their future redemption, we should suppose the Church to have been promised a happy, quiet, and completely peaceful state, after the people had returned from captivity. But history testifies how very differently it turned out. For the faithful must have grown weary and have fallen away unless they had been admonished of the various disturbances which were at hand. This, then, is the first reason why God revealed to his Prophet what we shall soon see; namely, that three monarchies yet remained, each of which should succeed the former, and that during them all the faithful should endure permanently and constantly in reliance on the promises, although they should see the whole world shaken, and severe and distressing convulsions prevailing everywhere. For this reason, Daniel's vision concerning the four empires is here set forth. Perhaps it will be better to defer the summary of it till the Prophet begins to treat of each beast separately. But with regard to the two first verses, we must observe the time of the dream.

Before the Medes and Persians transferred the Chaldean empire to themselves, the Prophet was instructed in this subject, that the Jews might recognise the partial fulfilment of what God had so often promised themselves and their fathers. For if their enemies had possessed Babylon without any new prediction, the Jews perhaps would not have been so attentive to those prophecies which had been long ago uttered in their favour. Hence God wished to refresh their memories, and then, when they saw the fall of that empire which all thought to be impregnable, they would perceive the government of God's secret counsels, and the partial, if not the complete fulfilment of what he had testified by their prophets. He says—*he saw a dream.* When he previously spoke of the dream of King Nebuchadnezzar he mentioned a vision, but not for the same reason, because the unbelieving when seeing do not observe. They perceive something indeed, dimly and without distinctness, while their thoughts immediately fade away. The Prophet's method was different; because he not only dreamed, but saw a distinct vision, and thus could profitably deliver to others what he had received. The Prophet then expresses something peculiar by this phrase, for we know how prophets usually attribute such visions to God, when they perceive the secrets of heaven, not with the eyes of flesh, but by the illumination and intelligence of the Spirit. He adds—*visions of his head were on his bed;* thus the dream would have more weight, and lest we should think any confusion existed in Daniel's brain. Thus he expresses how he saw whatever the Lord wished him to know in a dream with a calm mind. He afterwards adds—*Then he wrote the dream, and explained the meaning of the words.* By this phrase he teaches us how his seeing the vision was not for his own sake personally, but for the common edification of the Church. Those who suppose Daniel to have leapt suddenly from his bed, lest he should forget the dream, offer a vain and frivolous comment. Daniel rather wished to bear witness to this vision as not peculiar to himself, but common to God's elect people; and hence not only to be celebrated orally, but to be delivered to posterity for a perpetual remembrance. We must bear in mind these two points; first, Daniel wrote this prophecy that the knowledge of it might ever be celebrated among the faithful; and then, he considered the interests of posterity, and so left the vision written. Both these points are worthy of notice to induce us to pay greater attention to the vision, since it was not delivered for a single individual; but God chose Daniel as his minister, and as the herald and witness of this oracle. Hence we see how it concerns us; it was not teaching for any single age, but it extends to us, and ought to flourish till the end of the world. He repeats the same thing by adding—*he explained the sense of the words.* For those who separate these two clauses, seem to stumble on plain ground.[1] *Daniel* then *spoke* and *said*—This has no reference to words, but to writing; as if the Prophet had said, I have discharged my duty; since he knew that what we shall afterwards see concerning the four monarchies was

---

[1] The phrase in the Latin text is a proverb: *nodum quærere in scyrpo.* The French is correct in its interpretation: *chercher de la difficulté où il n'y en a point.* Both Ennius and Terence use the proverb.— *Ed.*

not divinely entrusted to him for the sake of suppressing anything made known, but he rather felt himself a chosen instrument of God, who was thus suggesting to the faithful material for trust and endurance. *He spoke*, therefore, and *explained;* that is, when he desired to promulgate this oracle, he bore witness to there being no difference between himself and God's Church in this announcement; but as he had been an elect and ordained teacher, so he delivered what he had received, through his hands. Hence Daniel not only commends his own faith, but excites all the pious to anxiety and attention, lest they should despise what God had pronounced through his mouth.

He repeats again, *He saw in his vision during the night.* Again, I say, Daniel affirms that he brought forward nothing but what God had authoritatively delivered to him. For we know that in the Church all human traditions ought to be treated as worthless, since all men's wisdom is vanity and lies. As God alone deserves to be listened to by the faithful, so Daniel here asserts that he offers nothing of his own by dreaming in the ordinary way, but that the vision is sure, and such as cannot deceive the pious.

He afterwards adds, *Behold! the four winds of heaven fought in a great sea.* I much prefer this rendering. Interpreters differ respecting the winds, but the genuine sense appears to me to be this; Daniel assumes a simile universally known, for on solid ground any such turbulent concussion is seldom heard of as at sea, when any mighty tempest arises. Without doubt, he here proposes the image of a raging sea to warn the faithful against dreadful commotions at hand, just as if the sea were agitated with storms and raging with tempests on all sides. This is the meaning of the phrase. Hence he names *four winds*, to shew the faithful how the motion which should shatter the globe should not be single and simple, but that various storms should arise together on all sides—exactly as it happens. We may sometimes see the earth moved just as if a tempest were tossing about the sea in all directions, but the motion will yet be single. But God wished to shew his Prophet not only a simple concussion, but many and different ones, just as if all the winds were to meet in one general conflict.   Philosophers, indeed, enumerate more winds than four when they desire to treat of the number with precision, but it is the common phrase to speak of four winds blowing from the four quarters or regions of the globe.   The sense, however, is clear and by no means forced—the world being like a troubled sea, not agitated by a single storm or wind, but by different conflicting blasts, as if the whole heavens conspired to stir up commotions.   This vision at the first glance was very bitter to the faithful, because they counted the years prescribed to them by Jeremiah; the seventieth year was now at hand, and God had then promised them an end of their troubles.   Now God announces that they must not indulge in the hope of rest and joy, but rather prepare themselves for sustaining the rush of the fiercest winds, as the world would be everywhere agitated by different storms. They might perhaps suspect God of not performing his promises, but this ought to be sufficient for appeasing their minds and propping them up with the hope of redemption, when they saw nothing happen either rashly or by chance. Again God came to meet their temptations lest their courage should fail, by teaching them that the method of their redemption was not quite so easy as they had previously conceived from former predictions.   God indeed had not changed his plans, for although a long period had elapsed since he spoke by Isaiah and the other prophets, yet he wished to prepare the Jews against delay, lest it should break down the courage which would be required to meet such great afflictions.   But when redemption really approached, then God explained its method more fully and familiarly, and shewed how great and severe were the remaining struggles.   Hence the faithful, instructed by such prophecies, would contend strenuously and yet proceed constantly in their course of faith and patience. It now follows,—

3. And four great beasts came up from the sea, diverse one from another.

3. Et quatuor bestiæ magnæ prodibant e mari, diversæ hæc ab illa.[1]

After Daniel had beheld these great commotions which

[1] That is, differing among themselves.—*Calvin.*

were shaking the earth in different parts, another vision was offered to him. What has already been said concerning the troubled sea and the conflict of the winds, is extended to the four monarchies, concerning which we shall now treat. A certain preparation is intended when God offers to the eyes of his Prophet a turbulent sea produced by the conflict of the winds. Just as if he should say—after these troubles others shall spring up; thus men will wait for peace and tranquillity in vain, for they must suffer under fresh agitations. Now, the kind of trouble is expressed, by the words, *four beasts proceed out of the sea.* Hence that concussion, those storms, and that confused disturbance of the whole world through one kingdom succeeding to another. It can scarcely happen that any kingdom can perish without involving others in its ruin. A single edifice can scarcely fall without the crash being heard far and wide, and the earth seeming to gape at its overthrow. Then, what must happen when the most powerful monarchies so suddenly perish? Hence in this verse Daniel shews how the world is like a troubled sea, since violent changes among its empires were then at hand. The comparison of empires to beasts is easily explained. We know how God's glory and power are resplendent in all kingdoms, if they are rightly conducted after the law of equity. But since we often see the truth of what was said to Alexander,—The greatest kingdoms are the greatest robberies, and very few absorb the whole power in a great empire, and exercise a cruel and excessive tyranny. Here the Prophet compares empires to great and savage beasts, of which he will afterwards treat. Now we understand the meaning of the words: and we may learn this lesson from what usually happens in the empires of the world; in themselves, as I have said, they are most beautiful reflections of the divine wisdom, virtue, and justice, although those who obtain supreme sway very rarely acknowledge themselves divinely created for the discharge of their office. As, therefore, kings are mostly tyrants, full of cruelty and barbarity, and forgetful of humanity, the Prophet marks this vice as springing from themselves and not from the sacred ordinance of God. Let us proceed,—

4. The first *was* like a lion, and had eagle's wings: I beheld till the wings thereof were plucked, and it was lifted up from the earth, and made stand upon the feet as a man, and a man's heart was given to it.

4. Prima sicut leo,[1] et alæ aquilæ ei: vidi donec evulsæ sunt alæ ejus, et sublata fuit e terra, et super pedes *suos* quasi homo stetit, et cor hominis datum est ei.

It is clear that the four monarchies are here depicted. But it is not agreed upon among all writers which monarchy is the last, and which the third. With regard to the first, all agree in understanding the vision of the Chaldean Empire, which was joined with the Assyrian, as we saw before. For Nineveh was absorbed by the Chaldeans and Babylonians; but the Prophet discourses at length of the Assyrian and Chaldean Empire, which was then flourishing. No one, however, would have thought it so near its end; and on the very night on which Belshazzar was slain, we saw how securely and proudly he was immersed in his pleasures, and what great and listless security existed throughout the city. This monarchy then ought to be set before us in the first place. As in the second chapter that empire was called the golden head of the statue, so also it is now called a lion; that is, it is compared to a generous animal. It is comprehended under the image of a beast, and its fierceness and atrocity, as I have said, is hereby denoted; but with respect to the other kingdom, some superiority is granted to it, since the world is always growing worse and worse. And although Cyrus was a very prudent prince, yet he did not reach the temperance of former ages; for his ambition, avarice, and cruelty were insatiable. For Isaiah also, when he speaks of the Persians, says, They desire neither silver nor gold, but thirst after human blood. (Chap. xiii. 17.)

We perceive then the reason why the Prophet says, *The first beast offered to me was like a lion*, because greater integrity flourished under the Chaldeans than when all the empires were mixed together, and the Persians subdued both the Chaldeans and the Medes. For it is evident from all histories that they were a barbarous and fierce nation. They were indeed showy in their praise of virtue, since they spent their lives in austerity, and despised all luxuries,

---

[1] The first beast like a lion.—*Calvin.*

and were exceedingly temperate in their living; but their ferocity and brutal cruelty rendered them detestable. *The first beast* then *was like a lion,* says he, *and had eagle's wings;* that is, although it was a lion, yet it had wings. This refers to its swiftness, since we know in how short a time the Assyrians increased their monarchy, for they had previously subdued the Chaldeans, just like a lion for swiftness. For a lion has force, spirit, and cruelty for committing injuries. Besides, the Prophet saw a winged lion, since they not only increased their empire by their own strength, but suddenly extended their wings in every direction. We see, then, how strength and power are denoted on the one hand, and the greatest speed on the other. He afterwards adds, *Their wings were dragged or torn off.* For when the Chaldeans desired to stretch beyond their bounds, the Lord restrained them within due limits, and checked their continual victories. Their wings were then torn off, when God restrained them by the check of a bridle, lest they should wander as freely as they had formerly done.

The Prophet then adds, *This beast was raised from the earth,* implying the cessation of the empire. For neither the Chaldeans nor the Assyrians were entirely destroyed; but their glory was completely taken away. The face of the beast no longer appeared, when God transferred that monarchy to the Medes and Persians. Hence the Prophet adds, *It stood upon its feet, and the heart of a man was given to it.* By this form of expression, he means to imply the reduction of the Assyrians and Chaldeans to their ordinary condition, and that they were no longer like a lion, but like private men deprived of their power and strength. Hence the expression, *a man's heart was given to them,* is not intended by way of praise, but by "a man" he intends any private person; as if he had said, the aspect of the Chaldeans and Assyrians was no longer terrible, since, while their sway prevailed, all men dreaded their power. Hence God removed from the world the face of that beast, and substituted that of a man, and made them stand upon their feet. Formerly they flew about in the air, and despised the earth as far beneath their feet, but God makes them *stand upon*

their feet ; that is, not conduct themselves after their customary and former manner, but simply on the common level,
after God had deprived them of their empire. This, in my
judgment, is the simple meaning of the Prophet. Should
there be any necessity, we shall afterwards confirm the
remarks which we now run through but cursorily. It follows :—

5. And behold another beast, a second, like to a bear, and it raised up itself on one side, and *it had* three ribs in the mouth of it be-tween the teeth of it : and they said thus unto it, Arise, devour much flesh.	5. Et ecce bellua, *bestia*, poste-rior altera¹ similis urso (*inquit*) et surrexit ad latus unum : et tres costæ in ore ejus inter dentes ejus : et sic dicebant ei,² Surge, comede carnem multam.

Here the Prophet proclaims how he was instructed by a
dream concerning the second beast. If we will only judge
by the event, this beast doubtless represented the kingdom
of the Medes and Persians, although the Prophet specifies
the Persians, as the Medes had long ago submitted to their
yoke. *Behold*, says he, *another beast like a bear.* We know
a bear to be a mean and foul animal, slothful and inert, as
well as cruel. In comparing the bear with the lion, its appearance is foul and displeasing, while the lion is remarkable
for beauty, although it is formidable. He compares the
Persians to a bear, on account of their barbarity, since we
have already pronounced that nation fierce and savage.
Then, again, the Persians were not civilized like the Assyrians
and Chaldeans, who dwelt in the most beautiful region in
the whole world, and in a most lovely country like a most
noble theatre ; but the Persians lay hid like wild beasts in
their caves. They dwelt among their mountains, and lived
like the brutes. Hence the Prophet compares them very
appositely to a bear ; nay, God shewed this form to his
Prophet. He afterwards adds, *It stood on one side.* Some
think this to have been added to express the more contracted
dominion of the Medes and Persians, but this opinion is unsuitable. We know how extensive was the sway of the
Medes before they came under the power of Cyrus and the

¹ That is, the second beast followed the first.—*Calvin.*
² That is, " Thus it was said to it ;" for this word is taken indefinitely.
—*Calvin.*

Persians. By themselves the Medes were most powerful; then the Persians were added, and afterwards Cyrus seized upon the possessions of the Chaldean monarchy. He possessed even the keys of Egypt, reigned in Syria, held Judea, and extended beyond the sea, till at length he was conquered by the Scythians. When, therefore, it is said, *he stood on one side*, the obscure origin of his kingdom is intended, for the fame of the Persians was included within their mountains until Cyrus acquired for them a name by his exploits. For he was a brave warrior, and deservedly eclipsed the glory of all others. Hence, at first *this beast stood on one side;* that is, the Persians were without fame or reputation; they had no wealth, and never emerged from their lurking-places. We see how this particular is restricted to their origin in consequence of its obscurity.

The Prophet then adds: *Three ribs were in the beast's mouth between its teeth ; and it was thus proclaimed, Arise, eat much flesh !* Those who understand three definite kingdoms by the three ribs, seem to refine far too minutely. I think the number indefinite, because this beast had bitten by its mouth not one rib but more; because the Persians, as we have said, drew to themselves the power of the Medes, and afterwards subdued the Assyrians and Chaldeans, and Cyrus also subdued many nations, until all Asia Minor acknowledged his authority. When, therefore, the Prophet speaks of three ribs, it implies the insatiable nature of this beast, since it was not content with a single body, but devoured many men together. For, by "many ribs," he means much prey. This is the whole sense. I do not hesitate to explain the following words, *it was said to the beast,* of angels, or of God himself. Some prefer to understand this of the stimulus by which Cyrus was instigated to cruelty. But since God exhibits to his Prophet the image of his Providence, what I have lately suggested becomes very probable, namely, *it was said to the beast, Arise, eat much flesh;* not because God was the author of cruelty, but since He governs by His secret counsel the events which men carry on without method, His authority is here deservedly placed before our eyes; for Cyrus would not have penetrated so swiftly into different regions, and have drawn to himself so many empires, and subjugated so many powerful nations, had not God wished to punish the world, and had made Cyrus the instrument of slaughter.   As therefore Cyrus executed God's vengeance by shedding so much human blood, the Prophet declares it to have been said to him, *Arise, and eat flesh.* In one respect God was not pleased by the slaughter of so many nations by Cyrus, and by the increase of one man's power and tyranny through so much human bloodshed ; but in another respect God is said to have commanded the conduct of Cyrus, since he wished to punish the world for its ingratitude, to which the most desperate obstinacy and rebellion were added.   There was no remedy for these vices ; hence God entrusted Cyrus with the duty of executing His judgment.   I am compelled to stop here.

PRAYER.

Grant, Almighty God, since thou exposest us to various distresses in this world, for the purpose of exercising our faith and patience: Grant, I say, that we may remain tranquil in our station, through reliance on thy promises.   When storms gather around us on all sides, may we never fall away and never despond in our courage, but persevere in our calling.   Whatever may happen, may we recognise thee as carrying on the government of the world, not only to punish the ingratitude of the reprobate, but to retain thine own people in thy faith and protection, and preserve them to the end.   May we bear patiently whatever changes may happen to us, and may we never be disturbed or distressed in our minds, till at length we are gathered into that happy rest, where we shall be free from all warfare and all contests, and enjoy that eternal blessedness which thou hast prepared for us in thine only begotten Son.—Amen.

Lecture Thirty-Third.

6. After this I beheld, and lo another, like a leopard, which had upon the back of it four wings of a fowl: the beast had also four heads ; and dominion was given to it.

6. Post hoc vidi,[1] et ecce alia, *bestia scilicet*, sicut pardus, *similis pardo*, et alæ quatuor avis super dorsum ejus, et quatuor capita bestiæ : et potestas data est ei.

DANIEL has already spoken of two empires, namely, the

---

[1] That is, a vision was offered to me.—*Calvin*

Chaldean and Persian. Interpreters agree in the necessity for referring this vision to the Macedonian Empire. He compares this kingdom to a leopard, or, as some translate, a panther, since Alexander obtained his great power through swiftness alone ; and although it is not by any means a striking animal, yet it managed by its remarkable speed to subdue the whole East. Others bring forward many points of likeness, in which the Grecian character is in accordance with the nature of the leopard. But I fear these *minutiœ* have but little weight : it is sufficient for me that the Spirit treats here of the third empire. It was not of any importance at first, and could neither terrify distant regions, nor acquire subjects by its own worthiness. It then became like some swift animal, if I may say so, since the swiftness of Alexander is notorious ; but he did not excel in either prudence, or gravity, or judgment, or in any other virtues. Mere rashness seized upon him ; and even if he had never tasted wine, his ambition would have intoxicated him. Hence Alexander's whole life was drunken ; there was neither moderation nor composure in him. We see, then, how suitably this answers to the character of Alexander, although this is also extended to his successors, all of whom partook largely of the nature of their prince. Daniel says, therefore, *A beast appeared to him like a leopard.*

He also says, *It had four wings on its back, and four heads.* Some persons, as I think perversely, distinguish between the wings and the heads. They suppose the kingdom to be depicted as winged because Alexander seized upon many kingdoms in a short period ; but the more simple sense is, this beast had four wings and four heads, because Alexander had scarcely completed his victories when he died, contrary to all expectation ; and after his death, every one seized a portion of the prey for himself. This, however, is certain : after the chief generals of his army had contended for many years, all histories agree in stating that the supreme power centred in four. For Seleucus obtained Asia Major, and Antigonus Asia Minor, Cassander was king of Macedon, and was succeeded by Antipater, while Ptolemy the son of Lagus became the ruler of Egypt. They had agreed indeed otherwise among themselves; for Alexander had a son by Roxana, the daughter of Darius; he had a brother, Aridæus, who grew up to manhood, but was epileptic and of weak intellect. Then, since the generals of Alexander were cunning, they acted on this pretext, that all should swear allegiance to their young ward, and then to Aridæus, in case their ward should die before he was of age.[1] Then Lysimachus was set over the treasury, and another commanded the forces, and others obtained various provinces. Fifteen or twenty leaders divided among themselves both offices and power, while no one dared to assume the name of king. For Alexander's son was the lawful king, and his successor was that Aridæus of whom I have spoken. But they soon afterwards united; and that was an admirable specimen of God's Providence, which alone is sufficient to prove that passage of Scripture: He who sheds man's blood, by man shall his blood be shed. (Gen. ix. 6.) For none of Alexander's generals escaped in safety except those four whom we have mentioned. His mother, at the age of eighty, suffered a violent death; his wife, Roxana, was strangled; his son perished miserably; Aridæus, his brother, a man of no intellect, and almost on a level with the brutes, was slain with the rest—in truth, the whole family of Alexander suffered violent deaths. With respect to the generals, they perished in battles, some of them being betrayed by their soldiers, and others the victims of their own negligence; and yet, although they expected a sanguinary end, they did not escape it. But four only survived, and so the whole empire of Alexander was divided into four parts. For Seleucus, whose successor was Antiochus, obtained Upper Asia, that is, the eastern empire; Antigonus, Asia Minor, with a part of Cilicia, and Phrygia, and other neighbouring regions; Ptolemy seized upon Egypt and a part of Africa; Cassander and then Antipater were kings of Macedon. By *four wings* and *four heads*, Daniel means that partition which was made immediately after the death of Alexander. Now, therefore,

---

[1] The Latin text in the Geneva edition of 1617 has "*populi*" where it ought to be "*pupilli*." That of 1569 is correct in reading "*pupilli*." —*Ed.*

we understand what God shewed to his Prophet under this vision, when he set before him the image of a leopard with four wings and heads.

He says, *Power was given to the beast,* because the success of Alexander the Great was incredible. For who would have thought, when he was crossing the sea, that he would have conquered all Asia and the East? He led with him 30,000 men, and did not undertake the war on his own responsibility alone, but by various arts, he procured the nomination to the leadership of Greece from the Free States. Alexander was, therefore, a kind of mercenary of the Greeks, and was unable to lead with him more than 30,000 men, as we have said. He engaged in battle with 150,000, then with 400,000, and then with almost a myriad. For Darius in his last battle had collected above 800,000 men besides camp-followers, so that there were almost a million with him. Alexander had already drawn to himself some auxiliaries from the foreign nations whom he had conquered; but he could not trust them : hence his whole strength lay in these 30,000, and on the day on which he conquered Darius, he was so overcome by sleep that he could scarcely be aroused. The historians who extol his prudence, excuse this by recording his sleeplessness during the preceding night ; besides, all agree in stating him to have been apparently dead, and when all his generals approached they could scarcely wake him up, and then they purposely raised a shout around his tent, though no one dared to enter. Alexander had scarcely wiped his eyes, when Darius fled ; hence the Prophet's statement is true—*a beast's power was given to him,* since this happened beyond every natural expectation and every human opinion, as by his aspect alone he could frighten all Greece, and lay prostrate so large an army. He states this of the Third Empire. I will not repeat here all that can be said and can be gathered from history ; for many things must be put off till the eleventh chapter. I will therefore briefly compress whatever points seem necessary for the interpretation of the passage. It now follows,—

7. After this I saw in the night-visions, and behold a fourth beast, dreadful and terrible, and strong exceedingly; and it had great iron teeth: it devoured and brake in pieces, and stamped the residue with the feet of it: and it *was* diverse from all the beasts that *were* before it; and it had ten horns.

7. Postea, *post hoc*, vidi, *hoc est, videbam*, in visionibus noctis; et ecce bestia quarta formidabilis, et metuenda,[1] et fortis valde: et dentes ferri, *hoc est, ferrei*, illi magni: comedens et conterens, et reliquum pedibus conculcans: et ipsa diversa *erat* ab omnibus bestiis prioribus, et cornua decem illi.

There is greater difficulty in this Fourth Monarchy. Those who are endued with moderate judgment, confess this vision to be fulfilled in the Roman Empire; but they afterwards disagree, since what is here said of the fourth beast many transfer to the Pope, when it is added a Little Horn sprang up; but others think the Turkish kingdom is comprehended under the Roman. The Jews for the most part incline this way, and they are necessarily compelled to do so, since Daniel will afterwards add—I saw the throne of the Son of Man; since it is clear, from this prediction, that Christ's kingdom was erected by the overthrow of the Roman dominion, the Jews turn round, and, as I have said, join the Turkish monarchy with the Roman, since they do not find their Christ according to their imagination. And there are some of our writers who think this image ought not to be restricted to the Roman Empire, but ought to include the Turkish. In my view, there is nothing probable in that opinion; I have no doubt that in this vision the Prophet was shewn the figure of the Roman Empire, and this will be more apparent as we go on.

He says *a fourth beast appeared.* He gives it no fixed name, because nothing ever existed like it in the world. The Prophet, by adding no similitude, signifies how horrible the monster was, for he formerly compared the Chaldean Empire to a lion, the Persian to a bear, and the Macedonian to a leopard. In these comparisons there was something natural; but when he descends to the fourth beast, he says, it was *formidable in its aspect, and terrible, and very brave* or strong, and without any addition calls it "a beast." We see then his wish to express something prodigious by this fourth beast, as there is no animal so fierce or cruel in the

[1] That is, which can strike terror.—*Calvin.*

world which can in any way represent with sufficient strength the nature of this beast. *Behold,* therefore, *the fourth beast which was formidable, and fearful, and very strong.* We know of no such Monarchy before this. Although Alexander subdued the whole of the East, his victory, we are sure, was not stable. He was content with fame alone ; he granted liberty to all people ; and as long as they flattered him, he sought nothing else. But we know the Romans to have been masters even as far as Babylon ; we know the following countries to have been subdued by them : Asia Minor, Syria, Cilicia, Greece, and Macedon, both the Spains, Gaul, Illyricum, and part of Germany. At length Britain was subjugated by Julius Cæsar. No wonder this beast is called formidable and very strong ! For before Julius Cæsar became master of the Empire, the whole Mediterranean Sea was in all its parts under subjection to the Roman Empire. Its amazing extent is well known. Egypt had indeed its own kings, but they were tributary ; whatever edicts the Romans decreed, they were executed immediately in Egypt. Minor sovereigns existed in Asia Minor as a kind of spies, but this state of things we shall treat presently. It is also well known that they possessed supreme power throughout the Mediterranean Sea, and that by the conquest of Mithridates. Pompey reduced Pontus under his dominion. In the East affairs were all at peace. The Medes and Persians gave them some trouble, but they never moved unless they were provoked. The Spains were not yet accustomed to the yoke, but we know that there were always two prætors there. Julius Cæsar was the first who entered Britain after subduing Gaul. Hence we see how far and wide the Romans extended their power, and with what immense cruelty. Hence Daniel calls this beast *formidable and very strong.*

He afterwards adds, *It had large iron teeth.* This ought to be referred to its audacity and insatiable greediness. We see how completely free their nation was from the fear of death, for they were so hardened that if any one deserted his rank for the sake of avoiding danger, he was afterwards branded with such marks of infamy, that he was compelled either to strangle himself or to incur a voluntary death! There was, then, a certain brutal cruelty in that nation, and we also know how insatiable they were. For this reason Daniel says *they had large iron teeth.* He adds, *it consumed, and broke to pieces, and trod the remnant under foot.* These things are spoken allegorically, not only because this vision was offered to the holy Prophet, but also because God wished to paint a kind of living image, in which he might shew the peculiar characters of each government. For we know how many lands the Romans had consumed, and how they transferred to themselves the luxuries of the whole world, and whatever was valuable and precious in Asia Minor, and Greece, and Macedonia, as well as in all islands and in Asia Major—all was swept away—and even this was insufficient to satisfy them! This, then, is the ravenousness of which the Prophet now speaks, *since they consumed,* says he, *and rubbed to pieces with their teeth.* He adds, *they trod the remnant under their feet*—a metaphor worthy of notice, as we know they were accustomed to distribute the prey which they could not carry with them. They devoured and tore with their teeth the treasures and costly furniture and everything else; for their supplies were provided by tributes which produced large sums of money. If there was any portion of the Mediterranean which they could not defend without keeping a permanent garrison there, we know how they engaged the services of tributary kings. Thus the kingdom of Eumenes increased to a great extent till the time of his grandson Attalus, but they bestowed it partly on the Rhodians, and partly on the Cyprians and others. They never remunerated those allies who almost exhausted their own possessions in aiding them, out of their own resources, but enriched them with the spoils of others; and they not only seized upon the property of one city and bestowed it on another, but they set up their lands for sale. Thus, the liberty of the Lacedæmonians was betrayed to the tyrant Nabis. They also enriched Masinissa with so much wealth, that they acquired Africa for themselves by his means. In fine, they so sported with kingdoms in seizing and giving them away, that they rendered provinces tranquil by the wealth and at the expense of others. This was remarkably conspicuous in the case of Judea, where they created out of nothing Ethnarchs and Tetrarchs and kings, who were nothing but their satellites—and that too but for a moment. For as soon as any change occurred, they retracted what they had given as easily as they bestowed it. Hence, this their cunning liberality is called treading under foot; for that remnant which they could not devour and consume with their teeth *they trod under foot,* as they kept all those whom they had either enriched or increased subject to themselves. Thus we see with what servility they were flattered by those who had obtained anything through their generosity. And how degrading was the slavery of Greece from the time the Romans entered the country! for as each state acquired any new territory, it erected a temple to the Romans. They also sent their ambassadors there to act as spies, who, under the pretence of punishing the neighbouring people for plotting against them, enriched themselves by plunder. Thus the Romans held under their feet whatever they had given to others. We see then how suitably and properly the Prophet speaks, when he says, the Romans trod down the remnant; for whatever they could not consume, and what their voraciousness could 'not devour, *they trod under their feet.*

He adds afterwards, *And this beast differed from all the former ones, and had ten horns.* When he says, *this beast was different from the rest,* he confirms what we formerly said, namely, this was a horrible prodigy, and nothing could be compared to it in the nature of things. And surely if any one attentively and prudently considers the origin of the Romans, he would be astonished at their remarkable progress to such great power; for it was an unusual monster, and nothing like it had ever appeared. Interpreters treat in various ways what the Prophet subjoins respecting *the ten horns.* I follow a simple and genuine opinion, namely, the Prophet means this Empire to belong to more persons than one. For the angel will afterwards assert the ten horns to be kings; not that so many kings ruled at Rome, according to the foolish dream of the Jews, who are ignorant of all

things ; but the Prophet here distinguishes the Fourth
Monarchy from the rest, as if he had said it should be a
popular government, not presided over by one king, but
divided into many heads.   For they even divided provinces
among themselves, and made treaties with each other, so
that one was governor of Macedonia, another of Cilicia, and
another of Syria.   Thus we see how numerous the kingdoms
were.   And with regard to the number ten, we know this to
be a frequent and usual form of speech in Scripture, where
ten signifies many.   When plurality is denoted, the number
ten is used.   Thus when the Prophet states the fourth beast
to have ten horns, he means, there were many provinces so
divided, that each ruler, whether proconsul or prætor, was
like a king.   For the supreme power was given to them,
while the city and Italy were given up to the consuls.   The
consul could indeed write to the provinces and command
whatever he pleased ; then he could elevate to honour whom
he pleased for the sake of favour and friendship ; but each of
the prætors and proconsuls when he obtained a province,
became a kind of king, since he exercised the supreme
power of life and death over all his subjects.   We need not
be too anxious about the number, as we have already explained it.   Those who reckon the Roman provinces make
great mistakes ; they omit the principal one ; they make
only one of Spain, and yet we know there were two.   They
do not divide Gaul, yet there were always two proconsuls
there, except under Julius Cæsar, who obtained the command
of both Gauls.   So also they speak of Greece, and yet
neither a proconsul nor a prætor was ever sent into Greece.
Finally, the Prophet simply means that the Roman Empire
was complex, being divided into many provinces, and these
provinces were governed by leaders of great weight at Rome,
whose authority and rank were superior to others.   Proconsuls and prætors obtained the provinces by lot, but favour
frequently prevailed, as the histories of those times sufficiently assure us.   Let us proceed,—

8. I considered the horns, and,   8. Intelligebam[1] ad cornua : et
behold, there came up among them   ecce cornu aliud parvum exortum

---

[1] That is, I was attentive.— *Calvin.*

another little horn, before whom there were three of the first horns plucked up by the roots: and, and, be-hold, in this horn *were* eyes like the eyes of man, and a mouth speaking great things.

fuit inter alia: et tria ex cornibus prioribus ablata sunt e facie ejus: et ecce oculi quasi oculi hominis in cornu illo, et os loquens grandia.

Daniel proceeds with his description of the fourth beast. First, he says, *he was attentive*, with the intention of rousing us to serious meditation. For what is said of the fourth beast, was remarkably memorable and worthy of notice. This, then, is the reason why God struck the heart of his servant with wonder. For the Prophet would not have given his attention to the consideration of the fourth beast, unless he had been impelled to it by the secret instinct of God. The Prophet's attention, then, sprang from a heavenly impulse. Wherefore it is our duty not to read carelessly what is here written, but to weigh seriously and with the greatest diligence what the Spirit intends by this vision. *I was attentive*, therefore, says he, *to the horns, and behold one small one arose among them.* Here interpreters begin to vary; some twist this to mean the Pope, and others the Turk; but neither opinion seems to me probable; they are both wrong, since they think the whole course of Christ's kingdom is here described, while God wished only to declare to his Prophet what should happen up to the first advent of Christ. This, then, is the error of all those who wish to embrace under this vision the perpetual state of the Church up to the end of the world. But the Holy Spirit's intention was completely different. We explained at the beginning why this vision appeared to the Prophet — because the minds of the pious would constantly fail them in the dreadful convulsions which were at hand, when they saw the supreme dominion pass over to the Persians. And then the Macedonians broke in upon them, and acquired authority throughout the whole of the East, and afterwards those robbers who made war under Alexander suddenly became kings, partly by cruelty and partly by fraud and perfidy, which created more strife than outward hostility. And when the faithful saw all those monarchies perish, and the Roman Empire spring up like a new prodigy, they would lose their courage in such confused and turbulent changes. Thus this vision was presented to the Prophet, that all the children of God might understand what severe trials awaited them before the advent of Christ. Daniel, then, does not proceed beyond the promised redemption, and does not embrace, as I have said, the whole kingdom of Christ, but is content to bring the faithful to that exhibition of grace which they hoped and longed for.

It is sufficiently clear, therefore, that this exhibition ought to be referred to the first advent of Christ. I have no doubt that *the little horn* relates to Julius Cæsar and the other Cæsars who succeeded him, namely, Augustus, Tiberius, Caligula, Claudius, Nero, and others. Although, as we said before, the counsel of the Holy Spirit must be attended to, which leads the faithful forwards to the beginning of the reign of Christ, that is, to the preaching of the Gospel, which was commenced under Claudius, Nero, and their successors. He calls it *a little horn*, because Cæsar did not assume the name of king; but when Pompey and the greater part of the senate were conquered, he could not enjoy his victory without assuming to himself supreme power. Hence he made himself tribune of the people and their dictator. Meanwhile, there were always Consuls; there was always some shadow of a Republic, while he daily consulted the senate and sat in his seat while the consuls were at the tribunals. Octavius followed the same practice, and afterwards Tiberius also. For none of the Cæsars, unless he was consul, dared to ascend the tribunal; each had his own seat, although from that place he commanded all others. It is not surprising, then, if Daniel calls the monarchy of Julius and the other Cæsars *a little horn*, its splendour and dignity were not great enough to eclipse the majesty of the senate; for while the senate retained the name and form of honour, it is sufficiently known that one man alone possessed the supreme power. He says, therefore, *this little horn was raised among the ten others.* I must defer the explanation of what follows, viz., *three of these ten were taken away.*

PRAYER.

Grant, Almighty God, since thou hast formerly admonished thy servants, that thy children, while they are pilgrims in this world, must be familiar with horrible and cruel beasts, if the same thing should happen to us, that we may be prepared for all contests. May we endure and overcome all temptations, and may we never doubt thy desire to defend us by thy protection and power, according to thy promise. May we proceed through the midst of numberless dangers, until after accomplishing the course of our warfare, we at length arrive at that happy rest which is laid up for us in heaven by Christ our Lord.— Amen.

Lecture Thirty-Fourth.

THREE things remain to be explained by us in expounding the Fourth Beast. First of all, *Three horns were taken away from its face;* Secondly, *The little horn,* which rose among the ten, *appeared with human eyes;* Thirdly, *It spoke magnificently,* or uttered swelling words. With regard to the three horns, it is sufficiently evident from the testimony of the angel that they were three kings; not because this ought to be referred to persons, as I yesterday disproved, but because the Romans were accustomed to send to each province, rulers like kings who there exercised the supreme authority. Those who extend this prophecy to the end of Christ's kingdom, think that a dispersion which happened about three or five hundred years after the death of Christ is intended; but they are greatly mistaken. Clearly enough the whole strength of the Roman Empire was exhausted and the provinces gradually cut off, till it became a kind of mutilated body; but we yesterday shewed the incorrectness of any explanation of this oracle, except concerning the state of the Church at the first Advent of Christ and the preaching of the Gospel. At that time, it is well known, nothing had been subtracted from the boundaries of the Empire. For Julius Cæsar was formidable not only to the Gauls, but also to the Germans; and besides this, the affairs of the East were at peace. After his death, although Octavius or Augustus had suffered two very destructive slaughters, especially under Quintilius Varus, who had been sent into Germany with a powerful army, yet he also extended the boundaries of the Empire, especially in the East. He also subdued the whole of Spain, where no commotions afterwards took place. As, therefore, at that period no province had been cut off from the Roman Empire, what is the meaning of the expression, *Three horns were cut off and removed from the face of the beast ?* The solution is not difficult. Only let us observe how the little horn is compared with the first stature of the beast. It first appeared with ten horns ; when the little horn arose its figure was changed. The Prophet then says—a part of the horns was cut off, as the senate then ceased to create proconsuls. For we know how Augustus assumed to himself certain provinces, and he did this for the purpose of creating presidents at his own will, and of constituting a strong force, ever at hand, should any one rebel against him. For he did not care so much about provinces as about an army, should any tumult arise. He was desirous, therefore, of throwing a bridle over them all, lest any one should dare to attempt a revolution. Whatever was thus added to *the little horn* was taken from the ten horns, that is, from the whole body, as the state of the monarchy was entirely changed. There is nothing forced in this exposition. We must also contend for a definite or fixed number being put for an uncertain one ; as if the Prophet had said—a part of the power of the beast was abstracted after the rising of the little horn. Thus much for the first clause.

He now adds, *The eyes in this small horn were like those of men ;* and then, *it spoke mighty things.* With respect to the eyes, this expression implies—the form of a human body was exhibited, because the Cæsars did not abolish the senate nor change at once the whole form of the government ; but, as we yesterday said, they were content with power ; and as to splendour, titles, and pomp, they readily left these to the consuls and the senate. If any one considers the manner in which those Cæsars, who are doubtless intended by *the*

little horn, conducted themselves, their conduct will appear
like a human figure. For Julius Cæsar pretended, although
he was dictator, to obey the senate's authority, and the
consuls asked the opinion of the senators, after the ancient
manner. He sat in the midst, and permitted many things
to be decreed without interposing his will. Augustus also
abused the shadow of the tribunitial power only for the
purpose of ruling the Empire. Thus he submitted to the
consuls; and when he wished to be elected to that office, he
became a candidate with the other competitors, and put on
the white robe like a private citizen. Tiberius also was a
great pretender, and while plotting schemes of tyranny, was
neither open nor ingenuous in his plans. So also *the eyes of
a man appeared in the little horn,* that is, after this change
took place and the senate and people were deprived of their
liberty. He who held the government of the republic was
not formidable, as an entire beast, but was like a private
man as to outward form.

The Prophet adds, *The small horn had a loud sounding
mouth.* For although, with the view of conciliating favour,
the Cæsars conducted themselves like men, we know how
atrociously they threatened their enemies, and how imperi-
ously they either hindered or committed whatever they
lusted, as it seemed good to them. There was, then, a great
difference between their mouth and their eyes. For, as we
already said, the splendour and dignity of the empire
was in the power of the consuls and senate at the beginning.
Meanwhile, by insidious arts, the Cæsars drew towards
themselves the whole power, till no one dared to do anything, except at their bidding. Many interpreters explain
this as blasphemy against God, and impiety; and the angel
will touch upon this point at the close of the chapter. But
if we weigh the whole expression judiciously, what I say
will appear correct, and the loud speaking here mentioned by
the Prophet will signify, that pride with which the Cæsars
were puffed up, imposing silence on all men and allowing no
one to open their mouths contrary to their will. The
Prophet's words are very well explained by this fact; for *the
three horns being removed from the ten,* means some part of

the empire was separated from the main body ; then, *the small horn being endued with human eyes,* implies a kind of modesty, as the Cæsars acted like private persons, and left outward shew with the senate and people ; and thirdly, *when the mouth of the little horn spoke swellingly,* trepidation seized upon all the Romans, and especially whoever enjoyed any reputation, hung upon the nod of the Cæsars, who imposed the vilest slavery, and received the foulest and most shameful flattery from the whole senate.　It now follows,—

9. I beheld till the thrones were cast down, and the Ancient of days did sit, whose garment *was* white as snow, and the hair of his head like the pure wool : his throne *was like* the fiery flame, *and* his wheels *as* burning fire.

9. Videbam usque dum throni erecti sunt,[1] et Antiquus, *senex,* dierum sedit : vestimentum ejus quasi nix candidum, et capillus capitis ejus quasi lana munda, solium ejus scintillæ ignis, rotæ ejus ignis ardens.

Daniel now relates how he saw another figure, namely, God sitting on his throne to exercise judgment.　We shall see it afterwards concerning Christ, but Daniel now teaches only the appearance of God in his character of a judge. This was the reason why many persons extend this prophecy to the second Advent of Christ—an interpretation by no means correct, as I shall shew more copiously in the proper place.　But first it is worth while to consider here, why he says—*the Ancient of days,* meaning the eternal Deity himself, *ascended the throne of judgment.*　This scene seems unnecessary, because it is the peculiar office of God to govern the world ; and as we know this cannot be done without upright judgment, it follows that God has been a perpetual judge from the creation of the world.　Now, even a moderate acquaintance with the Scriptures shews how well this passage suits us by appealing to our senses ; for unless God's power is made conspicuous, we think it either abolished or interrupted.　Hence those forms of expression which occur elsewhere ; as, "How long art thou silent, O Lord ; and how long wilt thou cease from us ?" (Ps. xiii. 1 ; ix. 7, and elsewhere,) and—God ascends his throne—for we

---

[1] Or removed ; for the word רמיו, *remiv,* is expounded by interpreters in two senses ; verbally, " until they took away thrones or erected them aloft."—*Calvin.*　" The word may be rendered ' were pitched,' or set down, for the reception of Deity and his assessors the saints."—*Wintle.*

should not acknowledge him as a judge, unless he really and experimentally proved himself such. This then is the reason why Daniel says God himself was seated in judgment.

But before we proceed further, we must observe the sense in which he says—thrones were either erected or cast down —for the word רום, *rum*, can be taken in either sense. Those who translate it, "Thrones were removed," interpret it of the Four Monarchies already mentioned. But for my part, I rather incline to a different opinion. If any one prefers explaining it of these Monarchies, I do not contend with him, for that sense is probable ; and as far as the pith of the matter is concerned, there is not much difference. But I think the thrones or seats are here placed to exhibit the divine judgment, because the Prophet will immediately represent myriads of angels standing before God. We know how often angels are adorned with this title as if they were assessors of Deity ; and the form of speech which Daniel uses when he says, "The judgment was set," will also agree with this. He speaks here of assessors with the judge, as if God did not sit alone, but had councillors joined with him. In my opinion the most suitable explanation is,—thrones were created for the Almighty to sit on with his councillors ; not implying his need of any council, but of his own goodwill and mere favour he dignifies angels with this honour, as we shall see immediately. Daniel therefore describes, after our human fashion, the preparations for judgment ; just as if any king should go publicly forth for the purpose of transacting any business of moment, and should ascend his tribunal. Councillors and nobles would sit around him on both sides, not partaking of his power, but rather increasing the splendour of his appearance. For if the king alone should occupy the whole place, the dignity would not be so magnificent as when his nobles, who depend upon him, are present on all sides, because they far surpass the ordinary multitude. Daniel, therefore, relates the vision presented to him in this form ; first, because he was a man dwelling in the flesh ; and next, he did not see it for himself personally, but for the common benefit of the whole Church. Thus God wished to exhibit a representation which might infuse into the Prophet's mind and into those of all the pious, a feeling of admiration, and yet might have something in common with human proceedings. *Thrones, therefore, he says, were erected;* afterwards, *the Ancient of days was seated.* I have already expounded how God then began to seat himself, as he had previously appeared to be passive, and not to exercise justice in the world. For when things are disturbed and mingled with much darkness, who can say, " God reigns ?" God seems to be shut up in heaven, when things are discomposed and turbulent upon earth. On the other hand, he is said to ascend his tribunal when he assumes to himself the office of a judge, and openly demonstrates that he is neither asleep nor absent, although he lies hid from human perception.

This form of speech was very appropriate for denoting the coming of Christ. For God then chiefly displayed his supreme power, as Paul cites a passage from the Psalms, (lxviii. 8, in Eph. iv. 8,) " Thou hast ascended on high." When the subject treated is the first coming of Christ, it ought not to be restricted to the thirty-three years of his sojourn in the world, but it embraces his ascension, and that preaching of the gospel which ushered in his kingdom ;— this will be said again more clearly and copiously. Daniel appropriately relates how God was seated when the first advent of Christ is depicted, since the majesty of God shone in the person of Christ; for which reason he is called " The invisible image of God and the character of his glory," (Heb. i. 3 ;) that is, of the substance or person of the Father. God therefore, who had seemed for so many ages not to notice the world nor to care for his elect people, ascended his tribunal at the advent of Christ. To this subject the Psalms, from the 95th to the 100th, all relate—" God reigns, let the earth rejoice ;" " God reigns, let the islands be afraid." In truth, God had not dwelt in complete privacy before Christ's advent ; but the empire which he had erected was hidden and unseen, until he shewed forth his glory in the person of his only begotten Son. *The Ancient of days,* therefore, *was seated.*

He now says, *His raiment was white like snow: the hair
of his head was like pure wool.* God here shews himself to
his Prophet in the form of man. We know how impossible
it is for us to behold God as he really exists, till we ourselves
become like him, as John says in his canonical epistle.
(1 John iii. 2.) As our capacity cannot endure the fulness of that surpassing glory which essentially belongs to
God, whenever he appears to us, he must necessarily put
on a form adapted to our comprehension. God, therefore,
was never seen by the fathers in his own natural perfection;
but as far as their capacities allowed, he afforded them a
taste of his presence for the sure acknowledgment of his
Deity; and yet they comprehended him as far as it was
useful for them and they were able to bear it. This is the
reason why God appeared *with a white garment,* which is
characteristic of heaven; and *with snowy hair,* like white
and clean wool. To the same purpose is the following: *His
throne was like sparks of fire,* that is, like glowing fire; *his
wheels were like burning fire.* God in reality neither occupies any throne, nor is carried on wheels; but, as I already
said, we ought not to imagine God in his essence to be like
any appearance to his own Prophet and other holy fathers,
but he put on various appearances, according to man's comprehension, to whom he wished to give some signs of his
presence. I need not dwell longer on these forms of speech,
though subtle allegories are pleasing to many. I am satisfied with holding what is solid and sure. It now follows:—

10. A fiery stream issued and came
forth from before him: thousand
thousands ministered unto him, and
ten thousand times ten thousand
stood before him: the judgment was
set, and the books were opened.

10. Fluvius[1] ignis fluebat, et exi-
bat a præsentia ejus, *vel a conspectu:*
millia millium[2] ministrabant ei: et
decies millia decies millium[3] coram
ipso stabant: judicium sedit, et libri
aperti sunt.

Daniel proceeds with what he commenced in the former
verse. He says a splendour or stream of fire; for נהר, *neher,*
may be used in both senses, since נהר, *neher,* signifies both
" to flow" and " to shine." Yet, since he previously spoke

---

[1] Some, the light or splendour.—*Calvin.*
[2] That is, millions.—*Calvin.*
[3] That is, myriads of myriads, or a hundred million.—*Calvin.*

of splendour, the word " stream" will suit the passage very
well ; for a *fiery stream issued from the presence of God,*
which both inundated and burnt up the land.   Without
doubt God wished to inspire his Prophet with fear for the
purpose of arousing him the better, as we never sufficiently
comprehend his majesty unless when humbled ; and we cannot experience this humility without fear.   This is the reason why God always shews something terrible when he appears to his servants, not merely to create astonishment, but
to excite their fear and reverence.   Hence God seems to
have considered this point in this vision, when *the stream
took its rise from his appearance, even a river of flame.*
Afterwards he adds, *numberless attendants stood before him.*
Without the slightest doubt, the Prophet here speaks of
angels : he says there were *thousands of thousands,* or ten
times a hundred thousand ; and again, *ten thousand times ten
thousand,* that is, ten thousand myriads.   Here the numbers
are not reckoned, but God signifies his having at hand the
greatest forces obedient to his will, and far surpassing any
armies which the greatest and most powerful princes collect.
This passage teaches us that angels were created for the
purpose of receiving and executing the commands of God,
and of being the ministers of God, as it were his hands in
heaven and in earth.   As regards numbers, no wonder many
myriads are enumerated by the Prophet.   Christ said, " Can
I not ask the Father and he will send a legion ?" (Matt.
xxvi. 53.)   So, in this passage, Daniel says there were
numberless angels under God's hand, and there was no need
of collecting armies after the manner of princes, since they
are always present and intent on obedience.   Thus they immediately fulfil all his commands, as angels run swiftly
throughout heaven and earth.   We also perceive the supreme
power of the Almighty denoted here, as if the Prophet had
said—God is not like a king or a judge merely by title, but
he possesses the greatest and most unlimited power ; he has
myriads of satellites ever at hand for the purpose of fulfilling and executing his supreme will.   And in this sense he
says, *they stood before him.*   He uses the word for ministry
or service, and afterwards adds, *to stand.*   For ministers can-

not always render their service as quickly as their rulers desire. But the angelic method is different. Not only are they prepared to obey, but in a moment they understand what God wishes and commands without needing time for compliance. We see even the greatest princes cannot immediately carry out their decrees, because their ministers are not always at hand. But there is no necessity for dwelling longer upon angels. Daniel adds, *The judgment was fixed, and the books were opened.* Although God alone is eminent and conspicuous above the angels, and the height of their glory and dignity does not obscure the supreme empire of the Almighty, yet, as we have formerly said, he deems them worthy of the honour of being placed as councillors on each side of him, and that for the sake of illustrating his own majesty. For we have stated that nobles do not sit at the side of monarchs to diminish his majesty or to attract it to themselves, but rather to reflect the magnitude and power of the monarch more fully. This is the reason why the Prophet joins angels with God, not as allies, but simply as his councillors.

I refer the phrase, *the books were opened,* to the preaching of the gospel. Although God was recognised in Judea, as it is said in the 76th Psalm, (ver. 2,) yet this acknowledgment was but slight and involved in many figures. God was revealed through enigmas until Christ's coming ; but then he manifested himself truly, just like opening books previously shut. There is therefore a contrast to be observed here between that obscure season which preceded the coming of Christ, and the clearness which now shines under the gospel. Because, therefore, God was plainly made known after the Sun of righteousness arose, according to the Prophet Malachi, (chap. iv. 2,) this is the reason why the books are now said *to have been opened at that season.* Meanwhile, we confess that God was not altogether hidden, nor did he speak from concealment, but this is said comparatively by the Prophet, as the books were opened whenever God openly appeared as the Judge, Father, and Preserver of the world, in the person of his only begotten Son. It afterwards follows :—

11. I beheld then, because of the voice of the great words which the horn spake : I beheld *even* till the beast was slain, and his body destroyed, and given to the burning flame.

11. Videbam tunc, propter vocem[1] sermonum grandium, quos cornu proferebat, videbam usque dum occisa fuit bestia, et abolitum corpus ejus, et data fuit incendio ignis.

Since the presumptuous speaking of the little horn terrified the Prophet, he now says he was *attentive in considering this portion.* He next says, *The beast was slain, and his body was consumed by the burning of fire.* This ought clearly to be referred to the end of the Roman empire. For, from the time when foreigners obtained the mastery, the fourth beast ceased to flourish. The name was always retained, yet with great mockery of that ancient monarchy. I now omit all mention of Caligula, Nero, Domitian, and similar monsters. But when Spaniards and Africans acquired the absolute sway, can we call Rome any longer the mistress of the world? Surely this would be foolish indeed ! To this very day the Germans also say they possess the Roman empire ; but while the title of empire has passed to the Germans, clearly enough Rome is at this very day in slavery. For as to the Pope having erected his own throne there, this empire is unworthy of the name of monarchy ; but whatever be our view of this point, for about 1500 years the Romans have been in bondage as slaves to foreign princes. For, after the death of Nero, Trajan was his successor, and from that time scarcely a single Roman obtained the empire ; and God branded it with the most disgraceful marks of ignominy, when a swine-herd was created emperor, and that too by the lust of the soldiery ! The senate retained its name till then ; but if it pleased the soldiers to create any one a Cæsar, the senate was immediately compelled to submit to their dictation. Thus, the Prophet with great propriety says, *The beast was slain* shortly after the promulgation of the gospel. Then the presumptuous speaking of *the little horn* was at an end, and *the fourth beast* was extinct about the same time.

[1] That is, I was gazing upon that vision still : it signifies the attention of the mind, and that not after a human method, but as if he had been caught up aloft in a prophetic spirit. Thus he says his senses were fixed upon that vision—" on account of the voice," therefore, or " through the voice."—*Calvin.*

For then no Roman became an Emperor who claimed for himself any share of power ; but Rome itself fell into disgraceful slavery, and not only foreigners reigned there most shamefully, but even barbarians, swine-herds, and cow-herds ! All this occurred in fulfilment of what God had shewn to his Prophet, namely, after the coming of Christ and the opening of the books, that is—after the knowledge which shone upon the world through the preaching of the gospel—the destruction of that fourth beast and of the Roman empire was close at hand.

PRAYER.

Grant, Almighty God, whatever revolutions happen daily in the world, that we may always be intent on the sight of thy glory, once manifested to us in thy Son. May the splendour of thy majesty illuminate our hearts, and may we pass beyond the visible heavens, the sun, the moon, and every shining thing; and may we behold the blessedness of thy kingdom, which thou proposest to us in the light of thy Gospel. May we walk through the midst of the darkness and afflictions of the world, content with that light by which thou invitest us to the hope of the eternal inheritance which thou hast promised us, and acquired for us by the blood of thine only begotten Son.—Amen.

Lecture Thirty-Fifth.

12. As concerning the rest of the beasts, they had their dominion taken away : yet their lives were prolonged for a season and time.

12. Et reliquis bestiis abstulerant potestatem, *vel dominationem,* et longitudo in vita data illis fuerat usque ad tempus et tempus.

WITHOUT doubt the Prophet refers to what ought to come first in order, as the empires of which he is speaking were extinct before the Roman.   Hence these verbs ought to be taken in the pluperfect tense, because the power had been already removed from the other three beasts.   For the Hebrews were accustomed to repeat afterwards anything which had been omitted, and they do not always observe the order of time in their narratives.   Thus, after he had said the fourth beast was slain and consumed by burning, he now adds what he had omitted concerning the remaining three, namely, *their dominion had been taken from them.* He adds also what is worthy of notice, *Length,* or continuance, *in life was granted to them even for a time and a time.* There are two different words used here, but they signify one and the same thing, namely, a convenient time. Here the Prophet understands how nothing happens accidentally, but all things are carried on in the world in their own time, as God has decreed them in heaven. Perhaps when the subject-matter of the discourse is *length of life,* it signifies the protracted period of these afflictions, as they should not pass away suddenly like clouds. Not only severe but lengthened trials are said to await the faithful, which must afflict their minds with weariness, unless the hope of a better issue propped them up. Thus, the Holy Spirit predicts how God would at length deliver his Church when he had exercised its patience for a length of time. From *the rest of the beasts power was taken away.* The copula in the word וארכה, *ve-arkeh,* " and length," may be resolved in this way—" because length in life ;" as if he had said, The trials by which the sons of God were to be oppressed should not be perpetual, because God had prescribed and defined a fixed period. *A continuance,* therefore, *in life was granted to them,* namely, *for a time and a time.* The copula may be treated as " an adversative particle ;" as if he had said, " although a continuance," that is, although the people should not immediately escape from those sorrowful cares which oppressed them, yet God's opportunity would at length arrive, that is, the time at which it pleased God to redeem his own Church. But the former exposition seems more genuine and more consistent, because length of time has its own limits and boundaries. There is also a contrast between the words ארכה, *arkeh,* " length," and זמן, *zemen,* " time," and עדן, *gneden,* " time," because length or " prolonging" has reference to our perceptions ; for when we are suffering pain, the greatest speed seems delay. Thus, any one in anxiety for an improved state of things counts every moment, and is so flagrant in his desires as to call the Almighty in question for any delay. As, then, the impatience of men is so great, when they are expecting with anxiety this freedom from adversity, the Prophet says, in

the ordinary acceptation of the phrase, *length of time was
granted to the beasts ;* but he opposes a fit time ; as if he had
said—They act preposterously who thus indulge their own
passions.   Since God has fixed his own time, they require
patience, and need not reckon the years ; but this one thing
must be concluded, when the Lord pleases he will not delay
his help.   This, therefore, is the full sense of the verse.   It
follows :—

13. I saw in the night-visions, and, behold, *one* like the Son of man came with the clouds of heaven, and came to the Ancient of days, and they brought him near before him.	13. Videbam in visionibus noctis: et ecce in nubibus[1] cœli, *vel cœlorum,* tanquam Filius hominis veniebat, et usque ad Antiquum dierum venit, et coram eo repræsentarunt.[2]

After Daniel has narrated how he saw God on the throne
of judgment, openly exercising his power and laying open to
the world what was formerly hidden from it, namely, his
supreme authority in its government, he now adds the second
part of the vision, *As it were the Son of man appeared in
the clouds.*   Without doubt this is to be understood of Christ,
and the Jews, perverse as they are, are ashamed to deny it,
although they differ afterwards about Christ.   But the object of this vision was to enable the faithful certainly to expect the promised Redeemer in his own time.   He had been
endued with heavenly power, and was seated at his Father's
right hand.   Hence Daniel says, *He was intent on these
nightly visions.*   And this repetition is by no means superfluous, as it informs us of the Prophet's alertness when God
shews himself present.   Daniel expresses this fully in his
own words, for he roused himself when he perceived important, and rare, and singular matters set before him.   This
attentive disposition of the Prophet ought to stir us up to
read his prophecy without listlessness, and with awakened
minds earnestly to derive from heaven true and sincere intelligence.   *I was,* then, says he, *attentive in visions of the
night, and beheld as it were the Son of man.*   I have already
said this passage cannot be otherwise taken than concerning

[1] For ﬠﬦ, *gnem,* is taken in this passage in Chaldee, like ﬢ, *be.* This
usage is customary : hence " in the clouds."—*Calvin.*

[2] Verbally, " made him approach."—*Calvin.*   The Latin text of 1561
has " eum" at the end of the verse, and the French translation implies it.
See the DISSERTATIONS at the end of this volume.—*Ed.*

Christ. We must now see why he uses the word "like" the Son of man ; that is, why he uses the letter כ, *ke,* the mark for likeness. This might be twisted in favour of the folly of the Manichees, who thought Christ's body to be only imaginary. For, as they wrest the words of Paul, and pervert their sense, that Christ was in likeness as a man, (Phil. ii. 7,) so also they may abuse the Prophet's testimony, when Christ is not said to be a man but only like one. With respect to Paul's words, he is not speaking of the essence of his human nature, but only of his state ; for he is speaking of Christ being made man, of his condition being humble and abject, and even servile. But in the passage before us the reason is different. For the Prophet says, *He appeared* to him *as the Son of man,* as Christ had not yet taken upon him our flesh. And we must remark that saying of Paul's : When the fulness of time was come, God sent his Son, made of a woman. (Gal. iv. 4.) Christ then began to be a man when he appeared on earth as Mediator, for he had not assumed the seed of Abraham before he was joined with us in brotherly union. This is the reason why the Prophet does not pronounce Christ to have been man at this period, but only like man ; for otherwise he had not been that Messiah formerly promised under the Law as the son of Abraham and David. For if from the beginning he had put on human flesh, he would not have been born of these progenitors. It follows, then, that Christ was not a man from the beginning, but only appeared so in a figure. As also Irenæus[1] says : This was a " prelude," he uses that word. Tertullian also says : " Then the Son of God put on a specimen of his humanity."[2] This was a symbol, therefore, of Christ's future flesh, although that flesh did not yet exist. We now see how suitably this figure agrees with the thing signified, wherein Christ was set forth as the Son of man, although he was then the eternal Word of God.

It afterwards follows, *He came to the Ancient of days.*

---

[1] The Latin translation of Irenæus is "*præludium.*" The French here has "*une approche et entree,*" and then adds, " He uses a word which we cannot translate into French." It means a preface or introduction.—*Ed.*

[2] Tertullian's words are, " Tunc præluxit Filius Dei humanitate sua." —*Ed.*

This, in my judgment, ought to be explained of Christ's ascension; for he then commenced his reign, as we see in numberless passages of Scripture. Nor is this passage contrary to what the Prophet had previously said—he saw the Son of man in the clouds. For by this expression he simply wishes to teach how Christ, although like a man, yet differed from the whole human race, and was not of the common order of men; but excelled the whole world in dignity. He expresses much more when he says, in the second clause, *He came even unto the Ancient of days.* For although the Divine Majesty lay hid in Christ, yet he discharged the duty of a slave, and emptied himself, as Paul says, (Phil. ii. 7.) So also we read in the first chapter of John, (John i. 14,) Glory appeared in him as of the only begotten Son of God; that is, which belongs to the only begotten Son of God. Christ, therefore, thus put off his glory for the time, and yet by his miracles and many other proofs afforded a clear and evident specimen of his celestial glory. He really appeared to Daniel in the clouds, but when he ascended to heaven, he then put off this mortal body, and put on a new life. Thus Paul also, in the sixth chapter to the Romans, says, he lives the life of God, (verse 10;) and other phrases often used by our Lord himself agree very well with this, especially in the Evangelist John, "I go to the Father:" "It is expedient for me to go to the Father, for the Father is greater than I," (chap. xvi. 7; xiv. 28;) that is, it is expedient for me to ascend to that royal tribunal which the Father has erected for me by his eternal counsel, and thus the whole world will feel the supreme power to have been entrusted to me. Now, therefore, we understand the full meaning of the Prophet's words.

But as there are many fanatics who wrest what has been said of the person of the Mediator, as if Christ were not the true God, but had a beginning from the Father at some definite period of time, we must observe how the Prophet's expression suits neither the human nor the divine nature of Christ properly speaking, but a Mediator is here set before us who is God manifest in flesh. For if we hold this principle that Christ is described to us, not as either the word of God, or the seed of Abraham, but as Mediator, that is, eternal God who was willing to become man, to become subject to God the Father, to be made like us, and to be our advocate, then no difficulty will remain. Thus he appeared to Daniel like the Son of man, who became afterwards truly and really so. He was in the clouds, that is, separated from the common lot of mankind, as he always carried with him some marks of deity, even in his humility. *He now arrives at the Ancient of days,* that is, when he ascends to heaven, because his divine majesty was then revealed. And hence he says, It is expedient for you, for me to go to the Father, because the Father is greater than I. (John xiv. 28.) Christ here detracts nothing from his deity, but as his nature was not known in the world, while his divine majesty lay hid in the form of a servant, he calls the Father simply God ; as if he had said, If I remain with you upon earth, what would the presence of my flesh profit you ? But when I ascend to heaven, then that oneness which I have with the Father will become conspicuous. When, therefore, the world shall understand that I am one with the Father, and that the Deity is one, the hope of all the pious will become more firm and unconquered against all temptations ; for they will know themselves to be equally under the protection of both God and man. If, therefore, Christ were always dwelling upon earth, and had borne witness a thousand times to his being given to us by his Father as the guardian of our salvation, yet there always would have been some hesitation and anxiety. But when we know him to be seated at his Father's right hand, we then understand him to be truly God, because all knees would not be bent before him, unless he had been the eternal God. We must hold that passage of Isaiah, (chap. xlii. 8,) As I live, saith the Lord, my glory I will not give to another. As, therefore, God's glory can never be transferred to either man or any other creature, the true unity and nature of God necessarily shines forth in the human nature of Christ, for every knee is bent before him. Now, therefore, we understand the sense in which the Prophet says, Christ *came as the Son of man,* that is, like a man, *even to the Ancient of days.* For after Christ had passed

through the period of his self-abasement, according to Paul,
(Phil. ii. 7,) he ascended into heaven, and a dominion was
bestowed upon him, as the Prophet says in the next verse.
This passage, then, without the slightest doubt, ought to be
received of Christ's ascension, after he had ceased being a
mortal man. He says, *He was represented before God*,
namely, because he sits at his right hand. It follows,—

14. And there was given him dominion, and glory, and a kingdom, that all people, nations, and languages, should serve him: his dominion *is* an everlasting dominion, which shall not pass away, and his kingdom *that* which shall not be destroyed.	14. Et ei data *fuit* potestas, et gloria, *vel, decus*, et regnum: et omnes populi, nationes, et linguæ ei servient: potestas ejus potestas seculi, *æterna*, quæ non auferetur, et regnum ejus non corrumpetur.[1]

The Prophet confirms and explains more clearly in this
verse what he had said in the former one. For we may collect from it how the personage previously mentioned arrived
at the Ancient of days, who is God, namely, *because power
was given to him.* For although Christ truly ascended into
heaven, (Matt. xxviii. 18,) yet we ought clearly to weigh
the purpose of his doing so. It was to acquire the supreme
power in heaven and in earth, as he himself says. And Paul
also mentions this purpose in the first and second chapters
of the Ephesians. (Chap. i. 21 ; ii. 7.) Christ left the world
and ascended to the Father; first, to subdue all powers to
himself, and to render angels obedient; next, to restrain
the devil, and to protect and preserve the Church by his
help, as well as all the elect of God the Father. So, therefore, Daniel now proceeds with what he formerly said concerning the approach of Christ to God. Thus the madness
of those who argue against Christ being true and eternal
God, because he is said to have come to the Ancient of days,
is refuted. First of all, as we have said, this is understood
of the person of the Mediator; next, all doubt is taken away
when the Prophet adds, *Power was given unto him.* Behold,
therefore, a certain explanation. We will not say it was
bestowed with relation to his being, and being called God.
It was given to him as Mediator, as God manifest in flesh,
and with respect to his human nature. We observe how

[1] Or, shall not be abolished.—*Calvin.*

well all these things agree, when the Prophet here says, *The chief power was given to Christ.* We must hold therefore its reference to that manifestation, because Christ was from the beginning the life of men, the world was created by him, and his energy always sustained it, (John i. 4;) but power was given to him to inform us how God reigned by means of his hand. If we were required to seek God without a Mediator, his distance would be far too great, but when a Mediator meets us, and offers himself to us in our human nature, such is the nearness between God and us, that our faith easily passes beyond the world and penetrates the very heavens. For this reason, therefore, *All power, honour, and kingdom was* given to Christ. He adds also, *All nations shall serve him,* that is, they may serve him ; for the copula ought to be translated thus,—*That all nations, people, and tongues should serve him.* We have shewn how this ought properly to be understood of the commencement of the reign of Christ, and ought not to be connected with its final close, as many interpreters force and strain the passage. Meanwhile we must add, that the events which the Prophet here narrates are not yet complete ; but this ought to be familiar to all the pious, for whenever the kingdom of Christ is treated of, his glory is magnificently extolled, as if it were now absolutely complete in all its parts. It is not surprising, if according to the frequent and perpetual usage of Scripture, the Prophet should say *power was given* to Christ, to subdue all people, nations, and languages to himself, as it is said in Ps. cx. 1,—Jehovah said to my Lord, Sit thou on my right hand, until I make thy enemies the footstool of thy feet. We see, then, how Christ was raised to his own empire to govern his Church in the name and with the power of his Father, while at the same time many enemies rise up against him. Still the obstinacy of the devil and of all impious men continues, although Christ governs heaven and earth, and is the supreme king before whom every knee is bent. We also know how marked the difference is between the beginning of his kingdom and its final completion. Whatever the meaning, this vision suits very well with many assertions of Christ, where he bears witness to the power

given him by the Father.   (Matt. xxviii. 18, and elsewhere.)
He does not here speak of the last judgment, but is only
teaching us the object of his ascension to heaven.

This view the Prophet confirms by saying, *his dominion
is the dominion of an age, which is not taken away, and his
kingdom can never be corrupted* or abolished.   For by these
words he teaches familiarly and openly, why Christ is the
Supreme King, namely, for the perpetual government of his
Church in this world.   We ought to look up to heaven in
very deed whenever the state of the Church is under consideration, since its happiness is neither earthly, nor perishable, nor temporary, though nothing sublunary is either firm
or perpetual.   But when the Prophet says Christ's dominion
is eternal, he doubtless signifies the constant endurance of
his monarchy even to the end of the world, when he shall
gather his people together to a happy life and an eternal
inheritance.   Although, therefore, celestial immortality is
comprehended under these words, yet in a former passage
the Prophet pointed out the perpetual existence of the
Church in this world, because Christ will defend it, although
daily subject to numberless causes of destruction.   And who
would not assert the almost daily perishing of the Church,
if God did not wonderfully preserve it by the hand of his
only begotten Son?   Hence it is correct to understand the
phrase, *His kingdom shall be the kingdom of an age.*   And
thus we receive no common consolation, when we see the
Church tossed about amidst various fluctuations, and almost
buried and devoured by continual shipwrecks, yet Christ is
ever stretching forth his hand to preserve it, and to save it
from every sorrowful and horrible species of destruction.   It
now follows,—

15. I Daniel was grieved in my
spirit in the midst of *my* body, and
the visions of my head troubled me.

16. I came near unto one of them
that stood by, and asked him the
truth of all this. So he told me,

15. Succisus fuit spiritus meus
mihi Danieli,[1] in medio corporis,[2] et
visiones capitis mei terruerunt me.

16. Accessi ad unum ex his qui
aderant, et sciscitatus sum ex eo
veritatem super his omnibus : et

[1] Or vanished, or my spirit was wanting to me, Daniel.—*Calvin.*

[2] Or "sheath," properly; but here this noun is transferred metaphorically
to the body.—*Calvin.*   Aben-Ezra calls the body "the sheath" of the
mind.—*Ed.*

and made me know the interpreta-   dixit mihi, et enarrationem sermo-
tion of the things.   num patefecit mihi.

Daniel says, his spirit was either cut off or vanished, as if
he suffered some mental deficiency.   In this way God wished
to communicate to his servant the magnitude of the vision.
And he inspires us also with reverence for this vision, lest
we should treat it coldly and commonly.   But we ought to
understand how God opens up to Daniel, his servant, and to
us by his assistance and ministry, these mysteries which
cannot be otherwise comprehended by our human senses.
For if Daniel, whom we know to have been a remarkable
Prophet, felt his spirit to be so deficient and nearly vanishing away, surely we who as yet know so little of God's mysteries, nay, who have scarcely tasted their first rudiments,
never can attain so great a height, unless we overcome the
world and shake off all human sensations.   For these things
cannot be perceived by us unless our minds are clear and
completely purified.

He says, therefore, in the first place, *his spirit was cut off*,
or vanished, *in the midst of his body;* as if he had said he
was almost lifeless and nearly dead.   And he added, as a
reason, *the visions of his head had frightened him.*   No one
can faint away—an event which sometimes happens—without a cause.   When that terror called a panic seizes upon
some persons, we observe how they become deprived of self-
possession, and lie almost lifeless.   But Daniel, to shew himself separate from such persons, says *he was frightened* or
disturbed *by visions of his head;* as if he had said, he was
not disturbed without occasion, but it was caused by the
mystery of which the vision had been offered to him.   He
came to one of those standing by.   He had said a short time
before, ten thousand times ten thousand were at the right
hand of the tribunal of God.   Without the slightest doubt,
the Prophet asked one of these angels.   And here we must
notice his modesty and docility in flying to some instructor,
because he was conscious of his own ignorance and found no
other remedy.   At the same time, we are taught by the
Prophet's example not to reject all visions, but to seek their
interpretation from God himself.   Although God in these

days does not address us by visions, yet he wishes us to be content with his Law and Gospel, while angels do not appear to us, and do not openly and conspicuously descend from heaven ; but, since Scripture is obscure to us, through the darkness in which we are involved, let us learn not to reject whatever surpasses our capacity, even when some dark veil envelops it, but let us fly to the remedy which Daniel used, not to seek the understanding of God's word from angels, who do not appear to us, but from Christ himself, who in these days teaches us familiarly by means of pastors and ministers of the gospel.   Now, as a supreme and only Master has been given us from the Father, so also he exercises the office of teacher by his own ministers whom he set over us.   (Matt. xxiii. 8, 10.)   Therefore, as Daniel approached the angel who was near him, so we are daily commanded to approach those who have been entrusted with the gift of interpretation, and who can faithfully explain to us things otherwise obscure.   Our confidence, too, ought to be increased by what follows directly : *The angel spoke, and opened the interpretation of the words.*   Daniel here shews his modesty and humility not to have been in vain, as God commanded the angel to explain all obscurities.   So, without doubt, Christ will at this time satisfy our prayers, if we are truly his disciples ; that is, if, after those mysteries which surpass and absorb all our senses have terrified us, we fly to that order which he has prescribed for us, and seek from faithful ministers and teachers the interpretation of those things which are difficult and obscure, and entirely concealed from us.

PRAYER.

Grant, Almighty God, since the faith of the fathers was supported by obscure shadows, by which thou didst wish it to be nourished, until thy Son was manifestly revealed to us in the flesh : Grant, I pray thee, at this day, after he has appeared to us as the best and most perfect teacher, and explained thy counsels to us familiarly, that we may not be either so dull or so careless as to allow the great clearness of the manifestation of thyself offered us in the Gospel to escape from our grasp.   May we be so directed towards life eternal, until after the performance of our course in this present life, and the removal of all obstacles which Satan places in our way, either to delay us or turn us aside, we may at length arrive at the enjoyment of that blessed life in which Christ, thine only begotten Son, has preceded us.   May we thus be co-heirs with him, and as thou hast appointed him sole inheritor, so may he gather us unto the secure inheritance of a blessed immortality.—Amen.

Lecture Thirty=Sixth.

17. These great beasts, which are four, *are* four kings, *which* shall arise out of the earth.

18. But the saints of the most High shall take the kingdom, and possess the kingdom for ever, even for ever and ever.

17. Hæ bestiæ magnæ quas vidisti quatuor, *sunt* quatuor regna, *quæ* exsurgent e terra.

18. Et sortientur, *obtinebunt,* regnum sanctorum excelsorum : et possidebunt regnum usque in seculum, et usque in seculum seculorum.

HERE the angel answers Daniel concerning the four beasts which had been shewn him in the vision.   He says, therefore, *Four kingdoms arose,* and by the name kingdom he means monarchy ; for we know that the Persians had many kings until Alexander transferred to himself the empire of the East.   Although Cyrus had seven or eight successors, yet the Persian empire continued through them all.   And as we saw before, although whatever Alexander had acquired by his arms was divided among his four successors, yet it still remained the Macedonian kingdom.   The same thing must be said concerning the fourth kingdom.   Although we know consuls to have been created yearly at Rome, yet that government lasted till Julius Cæsar destroyed it, and consumed the strength of the empire, so as to surpass by his power the splendid altitude which had been long and widely conspicuous in the world.   Hence the angel replied, *By the four beasts four kingdoms* are denoted : he says, *shall arise ;* and yet the Chaldean had long ago arisen, and was now verging under Belshazzar to its fall.   But it was proposed by the angel to teach the Prophet and all the people that there was no reason why revolutions should disturb them too much.   The Israelites then saw themselves lying as if dead, yea, actually buried and concealed under the earth.

For exile was to them equivalent to the tomb. For this reason, then, the angel announces *the springing up of four kingdoms,* while the first was then flourishing ; but, as I have already said, this suits very well with the scope and object of the prophecy. He had formerly said *from the sea,* but the word "sea" is used metaphorically, since the condition of the earth was turbulent through many ages. As, therefore, nothing was stable, God appropriately set forth the whole world under the figure of the sea. He afterwards adds, *They will obtain the kingdom of the holy lofty ones.* Here interpreters vary considerably, because, as I have before explained it, some take this prophecy to relate to the kingdom of Turkey, others to the tyranny of the Pope of Rome, and extend what the Prophet here says to the final judgment. There is nothing surprising, then, in this diversity of opinion shewing itself more fully in the various details. By *sacred holy ones* some understand angels ; but there is still much controversy about the words, for the noun *of saints* is "in regimen," as if the Prophet had said saints of lofty ones, properly speaking.[1] Similar passages justify those who take it "in the absolute state." But if we follow the grammatical construction, we cannot explain it otherwise ; but the former noun may be put in a state of regimen, as we have said. And I embrace this opinion. Some refer it to the one God, but I think this a profane way of expression. I have no doubt about the Prophet meaning sons of God by *sacred lofty ones,* because, though they are pilgrims in the world, yet they raise their minds upwards, and know themselves to be citizens of the heavenly kingdom. Hence by the word עליונין, *gnelionin,* "lofty ones," I have no doubt the Prophet means heavenly powers ; that is, whatever we can conceive of divinity, and whatever is exalted above the world. I will now give my reasons shortly why I like this sense the best.

If we call *the holy lofty ones* God himself, what sense can

---

[1] The Latin here refers to the Hebrew construction. The French translation has expressed Calvin's meaning without keeping close to the words. *Les saincts des souverains* is the French reading of the Hebrew regimen. See DISSERTATIONS at the end of this volume.—*Ed.*

we elicit from the passage? Did the Chaldeans and the rest of the monarchies usurp and transfer to themselves the power of God? There is some truth in this, because all who domineer without submitting to the one God despoil him of his peculiar honour, and are rather robbers than kings. But the Prophet, in my opinion, understood something else from the angel, namely, that the Church should lose all form and dignity in the world during the flourishing of these four monarchies. We know the sons of God to be heirs of the world; and Paul, when speaking of the promise given to Abraham, says, he was chosen by God as heir of the world. (Rom. iv. 13; Heb. i. 2.) And this doctrine is sufficiently known—the world was created for the sake of the human race. When Adam fell from his lawful rights, all his posterity became aliens; God deprived them of the inheritance which he had designed for them. Now, therefore, our inheritance must be restored through Christ, for which reason he is called the only heir of the world. Thus it is not surprising if the angel says that tyrants, when they exercise supreme dominion, assume and arrogate to themselves the peculiar property of the sacred lofty ones, meaning the people of God. And this suits very well with the assertions of the present passage concerning the Church being deprived of its dignity, eminence, and visibility in the world. For then God's people were like a putrid carcase, the limbs of which were separated and dispersed on all sides, without any hope of restoration. Lastly, although by the permission of Darius, and the edict and liberality of Cyrus, some portion of them returned to their country, yet what was that nominal return? They had but a precarious dwelling in the inheritance divinely promised them; they were pressed on all sides by their enemies, and were subject to the lust and injustice of them all. For the Church had no empire under the Persians. After the third change we know how miserably they were afflicted, especially under Antiochus. That nation was always opposed to them, but then they were almost reduced to extremities, when Antiochus endeavoured furiously to abolish the whole law and worship of God. Under the Macedonian kingdom the Jews were in constant slavery; but when the Roman army penetrated those regions, they felt the horrible tyranny of the fourth beast, as we have already seen. Lastly, it is sufficiently evident from the continual history of those times, that the sons of God were always under the yoke, and were not only cruelly but ignominiously treated.

Thus this prophecy was fulfilled, namely, *The four beasts took upon themselves the empire which properly belonged to the sacred lofty ones;* that is, to God's elect sons, who, though dwellers on earth, are dependent on heaven. In this interpretation I see nothing forced, and whoever prudently weighs the matter will, as I hope, recognise what I have said as the meaning of the Prophet. The latter clause now follows: *They shall obtain the kingdom,* says he, *for ever, and even for ever and ever.* A difficult question arises here, because by these words Daniel, or the angel addressing him, seems to express a perpetual condition under these four monarchies. Belshazzar was the last king of the Babylonian dynasty, and at the period of this vision the overthrow of that monarchy was at hand. With regard to the Persian kings, there were only eight of them besides Cyrus. And concerning Alexander we know a sudden change happened; the terror of him spread abroad like a storm, but it vanished away after it had affected all the people of the East. The Macedonian kingdom also suffered a concussion, when those leaders began to disagree among themselves who had obtained from Alexander authority and rank; and at length the kingdom became fourfold, as we have already stated, and shall mention again. Now if we count the years, the length of those monarchies was not so great as to justify the epithet "perpetual." I reply, this must be referred to the sensations of the pious, to whom that delay seemed specially tedious, so that they would have pined away in their miseries, had not this prophecy in some way relieved them. We see at the present moment how great is the fervour of desire when reference is made to the help of God; and when our minds have been heated with desire, they immediately decline to impatience. It thus happens that the promises of God do not suffice to sustain us, because nothing is more difficult than to bear long delay. For if the Church in our time had been oppressed for a hundred years, what constancy would have been discerned in us? If a whirlwind arises, we are astonished, and cry out, "What next? what next?" Three or four months will not have elapsed before all men enter upon a strife with God and expostulate with him, because he does not hasten at once to bring assistance to his Church. We are not surprised, then, at the angel here assigning one age, or even an "age of ages," to tyrants under whom the Church should be oppressed. Although I do not doubt the reference to the fulness of times, as we know Christ to have been the end of the Law, and as his advent drew nearer, so God admonished the faithful to carry forward their own expectations to the advent of their Redeemer. When, therefore, the angel uses the phrase *one age and an age of ages,* I have no doubt that he defined the time for the elect, to strengthen them in patiently bearing trouble of all kinds, as this had been divinely decreed ; for the four beasts were to reign not only for a few years, but for *continual ages ;* that is, until the time of renovation had arrived for the world, when God completely restored his Church. Let us proceed :—

19. Then I would know the truth of the fourth beast, which was diverse from all the others, exceeding dreadful, whose teeth *were of* iron, and his nails *of* brass; *which* devoured, brake in pieces, and stamped the residue with his feet;

20. And of the ten horns that *were* in his head, and *of* the other which came up, and before whom three fell; even *of* that horn that had eyes, and a mouth that spake very great things, whose look *was* more stout than his fellows.

19. Tunc optavi ad veritatem[1] de bestia quarta, quæ erat diversa ab omnibus aliis, terribilis valde, cujus dentes *erant* ferri, *ferrei,* et ungues æris, *ærei,* comedens et conterens, et residuum pedibus suis conculcans.

20. Et super cornibus decem, *de cornibus decem,* quæ *erant* in capite ejus, et de postremo quod surgebat, et *quod* ceciderant ex prioribus tria : et *quod* cornu illi *erant* oculi, et os loquens grandia : et aspectus ejus magnus præ sociis.[2]

Here the Prophet interrogates the angel concerning the Fourth Beast more attentively and carefully ; as we formerly saw him touched with greater admiration on beholding the beast which was formidable beyond the other three, so that neither a name nor representation could be found for it.

---

[1] This word לִצְבָא, *litzba,* is usually explained to mean "for the truth," that is, I desired to know.—*Calvin.* The *Vulgate* has "diligentius discere." *Wintle,* "accurate information."

[2] That is, "beyond the other beasts."—*Calvin.*

As, therefore, God displayed something great under the image of the fourth beast, he caused his Prophet to wake up to understand the mystery of it. For this reason he now interrogates the angel; for he says *he wished for the truth* concerning the fourth beast, and he also repeats what we saw before, namely, *its being different from the others.* And surely the subjugation of so many kings by the Romans was a difference worthy of notice. Let us think upon the origin of that nation ;—a few robbers seizing upon a desert spot, growing great by brutal audacity and force, until they reduced all their neighbours under their power. Then they crossed the sea, and added first one province, and then another to their sway. And when the kingdom of Macedon came within their power, this was indeed portentous. At length they became masters throughout the whole circuit of the Mediterranean, and there was no corner which did not receive their yoke ; and this could never have been imagined by human apprehension.

It is said then, *this beast was different from the others, and very terrible.* In the same sense *its teeth* are called *iron*, and *its claws brazen.* No mention had hitherto been made of the claws ; the Prophet had spoken only of iron teeth, but he now adds *brazen claws*, as if he had said, This beast shall be endued with such savage madness, as not only to attack all things by its unusual violence, but to tear, lacerate, and devour all things ; as he repeats again what he had said, *eating and destroying and treading under foot the remainder.* As I have already explained all these points, I am unwilling to consume your time in vain and to confuse you with useless repetitions. *I asked also*, said he, *concerning the ten horns which were upon its head.* And this is the reason why I must cut the subject off shortly here, as the angel's reply will follow directly. The Prophet, therefore, is now, without doubt, placed under a celestial impulse, because God was unwilling to teach him only as a private person ; he was to be a witness and herald of so great a mystery ; and we may at this day learn from his writings, which are of the utmost use to us when we become fully acquainted with them.

He says, therefore, *He also inquired about the ten horns which were on the head of the beast, and of the other horn which had arisen*, meaning the small one, *and concerning the three horns falling from the face of the beast.* We have shewn how provinces were denoted by the ten horns, and how the difference between the Roman Empire and other monarchies was pointed out, because there never was one supreme ruler at Rome, except when Sylla and Marius exercised their usurped authority—but each for only a short time. Here then the continual state of the Roman Empire is under review, for it was not simply a single animal, as it had ten horns. A finite number is put for an indefinite one. With regard to the little horn, I said it referred to the Cæsars, who attracted the whole government of the state to themselves, after depriving the people of their liberty and the senate of their power, while even under their sway some dignity was continued to the senate and some majesty retained by the people. We have explained also how the three horns were broken; that is, how craftily the Cæsars infringed upon and diminished the strength of both people and senate. Lastly, we have accounted for this little horn being displayed with human eyes, since the Cæsars exercised their dominion with cunning, when they pretended to be only tribunes of the people, and allowed the ensigns of empire to remain in the hands of the consuls; for when they came into the senate, they sat in a lowly situation in curule seats prepared for the tribunes. As, therefore, they tyrannized with such cleverness and cunning, instead of by open violence, they are said to be endowed with the eyes of a man. Then as to the tongue, the sense is the same; for although they always professed the consular power to be supreme in the state, yet they could not restrain themselves, but vomited forth many reproachful speeches. On the one side, we see them remarkable for eyes, and on the other, for the tongue. *And its aspect was terrible beyond its companions.* This seems not to belong peculiarly to the little horn which had arisen among the ten, but rather to the fourth beast. But if any one wishes to understand it of the little horn, I will not contest the point, as it will thus make tolerable sense. But I rather embrace my former opinion, for it is not surprising to find the Prophet after his discourse on the little horn, returning to the beast himself.

21. I beheld, and the same horn made war with the saints, and prevailed against them;	21. Vidi, et cornu illud faciebat prælium cum sanctis, et prævaluit illis.
22. Until the Ancient of days came, and judgment was given to the saints of the most High; and the time came that the saints possessed the kingdom.	22. Donec venit Antiquus dierum, et judicium datum est sanctis excelsorum, et venit tempus, et regnum acceperunt sancti.

The Prophet now adds what he had omitted. The angel does not yet answer him, but as he had not sufficiently expressed how the little horn waged war with the sons of God, he now supplies the omission. He says, therefore, *he saw* —this ought to be received by way of correction; *I saw*, says he, meaning it was shewn me in a vision, how the little horn *made war with the saints so as to prevail against them.* Clearly enough other tyrants assailed the elect people of God with far greater injury. Hence many refer this to Antiochus Epiphanes, who was hostile to the Jews beyond all others, and was utterly determined to blot out the name of the God of Israel. And we know how often he raised powerful armaments to extinguish both the people and the worship of God. As, therefore, the cruelty of Antiochus was so severe against the Israelites, many think his image to have been exhibited to the Prophet as the little horn, and what we shall afterwards see about "the time," and "times," and "half-a-time," they explain of the three years and a half during which the Temple was in ruins, and the people thereby prevented from offering sacrifices. As, therefore, their religion was then interrupted, they think that tyranny was denoted, by which the people were prohibited from testifying their piety. But although this opinion is plausible, and at first sight bears upon the face of it the appearance of truth, yet if we weigh all things in order, we may easily judge how unsuitable it is to Antiochus. Why, therefore, does the Prophet say—*the little horn waged war with the saints?* Antiochus certainly made war against the Church, and so did many others; the Egyptians, we know, often broke in and spoiled the Temple and the Romans too, before the monarchy of the Cæsars. I reply, this is spoken comparatively, because no war was ever carried on so continuously and professedly against the Church, as those which occurred after the Cæsars arose, and after Christ was made manifest to the world; for the devil was then more enraged, and God also relaxed the reins to prove the patience of his people. Lastly, it was natural for the bitterest conflicts to occur when the redemption of the world was carried out; and the event clearly shewed this. We know first of all, by horrid examples, how Judea was laid waste, for never was such cruelty practised against any other people. Nor was the calamity of short duration; we are well acquainted with their extreme obstinacy, which compelled their enemies to forget clemency altogether. For the Romans desired to spare them as far as possible, but so great was their obstinacy and the madness of their rage, that they provoked their enemies as if devoting themselves to destruction, until that dreadful slaughter happened, of which history has sufficiently informed us. When Titus, under the auspices of his father Vespasian, took and destroyed the city, the Jews were stabbed and slaughtered like cattle throughout the whole extent of Asia. Thus far, then, it concerns the Jews.

When God had inserted the body of the Gentiles into his Church, the cruelty of the Cæsars embraced all Christians; thus the little horn waged war with the saints in a manner different from that of the former beasts, because the occasion was different, and the wrath of Satan was excited against all God's children on account of the manifestation of Christ. This, then, is the best explanation of *the little horn waging war against the saints.* Thus he says, *It must prevail.* For the Cæsars and all who governed the provinces of the empire raged with such extreme violence against the Church, that it almost disappeared from the face of the earth. And thus it happened, that the little horn prevailed in appearance and in general opinion, as, for a short time, the safety of the Church was almost despaired of.

It now follows, *Until the Ancient of days came, judgment was given to the saints of the lofty ones.* No doubt the Prophet says God came in the same sense as before; namely, when he erected his tribunal and openly appeared as the judge of the world in the person of Christ. He does not here set before us the Son of man, as he did before, but yet a fuller explanation of this passage is to be sought in the former one. *God* then is said *to have come*, when he put forth his power in supplying the needs of the Church, as by a common figure he is said to be at a distance from us, and to sleep or to be reposing, when he does not shew himself openly as our deliverer. So, on the other hand, he is said to come to us, when he openly proves his constant care of us. Under this figure Daniel now says he beheld the appearance of God himself. *The Ancient of days then came.* If we ask when, we have the reply at hand; it was immediately after the promulgation of the gospel. Then God stretched forth his hand for his Church, and lifted it out of the abyss. For since the Jewish name had been for a long time hated, and all people desired to exterminate the Jews from the world, Christ's advent increased this hatred and cruelty; and the license to injure them was added, as they thought Christ's disciples were plotting a change of government, and wished to overthrow the existing state of things; as in these days all the pious suffer grievously under this false imputation. God, therefore, is said to have come, when the doctrine of the gospel was more and more promulgated, and some rest granted to the Church. Thus, by this repose, *the saints received the kingdom* which had been taken from them; that is, the kingdom of God and of the saints obtained some fame and celebrity in the world, through the general diffusion of the doctrine of piety, in every direction. Now, therefore, we understand what Daniel wished to convey by the phrase, *The Ancient of days came, and judgment was given to the saints of the lofty ones.* The remainder tomorrow.

PRAYER.

Grant, Almighty God, since thou provest our faith and constancy by many trials, as it is our duty in this respect and in all others, to submit to thy will: Grant, I pray, that we may not give way to the many attacks by which we are tossed about. For we are assailed on all sides by Satan and all the impious, and while their fury is ever burning and raging cruelly against us, may we never yield to it.   May we proceed in our warfare, in reliance on the unconquered might of the Spirit, even though impious men prevail for a season.   May we look forward to the advent of thy only-begotten Son, not only when he shall appear at the last day, but also whenever it shall please thee for him to assist thy Church, and to raise it out of its miserable afflictions.   And even if we must endure our distresses, may our courage never fail us, until at length we are gathered into that happy rest, which has been obtained for us through the blood of the same, thine only-begotten Son.—Amen.

Lecture Thirty=Seventh.

WE yesterday began to explain how *judgment was given to the saints* at the commencement of the gospel era.   For we know how very partial even in those times was the Church's tranquillity.   Because when it was free from external persecution and the shedding of blood, domestic enemies arose who proved far more injurious.   Thus the kingdom of Christ never flourished in the world, so as to have anything in common with those empires, in which great splendour and pomp were apparent.   But God wished to propose this solace to his Prophet, by shewing him the future reputation of the Church and its elevation to some degree of honour after emerging from obscurity, so that the elect dared openly to give homage to Christ, and to profess true and sincere piety. Hence by judgment being given to the saints, the Prophet means the restoration of the right of which they had been deprived, and their obtaining the kingdom at the same time, as the Church no longer lay prostrate as before the advent of Christ.   For the promulgation of the gospel was at length free, as we shall immediately see.   Let us proceed to the context,—

23. Thus he said, The fourth beast shall be the fourth kingdom upon earth, which shall be diverse

23. Sic dixit,[1] Bestia quarta, regnum quartum erit in terra, quod erit diversum ab omnibus regnis:

[1] The expression seems concise, but because he had formerly added what had been omitted, for the purpose of connecting the history, he repeats again, "the angel said so," namely, " as to that portion of the vision, thus spake the angel."—*Calvin.*

from all kingdoms, and shall devour the whole earth, and shall tread it down, and break it in pieces.

et vorabit[1] totam terram, et conteret,[2] et comminuet eam.

24. And the ten horns out of this kingdom *are* ten kings *that* shall arise : and another shall rise after them ; and he shall be diverse from the first, and he shall subdue three kings.

24. Et cornua decem ab illo regno, decem Reges sunt, qui exorientur, *qui surgent*, et aliud postremum surget post illos *Reges*,[3] et ipse[4] erit diversus a superioribus,[5] et tres Reges affliget.

This reply of the angel is subject to the same obscurity as the vision itself, but it ought to be sufficient to calm the minds of the faithful to know that various changes should arise and shake the whole earth ; for as many troubles were prepared for the saints, so also they were braced up to fortitude and endurance.   For God was not willing fully to explain what he had shewn to his Prophet; he only wished to set before him this conclusion—a kingdom shall arise completely different from all others.   Thus the angel says, The Fourth Beast signifies *a fourth kingdom, which shall differ from all the kingdoms.*   Previously to that period, no state was so extensive in its sway.   For although the Spartans and Athenians performed illustrious and memorable exploits, yet we know them to have been included within narrow boundaries ; and the ambition and wordy vanity of the Greeks caused them to celebrate those wars which were scarcely of any consequence, as we learn even from their own histories.   Whichever way we take this, Sparta obtained with difficulty the second rank in Greece, as Athens did the first.   As far as concerns the Roman Empire, we know it to have been more extensive and powerful than the other monarchies.   When all Italy came under their sway, this was sufficient for any noble monarchy ; but Spain, Sicily, part of Greece, and Illyricum were added, and afterwards all Greece and Macedon, Asia Minor, Africa, and all the islands ; for by one word they expelled the king of Cyprus, and sold his goods by public auction.   When the dregs of the people were collected, Claudius made a law for the banishment of

[1] Some translate it in the passive, " lest any change be made."—*Calvin.*
[2] Some translate, " shall rub to pieces," but the sense is the same.—*Calvin.*
[3] Or, after those horns.—*Calvin.*
[4] King, or the horn itself, shall be different.—*Calvin.*
[5] Which is denoted by the horn.—*Calvin.*

the king of Cyprus, and this he accomplished by his single voice, without the use of force at all.   No wonder then that God foretold *how different this kingdom should be from all the others;* it had no single head ; the senate had the chief authority, though all power was centred in the people. There was therefore a kind of mingled confusion, since the government of Rome was never settled.   And if we weigh all things prudently, it was neither a republic nor a kingdom, but a confused compound, in which the people exercised great power in a tumultuous way, and the senate oppressed the people as much as it could.   There were three ranks— the senatorian, the equestrian, and the plebeian, and that mixture made the kingdom like a monster.   The angel, therefore, announces *the fourth kingdom as different from the others.*

He afterwards confirms what we said before ; *it will fall,* says he, *and break to pieces, and tread down the whole earth.* This was fulfilled after Gaul and Britain were subdued, Germany partially subjugated, and Illyricum, Greece, and Macedon, reduced to submission.   At length they penetrated to Asia, and Antiochus was banished beyond the Taurus ; his kingdom afterwards became their prey, then they obtained possession of Syria.   The kings of Egypt were their allies, and yet became dependent upon their nod ; the sovereign dared not appoint an heir, without consulting their pleasure.   As, therefore, they ruled supremely so long and so widely, they fulfilled this prophecy by *devouring the whole earth.*   For such lust for dominion never existed before ; wars were heaped upon wars, they were alike greedy of the blood of others, and by no means sparing of their own.   The whirlpool was insatiable, while it absorbed the whole world, and their pride crushed it and trampled it under foot. Cruelty was added to pride, for all looked up to the Romans, and conciliated the favour of Rome by flattery, for the purpose of raging savagely against their own people.   By these arts almost the whole of Greece perished.   For they knew how many innocent persons everywhere perished in every city, a kind of diversion which delighted them ; they were fully aware how easy it was to attract all the power of the

whole world to themselves, when it was able to put forth
neither strength, nor skill, nor power against them. For
their nobles were constantly at variance; sometimes one
faction and sometimes another was supreme, and thus the
splendour of every city easily and gradually diminished.
Thus all Greece was spoiled, and the Romans exercised their
dominion there without difficulty, as over brute beasts. We
may say the same of Asia also. We are not surprised then
at the angel saying, *the earth would be trodden down and
trampled on by this fourth beast.*

He afterwards adds, *The ten horns are the ten kings which
should arise.* These Ten Kings are clearly comprehended
under one empire, and there is no question here of separate
persons. In the Persian kingdom, we observed many kings,
and yet the image of the second beast was single, while it
embraced all those kings until the change occurred. So also
now, when treating of the Romans, the Prophet does not
assert that ten kings should succeed each other in regular
order, but rather the multiform nature of the kingdom, under
more heads than one. For the royal office belonged to the
senators or leading citizens, whose authority prevailed very
extensively both with the senate and the people. And with
reference to the number, we said the plural number only was
denoted, without any limitation to the number ten. The
conclusion is as follows,—this kingdom should be like a single
terrible animal bearing many horns, since no single king held
the chief sway there, as was customary by common usage in
other lands, but there should be a mixture, like many kings
in place of one holding the pre-eminence. The fulfilment
of this is sufficiently known from the history of Rome; as
if it had been said, there should not be any single king at
Rome, as of Persia and other nations, but many kings at the
same time, alluding to the mixture and confusion in which
the supreme authority was involved.

The Little Horn follows : *A king shall arise,* says he, *different from those former ones, and shall afflict three kings.* We
shewed how unintelligible this becomes, unless we refer it
to the Cæsars to whom the monarchy passed ; for after long
and continued and intestine strife, the whole power passed

over to the Triumvirate.   A conspiracy was entered into by
Lepidus, Mark Antony, and Octavius.   Octavius was then
all but a boy, having scarcely arrived at manhood, but all
the veteran soldiers were in his favour, in consequence of the
name of Julius Cæsar and his adoption by him.   Hence he
was received by the other two into that alliance, of which
Lepidus was the first, and Antony the second.   At length
discords arose among them, and Lepidus was deprived of his
place in the triumvirate, and lived, as if half-dead, while his
life was only spared to him because he was raised to the
office of chief priest.

Reverence for the priesthood restrained Antony from
putting him to death, as long as he was content to live in
privacy and retirement.   Octavius at length became supreme,
but by what artifice?   We said Julius Cæsar took no more
upon himself than the office of dictator, while consuls were
annually elected as usual.   He did not strain the power of
the dictatorship beyond moderation, but he so restrained
himself, that some popular rights might seem still to flourish.
Octavius also followed the cunning of his uncle and adopted
father.   The same conduct will be found in the other Cæsars,
though there were many differences between them.   As the
shadow of a republic yet remained, while the senate was held
in some degree of reverence, it is not surprising, if the angel
predicts that the beast should survive, *when another small
horn should arise different from the others.*

He adds, *And shall afflict the three kings.*   I have explained this point by the slight change which the Cæsars
effected in the provinces, for if any of the provinces were
warlike, strong armies and veteran soldiers were usually
sent there.   The Cæsars took these to themselves, while
some executive management was left to the senate with
regard to the other provinces.   Lastly, by this form of
speech, the angel portrays the coming dominion of the little
horn, and its diminishing the strength of the former ones:
and yet the beast should remain apparently entire; thus,
the effigy of the republic was preserved, as the people were
always designated—in the forum, by the high-sounding name,
Romans, and in battle, as fellow-soldiers.   Meanwhile,

although the name of the Roman empire was so celebrated, and its majesty was in every one's mouth, the supreme authority was in the possession of one little horn which lay concealed, and dared not openly raise its head. This, then, is the pith of the interpretation of what the angel here sets before us. It follows,—

25. And he shall speak *great* words against the most High, and shall wear out the saints of the most High, and think to change times and laws: and they shall be given into his hand, until a time and times and the dividing of time.	25. Et sermones ad regionem, *vel ad latus*, excelsi loquetur, et sanctos excelsorum conteret, et putabit ad mutandum[2] tempora et legem : et tradetur in manum ejus usque ad tempus, et tempora, et divisionem temporis.

The angel now explains a little more clearly what the Prophet had formerly touched upon but briefly, namely, this last king should be a manifest and professed enemy to the Church. We yesterday shewed how miserably and cruelly the Church had been harassed by many tyrants. And if we compare these tyrants with each other, we shall find the Church to have been much more heavily afflicted after Christ's advent, and to have been opposed by the Cæsars in open warfare. The occasion arose in this way. The doctrine of the Gospel had been dispersed through almost all the provinces of the empire. The Jewish name was hateful ; and the novelty of the teaching added greatly to that unpopularity. Men thought the Jews had invented a new deity for themselves—even Christ, as their language seemed to imply the worship of a new divinity. As, therefore, some material for rage against the pure worship of God was afforded them, the Cæsars became more and more stirred up to carry on war against the elect, and to oppress the Church. It was not their fault if they did not extinguish the whole light of the celestial doctrine, abolish true religion, and banish the knowledge of God from the world. This agrees very well with what Daniel relates of this king becoming so headstrong, as to *utter words against the most High God.* Some translate it, on the part of the most High, but I know no reason for their doing so. לצד, *letzed,* signi-

---

[1] Others translate, " shall consume, afflict."—*Calvin.*
[2] That is, he shall think with himself to change.—*Calvin.*

fies on the side or the region. The equivalent phrase is this ; so great should be the pride of this new king, who did not exercise his power openly but by hidden deceit, that he should sit as it were on the side of God and in opposition to him. This means he should be manifestly God's enemy. Those who understand this of Antichrist, think their opinion confirmed by the conduct of other tyrants who carried on their warfare against God with arms and violence, but not by words. But the Prophet does not speak so subtlely here. For by *words* he does not here mean doctrine, but that verbal boasting by which the Cæsars dared to promulgate their edicts throughout the whole world, urging all the proconsuls to punish the Christians, and not to permit that impious and cursed sect to flourish ; and thus terrors flew about throughout the whole world. What Daniel now relates was then fulfilled, namely, *the utterance of words of defiance against God ;* for those tyrants thought their own edicts, without the armament of soldiers, would be sufficient to extinguish the memory of Christ. Thus, also, true piety was disgracefully traduced, and the very name of Christ lacerated by horrible reproaches, as historians have amply informed us.

This explanation, therefore, is most suitable *to the little horn speaking* or uttering *words against the most High. He shall afflict*, says he, *the saints of the lofty ones.* We have already briefly explained the meaning of this expression, according to its grammatical construction. By saints he doubtless means sons of God, or his elect people, or the Church. He calls these " saints of lofty ones," because as elect they depend upon heaven ; and although they are pilgrims in the world, yet their life is in heaven, where the eternal inheritance remains for them which was obtained by Christ. As, therefore, their treasure is now heaven, they deservedly boast of being citizens of heaven, and allies and brethren of angels. Thus they are properly called " saints of lofty ones ;" they are separated from the world, and know themselves to live here day by day until they arrive at firm and enduring repose. We know this to have been fulfilled, because overwhelming terror fell upon all the pious, and the

Church almost perished, while multitudes who were suspected of being Christians were subjected to cruel tortures. The prevalence of this universal license for persecuting all the pious explains how the saints were then afflicted by the small horn.

The Prophet or rather the angel next says, *He will think,* or meditate, *to change time and law, and they shall be delivered into his hand.* As to the time here spoken of, many refer it to holy days. But we may understand it generally of the small horn overthrowing whatever was formerly customary in the world ; and thus also I interpret the word רת, *reth,* not the Law of God or the Gospel, but any rites, customs, and institutions. While interpreters are contending about this word, some referring it to the Decalogue, and others to the preaching of the Gospel, I think the simple sense of the Prophet to be this : the Cæsars perverted all laws, both human and divine. We have seen how they attempted this, and how far they accomplished it. It is not surprising then if the Prophet assigns this unbridled audacity to this last king, *who thought to change whatever had been formerly ordained in the world.* And for this reason it had been formerly said this horn should be furnished with human eyes ; and next, should speak mightily, thundering horribly, and inspiring all men with fear through its voice alone. We know this to have been represented as in a glass, if we consider how far the Cæsars proceeded in their arrogance. First, as to Octavius, while he restrained himself within due bounds politically, he suffered himself to be adored as a god, and altars to be erected to him ; he wished the public to be persuaded of his deity, and celebrated a banquet in which he sat among the superior deities. Tiberius neglected religious ceremonies entirely, and yet we see how he despised all men. Although he was of an obtuse disposition, in his daring he was extreme, and was all the while craftily deceiving the senate. Next, as to Caligula, he threatened Jupiter in this way,—" What ! thou art an exile here and I a native : I will banish thee into Greece thy native place." He often inflicted blows upon the statue of Jupiter, and not content with the name of a god, he ordered the chief sacrifices to be offered to himself. This diabolic fury increased in Domitian. And considering the Cæsars as men, what was their character? One of them said, " I wish the Roman people had but one neck." He enjoyed the slaughter of the senate as a sport, and wished to make his horse a consul. How disgraceful was such conduct! We see, then, how this prediction was not uttered without a cause ; namely, so great should be the arrogance of the small horn that it would dare to change and turn into a new chaos all " law," meaning all order of every kind, and " times," meaning the very series and nature of all things. The Prophet then says *he thought.* He does not express the result, but simply signifies the arrival of the small horn at such a degree of madness as to suppose it could draw down the sun from heaven, turn light into darkness, and leave nothing entire, nothing in order, throughout the world. Those occurrences really happened in accordance with this prophecy. I cannot enter into details here. I should have to detain you many days or even months with citing history ; I can only touch shortly upon what is necessary for explaining the Prophet's words and the meaning of his prediction.

They shall be delivered into his hands means,—however the small horn should leap forward in desperate fury, yet God should always rule over him, and nothing should happen without his permission. It was God then who delivered into the hands of that king the saints, the political government, and the institutions of piety, allowing him to pour out promiscuously human blood, to violate every national right, and to ruin as far as possible all religion. It brings us then no little comfort to know when God's permission is given to tyrants to harass the Church and interfere with his lawful worship ; for if we were left to the mercy of their lusts, how distressing would be the universal confusion! But he succours us, as the angel says, when tyrants assail us and disturb all order by their horrible licentiousness and cruel rage against the miserable and the innocent : he succours us, I say, so that they are unable to move a finger against us without God's permission. We are not permitted to know why God relaxes the rein in favour of the enemies of his

Church ; perhaps it is to prove and try the patience of his people. It is sufficient for us, if, when tyrants scheme and plot in every way, they are unable to do anything without the divine permission.

But a greater consolation is added in the last clause, *even for a time and times, and the division of a time,* or half, as some translate it ; it is properly a division. Interpreters differ widely about these words, and I will not bring forward all their opinions, otherwise it would be necessary to refute them. I should have no little trouble in refuting all their views, but I will follow my own custom of shortly expressing the genuine sense of the Prophet, and thus all difficulty will be removed. Those who consider a "time" to mean a "year," are in my opinion wrong. They cite the forty-two months of the Apocalypse, (chap. xiii. 5,) which make three years and a half ; but that argument is not conclusive, since in that case a year will not consist of 365 days, but the year itself must be taken figuratively for any indeterminate time. It is better then to keep close to the Prophet's words. A "time," then, is not put for a certain number of months or days, nor yet for a single year, but for any period whose termination is in the secret counsel of God. *They shall be given,* then, *for a time,* says he, and afterwards adds *times ;* that is, for a continuance of times ; and again, *even to a section* or division *of a time ;* meaning, these calamities should come to an end whenever God, in mercy to his Church, should restrain those tyrants by his wrath against them. As long, therefore, as the cruelty of the Cæsars oppressed God's Church, it was committed into their hands. We have already seen how many Cæsars were enemies of the true Church. First of all, Nero raged most cruelly, for he burnt some thousands of Christians at Rome, to extinguish the infamy which raged against himself. The people could not endure his barbarity ; for, while the fourth part of the city was destroyed by fire, he was enjoying his pleasure and rejoicing in so mournful a spectacle ! As he feared the popular tumult against himself, he laid hold of many Christians, and offered them to the people as a kind of expiation. Those who followed him did not cease to pour forth innocent blood, and those who seemed to be endued with some degree of clemency and humanity were all at length seized with a diabolic fury. Trajan was esteemed a very excellent prince, and yet we know how he commanded the Christians everywhere to be slain, since he thought them obstinate in their error.   And others were more savage still.   No wonder, therefore, the angel predicts, *even for a time, and times, and the division of a time,* that license would be given to the tyrants and enemies of the Church to pervert all things, to despise God, and set aside all justice, and to execute a cruel and barbarous slaughter.   This ought to be predicted for two reasons : first, lest through length of time the faithful should fall away, because when " the time"—a space of about ten years—had passed, they would come to *the times,* consisting of about fifty or a hundred years.

This, then, was one reason why God admonished the faithful *concerning the time and times.*   But he wished also to mitigate their sorrow by adding *half a time,* thus promising some moderation and ending to such great calamities.   The language of our Lord to his Apostles concerning the various commotions of the earth, corresponds very well with this view. " There shall arise wars and rumours of wars, and no end as yet," says he.   He announces them as the preludes to greater evils, when the whole of Judea should be devastated with wars and other slaughters.   He afterwards adds, " Unless those days had been shortened."   (Matt. xxiv. 6 ; Mark xiii. 7 ; Luke xxi. 9.)   This shortening of the days is here noticed as if the Lord cut short a continued succession of them.   For when the possession of the tyranny appeared fierce, then suddenly and beyond the expectation of all, God at length snatched away his Church, and then the evangelical doctrine emerged, and was celebrated everywhere.   God, therefore, then shortened the days on account of his own elect, and this is understood by the last clause, *a division of a time.* I will defer the rest till to-morrow.

PRAYER.

Grant, Almighty God, since we must be daily exercised by various contests, that we may never yield to the infirmities of the flesh, and never forget thy holy calling.   Animate us, we pray thee, for all hostile engagements; may we stand unbroken against all the assaults of Satan and the wicked; and thus give ourselves up and devote ourselves to thee.   May we never hesitate to suffer death itself, if necessary, and even to offer ourselves daily to various kinds of death, until we shall have discharged our warfare, and enjoy that happy and eternal rest which thou hast prepared for us in thine only-begotten Son.—Amen.

Lecture Thirty=Eighth.

26. But the judgment shall sit, and they shall take away his dominion, to consume and to destroy *it* unto the end.	26. Et judicium sedebit, et potestatem ejus auferent ad dissipandum et perdendum,[1] usque in finem.

THE angel now answers Daniel concerning the death of the fourth beast.   For we said when the Cæsars had transferred the empire to themselves, the strength of the senate and of the people was enervated; but because the name still remained, the fourth beast is not said to have been slain until foreigners disgracefully became masters of Rome.   For if the Romans had been conquered a hundred times over by professed enemies, they would not have suffered such disgrace as when obscure and low-born men exercise a cruel and barbarous tyranny; for then neither the senate nor the people enjoy any authority.   The angel thus marks the time correctly at which the fourth beast was to fall, when the Spaniards, the Africans, and other barbarians, who were even always unknown in their own country, were raised to the highest honours beyond the expectation of mankind.   For their lust oppressed the whole state; they beheaded the most noble senators, and appointed in their stead the meanest of men, in token of their spirit of ignominy.   *Then the fourth beast was slain;* and this is the explanation of this portion of the angel's reply.   He says also, *Judgment shall then sit;* that is, God shall again restore to order all this confusion, and the world shall feel his Providence ruling over the earth and the human race.   For when all things are allowed to proceed without punishment, and neither justice nor honesty are held

[1] That is, to dissipate and blot out.—*Calvin.*

in any account, God is then supposed to be enjoying his ease in heaven, and to be forgetful of the human race.   Hence, in opposition to this, he is said to ascend a tribunal as often as we really and experimentally feel his care over us.   Thus the restoration is here called a sitting in judgment, when the Roman empire was blotted out, and God executed the penalty of such great and such unbridled ferocity as that already recorded.   As this phrase is very common and of frequent use in Scripture, I will not continue the explanation.

The judgment, then, *shall be set;* that is, after all things have been long involved in darkness, new light shall burst forth, and men shall readily acknowledge the sway of the Almighty.   *And power*, says he, *shall they take away from the beast for dissipating and destroying even to the end.*   Here the angel announces the final overthrow of the fourth beast. Respecting the plural number of the verb, we have already mentioned the opinion of some who refer it to more angels than one, but it is better to understand it more simply, as an absolute and indefinite form of expression.   And yet I do not object, as I before stated, to the view of those who take it of angels, yet I fear this is too refined ; I prefer the simpler view as being free from all controversy.   The sense, then, is this : When the beast shall have raged cruelly for a length of time, and especially the little horn, God shall discharge the duty of a judge, and the beast, with this small horn, shall be removed out of the way.   The angel adds next, There shall be no hope of any new life similar to that of many kingdoms which often fall at one period and rise again at another ; but he here announces the final slaughter, as if he had said, the wound is incurable and deadly.   It now follows :—

27. And the kingdom and dominion, and the greatness of the kingdom under the whole heaven, shall be given to the people of the saints of the most High, whose kingdom *is* an everlasting kingdom, and all dominions shall serve and obey him.

27. Et regnum, et potestas, et magnitudo regni sub toto cœlo dabitur populo sanctorum excelsorum.   Regnum ejus regnum seculi, *hoc est, perpetuum,* et omnes potestates ei servient, atque obedient.

This verse assures us how these predictions concerning the destruction of the beast regard the Church's safety.

Thus the faithful might know themselves noticed by God, and how the changes which successively happened tended to the same end—the acknowledgment on the part of the pious of their continuance under the care and guardianship of God. For any discussion of the four monarchies would have been cold and useless, unless there had been added God's peculiar care of his own Church, and his conducting the affairs of the world for the safety of his people. As we have said in other places, God's elect people are of more consequence than all the kingdoms which are conspicuous in the world. (Isa. xliii. 3.) This, then, is the sense of the words. If we separate this verse from its context, the prophecy will still have its use. We may elicit from it how all things which seem stable in the world are yet perishable, and nothing is so firm as not to be subject every moment to constant variation. But the chief intention of this prediction is, as I have said, to shew the relation of all events to the safety of the pious. When, therefore, all things seem carried away by the blind impulse of chance, we ought always to contemplate God as watching for his Church, and tempering all storms and all commotions to the service and safety of the pious, who rest upon his Providence. These two things, then, are mutually in accordance, namely, *the slaying of the fourth beast, and the giving of the kingdom and authority to the people of the saints.* This does not seem to have been accomplished yet ; and hence many, nay, almost all, except the Jews, have treated this prophecy as relating to the final day of Christ's advent. All Christian interpreters agree in this ; but, as I have shewn before, they pervert the Prophet's intention. As to the Jews, theirs is no explanation at all, for they are not only foolish and stupid, but even crazy.[1] And since their object is the adulteration of sound doctrine, God also blinds them till they become utterly in the dark, and both trifling and childish ; and if I were to stop to refute their crudities, I should never come to an end.

This prophecy does not seem to be accomplished at the de-

---

[1] Calvin's expression is here proverbial ; the French translates *ils n'en approchent ne pres ne loin ;* the Latin being, *neque cœlum neque terram attingunt.*—*Ed.*

struction of the beast; but this is easily explained. We
know how magnificently the prophets speak of Christ's kingdom, and adore his dignity and glory with splendid eulogies;
and although these are not exaggerated, yet if judged of by
human perceptions, you would surely think them exceedingly
extravagant, and find neither solidity nor firmness in their
words. And no wonder: for Christ's kingdom and his
dignity cannot be perceived by carnal eyes, nor even comprehended by the human intellect. Let those who appear
the most sagacious of men combine together all their clear-
sightedness, yet they can never ascend to the height of
Christ's kingdom, which surpasses the very heavens. Nothing
is more contrary to our natural judgment than to seek life in
death, riches in poverty and want, glory in shame and disgrace—to be wanderers in this world, and at the same time
its heirs! Our minds cannot naturally comprehend these
things. No wonder, then, if mortals judge erroneously of
Christ's kingdom, and are blind in the midst of light. Still
there is no defect in the Prophet's expressions, for they de-
pict for us the visible image of Christ's kingdom, and ac-
commodate themselves to our dulness. They enable us to
perceive the analogy between things earthly and visible, and
that spiritual blessedness which Christ has afforded to us,
and which we now possess through hope in him. For while
we only hope, our happiness is concealed from us; it is not
perceptible by our eyes or by any of our senses.

Let us now return to the passage. Daniel first of all says,
*A kingdom, and power, and extensive dominion, shall be
given to the people of the holy ones.* This was partially fulfilled when the Gospel emerged from persecution: then the
name of Christ was everywhere celebrated and held in honour
and esteem, while previously it had been the subject of the
greatest envy and hatred. For nothing had been more
hated and detested for many years than the name of Christ.
God, therefore, then gave the kingdom to his people, when
he was acknowledged as the Redeemer of the world throughout its many changes, after having been formerly despised
and utterly rejected. I may here remark again, and impress
upon the memory what I have frequently touched upon,

namely, the custom of the Prophets, in treating of Christ's
kingdom, to extend their meaning further than its first be-
ginnings ; and they do this while they dwell upon its commencement.   Thus Daniel or the angel does not predict here
occurrences connected with the advent of Christ as Judge of
the world, but with the first preaching and promulgation of
the Gospel, and the celebration of the name of Christ.   But
this does not prevent him from drawing a magnificent picture of Christ's reign, and embracing its final completion.
It is sufficient for us to perceive how God begins to give the
kingdom to his elect people, when, by the power of his Spirit,
the doctrine of the holy Gospel was everywhere received in
the world.   The sudden change which it occasioned was incredible, but this is a customary result ; for, when anything
is predicted, we think it a fable and a dream, and when God
performs what we never would have thought of, the event
appears to us trifling, and we treat it as of no moment.   For
example, when the preaching of the Gospel commenced, no
one would have thought its success could have been so great
and so prosperous ; nay, two hundred years before Christ
was manifest, when religion was almost blotted out, and the
Jews were execrated by the whole world, who would have
thought the Law would spring from Zion ?   Yet God erected
his sceptre there.   The dignity of the kingdom had vanished,
the offspring of David was extinct.   For the family of Jesse
was but a trunk, after the simile used by the prophet Isaiah.
(Chap. xi. 1.)   If any one had asked all the Jews one after
another, no one would have believed the possibility of those
events which accompanied the preaching of the Gospel ; but
at length the dignity and virtue of the kingdom of David
shone forth in Christ.   Yet it vanishes before our eyes, and
we seek new miracles, as if God had not sufficiently proved
himself to have spoken by his prophets !   Thus we observe
how the Prophet keeps within bounds when he says, *A kingdom, and a power, and a magnitude of empire was given to
the people of the saints.*

He adds, *An empire under the whole heavens.*   Here the
Rabbi Abarbinel, who thinks himself superior to all others,
rejects our idea of the spiritual reign of Christ as a foolish

imagination.   For the kingdom of God, he says, is established under the whole heavens, and is given to the people of the saints.   If it is established under heaven, says he, it is earthly, and if earthly, therefore not spiritual.   This seems in truth a very subtle argument, as if God could not reign in the world except as an ordinary mortal.   As often as Scripture says " God reigns," according to this argument God must be transfigured into human nature, otherwise there will be no kingdom of God except it is earthly, and if earthly it is temporal, and therefore perishable.   Hence we must infer that God changes his nature.   His kingdom, then, will consist in opulence, and military power and parade, and the common luxuries of life, so that God will become unlike himself.   We perceive the puerile trifling of those Rabbis who pretend to glory in their ingenuity, to the total destruction of the whole teaching of piety.   They intend nothing else than to adulterate the purity of Scripture by their foul and senseless comments.   But we know the reign of God and of Christ, although existing in the world, not to be of it, (John xviii. 36 ;) the meaning of the two expressions is exactly the opposite.   God, therefore, still exercises his heavenly reign in the world, because he dwells in the hearts of his people by his Spirit.   While God held his seat at Jerusalem, was his kingdom merely an earthly and corruptible one ?   By no means, for by the possession of an earthly habitation he did not cease to be in heaven also.   Thus the angel instructed the Prophet concerning the saints who are pilgrims in the world, and yet shall enjoy the kingdom and possess the greatest power under heaven.   Hence also we correctly conclude, that this vision ought not to be explained of the final advent of Christ, but of the intermediate state of the Church.   The saints began to reign under heaven, when Christ ushered in his kingdom by the promulgation of his Gospel.

Another point must be noticed,—what belongs to the head is transferred to the body.   There is nothing new in this, as the supreme power is constantly promised by the Prophets to the Church, especially by Isaiah, who often predicts its complete supremacy.   The Papists seize upon such testimo-

nies to clothe themselves in the spoils of God, as if God had
resigned his right to them! But they are immersed in the
same error with the Jews, who swell with pride whenever
such dignity is promised to the elect people, as if they could
remain separate from God and yet obtain the right of treading the whole world under foot. The Papists also do exactly
the same. We, however, must be guided by a very different
rule, namely, in consequence of the intimate union between
Christ and his Church, the peculiar attribute of Christ himself is often transferred to his body. Not that the Church
reigns by itself; but Christ, as its only supreme head, obtains dominion therein, and not for his own private advantage
—for what need has he of this dominion? but for the common safety of all its members. Wherefore Christ is our
King, and he designs to erect his throne in the midst of us;
he uses nothing for his own advantage, but communicates
all things to us, and renders them useful to us; hence, we
are deservedly called kings, because he reigns, and as I
have already said, language which is exclusively appropriate to him, is transferred to us in consequence of the intimate communion existing between the head and the
members.

This is also the sense of the phrase here added by the
Prophet, *All powers shall serve and obey it.* I have no doubt
the angel here confirmed Isaiah's prophecy, as the Holy
Spirit, the better to confirm and strengthen the faith of the
pious, often reconciles one Prophet with another, and thus
their mutual agreement becomes the seal of their truth. It
is said in Isaiah, The kingdom and the land which will not
serve thee, shall be destroyed: kings shall come and adore
thee, the people shall offer thee gifts. (Chap. lx. 12.) In
the Psalms it is said, "Kings shall assemble together, to
serve God." (Ps. cii. 22.) And Isaiah treats very fully on
the empire of the Church. The angel now repeats the same
thing, to add, as I have said, greater confidence and authority to the prophecy of Isaiah. Meanwhile, we observe how
completely all the Prophets agree, and at the same time we
interpret these words of the kingdom of Christ, from the
period at which the teaching of the gospel was rendered re-

markably conspicuous; for then God's royal sceptre went forth from Jerusalem, and shone far and wide, while the Lord was extending his hand and his authority over all the regions of the world. As all these important events tended to the common salvation of the Church, it is said, *The kingdom shall belong to the holy people.* As to the phrase, *The saints of the high ones,* I have already explained why the Prophet applies this phrase to the faithful, and why the angel also does the same; namely, because God separated them from the world, and they were always looking upwards and drawing all their hopes from above. Then, as to the Rabbi whom I cited, he twists this passage, and tries to shew that the Prophet did not speak of Christ, when he says he saw the figure of the Son of man. But this is complete trifling, for he asserts the Son of man to mean "the people of the saints," and thus the phrase would have no reference to Christ, but to the whole offspring of Abraham. We must not be surprised at the shameful ignorance of these Rabbis, and at their blundering at the very rudiments, since they do not acknowledge the necessity for a Mediator, through whom alone the Church can obtain any favour before God. They boast in what we also allow—in the sons of Abraham being the elect, and in this title as availing to render them a holy people, and heirs of God, and a kingdom of priests. This is true, but on what was their covenant of adoption founded but on Christ? Hence their separating the Church from the Mediator, is like leaving a mutilated body apart from its disjoined head. Besides, from what the Prophet stated before about the Son of man, his subject is evidently changed in this verse. He stated there, power was given to the Son of man after he had arrived at the Ancient of days, and the Son of man, or at least his likeness, appeared in the clouds. First of all, we must notice this likeness, as it were the Son of man, as we have already explained the vision. Surely Abraham's posterity were really men, but the vision offered to the Prophet was but a similitude; as Christ had not yet put on our flesh, this was only a prelude to his future manifestation in the flesh. Here he speaks openly and without a figure of *the people of the saints,* and this prophecy depends upon the former one. For unless Christ were seated at his Father's right hand, and had obtained supreme dominion, causing every knee to bend before him, the Church could never exercise its power. Thus we observe how all things mutually agree among each other.

As, however, it is certain that many have perseveringly rebelled against God and the teaching of his gospel, it may seem absurd for the angel to pronounce all the powers of the world obedient and submissive. But it is worth while to study the customary methods of scriptural expression. For instance, by the phrase "all people," the Spirit does not mean every single person, but simply some out of every nation who should submit to Christ's yoke, acknowledge him to be king, and obediently obey his Church. How often do these sentiments occur in the prophets? All nations shall come—all kings shall serve. At that time no king existed who was not professedly an enemy of true piety, and who did not desire the abolition of the very name of his law. The prophets enlarge thus magnificently on the future restoration of this kingdom, as we have stated before, in consequence of the event being so utterly incredible. So, also, in this place *all powers*, says he, *shall serve and obey him;* that is, no power shall so boast in its loftiness, as not willingly to become subject to the Church, although at present all so fully despise it; nay, while they rage with all their might against the most wretched Church, and while they tread it most ignominiously under foot, even then they shall be subject to it. This we know to have been amply fulfilled. Some persons foolishly press beyond their meaning words of universal import, as when Paul says, God wishes all to be saved. Hence, they say, no one is predetermined for destruction, but all are elect, that is, God is not God. (1 Tim. ii. 4.) But we are not surprised at such madness as this, corrupting the impious and profane, who desire by their cavils to promote disbelief in all the oracles of the Spirit. Let us clearly comprehend the frequency of this figure of speech; when the Holy Spirit names "all," he means some out of all nations, and not every one universally.

28. Hitherto *is* the end of the matter. As for me Daniel, my cogitations much troubled me, and my countenance changed in me: but I kept the matter in my heart.

28. Hucusque finis sermonis,[1] mihi Danieli,[2] multum cogitationes meæ terruerunt me, et vultus meus mutatus est super me, *vel, in me*, et sermonem servavi,[3] in corde meo.

In this verse Daniel first says the vision was concluded, and thus the faithful might rest satisfied in looking for nothing beyond it. For we know how restless are the fancies of mankind, and how insane a disease is a vain curiosity. God is aware of what is useful for our information, and so he adopts his method of teaching to our capacity and profit. Yet we are volatile and insatiable, saying, Why is not this added? why does God stop here? why does he not proceed further? As, therefore, human ingenuity is so inflamed and intemperate, Daniel here deservedly says, *an end was put to the vision,* to cause all the elect to acquiesce in it and be contented with this partial knowledge. He afterwards adds, *he was disturbed in his thoughts, and his countenance was changed;* for he was afraid lest the pious should think this vision a mere vanished spectre. It was of the greatest importance to distinguish this vision from any frivolous imagination. Daniel, therefore, to shew how the scene proposed to his notice was a divine revelation, expresses clearly how he *was terrified in his thoughts.* This occurred, because God wished to stamp upon his heart the certainty of the prophecy. To the same purpose is *the change of countenance.* He adds, *he laid up the discourse in his heart,* to assure us of his being a faithful interpreter; for if we suspected him of negligence, we should not receive with reverence the message he delivered in these words, as really proceeding from God. But when Daniel affirms that he discharged the duty of a faithful servant, who *kept the whole discourse in his heart,* additional authority is added to his teaching. In conclusion, we must remember two points; first, the celestial revelation made known to the Prophet to prove him a servant and messenger of God to us; and secondly, the faithful discharge of his duties, as *he laid up in his heart* what he had received, and

---

[1] Or, as yet there is an end of the discourse.—*Calvin.*
[2] Or, as far as I, Daniel, am concerned.—*Calvin.*
[3] Or, I have laid it up to be kept.—*Calvin.*

thus delivered it through his own hands to the Church at large. Another vision follows:—

CHAPTER EIGHTH.

1. In the third year of the reign of King Belshazzar a vision appeared unto me, *even unto* me Daniel, after that which appeared unto me at the first.

1. Anno tertio regni Beltsazar Regis, visio visa fuit, *visio apparuit,* mihi, mihi *inquam* Danieli postquam apparuerat mihi in principio.[1]

Here Daniel relates another vision, differing from the former as a part from the whole. For God wished to shew him first what various changes should happen before Christ's advent. The second redemption was the beginning of a new life, since God then not only restored afresh his own Church, but as it were created a new people; and hence the departure from Babylon and the return to their country are called the second birth of the Church. But as God at that time afforded then only a taste of true and solid redemption, whenever the prophets treat of that deliverance, they extend their thoughts and their prophecies as far as the coming of Christ. God therefore, with great propriety, shews the Four Monarchies to his Prophet, lest the faithful should grow weary in beholding the world so often convulsed, and all but changing its figure and nature. Thus they would be subject to the most distressing cares, become a laughing-stock to their enemies, and ever remain contemptible and mean, without the power to help themselves, under these constant innovations. The faithful, then, were forewarned concerning these Four Monarchies, lest they should suppose themselves rejected by God and deprived altogether of his care. But now God wished to shew only one part to his Prophet. As the destruction of the Babylonian empire was at hand, and the second kingdom was approaching, this dominion also should speedily come to its close, and then God's people should be reduced to the utmost extremity. And the chief object of this vision is to prepare the faithful

[1] That is, in addition to the vision which was offered me before.— *Calvin.*

to bear patiently the horrible tyranny of Antiochus, of which the Prophet treats in this chapter. Now, therefore, we understand the meaning of this prophecy, where God speaks of only two Monarchies, for the kingdom of the Chaldees was soon to be abolished : he treats first of the Persian kingdom ; and next, adds that of Macedon, but omits all others, and descends directly to Antiochus, king of Syria. He then declares the prevalence of the most wretched confusion in the Church ; for the sanctuary should be deprived of its dignity, and the elect people everywhere slain, without sparing even innocent blood. We shall see also why the faithful were informed beforehand of these grievous and oppressive calamities, to induce them to look up to God when oppressed by such extreme darkness. And at this day this prophecy is useful to us, lest our courage should fail us in the extreme calamity of the Church, because a perpetual representation of the Church is depicted for us under that calamitous and mournful state. Although God often spares our infirmities, yet the Church is never free from many distresses, and unless we are prepared to undergo all contests, we shall never stand firm in the faith. This is the scope and explanation of the prophecy. I will defer the rest.

PRAYER.

Grant, Almighty God, since thou formerly didst permit thy servants to maintain their courage in the midst of so many and such heavy commotions, that we may reap the same edification from these prophecies : and since we have fallen upon the fulness of times, may we profit by the examples of the ancient Church, and by the pious and holy admonitions which thou hast set before us. Thus may we stand firm and unconquered against all the attacks of Satan, and the world, and the impious, and so may our faith remain impregnable, until at length we enjoy the fruit of its victory in thy heavenly kingdom, through Christ our Lord.— Amen.

Lecture Thirty=Ninth.

I HAVE written a short preface to this vision, which is here described for us in this eighth chapter, to enable you to comprehend its contents, and to perceive the object for which it was offered to the Prophet. As to the time, we must remember that the Prophet was informed of the victory of Cyrus and Darius while the Babylonian monarchy was still standing and flourishing. Although Cyrus had already made great progress, and begun to lay waste the Chaldean territories, yet Belshazzar, as we have already seen, was carelessly enjoying his festivities. No one ever thought Cyrus would become the conqueror of so great a monarchy, for Belshazzar would not collect a great army to defend the boundaries of his kingdom. He thought he should repel all the endeavours of Cyrus as easily as possible ; and the greater his violence the more King Belshazzar hoped to overthrow him. Now God wished to shew his servant these future events. First of all, the immediate change is revealed ; and next the calamity to follow ultimately is made known— the calamity, I mean, of the Church under King Antiochus and his successors. The Prophet therefore says :—

2. And I saw in a vision; (and it came to pass, when I saw, that I *was* at Shushan *in* the palace, which *is* in the province of Elam;) and I saw in a vision, and I was by the river of Ulai.

3. Then I lifted up mine eyes, and saw, and, behold, there stood before the river a ram which had *two* horns : and the *two* horns *were* high; but one *was* higher than the other, and the higher came up last.

2. Vidi in visione : et fuit cum viderem, ut ego essem in Susan,[1] quæ est in Elam provincia. Vidi in visione, et ecce eram super fluvium Ulai.

3. Et extuli oculos meos, et vidi : et ecce aries unus stabat coram fluvio,[2] et ei cornua duo, et cornua erant excelsa, et unum excelsius altero, et excelsum hoc ascendebat retro.

Without any doubt, the Prophet here recognised a new empire as about to arise, which could not happen without Babylon being reduced to slavery. Hence it would tend in no slight degree to alleviate the cares of the pious, and to mitigate their sorrows, when they saw what they had previously thought incredible, namely, the approaching destruction of that horrible tyranny under which they had been so cruelly oppressed. And if the liberty of returning to their country was not immediately granted to the people, it would be no small consolation to behold God's judgment against

---

[1] הבירה, *hebireh*, which some translate citadel, or palace, or royal residence.—*Calvin.*

[2] That is, on the river's bank.—*Calvin.*

the Chaldeans as foretold by the prophets. We must now examine the Prophet's language. *I have seen in a vision,* says he. This word חֲזוֹן, *chezon,* a "vision," is added to shew us that the ram of which mention is made was not seen by the eyes of the body. Hence this was a heavenly oracle, and ought to have raised the beholder above all human sensations, to enable him to discern from a lofty watch-tower what was hidden from the rest of mankind. He did not see then what ordinary men might behold, but God shewed in a vision things which no mortal senses could apprehend. He next adds, *The vision was shewn to me, Daniel, and I happened,* says he, *when I saw it, to be in Shushan.* Some think Daniel to be then dwelling in Persia, but this view is by no means probable; for who could persuade the holy Prophet of God, who had been led captive with the rest and was attached to the king of Babylon, to depart as if he had been entirely his own master, and to go into Persia when the Persians were then open enemies? This is not at all likely; and I wonder what can induce men to adopt this comment, so contrary to all reason. For we need not dispute about a matter by no means obscure if we weigh the Prophet's words, as he removes all doubt by saying *he was in Shushan when he saw,* that is, when he was caught up by the prophetic spirit beyond himself and above the world. The Prophet does not say he dwelt in Shushan, or in the neighbourhood, but he was there in the vision only. The next verse, too, sufficiently shews him to have then been in Chaldea—in the third year, he says, of the reign of King Belshazzar. By naming the king, he clearly expresses that he then dwelt under his power and dominion. It is clearly to be gathered from these words, without the slightest doubt, that the Prophet then dwelt in Chaldea. And perhaps Babylon had been already besieged, as we saw before. He says *he was in the palace at Shushan.* I know not how I ought to translate this word הַבִּירָה, *hebireh,* as I see no reason for preferring the meaning "palace" to that of "citadel." We are sure of the nobility and celebrity of the citadel which was afterwards the head of the East, for all nations and tribes received from thence their laws, rights, and judgments. At the same time, I think this citadel was not then built, for its empire over the Persian territory was not firmly established till the successors of Cyrus. We may perhaps distinguish Shushan from Persia at large, yet as it is usually treated as a part of that kingdom, I will not urge the distinction. The country is, however, far milder and more fertile than Persia, as it receives its name from being flowery and abounding in roses. Thus the Prophet says *he was there in a vision*.

He afterwards repeats this : *I saw in a vision, and behold I was near the river Ulai*. The Latin writers mention a river Eulæus, and as there is a great similitude between the words, I have no hesitation in understanding Daniel's language of the Eulæus. The repetition is not superfluous. It adds certainty to the prophecy, because Daniel affirms it not to have been any vanishing spectre, as a vision might be suspected to be, but clearly and certainly a divine revelation, as he will afterwards relate. He says, too, *he raised his eyes upwards*. This attentive attitude has the same meaning, as experience informs us how often men are deceived by wandering in erroneous imaginations. But Daniel here bears witness to his raising his eyes upwards, because he knew himself to be divinely called upon to discern future events.

He next subjoins, *And behold a ram stood at the bank of the river, and it had horns*. He now compares the empire of Persia and Media to a ram. It ought not to seem absurd that God proposed to his servant various similitudes, because his duty was to teach a rude people in various ways ; and we know this vision to have been presented before the Prophet, not for his private instruction only, but for the common advantage of the whole people. I do not think we need scrupulously inquire why the Persian kings are called rams. I know of no valid reason, unless perhaps to institute a comparison between them and Alexander of Macedon and his successors. If so, when God, under the image of a ram, exhibits to his Prophet the Persian empire, he does not illustrate its nature absolutely, but only by comparison with that of Alexander. We are well aware of the opposition between these two empires. The Persian monarchy is called " a ram," with reference to the Macedonian, which, as we shall afterwards see, bears the name of "he-goat" with respect to its antagonist. And we may gather the best reason for this comparison in the humble origin of the kings of Persia. With great propriety, then, Cyrus, the first ruler of this empire, is here depicted for us under the form or image of a ram. His "horn" produced a concussion through the whole earth, when no one expected anything to spring from a region by no means abounding in anything noble. And as to Alexander, he is called a "he-goat," with respect to the "ram," as being far more nimble, and yet more obscure in his origin. For what was Macedon but a mere corner of Greece? But I do not propose to run the parallel between these points; it is sufficient that God wishes to shew to his Prophet and to the whole Church, how among the Persians, unknown as they were, and despised by their neighbours, a king should arise to consume the Median power, as we shall soon see, and also to overthrow the Babylonian monarchy. *Behold*, therefore, says he, *a ram stood before the river*, or at the bank of the river, since Cyrus subdued both the Medes and his grandfather, as historians inform us. Cyrus then rushed forth from his own mountains *and stood at the bank of the river*. He also says, *He had two horns*. Here the Prophet puts two horns for two empires, and not by any means for two persons. For although Cyrus married the daughter of Cyaxares his uncle, yet we know the Persian empire to have lasted a long time, and to have supplied historians with a long catalogue of kings. As Cyrus had so many successors, by the two horns God doubtless shewed his Prophet those two empires of the Medes and Persians united under one sovereignty. Therefore, when the ram appeared to the Prophet, it represented both kingdoms under one emblem.

The context confirms this by saying, *The two horns were lofty, one higher than the other, and this was raised backwards*. The two horns were lofty; for, though the Persian territory was not rich, and the people rustic and living in woods, spending an austere life and despising all luxuries, yet the nation was always warlike. Wherefore the Prophet says this horn *was higher than the other*, meaning, than the empire of the Medes. Now Cyrus surpassed his father-in-law Darius in fame, authority, and rank, and still he always permitted Darius to enjoy the royal majesty to the end of his life. As he was an old man, Cyrus might easily concede to him the highest office without any loss to himself. With respect then to the following period, Cyrus was clearly pre-eminent, as he was certainly superior to Darius, whom Xenophon calls Cyaxares. For this reason, then, *this horn was higher.* But meanwhile the Prophet shews how gradually Cyrus was raised on high. The horn rose *backwards;* that is, "afterwards"—meaning, although the horn of the Median kingdom was more illustrious and conspicuous, yet *the horn which rose afterwards* obscured the brightness and glory of the former one. This agrees with the narratives of profane history: for every reader of those narratives will find nothing recorded by Daniel which was not fulfilled by the event. Let us go on :—

4. I saw the ram pushing westward, and northward, and southward ; so that no beasts might stand before him, neither *was there any* that could deliver out of his hand ; but he did according to his will, and became great.	4. Vidi arietem ferientem Occasum et Aquilonem, *Septentrionem* et Meridiem : et nullæ bestiæ consistebant coram ipso,[1] et nemo eripiens e manu ejus,[2] itaque fecit secundum arbitrium suum, et magnificatus est.

The Prophet now shortly sketches the great success which should attend this double kingdom. He says, *The ram struck all the nations towards the west, and north, and south.* The Persian and Median territory lay to the east of Babylon and Egypt, Syria, Asia Minor, and Greece. This, without doubt, is extended to all the successors of Cyrus, who are recorded as having convulsed the whole world. Cyrus himself was shortly afterwards cruelly and basely slain, according to many historians, although Xenophon affirms that he died in his bed. But I have before warned you not to put your trust in that writer, although most excellent, since, under the image of that king, he wished to set before us an example of perfect manliness ; and hence he brings him forward as discoursing on his deathbed, and exhorting his sons

[1] Or, before his face.—*Calvin.*
[2] There was none to snatch it from his hand.—*Calvin.*

to kingly virtues. Whichever is the true account, Cyrus was clearly overtaken in the midst of his career. In this way God wished to chastise his insatiable cupidity, a vice in which he resembled Alexander. As to his successors, they excited such commotions in the whole world as to stir up heaven and earth. Xerxes alone said he could bind the sea with fetters! and we know the greatness of the army which he commanded; and this passage treats not only of one king, but of all those of Persia. As they obtained a dominion so far and wide, their ambition and pride always inflamed them, and there was no end to their warfare till they had subdued the distant boundaries of the world. We are acquainted too with their numerous attempts to destroy the liberty of Greece. All this the Prophet embraces in but few words. God also wished to give his Prophet a short glance into futurity, as far as such knowledge could be useful. *I saw*, then, says he, *a ram*, namely, a beast which possessed a double horn, representing the Medes and Persians united in the same sovereignty.

He struck the west, and the north, and the south, so that no beasts could stand before him. As the Persian kingdom is here depicted under the image of a ram, all kings and people are called "beasts." Thus, *no beasts stood before him, and no one could deliver out of his hand.* It is well known, indeed, how Xerxes and others failed in their attacks, and how many wars the Monarchs of Persia attempted in which they were conquered by the Greeks; but still their conquerors were in no better condition, as they were compelled to seek peace like suppliants. So great became the power of the Persians, that they inspired all nations with fear. For this reason the Prophet says, *he did according to his pleasure*, not implying the complete success of these Monarchs according to their utmost wishes, for their desires were often frustrated, as we have already narrated on the testimony of historical evidence. Still they were always formidable, not only to their neighbours who submitted to their yoke, but to the most distant nations, as they crossed the sea and descended from Asia upon Greece. In the last word, he expresses this fact,—the *ram became mighty*. For the Per-

sian king became the greatest of all Monarchs in the world,
and it is sufficiently notorious that no one could add to his
dignity and strength.   It follows :—

5. And as I was considering, behold, an he-goat came from the west, on the face of the whole earth, and touched not the ground; and the goat *had* a notable horn between his eyes.	5. Et ego eram intentus,[1] ecce, *inquit*, hircus caprarum venit ab Occasu,[2] super faciem totius terræ, neque tamen attingebat terram,[3] et hirco cornu illustre *erat* inter oculos ejus.
6. And he came to the ram that had *two* horns, which I had seen standing before the river, and ran unto him in the fury of his power.	6. Et venit ad arietem, cui erant cornua duo,[4] quem videram stantem in ripa fluvii,[5] et cucurrit ad eum cum furore fortitudinis suæ.

Here another change is shewn to the Prophet, namely,
Alexander's coming to the east and acquiring for himself
the mighty sway of the Persians, as afterwards happened.
With the view, then, of procuring confidence for his prediction, he says, *he was attentive.*   He doubtless dwells upon
the reverence with which he received the vision to exhort
us to the pursuit of piety, and also to modesty and attention.
The Prophet, therefore, was not carried away in imagination
by a dream which could be called in question ; he knew this
vision to have been set before him by God, and acknowledged
his duty to receive it with modesty and humility.   Wherefore, *I was attentive, and behold a he-goat came forth from
the west,* says he.   The situation of Macedon with respect to
Persia must be noticed.   As the Greeks were situated to the
west of Persia, the Prophet says, *the he-goat came from the
west, and went over the surface of the whole earth.*   These
words signify the very extensive dominion of Alexander, and
the terror of surrounding nations.   His arrival in Asia with
a very insignificant army is well known.   He thought 30,000
men sufficient, after he had been created their general by the
States of Greece.   Hence, the passage is to be understood
not of numbers, but of the terror inspired on all sides ; for,
although he advanced with but a moderate force, yet he terrified the whole earth.

[1] That is, I attended or was attentive.—*Calvin.*
[2] From the west.—*Calvin.*
[3] It did not touch the ground.—*Calvin.*
[4] Which was possessed of two horns, or verbally, " master of horns."—
Calvin.
[5] Before the river.—*Calvin.*

But he did not touch the ground, says he.   This refers to his swiftness, for he rather flew than travelled either on foot or by sea, so incredible was his speed in this expedition. For if any one had galloped through regions completely at peace, he could not have passed through Asia more speedily. Hence a he-goat was shewn to the Prophet *who did not touch the ground,* that is, who was borne along with a rapid impulse, like that of lightning itself. *And the goat had a horn,* says he, *between its eyes—a remarkable horn.* We know how much glory Alexander acquired for himself in a short time, and yet he did not undertake the war in his own name, or on his own responsibility, but he used every artifice to obtain from the Grecian States the office of general-in-chief against the Persians, as perpetual enemies.   We are well acquainted with the hostility of the Persians to the Greeks, who, though often compelled to retreat with great disgrace, and infamy, and loss of troops, still kept renewing the war, as they had abundance of men and of pecuniary resources.   When Alexander was created general of the whole of Greece, *he had a remarkable horn between his eyes;* that is, he took care to have his title of general made known to increase his personal authority.   Besides, it was sufficiently prominent to constitute him alone general of the whole army, while all things were carried on according to his will, as he had undertaken the war.   This, then, is the reason why the Prophet says, *the horn was visible between the eyes of the goat.* It follows, *It came to the ram, which had two horns;* that is, it came against the king of the Medes and Persians.   Cyrus also had seized on Babylon, and had subdued many kings, but two horns are assigned to the ram, since the Persian kings had united the Medes in alliance to themselves.   Hence *one he-goat with his horn came against the ram which had two horns, and ran against it in the ardour of its bravery.*   Thus the perseverance of Alexander is denoted, as he hastened so as to surpass all expectation by the speed of his arrival.   For Darius continued in security, although he had collected a large army, but Alexander *rushed forwards in the boldness of his strength,* and surrounded the enemy by his celerity.   It follows :—

7. And I saw him come close unto the ram, and he was moved with choler against him, and smote the ram, and brake his two horns; and there was no power in the ram to stand before him, but he cast him down to the ground, and stamped upon him : and there was none that could deliver the ram out of his hand.

7. Et vidi appropinquantem ad arietem, et exasperantem seipsum,[1] percussit arietem, et confregit duo cornua ejus, et non fuit virtus in ariete ad standum coram facie ejus, et dejecit eum in terram,[2] et calcavit eum : et non fuit qui erueret arietem e manu ejus.

Here God shews to his Prophet the victory of Alexander, by which he subdued almost the whole east. Although he encountered many nations in battle, and especially the Indians, yet the name of the Persian empire was so celebrated in the world, that the dignity of others never approached it. Alexander, therefore, by conquering Darius, acquired nearly the whole east. God shewed his Prophet the easiness of his victory under this figure. *I looked,* says he, *when he approached the ram.* Darius was fortified by both the distance of his stations and the strength of his fortifications ; for many of his cities were impregnable, according to the common opinion of mankind. It was incredible, then, that the he-goat should approach the ram, surrounded as he was on all sides by such strong and such powerful garrisons. But the Prophet says *he approached the ram,* and then, *he exasperated himself against him.* This applies to Alexander's furious assaults. We are well acquainted with the keenness of his talents and the superiority of his valour; yet, such was his unbridled audacity, that his promptness approached rather to rashness than to regal bravery. For he often threw himself with a blind impulse against his foes, and it was not his fault if the Macedonian name was not destroyed ten times over. As, then, he rushed on with such violent fury, we are not surprised when the Prophet says *he was exasperated of his own accord.* *And he struck the ram,* says he. He conquered Darius in two battles, when the power of the Persian sway throughout Asia Minor was completely ruined. We are all familiar with the results of these hazardous battles, shewing the whole stress of the war to have rested on that engagement in which Darius was first conquered ; for when

---

[1] That is, when the he-goat approached the ram, and excited himself, or became savage against him.—*Calvin.*

[2] Threw him prostrate.—*Calvin.*

he had collected fresh forces, and engaged a second time, he despaired of his kingdom, was betrayed by his followers, and cruelly slain.   Thus *the he-goat struck the ram, and broke his two horns;* for Alexander acquired the Median as well as the Persian empire.

He says, *The ram had no strength to stand;* and although he had collected an immense multitude, yet that preparation was available for nothing but empty pomp.   For Darius was resplendent with gold, and silver, and gems, and he rather made a shew of these luxuries in warfare, than displayed manly and vigorous strength.   *The ram,* then, *had no power to stand before the he-goat.*   Hence, *he threw him prostrate on the earth, and trod him down; and no one was able to deliver out of his hand.*   Darius, indeed, was slain by his attendants, but Alexander trod down all his glory, and the dignity of the Persian empire, under which all the people of the east trembled.   We are aware also of the pride with which he abused his victory, until under the influence of harlots and debauchees, as some report, he tumultuously set fire to that most celebrated citadel of Susæ in a drunken fit. As he so indignantly trampled under foot the glory of the Persian monarchy, we see how aptly the events fulfilled the prophecy, in the manner recorded by all profane historians.

PRAYER.

Grant, Almighty God, since thou desirest us to be tossed about amidst many and various convulsions, that our minds may always look upwards towards heaven, where thou hast prepared for us certain rest and a tranquil inheritance beyond the reach of disturbance and commotion.   When the land through which we are on pilgrimage is in confusion, may we be so occupied during its storms, as to stand composed and grounded upon the faith of thy promises, until having discharged our warfare, we are gathered together into that happy rest, where we shall enjoy the fruit of our victory, in Christ Jesus our Lord.—Amen.

Lecture Fortieth.

8. Therefore the he-goat waxed very great : and, when he was strong, the great horn was broken; and for it came up four notable ones, toward the four winds of heaven.	8. Et hircus caprarum magnificatus est admodum : et cum in robore suo esset, fractum fuit cornu magnum, et prodierunt loco ejus illustria quatuor *alia*, versus quatuor ventos cœlorum.

THIS prophecy relates to the death of Alexander. We have explained how, under the image of a he-goat, the Macedonian empire is set before us, having its beginning in the person of Alexander, but by no means ending there, as the monarchy was divided into four parts. The angel said, or at least Daniel records his words,—*that he-goat increased to an immense magnitude*, because he wandered as it were in sport through almost the whole east, and at the same time subdued it ; *but when it was in its strength*, says he, *its great horn was broken.* By the great horn, he means the monarchy, which was solely in Alexander's power during his life, as he was the first and last monarch of his race. And in consequence of his generals, who had obtained dominion in the four quarters of the world, becoming kings, as we shall soon see, the word "he-goat" is not restricted to his person, but is extended to his successors. He himself is called "the great horn." Hence, *when the he-goat was in his strength, the great horn was broken.* For Alexander had arrived at the height of prosperity when he died. Whether he perished by disease or by poison is unknown, since historians report a great suspicion of foul-play. The angel does not notice his age, which was thirty-three years at his death, while he seemed to have been born for subduing the whole world, although he was so suddenly snatched away. But the angel regards those continued successes, since Alexander almost by a look subdued the whole east, as we have stated before, and hurried on rashly from place to place. Hence he perpetually gained fresh victories, though at the constant hazard of his life, as he had far more audacity than skill. *When he was in his strength*, says he ; meaning, after having subjugated the whole east. He had returned from India, and had determined to re-cross the sea, and to reduce Greece under his power; for the States had rebelled against him, and the Athenians had already collected a great army; but all the eastern States of Asia had been rendered subservient to Alexander when he died. The angel refers to this by the breaking of *the great horn.*

He afterwards adds, *In his place four conspicuous horns sprang up.* For he uses the noun חזות, *chezeveth,* "notable," as in yesterday's Lecture.[1] There were, therefore, four kingdoms which excelled, and each of them was celebrated and placed aloft. Nor is this superfluous, since we know how many became kings, who had enlisted in the service of Alexander with reputation and dignity. Perdiccas was the first, and all thought him to have been favoured with special honour by Alexander. When asked whom he wished for a successor, he replied, according to the greatness or pride of his spirit, "The person whom he considered most worthy of empire." He had a son by Roxana the daughter of Darius, as well as another son; then Aridæus his brother approached; yet he deemed no one worthy of the honour of being his successor, as if the world contained no equal to himself. His answer, then, was a proof of his pride. But when he was unable to speak, he took a ring from his hand and gave it to Perdiccas. Hence all conjectured that he had the preference in Alexander's judgment, and he obtained the supreme authority. After this, Eumenes was slain, who had served under him. Although he was an ally, he was judged as an enemy, and betrayed by his men; Lysimachus being slain on the other side. Fifteen generals were put to death. And as so many succeeded to the place of Alexander and exercised the royal authority, the angel correctly expresses how *four conspicuous horns sprang up in the place of one great one.* For after various conflicts and many fluctuations for fifteen years or thereabouts, Alexander's monarchy was at length divided into four parts.

[1] This noun is connected with חזון, *chezeven,* "vision," and is translated in our version variously. In Isaiah xxviii. 18, it is rendered by "agreement," and in ver. 5 of this chap., by "notable," and in the margin correctly by "of sight." Calvin's Latin "*illustre,*" is very suitable.—*Ed.*

Cassander, the son of Antipater, obtained the kingdom of Macedon, after slaying Olympias, the mother of Alexander, his sister, his sons, and his wife Roxana. This was a horrible slaughter, and if ever God offered a visible spectacle to the world, whereby he openly denounced the shedding of human blood, surely a memorable proof of this existed in the whole of Alexander's race ! Not a single one survived for twenty years after his death. Though his mother had grown old, she was not permitted to descend naturally to the grave, but was murdered. His wife, and son, and brother, and all his relations, shared her fate. And that slaughter was even yet more cruel, as no single leader spared the life of his companions, but each either openly attacked or craftily assailed his friend and confederate ! But omitting details, four kingdoms were at last left after such remarkable devastations. For Cassander, the son of Antipater, obtained Macedon and some part of Thrace, together with the cities of Greece. Seleucus became master in Syria ; Antigonus in Asia Minor, joining Phrygia, Paphlagonia, and all other Asiatic regions, after five or six generals were slain. Ptolemy became prefect of Egypt. This makes four horns, which the angel calls " conspicuous," for on the testimony of history, all the other principalities vanished away. Alexander's generals had divided among themselves many large and fertile provinces, but at length they were summed up in these four heads. He says, *by the four winds of heaven*, that is, of the atmosphere. Now the kingdom of Macedon was very far distant from Syria ; Asia was in the midst, and Egypt lay to the south. Thus, the he-goat, as we saw before, reigned throughout the four quarters of the globe ; since Egypt, as we have said, was situated towards the south ; but the kingdom of Persia, which was possessed by Seleucus, was towards the east and united with Syria ; the kingdom of Asia was to the north, and that of Macedon to the west, as we formerly saw the he-goat setting out from the west. It now follows,—

9. And out of one of them came forth a little horn, which waxed exceeding great, toward the south, and

9. Et ex uno illorum egressum est cornu unum parvum, et magnificatum fuit eximie versus Meri-

toward the east, and toward the   diem, et ad Orientem, et ad
pleasant *land*.   gloriam. [1]

Now God shews his Prophet what peculiarly concerned
the welfare of his Church.   For it was of very great importance to warn the Jews of the calamities which were about
to oppress them.   There is nothing which more torments
the minds of men than their becoming bewildered in false
imaginations, and thinking the world the sport of chance,
while they never ponder over the providence of God nor
reflect upon his judgments.   Hence, with this design, God
wished to teach the Prophet and all the pious the nature of
their future afflictions, since they would thus understand
how events never happened by chance, but all these scourges
proceeded from God ; for the same God both determines
and executes his decrees, as he also predicts future events.
For if nothing had been predicted, the pious would have
glided gently downwards to despair in consequence of their
heavy afflictions.   We know also how magnificently the
prophets extol the grace of God when they promise return
and deliverance.   Isaiah, too, has elsewhere spoken. to this
effect : Not in haste nor in tumult shall ye go forth, but
with a standard displayed.   Again, The wealth of all the
nations shall flow towards you ; kings shall come, and
submit, and bow the knee to thee.   (Chap. lii. 10 ; lv. 12 ;
lx. 6.)   The Jews were permitted to return to their own
land ; but we know how cruelly they were harassed by all
their neighbours, so that they did not dwell in that corner
of the world without the greatest difficulties.   The building
of both the city and the Temple was hindered by many
enemies, till at length they became tributary to the kings of
Syria.   Antiochus, indeed, who is here alluded to, advanced
with cruel tyranny against the people of God.   If this had
not been predicted, they would have thought themselves
deceived by the splendid promises concerning their return.
But when they perceived everything occurring according as
they had been opportunely forewarned, this became no slight

[1] Or, desire ; some translate it in the genitive, and understand " desirable land ;" for Judea was often called the desirable land, because God
of his own free-will chose to be worshipped there ; but we may receive it
simply for   glory."—*Calvin.*

solace in the midst of their woes ; they could then determine
at once how completely it was in the power of God to
relieve them from so many and such oppressive evils.　With
what intention, then, had God predicted all these things to
his Prophet Daniel ? clearly that the Jews might look forward to a happy result, and not give way to despair under
events so full of anxiety and confusion.　This, then, was the
utility of the prophecy, with reference to that particular
period.

When the Prophet says, *Out of one of those four horns a
little horn arose*, Antiochus Epiphanes is most distinctly
pointed out.　The title Epiphanes means " illustrious," as,
after the capture of his father, he was detained as a hostage
at Rome, and then escaped from custody.　Historians inform
us of his possessing a servile disposition, and being much
addicted to gross flattery.　As he had nothing royal or
heroic in his feelings, but was simply remarkable for cunning,
the Prophet is justified in calling him *the little horn*.　He
was far more powerful than his neighbours ; but *the horn* is
called *little*, not in comparison with the kingdoms of either
Egypt, or Asia, or Macedon, but because no one supposed he
would ever be king and succeed his father.　He was the
eldest of many brothers, and singularly servile and cunning,
without a single trait worthy of future royalty.　Thus he
was *the little horn* who escaped secretly and fraudulently
from custody, as we have already mentioned, and returned
to his native country, which he afterwards governed.

He now adds, *This horn was very mighty towards the south
and the east, and " the desire:"* for unless he had been checked
by the Romans, he would have obtained possession of Egypt.
There is a remarkable and celebrated story of Pompilius, who
was sent to him to command him to abstain from Egypt at the
bidding of the senate.　After he had delivered his message, Antiochus demanded time for deliberation, but Pompilius drew
a circle with the staff which he held in his hand, and forbade
him to move his foot until he gave him an answer.　Though
he claimed Egypt as his own by right of conquest, yet he
dared not openly to deny the Romans their request ; at first he
pretended to be merely the guardian of his nephew, but he

certainly seized upon the kingdom in his own name. However, he dared not oppose the Romans, but by changing his ground wished to dismiss Pompilius. They had been mutual acquaintances, and a great familiarity had arisen between them while he was a hostage at Rome ; hence he offered to salute Pompilius at the interview, but he rejected him disdainfully, and, as I have said, drew a line around him, saying, " Before you go out of this circle answer me ; do not delude me by asking time to consult with your councillors ; answer at once, otherwise I know how to treat thee." He was compelled to relinquish Egypt, although he had formerly refused to do so. The language of the Prophet, then, was not in vain, *The small horn became mighty towards the south,* that is, towards Egypt, *and the east;* for he extended his kingdom as far as Ptolemais. In the third place, he uses the word *glory;* that is, Judea, the sanctuary of God, which he had chosen as his dwelling, and desired his name to be invoked. Thus this small horn *extended itself to the glory,* or the land of glory or desire. There is nothing doubtful in the sense, though the interpretation scarcely agrees with the words. It afterwards follows :—

10. And it waxed great, *even* to the host of heaven ; and it cast down *some* of the host and of the stars to the ground, and stamped upon them.	10. Et magnificatum est *cornu illud parvum* ad exercitum cœlorum, et dejecit in terram ex illo exercitu, *nempe cœlesti,* et ex stellis, et calcavit eas.

Here Daniel continues the vision which he had received. We have already shewn the object of the Almighty to be the preparation of the faithful to bear serious calamities, because nothing new or unexpected should happen to them. Now, Daniel's dwelling upon this point is not surprising, for it becomes his duty to inform the faithful of the heavy calamities which were at hand, and thus to mould them to patience and equity. Thus he says, *The horn became magnificent, even to the army of the heavens.* Without the slightest doubt this figure marks the elect people of God. Although the Church often lies prostrate in the world, and is trodden under foot and buried, yet it is always precious before God. Hence the Prophet adorns the Church with this praise, not to obtain for it any honour before men, but because God has

separated it from the world, and provided a sure inheritance
in heaven.   Although the sons of God are pilgrims on earth,
and have scarcely any dwelling-place here, becoming like
castaways before men, yet they are nevertheless citizens of
heaven.   The usefulness of this teaching to us is apparent,
by its inducing us to bear it patiently whenever we are often
thrown prostrate on the ground, and whenever tyrants and
the despisers of God look down upon us with scorn.   Meanwhile our seat is laid up in heaven, and God numbers us
among the stars, although, as Paul says, we are as dung and
the offscouring of all things.   (1 Cor. iv. 13.)   In fine, God
here shews his Prophet, as in a mirror, the estimation in
which he holds his Church, however contemptible it is on
earth.   *That horn, then, was magnified before the army of
the heavens, and cast down some of that army upon the earth,
and trod them out of the stars.*   Exactly as if he proclaimed
the loosening of the reins from the tyrant, permitting him
to treat the Church with contempt, to tread it under foot,
and to draw down the stars from heaven, just as if God never
appeared for its protection.   For when God permits us to be
safe and secure in his hand, and pronounces it impossible to
prevail against his help, while tyrants harass and oppress
us by their lust, it is like drawing down stars from heaven.
God therefore, while he takes us under his guardianship,
does not offer us any succour, but dissembles as if he wished
to betray us to our enemies.   Nothing therefore is superfluous in these expressions of the Prophet—*The stars were
trodden down, and the heavenly army thrown down to earth.*
He now adds :—

11. Yea, he magnified *himself* even to the prince of the host, and by him the daily *sacrifice* was taken away, and the place of his sanctuary was cast down.

11. Et ad Principem exercitus magnificatum est,[1] et ab eo ablatum fuit juge,[2] et projectus fuit[3] locus sanctuarii ejus.

Daniel announces something still more atrocious here,
namely, the exaltation of the little horn against God.
Some take " the prince of the army" for the high-priest, as
princes are sometimes called כוהנים, *kuhnim,* as well as

[1] That is, proceeded even to the prince of the army.—*Calvin.*
[2] Namely, the sacrifice.—*Calvin.*   [3] Or, dissipated.—*Calvin.*

שרים, *serim ;* but that is too forced.   The true sense of the
passage imputes such arrogance and folly to Antiochus as to
urge him to declare war with the stars of heaven, implying
not only his opposition to God's Church, which is separate
from the world, but also his daring defiance of God himself and
his resistance to his power.   He not only exercised his cruelty
against the faithful, but profaned the temple itself, and
endeavoured to extinguish all piety, and to abolish the worship of God throughout Judea, as we shall explain more fully
in other passages.   As, therefore, Antiochus not only raged
against men, but used his utmost endeavours to overthrow
religion, Daniel relates how *that horn was raised up even
against the prince of the army.*   God is deservedly entitled
to this appellation, because he defends his Church, and
cherishes it under his wings.   This expression ought to be
explained not only of God's glory and empire, but also of his
paternal favour towards us, as he deigns to manifest his care
for us as if he were our Prince.

From him, says he, *was the perpetual sacrifice utterly
snatched away, and the place of his sanctuary cast down.*
These words are horrible in their import ; God was thus
spoiled of his rights, since he had chosen but a single corner
in the world for his special worship.   What heathen, then,
would not despise this forbearance of God, in permitting
himself to be deprived of his legitimate honour by that sor-
did tyrant ?   As we have already stated, Antiochus had
neither greatness of mind nor warlike courage, being skilful
only in cunning and in the basest acts of flattery.   Besides,
granting him to have comprised a hundred Alexanders in
his own person, what can be the Almighty's design in allowing his temple to be polluted, and all true sacrifices to cease
throughout the world ?   One corner alone, as we have lately
mentioned, was left where God wished to be worshipped, and
now Antiochus seizes upon the temple, and profanes and defiles it with the utmost possible indignity, thus leaving no
single place sacred to the Almighty.   For this reason I have
asserted the prophecy to appear very harsh.   The Prophet now
increases the indignity when he speaks of *the perpetual sacrifice.*   For God had often borne witness to his temple being

his perpetual "rest," or "station," or "seat ;" yet he is now ejected from this spot, as if exiled from the earth entirely. The temple could not exist without sacrifices, for the whole worship under the law was a kind of appendage to the temple. As God had promised the sacrifice should be perpetual and eternal, who would not assert, when Antiochus destroyed it, either all the promises to have been deceptive, or all authority to have departed from God, who failed to defend his right against that impious tyrant ? Surely this must have been a distressing calamity, overwhelming all the faithful ! And when even at this moment we read the prophecy, all our senses are horrified by its perusal. No wonder, then, that God forewarned his servant of such sorrowful events, and such incredible evils, to admonish his whole Church in due season, and to arm them against the severest temptations, which might otherwise strike down even the most courageous. *The sacrifice,* then, says he, *was snatched away from God himself, and the place of his sanctuary was cast down* or dissipated. It afterwards follows :—

| 12. And an host was given *him* against the daily *sacrifice* by reason of transgression, and it cast down the truth to the ground ; and it practised, and prospered. | 12. Et tempus[1] datum est super jugi *sacrificio* in scelere,[2] et projiciet veritatem in terram, et faciet,[3] et prospere aget. |

The Prophet mitigates the asperity which he now records. It seems absurd for God to allow such license to Antiochus, that his temple should be spoiled and all sacrifices and all worship exterminated. It is difficult to reconcile this, for the opinion will naturally creep in,—possibly God is constrained and deprived of power to subdue his foes. The Prophet therefore clearly states here how the license for vexing and oppressing the Church would never have been granted to Antiochus without God's permission. *Time,* therefore, *shall be given him,* says he. By the words, *time shall be given,* he refers to the will of God, meaning, the pious shall have no cause for desponding while they see all things

---

[1] Some translate " army," but I approve of the other sense, and shall give the reason by and bye.—*Calvin.*

[2] Or, on " account of wickedness," verbally, " time shall be given"—the future tense.—*Calvin.*

[3] That is, shall have execution prepared, as we commonly say.— *Calvin.*

disturbed and confused in every direction, as God will rule all these perplexities by his secret judgment. *Time, then, shall be given,* implying, Antiochus can do nothing by his unbridled and furious audacity, unless divinely permitted and previously limited. צבא, *tzeba,* signifies both "army" and "time," but the latter meaning is the most suitable here ; for when it is translated " an army shall be given him," the sense appears forced.   I more willingly embrace the sense of time being allowed ; that is, God will try the patience of his Church for a certain definite time, and will then bring their troubles to an end.   We know it to be impossible to sustain the spirits of the faithful, otherwise than by their expectation of a favourable termination, and by the hope of their emerging from the abyss of sorrow.   This, then, is the reason why God shews his Prophet by a vision the temporary duration of the sway of Antiochus.   *A period,* then, *shall be appointed to him over the perpetual sacrifice;* meaning, whatever he may intend, he shall not abolish the worship of God.   For, however he may exert himself, God will not permit the sacrifices to perish utterly and for ever ; he will restore them in his own time, as we shall afterwards see, and when we come to the close, we shall find the context flowing on in accordance with this meaning—*a time shall be given him over the continual sacrifice.*

He afterwards adds בפשע, *beph-sheng,* " in wickedness," or " in sin."   I prefer the simple translation " in sin" to "by sin," although different senses are elicited according to the different views of interpreters.   It is better to leave it to every one's free choice, and thus simply to translate " in wickedness" or " sin."   Some refer it to Antiochus, because he wickedly polluted God's temple, and abolished the sacrifices.   This sense is probable, but I will add others, and then say which of them I like best.   Some -understand " in sin" of the priests, because, through the perfidy of Jason, Antiochus entered the city, spoiled the temple, and introduced those abominations which exterminated all piety and divine worship.   (2 Macc. iv. 7.)   As Jason desired to snatch the priesthood from his brother Onias, he opened the gates to Antiochus ; then a great slaughter followed, in which all the

adherents of Onias were cruelly slain.   Afterwards Menelaus
expelled Jason again by similar perfidy.   Some translate
" by means of wickedness," as these priests induced Antiochus to exercise cruelty in the holy city, and to violate the
temple itself.   Others approach nearer the real sense, by
supposing the sacrifices to have ceased through wickedness,
because they were adulterated by the priests.   But this appears to me too restricted.   In my judgment, I rather incline
towards the view of those who take " wickedness" as a cause
and origin, thereby teaching the Jews how justly they were
punished for their sins.   I have already explained how properly the vision was limited as to time, and controlled by
God's permission and secret counsel.   The cause is here expressed ; for it might still be objected, " How happens it that
God submits himself and his sacred name to the ridicule of
the impious, and even deserts his own people ?   What does
he intend by this ?"   The Prophet, therefore, assigns this
cause—the Jews must feel the profanation of the temple, the
sad devastation of the whole city and their horrible slaughter, to be the reward due to their sins.   *A time, therefore,
shall be assigned over the perpetual sacrifice in sin ;* that is,
on account of sin.   We here see how God on the one hand
moderates the weight of the evils which pressed upon the
Jews, and shews them some kindness, lest sorrow, anxiety,
and despair should consume the wretched people ; on the
other hand, he humbles them and admonishes them to confess their sins, and then he urges them to apply their minds
to repentance, by stating their own sins to be the cause of
their afflictions.   He thus shews how the source of all their
evils was in the Jews themselves, while God's anger was provoked by their vices.   It is necessary to stop here till to-
morrow.

PRAYER.

Grant, Almighty God, as thou hast enlightened us by the teaching of thy Gospel, and set before our eyes thine only begotten
Son as a Sun of righteousness to rule us, and hast deigned to
separate us from the whole world, and to make us thy peculiar
people, and to prepare for us a certain seat in heaven : Grant,

I pray thee, that we may be heirs of eternal life. Grant us also, to be mindful of thy sacred calling, and to make our pilgrimage on earth with spirits looking upwards and tending towards thee. May we meditate upon the righteousness of thy kingdom, and be entirely devoted to thee. Do thou protect us by thy hand even to the end, and may we march boldly under thy standard, till at length we arrive at that blessed rest, where the fruit of our victory is laid up for us in Jesus Christ our Lord. —Amen.

Lecture Forty=First.

DANIEL here mentions one among the many crimes of Antiochus, *his casting down truth to the ground.* This clause ought to be joined with the former ; for Antiochus could not deprive God of his lawful worship without abolishing sound doctrine. The angel seems here to express the reason for the destruction of the sanctuary, because the worship of God depended upon the teaching of the law, which is here understood by the word "*truth.*" This passage then states that no religion is pleasing to God unless founded on truth ; for God, according to the uniform teaching of the Scriptures, does not desire to be worshipped according to man's caprice, but rather tries the obedience of men by prescribing what he demands and approves, lest men should pass over these bounds. We must here remark the union which Daniel now establishes between the overthrow and abolition of the worship of God, and the casting down of truth to the ground, when it neither obtains its proper rank, nor subdues all mortals to itself.

It may be read, he will cast down truth in the earth ; thus making a distinction between heaven and earth. And if we like to read it so, the sense will be—truth still remains stable although it perishes in the earth, because it has its station in heaven. Thus the sense would be—after the abolition of the worship of God, and the cessation of the sacrifices, piety could no longer exist among mortals. At length he adds, *he shall succeed and prosper.* The first word here implies execution. God wished on the whole to admonish his Church concerning the prosperous success of Antiochus, lest the faithful should be dispirited at beholding the impious tyrant so petulantly and wantonly polluting God's temple, and utterly destroying his religion, as if he had provoked God himself to the contest. For this conduct was equivalent to a direct declaration of war against God. For his success would trouble all the pious, as if the tyrant was superior to God himself. Hence this prediction would warn the faithful against the novelty or suddenness of anything which might occur. It follows,—

13. Then I heard one saint speaking, and another saint said unto that certain *saint* which spake, How long *shall be* the vision *concerning* the daily *sacrifice*, and the transgression of desolation, to give both the sanctuary and the host to be trodden under foot?

14. And he said unto me, Unto two thousand and three hundred days; then shall the sanctuary be cleansed.

13. Et audivi sanctum unum loquentem: dixit ergo sanctus unus mirabili, *dicemus postea de voce*, loquens, Quousque visio jugis *sacrificii*, et sceleris vastantis *ad* dandum,[1] et sanctuarium, et exercitus conculcatio.[2]

14. Et dixit mihi, ad vesperum, mane,[3] duo millia et trecenti *anni*: et justificabitur sanctuarium.

Here he expresses more clearly what I formerly said, unfolding God's intention of consoling and soothing the sorrows of the pious, lest they should sink under the severity of their trials, at the sight of an impious tyrant domineering in the sanctuary of God. Besides, the spot which God had promised should be his perpetual dwelling-place, was exposed to impious superstitions, for the idol of Jupiter Olympius was erected there, as the history of the Maccabees informs us. (2 Macc. i. 57; vi. 2.) God therefore wished to uphold his servants, lest too severe a temptation should overwhelm them, and lest trial in so many forms should cause them to yield and become deficient in piety through want of courage. But while Daniel is stupified through astonishment, God provides for his infirmity by means of an angel. Daniel

---

[1] Some translate, How long will the vision be permitted? but it ought rather to be treated by the rules of grammar—"How long will be allowed for the vision of the perpetual sacrifice and the devastating wickedness?"—*Calvin.*

[2] That is, for treading down. This word may be repeated.—*Calvin.*

[3] That is, until evening and morning. *Calvin.*—Wintle's notes on these verses are very explanatory, and agree on the whole with Calvin's comments. See DISSERTATION on this verse.—*Ed.*

himself, without doubt, inquired concerning the vision as we shall see he did afterwards; but here God desired to meet him, as he saw the holy man so overcome by fear as scarcely to dare to make any inquiry.   God, therefore, here affords no common proof of his paternal goodness and indulgence, in interposing and sending his angel to make inquiries in the Prophet's name.   He says, then, *he heard a holy one*, meaning an angel.   For, although God deigns to call the faithful while dwelling in the world by this honourable title, yet the superior purity of angels is familiar to us, as they are altogether free from the lusts of the flesh.   But we, alas! are detained in this prison-house, we are bound down in slavery to sin, and are polluted by much corruption.   The holiness of angels, however, is far greater than that of mortals, and thus this attribute of "holiness" is properly applied to them.   When Daniel was caught up by the prophetic spirit, he was separated from the society of men, and was admitted to that of angels.

An angel then said to the wonderful one.   The Hebrews often use this expression when they mean "whoever it may be"—*ploni almoni*, and apply it to places as well as persons. They use it also of any place unknown to them or concealed from them.   They treat the noun as compounded of two words, and many interpret it of any one unknown, but I think the word to be more emphatic than this.[1]   Daniel here brings forward an angel speaking, and adds dignity to his description by calling him "holy."   Without doubt, then, the person of whom the angel asked the question was his superior; it is not likely that he would be called "a certain one," while the angel is termed a holy one.   Reason, then, requires the expression to be applied to some angel whose glory was incomprehensible, or at least far superior to ordinary ones; for, as Daniel calls one angel "holy," so he would have called the rest, as we shall afterwards see.   When treating, however, of a distinct being, he uses the word פלמוני, *palmoni*, and its etymology guides us to its sense, as meaning something mysterious and incomprehensible.   Then, who

---

[1] Calvin means to imply that the Jews used these words to express the idea of the Latin phrase, "*omne ignotum pro magnifico.*"—*Ed.*

does not see that Christ is denoted, who is the chief of angels and far superior to them, all? In the ninth chapter of Isaiah, (verse 6,) he is called פלא, *pela,* "wonderful." The word in the text is a compound one, as we have said, but as פלא, *pela,* signifies "hidden" in Hebrew, as Christ is so called, and as in Judges iii. 1, God claims this name as peculiarly his own, all these points agree well together. The sense then is, an angel comes to Christ for the sake of Daniel and of the whole Church, and seeks from him as from the supreme teacher and master, the meaning of the declarations which we have just heard. We need not feel surprise at angels inquiring into futurity, as if it were unknown to them. It is the property of Deity alone to know all things, while the knowledge of angels is necessarily limited. Paul teaches us to wonder at the Church being collected out of profane and strange people; this was a mystery hidden from angels themselves, before God really shewed himself the father of the whole world. (Eph. iii. 10.) Hence, there is no absurdity in supposing angels to inquire into mysteries, as ignorance is not necessarily deserving of blame, and as God has not raised his creatures to his own level. It is his peculiar province to know all things, and to have everything under his eye. The angel desires to understand this mystery, not so much for his own sake as on account of the whole Church; for we know them to be our ministers, according to the clear testimony of the Apostle. (Heb. i. 14.) As they keep watch over us so carefully, it does not surprise us to find the angel inquiring so anxiously concerning this vision, and thus benefiting the whole Church by the hand of Daniel.

Meanwhile, we must notice, how Christ is the chief of angels and also their instructor, because he is the eternal Wisdom of God. Angels, therefore, must draw all the light of their intelligence from that single fountain. Thus angels draw us to Christ by their example, and induce us to devote ourselves to him through the persuasion that this is the supreme and only wisdom. If we are his disciples, being obedient, humble, and teachable, we shall desire to know only what he will make manifest to us. But the angel asks, *What is the meaning of the vision of the perpetual* sacrifice, *and of the sin?* that is, what is the object of the vision concerning the abrogation of the perpetual sacrifice, and concerning the sin which lays waste? As to the second point, we explained yesterday the various opinions of interpreters, some twisting it to Antiochus, who impiously dared to violate God's temple, and others to the priests. But we said the people were intended, lest many, as they are accustomed, should blame the Almighty for so heavily afflicting the Church. But God wished to bear witness to the origin of this devastation from the sins of the people. It is just as if the angel had said, How long will the sacrifices cease? How long will this vengeance, by which God will chastise the wickedness of his people, endure? For the sin is called devastating, through being the cause of that calamity. It is afterwards added, *how long will the sanctuary and the army be trodden down?* that is, how long will the worship of God, and true piety, and the people itself, be trodden down under this cruel tyranny of Antiochus? But this question has far more efficacy, than if the Prophet had said, as we saw yesterday, that the punishment should be uniform and temporal. It was now necessary to explain what had already been stated more clearly. Thus this question was interposed with the view of rendering Daniel more attentive, and of stirring up the people by this narrative to the pursuit of learning. For it is no common event when angels approach Christ for our sakes, and inquire into the events which concern the state and safety of the Church. As, therefore, angels discharge this duty, we must be worse than stony, if we are not urged to eagerness and carefulness in the pursuit of divine knowledge. We see, then, why this passage concerning the angel is interposed.

The phrase, *And he said to me,* now follows. This ought to be referred not to the angel inquiring, but to the Wonderful One. Whence we rather gather the great anxiety of the angel concerning the interpretation of the prophecy, not for his own sake, but for the common benefit of the pious. Respecting this Wonderful One, though I am persuaded he was the Son of God, yet whoever he was, he certainly does not reject the angel's request. Why then does he address

Daniel rather than the angel? Because the angel was not
seeking his own benefit, but took up the cause of the whole
Church, as we have shewn how angels are occupied in our
salvation. Thus also we see how the angel notices the Prophet's astonishment, when he was almost dead, and had not
thought of inquiring for himself, or at least did not dare to
break forth at once ; for he afterwards recovered himself, and
was raised up by the angel's hand, as we shall soon perceive.
The Wonderful One said to me—that is, the incomprehensible or the mysterious one said to me—*for two thousand three
hundred evenings and mornings, then the sanctuary shall be
justified.* Here the Hebrews are mutually at variance whether they ought to understand the number of years or of
months ; but it is surprising to perceive how grossly they are
deluded in so plain a matter. The expression, *to evening
and morning,* is not doubtful, since Christ clearly means two
thousand three hundred days ; for what else can the phrase,
morning and evening, signify? It cannot be used of either
years or months. Evidently we ought to understand natural
days here, consisting of twenty-four hours each. Those who
receive it of years and months are wretchedly mistaken, and
even ridiculous in their calculations. For some begin to
calculate the time from Samuel, they next descend to the
reign of Saul, and next to that of David ; and thus they
foolishly trifle, through not understanding the intention of
Christ, who wished his Church to be forewarned of the coming empires and slaughters, with the view of rendering
the faithful invincible, however sorely they may be oppressed
on all sides. Christ therefore wished to hold up a light to
direct all the elect through the approaching darkness under
the tyranny of Antiochus, and to assure them that in the
very depths of it they would not be deserted by the favour
of God. Hope would thus elevate their minds and all their
senses unto the promised termination. To what purpose,
then, do those interpreters speak of the reigns of Saul and
David? We see this to be altogether foreign and adverse to
the mind of Christ, and to the use of this prophecy. No less
absurd is the guess of those who prate about months. Their
refutation would occupy three or four hours, and would be a

waste of time, utterly profitless. It is sufficient to gather
this simple meaning from the words—Christ does not speak
here of years or months, but of days. We must now seek
the true interpretation of the passage from the whole context. We have shewn how impossible it is to explain this
prophecy otherwise than by Antiochus : the event itself
proves this to be its meaning. Blind indeed must be those
who do not hold this principle—the small horn sprang from
one of those remarkable and illustrious persons who came
forth in place of one very large horn. Boys even know this
by reading the accredited history of those times. As Christ
here alluded to the tyranny of Antiochus, we must observe
how his words accord with the facts.   Christ numbers 2300
days for the pollution of the sanctuary, and this period comprehends six years and about four months. We know the
Jews to have used lunar years as well as months. They
afterwards used intercalary periods, since twelve lunar months
did not correspond with the sun's course. The same custom
prevailed among both Greeks and Romans. Julius Cæsar
first arranged for us the solar year, and supplied the defect
by intercalary days, so that the months might accord with
the sun's course. But however that was, these days, as I
have said, fill up six years and three months and a half.
Now, if we compare the testimony of history, and especially
of the book of Maccabees, with this prophecy, we shall find
that miserable race oppressed for six years under the tyranny
of Antiochus. The idol of Olympian Jove did not remain in
the temple for six continuous years, but the commencement
of the pollution occurred at the first attack, as if he would
insult the very face of God. No wonder then if Daniel understood this vision of six years and about a third, because
Antiochus then insulted the worship of God and the Law ;
and when he poured forth innocent blood promiscuously,
no one dared openly to resist him. As, therefore, religion
was then laid prostrate on the ground, until the cleansing of
the temple, we see how very clearly the prophecy and the
history agree, as far as this narrative is concerned. Again,
it is clear the purifying of the temple could not have been
at the end of the sixth current year, but in the month כסלו,

keslu, answering to October or November, as learned men
prudently decide, it was profaned. For this month among
the Jews begins sometimes in the middle of October, and
sometimes at the end, according to the course of the moon ;
for we said the months and years were lunar. In the month
Keslu the temple was polluted ; in the month אדר, *Ader*,
about three months afterwards, near its close, the Maccabees
purged it. (1 Macc. iv. 36.) Thus the history confirms in
every way what Daniel had predicted many ages previously
—nay, nearly three hundred years before it came to pass.
For this occurred a hundred and fifty years after the death
of Alexander. Some time also had already elapsed, as there
were eight or ten kings of Persia between the deaths of Cyrus
and Darius. I do not remember any but the chief events
just now, and it ought it to be sufficient for us to perceive
how Daniel's predictions were fulfilled in their own season,
as historians clearly narrate. Without the slightest doubt,
Christ predicted the profanation of the temple, and this
would depress the spirits of the pious as if God had betrayed
them, had abandoned all care of his temple, and had given
up his election and his covenant entirely. Christ therefore
wished to support the spirit of the faithful by this prediction,
thereby informing them how fully they deserved these future
evils, in consequence of their provoking God's wrath ; and
yet their punishment should be temporary, because the very
God who announced its approach promised at the same time
a prosperous issue.

Respecting the phrase, *the sanctuary shall be justified,*
some translate it—" Then the sanctuary shall be expiated ;"
but I prefer retaining the proper sense of the word. We
know how usually the Hebrews use the word " justify" when
they speak of rights. When their own rights are restored to
those who have been deprived of them—when a slave has
been blessed with his liberty—when he who has been unjustly
oppressed obtains his cause, the Hebrews use this word
"justified." As God's sanctuary was subject to infamy by
the image of Olympian Jove being exhibited there, all respect for it had passed away ; for we know how the glory of
the temple sprang from the worship of God. As the temple

had been defiled by so great a disgrace, it was then "justified," when God established his own sacrifices again, and restored his pure worship as prescribed by the Law. *The sanctuary, therefore, shall be justified ;* that is, vindicated from that disgrace to which for a time it had been subject.   It follows :—

15. And it came to pass, when I, *even* I Daniel, had seen the vision, and sought for the meaning, then, behold, there stood before me as the appearance of a man.	15. Et factum est, cum viderem ego Daniel visionem, et quærerem intelligentiam, ecce stetit coram me quasi aspectus, *vel, species,* viri.

Daniel again confirms his original statement.   But before he descends to the interpretation, he makes a preface concerning the faithfulness and certainty of the oracle, lest the Church should hesitate to embrace his utterance as really proceeding from God.   In doing this, he uses no artifice as rhetoricians do ; but God wished to stir up both him and all the pious to meditate upon this prophecy, the knowledge of which was then so peculiarly necessary and useful.   He says, therefore, *when he sought the understanding of this vision, there appeared to him a form like that of a man.* Now God had anticipated this desire of the Prophet, by the answer which the angel received from Christ, who in reply had partly explained the sense of this vision.   Now Daniel, finding himself anticipated by God who did not wait for his inquiry, gathers courage, and trusting in God's readiness to furnish an answer, he wishes to learn the matter more clearly ; not that he was altogether ignorant of the subject, but he did not yet perceive with sufficient clearness what was useful to himself and the whole Church.   We see then, how the answer of Christ only afforded him a taste of the vision, and only urged him forwards towards the full comprehension of it.   Many are immediately satisfied with but moderate information, and as soon as they understand a portion of any subject, they reject every addition, and many too often settle down at the first elements, and their obstinacy prevents that complete knowledge which is necessary. Daniel therefore shews himself to be far distant from such fastidiousness, as he was rendered more attentive by hearing from Christ's lips the real object of the vision.   *When I was attentive I sought to understand it,* says he, *behold! there stood before my face* (or near it) *like the aspect of a man.* We ought probably to interpret this passage of Christ, who is now called like a man, as formerly. (Chap. vii. 13.) For he had not yet put on our flesh, so as to be properly entitled to the name of a man ; but he was here like a man, because he wished to allow the holy fathers a taste from which they might understand his future coming as Mediator, when he should put on human nature as God manifest in flesh. (1 Tim. iii. 16.) Thus Daniel speaks suitably as before when he says, Christ *appeared to him under the aspect of a man.*   But he adds to the same purpose,—

16. And I heard a man's voice between *the banks of* Ulai, which called, and said, Gabriel, make this *man* to understand the vision.	16. Et audivi vocem hominis in Ulai,[1] et clamavit, et dixit, Gabriel, doce hanc visionem.

He does not use the particle implying fitness, but says he heard the voice of a man, because he treats no longer of either a man or a figure, but of a voice. It is sufficient to say at once, he was like a man, not really so, but only under the image and appearance of one.   Christ therefore *appeared as a man,* and is called one, since Scripture often records how angels often appeared under the form of men, and are called indiscriminately, either angels or men. (Judg. xiii. 3, &c.) So in this place Daniel relates the appearance of a man, or the aspect of one, improperly indeed, but without any danger of mistake ; for he afterwards admonishes the faithful, how this person was not clothed with the substance of flesh, but had only a human form and aspect. *I heard then a human voice in the midst of the river.*   We gather from this that the same person is here intended of whom mention was lately made, because he commands the angel ; whence this can be referred to Christ alone.

Gabriel, says he, *teach him.*   We observe the speaker from the midst of the river here commanding Gabriel, as if superior to him.   For Gabriel as the name of an angel, is sufficiently known from other passages of Scripture ; (Luke i. 19, 26 ;) and its etymology, " The strength of God," is very

---

[1]   That is, between the two banks of the river.—*Calvin.*

suitable to this meaning. Without any doubt, the angel here receives his commands from Christ. Thus, we see the supreme power and authority represented under the form and aspect of a man, as well as obedience pourtrayed in Gabriel, who discharges the duty enjoined upon him. From this Christ's divinity is inferred, as he could not issue orders to angels, without either having special authority, or being God himself. But when the phrase "like a man" is used, we are taught his manifest superiority to man. And what does this imply? not angelic nature but divine. Christ by thus presenting himself under a human form, shews, by a kind of foreshadowing, how he would become a man, when the fulness of time arrived. Then he would really manifest himself as the head of the Church, and the guardian of the salvation of the pious. For he proves himself to have power over all angels, when he orders Gabriel to discharge the office of the Prophet's instructor. We will put off the remainder.

PRAYER.

Grant, Almighty God, since in these days the earth is full of defilements which pollute the sacred worship of thy name, as there is scarcely a corner of the world which Satan has not corrupted, and as thy truth is everywhere adulterated, that we may persevere and remain stedfast in our course of piety. May we always be attentive to that light which thou didst first set before us in the Law, and which shines upon us now more fully under the Gospel. May we never become plunged into that darkness in which we see the world wrapt up, and in which those who seem to be themselves most acute are still involved. Grant us always to follow that life which thou shewest us, until we arrive at that goal which thou hast set before us, and to which thou daily invitest us by thine only-begotten Son.—Amen.

Lecture Forty=Second.

17. So he came near where I stood; and when he came, I was afraid, and fell upon my face: but he said unto me, Understand, O son

17. Et venit ad stationem meam: et cum veniret territus sum, et cecidi super faciem meam: tunc dixit ad me, **Intellige**, fili

of man; for at the time of the end   hominis, quia ad tempus finis
shall be the vision.   visio.[1]

I will not repeat what I have already explained. I will
proceed with what I had commenced, namely, the Prophet's
need of instruction, because he could not understand the
vision without an interpreter; wherefore the angel was
ordered to explain this revelation of God more fully. But
before he narrates this, he says, *he was frightened at the
approach of the angel.* Without doubt, this reverence was
always present to his mind. Whenever he perceived himself called or taught by God, he was doubtless struck with
fear; but here some special feeling is expressed, as God
desired to influence his mind to set us an example, and to
render us more attentive. Here Daniel explains his own
mind to us, commending the magnitude and importance of
the vision, lest we should read with carelessness what he
will afterwards relate, and not treat the occasion with sufficient seriousness. For God used the angel as his servant to
explain his intention to the Prophet; at the same time he
inwardly touched his mind by his Spirit to shew us the way,
and thus he would not only train us to docility, but also to
fear. He says, then, *he was frightened and fell down.* This,
as I have said, was usual with the Prophet, as it ought to
be with all the pious. Paul also, in celebrating the effect
and power of prophecy, says, if any unbelievers should enter
into the assembly and hear a prophet speaking in God's
name, he would prostrate himself, says he, upon his face.
(1 Cor. xiv. 25.) If this happened to unbelievers, how great
will be our dulness, unless we receive most reverently and
humbly, what we know to have been uttered by the mouth
of God? Meanwhile, we should remember what I have
lately touched upon,—the importance of the present oracle
as here commended to us by the Prophet; *for he fell upon
his face through his fright,* as he will repeat in the next verse.

Nor is the following exhortation superfluous; *understand,*
says he, *O son of Adam.* It would be of little use to us to be
moved and excited for a time, unless our minds were afterwards
composed for hearing. For many are touched by fear when

---

[1] Or, at the time of the end of the vision.—*Calvin.*

God appears to them; that is, when he compels them to feel the force and power of his sway; but they continue in their stupidity, and thus their fright is rendered profitless. But Daniel here makes a difference between himself and the profane, who are only astonished and by no means prepared for obedience. At the same time, he relates how his own excitement was effected by the assistance of the angel. The fear, then, of which we have lately made mention, was a preparation for docility; but this terror would have been useless by itself, unless it had been added, *that he might understand.* We ought to understand how piety does not consist merely in acknowledging the fear of God, but obedience is also required, preparing us to receive with tranquil and composed feelings whatever we shall be taught. We ought diligently to observe this order.

It now follows : *Because there shall be an end of the vision at a fixed time.* Some join לעת־קץ, *legneth-ketz,* making the sense "at the end of the time," קץ, *ketz,* in this sense being in the genitive case by way of an epithet, as the Hebrews commonly use it. They elicit this sense—the vision shall be for a prefixed time. But others prefer—the end of the vision shall be for a time. I think this latter sense is better, as the former seems to me forced. On the whole, it is not of much consequence, yet as that form of expression is the easier, namely, the end or fulfilment of the vision should be at a definite time, I had rather follow that interpretation. The angel asserts, then, that this was no vain speculation, but a cause joined with its effect, which should have its completion at a stated period. *There shall be an end,* then, *of the vision in its time ;* meaning, what you now behold shall neither vanish away nor be destroyed, but its end shall happen when the time shall arrive which God has determined. קץ, *ketz,* is often taken in this sense. Hence *there shall be an end of the vision ;* that is, the vision shall be completed when the fitting time shall arrive. We ought to bear in mind this exhortation of the angel, because unless we are certainly persuaded of the fixedness of anything when God speaks, we shall not be ready to receive whatever he pronounces. But when we are convinced of this saying, God never separates his hand from his mouth—meaning, he is never unlike himself, but his power follows up his word, and thus he fulfils whatever he declares ; this becomes a sure and firm foundation for our faith.   This admonition of the angel ought to be extended generally to the whole of Scripture, since God does not throw words into the air, according to the common phrase.   For nothing happens rashly, but as soon as he speaks, his truth, the matter itself and its necessary effect, are all consistent.   It follows :—

18. Now, as he was speaking with me, I was in a deep sleep on my face toward the ground: but he touched me, and set me upright.	18. Et cum loqueretur mecum, sopitus corrui super faciem meam in terram, et tetigit me,[1] et restituit me super stationem meam.[2]

The Prophet repeats what he had said, namely, how he had been frightened by the magnitude of this vision ; meanwhile, he was raised up by the angel, lest he should remain in that state of stupor.   Yet these two clauses must be noticed : Daniel was astonished at the outset, for he could not otherwise be sufficiently composed to listen to the angel's voice ; but at the same time another clause is added, stating, the angel set him upright in his place.   Whenever God addresses us, we must necessarily be subject to fear and dread, to produce humility, and to render us docile and obedient.   Fear s the true preparation for obedience ; but, as we formerly said, another feeling ought to follow ; namely, as God has previously prostrated and cast us down, he will also raise us up, thereby preparing us for listening ; and this disposition cannot arise except our minds are sedate and composed. The Prophet then expresses both these states of mind here. This, as I have said, is common to all the pious ; but a peculiarity is noticed here, lest the readers of the vision should become torpid, and receive it carelessly ; for they ought to collect all their senses, conscious of their inability to understand it, unless the fear of God should precede, and thus form the mind for obedience.   *While he was speaking with me,* therefore, *I fell into a swoon with my face upon the ground ;*

[1] Some translate, " approached me," an interpretation which is tolerable. —*Calvin.*

[2] Verbally, "upon my standing," as in old French, " en mon estre."— *Calvin.*

that is, I lay astonished, *and he touched me.*   I have already stated the opinion of others, that the angel approached him, but it is only tolerable.   He now adds:—

19. And he said, Behold, I will make thee know what shall be in the last end of the indignation: for at the time appointed the end *shall be.*	19. Et dixit, Ecce ego docebo te¹ quod erit in fine iræ: quia ad præfixum, *vel, statutum tempus finis.*

Those who read the noun *ketz,* " end," in the genitive case in verse 17, understand in this place the word "vision" again, as if the Prophet had said, " At the time of the end there shall be a vision." But as מוֹעֵד, *mevegned,* or *moed,* signifies a " time fixed and settled beforehand," there is nothing superfluous in that method of speech ; then *ketz,* as I have said, is properly taken for the effect itself, and it would be harsh and far-fetched to say " at the time of the end there shall be a vision," in the sense of the filling up of the vision. For this word expresses all which such interpreters wish it to imply.   Besides, all are agreed as to the matter itself, since the angel bears witness to his being the interpreter chosen by God, who explains futurity to the Prophet.   *Behold,* therefore, says he, *I will explain to thee.*   He here acquires confidence for himself from his office, as he had accepted the commands divinely laid upon him.   And we should remark this also, since our faith will never rest or become firm unless the authority on which it is founded be fixed.   As then the angel declares himself to be executing an office divinely enjoined upon him, ought we to put confidence in men who conduct themselves with rashness, and, though they assume authority in God's name, yet have no certain and lawful calling ?   We may learn, then, how neither angels nor men ought to be held in such honour as to induce us to receive whatever they bring forward, unless the Almighty has appointed them to be his ministers and interpreters.

He then says, *I will announce to thee what shall happen even at the end of the wrath.*   Without doubt, the angel asserts by this phrase the suddenness of God's wrath.   We are aware how instantaneously on the return of the people their

Or, I will open to thee, or verbally, make thee know.—*Calvin.*

enemies attacked them in Judea, and never ceased to inflict upon them numberless troubles. Wherefore, as soon as the Jews had returned from exile, God began to exercise them in various ways, and not without sufficient reason. Every one privately studied his own interests, but without any regard for the temple and any desire for the worship of God, and thus they were given up to avarice and caprice. They also defrauded God himself in tithes and offerings, as is evident from the prophets Malachi and Haggai. (Chap. i. 12 ; iii. 8.) From that period God began to punish them, but deferred his vengeance till the time of Antiochus. The angel, therefore, calls *the end of the vengeance* that severer punishment which God inflicted after the people had abused his forbearance. Therefore *I will teach thee*, or lay before thee, *what shall happen at the close of the vengeance, because*, says he, *it shall be the time of the end.* He here repeats what he had said concerning the effect of the prophecy, meaning, the fulfilment should take place at its own appointed season. We must now notice the noun *moed*, because it is here opposed to our fervour and intemperance. Haste in desiring anything leads, as they say, to delay ; for as soon as God bears witness to anything, we wish it to be fulfilled at the very first moment, and if he suspend its execution only a very few days, we not only wonder but cry out with vexation. God, therefore, here admonishes us by his angel that he has a settled time, and thus we are to learn to put a bridle on ourselves, and not to be rash and unseasonably hasty, according to our usual habit. We ought, then, to remember the explanation given, and perceive how the effect of the vision is shewn here, and thus it will obtain from us its just reverence. It follows :—

20. The ram which thou sawest having *two* horns *are* the kings of Media and Persia.

21. And the rough goat *is* the king of Grecia : and the great horn that *is* between his eyes *is* the first king.

20. Et aries quem vidisti habentem duo cornua, reges sunt Medorum et Persarum.

21. Et hircus capræ, *qui natus erit ex hirco*, rex Græciæ, et cornu magnum quod erat inter oculos ejus, est rex primus.

By the word "Javan" the Hebrews designate not only the Greeks but the Macedonians, and the whole of that tract which is divided by the Hellespont, from Asia Minor as far as Illyricum. Therefore the meaning is—the king of Greece.

22. Now that being broken, whereas four stood up for it, four kingdoms shall stand up out of the nation, but not in his power.

22. Et confractum est,[1] et extiterunt quatuor, *cornua scilicet*, loco ejus: quatuor regna a gente exsurgent, *vel, existent*, et non pro fortitudine illius.

23. And in the latter time of their kingdom, when the transgressors are come to the full, a king of fierce countenance, and understanding dark sentences, shall stand up.

23. Et in fine regni illorum, ubi perfecti fuerint scelerati, existet rex præfractus facie,[2] et intelligens ænigmata.

Hence Luther, indulging his thoughts too freely, refers this passage to the masks of Antichrist, but we shall treat this point afterwards.[3]

24. And his power shall be mighty, but not by his own power: and he shall destroy wonderfully, and shall prosper, and practise, and shall destroy the mighty and the holy people.

24. Et roborabitur fortitudo ejus, et non in fortitudine sua,[4] et mirabilia[5] evertet, prosperabitur, et efficiet, et perdet, *repetit idem verbum*, robustos, et populum sanctorum.

25. And through his policy also he shall cause craft to prosper in his hand; and he shall magnify *himself* in his heart, and by peace shall destroy many: he shall also stand up against the Prince of princes; but he shall be broken without hand.

25. Et pro intelligentia sua prosperabitur dolus in manu ejus, et in corde suo magnificabit se, et in pace perdet multos, *vel, fortes,* et contra Principem principum stabit, *vel, exsurget*, et absque manu frangetur.

We have previously given a brief explanation of all these subjects. But here the angel removes all doubt, lest we should still anxiously inquire the meaning of the ram which Daniel saw, and of the he-goat which followed and prostrated the ram. The angel, therefore here pronounces the ram to represent two kingdoms, which coalesced in one. Cyrus, as we have said, granted it for a time to his father-in-law Cyaxares, but yet drew the whole power to himself, and the Persians began to extend their sway over all the

---

[1] That is, the horn was broken.—*Calvin.*

[2] Verbally, "in faces."—*Calvin.*

[3] The English reader may consult Michelet's Life of Luther. *Hazlitt's Ed.*, 1846, pp. 455, 459.

[4] Or, according to his fortitude; we shall treat this phrase also.—*Calvin.*

[5] That is, "in wonderful ways," "wonderfully;" the noun being used in the place of the adverb.—*Calvin.*

realms of the East. But God in this vision had respect to
the beginning of that monarchy. When, however, the Persians and Medes were united, then the ram bore two horns ;
then the he-goat succeeded, and he threw down the ram, as
we have already seen. In that he-goat there was first one
great horn and then four small ones. The angel then answers concerning the he-goat representing the kingdom
of the Greeks. There is not the slightest doubt here, since
Alexander seized upon the whole East, and thus the Persian
monarchy was utterly destroyed. In the he-goat, therefore,
the kingdom of Greece or Macedon was displayed, but the
horns will mark something special.

That great horn, says Daniel, *was the first king,* namely,
Alexander ; afterwards four smaller horns arose in his place.
We have already explained these. For when much blood
had been shed, and the greater part of the leaders had been
slain, and after the followers of Alexander had mutually
attacked and destroyed each other, those who remained divided his dominions among themselves. Cassander the son
of Antipater obtained Macedon ; Seleucus, Syria ; Ptolemy,
Egypt ; and Antigonus his own fourth share. In this way
the smaller horns succeeded Alexander, according to the clear
testimony of profane history. From the frequency with
which God sets this prophecy before us, we gather his intention of giving us a conspicuous sign of his majesty. For
how could Daniel conjecture future events for so long a period
before they happened ? He does not pronounce mere enigmas, but narrates things exactly as if they were already
fulfilled. At the present time Epicureans despise the Scriptures and laugh at our simplicity, as if we were too credulous. But they rather display their own prodigious madness
and blindness, by not acknowledging the prediction of Daniel
to be divine. Nay, from this prophecy alone we may prove
with certainty the unity of God. If any one was inclined to
deny that first principle, and utterly reject the doctrine of
his divinity, he might be convinced by this single prophecy.
Not only is this subject treated here, but Daniel points with
his finger to the God of Israel as the only one in whose hand
and will are all things, and from whom nothing either escapes

or is concealed.   From this prophecy alone the authority of Scripture is established by proofs perfectly sure and undoubted, as the Prophet treats with perfect clearness events at the time unknown, and which no mortal could ever have divined.

First of all he says, *The ram which thou sawest, having two horns, means the kings of the Medes and Persians.*   This had not then occurred, for that ram had not yet risen and seized upon Babylon, as we have stated already.   Thus Daniel was raised up as it were to heaven, and observed from that watch-tower things hidden from the minds of men.   He afterwards adds, *The he-goat is the king of Greece.*   Philip, the father of Alexander, although a strenuous and a most skilful warrior, who surpassed all the kings of Macedon for cleverness, yet, superior as he was, never dared to cross over the sea.   It was sufficient for him if he could strengthen his power in Greece, and render himself formidable against his neighbours in Asia Minor.   But he never dared to attack the power of Persia, or even to harass them, and much less to overcome the whole East.   Alexander, inflamed rather by rashness and pride than by good judgment, thought nothing would prove difficult to him.   But when Daniel saw this vision, who ever would have thought of any king of Greece invading that most powerful monarchy, and not only seizing upon the whole of Asia, but obtaining sway in Egypt, Syria, and other regions?   Although Asia Minor was an extensive region, and well known to be divided into many rich and fertile provinces, yet it was but a small addition to his immense empire.   Nay, when Nineveh was conquered by Babylon, and the Chaldeans became masters of Assyria, this also was an addition to the Persian monarchy. We are familiar with the amazing riches of the Medes, and yet they were entirely absorbed.   Darius drew with him 800,000 men, and quite buried the earth under his army. Alexander met him at the head of 30,000.   What comparison was there between them !   When Xerxes[1] came to Greece he brought with him 800,000 men, and threatened to put fetters upon the sea ; yet Daniel speaks of this incredible

---

[1] The Edit. Gen., 1617, read *Merces* incorrectly: that of Vincent, 1571, and the French of Perrin, 1569, are correct, as in the text.—*Ed.*

event just as if it had already taken place, and were matter
of history.   These points must be diligently noticed that the
Scriptures may inspire us with the confidence which they
deserve.

The great horn, says he, *which was between his eyes was
the first king, and when it was broken, four others sprang up.*
Alexander, as we have mentioned, perished in the flower of
his age, and was scarcely thirty years old when he died,
through the influence of either poison or disease.   Which of
the two is uncertain, although great suspicion of fraud at-
taches to the manner of his death ; and whichever way it
happened, that horn was broken.   In his place there arose
four horns, *which sprang up,* says he, from that nation.
Here we must notice this, since I very much wonder what
has come into some persons' minds, to cause them to translate it "from the nations," and yet these are persons skilled
in the Hebrew language.   First, they shew great ignorance
by changing the number, and next, they do not comprehend
the intention of the angel.   For he confirms what he formerly said concerning the unity of the kingdom and its
division into four parts, and he assigns the reason here.
They shall spring, says he, from *a nation,* meaning the
Greeks, and all from a single origin.   For by what right did
Ptolemy obtain the empire ? solely by being one of Alexander's generals.   At the beginning, he dared not use the
royal name, nor wear the diadem, but only after a lapse of
time.   The same is true of Seleucus, and Antigonus, and
Cassander.   We see, then, how correctly the kingdom of the
Greeks is represented to us under the figure of a single
beast, although it was immediately dispersed and torn into
four parts.   The kingdoms, then, which sprang from *the
nation,* meaning Greece, *shall stand, but not in full strength.*
The copula is here taken in the sense of " but ;" *the four
kingdoms* shall stand, *but not by his strength,* for Alexander
had touched upon the Indian sea, and enjoyed the tranquil
possession of his empire throughout the whole east, having
filled all men with the fear of his industry, valour, and speed.
Hence, the angel states the four horns to be so small, that
not one of them should be equal to the first king.

And at the end of their reign, when the wicked shall be at their height, one king shall stand. By saying at the end of their kingdom, he does not mean to imply the destruction of the four kingdoms had ceased. The successors of Antiochus were not directly cast down from their sway, and Syria was not reduced into a province till about eighty or a hundred years after Antiochus the Great had been completely conquered. He again left heirs, who, without doubt, succeeded to the throne, as we shall see more clearly in the eleventh chapter. But this point is certain—Perseus was the last king of Macedon, and the Ptolemies continued to the times of Julius Cæsar and Augustus, and we are well aware how completely Cleopatra was conquered and ruined by Antony. As women succeeded to the throne, we could not place the destruction of the Macedonian empire under Antiochus Epiphanes. But the angel means, *at the end of their kingdom,* when they had really come to the close of their reigns, and their final ruin was at hand. For when Antiochus Epiphanes returned to his country, he seemed to have re-established his power, though it very soon afterwards began to die away. Similar circumstances also happened to Egypt and to Macedon, for the reign of all their kings was precarious, and although not directly overthrown, yet they depended on the Romans, and thus their royal majesty was but fleeting. *At the end,* therefore, *of their kingdom,* that is, when they arrived at the height, and their fall led them on to ruin, then, says he, *when the wicked were consummated* or *perfected.* Some apply this to the professed and outward enemies of the Church, but I rather approve of another opinion, which supposes the angel to be speaking of the impious, who provoked God's wrath, till it became necessary for grievous and severe penalties to be inflicted on the people, to whom God had so magnificently promised a happy and a tranquil state. This, however, was no common temptation, after the prophets had treated so fully of the happy and prosperous state of the people after their return from captivity, to behold the horrible dispersion, and to witness these tyrants making their assault not only upon men, but upon the temple of God itself. Wherefore the angel, as before, fortifies the

Prophet and all the rest of the pious against this kind of trial, and shews how God had not changed his counsels in afflicting his Church, to which he had promised tranquillity, but had been grievously provoked by the sins of the people. He then shews the urgent necessity which had compelled God to exercise this severity. When, therefore, *the impious had come to their height,* that is, when they had arrived at the highest pitch, and their intolerable obstinacy had become desperate. We perceive how the angel here meets the trial, and instructs the pious beforehand, unfolding to them the inviolability of God's word, while the people's impiety compelled him to treat them severely, although he had determined to display liberality in every way. Then, he says, *a king shall stand with a fierce countenance.* But the rest tomorrow.

PRAYER.

Grant, Almighty God, since we see thy Church throughout all ages to have been exercised by the Cross in various ways, and with constant suffering, that we also may prepare ourselves for undergoing whatever thou mayest lay upon us. May we learn also to consider our sins as the cause of whatever adversity happens to us; may we consider thee to be not only faithful in all thy promises, but also a Father—propitious to those wretched ones who suppliantly fly to thee for pardon. When we are humbled under thy powerful hand, may we be raised up by the hope of eternal salvation which is prepared for us. Thus may we look for a happy and joyful termination of all our contests, until we enjoy the fruit of our victory in thy heavenly kingdom, as it has been obtained for us by the blood of thine only-begotten Son.—Amen.

Lecture Forty=Third.

AFTER the angel had explained the Grecian monarchy, he records the future origin of a king who should be *hard of face.* Without the slightest doubt, he implies the iniquity of Antiochus by this phrase. He was notoriously destitute of any nobleness of mind, and remarkable for low cunning, and to this disposition was added an impudence which faltered at nothing. This is the sense in which I take the words *hard of face*. The following phrase asserts his cunning, when it says, *he shall be skilled in enigmas*. This is equivalent to saying, he should excel in cunning, and should not be easily deceived. By these two epithets he does not compliment, but rather defames Antiochus Epiphanes, by representing him as hardened as the wicked usually are, without the slightest particle of either reason, or equity, or shame. He next blames his craftiness and deceit, by stating he should be *skilled in enigmas*. He afterwards adds, *his power shall be strengthened, and yet not by his own might*. Some are of opinion that Antiochus Epiphanes is here compared to Alexander, as the angel had previously stated the inferiority of the four kings to the first; for they were prefigured by four small horns. For the most powerful of them all did not reign over a fifth part of the dominions which Alexander had acquired for himself by violence and war. Others, again, explain this passage as if the power of Antiochus would be great, but still very unlike that of Alexander, and far inferior to it, according to the sense, *not in his*, i.e., Alexander's, *strength*. Many, however, refer this to Antiochus, although they do not agree among themselves. Some, again, want a kind of correction, as if the angel implied that the power of Antiochus should be great, but not quite openly so. Hence *his valour shall be strengthened*, not meaning by "valour" that heroic spirit with which kings are usually endowed, nor any increase in magnanimity; nor yet that Antiochus should imitate such monarchs as these, but his strength should lie concealed. He should creep on by clandestine acts, and not contend in open battle according to the practice of those who excel in courage; he should secretly try many schemes, and thus stealthily extend his empire. This makes a tolerable sense. Others, again, think this ought to be referred to God, since the strength of Antiochus was not the result of his own industry or valour, but of the judgment of God, who armed him with it, because he wished to use him as a scourge to execute his punishments on the Jews. His fortitude, therefore, shall be strengthened, yet not by his own valour, as this entirely depended on the just designs and vengeance of God. Although this last sense is more profitable, and contains much useful instruction, yet I fear it is distorted. And thus the last clause is either a correction of the preceding words, meaning—" because he should not increase with ingenuous earnestness," or else, the angel is still comparing his strength with the power of Alexander. *His power*, therefore, *shall be strengthened*, and yet not bear comparison with Alexander's; or, his power shall be strengthened, but not by habits of war nor by open magnanimity, but he shall grow great by fraudulent and clandestine arts; because he was on the one hand most impious, and on the other, of a servile disposition, as we have formerly said.

It follows, *He shall make wonderful havoc, and shall prosper, and shall proceed*, that is, shall execute, *and shall destroy the strong, and the people of the saints.* By עצומים, *gnetzumim*, I understand not only the Jews, but also other neighbouring nations; as if the angel had said, Antiochus shall be conqueror wherever he shall extend his arms, until at length he shall subdue Judea, and miserably afflict the people of God. Wherefore, *he shall strike or destroy the brave, and the people of the saints*, that is, the holy people, as we saw before. *And according to his understanding shall his craftiness prosper in his hand.* The conjunction " and " may be here superfluous; in this sense the passage is usually received, thus reading it on in one context; according to his understanding he shall prosper, although there is the conjunction " and " in the way, but this is frequently superfluous in Hebrew. It means, *deceit shall prosper in his hand.* Here the angel confirms the former assertion respecting the servile cunning of Antiochus, as he did not act with ingenuous manliness, but with his audacity and hardihood he united malicious arts and craftiness unworthy of a king. *Craft*, therefore, *shall prosper in his hand, and that, too, as far as he understands it.* Some suppose the sharpness of Antiochus to be noticed here, as if the angel had said, Craftiness shall prosper in his hand, in consequence of his possessing superior ability and penetration. But the passage may be suitably explained in this way,—Antiochus shall act prosperously according to his mental perception, and shall be so assisted by his craftiness, as to obtain whatever he shall grasp at.

It follows next, *He shall magnify himself in his heart*, or he shall raise himself, and bear himself magnificently; although this expression implies boasting and pride, and is taken in a disadvantageous sense. *He shall be insolent, therefore, in his heart.* The angel seems to distinguish here between the scheming and penetration of Antiochus, and his pride of heart; for, although he should obtain great victories, and should subdue many nations according to his desires, yet he would oppress the Jews, and *then should be magnified in heart;* that is, should be puffed up with greater pride than before, on account of those continuous successes. *And in peace he shall destroy many*, or the brave; for the word רבים, *rabbim*, signifies either. Some translate, on account of his prosperity, because the Lord wished to relax the reins, so that no one should hinder the course of his victories. On account, then, of that success, he shall destroy many. Profane men, indeed, who understand nothing of God's providence, have said that fortune and chance prevail more in war than skill or arms; but the success of generals does not spring from either chance or fortune, but as God pleases to conduct the affairs of the world in various ways, so in some cases the evil and unskilful warriors succeed, while others make many fruitless efforts and trials, although they are superior in counsel, and are provided with the very best ornaments. But I rather incline to another sense which interpreters do not mention; namely, Antiochus should destroy and lay waste many nations without any trouble, with the greatest ease, and as it were in sport. Wherefore the Prophet signifies, or the angel who addresses the Prophet, that Antiochus should be the conqueror of many nations, not only because he should be endowed with great cunning, and should carry on the war more by treachery than by open violence, but as it is reported of Timotheus the Athenian general: He will take cities and lands, and subject them to himself, through fortune spreading her net for him while he is indulging in sleep. The angel, therefore, seems to point out this listlessness, by predicting much devastation by the hand of Antiochus in apparent ease and calmness. Others expound it thus,—nations shall be laid waste by that robber which have given him no occasion for attack, because they have never stirred up any hostility against him; but when they attempt to cultivate peace, he wearies them without the slightest pretext. But this interpretation seems to me forced.

He afterwards adds, *And against the Prince of princes he shall stand,* or rise up, *and he shall be destroyed without hand,* or shall be ruined. The ‫ו‬, *vau,* is put adversatively; *yet* he shall be destroyed without hand. This was far more galling to the Prophet, and to the whole people, for the angel to predict the contests of Antiochus, not only with mortals, but with God himself. Some understand ‫שׁר־שׂרים‬, *sar-sarim,* of the high priest, but this is too confined and spiritless. I have not the least doubt that God is here meant by the *Prince of princes.* Wherefore the complete sense is,—Antiochus should be not only bold, and cruel, and proud towards men, but this madness and fury should proceed so far as to lead him to attack and resist God. This is the full sense. But a consolation is soon added, when the angel says, *he should be destroyed without hand.* It would, indeed, have been almost intolerable for the Jews to hear only of the insolence of Antiochus in contending against God, unless this correction had been added—the end of the contest must be the self-destruction of Antiochus by his own impiety. *He shall be destroyed* then. But how? *without hand,* says he. For after subduing so many nations, and after obtaining whatever he wished, what more could be hoped for as far as man is concerned? Who would dare to rise up against him? Clearly enough, if the kings of Syria had been content with their own boundaries, they need not have feared any one, for no enemy would have molested them; but they provoked the Romans to attack them, and when they wished to invade Egypt, they did not prosper in their attempts. Whichever be the meaning, the angel here announces the sufficiency of the divine power without any human aid, for the destruction and overthrow of Antiochus. Some think this prophecy refers to Antichrist, thus they pass by Antiochus altogether, and describe to us the appearance of Antichrist, as if the angel had shewn to Daniel what should happen after the second renovation of the Church. The first restoration took place when liberty was restored to the people, and they returned from exile to their native land, and the second occurred at the advent of Christ. These interpreters suppose this passage to unfold that devastation of the Church which should take place after the coming of Christ, and the promulgation of the gospel. But as we have previously seen, this is not a suitable meaning, and I am surprised that men versed in the Scriptures should so pour forth clouds upon clear light. For, as we said yesterday, nothing can be clearer, or more perspicuous, or even more familiar, than this prophecy. And what is the tendency of ascribing so violently to Antichrist what even mere children clearly see to be spoken of Antiochus, except to deprive Scripture of all its authority? Others speak more modestly and more considerately, when they suppose the angel to treat of Antiochus for the purpose of depicting in his person the figure of Antichrist. But I do not think this reasoning sufficiently sound. I desire the sacred oracles to be treated so reverently, that no one may introduce any variety according to the will of man, but simply hold what is positively certain. It would please me better to see any one wishing to adapt this prophecy to the present use of the Church, and to apply to Antichrist by analogy what is said of Antiochus. We know that whatever happened to the Church of old, belongs also to us, because we have fallen upon the fulness of times.

No doubt the Holy Spirit wished to teach us how to bear our cross by making use of this example, but as I have already said, it seems to me far too frivolous to search for allegories. We should be content with true simplicity, and transfer to ourselves whatever occurred to the ancient people. (1 Cor. x. 11.) With how much reason does the Apostle say there should be false teachers in the kingdom of Christ, as there were formerly false prophets! (2 Pet. ii. 1.) So we must determine, that the devil, who was a murderer from the beginning, will always find those whom he will stir up and impel to persecute the Church. The devil contends at this very day, not only by fallacious doctrines, and impious errors, and impostures, but also by cruel tyranny, as he inflames many impious men to madness, and thus harasses the sons of God. As the Jews ought not to quail under the calamities which oppressed them, through Daniel's predictions concerning Antiochus, so the same doctrine ought in these days to fortify us, lest the novelty of our calamities should appal us, when the Church is oppressed by heavy burdens, and tyrants rage and storm, with fire and sword. (Rom. viii. 28.) For the fathers experienced similar trials, to whom Christ had not then pointed out the way of life, and who did not comprehend so clearly as we do our duty to be conformed to the only-begotten Son of God, because he is the first-born in the Church ; he is our head and we are his members. This was not so fully unfolded to those holy men, who still endured under so many afflictions, when they might suppose the Church completely buried, as it is certainly surprising that they did not yield a hundred times over to so many and such dreadful calamities. Therefore this doctrine will be best accommodated to our instruction, if we are convinced of the justice of our condition not being better than that of the fathers. What, therefore, happened to them ? *These wicked ones should be destroyed,* namely, the Jews, who professed themselves to be the elect people of God, and the holy family of Abraham, and in numberless ways had obstinately provoked God's wrath ; thus the Church was miserably harassed. Antiochus, especially, like a sweeping tempest, reduced all things to ruin, till the people felt themselves utterly undone, and to all human appearance were without the slightest hope. As God punished so severely the wickedness of his ancient people, it does not surprise us when we feel his present chastisements, as in these days the land is full of sinfulness, and we do not cease perpetually and purposely to provoke God's wrath. (1 Thess. iii. 3.) Lastly, to avoid the penalty due to our sins, let us consider the end of our calling, the subjection of our whole life to the cross. This is the warfare to which our heavenly Father destines us. As this is our lot, we ought to look into this mirror, and there behold the perpetual condition of the

Church. It is therefore no matter of surprise, if, instead
of one Antiochus, God should raise up many who are hardened and invincible in their obstinacy, and in their cruelty
make many attempts with clandestine arts, and plot for the
destruction of the Church.   If the fathers experienced this,
it does not surprise us, if we in these days undergo similar
sufferings.   This, I say, is a useful analogy, and does not
distort the simple sense of Scripture.   Now, let us go on,—

26. And the vision of the evening and the morning which was told *is* true: wherefore shut thou up the vision; for it *shall be* for many days.	25. Et visio matutina et vesper-tina quæ pronuntiata fuit, veritas est, Tu ergo obsigna, *vel claude,* visionem, quia ad dies multos *pro-tenditur.*

The angel again confirms the assertion that no part of
this vision was shewn to the Prophet in vain, because not
even the slightest portion of it should fail of its effect.   The
necessity of this method of confirming our faith is notorious,
because, although the events may be well known to us, yet
we cannot acquiesce in God's word, unless he should testify
so repeatedly to the truth of his assertions, and sanction by
such repetition whatever appears to us ambiguous.   When
it becomes perfectly obvious that the angel discourses upon
obscure events, and such as were utterly incredible at the
time, it does not surprise us when he announces again, that
the Prophet had seen nothing which God would not accomplish.   *This vision,* therefore, says he, *is truth.*   He calls it
" the vision of the evening and morning," because while the
angel was treating of the six years and almost a half, he
used this form of speech.   And we said this was purposely
expressed, lest any one should extend it to years or
months, as some did ; as if the angel had said,—Behold !
by calculating single days up to six years and about a
half, the completion of this prophecy when the Temple shall
be cleansed, shall be accurately discovered.   Again it is
asserted, that the vision is certain, because God had computed day by day the time of the profanation of the Temple
until the period of its cleansing.   *Do thou,* therefore, says
he, *seal* or close *the vision, because it is for many days.*   It
may surprise us why God should wish what he had explained
to his servant to remain concealed.   For Daniel was not

instructed in futurity for his own private advantage, but for the common usefulness of the whole people. It seems, therefore, contrary to his office to be commanded to close up the vision, and to keep it in complete obscurity. But the angel means, if the greater part of the people should reject this prophecy, this formed no reason why Daniel should hesitate. *Be thou, therefore, the guardian of this prophecy,* as if God had deposited a treasure in the hands of his servant, and had said, " Pay no regard to any who despise this prophecy ; many may deride thee, and others think thou art narrating fables, and very few will have confidence in thee : but do not relax on this account, but faithfully guard this treasure," *since it is for many days;* that is, although its effect is not immediately apparent, because God will suspend for some time the punishments of which it treats, and will not restore the Temple all at once, nor wrest his people immediately out of the hand of the tyrant. In consequence, then, of his deferring his judgments as well as his pity for many days, *do thou close up this vision,* that is, keep it to thyself, as if thou art alone. Thus God does not simply command his Prophet to be silent, or to conceal what he had learnt, but rather confirms him in his consistency, lest he should estimate this prophecy according to the ordinary opinions of his countrymen. And at the same time he shews, that though the Jews did not pay attention to what Daniel announced to them, yet nothing whatever should be in vain. It follows,—

27. And I Daniel fainted, and was sick *certain* days: afterward I rose up, and did the king's business ; and I was astonished at the vision, but none understood *it*.	27. Et ego Daniel deliquium passus sum, *vel, fractus sum,* et ægrotavi dies,[1] et surrexi,[2] feci opus regis,[3] et obstupui propter visionem : neque intelligens.[4]

Again, Daniel shews himself to have been so touched with the secret instinct of God, that he knew for certain this vision to have been divinely presented to him. For God wished so to affect his servant, that he might embrace with greater reverence what he both heard and saw. I have

---

[1] That is, for a time.—*Calvin.*   [2] That is, after I rose up.—*Calvin.*
[3] That is, I discharged my duty to which the king had appointed me.—*Calvin.*
[4] That is, there is no one who could understand.—*Calvin.*

already referred to our want of attention in listening to God's word as it deserves, unless some kind of fear precedes it which may rouse our minds by some means from their torpor ; but this prophecy had a special intention.   In an ordinary case, God did not humble his servant ; but by the disease which is here mentioned, he wishes to shew how this prediction related to some event of serious magnitude. Daniel, therefore, states *himself to have been astonished, as if suffering under some defect, and afflicted by disease.*   This disease did not happen to the Prophet naturally, but it fell upon him in consequence of his being suddenly terrified. And he afterwards shews this, by saying, no one understood the prediction.   Here, then, he admonishes all the pious, neither to hear nor read this narrative with carelessness, but to summon up their utmost attention, and to perceive that God here shews them things of the greatest importance, and which vitally concern their salvation.   This forms a reason why Daniel ought to suffer dejection and to be afflicted by disease.   He next says, *he returned to the king's business,* meaning his ordinary occupation.   We infer from this expression, the grievous error of those who think him to have been in Persia at this period, because he could not return to his duties, unless he were present in the king's palace.   But why is this added?   To assure us that the Prophet was not drawn off from the duties which the king had assigned to him, although God had chosen him to perform the peculiar office of Prophet and teacher of his Church. This is a rare instance, and ought not to be drawn into a precedent, according to the usual phrase.   Which of us, for instance, would be sufficient for those duties of political government assigned to Daniel, and also for those incumbent upon a pastor and teacher?   But God made use of his servant Daniel in an extraordinary way, because he had many reasons for wishing him occupied in the king's palace. We have previously seen how God's glory was illustrated by his position, for Daniel admonished Belshazzar of his approaching death, when his enemies had already partially captured the city.   And the utility of this was proved by Cyrus and Darius sparing the Jews.   As long as the

Chaldeans held the supreme power, Daniel was of no slight benefit to those miserable exiles ; for even if he lived under cruel tyrants, yet he had some authority remaining, and this enabled him to alleviate many of the sufferings of his nation. God, therefore, was consulting the advantage of the whole people, when he desired Daniel to proceed in the course of his usual duties. Besides this, he wished to confer upon him the extraordinary gift of prophecy, an endowment, as I have said, peculiar to Daniel. It now follows,—

CHAPTER NINTH.

1. In the first year of Darius the son of Ahasuerus, of the seed of the Medes, which was made king over the realm of the Chaldeans ;
2. In the first year of his reign, I Daniel understood by books the number of the years, whereof the word of the Lord came to Jeremiah the prophet, that he would accomplish seventy years in the desolations of Jerusalem.
3. And I set my face unto the Lord God, to seek by prayer and supplications, with fasting, and sackcloth, and ashes.

1. Anno uno, *id est, primo,* Darii filii Assueri e semine Medorum, qui rex fuit constitutus,[1] in regno Chaldaico.
2. In anno primo, *inquam,*[2] regni illius, ego Daniel intellexi in libris numerum annorum, de quibus fuerat sermo Jehovæ ad Jeremiam prophetam,[3] ad implendum desolationem Jerusalem annos septuaginta.
3. Et levavi faciem meam ad Dominum Deum, ut quærerem oratione et precationibus,[4] cum jejunio, sacco, et cinere.

In this chapter Daniel will explain to us two things. First, how very ardently he was accustomed to pray when the time of redemption, specified by Jeremiah, drew nigh ; and next, he will relate the answer he received from God to his earnest entreaties. These are the two divisions of this chapter : First, Daniel informs us how *he prayed when he understood from books the number of the years.* Whence we gather, that God does not here promise his children earthly blessings, but eternal life, and while they grow torpid and cast aside all care and spiritual concern, he urges them the more earnestly to prayer. For what benefit do God's pro-

---

[1] Verbally, was crowned, *i.e.,* was king.—*Calvin.*
[2] [3] He repeats the words, the first year.— *Calvin.*
    Some translate the word בינתי, *binthi,* I was attentive, I diligently considered, but this is of little consequence as to the sense.—*Calvin.*
[4] Some take "prayers and supplications" for the accusative case.—*Calvin.*

mises confer on us, unless we embrace them by faith? But prayer is the chief exercise of faith. This observation of Daniel's is worthy of notice; *he was stimulated to prayer because he knew from books the number of the years.* But I will defer the rest till to-morrow.

PRAYER.

Grant, Almighty God, as in these days thou hast called us to a similar lot to that which the fathers under the Law formerly experienced, and as thou didst confirm them in patience, and arm them for constancy in warfare, and render them superior in all conflicts with Satan and the world: Grant, I pray thee, that we at this day, whom thou wishest to be joined to them, may become proficients in thy word. May we look forward to bearing the cross throughout our whole life. May we be prepared for the contest, and prefer miserable affliction under the standard of the cross, to spending a secure and luxurious life in our own enjoyments, and thus becoming deprived of that hope of victory which thou hast promised us, and whose fruit thou hast laid up for us in heaven, through Jesus Christ our Lord.—Amen.

Lecture Forty-Fourth.

WE began to say yesterday, that the faithful do not so acquiesce in the promises of God as to grow torpid, and become idle and slothful through the certainty of their persuasion that God will perform his promises, but are rather stimulated to prayer. For the true proof of faith is the assurance when we pray that God will really perform what he has promised us. Daniel is here set before us as an example of this. For when he understood the time of deliverance to be at hand, this knowledge became a stimulus to him to pray more earnestly than he was accustomed to do. It is clear then, as we have already seen, that the Prophet was diligent and anxious in this particular. He did not deviate from his usual habit when he saw the greatest risk of being put to death; for while the king's edict prohibited every one from praying to God, he still directed his face towards Jerusalem. This was the holy Prophet's daily habit. But we shall perceive the extraordinary nature of his present prayer, when he says, he prayed in dust and ashes. From this it appears, how God's promise stirred him up to supplication, and hence we gather what I have lately touched upon,—that faith is no careless speculation, satisfied with simply assenting to God. For the stupid seem to assent by outward hearing, while true faith is something far more serious. When we really embrace the grace of God which he offers us, he meets us and precedes us with his goodness, and thus we in time respond to his offers, and bear witness to our expectation of his promises. Nothing, therefore, can be better for us, than to ask for what he has promised. Thus in the prayers of the saints these feelings are united, as they plead God's promises wherein they intreat him. And we cannot possibly exercise true confidence in prayer, except by resting firmly on God's word. An example of this kind is here presented to us in Daniel's case. When *he understood the number of the years to be at hand of which God had spoken by Jeremiah,* he applied his mind to supplication. It is worth while to notice what I have mentioned:—Daniel is not here treating of his daily prayers. We may easily collect from the whole of his life, how Daniel had exercised himself in prayer before Jeremiah had spoken of the seventy years. Because he knew the time of redemption to be at hand, he was then stimulated to more than his usual entreaties. He expresses this, by saying, *in fasting, and sackcloth, and ashes.* For the saints were not accustomed to throw ashes over their heads every day, nor yet to separate themselves for prayer, by either fasting or putting on sackcloth. This action was rare, used only when God gave some sign of his wrath, or when he held out some scarce and singular benefit. Daniel's present prayer was not after his usual habit, but when he put on sackcloth and sprinkled himself with ashes, and endured fasting, he prostrated himself suppliantly before God. He also pleaded for pardon, as we shall afterwards see, and begged the performance of what the Almighty had surely promised.

From this we should learn two lessons: First, we must perseveringly exercise our faith by prayers; next, when

God promises us anything remarkable and valuable, we
ought then to be the more stirred up, and to feel this expectation as a sharper stimulus. With reference to the fasting,
and sackcloth, and ashes, we may shortly remark, how the
holy fathers under the Law were in the habit of adding
extraordinary ceremonies to their prayers, especially when
they wished to confess their sins to God, and to cast themselves before him as thoroughly guilty and convicted, and as
placing their whole hope in their supplication for mercy.
And in the present day the faithful are justified in adding
certain external rites to their prayers ; although no necessity
either can, or ought to be laid down beforehand in this
case. We know also, the Orientals to be more devoted to
ceremonies than we are ourselves. And this difference must
be noticed between the ancient people and the new Church,
since Christ by his advent abolished many ceremonies. For
the fathers under the Law were, in this sense, like children,
as Paul says. (Gal. iv. 3.) The discipline which God had
formerly instituted, involved the use of more ceremonies
than were afterwards practised. As there is this important
difference between our position and theirs, whoever desires
to copy them in all their actions, would rather become the
ape than the imitator of antiquity. Meanwhile, we must
notice that the reality remains for us, although external
rites are abolished. Two kinds of prayer, therefore, exist ;
one which we ought to practise daily, in the morning, evening, and if possible, every moment ; for we see how constancy
in prayer is commended to us in Scripture. (Luke xviii. 1 ;
Rom. xii. 12 ; 1 Thess. v. 17.) The second kind is used,
when God denounces his wrath against us, or we have need
of his special aid, or seek anything unusual from him. This
was Daniel's method of praying when he put on sackcloth,
and sprinkled himself with ashes. But as I have treated
this subject elsewhere, I now use greater brevity.

When Daniel perceived the period of deliverance at hand,
he not only prayed as usual, but left all his other occupa-
tions for the purpose of being quite at ease and at leisure,
and thus he applied his mind exclusively to prayer, and
made use of other aids to devotion. For the sackcloth and

the ashes availed far more than mere outward testimony; they are helps to increase our ardour in praying, when any one feels sluggish and languid. It is true, indeed, that when the fathers under the Law prayed with sackcloth and ashes, this appearance was useful as an outward mark of their profession. It testified before men, how they came before God as guilty suppliants, and placed their whole hope of salvation in pardon alone. Still this conduct was useful in another way, as it stirred them up more eagerly to the desire to pray. And both these points are to be noticed in Daniel's case. For if the Prophet had such need of this assistance, what shall be said of our necessities? Every one ought surely to comprehend how dull and cold he is in this duty. Nothing else, therefore, remains, except for every one to become conscious of his infirmity, to collect all the aids he can command for the correction of his sluggishness, and thus stimulate himself to ardour in supplication. For when Daniel, according to his daily custom, prayed so as to run the risk of death on that very account, we ought to gather from this, how naturally alert he was in prayer to God. He was conscious of the want of sufficiency in himself, and hence he adds the use of sackcloth, and ashes, and fasting.

I pass by what might be treated more diffusely—how fasting is often added to extraordinary prayers. We conclude also, how works by themselves fail to please the Almighty, according to the fictions of the Papists of these days, and also to the foolish imaginations of many others. For they think fasting a part of the worship of God, although Scripture always commends it to us for another purpose. By itself it is of no consequence whatever, but when mingled with prayers, with exhortations to penitence, and with the confession of sinfulness, then it is acceptable, but not otherwise. Thus, we observe Daniel to have made use of fasting correctly, not as wishing to appease God by this discipline, but to render him more earnest in his prayers.

We must next notice another point. Although Daniel was an interpreter of dreams, he was not so elated with confidence or pride as to despise the teaching delivered by other prophets. Jeremiah was then at Jerusalem, when Daniel was dragged into exile, where he discharged the office of teacher for a long period afterwards, so that Babylon became a kind of pulpit.[1] And Ezekiel names him the third among the most excellent servants of God, (chap. xiv. 14,) because Daniel's piety, integrity, and holiness of life, were even then celebrated. As to Jeremiah, we know him to have been either just deceased in Egypt, or perhaps to be still living, when this vision was offered to Daniel, who had perused his prophecies previously to this occasion. We observe also, the great modesty of this holy man, because he exercised himself in reading the writings of Jeremiah, and was not ashamed to own how he profited by them. For he knew this prophet to have been appointed to instruct himself as well as the rest of the faithful. Thus he willingly submitted to the instruction of Jeremiah, and ranged himself among his disciples. And if he had not deigned to read those prophecies, he would have been unworthy to partake of the promised deliverance. As he was a member of the Church, he ought to have been a disciple of Jeremiah, so in like manner, Jeremiah would not have objected to profit in his turn, if any prophecy of Daniel's had been presented to him. This spirit of modesty ought to flourish among the servants of God, even if they excel in the gift of prophecy, inducing them to learn from each other, while no one should raise himself above the common level. While we are teachers, we ought at the same time to continue learners. And Daniel teaches us this by saying, *he understood the number of years in books, and the number was according to the word of Jehovah to the prophet Jeremiah.* He shews why he exercised himself in the writings of Jeremiah,— because he was persuaded that God had spoken by his voice. Thus it caused him no trouble to read what he knew to have proceeded from God.

We must now remark THE TIME OF THIS PROPHECY—*the first year of Darius.* I will not dwell upon this point here, be-

---

[1] A turn of expression rather unexpected. The Latin text is *quasi suggestus ;* and both the French editions translate *comme une chaire pour prescher.—Ed.*

cause I had rather discuss the years when we come to the second part of the chapter. I stated yesterday that this chapter embraced two principal divisions. Daniel first records his own prayer, and then he adds the prediction which was brought to him by the hand of the angel. We shall next speak of the seventy years, because the discussion will then prove long enough. I will now touch but briefly upon one point—the time of redemption was at hand, as the Babylonian monarchy was changed and transferred to the Medes and Persians. In order to render the redemption of his people the more conspicuous, God desired to wake up the whole East after the Medes and Persians had conquered the Babylonians. Cyrus and Darius published their edict about the same time, by which the Jews were permitted to return to their native country. *In that year*, therefore, meaning the year in which Darius began his reign. Here it may be asked, Why does he name Darius alone, when Cyrus was far superior to him in military prowess, and prudence, and other endowments ? The ready answer is this, Cyrus set out immediately on other expeditions, for we know what an insatiable ambition had seized upon him. He was not stimulated by avarice, but by an insane ambition, and never could rest quiet in one place. So, when he had acquired Babylon and the whole of that monarchy, he set out for Asia Minor, and harassed himself almost to death by continual restlessness. Some say he was slain in battle, while Xenophon describes his death as if he was reclining on his bed, and at his ease was instructing his sons in what he wished to have done. But whichever be the true account, all history testifies to his constant motion from place to place. Hence we are not surprised at the Prophet's speaking here of Darius only, who was more advanced in age and slower in his movements through his whole life. It is sufficiently ascertained that he was not a man fond of war ; Xenophon calls him Cyaxares, and asserts him to have been the son of Astyages. We know, again, that Astyages was the maternal grandfather of Cyrus ; and thus this Darius was the uncle as well as father-in-law of Cyrus, as the mother of Cyrus was his sister. When the Prophet calls his father Ahasuerus, it need not occasion us any trouble, as the names vary very much when we compare the Greek with the Hebrew. Without the slightest doubt, Astyages was called Ahasuerus, or at least one was his name and the other his surname. All doubt is removed by the expression, *Darius was of the seed of the Medes.* He distinguishes here between the Medes and Persians, because the Medes had seized upon rich and splendid territories, stretching far and wide on all sides, while the Persians were shut up within their own mountains, and were more austere in their manner of life. But the Prophet here states of this Darius his Median origin, and adds another circumstance, namely, *his obtaining the kingdom of the Chaldees.* For Cyrus allowed him to be called king, not only on account of his age and of his being both his uncle and father-in-law, but because he would not attempt anything against his authority. He knew he had no heir who might in future become troublesome to him. Cyrus therefore yielded the empty title to his father-in-law, while the whole power and influence remained completely within his own grasp.

He says, then, *When I understood in books the number of the years for filling up the desolation of Jerusalem,* namely, *seventy years.* This prophecy is found in the 25th chapter of Jeremiah, and is repeated in the 29th. God fixed beforehand seventy years for the captivity of his people, as it was a grievous trial to be cast out of the land of Canaan, which had been granted them as a perpetual inheritance. They remembered those celebrated sentences, "This shall be my rest for ever," and "Ye shall possess the land for ever." (Ps. cxxxii. 14.) When they were cast out and dispersed throughout the various countries of the earth, it seemed as if the covenant of God had been abolished, and as if there was no further advantage in deriving their origin from those holy fathers to whom their land had been promised. For the purpose of meeting these temptations, God fixed beforehand a set time for their exile, and Daniel now recurs to this prediction. He adds, *Then I raised my face.* It is properly אתנה, *ath-neh,* I placed ; but as some interpreters seem to receive this word too fancifully, as if Daniel had then looked towards the sanctuary, I prefer rendering it, *He raised his face to God.* It is quite true that while the altar was standing, and the ark of the covenant was in the sanctuary, God's face was there, towards which the faithful ought to direct both their vows and prayers ; but now the circumstances were different through the temple being overthrown. We have previously read of Daniel's praying and turning his eyes in that direction, and towards Judea, but his object was not a desire to pray after the manner of his fathers. For there was then neither sanctuary nor ark of the covenant in existence. (Chap. vi. 10.) His object in turning his face towards Jerusalem was openly to shew his profession of still mentally dwelling in that land which God had destined for the race of Abraham. By that outward gesture and ceremony the Prophet claimed possession of the Holy Land, although still a captive and an exile. With regard to the present passage, I simply understand it to mean, he raised his face towards God. *That I might inquire,* says he, *by supplication and prayers.* Some translate, that I might seek supplication and prayer. Either is equally suitable to the sense, but the former version is less forced, because the Prophet sought God by supplication and prayers. And this form of speech is common enough in Scripture, as we are said to seek God when we testify our hope of his performing what he has promised. It now follows :—

4. And I prayed unto the Lord my God, and made my confession, and said, O Lord, the great and dreadful God, keeping the covenant and mercy to them that love him, and to them that keep his commandments.

4. Et oravi Jehovam Deum meum, et confessus sum,[1] et dixi, Quæso Domine Deus magne et terribilis, custodiens fœdus et misericordiam diligentibus ipsum, et custodientibus præcepta ejus.

Here Daniel relates the substance of his prayer. He says, *He prayed and confessed before God.* The greater part of this prayer is an entreaty that God would pardon his people. Whenever we ask for pardon, the testimony of repentance ought to precede our request. For God announces that he will be propitious and easily entreated when men seriously and

[1] The same word in Hiphil signifies to celebrate God's praises, but it is here taken for confessing a fault.—*Calvin.*

heartily repent. (Is. lviii. 9.) Thus confession of guilt is one method of obtaining pardon ; and for this reason Daniel fills up the greater part of his prayer with the confession of his sinfulness. He reminds us of this, not for the sake of boasting, but to instruct us by his own example to pray as we ought. He says, therefore, *he prayed and made confession.* The addition of "my God" to the word Jehovah is by no means superfluous. *I prayed,* he says, *to my God.* He here shews that he did not utter prayers with trembling, as men too often do, for unbelievers often flee to God, but without any confidence. They dispute with themselves whether their prayers will produce any fruit ; Daniel, therefore, shews us two things openly and distinctly, since he prayed with faith and repentance. By the word confession he implies his repentance, and by saying *he prayed to God,* he expresses faith, and the absence of all rashness in throwing away his prayers, as unbelievers do when they pray to God confusedly, and are all the while distracted by a variety of intruding thoughts. *I prayed,* says he, *to my God.* No one can use this language without a firm reliance on the promises of God, and assuming that he will prove himself ready to be entreated. He now adds, *I entreat thee, O Lord.* The particle אנא, *ana,* is variously translated ; but it is properly, in the language of grammarians, the particle of beseeching. *O Lord God,* says he, *great and terrible.* Daniel seems to place an obstacle in his own way by using this language ; for such is the sanctity of God that it repels us to a distance as soon as we conceive it in the mind : wherefore this terror seems to be removed when we seek a familiar approach to the Almighty. One might suppose this method of prayer by no means suitable, as Daniel places God before his eyes as great and formidable. It seems something like frightening himself ; yet the Prophet deserves a due moderation, while on the one hand he acknowledges God to be great and terrible, and on the other he allows him *to keep his covenant towards those who love him and obey his statutes.* We shall afterwards see a third point added—God will receive the ungrateful and all who have departed from his covenant. The Prophet joins these two things together.

With reference to the epithets *great and terrible*, we must maintain what I have already stated, namely, the impossibility of our praying rightly, unless we humble ourselves before God ; and this humility is a preparation for repentance. Daniel, therefore, sets before himself the majesty of God, to urge both himself and others to cast themselves down before the Almighty, that, in accordance with his example, they may really feel penitent before him. *God*, therefore, says he, *is great and terrible*. We shall never attribute just honour to God unless we become cast down, as if dead, before him. And we ought diligently to notice this, because we are too often careless in prayer to God, and we treat it as a mere matter of outward observance. We ought to know how impossible it is to obtain anything from God, unless we appear in his sight with fear and trembling, and become truly humbled in his presence. This is the first point to be noticed. Then Daniel mitigates the asperity of his assertion by adding, *keeping his covenant, and having pity upon those who love him.* Here is a change of person : the third is substituted for the second, but there is no obscurity in the sense ; as if he had said, *Thou keepest thy covenant with those who love thee and observe thy statutes.* Here Daniel does not yet fully explain the subject, for this statement is too weak for gaining the confidence of the people ; they had perfidiously revolted from God, and as far as related to him, his agreement had come to an end. But Daniel descends by degrees and by sure steps to lay a foundation for inspiring the people with assured trust in the lovingkindness of God. Two points are embraced in this clause : first of all, it shews us there is no reason why the Jews should expostulate with God or complain of being too severely treated by him. Daniel, therefore, silences all expressions of rebellion by saying, *Thou, O God, keepest thy covenant.* We must here notice the real condition of the people : the Israelites were in exile ; we know how hard that tyranny was—how they were oppressed by the most cruel reproaches and disgrace, and how brutally they were treated by their conquerors. This might impel many to cry out, as doubtless they really did, " What does God want with us ? What the better are we for being chosen as his peculiar people ? What is the good of our adoption if we are still the most miserable of all nations ?" Thus the Jews might complain with the bitterest grief and weariness of the weight of punishment which God had inflicted upon them. But Daniel here asserts his presenting himself before God, not to cavil and murmur, but only to entreat his pardon. For this reason, therefore, he first says, *God keeps his covenant towards all who love him ;* but at the same time he passes on to pray for pardon, as we shall afterwards perceive. We shall treat of this covenant and the Almighty's lovingkindness in the next Lecture.

PRAYER.

Grant, Almighty God, as at the present time thou dost deservedly chastise us for our sins, according to the example of thine ancient people, that we may turn our face to thee with true penitence and humility : May we throw ourselves suppliantly and prostrately before thee ; and, despairing of ourselves, place our only hope in thy pity which thou hast promised us. May we rely on that adoption which is founded on and sanctioned by thine only-begotten Son, and never hesitate to come to thee as a father whenever we fly to thee. Meanwhile, do thou so thoroughly affect our minds, that we may not only pray to thee as a matter of duty, but truly and seriously take refuge in thee, and be touched with a sense of our sins, and never doubt thy propitious disposition towards us, in the name of the same thy Son our Lord.—Amen.

Lecture Forty=Fifth.

In the last Lecture Daniel said that *he prayed and confessed.* Now, in narrating the form of his prayer, he begins by confession. We must notice this, to enable us to understand the scope which Daniel had in view, as well as the special object of his prayer. This is the kind of beginning which he makes,—the people are guilty before God, and suppliantly pray for pardon ; but before the Prophet comes to this entreaty, he confesses how the people were most severely and justly chastised by the Lord, as they had so

grievously and variously provoked his anger. First of all,
he calls God terrible, for I have recited and translated his
words. When the Prophet desires to attract God's favour
towards himself, he begins by bringing forward his majesty.
By these words he stirs up himself and the rest of the faithful to reverence, urging them to approach the presence of
God with submission, to acknowledge themselves utterly
condemned, and to be deprived of all hope except in the mere
mercy of God. He calls him, therefore, *great and terrible*,
in order to humble the minds of all the pious before God, to
prevent their aspiring to any self-exaltation, or being puffed
up with any self-confidence. For, as we have said elsewhere,
the epithets of God are at one time perpetual, and at another
variable, with the circumstances of the subject in hand.
God may always be called great and terrible; but Daniel
calls him so here, to stir up himself and all others to humility
and reverence, as I have previously remarked. Then he
adds, He is faithful in keeping his covenant and in shewing
pity towards all his true worshippers. I have referred to a
change of person in this clause, but it does not obscure the
sense or render it in any way doubtful. I have explained
how these words also testify to the absence of all cause why
the people should murmur or complain of being treated too
harshly. For where the faithfulness of God to his promises
has once been laid down, men have not the slightest reason
to complain when he treats them less clemently, or frustrates
them because they are found fallacious and perfidious; for
God always remains true to his words. (1 Cor. i. 9 ; x. 13 ;
2 Thess. iii. 3.) In this sense Daniel announces that *God keeps
his covenant towards all who love him.* We must next notice
how he adds the word "pity" to "covenant." He does not
put these two words as differing from each other, ברית,
berith, and חסד, *chesed*, but unites them together, and the
sentence ought to be understood by a common figure of
speech, implying that God made a gratuitous covenant which
flows from the fountain of his pity. What, therefore, is this
agreement or covenant and pity of God? The covenant
flows from God's mercy ; it does not spring from either the
worthiness or the merits of men ; it has its cause, and sta-

bility, and effect, and completion solely in the grace of God. We must notice this, because those who are not well versed in the Scriptures may ask why Daniel distinguishes mercy from covenant, as if there existed a mutual stipulation when God enters into covenant with man, and thus God's covenant would depend simply on man's obedience. This question is solved when we understand the form of expression here used, as this kind of phrase is frequent in the Scriptures. For whenever God's covenant is mentioned, his clemency, or goodness, or inclination to love is also added. Daniel therefore confesses, in the first place, the gratuitous nature of the covenant of God with Israel, asserting it to have no other cause or origin than the gratuitous goodness of God. He next testifies to God's faithfulness, for he never violates his agreement nor departs from it, as in many other places God's truth and faithfulness are united with his clemency. (Ps. xxxvi. 6, and elsewhere.) It is necessary for us to rely on God's mere goodness, as our salvation rests entirely with him, and thus we render to him the glory due to his pity, and thus it becomes needful for us, in the second place, to obtain a clear apprehension of God's clemency. The language of the Prophet expresses both these points, when he shews how God's covenant both depends upon and flows from his grace, and also when he adds the Almighty's faithfulness in keeping his agreement.

He adds, *Towards those who love thee and keep thy commandments.* We must diligently notice this, because Daniel here drives away the whole people from the defence which many might put forward, as hypocrites willingly become angry with God ; nay, boldly reproach him because he does not either pardon or indulge them. Daniel, therefore, to check this pride and to cut off every pretence for strife on the part of the impious, says, *God is faithful towards all who love him.* He admonishes us thus : God is never severe unless when provoked by the sins of men ; as if he had said, God's covenant is firm in itself ; when men violate it, it is not surprising if God withdraws from his promises and departs from his agreement, on perceiving himself treated with perfidy and distrust. The people, therefore, are here obliquely condemned, while Daniel testifies to God's *constancy in keeping his promises*, if men on their part act with good faith towards him. On the whole, he shews how the people were in fault, when God altered his usual course of kind and beneficent treatment, and put in force instead his severest vengeance, when the people were expelled from the land of Canaan which was their perpetual inheritance. Daniel here explains how all blame must be removed from God, as the people had revolted from him, and by their perfidy had violated their compact. We see, therefore, how he throws the blame of all their calamities upon the people themselves, and thus absolves God from all blame and all unjust complaints. Besides, the Prophet shews how the special object of the worship of God is to induce us to love him. For many observe God's law after the manner of slaves ; but we ought to remember this passage, God loveth a cheerful giver. (2 Cor. ix. 7.) When, therefore, hypocrites are violently drawn towards obedience, the Prophet here distinguishes between the true worshippers of God and those who discharge their duty only in a perfunctory manner, and not from the heart. He asserts the principle of worshipping God to be a diligent love of him, and this sentiment frequently occurs in the writings of Moses. (Deut. x. 12.) We must hold, therefore, the impossibility of pleasing God by obedience, unless it proceeds from a sincere and free affection of the mind. This is the very first rule in God's worship. We must love him ; we must be prepared to devote ourselves entirely to obedience to him, and to the willing performance of whatever he requires from us. As it is said in the Psalms, (Ps. cxix. 24,) Thy law is my delight. And again, in the same Psalm, David states God's law to be precious to him beyond gold and silver, yea, pleasing, and sweet beyond even honey. (Ver. 72, 103.) Unless we love God we have no reason for concluding that he will approve of any of our actions : all our duties will become corrupt before him, unless they proceed from the fountain of liberal affection towards him. Hence the Prophet adds, *To those who keep his statutes.* External observance will never benefit us, unless the love of God precede them. But we must notice this also in its turn;—God cannot be sincerely loved by us unless all our outward members follow up this affection of the soul.   Our hands and all that belong to us will be kept steady to their duty, if this spontaneous love flourish within our hearts.   For if any one asserts his love of God a thousand times over, all will be discovered to be vain and fallacious, unless the whole life correspond with it.   We can never separate love and obedience   It now follows :—

5. We have sinned, and have committed iniquity, and have done wickedly, and have rebelled, even by departing from thy precepts, and from thy judgments:

6. Neither have we hearkened unto thy servants the prophets, which spake in thy name to our kings, our princes, and our fathers, and to all the people of the land.

7. O Lord, righteousness *belongeth* unto thee, but unto us confusion of faces, as at this day ; to the men of Judah, and to the inhabitants of Jerusalem, and unto all Israel, *that are* near, and *that are* far off, through all the countries whither thou hast driven them, because of their trespass that they have trespassed against thee.

5. Peccavimus, et inique egimus et improbe nos gessimus, et rebellavimus, et recessimus a præceptis tuis, et judiciis tuis.[1]

6. Et non auscultavimus servis tuis prophetis, qui loquuti sunt in nomine tuo ad reges nostros, principes nostros, et patres nostros, et ad populum terræ.

7. Tibi domine justitia, et nobis pudor vultus,[2] sicuti hodie viro Jehudah,[3] et incolis Jerusalem, et toti Israeli, propinquis, et longinquis, in omnibus terris, quo expulisti eos, ob transgressiones,[4] quibus transgressi sunt contra te.

Daniel here continues his confession of sin.   As we have already stated, he ought to begin here, because we must remark in general the impossibility of our pleasing God by our prayers, unless we approach him as criminals, and repose all our hopes on his mercy.   But there was a special reason for the extraordinary nature of the Prophet's prayers, and his use of fasting, sackcloth, and ashes.   This was the usual method of confession by which Daniel united himself with the rest of the people, for the purpose of testifying throughout all ages the justice of the judgment which God had exercised in expelling the Israelites from the promised land, and totally disinheriting them.   Daniel, therefore, insists upon this point.   Here we may notice, in the first place, how

[1] Or, we have revolted from thy precepts and thy judgments.—*Calvin.*
[2] Verbally, of faces.—*Calvin.*   [3] That is, to all the Jews.—*Calvin.*
[4] Or, on account of transgressions.—*Calvin.*

prayers are not rightly conceived, unless founded on faith
and repentance, and thus not being according to law, they
cannot find either grace or favour before God. But great
weight is to be attached to the phrases where Daniel uses
more than a single word in saying the people acted impiously.
He puts חטאנו, *chetanu, we have sinned,* in the first place,
as the word does not imply any kind of fault, but rather a
serious crime or offence. We, therefore, have sinned; then
we have done wickedly; afterwards *we have acted impiously;*
for רשע, *reshegn,* is stronger than חטא, *cheta.* We have
done wickedly, we have been rebellious, says he, *in trans-
gressing thy statutes and commandments.* Whence this
copiousness of expression, unless Daniel wished to stimulate
himself and his whole people to penitence? For although
we are easily induced to confess ourselves guilty before God,
yet scarcely one in a hundred is affected with serious re-
morse; and those who excel others, and purely and reverently fear God, are still very dull and cold in recounting
their sins. First of all, they acknowledge scarcely one in a
hundred; next, of those which do come into their minds,
they do not fully estimate their tremendous guilt, but rather
extenuate their magnitude; and, although they perceive
themselves worthy of a hundred deaths, yet they are not
touched with their bitterness, and fear to humble themselves
as they ought, nay, they are scarcely displeased with themselves, and do not loathe their own iniquities. Daniel,
therefore, does not accumulate so many words in vain, when
he wishes to confess his own sins and those of the people.
Let us learn then how far we are from penitence, while we
only verbally acknowledge our guilt; then let us perceive
the need we have of many incentives to rouse us up from
our sloth; for although any one may feel great terrors and
tremble before God's judgments, yet all those feelings of
dread vanish away too soon. It therefore becomes necessary to fix God's fear in our hearts with some degree of violence. Daniel shews us this when using the phrase, *The
people have sinned; they have acted unjustly; they have conducted themselves wickedly and become rebellious, and declined
from the statutes and commandments of God.* This doctrine,

therefore, must be diligently noticed, because, as I have said, all men think they have discharged their duty to God, if they mildly profess themselves guilty before him, and acknowledge their fault in a single word.   But as real repentance is a sacred thing, it is a matter of far greater moment than a fiction of this kind.   Although the multitude do not perceive how they are only deceiving themselves when they confess a fault, yet in the meantime they are only trifling with God like children, while some say they are but men, and others shelter themselves in the crowd of offenders. "What could I do? I am but a man; I have only followed the example of the many."   Lastly, if we examine carefully the confessions of men in general, we shall always find some latent hypocrisy, and that there are very few who prostrate themselves before God as they ought.   We must understand, therefore, this confession of Daniel's as stimulating himself and others to the fear of God, and as laying great stress upon the sins of the people, that every one may feel for himself real and serious alarms.

Then he shews how *impiously, and wickedly, and perfidiously the Israelites had rebelled,* and how *they had declined from God's statutes and commandments.*   Daniel enlarges upon the people's fault, as they had no pretext for their ignorance after they had been instructed in God's law. They were like a man who stumbles in broad daylight.   He surely is without excuse who raises his eyes to heaven or closes them while he walks, or casts himself forward with blind impulse, for if he fall he will find no one to pity him. So Daniel here enlarges upon the people's crime, for the law of God was like a lamp pointing out the path so clearly that they were wilfully and even maliciously blind.   (Ps. cxix. 105.)   Unless they had closed their eyes, they could not err while God faithfully pointed out the way in which they ought to follow and persevere.   This is the first point.   But we ought to gather another doctrine from this passage, namely, there is no reason why men should turn away entirely from God, even if they have transgressed his commands, because, although they please both themselves and others, and think they have obtained the good opinion of the whole world, yet this will avail men nothing if they decline from God's commandments and statutes. Whoever, therefore, has the law in his hands, and turns aside in any direction, although he may use the eloquence of all the rhetoricians, yet no defence will be available. This perfidy is surely without excuse—to disobey the Almighty as soon as he shews us what he approves and what he requires. Then, when he forbids anything, if we turn aside ever so little from his teaching, we are perfidious and wicked, rebellious and apostate. Lastly, this passage proves that there is no rule of holy, pious, and sober living except a complete performance of God's commandments. For this reason he puts *statutes and judgments* to shew that the people did not sin in ignorance. He might have concluded the sentence in one word : we have departed from thy commandments; but he joins judgment to commands. And why so ? To point out how easy and clear and sufficiently familiar was God's institution, if the Israelites had only been teachable. Here we may notice the frequent recurrence of this repetition. The unskilful think these synonyms are heaped together without an object, when statutes, judgments, laws, and precepts are used, but the Holy Spirit uses them to assure us that nothing shall be wanting to us if we inquire at the mouth of God. He instructs us perfectly in regulating the whole course of our lives, and thus our errors become knowing and wilful, when God's law has been clearly set before us, which contains in itself a perfect rule of doctrine for our guidance.

He afterwards adds, *We have not obeyed thy servants the prophets who have spoken in thy name.* We ought also diligently to notice this, because the impious often wickedly fail to discern the presence of God, whenever he does not openly descend from heaven and speak to them by angels ; and so their impiety is increased throughout all ages. Thus, in these days, many think themselves to have escaped, by boasting in the absence of any revelation from heaven : the whole subject, they say, is full of controversy ; the whole world is in a state of confusion ; and what do the teachers of the Church mean by promoting such strife among each other ? Then they boast and think as they please, and are blind of

their own accord. But Daniel here shews how no turning
to God is of the slightest avail, unless he is attended to
when he sends his prophets, because all who despise those
prophets *who speak in the name of the Lord* are perfidious
and apostate, wicked and rebellious. We see, then, the
suitability of this language of Daniel, and the necessity of
this explanation : *The people were wicked, unjust, rebellious,
and impious, because they did not obey the prophets.* He
does not assert that this wicked, impious, contumacious,
and perfidious character of the people arises from their not
listening to God thundering from heaven, or to his angels
when sent to them, but because they did not obey his prophets. Besides this, he calls the prophets *servants of God who
speak in his name.* He distinguishes between true and false
prophets ; for we know how many impostors formerly abused
this title in the ancient Church ; as in these days the dis-
turbers of our churches falsely pretend to the name of God,
and by this audacity many of the simple are deceived.
Daniel, therefore, distinguishes here between the true and
false prophets, who everywhere boast in their divine election
to the office of teachers. He speaks here of the effect,
treating all these boastings as vain and foolish, for we are
not ignorant of the manner in which all Satan's ministers
transform themselves into angels of light. (2 Cor. xi. 14.)
Thus the evil as well as the good speak in God's name ; that
is, the impious no less than the righteous teachers put forth
the name of God ; but here, as we have said, Daniel refers
to the effect and the matter itself, as the phrase is. Thus
when Christ says, When two or three are gathered together
in my name, (Matt. xviii. 20,) this is not to be applied to
such deceptions as are observable in the Papacy, when they
proudly use God's name as approving certain assemblies of
theirs. It is no new thing, then, for a deceiving Church to
hide its baseness under this mask. But when Christ says,
Where two or three are assembled in my name, this refers to
true and sincere affection. So also Daniel in this passage
says, *True prophets speak in God's name ;* not only because
they shelter themselves under this name for the sake of its
authority, but because they have solid proofs of the exercise

of God's authority, and are really conscious of their true vocation.

He afterwards adds, *To our kings, our nobles, our fathers, and all the people of the land.* Here Daniel lays prostrate every high thing in this world with the view of exalting God only, and to prevent any pride rising in the world to obscure his glory, as it otherwise would do. Here, then, he implicates *kings, princes, and fathers* in the same guilt ; as if he had said, all are to be condemned without exception before God. This, again, must be diligently noticed. For we see how the common people think everything permitted to them which is approved by their kings and counsellors. For in the common opinion of men, on what does the whole foundation of right and wrong rest, except on the arbitrary will and lust of kings ? Whatever pleases kings and their counsellors is esteemed lawful, sacred, and beyond all controversy ; and thus God is excluded from his supreme dominion. As, therefore, men thus envelop themselves in clouds, and willingly involve themselves in darkness, and prevent their approach to God, Daniel here expresses how inexcusable all men are who do not obey the Prophets, even if a thousand kings should obstruct them, and the splendour of the whole world should dazzle them. By such clouds as these God's majesty can never be obscured ; nay more, this cannot offer the slightest impediment to God's dominion or hinder the course of his doctrine. These points might be treated more copiously : I am only briefly explaining the Prophet's meaning, and the kind of fruit which ought to be gathered from his words. Finally, it is a remarkable testimony in favour of the Prophet's doctrine, when kings and their counsellors are compelled to submit, and all the loftiness of the world is brought under subjection to the prophets, as God says in Jeremiah, (chap. i. 10,) Behold ! I have set thee above kingdoms, and above the empires of this world, to destroy and to build up, to plant and to root out. There God asserts the authority of his teaching, and shews its superiority to everything in the world ; so that all who wish to be free from it, as if endowed with some peculiar privilege, are both foolish and ridiculous. This, then, must be noticed in the Prophet's

words, when he says, *God spoke by his prophets to kings,
princes, and fathers.* Respecting the "fathers," we see how
frivolous is the excuse of those who use their fathers as a
shield in opposing God. For here Daniel unites both fathers
and children in the same guilt, and shews how all equally
deserve condemnation, when they do not listen to God's prophets, or rather to God speaking by means of his prophets.

He next subjoins, *To thee, O Lord, belongs righteousness,
and to us confusion of face, as it is at this day.* The meaning
is, God's wrath, which he manifests towards his people, is
just, and nothing else remains but for the whole people to
fall down in confusion, and candidly acknowledge itself deservedly condemned. But this contrast which unites opposite clauses, ought also to be noticed, because we gather from
the Prophet's words that God can neither be esteemed just
nor his equity be sufficiently illustrious, unless when the
mouths of men are closed, and all are covered and buried in
disgrace, and confess themselves subject to just accusation,
as Paul also says, Let God be just, and let all men's mouths
be stopped, (Rom. iii. 4, 26 ;) that is, let men cease to cavil
and to seek any alleviation of their guilt by their subterfuges. While, therefore, men are thus cast down and prostrate, God's true glory is illustrated. The Prophet now
utters the same instruction by joining these two clauses, of
opposite meanings, *Righteousness is to thee, but shame to
us.* Thus we cannot praise God, and especially while he
chastises us and punishes us for our sins, unless we become
ashamed of our sins, and feel ourselves destitute of all righteousness. Lastly, when we both feel and confess the equity
of our condemnation, and when this shame seizes upon our
minds, then we begin to confess God's justice ; for whoever
cannot bear this self-condemnation, displays his willingness
to contend against God. Although hypocrites apparently
bear witness to God's justice, yet whenever they claim anything as due to their own worthiness, they at the same time
derogate from their judge, because it is clear that God's
righteousness cannot shine forth unless we bury ourselves in
shame and confusion. *According as at this day,* says Daniel.
He adds this to confirm his teaching ; as if he had said, the

impiety of the people is sufficiently conspicuous from their punishment. Meanwhile, he holds the principle that the people were justly chastised ; for hypocrites, when compelled to acknowledge God's power, still cry out against his equity. Daniel joins both points together : thus, God has afflicted his people, and this very fact proves them to be wicked and perfidious, impious and rebellious. *As it is at this day*, meaning, I will not complain of any immoderate rigour, I will not say thou hast treated my people cruelly ; for even if the punishments which thou hast inflicted on us are severe, yet thy righteousness shines forth in them : I therefore confess how fully we deserve them all. *To a man of Judah*, says he. Here Daniel seems to wish purposely to strip the mask off the Israelites, under which they thought to hide themselves. For it was an honourable title to be called a Jew, an inhabitant of Jerusalem, an Israelite. It was a sacred race, and Jerusalem was a kind of sanctuary and kingdom of God. But now, says he, though we have hitherto been elevated aloft so as to surpass the whole world, and though God has deigned to bestow upon us so many favours and benefits, yet confusion of face is upon us : let our God be just. Meanwhile, let all these empty boastings cease, such as our deriving our origin from holy fathers and dwelling in a sacred land ; let us no longer cling to these things, says he, because they will profit us nothing before God. But I see that I am already too prolix.

PRAYER.

Grant, Almighty God, as no other way of access to thee is open for us except through unfeigned humility, that we may often learn to abase ourselves with feelings of true repentance. May we be so displeased with ourselves as not to be satisfied with a single confession of our iniquities ; but may we continue in the same state of meditation, and be more and more penetrated with real grief. Then may we fly to thy mercy, prostrate ourselves before thee in silence, and acknowledge no other hope but thy pity and the intercession of thine only-begotten Son. May we be so reconciled to thee, as not only to be absolved from our sins, but also governed throughout the whole course of our life by thy Holy Spirit, until at length we enjoy the victory in every kind of contest, and arrive at that blessed rest which thou hast prepared for us by the same our Lord Jesus Christ.—Amen.

Lecture Forty=Sixth.

8. O Lord, to us *belongeth* confusion of face, to our kings, to our princes, and to our fathers, because we have sinned against thee.

8. Jehovah, nobis pudor faciei, regibus nostris, principibus nostris, et patribus nostris, quia peccavimus in te.

IN this verse Daniel completes his own confession. We have stated the beginning of his prayer to be this : He threw himself before God as a criminal, with the whole people, and prayed earnestly for pardon. It was his duty to begin in this way : he had previously named the whole people ; he now speaks of *kings, princes, and fathers*, and thus comprehends the common people. Besides, kings are accustomed to absolve themselves and those who approach their presence from all ordinary laws ; wherefore Daniel uses the phrase, *kings, princes, and fathers.* While he treated of the people, he shewed how those at a distance, as well as those at home, were equally subject to God's wrath, because, had he executed his vengeance equitably on all, no one was so free from wickedness as to be free from punishment. God had not driven all the Jews into either Chaldea or Assyria, and many had remained in the neighbouring nations. Yet Daniel denies them any diminution of their guilt, although they had been treated more humanely by God, who had spared them some portion of their suffering. We are taught by this passage, that the crimes or guiltiness of men are not always to be estimated by the amount of their punishment. For God acts very mildly with some who deserve yet greater severity ; and if he does not entirely spare us, he partially remits his rigour towards us, either to allure us to repentance, or for some reasons hitherto unknown to us. Whatever the reason may be, even if God does not openly punish us all, this ought neither to lead us to excuse ourselves, nor to any self-indulgence, because we do not experience the same severity from God. The conclusion to be drawn is this, all the Israelites are justly afflicted, because, from first to last, all have conducted themselves impiously. For Daniel repeats the word which does not signify declension merely, but to act with gross wickedness ; as if he had said, the Israelites deserved no common punishment, and thus it should not surprise us when God executes such dreadful vengeance against them.   It follows :—

9. To the Lord our God *belong* mercies and forgivenesses, though we have rebelled against him.

9. Domino Deo nostro miserationes, et veniæ,[1] quamvis rebelles fuerimus in ipsum.[2]

Daniel here betakes himself to God's mercy as to a sacred asylum ; for it is not sufficient to acknowledge and confess our sins, unless we are supported by a confidence of our obtaining pardon from God's mercy. We see numbers who use great prolixity in bearing witness to the truth, that they richly deserve all kinds of punishment ; but no good result arises from this, because despair overwhelms them and plunges them into an abyss. Recognition of a fault is in truth without the slightest profit, unless with the addition of the hope of pardon. Daniel, therefore, after candidly confessing the treatment which the whole people had received from God to have been deserved, although so severe and harsh, still embraces his pity. According to the common saying, this is like a drowning man catching at a straw. We observe also how David makes use of the same principle : There is forgiveness with thee that thou mayest be feared. (Ps. cxxx. 4.) And this moderation must be diligently marked, because Satan either lulls us into torpid security, or else so agitates us as utterly to absorb our minds in sorrow. These two artifices of Satan are sufficiently known to us. Hence that moderation which I have mentioned must be maintained, lest we should grow torpid in the midst of our vices, and so indulge in contempt of God as to induce forgetfulness of him. Then, on the other hand, we ought not to be frightened, and thus close against us the gate of hope and

---

[1]   סלח, *selech*, signifies " to pardon." It is translated " propitiations," but there is no doubt about the sense.—*Calvin.*

[2]   Or, because they are rebellious ; for the particle כי, *ki*, is properly causal ; but it appears from many passages of Scripture to be taken adversatively, which seems to suit this passage better.—*Calvin.*

pardon. Daniel, therefore, here follows the best arrangement, and prescribes the same rule for us. For, in confessing the people's wickedness, he does not entirely throw away the hope of pardon, but supports himself and others with this consolation—God is merciful. He rests this hope of pardon on the very nature of God ; as if he had said, there is nothing so peculiar to God as pity, and hence we ought never to despair. *To God,* says he, *belong mercies and forgivenesses.* No doubt Daniel took this phrase from Moses, especially from that remarkable and memorable passage where God pronounces himself a severe avenger, yet full of mercy, inclined to clemency and pardon, and exercising much forbearance. (Exod. xxxiv. 6.) As, therefore, Daniel held the impossibility of God putting away his affectionate feelings of pity, he takes this as the main point of his teaching, and it becomes the chief foundation for his hopes and his petition for pardon. He argues thus, *To God belong loving-kindnesses ;* therefore, as he can never deny himself, he will always be merciful. This attribute is inseparable from his eternal essence ; and however we have rebelled against him, yet he will never either cast away nor disdain our prayers.

We may conclude from this passage that no prayers are lawful or rightly composed unless they consist of these two members. First, all who approach God ought to cast themselves down before him, and to acknowledge themselves deserving of a thousand deaths ; next, to enable them to emerge from the abyss of despair, and to raise themselves to the hope of pardon, they should call upon God without fear or doubt, and with firm and stable confidence. This reliance upon God can have no other support than the nature of God himself, and to this he has borne ample testimony. With respect to the close of the verse, it may be explained in two ways : *Because, or although, we are rebellious against him.* I have stated that I rather approve of taking the particle כִּי, *ki,* in the sense of opposition. *Although* we have rebelled against God, *still* he will be entreated, and never will be unmindful of his pity. If any one prefers taking it in a causal sense, it will suit tolerably well ; as if Daniel had said, the people have no other hope left but the mercy of God, as they have been convicted of sin over and over again. *Because* we have acted wickedly towards him, what is left for us but to throw ourselves with all our trust upon the clemency and goodness of God, since he has borne witness to his being propitious to sinners who truly and heartily implore his favour? It now follows:—

10. Neither have we obeyed the voice of the Lord our God, to walk in his laws, which he set before us by his servants the prophets.	10. Et non auscultavimus voci Jehovæ Dei nostri, ut ambularemus in legibus ejus, quas proposuit coram facie nostra per manum servorum suorum prophetarum.

Here, again, Daniel shews how the Israelites provoked God's anger against them by the wickedness of their conduct. He points out one special kind of sin and method of acting wickedly, namely, despising the teaching which proceeded from God as its author, and was expounded to them by his prophets. We must diligently notice this, as we have previously advised; for although no one is excusable before God by the pretext of ignorance, yet we perceive how our wickedness is aggravated when we knowingly and wilfully make a point of rejecting what God commands and teaches. Daniel, therefore, enlarges upon the people's crime by adding the circumstance, *they would not hear the prophets.* Everything which would have been a fault in the Chaldeans or Assyrians was the most grievous wickedness in the elect people. Their obstinacy was the more provoking, because while God had pointed out the way by his prophets, they had turned their backs upon him. *We have not heard.* Clearly enough this verse is added by way of explanation, as Daniel might express the reason for their wickedness. Therefore he calls the laws of God "doctrine," which consists of many parts; for it is certain that nothing was omitted by God which was useful to be known, and thus he had embraced the whole perfection of justice in his discourse. He is treating here not only the law of Moses, but the teaching of the prophets, as the words clearly point out; and the noun תורה, *torah*, "law," is to be taken for "doctrine." It is just as if Daniel had said, God was rejected when he wished to rule his people by his prophets. But the plural number seems to denote what I have stated, namely, that the perfection of doctrine was comprehended in the prophets; for God omitted nothing while he completed the revelation of whatever was needful for the guidance of the life. Yet this was rendered entirely useless by the perverseness of the people's nature, apparent in their rejection of all God's laws.

Daniel confirms this sentiment by adding, *Those laws were set before the people.* This shews how everything was supplied to the people, since God had familiarly delivered to them whatever was needful for the utmost degree of piety and justice. For this phrase, *to put anything before one's face,* means to deliver all useful knowledge openly, perspicuously, and lucidly, and with great familiarity and skilfulness. Thus nothing is left doubtful or complicated, nothing remains obscure, unconnected, or confused. As, therefore, God had unfolded the whole scope of righteousness by his law, the people's impiety was the more severe and detestable, because they would not receive benefit from such familiar instruction. The Prophet intends by these words to shew how such wilful sinners were worthy of double punishment. They are first convicted of contumacy because they had no pretext for their ignorance; they made an open and furious assault upon God, for although the way was pointed out to them, yet they turned aside in all directions, and threw themselves headlong. We must remember what I have previously touched upon, namely, the value of an external ministry, because we are aware how the ancient people, when rebellious against the prophets, were accustomed to pretend that they did not really despise God. As, therefore, hypocrites think their sins are concealed by a covering of this kind, Daniel clearly expresses that God is despised in his prophets, although he neither descends from heaven nor sends down his angels. And this is the meaning of the expression, *the prophets were the servants of God;* it declares how they taught nothing either rashly or in their own name or by their own impulse, but faithfully executed the Almighty's commands. It follows:—

11. Yea, all Israel have trans-   11. Et totus Israel transgressi

gressed thy law, even by departing, that they might not obey thy voice; therefore the curse is poured upon us, and the oath that *is* written in the law of Moses the servant of God, because we have sinned against him.

sunt legem tuam, et defecerunt,[1] ne auscultarent voci tuæ. Ideo,[2] effusa est super nos,[3] maledictio[4] et jusjurandum, quod scriptum est in lege Mosis servi Dei, quia peccavimus contra ipsum.

Daniel again confirms what I formerly said concerning the punishment being most justly inflicted upon the people. They had no cause for the slightest complaint of any excess of severity on the part of God. He now says, *All Israel had sinned.* He does not enumerate the separate ranks of the people as he did before, but he pronounces all to be transgressors in one single word, as they had broken God's law from the least to the greatest. He uses sometimes the second and sometimes the third person, as a mark of his vehemence and ardour, since Daniel now speaks for the whole world, and then prostrates himself before God, and prepares to approach his tribunal. It is just as if at one time he were to confess himself guilty before God and angels, and next to ascend a theatre and testify to his own infamy and that of the whole people before all mankind. *In revolting,* he says, *so as not to hear.* By these words Daniel expresses the determined obstinacy of the people, implying—this was not occasioned by either error or ignorance ; nay, even sloth was not the cause of Israel's wilful blindness and inattention to God's precepts, but was only the beginning of this act of rebellion. *In revolting,* therefore, *so as not to hear thy voice.* We now understand the Prophet's meaning. He was not content with the simple condemnation of the people, but he wished to mark distinctly the various forms of rebellion, to impress the Israelites with a fuller sense of the grievous manner in which they had provoked God's wrath. Not only had they departed from the right course through negligence or folly, but they had knowingly transgressed God's law. We must carefully notice this. Although hypocrites testify themselves to be prepared for obedience, if only they can be

---

[1] Verbally, receded or declined.—*Calvin.*
[2] The copula here has an inferential force.—*Calvin.*
[3] Or, distilled ; for נתך, *nethak*, has both meanings.—*Calvin.*
[4] Some translate, " execration."—*Calvin.*

quite sure that God is speaking to them, yet they are certainly held back by some hidden depravity from coming openly to the light.   And whenever God's word is put before us, whoever does not prove himself of a docile disposition, even if he should swear a hundred times over that he is perplexed and must decline embracing the teaching proposed to him, because he is doubtful whether God speaks to him or not, he lies ; and the truth of Daniel's assertion will always be made clear ; for all who do not hear God when he speaks to them are backsliders and inwardly perverse, and by the depravity of their nature place a veil before themselves which obscures their perceptions, and then their own minds prevent them from becoming obedient to God.

He next adds, *For this cause the curse of which Moses had written is poured down upon us.* By this circumstance he enlarges upon the people's crime, because they had long ago been warned of the impending judgments, and yet they closed their eyes and despised both threats and instruction.   This was the very height of wickedness ; for the Israelites were untractable, although God stretched out his hand towards them, pointed out the way of safety, and taught them faithfully whatever was useful for them ; but this only increased their perverseness, while they treated his threatenings as if utterly worthless.   Besides this, they added contempt of his teaching to ridiculing his threats, as they thought either that God was deluding them when he announced by Moses his coming vengeance unless they obeyed his law, or else they imagined it all invented by Moses, and that God could not possibly execute his threats.   Thus the people are convicted of desperate impiety, as they neither attended to the teaching of the Almighty nor believed in the authority of his threatenings.   If a father threatens his son, or a master his servant, the vengeance will be just, as the comic poet says, Do not say you have not been warned. (Terence Andria, Act i. Scene 2.)   As God had predicted for so many ages that the Israelites should not be unpunished if they transgressed the law, this proves how completely unmanageable they were.   (Lev. xxvi. ; Deut. xxviii.)   And when he says *the curse was poured out* or distilled, he confesses how the wrath of God inundated the whole people like a deluge, although it was completely under control. For God had predicted what he intended to do by the mouth of Moses, and whoever reads those curses which Moses denounces against transgressors of the law, will confess them to be by no means immoderate. When, therefore, execution really occurs, must we not acknowledge the shining forth of God's justice without the slightest possibility of blame? I have stated that the word שבועה, shebugneh, is explained by some as an "oath," and by others a "curse:" it properly means a curse, and is deduced from the word שבוע, shebugn, which seems to be taken in an extraordinary sense, because this word properly means *seven*, and the word derived from it means to "swear," through the practice of bringing forward a certain number of witnesses; and hence the noun means an oath. But because a curse is often interposed, and the swearer calls God to witness against himself if he fails to perform his verbal engagement, some interpreters elicit the sense of a curse being poured out. But there may be some change of construction here, and so I willingly interpret it. *The curse and the oath*, then, *are poured out;* that is, the curse which God has sanctioned by an oath, by a figure of speech well known to grammarians under the name of *hypallage*. The curse, therefore, was sworn by the mouth of God himself; and we know how threats cause more terror by being confirmed by an oath, just as God, on the other hand, adds strength to the promises of his favour.

He adds afterwards, *Because we have acted wickedly against him.* By this expression, Daniel shortly but clearly affirms that the people have no cause for complaint, as their calamities were the result of neither accident nor chance. They might behold the very source of their evils in the law of God. Had there been no predictions of this kind, the Israelites might have doubted and even disputed with themselves, as to the origin and cause of their being enslaved by their enemies, and of their being cast out with the utmost contempt and cruelty into distant lands. They might then have inquired into the causes of their evils, as if they were entirely unknown. But when the law of Moses was before their eyes, and God had therein sworn that he would perform the very threatenings just as they had happened, no further doubt could possibly remain. This, then, is the summary of Daniel's meaning; the very denunciation of these punishments was sufficient to condemn the Israelites, because their sins were brought home to them over and over again, when God fulfilled against them, what he had formerly predicted by his servant Moses. It follows,—

12. And he hath confirmed his words, which he spake against us, and against our judges that judged us, by bringing upon us a great evil: for under the whole heaven hath not been done as hath been done upon Jerusalem.	12. Et stabilivit sermonem suum, quem loquutus fuerat super nos, et super judices nostros, qui nos judicarunt,[1] ut adduceret super nos malum magnum quod non factum est sub toto cœlo, sicut factum est[2] in Jerusalem.

Daniel pursues the same sentiment, shewing how the Israelites had no cause whatever for expostulating with God on account of their being so heavily afflicted, and no reason for doubting either its origin or intention. For now all had come to pass exactly as it had been long ago predicted. *God*, therefore, *has stirred up his word against us;* as if he had said, there is no reason why we should strive with God, for we behold his truthfulness in the punishments which he has inflicted upon us, and his threats are no mere vain scarecrows, or fabulous inventions manufactured to frighten children. God now really proves how seriously he had spoken. What then is the use of our turning our backs upon him, or why should we seek vain excuses when God's truthfulness shines brightly in our destruction? Do we wish to deprive God of his truthfulness? surely whatever our earnestness we shall never succeed. Let, therefore, this suffice to condemn us,—God has predicted everything which occurs, and thus effectually and experimentally proves himself an avenger. *God*, therefore, *ratified his word;* that is, God's word would have remained without the slightest efficacy and vigour, unless this curse had been suspended over our head; but while we lie prostrate and almost buried under our calamities, God's word is borne aloft; that is, God

---

[1] That is, against our judges and rulers who governed us; for the Hebrews use " to judge," as signifying " to govern."—*Calvin.*

[2] That is, as it happened.—*Calvin.*

makes his truthfulness conspicuously visible, which otherwise would scarcely be perceptible at all.   Unless God
punished the wickedness of men, who would not treat the
threatenings of his law as childish ?   But when he demonstrates by certain proofs the very best reasons for terrifying
mankind, efficacy and vigour are immediately imparted to
his words.   Besides this, Daniel here intends to cast off all
subterfuges, and to cause the people candidly to acknowledge, and really to feel themselves justly afflicted.   He
says, *against us and against our judges, who judged us.*
Again, Daniel throws down all haughtiness of the flesh,
with the view of exalting God alone and of preventing any
mortal splendour from obscuring the authority of the Law.
For we know how the common people think they have a
shield for the defence of all their crimes, when they can
quote the example of kings and judges.   At this very day,
whenever we argue against the superstitions of the Papacy,
they say, "Well! if we do make a mistake, yet God has
set over us both kings and bishops who rule us after their
manner, why then should we be blamed when we have God's
command for following those who are endued with power
and dignity ?"   As, therefore, the vulgar generally catch at
a subterfuge like this, Daniel again affirms, that although
those who transgress God's law are endowed with great
worldly authority, yet they are not exempt from either
blame or punishment, nor can the ordinary multitude be
excused if they follow their example.   Therefore, *as he had
spoken by Moses against our judges who judged us,* he says ;
that is, although power had been conferred upon them for
ruling us, yet the whole ordination of it is from God : yet
after they had utterly abused their government, and violated
God's justice, and thus had endeavoured to draw down God,
if possible, from his elevation, Daniel asserts that their
loftiness will by no means shelter them from the consequences of transgression.

He afterwards adds, *To bring upon us a great evil, which
has never happened under the whole heavens, as it has now
occurred at Jerusalem.*   Here Daniel foresaw an objection
which had some slight force in it.   Although God had

deservedly punished the Israelites, yet when he displayed his anger against them more severely than against other nations, he might seem forgetful of his equity.   Daniel here removes all appearance of incongruity, even if God is more severe against his elect people then against profane nations, because the impiety of this people was far greater than that of all others on account of their ingratitude, contumacy, and impracticable obstinacy, as we have already said.   Since the Israelites surpassed all nations in malice, ingratitude, and all kinds of iniquity, Daniel here declares how thoroughly their disastrous afflictions were deserved.   Again, we are here reminded, whenever God severely chastises his Church, of that principle to which we must return, namely, our impiety is the more detestable to God the nearer he approaches us ; and the kinder he is to us, the more chargeable we are, unless in our turn we prove ourselves grateful and obedient.   This state of things ought not to seem troublesome to us, as vengeance begins at the house of God, and he puts forth examples of his wrath against his own people far more tremendous than against others ; this, I say, we ought not to take ill, as I have already explained the reason of it.   It does not surprise us to find the Gentiles groping in darkness, but when God shines upon us and we resist him with determined wilfulness, we are doubly impious.   This comparison, therefore, must be noticed, as evil was poured out upon Jerusalem ; meaning, no similar punishment was inflicted upon other nations, for *what happened to Jerusalem*, says Daniel, *never occurred under the whole heaven*.   It follows,—

13. As *it is* written in the law of Moses, all this evil is come upon us : yet made we not our prayer before the Lord our God, that we might turn from our iniquities, and understand thy truth.

13. Sicuti scriptum est in lege Mosis, totum malum hoc venit super nos, et non deprecati sumus faciem Jehovæ Dei nostri, ut reverteremur ab iniquitatibus nostris, et attenti essemus ad veritatem tuam.

He repeats what he had already said, without any superfluity, shewing how God's judgments are proved by their effects, as the law of Moses contains within it all the penalties which the Israelites endured.   As, therefore, so manifest an agreement existed between the law of God and the people's experience, they ought not to become restive, and to have sought every kind of subterfuge without profit. By this alone God sufficiently proved himself a just avenger of their crimes, because he had predicted many ages before what he had afterwards fully carried out. This is the object of the repetition, when Daniel says the people felt the justice of the penalties denounced against them in the law of Moses, for in the meantime he adds, *we have not deprecated the face of God.* Here he severely blames the people's hardness, because even when beaten with stripes they never grew wise. It is said—fools require calamities to teach them wisdom. This, therefore, was the height of madness in the people to remain thus stubborn under the rod of the Almighty, even when he inflicted the severest blows. As the people were so obstinate in their wickedness, who does not perceive how sincerely this conduct was to be deplored? *We have not deprecated,* therefore, *the face of our God.* This passage teaches us how the Lord exercises his judgments by not utterly destroying men, but holding his final sentence in suspense, as by these means he wishes to impel men to repentance. First of all, he gently and mercifully invites both bad and good by his word, and adds also promises, with the view of enticing them; and then, when he observes them either slow or refractory, he uses threatenings with the view of arousing them from their slumber; and should threats produce no effect, he goes forth in arms and chastises the sluggishness of mankind. Should these stripes produce no improvement, the desperate character of the people becomes apparent. In this way, God complains in Isaiah of their want of soundness; the whole body of the people is subject to ulcers from the head to the sole of the foot, (chap. i. 6;) and yet he would lose all his labour, through their being utterly unmanageable. Daniel now asserts the existence of the same failing in the people, while he states the Israelites to be so untouched by a sense of their calamites, as never to supplicate for pardon. I cannot complete the remainder to-day.

PRAYER.

Grant, Almighty God, that we may learn seriously to consider in how many ways we become guilty before thee, especially while we daily continue to provoke thy wrath against us.   May we be humbled by true and serious repentance, and fly eagerly to thee, as nothing is left to us but thy pity alone; when cast down and confounded, and reduced to nothing in ourselves, may we fly to this sacred anchor, as thou art easily entreated, and hast promised to act as a father of mercies to all sinners who seek thee.   Thus may we approach thee with true penitence, and relying on thy goodness, never doubt the granting of our requests; and being freed by thy mercy from the tyranny of Satan and of sin, may we be governed by thy Holy Spirit, and so directed in the way of righteousness as to glorify thy name throughout our lives, till we arrive at that happy and immortal life which we know to be laid up in heaven for us, by Christ our Lord.—Amen.

Lecture Forty-Seventh.

In yesterday's Lecture we dwelt on the Prophet's enlarging upon the people's crime, in resisting the impression made by God's chastisements; but now he more clearly demonstrates the kind of obstinacy displayed.   For *they did not turn away from their iniquities, and were not attentive to God's truth.*   He had said before, *we have not deprecated the anger of God.*   But here he expresses something more, namely, allowing the existence of some pretence to prayer, there was no real sincerity.   We know how impiously hypocrites abuse God's name, and pretend to the outward form of prayer, and even to the greatest fervour, but there is no reality in their prayers.   Thus the Prophet has good reason for uniting what ought never to be separated, and then convicts the Israelites of obstinacy, because they did not flee suppliantly to God's mercy with repentance and faith.   There was, doubtless, some form of piety left among the people; but Daniel here estimates prayers according to God's word, and thus puts these two things before us, namely, repentance and faith.   We must diligently notice this.   For nothing is more common than an earnest supplication for pardon when the signs of God's wrath are apparent; this was always customary among all nations and at all times, and yet there existed neither repentance nor faith. Hence their prayers became mere falsehood and vanity. This is the meaning of the Prophet's language when he says, *We have not asked at the face of Jehovah our God, by turning away from our iniquities,* (or that we may return,) *and by being instructed in thy truth.* Finally, we may gather from this passage what the rule of pious and acceptable prayer really is; first, we must be displeased with ourselves for our sins; next, we must regard the threats and promises of the Almighty. As to the first member of the sentence, experience teaches us how rashly many break forth into prayer, even when their evil conduct rises up professedly against God. On the one hand, they are so enraged as not to hesitate to engage in warfare with God, and yet they pray unto him, because terror seizes upon their minds and compels them to submit themselves to God. The Prophet, therefore, here shews the utter inutility of that outward shew and perverse mixture of noise and flattery, because God cannot approve of any prayers, unless they spring equally from repentance and faith. When he says, *the people were not attentive to God's truth,* in my opinion this is extended equally to threats and promises, and faith apprehends both God's pity and his judgments. For, surely, it cannot be otherwise, when terror rouses the pious to fly to God's mercy. As, therefore, God embraces each quality in his word, as he cites all who have sinned to his own tribunal, and then gives them a hope of reconciliation, if the sinner is really converted to him; so also Daniel, by saying, *the Israelites were not attentive to God's truth,* doubtless had respect to both objects, namely, their want of sufficient consideration of God's judgments, and next, their stupidity in despising his pity when plainly set before them. On the whole, this passage shews us the impossibility of our prayers being pleasing to God, unless they flow from true repentance and faith; that is, when we heartily feel our wickedness, we then flee to God's mercy and rely upon his promises. Hence we discover three things to be necessary to render God propitious to us; first, dissatisfaction with ourselves which occasions sorrow, through our being conscious of our sins, and of our having provoked God's anger. This is the first point. Secondly, faith must necessarily be added. Lastly, prayer must follow as a proof of our repentance and faith. When men remain without repentance and faith, we observe how God's name is profaned although we conceive and utter many prayers, at the very time when the two principal dispositions are entirely wanting. Now let us proceed,—

14. Therefore hath the Lord watched upon the evil, and brought it upon us: for the Lord our God *is* righteous in all his works which he doeth: for we obeyed not his voice.	14. Et vigilavit Jehovah super malum, et immisit illud[1] super nos: quia justus est Jehovah Deus noster in omnibus operibus suis, quæ fecit, *hoc est, facit,* et non auscultavimus voci ejus.

Daniel confirms what he had formerly said respecting the slaughter which afflicted the Israelites not being the offspring of chance, but of the certain and remarkable judgment of God. Hence he uses the word שָׁקַד, *seked,* which signifies to watch and to apply the mind attentively to anything. It is properly used of the guards of cities, who keep watch both by night and by day. This phrase does not appear to me to imply haste, but rather continual carefulness. God often uses this metaphor of his watching to chastise men who are far too eager to rush into sin. We are familiar with the great intemperance of mankind, and their disregard of all moderation whenever the lusts of the flesh seize upon them. God on the other hand says he will not be either slothful or neglectful in correcting this intemperance. The reason for this metaphor is expressed in the forty-fourth chapter of Jeremiah, where men are said to burst forth and to be carried away by their appetites, and then God is continually on the watch till the time of his vengeance arrives. I have mentioned how this word denotes rather continual diligence than hasty swiftness; and the Prophet seems here to imply that although God had endured the people's wickedness, yet he had at length really performed his previous threatenings, and was always on the watch, and rendering it impossible for the people to escape his judgments upon the wickedness

---

[1] Made it come.—*Calvin.*

in which they indulged.   Therefore *hath Jehovah closely at-*
tended to the calamity, and caused it to come upon us, says
he.   With the view of comprehending the Prophet's intention more fully, we must notice what God pronounces by
Jeremiah in the Lamentations, (chap. iii. 38,) where he
accuses the people of sloth, because they did not acknowledge
the justice of the punishments which they suffered; he blames
them in this way : Who is he who denies both good and evil
to proceed from the mouth of God ; as if he were pronouncing a curse against those who are ignorant of the origin of
calamities from God, when he chastises the people.   This
sentiment is not confined to a single passage.   For God often
inveighs against that stupidity which is born with mankind,
and leads them to attribute every event to fortune, and to
neglect the hand of the smiter.   (Isaiah ix. 13.)   This kind of
teaching is to be met with everywhere in the prophets, who
shew how nothing can be worse than to treat God's judgments as if they were accidents under the influence of chance.
This is the reason why Daniel insists so much upon this
point.   We know also what God denounces in his law : If
ye have walked against me rashly, I also will rashly walk
against you, (Lev. xxvi. 27, 28 ;) that is, if ye do not cease
to attribute to fortune whatever evil ye suffer, I will rush
against you with closed eyes, and will strive with you with
similar rashness ; as if he had said, If ye cannot distinguish
between fortune and my judgments, I will afflict you on all
sides, both on the right hand and on the left, without the
slightest discretion ; as if I were a drunken man, according
to the expression, With the perverse, thou wilt be perverse.
For this reason Daniel now confesses, *God watched over the*
calamity, so as to bring down all those afflictions by which
the people was oppressed.

In this passage we are taught to recognise God's providence in both prosperity and adversity, for the purpose of
stirring us up to be grateful for his benefits, while his punishments ought to produce humility.   For when any one explains these things by fortune and chance, he thereby proves
his ignorance of the existence of God, or at least of the
character of the Deity whom we worship.   For what is left

for God if we rob him of his providence?   It is sufficient here just to touch on these points which are often occurring, and of which we usually hear something every day.   It is sufficient for the exposition of this passage to observe how the Prophet incidentally opposes God's judgment and providence to all notions of chance.

He next adds, *Jehovah our God is just in all his works.* In this clause the Prophet confirms his former teaching, and the phrase, *God is just,* appears like rendering a reason for his dealings ; for the nature of God supplies a reason why it becomes impossible for anything to happen by the blind impulse of fortune.   God sits as a judge in heaven ; whence these two ideas are directly contrary to each other.   Thus if one of the following assertions is made, the other is at the same time denied ; if God is the judge of the world, fortune has no place in its government ; and, whatever is attributed to fortune is abstracted from God's justice.   Thus we have a confirmation of our former sentence by the use of contraries or opposites ; for we must necessarily ascribe to God's judgment both good and evil, both adversity and prosperity, if he governs the world by his providence, and exercises the office of judge.   And if we incline in the least degree to fortune, then God's judgment and providence will cease to be acknowledged.   Meanwhile, Daniel not only attributes power to God, but also celebrates his justice ; as if he had said, he does not arbitrarily govern the world without any rule of justice or equity, but *he is just.*   We must not suppose the existence of any superior law to bind the Almighty ; he is a law unto himself, and his will is the rule of all justice ; yet we must lay down this point ; God does not reign as a tyrant over the world, while in the perfection of his equity, he performs some things which seem to us absurd, only because our minds cannot ascend high enough to embrace a reason only partially apparent, and almost entirely hidden and incomprehensible in the judgments of God. Daniel, therefore, wished to express this by these words, *Jehovah our God,* says he, *is just in all the works which he performs.*   The meaning is, the people would not have been so severely chastised and afflicted with so many miserable calamities, unless they had provoked God's wrath; this might be easily collected from the threatenings which God had denounced many ages beforehand, and which he at that time proved in real truth to be in no degree frivolous. Next, a second part is added, as not only God's power but his justice shines forth in the slaughter of the people; and I have touched briefly on each of these points, as far as it was necessary for explanation. But we must notice the Prophet's allusion in these words to those numerous trials which had fallen upon the faithful for the purpose of proving their faith. They perceived themselves the most despised and miserable of mortals; the peculiar and sacred people of God was suffering under the greatest reproach and detestation, although God had adopted them by his law with the intention of their excelling all other people. While, therefore, they perceived themselves drowned in that deep whirlpool of calamities and disgrace, what would they suppose, except that God had deceived them, or that his covenant was utterly annihilated? Daniel, therefore, establishes the justice of God in all his works for the purpose of meeting this temptation, and of confirming the pious in their confidence, and of inducing them to fly to God in the extremity of their calamities.

He adds, as a reason, *Because they did not listen to his voice.* Here, again, he points out the crime of the people who had not transgressed through ignorance or error, but had purposely taken up arms against God. Whenever God's will is once made known to us, we have no further excuse for ignorance; for our open defiance of the Almighty arises from our being led away by the lusts of the flesh. And hence we gather how very detestable is the guilt of all who do not obey God's voice whenever he deigns to teach us, and who do not instantly acquiesce in his word. It now follows,—

15. And now, O Lord our God, that hast brought thy people forth out of the land of Egypt with a mighty hand, and hast gotten thee renown, as at this day; we have sinned, we have done wickedly.

15. Et nunc Domine Deus noster, qui eduxisti populum tuum e terra Ægypti cum manu forti, et fecisti, *comparasti,* tibi nomen secundum diem hanc,[1] peccavimus, impie egimus.

[1] That is, as the event itself pointed out.—*Calvin.*

16. O Lord, according to all thy righteousness, I beseech thee, let thine anger and thy fury be turned away from thy city Jerusalem, thy holy mountain: because for our sins, and for the iniquities of our fathers, Jerusalem and thy people *are become* a reproach to all *that are* about us.

17. Now therefore, O our God, hear the prayer of thy servant, and his supplications, and cause thy face to shine upon thy sanctuary *that is* desolate, for the Lord's sake.

16. Domine secundum omnes justitias tuas avertatur, quæso, ira tua, et excandescentia tua ab urbe tua Jerusalem, monte sanctitatis tuæ: quoniam ob peccata nostra, et ob iniquitates[1] patrum nostrorum, Jerusalem, et populus tuus est in probrum cunctis vicinis[2] circuitibus nostris.[3]

17. Et nunc audias, Deus noster, precationem servi tui, et orationem ejus atque illumina faciem tuam[4] super sanctuarium tuum, quod vastatum est, *vel*, *desolatum*, propter Dominum.

After Daniel has sufficiently confessed the justice of those judgments which God had inflicted upon the people, he again returns to beg for pardon. First, he would conciliate favour for himself; next, he would stir up the minds of the pious to confidence, and so he sets before them that proof of grace which ought to avail to support the minds of the pious even to the end of the world. For when God led his people out of Egypt, he did not set before them any momentary benefit merely, but he bore witness to the adoption of the race of Abraham on the condition of his being their perpetual Saviour. Therefore, whenever God wishes to gather together those who have been dispersed, and to raise their minds from a state of despair to cheerful hope, he reminds them of his being their Redeemer. I am that God, says he, who led you out of Egypt. (Lev. xi. 45, and often elsewhere.) God not only commends his own power in such passages, but denotes the object of their redemption ; for he then received his people under his care on the very ground of never ceasing to act towards them with the love and anxiety of a father. And when in their turn such anxiety seized upon the faithful as to lead them to apprehend their own utter desertion by God, they are in the habit of seizing upon this shield—God did not lead our fathers out of Egypt in vain. Daniel now follows up this reasoning: *Thou, O Lord our God,* says he, *who hast led forth thy*

[1] Or, in our sins and iniquities.—*Calvin.*
[2] Verbally, " all."—*Calvin.*
[3] That is, those who are in our circuit.—*Calvin.*
[4] That is, make thy face to shine.—*Calvin.*

people; as if he had said, he called upon God, because by
one single proof he had testified to all ages the sacred character of the race of Abraham. We observe, then, how he
stirs up himself and all the rest of the pious to prayer, because by laying this foundation, he could both complain
familiarly, and fearlessly request of God to pity his people,
and to put an end to their calamities. We now understand
the Prophet's meaning, when he says, *the people were led
forth from Egypt.*

He afterwards adds another cause, *God then acquired renown for himself, as the event evidently displayed.* He here
joins God's power with his pity, implying, when the people
were led forth, it was not only a specimen of paternal favour
towards the family of Abraham, but also an exhibition of
divine power. Whence it follows, his people could not be
cast off without also destroying the remembrance of that
mighty power by which God had acquired for himself renown.
And the same sentiment often occurs in the prophets when
they use the argument :—If this people should perish, what
would prevent the extinction of thy glory, and thus whatever
thou hadst conferred upon this people would be buried in
oblivion ? So, therefore, Daniel now says, *By bringing thy
people from the land of Egypt, thou hast made thyself a name;*
that is, thou hast procured for thyself glory, which ought to
flourish through all ages unto the end of the world. What,
then, will occur, if the whole of thy people be now destroyed?
He next adds, *We have done impiously, and have acted
wickedly.* In these words Daniel declares how nothing was
left except for God to consider himself rather than his
people, as by looking to them he would find nothing but
material for vengeance. The people must necessarily perish,
should God deal with them as they deserved. But Daniel
here turns away God's face by some means from the people's
sins, with the view of fixing his attention on himself alone
and his own pity, and on his consistent fidelity to that perpetual covenant which he had made with their fathers.

Lastly, he would not permit that redemption to fail which
was an illustrious and eternal proof of his virtue, favour,
and goodness. Hence he subjoins, *O Lord, may thine anger*

be averted according to all thy righteousness, and thine indig-
nation from thy city Jerusalem, the mountain of thy holiness.
We observe how Daniel here excludes whatever merit there
might be in the people.   In reality they did not possess any,
but I speak according to that foolish imagination which men
can scarcely put off.   They always take credit to themselves,
although they are convicted of their sins a hundred times
over, and still desire to conciliate God's favour by pleading
some merit before God.   But here Daniel excludes all such
considerations when he pleads before God his own justice,
and uses the strong expression, *according to all thy righteous-*
ness.   Those who take this word "righteousness" to mean
"judgment," are in error and inexperienced in interpreting
the Scriptures ; for they suppose God's justice to be opposed
to his pity.   But we are familiar with God's righteousness
as made manifest, especially in the benefits he confers on us.
It is just as if Daniel had said, that the single hope of the
people consisted in God's having regard to himself alone, and
by no means to their conduct.   Hence he takes the righteousness of God for his liberality, gratuitous favour, consistent fidelity, and protection, which he promised his servants:
O God, therefore, he says, *according to all thy promised*
mercies ; that is, thou dost not fail those who trust in thee,
thou dost promise nothing rashly, and thou art not accustomed to desert those who flee to thee ; oh ! by thy very
justice, succour us in our distress.   We must also notice the
universal particle " all," because when Daniel unites so many
sins which might drown the people in an abyss a thousand
times over, he opposes to this *all* God's promised mercies.
As if he had said, although the number of our iniquities is
so great that we must perish a hundred times over, yet thy
promised mercies are far more numerous, meaning, thy justice surpasses whatever thou mayest find in us of the deepest
dye of guilt.

He says, again, *Let thine anger be turned away, and thy*
burning wrath from thy city Jerusalem, and from thy holy
mountain.   In joining together anger and burning wrath,
the Prophet does not imply any excess on the part of God,
as if he revenged the sins of the people too severely, but he

again represents the aggravation of their wickedness, causing him to become so angry with them as to lay aside his usual character, and to treat their adoption as vain and fruitless. Daniel does not complain in this case of the severity of the punishment, but rather condemns himself and the rest of the people for causing a necessity for such severe measures. Once more, he sets before God the holy mountain which he had chosen, and in this way averts his countenance from judgment, lest he should reckon with them for so many sins, by which God was deservedly incensed. Here, therefore, God's election is interposed, because he had consecrated Mount Zion to himself, and desired to be worshipped there, where also his name should be celebrated and sacrifices offered to him. In this respect, therefore, Daniel obtains favour for himself before God, and, as I have said, he excludes all other considerations.

He next adds, *Because on account of our sins, and the iniquities of our fathers, Jerusalem and thy people are a reproach to all our neighbours.* By another argument, the Prophet desires to bend God to pity; for Jerusalem as well as the people were a disgrace to the nations; yet this caused equal disgrace to fall upon God himself. As, therefore, the Gentiles made a laughing-stock of the Jews, they did not spare the sacred name of God; nay, the Jews were so despised, that the Gentiles scarcely deigned to speak of them, and the God of Israel was contemptuously traduced, as if he had been conquered, because he had suffered his temple to be destroyed, and the whole city Jerusalem to be consumed with burning and cruel slaughter. The Prophet, therefore, now takes up this argument, and in speaking of the sacred city, doubtless refers to the sacredness of God's name. His language implies,—Thou hast chosen Jerusalem as a kind of royal residence; it was thy wish to be worshipped there, and now this city has become an object of the greatest reproach to our neighbours. Thus he declares how God's name was exposed to the reproaches of the Gentiles. He afterwards asserts the same of God's people, not by way of complaint when the Jews suffered these reproaches, for they deserved them by their sins, but the language is emphatic, and yet they were God's people.   God's name was intimately bound up with that of his people, and whatever infamy the profane cast upon them, reflected chiefly on God himself. Here Daniel places before the Almighty his own name ; as if he had said, O Lord ! be thou the vindicator of thine own glory, thou hast once adopted us on this condition, and may the memory of thy name be ever inscribed upon us ; permit us not to be so reproachfully slandered, let not the Gentiles insult thee on our account.   And yet he says this was done *on account of the iniquities of the people and of their fathers ;* by which expression he removes every possibility of doubt. Oh ! how can it happen, that God will so lay his people prostrate ?   Why has he not spared at least his own name ! Daniel, therefore, here testifies to his being just, because the iniquity of the people and of their fathers had risen so high, that God was compelled to exercise such vengeance against them.

His next prayer is, *Do thou who art our God hear the prayer of thy servant, and his supplications, and cause thy face to shine forth.*   In these words Daniel wrestles with distrust, not for his own sake privately, but for that of the whole Church to whom he set forth the true method of prayer.   And experience teaches all the pious how necessary this remedy is in those doubts which break into all our prayers, and make our earnestness and ardour in prayer grow dull and cold within us, or at least we pray without any composed or tranquil confidence, and this trembling vitiates whatever we had formerly conceived.   As, therefore, this daily happens to all the pious when they leave off the duty of prayer for even a short period, and some doubt draws them off and shuts the door of familiar access to God, this is the reason why Daniel so often repeats the sentence, *Do thou, O Lord, hear the prayer of thy servant.*   David also inculcates such sentiments in his prayers, and has the greatest necessity for acting so.   And those who are truly exercised in praying feel how God's servants have good cause for such language whenever they pray to him.   But I will complete the rest to-morrow.

PRAYER.

Grant, Almighty God, as thou hast deigned to gather us once among thy people, and hast wished us also to bear thy name, and that of thine only-begotten Son; although we so often provoke thine anger by our sins, and never cease to heap evil upon evil: Grant that we may never be exposed as a laughing-stock and spectacle, to the disgrace of thy sacred name. As, therefore, thou now seest the impious seizing all occasions of grossly slandering thyself, and thy sacred gospel, and the name of thine only-begotten Son, do not permit them, I pray thee, petulantly to insult thee. May thy Spirit so govern us, that we may desire to glorify thy name. May it be glorified in spite of Satan and all the impious, until we are gathered into that celestial kingdom which thou hast promised us in the same Christ our Lord.— Amen.

Lecture Forty-Eighth.

WE yesterday commenced our comment on the passage in which Daniel asks the Almighty *to make his face to shine upon his own sanctuary.* We are well aware how often this expression occurs in the Scriptures, where God is said to manifest his opposition by hiding his face, when he does not assist his own people, but hides himself as if he were forgetful of them. As Scripture everywhere compares our calamities and adversities to darkness, therefore God in whose favour our happiness is placed is said to hide his face when he does not succour us; and again, he is said to render his face bright and conspicuous, when he gives us some sign of his parental favour. God seemed for a long time to have deserted his sanctuary, and therefore the Prophet prays him *to make his face to shine.* We must remark his expression; *upon thy sanctuary which is laid waste.* We gather from it, that although the Prophet saw all things lost in a carnal sense, yet he neither despaired nor desisted from his prayers. And this rule must be noticed,—God's grace is not to be estimated by the present aspect of things, because he often shews himself angry with us. Our carnal reason must be overcome, if we wish to pray to God in adversity, as the

Prophet here teaches us by his own example. For the sanctuary was cut off; its very devastation might have formed an excuse to Daniel and all the pious for offering their prayers no longer. What success could be hoped for in such a deplorable state of affairs? Daniel by this circumstance shews how he struggled on without allowing any obstacle to interrupt the course of his prayer. He adds, *for the Lord's sake;* all the Hebrew doctors agree that the word אֲדֹנִי, *Adoni,* when written with the great point *kametz,* is taken for God alone; but in certain passages of Scripture it is as clearly used for the Mediator also. And very probably it has this sense here; although the Hebrews use this form *for God's sake,* or for thy sake, when they make a direct appeal to the Deity, yet I confess they often use the third person. But what necessity is there for flying to this harsher form of speech, when the other sense appears more appropriate to the passage? He will afterwards say, on account of thee, my God; but he says here, *for the Lord's sake.* If, however, I had to contend with a person of a captious disposition, I confess I could not convince him from this passage; but if we weigh the Prophet's words without contention, we shall rather incline to this view of the subject. Here, therefore, he sets before God the Mediator by whose favour he hopes to obtain his request. Still, if any one prefers to apply this to God, let him retain his opinion. Let us now proceed,—

18. O my God, incline thine ear, and hear; open thine eyes, and behold our desolations, and the city which is called by thy name: for we do not present our supplications before thee for our righteousness, but for thy great mercies.

18. Inclina Deus mi, aurem tuam, et audi: aperi oculos tuos, et respice desolationes nostras,[1] et civitatem super quam invocatum est nomen tuum, super eam,[2] quia non propter justitias nostras nos prosternimus preces nostras coram facie tua, sed propter misericordias tuas[3] multas, *vel, magnas.*

This short clause breathes a wonderful fervour and vehemence of prayer; for Daniel pours forth his words as if he were carried out of himself. God's children are often in an ecstasy in prayer; they moan and plead with God, use various modes of speech and much tautology, and cannot satisfy

[1] Or, devastations.—*Calvin.*
[2] The words *super eam,* "upon it," are redundant.—*Calvin.*
[3] Or, on account of thy compassions.—*Calvin.*

themselves. In forms of speech, indeed, hypocrites are sometimes superior; they not only rival God's sincere worshippers, but are altogether carried along by outward pomps, and by a vast heap of words in their prayers, they arrive at much elegance and splendour, and even become great rhetoricians. But Daniel here only displays some portion of his feelings; there is no doubt of his wishing to bear witness to the whole Church how vehemently and fervently he prayed with the view of inflaming others with similar ardour. In this verse, he says, *O my God, incline thine ear and hear.* It would have been sufficient simply to have said, hearken; but as God seemed to remain deaf notwithstanding so many prayers and entreaties, the Prophet begs him to incline his ear. There is a silent antithesis here, because the faithful had seemed to be uttering words to the deaf, while their groans had been continually carried upwards to heaven during seventy years without the slightest effect. He adds next, *open thine eyes and see.* For God's neglecting to answer must have cast down the hopes of the pious, because the Israelites were treated so undeservedly. They were oppressed by every possible form of reproach, and suffered the most grievous molestation in their fortunes as well as in everything else. Yet God passed by all these calamities of his people, as if his eyes were shut; and for this reason Daniel now prays him to open his eyes. It is profitable to notice these circumstances with diligence, for the purpose of learning how to pray to God; first, when at peace and able to utter our petitions without the slightest disquietude, and next, when sorrow and anxiety seize upon all our senses, and darkness everywhere surrounds us; even then our prayers should be steadily continued in the midst of these great obstacles. And we gather at the same time, while God presses us to the very extremity of our lives, how we ought to be still more importunate, because the very object of this our severe affliction, is to awaken us amidst our slothfulness. Thus it is said in the Psalms, (xxxii. 6,) The saint will approach thee in an accepted time. Our opportunity arises when the very last necessities overwhelm us, because God then stirs us up, and, as I have said, corrects our slowness. Let us learn, therefore, to accustom ourselves to vehemence in prayer whenever God urges and incites us by stimulus of this kind.

He next says, *Look upon our desolations*—of this we have already said enough—*and on the city on which thy name is called.* Again Daniel sets before himself the sure foundation of his confidence,—Jerusalem had been chosen as God's sanctuary. We know God's adoption to have been without repentance, as Paul says. (Rom. xi. 29.) Daniel, therefore, here takes the very strongest method of appealing to God's honour, by urging his wish to be worshipped on Mount Zion, and by his destining Jerusalem for himself as a royal seat. The phrase, to be called by God's name, means, reckoning either the place or the nation as belonging to God. For God's name is said to be called upon us, when we profess to be his people, and he distinguishes us by his mark, as if he would openly shew to the eyes of mankind his recognition of our profession. Thus God's name was called upon Jerusalem, because his election had been celebrated already for many ages, and he had also gathered together one peculiar people, and pointed out a place where he wished sacrifices to be offered.

He adds afterwards, *Because we do not pour forth our prayers before thy face upon or through our own righteousness,* (כִּי, *ki,* " but," is in my opinion put adversatively here,) *but on account of thy many or great mercies.* Daniel more clearly confirms what was said yesterday, shewing how his hope was founded in God's mercy alone. But I have stated how he expresses his meaning more clearly by opposing two members of a sentence naturally contrary to each other. *Not in our righteousness,* says he, *but in thy compassions.* Although this comparison is not always put so distinctly, yet this rule must be held—whenever the saints rely upon the grace of God, they renounce at the same time all their merits, and find nothing in themselves to render God propitious. But this passage must be diligently noticed, where Daniel carefully excludes whatever opposes God's gratuitous goodness ; and he next shews how, by bringing forward anything of their own, as if men could deserve God's grace, they diminish in an equal degree from his mercy. Daniel's words also contain another truth, manifesting the impossibility of reconciling two opposite things, viz., the faithful taking refuge in God's mercy, and yet bringing anything of their own and resting upon their merits. As, therefore, a complete repugnance exists between the gratuitous goodness of God and all the merits of man, how stupid are those who strive to combine them, according to the usual practice of the Papacy! And even now, those who do not yield willingly to God and his word, wish to throw a covering over their error, by ascribing half the praise to God and his mercy, and retaining the remainder as peculiar to man. But all doubt is removed when Daniel places these two principles in opposition to each other, according to my former remark —the righteousness of man and the mercy of God. Our merits, in truth, will no more unite with the grace of God than fire and water, mingled in the vain attempt to seek some agreement between things so opposite. He next calls these mercies " great," as we previously remarked the use of a great variety of words to express the various ways in which the people were amenable to his judgment. Here, therefore, he implores God's mercies as both many and great, as the people's wickedness had arrived at its very utmost pitch.

As to the following expression, *The people pour down their prayers before God,* Scripture seems in some degree at variance with itself, through the frequent use of a different metaphor, representing prayers as raised towards heaven. This phrase often occurs,—O God, we elevate or raise our prayers to thee. Here also, as in other places, the Spirit dictates a different form of expression, representing the faithful as casting down upon the ground their vows and prayers. Each of these expressions is equally suitable, because, as we said yesterday, both repentance and faith ought to be united in our prayers. But repentance throws men downwards, and faith raises them upwards again. At the first glance these two ideas do not seem easily reconciled ; but by weighing these two members of a true and logical form of speech, we shall not find it possible to raise our prayers and vows to heaven, without depressing them, so to speak, to the very

lowest depths.   For on the one hand, when the sinner comes
into the presence of God, he must necessarily fall completely
down, nay, vanish as if lifeless before him.   This is the
genuine effect of repentance.   And in this way the saints
cast down all their prayers, whenever they suppliantly acknowledge themselves unworthy of the notice of the Almighty.   Christ sets before us a picture of this kind in the
character of the publican, who beats on his breast and begs
for pardon with a dejected countenance.   (Luke xviii. 13.)
Thus also the sons of God throw down their prayers in that
spirit of humility which springs from penitence.   Then they
raise their prayers by faith, for when God invites them to
himself, and gives them the witness to his propitious disposition, they raise themselves up and overtop the clouds, yea,
even heaven itself.   Whence this doctrine also shines forth,
Thou art a God who hearest prayer, as we read in the Psalms.
(Ps. lxv. 2.)   In consequence of the faithful determining
God to be propitious, they boldly approach his presence, and
pray with minds erect, through an assurance that God is
well pleased with the sacrifice which they offer.   It follows :

19. O Lord, hear; O Lord, forgive ; O Lord, hearken and do; defer not, for thine own sake, O my God : for thy city and thy people are called by thy name.

19. Domine audi, Domine propitius esto, Domine attende, *vel, animad-verte,* et fac ne moreris propter te, Deus mi, quia nomen tuum invocatum est super urbem tuam, et super populum tuum.

Here vehemence is better expressed, as I have previously
observed.   For Daniel does not display his eloquence, as
hypocrites usually do, but simply teaches by his example the
true law and method of prayer.   Without doubt, he was
impelled by singular zeal for the purpose of drawing others
with him.   God, therefore, worked in the Prophet by his
Spirit, to render him a guide to all the rest, and his prayer
as a kind of common form to the whole Church.   With this
intention, Daniel now relates his own conceptions.   He had
prayed without any witness, but he now calls together the
whole Church, and wishes it to become a witness of his zeal
and fervour, and invites all men to follow this prescription,
proceeding as it does not from himself but from God.   *O
Lord, hear,* says he ; and next, *O Lord, be propitious.*   By

this second clause he implies the continual and intentional deafness of the Almighty, because he was deservedly angry with the people.　And we ought to observe this, because we foolishly wonder at God's not answering our prayers as soon as the wish has proceeded from our lips.　Its reason, too, must be noticed.　God's slowness springs from our coldness and dulness, while our iniquities interpose an obstacle between ourselves and his ear.　*Be thou*, therefore, *propitious, O Lord, that thou mayest hear*.　So the sentence ought to be resolved.　He afterwards adds, *O Lord, attend*.　By this word Daniel means to convey, that while the people had in many ways and for a length of time provoked God's anger, they were unworthily oppressed by impious and cruel enemies, and that this severe calamity ought to incline God to pity them.　*O Lord*, therefore, he says, *attend and do not delay*.　Already God had cast away his people for seventy years, and had suffered them to be so oppressed by their enemies, as to cause the faithful the utmost mental despondency.　Thus we perceive how in this passage the holy Prophet wrestled boldly with the severest temptation.　He requests God not *to delay* or put off.　Seventy years had already passed away since God had formally cast off his people, and had refused them every sign of his good will towards them.

The practical inference from this passage is the impossibility of our praying acceptably, unless we rise superior to whatever befalls us ; and if we estimate God's favour according to our own condition, we shall lose the very desire for prayer, nay, we shall wear away a hundred times over in the midst of our calamities, and be totally unable to raise our minds up to God.　Lastly, whenever God seems to have delayed for a great length of time, he must be constantly entreated *not to delay*.　He next adds, *For thine own sake, O my God*.　Again, Daniel reduces to nothing those sources of confidence by which hypocrites imagine themselves able to obtain God's favour.　Even if one clause of the sentence is not actually the opposite of the other, as it was before, yet when he says, *for thy sake*, we may understand the inference to be,—therefore not for our own sakes.　He confirms this view by the remainder of the context, *For thy sake, O my God, because thy name has been invoked upon thy city,* says he, *and upon thy people.*   We observe, then, how Daniel left no means untried for obtaining his request, although he relied on his gratuitous adoption, and never doubted God's propitious feelings towards his own people.   He finds indeed no cause for them either in mortals or in their merits, but he wishes mankind perpetually to behold his benefits and to continue steadfast to the end.   It follows :—

20. And whiles I was speaking, and praying, and confessing my sin, and the sin of my people Israel, and presenting my supplication before the Lord my God for the holy mountain of my God;

21. Yea, whiles I *was* speaking in prayer, even the man Gabriel, whom I had seen in the vision at the beginning, being caused to fly swiftly, touched me about the time of the evening oblation.

20. Et adhuc ego loquens,[1] et precarer, et confiterer peccatum meum, et peccatum populi mei Israel, et prosternerem,[2] precationem meam coram Jehova Deo meo, super montem[3] sanctuarii Dei mei.

21. Cum, inquam, loquerer in precatione mea, tunc vir Gabriel quem videram in visione principio volantem volatu, tetigit me circa tempus oblationis vespertinæ.

As to the translation, some take it as I do ; others say "flying swiftly," implying fatigue and alacrity.   Some derive the word for "flying" from עוּף, *gnof,* which signifies to fly, and they join it with its own participle, which is common in Hebrew ; others again think it derived from יעף, *yegnef,* signifying to fatigue, and then explain it metaphorically as flying hastily.[4]

Here Daniel begins to shew us that his prayers were by no means useless, nor yet without their fruit, as Gabriel was sent to elevate his mind with confidence, and to lighten his grief by consolation.   He next sets him forth as a minister of the grace of God to the whole Church, to inspire the faithful with the hope of a speedy return to their country, and to encourage them to bear their afflictions until God should open a way for their return.   Next, as to ourselves, we need not wonder at God's refusing at times an answer to our prayers, because those who seem to pray far better than

[1] That is, while I was yet speaking.—*Calvin.*
[2] Or, made to fall; the same word as before.—*Calvin.*
[3] That is, on account of, or for the sake of, the mountain.—*Calvin.*
[4] See Wintle's clear and comprehensive note *in loc.*—*Ed.*

the rest scarcely possess a hundredth part of the zeal and
fervour required.   On comparing our method of prayer with
this vehemence of the Prophet, surely we are in truth very
far behind him ; and it is by no means surprising, if, while
the difference is so great, the success should be so dissimilar.
And yet we may be assured that our prayers will never be
in vain, if we follow the holy Prophet at even a long interval.   If the limited amount of our faith hinders our prayers
from emulating the Prophet's zeal, yet God will nevertheless
listen to them, so long as they are founded in faith and
penitence.   Daniel says, therefore, *While I was as yet speaking, and praying, and confessing my sin and the sin of my
people Israel.*   First of all, we must notice how the Holy
Spirit here purposely dictated to the Prophet, how God's
grace would be prepared for and extended to all the wretched
who fly to it and implore it.   The Prophet, therefore, shews
why we are so destitute of help, for if pain occasions so much
groaning, yet we never look up to God, from whom consolation is always to be sought in all evils.   He thus exhorts us
to the habit of prayer by saying his requests were heard.
He does not bring forward any singular example, but, as I
have already said, he pronounces generally that the prayers
of those who seek God as a deliverer will never be either
vain or unfruitful.   I have shewn how our supplications do
not always meet with either the same or equal attention, since
our torpor requires God to differ in the help which he supplies.   But in this way the Prophet teaches us how those
who possess true faith and repentance, however slight, will
never offer up their prayers to God in vain.

He next adds what is necessary to conciliate God's favour,
namely, that men should anticipate God's judgment by condemning themselves.   So he asserts, *He confessed his sin and
that of his people.*   He does not speak here of one kind of
sin, but under the word חטא, *cheta,* he comprehends all
kinds of wickedness ; as if he had said, when I was confessing myself as steeped in sin and drowned in iniquity, I confessed the same on behalf of my people.   We must notice
also the phrase, *the sin of my people Israel.*   He might have
omitted this noun, but he wished to testify before God to the

Church being guilty and without the slightest hope of abso-
lution, unless God, whom they had so deservedly offended,
was graciously pleased to reconcile them to himself. But
the first clause is more worthy of notice, where Daniel relates the confession of his own sins before God. We know
what Ezekiel says, or rather the Spirit speaking through his
mouth. (Chap. xiv. 14.) For God names the three most
perfect characters which had then existed in the world, and
includes Daniel among them, although he was then living.
Although Daniel was an example of angelic justice, and is
celebrated by so remarkable an honour, yet, if even he were
before me, and were to entreat me for this state, I would not
listen to him, but I would free him only on account of his
own righteousness. As, therefore, God so extols his own
Prophet, and raises him on high as if he were beyond all the
pollution and vices of the world, where shall we find a man
upon earth who can boast himself free from every stain and
failing ? Let the most perfect characters be brought before
us—what a difference between them and Daniel ! But even
he confesses himself a sinner before God, and utterly re-
nounces his own righteousness, and openly bears witness to
his only hope of salvation being placed in the mere mercy
of God. Hence Augustine with much wisdom often cites
this passage against the followers of Pelagius and Cœlestius.
We are well aware with what specious pretences these
heretics obscured God's grace, when they argued that God's
sons ought not always remain in prison, but to reach the
goal. The doctrine indeed is passable enough, that the sons
of God ought to be free from all fault, but where is such integrity really found? Augustine, therefore, with the greatest
propriety, always replied to these triflers by shewing that no
one ever existed so just in this world as not to need God's
mercy. For had there been such a character, surely the
Lord, who alone is a fitting judge, could have found him.
But he asserts his servant Daniel to be among the most perfect, if three only are taken from the beginning of the world.
But as Daniel casts himself into the flock of sinners, not
through any feigned pretence or humility, but when uttering
the fulness of his mind before God, who shall now claim for

himself greater sanctity than this ? *When, therefore, I confess my sins before the face of my God.* Here surely there
is no fiction, whence it follows that those who pretend to
this imaginary perfection are demons in human shape, as
Castalio and other cynics, or rather dogs like him.

We must therefore cling to this principle : no man, even
if semi-angelic, can approach God, unless he conciliates his
favour by sincere and ingenuous confession of his sins, as in
reality a criminal before God. This, then, is our righteousness, to confess ourselves guilty in order that God may gratuitously absolve us. These observations, too, respecting
the Israelites concern us also, as we observe from the direction which Christ has given us to say, Forgive us our tres-
passes. (Matt. vi. 12 ; Luke xi. 4.) For whom did Christ
wish to use this petition ? Surely all his disciples. If any
one thinks that he has no need of this form of prayer, and
this confession of sin, let him depart from the school of
Christ, and enter into a herd of swine.

He now adds, *Upon the mountain of the sanctuary of my
God.* Here the Prophet suggests another reason for his
being heard, namely, his anxiety for the common welfare and
safety of the Church. For whenever any one studies his
own private interests, and is careless of his neighbour's advantage, he is unworthy to obtain anything before God. If,
therefore, we desire our prayers to be pleasing to God, and
to produce useful fruit, let us learn to unite the whole body
of the Church with us, and not only to regard what is expedient for ourselves, but what will tend to the common welfare of all the elect people. *While, therefore,* says he, *I was
yet speaking, and in the midst of my prayer.* It appears
that Daniel prayed not only with his affections, but broke
forth into some outward utterance. It is quite true that this
word is often restricted to mental utterance ; for even when
a person does not use his tongue, he may be said to speak
when he only thinks mentally within himself. But since
Daniel said, *When I was yet speaking in my prayer,* he
seems to have broken forth into some verbal utterance ; for
although the saints do not intend to pronounce anything
orally, yet zeal seizes upon them, and words at times escape

them.   There is another reason also for this : we are naturally slow, and then the tongue aids the thoughts.   For these reasons Daniel was enabled not only to conceive his prayers silently and mentally, but to utter them verbally and orally.

He next adds, *Gabriel came ;* but I cannot complete my comments on this occurrence to-day.

PRAYER.

Grant, Almighty God, that we may learn more and more fully to probe ourselves, and to discover the faults of which we are guilty: nay, may the serious weight of our wickedness truly humble us when we come into thy sight, and call upon thee even from the lowest depths.   May we never cease to hope for thy grace ; may we be elevated by that hope to the highest heavens, and be firmly assured that thou wilt always prove thyself a propitious Father to us.   And as thou hast granted us a Mediator who may procure favour for us from thee, may we never hesitate to approach thee familiarly, through reliance on him.   Whenever our miseries induce us to despair, may we never succumb to it ; but with unconquered fortitude of mind, may we persevere in invoking thy name and imploring thy pity, until we perceive the fruit of our prayers, and after being freed from all warfare, may we at length arrive at that blessed rest which is laid up for us in heaven, by the same, Christ our Lord.—Amen.

Lecture Forty=Ninth.

In the last Lecture we explained the appearance of the angel to Daniel, who satisfied the eagerness of his desires. For he prayed with great earnestness when he perceived the time to have elapsed which God had fixed beforehand by the mouth of Jeremiah, while the people still remained in captivity.   (Chap. xxv. 11.)   We have shewn how the angel was sent by God to the holy Prophet, to alleviate his sorrow and to remove the pressure of his anxiety.   He called the angel *a man*, because he took the form of a man, as we have already stated.   One thing only remains—his saying, *the vision was offered to him about the time of the evening sacrifice.*   Already seventy years had passed away, during which

Daniel had never observed any sacrifice offered; and yet he still mentions sacrifices as if he were in the habit of attending daily in the Temple, which was not really in existence. Whence it appears how God's servants, though deprived of the outward means of grace for the present moment, are yet able to make them practically useful by meditating upon God, and the sacrifices, and other rites, and ceremonies of his institution. If any one in these days is cast into prison, and even prohibited from enjoying the Lord's Supper to the end of his life, yet he ought not on that account to cast away the remembrance of that sacred symbol; but should consider within himself every day, why that Supper was granted us by Christ, and what advantages he desires us to derive from it. Such, then, we perceive were the feelings of the holy Prophet, because he speaks of these daily sacrifices as if then in actual use. Yet we know them to have been abolished, and he could not have been present at them for many years, although during that period the Temple was standing. Now let us go forward,—

| 22. And he informed *me*, and talked with me, and said, O Daniel, I am now come forth to give thee skill and understanding. | 22. Et docuit me, et loquutus est mecum, et dixit, Daniel, nunc exivi ut te intelligere facerem intelligentiam.[1] |

Here the angel prepares the Prophet's mind by saying, *he came from heaven to teach him. I went forth*, says he, *to cause thee to understand.* For Daniel ought to understand from this angel's duty, what he ought himself to do. As God had deigned to honour him so highly by setting before him one of his angels as his master and teacher, the Prophet ought not to neglect so singular a favour, lest he should seem ungrateful to God. We now understand why the angel testifies to *his coming to teach the Prophet.* And we also ought to reflect upon this whenever we enter God's Temple, or read any passage of holy Scripture, and acknowledge teachers to be sent to us from God to assist us in our ignorance, and to interpret the Scriptures for us. We ought also to admit Scripture to be given to us to enable us to find there whatever would otherwise be hidden from us. For

[1] That is, that I may teach thee what is necessary to be known.—*Calvin.* See DISSERTATIONS at the end of this volume.—*Ed.*

God opens, as it were, his own heart to us, when he makes known to us his secrets by means of the Law, and the Prophets, and his Apostles also. Thus, Paul shews the gospel to be preached for the obedience of the faith, (Rom. i. 5;) as if he had said, we shall not escape with impunity, unless we obediently embrace the doctrine of the gospel; otherwise, we do our utmost to frustrate the designs of God and elude his counsels, unless we faithfully obey his word. It follows,—

23. At the beginning of thy supplications the commandment came forth, and I am come to shew *thee*; for thou *art* greatly beloved: therefore understand the matter, and consider the vision.

23. Principio precationum tuarum exivit verbum, et ego veni ut annuntiarem, quia tu desideriorum vir,[1] itaque intellige in sermone, et intellige in visione.

Here the angel not only exacts docility from the Prophet, but also exhorts him to greater attention. We shall afterwards perceive that this singular and extraordinary prophecy needed no common study. This is the reason why the angel not only commands Daniel to receive his message with the obedience of faith, but also to pay greater attention than usual, because this was an important and singular mystery. He states first of all—*the word went forth from the time when the Prophet began to pray.* I will not delay by reciting the opinions of others, because I think I understand the genuine sense of the passage; namely, God heard the prayers of his servant, and then promulgated what he had already decreed. For by the word "went forth" he expresses the publication of a decree which had formerly been made; it was then issued just as the decrees of princes are said to go forth when they are publicly spread abroad. God had determined what he would do, directly Daniel had ceased, for God's counsel would never fail of its accomplishment; but he here points out the impossibility of the prayers of his saints being in vain, because he grants them the very thing which he would have bestowed had they not prayed for them, as if he were obedient to their desires, and approved of their conduct. It is clear enough, that we can obtain nothing by our prayer, without God's previous determination to

[1] That is, thou art a man to be desired.—*Calvin.*

grant it; yet these points are not contrary to each other for God attends to our prayers, as it is said in the Psalms,— He performs our wishes, and yet executes what he had determined before the creation of the world. (Ps. cxlv. 19.) He had predicted by Jeremiah, (chap. xxv. 11,) as we have remarked before, the close of the people's exile in seventy years; Daniel already knew this, as he related at the beginning of the chapter, yet he did not relax in his prayers, for he knew that God's promises afford us no ground or occasion for sloth or listlessness. The Prophet, therefore, prayed, and God shews how his desires were by no means vain as they concerned the welfare of the whole Church. He next states—*the word went forth as soon as Daniel began to pray;* that is, as soon as he opened his lips he was divinely answered. He afterwards adds, *he came to make this known, because,* says he, *thou art a desirable man.* Some take the word "desirable" actively, as if Daniel glowed with intense zeal; but this is forced and contrary to the usage of the language. Without doubt, the Prophet uses the word in the sense of acceptance with God, and the majority of interpreters fully agree with me. The angel therefore announces his arrival on behalf of Daniel, because he was in the enjoyment of God's favour. And this is worthy of notice, for we gather from the passage the impossibilty of our vows and prayers acquiring favour for us before God, unless we are already embraced by his regards; for in no other way do we find God propitious, than when we flee by faith to his lovingkindness. Then, in reliance upon Christ as our Mediator and Advocate, we dare to approach him as sons to a parent. For these reasons our prayers are of no avail before God, unless they are in some degree founded in faith, which alone reconciles us to God, since we can never be pleasing to him without pardon and remission of sins. We observe also, the sense in which the saints are said to please God by their sometimes failing to obtain their requests. For Daniel was subject to continual groanings for many years, and was afflicted by much grief; and yet he never perceived himself to have accomplished anything worthy of his labours: he might really conclude all his labour to be utterly lost, after praying so often and so perseveringly without effect. But the angel meets him frankly and testifies to his acceptance with God, and enables him to acknowledge that he had not suffered any repulse, although he had failed to obtain the object of his earnest desires. Hence, when we become anxious in our thoughts, and are induced to despair through the absence of all profit or fruit from our prayers, and through the want of an open and immediate answer, we must derive this instruction from the angel's teaching,— Daniel, who was most acceptable to God, was heard at length, without being permitted to see the object of his wishes with his bodily eyes. He died in exile, and never beheld the performance of the Prophet's prophecies concerning the happy state of the Church, as if immediately preparing to celebrate its triumphs. At the end of the verse, as I have already mentioned, the angel stimulates Daniel to greater zeal, and urges him to apply his mind and all his senses attentively to understand the prophecy which the angel was commanded to bring before him. It now follows,—

24. Seventy weeks are determined upon thy people, and upon thy holy city, to finish the transgression, and to make an end of sins, and to make reconciliation for iniquity, and to bring in everlasting righteousness, and to seal up the vision and prophecy, and to anoint the most Holy.

24. Septuaginta hebdomades finitæ sunt super populum tuum, et super urbem tuam sanctam,[1] ad claudendum scelus, et obsignandum peccatum, et expiandam iniquitatem, et adducendam justitiam æternam, et obsignandam visionem,[2] et prophetiam, et ungendum sanctum sanctorum.[3]

This passage has been variously treated, and so distracted, and almost torn to pieces by the various opinions of interpreters, that it might be considered nearly useless on account of its obscurity. But, in the assurance that no prediction is really in vain, we may hope to understand this prophecy, provided only we are attentive and teachable according to the angel's admonition, and the Prophet's example. I do not usually refer to conflicting opinions, because I take no pleasure in refuting them, and the simple method which I adopt pleases me best, namely, to expound what I think

[1] Verbally, upon the city of thy holiness.—*Calvin.*
[2] The word חתם, *chethem*, "to seal," is repeated twice.—*Calvin.*
[3] Or, holiness of holiness, alluding to the Temple.—*Calvin.*

delivered by the Spirit of God. But I cannot escape the necessity of confuting various views of the present passage. I will begin with the Jews, because they not only pervert its sense through ignorance, but through shameful impudence. Whenever they are exposed to the light which shines from Christ, they instantly turn their backs in utter shamelessness, and display a complete want of ingenuousness. They are like dogs who are satisfied with barking. In this passage especially, they betray their petulance, because with brazen forehead they elude the Prophet's meaning. Let us observe, then, what they think, for we should condemn them to little purpose, unless we can convict them by reasons equally firm and certain. When Jerome relates the teaching of the Jews who lived before his own day, he attributes to them greater modesty and discretion than their later descendants have displayed. He reports their confession, that this passage cannot be understood otherwise than of the advent of Messiah. But perhaps Jerome was unwilling to meet them in open conflict, as he was not fully persuaded of its necessity, and therefore he assumed more than they had allowed. I think this very probable, for he does not let fall a single word as to what interpretation he approves, and excuses himself for bringing forward all kinds of opinions without any prejudice on his part. Hence, he dares not pronounce whether or not the Jewish interpreters are more correct than either the Greek or the Latin, but leaves his readers entirely in suspense. Besides, it is very clear that all the Rabbis expounded this prophecy of Daniel's, of that continual punishment which God was about to inflict upon his people after their return from captivity. Thus, they entirely exclude the grace of God, and blame the Prophet, as if he had committed an error in thinking that God would be propitious to these miserable exiles, by restoring them to their homes and by rebuilding their Temple. According to their view, the seventy weeks began at the destruction of the former Temple, and closed at the overthrow of the second. In one point they agree with us,—in considering the Prophet to reckon the weeks not by days but by years, as in Leviticus. (Chap. xxv. 8.) There is no difference between us and the Jews in numbering the years; they confess the number of years to be 490, but disagree with us entirely as to the close of the prophecy. They say—as I have already hinted—the continual calamities which oppressed the people are here predicted. The Prophet hoped the end of their troubles was fast approaching, as God had testified by Jeremiah his perfect satisfaction with the seventy years of captivity. They say also—the people were miserably harassed by their enemies again overthrowing their second Temple; thus they were deprived of their homes, and the ruined city became a sorrowful spectacle of devastation and disaster. In this way, I shewed how they excluded the grace of God; and to sum up their teaching shortly, this is its substance,—the Prophet is deceived in thinking the state of the Church would improve at the close of the seventy years, because seventy weeks still remained; that is, God multiplied the number in this way, for the purpose of chastising them, until at length he would abolish the city and the Temple, disperse their nation over the whole earth, and destroy their very name, until at length the Messiah whom they expected should arrive. This is their interpretation, but all history refutes both their ignorance and their rashness. For, as we shall afterwards observe, all who are endued with correct judgment will scarcely approve of this, because all historians relate the lapse of a longer period between the monarchy of Cyrus, and the Persians, and the coming of Christ, than Daniel here computes. The Jews again include the years which occurred from the ruin of the former Temple to the advent of Christ, and the final overthrow of their city. Hence, according to the commonly received opinion, they heap together about six hundred years. I shall afterwards state how far I approve of this computation, and how far I differ from it. Clearly enough, however, the Jews are both shamefully deceived and deceive others, when they thus heap together different periods without any judgment.

A positive refutation of this error is readily derived from the prophecy of Jeremiah, from the beginning of this chapter, and from the opinion of Ezra. That deceiver and impostor,

Barbinel, who fancies himself the most acute of all the Rabbis, thinks he has a convenient way of escape here, as he eludes the subject by a single word, and answers only one objection. But I will briefly shew how he plays with frivolous trifles. By rejecting Josephus, he glories in an easy victory. I candidly confess that I cannot place confidence in Josephus either at all times or without exception. But what conclusions do Barbinel and his followers draw from this passage? Let us come to that prophecy of Jeremiah which I have mentioned, and in which he takes refuge. He says, the Christians make Nebuchadnezzar reign forty-five years, but he did not complete that number. Thus he cuts off half a year, or perhaps a whole one, from those monarchies. But what is this to the purpose? because 200 years will still remain, and the contention between us concerns this period. We perceive then how childishly he trifles, by deducting five or six years from a very large number, and still there is the burden of 200 years which he does not remove. But as I have already stated, that prophecy of Jeremiah concerning the seventy years remains immovable. But when do they begin? From the destruction of the Temple? This will not suit at all.

Barbinel makes the number of the years forty-nine or thereabouts, from the destruction of the Temple to the reign of Cyrus. But we previously perceived the Prophet to be then instructed concerning the close of the captivity. Now, that impudent fellow and his followers are not ashamed to assert that Daniel was a bad interpreter of this part of Jeremiah's prophecy, because he thought the punishment completed, although some time yet remained. Some of the Rabbis make this assertion, but its frivolous character appears from this,—Daniel does not here confess any error, but confidently affirms that he prayed in consequence of his learning from the book of Jeremiah the completion of the time of the captivity. Then Ezra uses the following words,—When the seventy years were completed, which God had predicted by Jeremiah, he stirred up the spirit of Cyrus, king of Persia, to free the people in the first year of his monarchy. (Chap. i. 1.) Here Ezra openly states, that Cyrus gave the people liberty by the secret impulse of the Spirit. Had the Spirit of God become forgetful, when he hastened the people's return? For then we must necessarily convict Jeremiah of deception and falsehood, while Ezra treats the people's return as an answer to the prophecy. On the other hand, they cite a passage from the first chapter of Zechariah, (ver. 12,) Wilt thou not, O Lord, pity thy city Jerusalem, because the seventy years are now at an end? But here the Prophet does not point out the moment at which the seventy years were finished, but while some portion of the people had returned to their country by the permission of Cyrus, and the building of the Temple was still impeded, after a lapse of twenty or thirty years, he complains of God not having completely and fully liberated his people. Whether or not this is so, the Jews must explain the beginning of the seventy years from the former exile before the destruction of the Temple; otherwise the passages cited from Daniel and Ezra would not agree. We are thus compelled to close these seventy years before the reign of Cyrus, as God had said he should then put an end to the captivity of his people, and the period was completed at that point.

Again, almost all profane writers reckon 550 years from the reign of Cyrus to the advent of Christ.

I do not hesitate to suppose some error here, because no slight difficulty would remain to us on this calculation, but I shall afterwards state the correct method of calculating the number of years. Meanwhile, we perceive how the Jews in every way exceed the number of 600 years, by comprehending the seventy years' captivity under these seventy weeks; and then they add the time which elapsed from the death of Christ to the reign of Vespasian. But the facts themselves are their best refutation. For the angel says, *the seventy weeks were finished.* Barbinel takes the word חתך, *chetek,* for "to cut off," and wishes us to mark the continual miseries by which the people were afflicted; as if the angel had said, the time of redemption has not yet arrived, as the people were continually wretched, until God inflicted upon them that final blow which was a desperate slaughter. But when this word is taken to mean to "termi-

nate" or "finish," the angel evidently announces the conclusion of the seventy weeks here. That impostor contends
with this argument—weeks of years are here used in vain,
unless with reference to the captivity. This is partially
true, but he draws them out longer than he ought. Our
Prophet alludes to the seventy years of Jeremiah, and I am
surprised that the advocates of our side have not considered
this, as no one suggests any reason why Daniel reckons
years by weeks. Yet we know this figure to be purposely
used, because he wished to compare seventy weeks of years
with the seventy years. And whoever will take the trouble
to consider this likeness or analogy, will find the Jews slain
with their own sword. For the Prophet here compares God's
grace with his judgment ; as if he had said, the people have
been punished by an exile of seventy years, but now their
time of grace has arrived ; nay, the day of their redemption
has dawned, and it shone forth with continual splendour,
shaded, indeed, with a few clouds, for 490 years until the
advent of Christ. The Prophet's language must be interpreted as follows,—Sorrowful darkness has brooded over you
for seventy years, but God will now follow up this period by
one of favour of sevenfold duration, because by lightening your
cares and moderating your sorrows, he will not cease to prove
himself propitious to you even to the advent of Christ. This
event was notoriously the principal hope of the saints who
looked forward to the appearance of the Redeemer.

We now understand why the angel does not use the reckoning of years, or months, or days, but weeks of years, because
this has a tacit reference to the penalty which the people
had endured according to the prophecy of Jeremiah. On
the other hand, this displays God's great lovingkindness,
since he manifests a regard for his people up to the period
of his setting forth their promised salvation in his Christ.
Seventy weeks, then, says he, *were finished upon thy people,
and upon thy holy city.* I do not approve of the view of
Jerome, who thinks this an allusion to the rejection of the
people ; as if he had said, the people is thine and not mine.
I feel sure this is utterly contrary to the Prophet's intention.
He asserts the people and city to be here called Daniel's,

because God had divorced his people and rejected his city. But, as I said before, God wished to bring some consolation to his servant and all the pious, and to prop them up by this confidence during their oppression by their enemies. For God had already fixed the time of sending the Redeemer. The people and the city are said to belong to Daniel, because, as we saw before, the Prophet was anxious for the common safety of his nation, and the restoration of the city and Temple. Lastly, the angel confirms his previous expression —God listened to his servant's prayer, and promulgated the prophecy of future redemption. The clause which follows convicts the Jews of purposely corrupting Daniel's words and meaning, because the angel says, *the time was finished for putting an end to wickedness, and for sealing up sins, and for expiating iniquity.* We gather from this clause, God's compassionate feelings for his people after these seventy weeks were over. For what purpose did God determine that time? Surely to prohibit sin, to close up wickedness, and to expiate iniquity. We observe no continuance of punishment here, as the Jews vainly imagine; for they suppose God always hostile to his people, and they recognise a sign of most grievous offence in the utter destruction of the Temple. The Prophet, or rather the angel, gives us quite the opposite view of the case, by explaining how God wished to finish and close up their sin, and to expiate their iniquity He afterwards adds, *to bring in everlasting righteousness.* We first perceive how joyful a message is brought forward concerning the reconciliation of the people with God; and next, something promised far better and more excellent than anything which had been granted under the law, and even under the flourishing times of the Jews under David and Solomon. The angel here encourages the faithful to expect something better than what their fathers, whom God had adopted, had experienced. There is a kind of contrast between the expiations under the law and this which the angel announces, and also between the pardon here promised and that which God had always given to his ancient people; and there is also the same contrast between the eternal righteousness and that which flourished under the law.

He next adds, *To seal up the vision and the prophecy.* Here the word " to seal" may be taken in two senses. Either the advent of Christ should sanction whatever had been formerly predicted—and the metaphor will imply this well enough—or we may take it otherwise, namely, the vision shall be sealed up, and so finally closed that all prophecies should cease. Barbinel thinks he points out a great absurdity here, by stating it to be by no means in accordance with God's character, to deprive his Church of the remarkable blessing of prophecy. But that blind man does not comprehend the force of the prophecy, because he does not understand anything about Christ. We know the law to be distinguished from the gospel by this peculiarity,— they formerly had a long course of prophecy according to the language of the Apostle. (Hebrews i. 1.) God spake formerly in various ways by prophets, but in these last times by his only-begotten Son. Again, the law and the prophets existed until John, says Christ. (Matt. xi. 11-13; Luke xvi. 16; Luke vii. 28.) Barbinel does not perceive this difference, and as I have formerly said, he thinks he has discovered an argument against us, by asserting that the gift of prophecy ought not to be taken away. And, truly, we ought not to be deprived of this gift, unless God desired to increase the privilege of the new people, because the least in the kingdom of heaven is superior in privilege to all the prophets, as Christ elsewhere pronounces. He next adds, *that the Holy of holies may be anointed.* Here, again, we have a tacit contrast between the anointings of the law, and the last which should take place. Not only is consolation here offered to all the pious, as God was about to mitigate the punishment which he had inflicted, but because he wished to pour forth the fulness of all his pity upon the new Church. For, as I have said, the Jews cannot escape this comparison on the part of the angel between the state of the Church under the legal and the new covenants; for the latter privileges were to be far better, more excellent, and more desirable, than those existing in the ancient Church from its commencement. But the rest to-morrow.[1]

[1] See DISSERTATIONS at the end of this vol.—*Ed.*

PRAYER.

Grant, Almighty God, as through our extreme blindness, we cannot gaze upon open daylight, that we may be enlightened by thy Spirit. May we profit by all thy prophecies by which thou wishest to direct us to thine only-begotten Son; embrace him with true and certain faith, and remain obedient to him as our ruler and guide; and after we have passed through this world, may we at length arrive at that heavenly rest which has been obtained for us by the blood of the same thy Son.—Amen.

Lecture Fiftieth.

WE began yesterday to shew how foolishly the Rabbis corrupt by their comments this prophecy of which we are now treating; for they suppose the angel to be treating of the continual wrath of God which the Jewish people had partially experienced, and which was still to be of longer duration and greater severity, according to their supposition. We have explained how openly this is opposed to the words of Daniel, who here promises the return of God's favour to his people, and then shews the object and intention of the Holy Spirit. By this consolation he wished to lighten the sorrow of the holy man whom we have already seen to be extremely anxious about the state of the Church which he then perceived to be so deplorable. The phrase on which we have already commented confirms the same point, for the angel promises, at the arrival of the predicted period, *an end to sin and wickedness, and iniquity, because iniquity should then be expiated.* He next promises *the approach of eternal righteousness;* and lastly adds, *the sealing of the vision and prophecy, together with the spiritual anointing of the Holy of holies.* Every one admits this to be a promise of a blessing more excellent than anything under the law. No other interpretation can possibly be received than that which refers it to the advent of Christ, and the entire restoration of the Church of God. Other arguments follow. For the Prophet adds what I shall repeat again, for I must explain more fully what I now only casually run through.

25. Know therefore and understand, *that* from the going forth of the commandment to restore and to build Jerusalem, unto the Messiah the Prince, *shall be* seven weeks, and threescore and two weeks: the street shall be built again, and the wall, even in troublous times.

25. Cognosces ergo et intelliges,[1] ab exitu verbi de reditu,[2] et de ædificanda Jerosolyma usque ad Christum ducem hebdomadas septem, et hebdomadas sexaginta duas, et reducetur,[3] et re-ædificabitur platea,[4] et murus, idque in angustia temporum.

Daniel here repeats the divisions of time already mentioned. He had previously stated seventy weeks; but he now makes two portions, one of seven weeks, and the other of sixty-two. There is clearly another reason why he wished to divide into two parts the number used by the angel. One portion contains seven weeks, and the other sixty-two; a single week is omitted which will afterwards be mentioned. The Jews reject seven weeks from the rule of Herod to that of Vespasian. I confess this to be in accordance with the Jewish method of speech; instead of sixty-two and seven, they will say seven and sixty-two; thus putting the smaller number first. The years of man (says Moses) shall be twenty and a hundred, (Gen. vi. 3;) the Greeks and Latins would say, shall be a hundred and twenty years. I confess this to be the common phrase among the Hebrews; but here the Prophet is not relating the continuance of any series of years, as if he were treating of the life of a single man, but he first marks the space of seven weeks, and then cuts off another period of sixty-two weeks. The seven weeks clearly precede in order of time, otherwise we could not sufficiently explain the full meaning of the angel.

We shall now treat the sense in which *the going forth of the edict* ought to be received. In the meantime, it cannot be denied that the angel pronounces this concerning the edict which had been promulgated about the bringing back of the people, and the restoration of the city. It would, therefore, be foolish to apply it to a period at which the city was not restored, and no such decree had either been uttered or made public. But, first of all, we must treat what the

[1] Or, know and understand.—*Calvin.*
[2] Or, concerning the bringing back of the people.—*Calvin.*
[3] Or, the people shall return.—*Calvin.*
[4] A plain, from the word to spread.—*Calvin.*

angel says, *until the Christ, the Messiah.* Some desire to
take this singular noun in a plural sense, as if it were the
Christs of the Lord, meaning his priests ; while some refer
it to Zerubbabel, and others to Joshua. But clearly enough
the angel speaks of Christ, of whom both kings and priests
under the law were a type and figure. Some, again, think
the dignity of Christ lessened by the use of the word נגיד,
negid, "prince" or "leader," as if in his leadership there existed
neither royalty, nor sceptre, nor diadem. This remark is
altogether without reason ; for David is called a leader of
the people, and Hezekiah when he wore a diadem, and was
seated on his throne, is also termed a leader. (2 Sam. v. 2;
2 Kings xx. 5.) Without doubt, the word here implies superior excellence. All kings were rulers over the people of
God, and the priests were endowed with a certain degree of
honour and authority. Here, then, the angel calls Christ a
leader, as he far surpassed all others, whether kings or
priests. And if the reader is not captious, this contrast will
be admitted at once.

He next adds, *The people shall return or be brought back,
and the street shall be built, and the wall, and that, too, in
the narrow limit of the times.* Another argument follows,—
namely, after sixty-two weeks Christ shall be cut off. This
the Jews understand of Agrippa, who certainly was cut off
when Augustus obtained the empire. In this they seek only
something to say ; for all sound and sensible readers will be
perfectly satisfied that they act without either judgment or
shame, and vomit forth whatever comes into their thoughts.
They are quite satisfied when they find anything plausible
to say. That trifler, Barbinel, of whom I have previously
spoken, thinks Agrippa has just as much right to be called
a Christ as Cyrus ; he allows his defection to the Romans,
but states it to have been against his will, as he was still a
worshipper of God. Although he was clearly an apostate,
yet he treats him as by no means worse than all the rest,
and for this reason he wishes him to be called the Christ.
But, first of all, we know Agrippa not to have been a legitimate king, and his tyranny was directly contrary to the
oracle of Jacob, since the sceptre had been snatched away

from the tribe of Judah. (Gen. xlix. 10.) He cannot by any means be called Christ, even though he had surpassed all angels in wisdom, and virtue, and power, and everything else. Here the lawful government of the people is treated, and this will not be found in the person of Agrippa. Hence the Jewish arguments are altogether futile. Next, another statement is added, *he shall confirm the treaty with many.* The Jews elude the force of this clause very dishonestly, and without the slightest shame. They twist it to Vespasian and Titus. Vespasian had been sent into Syria and the East by Nero. It is perfectly true, that through a wish to avoid a severe slaughter of his soldiers, he tried all conditions of peace, and enticed the Jews by every possible inducement to give themselves up to him, rather than to force him to the last extremity. Truly enough, then, Vespasian exhorted the Jews to peace, and Titus, after his father had passed over to Italy, followed the same policy; but was this confirming the covenant? When the angel of God is treating events of the last importance, and embracing the whole condition of the Church, their explanation is trifling who refer it to the Roman leaders wishing to enter into a treaty with the people. They attempted either to obtain possession of the whole empire of the East by covenant, or else they determined to use the utmost force to capture the city. This explanation, then, is utterly absurd. It is quite clear that the Jews are not only destitute of all reason when they explain this passage of the continual wrath of God, and exclude his favour and reconciliation with the people, but they are utterly dishonest, and utter words without shame, and throw a mist over the passage to darken it. At the same time their vanity is exposed, as they have no pretext for their comments.

I now come to the ANCIENT WRITERS. Jerome, as I stated shortly yesterday, recites various opinions. But before I treat them singly, I must answer in few words, the calumny of that impure and obstinate Rabbi, Barbinel. To deprive the Christians of all confidence and authority, he objects to their mutual differences; as if differences between men not

sufficiently exercised in the Scriptures, could entirely overthrow their truth. Suppose, for instance, that I were to
argue against him, the absence of consent among the Jews
themselves. If any one is anxious to collect their different
opinions, he may exult as a conqueror in this respect, as
there is no agreement between the Rabbis. Nay, he does
not point out the full extent of the differences which occur
among Christians, for I am ready to concede far more than
he demands. For that brawler was ignorant of all things,
and betrays only petulance and talkativeness. His books
are doubtless very plausible among the Jews who seek
nothing else. But he takes as authorities with us, Africanus
and Nicolaus de Lyra, Burgensis, and a certain teacher
named Remond. He is ignorant of the names of Eusebius,[1]
Origen, Tertullian, Hippolytus, Apollinaris, Jerome, Augustine, and other similar writers. We here perceive how brazen
this prater is, who dares to babble about matters utterly
beyond his knowledge. But as I have stated, I allow many
differences among Christians. Eusebius himself agrees with
the Jews in referring the word " Christ" to the priests, and
when the angel speaks of the death of Christ, he thinks
the death of Aristobulus, who was slain, is intended here.
But this is altogether foolish. He is a Christian, you will
say ; true, but he fell into ignorance and error. The
opinion of Africanus is more to the point, but the time
by no means accords with that of Darius the son of Hystaspes, as I shall afterwards shew. He errs again on another
chapter, by taking the years to be lunar ones, as Lyranus
does. Without doubt, this was only a cavil of his ; through
not finding their own years suit, they thought the whole
number might be made up, by using intercalary years
together with the 490. For before the year was adjusted
to the course of the sun, the ancients were accustomed to
reckon twelve lunar months, and afterwards to add another.
The whole number of years may be made up according to
their imagination, if we add those additional periods to the
years here enumerated by the Prophet. But I reject this

---

[1] See this verse quoted in *Euseb.*, Hist. Ecc., lib. i. ch. 6 ; and the DIS-
SERTATIONS at the end of this vol., for an account of these writers.—*Ed.*

altogether. Hippolytus also errs in another direction ; for he reckons the seven weeks as the time which elapsed between the death and resurrection of Christ, and herein he agrees with the Jews. Apollinaris also is mistaken, for he thinks we must begin at Christ's birth, and then extends the prophecy to the end of the world. Eusebius also, who contends with him in a certain passage, takes the last week for the whole period which must elapse till the end of the world shall arrive. I therefore am ready to acknowledge all these interpretations to be false, and yet I do not allow the truth of God to fail.

How, therefore, shall we arrive at any certain conclusion ? It is not sufficient to refute the ignorance of others, unless we can make the truth apparent, and prove it by clear and satisfactory reasons. I am willing to spare the names of surviving commentators, and of those who have lived during our own times, yet I must say what will prove useful to my readers ; meanwhile, I shall speak cautiously, because I am very desirous of being silent upon all points except those which are useful and necessary to be known. If any one has the taste and the needful leisure to inquire diligently into the time here mentioned, Œcolampadius rightly and prudently admonishes us, that we ought to make the computation from the beginning of the world. For until the ruin of the Temple and the destruction of the city, we can gather with certainty the number of years which have elapsed since the creation of the world ; here there is no room for error. The series is plain enough in the Scriptures. But after this they leave the reader to other sources of information, since the computation from the overthrow of the Temple is loose and inaccurate, according to Eusebius and others. Thus, from the return of the people to the advent of Christ, 540 years will be found to have elapsed. Thus we see how impossible it is to satisfy sensible readers, if we only reckon the years in the way Œcolampadius has done.[1]

---

[1] See his Chronology at full length in his comment on this verse, lib. ii. p. 99. Edit. fol. 1567. The Editor ventures to recommend the readers of Calvin's Daniel, to peruse the judicious comments of Œcolampadius. They are worthy of more attention than they have received in England. See our DISSERTATIONS throughout.—*Ed.*

Philip Melancthon, who excels in genius and learning,
and is happily versed in the studies of history, makes
a double computation.   He begins one plan from the second
year of Cyrus, that is, from the commencement of the Persian
monarchy ; but he reckons the seventy weeks to be finished
about the death of Augustus, which is the period of the
birth of Christ.   When he arrives at the baptism of Christ,
he adds another method of reckoning, which commences at
the times of Darius : and as to the edict here mentioned,
he understands it to have been promulgated by Darius
the son of Hystaspes, since the building of the Temple was
interrupted for about sixty-six years.   As to this computation, I cannot by any means approve of it.   And yet I confess the impossibility of finding any other exposition of what
the angel says—*until Christ the Leader,* unless by referring
it to the baptism of Christ.

These two points, then, in my judgment, must be held as
fixed ; first, the seventy weeks begin with the Persian
monarchy, because a free return was then granted to the
people ; and secondly, they did not terminate till the baptism of Christ, when he openly commenced his work of
satisfying the requirements of the office assigned him by his
father.   But we must now see how this will accord with the
number of years.   I confess here, the existence of such great
differences between ancient writers, that we must use conjecture, because we have no certain explanation to bring
forward, which we can point out as the only sufficient one.
I am aware of the various calumnies of those who desire to
render all things obscure, and to pour the darkness of night
upon the clearest daylight.   For the profane and the sceptical catch at this directly ; for when they see any difference
of opinion, they wish to shew the uncertainty of all our
teaching.   So if they perceive any difference in the views of
various interpreters, even in matters of the smallest moment,
they conclude all things to be involved in complete darkness.
But their perverseness ought not to frighten us, because
when any discrepancies occur in the narratives of profane
historians, we do not pronounce the whole history fabulous.
Let us take Grecian history,—how greatly the Greeks differ

from each other? If any should make this a pretext for rejecting them all, and should assert all their narrations to be false, would not every one condemn him as singularly impudent? Now, if the Scriptures are not self-contradictory, but manifest slight diversities in either years or places, shall we on that account pronounce them entirely destitute of credit? We are well aware of the existence of some differences in all histories, and yet this does not cause them to lose their authority; they are still quoted, and confidence is reposed in them.

With respect to the present passage, I confess myself unable to deny the existence of much controversy concerning these years, among all the Greek and Latin writers. This is true: but, meanwhile, shall we bury whatever has already past, and think the world interrupted in its course? After Cyrus had transferred to the Persians the power of the East, some kings must clearly have followed him, although it is not evident who they were, and writers also differ about the period and the reigns of each of them, and yet on the main points there is a general agreement. For some enumerate about 200 years; others 125 years; and some are between the two, reckoning 140 years. Whichever be the correct statement, there was clearly some succession of the Persian kings, and many additional years elapsed before Alexander the Macedonian obtained the monarchy of the whole East. This is quite clear. Now, from the death of Alexander the number of years is well known. Philip Melancthon cites a passage from Ptolemy which makes them 292; and many testimonies may be adduced, which confirm that period of time. If any object,—the number of years might be reckoned by periods of five years, as the Romans usually did, or by Olympiads, with the Greeks, I confess that the reckoning by Olympiads removes all source of error. The Greeks used great diligence and minuteness, and were very desirous of glory: We cannot say the same of the Persian empire, for we are unable accurately to determine under what Olympiad each king lived, and the year in which he commenced his reign and in which he died. Whatever conclusion we adopt, my previous assertion is perfectly true,—if captious men are rebellious and darken the clear light of history, yet they cannot wrest this passage from its real meaning, because we can gather from both the Greek and Latin historians, the whole sum of the times which will suit very clearly this prophecy of Daniel. Whoever will compare all historical testimony with the desire of learning, and, without any contention, will carefully number the years, he will find it impossible to express them better than by the expression of the angel—seventy weeks. For example, let any studious person, endued with acuteness, experience, and skill, discover whatever has been written in Greek and Latin, and distinguish the testimony of each writer under distinct heads, and afterwards compare the writers together, and determine the credibility of each, and how far each is a fit and classical authority, he will find the same result as that here given by the Prophet. This ought to be sufficient for us. But, meanwhile, we must remember how our ignorance springs chiefly from this Persian custom ; whoever undertook a warlike expedition, appointed his son his viceroy. Thus, Cambyses reigned, according to some, twenty years, and according to others, only seven ; because the crown was placed on his head during his father's lifetime. Besides this, there was another reason. The people of the East are notoriously very restless, easily excited, and always desiring a change of rulers. Hence, contentions frequently arose among near relatives, of which we have ample narratives in the works of Herodotus. I mention him among others, as the fact is sufficiently known. When fathers saw the danger of their sons mutually destroying each other, they usually created one of them a king; and if they wished to prefer the younger brother to the elder, they called him "king" with the concurrence of their council. Hence, the years of their reigns became intermingled, without any fixed method of reckoning them. And, therefore, I said, even if Olympiads could never mislead us, this could not be asserted of the Persian empire. While we allow much diversity and contradiction united with great obscurity, still we must always return to the same point,—some conclusion may be found, which will agree with this prediction of the Prophet.

Therefore I will not reckon these years one by one, but will only admonish each of you to weigh for himself, according to his capacity, what he reads in history. Thus all sound and moderate men will acquiesce, when they perceive how well this prophecy of Daniel agrees with the testimony of profane writers, in its general scope, according to my previous explanations.

I stated that we must begin with the monarchy of Cyrus; this is clearly to be gathered from the words of the angel, and especially from the division of the weeks. For he says, *The seven weeks have reference to the repair of the city and temple.* No cavils can in any way deprive the Prophet's expression of its true force: *from the going forth of the edict concerning the bringing back of the people and the building of the city, until Messiah the Leader, shall be seven weeks;* and then, *sixty-two weeks* : afterward he adds, *After the sixty-two weeks Christ shall be cut off.* When, therefore, he puts *seven weeks* in the first place, and clearly expresses his reckoning the commencement of this period from the promulgation of the edict, to what can we refer these seven weeks, except to the times of the monarchy of Cyrus and that of Darius the son of Hystaspes? This is evident from the history of the Maccabees, as well as from the testimony of the evangelist John ; and we may collect the same conclusion from the prophecies of Haggai and Zechariah, as the building of the Temple was interrupted during forty-six years. Cyrus permitted the people to build the Temple ; the foundations were laid when Cyrus went out to the war in Scythia ; the Jews were then compelled to cease their labours, and his successor Cambyses was hostile to this people. Hence the Jews say, (John ii. 20,) Forty-six years was this Temple in building, and wilt thou build it in three days? They strive to deride Christ because he had said, Destroy this Temple, and I will rebuild it in three days, as it was then a common expression, and had been handed down by their fathers, that the Temple had occupied this period in its construction. If you add the three years during which the foundations were laid, we shall then have forty-nine years, or seven weeks. As the event openly shews the completion of what the angel had predicted to Daniel, whoever wishes to wrest the meaning of the passage, only displays his own hardihood.   And must we not reject every other interpretation, as obscuring so clear and obvious a meaning?   We must next remember what I have previously stated.   In yesterday's Lecture we saw that seventy weeks were cut off for the people; the angel had also declared the going forth of the edict, for which Daniel had prayed. What necessity, then, is there for treating a certainty as doubtful? and why litigate the point when God pronounces the commencement of this period to be at the termination of the seventy years proclaimed by Jeremiah?   It is quite certain, that these seventy years and seventy weeks ought to be joined together.   Since, therefore, these periods are continuous, whoever refers this passage to the time of Darius Hystaspes, first of all breaks the links of a chain of events all connected together, and then perverts the whole spirit of the passage ; for, as we yesterday stated, the angel's object was to offer consolation in the midst of sorrow.   For seventy years the people had been miserably afflicted in exile, and they seemed utterly abandoned, as if God would no longer acknowledge these children of Abraham for his people and inheritance.   As this was the Almighty's intention, it is quite clear that the commencement of the seventy weeks cannot be otherwise interpreted than by referring it to the monarchy of Cyrus.   This is the first point.

We must now turn to the SIXTY-TWO WEEKS ; and if I cannot satisfy every one, I shall still content myself with great simplicity, and I trust that all sound and humble disciples of Christ will easily acquiesce in this exposition.   If we reckon the years from the reign of Darius to the baptism of Christ, sixty-two weeks or thereabouts will be found to have elapsed.   As I previously remarked, I am not scrupulous to a few days or months, or even a single year; for how great is that perverseness which would lead us to reject what historians relate because they do not all agree to a single year ? Whatever be the correct conclusion, we shall find about 480 years between the time of Darius and the death of Christ.

Hence it becomes necessary to prolong these years to the baptism of Christ, because when the angel speaks of the last week, he plainly states, *The covenant shall be confirmed at that time*, and then *the Messiah shall be cut off*. As this was to be done in the last week, we must necessarily extend the time to the preaching of the Gospel. And for this reason Christ is called a " Leader," because at his conception he was destined to be king of heaven and earth, although he did not commence his reign till he was publicly ordained the Master and Redeemer of his people. The word "Leader" is applied as a name before the office was assumed ; as if the angel had said, the end of the seventy weeks will occur when Christ openly assumes the office of king over his people, by collecting them from that miserable and horrible dispersion under which they had been so long ground down. I shall put off the rest till to-morrow.

PRAYER.

Grant, Almighty God, since thy servants before the setting forth of thine only-begotten Son were sustained by those oracles which had not then been realized by the event, that we at this day may learn to put our trust in our Lord, who has so clearly revealed himself to us by his Gospel. May we stand so firm and constant in the faith of that Gospel, that we may never be tossed about by the disturbances and tumults of this world. May we ever proceed in the course of thy holy calling, till at length we are released from all contests, and arrive at that blessed rest which is laid up for us in heaven, by the same our Lord Jesus Christ.—Amen.

Lecture Fifty=First.

In yesterday's Lecture I explained my views of the seventy weeks. I now return to the words of the Prophet, on which I touched but briefly. He first says, *Seventy weeks have been cut off upon thy people, and upon the holy city.* By these words he implies first, the Israelites should be under the care and protection of God until the arrival of Christ ;

and next, Christ would come before the completion of the seventy years. The angel announces these two points, to assure the faithful of God's perpetual remembrance of his covenant, and to sustain them in the midst of all their anxieties and distresses. A remarkable passage now follows concerning the office of Christ. The angel foretells what they were to expect from Christ. First of all, he announces remission of sins ; for he points this out by the form of expression, *to prohibit* or close up *wickedness, to seal up sinfulness, and to expiate iniquity.* It does not surprise us to find the angel using many phrases in a matter of such importance. Such repetition in the language seems to us superfluous, but the knowledge of salvation is comprehended under this head. We are thus informed how God is reconciled to us by gratuitous pardon, and this is the reason why the angel insists on this subject by so many words. (Luke i. 77.) But we must remember what I said the day before yesterday—there is a tacit contrast between the remission now offered to us under the Gospel, and that formerly offered to the fathers under the Law. From the creation of the world no one could call upon God with a tranquil mind and with sure confidence, unless by relying upon the hope of pardon. For we know the door of mercy to be closed against us all through our being deservedly under God's wrath. Hence, unless the doctrine of gratuitous remission of sins shone forth, we should enjoy no liberty of calling upon God, and all hope of salvation would be at the same time extinct. It follows, therefore, the fathers under the Law had this benefit in common with us, namely, a certain persuasion of God's being propitious to them, and of his pardoning their transgressions. What, then, is the meaning of the phrase, Christ at his advent will seal up sins, and expiate iniquities ? Here, as I have said, a difference is shewn between the condition of the old and the new Church. The fathers indeed had hopes of remission of their sins, but their condition was inferior to ours in two respects. Their teaching was not so plain as ours, nor were their promises so full and steadfast. We excel them also in another respect. God bears witness to us that he is our Father, and so we flee to him with the utmost freedom and fearlessness ; and, in addition to this, Christ has already reconciled us to the Father by his blood. (Rom. viii. 15 ; Gal. iv. 6.) Thus we are superior to them, not only in our instruction, but in effect and completeness, since at this day God not only promises us the pardon of our sins, but testifies and affirms their entire blotting out and becoming abolished through the sacrifice of Christ his Son. This difference is openly denoted by the angel when he says, *Sins should be closed up and sealed, and iniquities also expiated* when Christ came. Hence we stated previously how something better was promised than the fathers experienced before the manifestation of Christ.

We here perceive the sense in which Christ *shut up sins, and sealed wickedness, and expiated iniquity ;* for he not only introduced the doctrine of gratuitous pardon, and promised that God would be entreated by the people, through his desire to pardon their iniquity, but he really accomplished whatever was needful to reconcile men to God. He poured forth his blood by which he blotted out our sins ; he also offered himself as an expiatory victim, and satisfied God by the sacrifice of his death, so as entirely to absolve us from guilt. Moses often uses the word חטא, *cheta*, when speaking of sacrifices ; but the angel here teaches us indirectly how all the expiations under the law were only figurative, and nothing but shadows of the future ; for, had sins been then really expiated, there would have been no need of the coming of Christ. As, therefore, expiation was suspended until the manifestation of Christ, there never was any true expiation under the law, but all its ceremonies were but shadowy representations. He afterwards adds, *To bring in eternal righteousness.* This righteousness depends on the expiation. For how could God reckon the faithful just, or impute righteousness to them, as Paul informs us, unless by covering and burying their sins, or purging them in the blood of Christ ? (Rom. iv. 11.) Is not God himself appeased by the sacrifice of his Son ? These phrases, then, must be united, *Iniquity shall be expiated, and eternal righteousness brought manifestly forward.* No righteousness will ever be found in mortal man, unless he obtain it from Christ; and if we use great accuracy of expression, righteousness cannot exist in us otherwise than through that gratuitous pardon which we obtain through the sacrifice of Christ. Meanwhile, Scripture purposely unites together remission of sins and righteousness, as also Paul says, Christ died for our sins, and rose again for our justification. (Rom. iv. 25.) His death procured satisfaction for us, so that we should not always remain guilty, nor be subject to the condemnation of eternal death, and then by his resurrection he procured righteousness for us, and also acquired eternal life. The reason why the Prophet here treats justice as perpetual or "of the ages," is this: the fathers under the Law were compelled to please God by daily sacrifices. There would have been no necessity for repeating sacrifices, as the Apostle admonishes us, if there had been any inherent virtue in a single sacrifice to appease the Almighty. (Heb. x. 1.) But since all the rites of the law tended to the same purpose of foreshadowing Christ, as the one and perpetual victim for reconciling men to God, daily sacrifices must necessarily be offered. Whence, as we formerly said, these satisfactions were plainly insufficient for procuring righteousness. Therefore Christ alone brought in eternal righteousness,—his death alone sufficed for expiating all transgressions. For Christ suffered, not only to satisfy for our sins, but he sets before us his own death in which we should acquiesce. Hence this eternal justice depends upon the enduring effect of the death of Christ, since the blood of Christ flowed as it were before God, and while we are daily purged and cleansed from our pollution, God is also daily appeased for us. We observe, then, how righteousness was not completely revealed under the law, but is now set before us under the Gospel. It follows, *To seal up the vision and the prophecy.*

This clause may have two senses, because, as I said before, Christ sealed up all visions and prophecies, for they are all yea and amen in him, as Paul says. (2 Cor. i. 20.) As, therefore, God's promises were all satisfied and fulfilled in Christ for the salvation of the faithful, so with propriety the angel affirms of his advent, *It shall seal up the vision and the prophecy.* This is one sense. The other is, the vision shall be sealed in the sense of its ceasing, as if the angel had said, Christ shall put an end to prophecies, because our spiritual position differs from that of the fathers. For God formerly spoke in many ways, as the Church had to pass through a variety of conflicting states and circumstances. But when Christ was manifested, we arrive at the close of prophetic times. Hence his advent is called the fulness of times, (Gal. iv. 4; Heb. i. 1;) and elsewhere Paul says, we have arrived at the last days, (1 Cor. x. 11,) since we are waiting for the second advent of Christ, and we have no need of fresh prophecies as formerly. Then all things were very obscure, and God governed his people under the dark shadow of a cloud. Our condition is in these days different. Hence we are not surprised at the angel pronouncing *all the visions and prophecies sealed up;* for the law and the prophets were until John, but from that time the kingdom of God began to be promulgated; that is, God appeared much more clearly than before. (Matt. xi. 13; Luke xvi. 16.) The very name of vision implies something obscure and doubtful. But now Christ, the Sun of righteousness, has shone upon us, and we are in meridian brightness; the Law appears only like a candle in the government of our life, because Christ points out to us in full splendour the way of salvation. Without doubt, the angel here wished us to distinguish between the obscure teaching of the Law, with its ancient figures, and the open light of the Gospel. Besides, the name "prophecy" is taken as well for the prophetic office as for the predictions delivered.

He afterwards adds, *To anoint the Holy of holies.* The angel here alludes to the rite of consecration which was observed under the Law; for the tabernacle with its appendages was consecrated by anointing. It is here shewn how the perfect and truly spiritual anointing was put off till the advent of Christ. He is himself properly and deservedly called the Holy One of holy ones, or the Tabernacle of God, because his body was really the temple of deity, and holiness must be sought from him. (Col. ii. 9.) The Prophet here reminds us of the anointing of the sanctuary under the Law being only a figure; but in Christ we have the true exhibition of the reality, although he was not visibly anointed with oil, but spiritually, when the Spirit of God rested upon him with all his gifts. Wherefore he says, (John xvii. 19,) For their sakes I sanctify myself.

It now follows, *Thou shalt know and understand, from the going forth of a word,* (or decree,) *for the bringing back of the people and the building of Jerusalem, until Christ the Leader, shall be seven weeks, and sixty-two weeks, and the people shall return,* (or be brought back,) *and the street shall be built, and the wall,* (or trench,) *and that too, in the narrow interval of the times ;* for thus I resolve the copula. As we have already said, the time which had been fixed beforehand for the perfect state of the Church is divided. In the first place, he puts seven weeks by themselves ; he then adds sixty-two weeks, and leaves one, of which we shall afterwards speak. He immediately explains why he separates the seven weeks from the rest, rendering every other interpreter unnecessary. Next, as to the going forth of the edict, we have stated how inadmissible is any interpretation but the first decree of Cyrus, which permitted the people freely to return to their country. For the seven weeks which make up forty-nine years clearly prove this assertion. From the beginning of the Persian monarchy to the reign of Darius the son of Hystaspes, the hostility of all the neighbouring nations to the Jews is notorious, especially in interrupting the building of their temple and city. Although the people had free permission to return to their country, yet they were there harassed by hostilities, and were almost induced to repine at this mark of God's favour. A great part of them preferred their former exile to a harassing and perplexing life spent among their most cruel foes. This is the reason why the angel informs them of the seven weeks to elapse after the people should be brought back, for they must not expect to spend their life in peace, and build their city and temple without any inconvenience ; for he announces the occurrence of this event *in the narrowness of the time.* By the word צוק, *tzok,* he does not mean " shortness," but rather signifies the anxious nature of the times, in consequence of the numerous troubles which all their neighbours should bring on the wretched people. It was worth while to support the pious by this previous admonition, lest they should cast away the desire of building the temple, or become utterly desponding through the weight of the afflictions which they must bear. We know what glowing predictions the prophets uttered concerning the happy state of the Church after its return ; but the reality was far different from this, and the faithful might have been quite drowned in despair unless the angel had raised their spirits by this prophecy. We thus perceive the great utility of this admonition, and at the same time it may be applied as a practical example to ourselves. Although God's loving-kindness to us was wonderful, when the pure Gospel emerged out of that dreadful darkness in which it had been buried for so many ages, yet we still experience the troubled aspect of affairs. The impious still ceaselessly and furiously oppose the miserable Church by both the sword and the virulence of their tongues. Domestic enemies use clandestine arts in their schemes to subvert our edifice ; wicked men destroy all order, and interpose many obstacles to impede our progress. But God still wishes in these days to build his spiritual temple *amidst the anxieties of the times ;* the faithful have still to hold the trowel in one hand and the sword in the other, as we find it in the book of Nehemiah, (chap. iv. 17,) because the building of the Church must still be united with many contests. It afterwards follows :—

26. And after threescore and two weeks shall Messiah be cut off, but not for himself : and the people of the prince that shall come shall destroy the city and the sanctuary; and the end thereof *shall be* with a flood, and unto the end of the war desolations are determined.

26. Et post hebdomadas sexaginta duas excidetur Christus, et nihil erit, et urbem et sanctuarium perdet populus ducis venientis, et finis ejus cum inundatione *erit, vel, in diluvio,* et ad finem belli definitio desolationum.

Here Daniel treats of the sixty-two weeks which elapsed between the sixth year of Darius and the baptism of Christ, when the Gospel began to be promulgated, but at the same time he does not neglect the seven weeks of which he had been speaking. For they comprehend the space of time which intervened between the Persian monarchy and the second edict which again granted liberty to the people after the death of Cambyses. *After the sixty-two weeks* which should succeed the seven former ones, *Messiah shall be cut off,* says he. Here the angel predicts the death of Christ. The Jews refer this to Agrippa, but this, as we have already observed, is utterly nugatory and foolish. Eusebius and others refer it to Aristobulus, but this is equally destitute of reason. Therefore the angel speaks of the only Mediator, as in the former verse he had said, *until Christ the Leader.* The extension of this to all the priesthood is both forced and absurd. The angel rather means this—Christ should then be manifest to undertake the government of his people ; or, in other words, until Messiah shall appear and commence his reign. We have already remarked upon those who erroneously and childishly explain the name " Leader," as if it were inferior in dignity to that of king. As the angel had used the name " Christ" in the sense of Mediator, so he repeats it in this passage in the same sense. And surely, as he had formerly treated of those singular marks of God's favour, by which the new Church was to surpass the old, we cannot understand the passage otherwise than of Christ alone, of whom the priests and kings under the Law were equally a type. The angel, then, here asserts, *Christ should die,* and at the same time he specifies the kind of death by saying, *nothing shall remain to him.* This short clause may be taken in various senses, yet I do not hesitate to represent the angel's meaning to be this—Christ should so die as to be entirely reduced to nothing. Some expound it thus,—the city or the people shall be as nothing to him ; meaning, he shall be divorced from the people, and their adoption shall cease, since we know the Jews to have so fallen away from true piety by their perfidy as to be entirely alienated from God, and to have lost the name of a Church. But that is forced. Others think it means, it shall be neither hostile nor favourable; and others, nothing shall remain to him in the sense of being destitute of all help ; but all these comments appear to me too frigid. The genuine sense, I have no doubt, is as follows,—the death of Christ should be without any attractiveness or loveliness, as Isaiah says. (Chap. liii. 2.) In truth, the angel informs us of the ignominious character of Christ's death, as if he should vanish from the sight of men through want of comeliness. *Nothing*, therefore, *shall remain to him*, says he ; and the obvious reason is, because men would think him utterly abolished.

He now adds, *The leader of the coming people shall destroy the city and the sanctuary.* Here the angel inserts what rather concerns the end of the chapter, as he will afterwards return to Christ. He here mentions what should happen at Christ's death, and purposely interrupts the order of the narrative to shew that their impiety would not escape punishment, as they not only rejected the Christ of God, but slew him and endeavoured to blot out his remembrance from the world. And although the angel had special reference to the faithful alone, still unbelievers required to be admonished with the view of rendering them without excuse. We are well aware of the supineness and brutality of this people, as displayed in their putting Christ to death ; for this event occasioned a triumph for the priests and the whole people. Hence these points ought to be joined together. But the angel consulted the interests of the faithful, as they would be greatly shocked at the death of Christ, which we have alluded to, and also at his ignominy and rejection. As this was a method of perishing so very horrible in the opinion of mankind, the minds of all the pious might utterly despond unless the angel had come to their relief. Hence he proposes a suitable remedy, *The leader of the coming people shall destroy the city and the sanctuary ;* as if he had said, There is no encouragement for the unbelievers to please and flatter themselves, because Christ was reduced to nothing after a carnal sense ; vengeance shall instantly overtake them ; *the leader of the coming people shall destroy both the city and the sanctuary.* He names a *coming leader*, to prevent the unbelievers from resting secure through self-flattery, as if God would not instantly stretch forth his hand to avenge himself upon them. Although the Roman army which should destroy the city and sanctuary did not immediately appear, yet the Prophet assures them of the arrival of a leader with an army which should occasion the destruction of both the city and the sanctuary. Without the slightest doubt, he here signifies that God would inflict dreadful vengeance upon the Jews for their murder of his Christ. That trifler, Barbinel, when desirous of refuting the Christians, says—more than two hundred years elapsed between the destruction of the Temple and the death of Christ. How ignorant he was! Even if we were to withhold all confidence from the evangelists and apostles, yet profane writers would soon convict him of folly. But such is the barbarity of his nation, and so great their obstinacy, that they are ashamed of nothing. As far as we are concerned, we gather with sufficient clearness from the passage how the angel touched briefly upon the future slaughter of the city and the destruction of the Temple, lest the faithful should be overwhelmed with trials in consequence of Christ's death, and lest the unbelievers should be hardened through this occurrence. The interpretation of some writers respecting the people of the coming leader, as if Titus wished to spare the most beautiful city and preserve it untouched, seems to me too refined. I take it simply as a leader about to come with his army to destroy the city, and utterly to overthrow the Temple.

He afterwards adds, *Its end shall be in a deluge.* Here the angel removes all hope from the Jews, whose obstinacy might lead them to expect some advantage in their favour, for we are already aware of their great stupidity when in a state of desperation. Lest the faithful should indulge in the same feelings with the apostates and rebellious, he says, *The end of the leader*, Titus, *should be in a deluge ;* meaning, he should overthrow the city and national polity, and utterly put an end to the priesthood and the race, while all God's favours would at the same time be withdrawn. In this sense *his end should be in a deluge.* Lastly, *at the end of the war a most decisive desolation.* The word נחרצת, *nech-retzeth,* " a completion," can scarcely be taken otherwise than as a noun substantive. A plural noun follows, שממות, *shemmoth,* " of desolations" or " devastations ;" and taken verbally it means " definite or terminated laying waste." The most skilful grammarians allow that the former of these words may be taken substantively for " termination," as if the angel had said : Even if the Jews experience a variety of

fortune in battle, and have hopes of being superior to their
enemies, and of sallying out and prohibiting their foes from
entering the city ; nay, even if they repel them, still the end
of the war shall result in utter devastation, and their destruction is clearly defined.   Two points, then, are to be noticed
here ; first, all hope is to be taken from the Jews, as they
must be taught the necessity for their perishing ; and secondly, a reason is ascribed for this, namely, the determination of the Almighty and his inviolable decree.   It afterwards follows :—

27. And he shall confirm the covenant with many for one week: and in the midst of the week he shall cause the sacrifice and the oblation to cease, and for the overspreading of abominations he shall make *it* desolate, even until the consummation, and that determined shall be poured upon the desolate.	27. Et roborabit[1] fœdus multis, hebdomade una : et dimidia hebdomade quiescere faciet[2] sacrificium, et oblationem : et super extensionem[3] abominationum obstupescet,[4] et ad finem, et ad determinationem stillabit super stupentem.

The angel now returns to Christ.   We have explained why
he made mention of the coming slaughter ; first, to shew the
faithful that they had no reason for remaining in the body
of the nation in preference to being cut off from it ; and
next, to prevent the unbelievers from being satisfied with
their obstinacy and their contempt of their inestimable blessings, by their rejecting the person of Christ.   Thus this
clause was interposed concerning the future devastation of
the city and temple.   The angel now continues his discourse
concerning Christ by saying, *he should confirm the treaty
with many for one week.*   This clause answers to the former,
in which Christ is called a Leader.   Christ took upon him
the character of a leader, or assumed the kingly office, when
he promulgated the grace of God.   This is the confirmation
of the covenant of which the angel now speaks.   As we have
already stated, the legal expiation of other ritual ceremonies
which God designed to confer on the fathers is contrasted
with the blessings derived from Christ ; and we now gather
the same idea from the phrase, the confirmation of the

---

[1] Shall confirm.—*Calvin.*   [2] Shall make to cease.—*Calvin.*
[3] Or, expansion, verbally, wing.—*Calvin.*
[4] Or, shall stupify, for some take it transitively.—*Calvin.*

covenant. We know how sure and stable was God's covenant under the law; he was from the beginning always truthful, and faithful, and consistent with himself. But as far as man was concerned, the covenant of the law was weak, as we learn from Jeremiah. (Chap. xxxi. 31, 32.) I will enter into a new covenant with you, says he; not such as I made with your fathers, for they made it vain. We here observe the difference between the covenant which Christ sanctioned by his death and that of the Jewish law. Thus God's covenant is established with us, because we have been once reconciled by the death of Christ; and at the same time the effect of the Holy Spirit is added, because God inscribes the law upon our hearts; and thus his covenant is not engraven in stones, but in our hearts of flesh, according to the teaching of the Prophet Ezekiel. (Chap. xi. 19.) Now, therefore, we understand why the angel says, *Christ should confirm the covenant for one week*, and why that week was placed last in order. In this week will he confirm the covenant *with many*. But I cannot finish this exposition just now.

PRAYER.

Grant, Almighty God, since all the treasures of thy goodness and indulgence were so liberally diffused, when thine only-begotten Son appeared, and are now daily offered to us through the Gospel: Grant, I say, that we may not deprive ourselves of such important blessings by our ingratitude. May we embrace thy Son with true faith; and enjoy the benefit of the redemption which he has procured for us. Being cleansed and purged by his blood, may we be acceptable in thy sight, and venture with full and certain confidence to call thee Father. May we fly to thy pity and assistance in all our miseries and troubles, until at length thou shalt gather us into that eternal rest, which has been obtained for us through the blood of thine only-begotten Son.— Amen.

Lecture Fifty-Second.

In the last Lecture we explained how *Christ confirmed the covenant with many during the last week;* for he gathered

together the sons of God from their state of dispersion when
the devastation of the Church was so horrible and wretched.
Although the Gospel was not instantly promulgated among
foreign nations, yet Christ is correctly said *to have confirmed
the covenant with many*, as the nations were directly called
to the hope of salvation. (Matt. x. 5.)   Although he forbade the disciples to preach the Gospel then to either the
Gentiles or Samaritans, yet he taught them that many sheep
were dispersed abroad, and that the time at which God
would make one sheep-fold was at hand.   (John x. 16.)
This was fulfilled after his resurrection.   During his lifetime
he began to anticipate slightly the calling of the Gentiles,
and thus I interpret these words of the Prophet, *he will confirm the covenant with many.*   For I take the word "many"
here, רבים, *rebim*, comparatively, for the faithful Gentiles
united with the Jews.   It is very well known that God's
covenant was deposited by a kind of hereditary right with
the Israelites until the same favour was extended to the
Gentiles also.   Therefore Christ is said not only to have renewed God's covenant with a single nation, but generally
with the world at large.   I confess, indeed, the use of the
word *many* for all, as in the fifth chapter of the Epistle to
the Romans, and in other places, (ver. 19,) but there seems
to be a contrast between the ancient Church, included within
very narrow boundaries, and the new Church, which is extended over the whole world.   We know how many, formerly
strangers, have been called from the distant regions of the
earth by the gospel, and so joined in alliance to the Jews as
to be all in the same communion and all reckoned equally
sons of God.

The Prophet now subjoins, *He will make to cease the sacrifice and offering for half a week.*   We ought to refer this to
the time of the resurrection.   For while Christ passed
through the period of his life on earth, he did not put an end
to the sacrifices; but after he had offered himself up as a
victim, then all the rites of the law came to a close.   By the
words "sacrifice and offering" the Prophet implies all ceremonies, a part being put for the whole; as if he had said,
after Christ had offered up one eternal sacrifice, all the cus-

tomary ceremonies of the Law were abolished; for otherwise
Christ's death would have been superfluous, had he not put
an end to all the old shadows of the Law.   Although the
sacrifices were continued for many years after Christ's death,
yet we can no longer call them "legitimate," for no reason
can be offered why the sacrifices of the Law should be pleasing to God, except their reference to that heavenly pattern
which Moses saw on the mount.   (Exod. xxv. 40.)   Hence,
after Christ had appeared and expiated all the sins of the
world, it became necessary for all sacrifices to cease.   (Heb.
viii. 5.)   This is the Prophet's intention when he says, *Christ
should cause the sacrifices to cease for half a week.*   He embraces two points at the same time; first, Christ really and
effectually put an end to the sacrifices of the Law; and
secondly, he proved it to the world in the preaching of the
Gospel by his Apostles.   We observe, then, the sense in which
God testified by his Prophet *the cessation of sacrifices after
Christ's resurrection.*   The veil of the temple was then rent
in twain; true liberty was proclaimed; the faithful might then
feel themselves to be full grown men, and no longer subject
to that government of childhood to which they had submitted
under the Law.

The second clause of the verse now follows: we have read
it before, but we now repeat it to refresh the memory.   *And
over the extension,* or expansion, *of abominations he shall
cause astonishment,* or stupefaction; *and even to consumption
and determination he shall pour himself upon the desolator.*
Some translate, It shall be poured or shall distil: we shall
treat the words afterwards.   The passage is obscure, and may
be rendered in a variety of ways, and consequently interpreters differ much from each other.   Some take כנף, *knaph,*
"a wing," for a "cherub;" then they change the numbers
from singular to plural, and think the Prophet alludes to
winged cherubim.   This gives those who adopt this rendering a two-fold method of explaining it.   Some say the
abomination shall be *above the wings,* that is, the ark of the
covenant, because the temple was profaned, and the abomination was so ruinous that it destroyed even the very cherubim.   Others take it causally—the abominations shall be for

the sake of the cherubim. But I leave these subtleties, as they do not seem to me to have any solidity. Others, again, follow the Greek version, as quoted by Christ in the 24th chapter of Matthew and elsewhere, although Christ seems rather to refer to the 12th chapter of our Prophet. But as these two passages refer to the same abomination, I will not insist on this point; I will only remark upon the translation of one word. Those who translate "the abominations of desolation" treat the words of Daniel too carelessly, for there is no grammatical dependence of one word on the other, or, technically speaking, no *state of regimen.* The preferable opinion is that which considers the word "wing" to mean extremity or extension. Others, again, treat "extremity" as if it meant a state of despair; as if the angel had said, on account of the extremity of the abominations, as evils should accumulate upon evils without end till matters came to the last pitch of despair. Others, again, explain "the wing of abominations" more simply for the expansion itself, as if the angel had stated, the temple shall be openly profaned, and the pollution shall be apparent far and wide.

Interpreters differ again about the words מְשֹׁמֵם, *mesmem,* and שֹׁמֵם, *sem-em,* usually translated "make desolate," and "desolation." Some take the former transitively, and others as neuter; the latter signifies to destroy and lay waste, and also to wonder and be astonished. I think these two words ought to be used in the same sense; as if the Prophet had said, all shall be astonished at the extent of the abominations; when they shall perceive the temple worship swept away as by a deluge, then they shall be mightily astonished. He afterwards adds the calamity which commenced when God shewed the pollution of the temple *shall distil* or pour itself *upon him who is astonished.* We will treat the occurrence itself to enable us to understand the sense of the words better. I have no hesitation in stating God's wish to cut off all hope of restoration from the Jews, whom we know to have been blinded by a foolish confidence, and to have supposed God's presence confined to a visible temple. As they were thus firmly persuaded of the impossibility of God's ever departing from them, they ought to be deprived of their false confidence, and no longer deceive themselves by such flattering hopes.   Thus the temporary pollution of the temple was shewn by Ezekiel. (Chap. x. 18.)   For when the prophets constantly proclaimed the approach of their enemies to destroy both the city and temple, the greater part of the people derided them.   In their opinion this would overthrow all their confidence in God, as if he had been false to his word, in promising them perpetual rest on Mount Zion. (Ps. cxxxii. 14.)   Here Ezekiel relates his vision of God sitting in the temple—he then vanished, and the temple was deprived of all its glory. This was but temporary.

But we are now treating of a profanation of the temple, which should prove, if I may use the phrase, eternal and irreparable.   Without the slightest doubt, this prophecy was fulfilled when the city was captured and overthrown, and the temple utterly destroyed by Titus the son of Vespasian. This satisfactorily explains the events here predicted.   Some consider the word "abominations" to be used metaphorically, and to signify the overthrow of the city ; but this seems to me forced.   Others explain it of the statue of Caligula erected in the temple ; and others again, of the standard of Tiberius, who ordered the eagles to be placed on the pinnacle of the temple.   But I interpret it simply of that profanation which occurred after the gospel began to be promulgated, and of the punishment inflicted upon the Jews when they perceived their temple subject to the grossest forms of desecration, because they were unwilling to admit the only-begotten Son of God as its true glory.   Others, again, understand the impious doctrines and superstitions, as well as the perverse errors with which the priests were imbued. But I think the passage marks generally the change which took place directly after Christ's resurrection, when the obstinate impiety of the people was fully detected.   They were then summoned to repentance ; although they had endeavoured to extinguish all hope of salvation through Christ, yet God stretched forth his hand to them, and tried whether their wickedness was curable or not.   After the grace of Christ had been obstinately rejected, then the *extension of abominations* followed ; that is, God overwhelmed the temple in desecration, and caused its sanctity and glory to pass utterly away.   Although this vengeance did not take place immediately after the close of the last week, yet God sufficiently avenged their impious contempt of his gospel, and besides this, he shews how he had no longer need of any visible temple, as he had now dedicated the whole world to himself from east to west.

I now return again to the explanation of the words separately.   The angel says, *Upon the extension of abominations, astonishment,* or astonishing ; for some think it an adjective, and others a substantive ; but the meaning is, *all should be stupified,* or astonished.   I do not altogether object to the meaning already referred to—namely, rendering the word " wing" as " extremity ;" for the sense will then be—when the abominations come to their height or extremity ; and the sense is the same, if we use the word " expansion." God intends to shew us the extensive range of the pollutions,—upwards, downwards, and all around, they should obscure and bury the temple's glory.   Hence *on account of the extremity* or *expansion of abominations there shall be astonishment,* for all shall be amazed.   The angel seems to oppose this stupor to pride ; for the Jews were thoroughly persuaded of God's being strictly bound to themselves, and of the impossibility of his being torn away from his own temple where he had fixed his eternal dwelling-place.   He predicts the approach of this amazement instead of their supine security.

He adds next, *And unto consumption.*   כלה, *keleh,* signifies " end" and " perfection," as well as "destruction."   I take it here for consumption or destruction.   *It shall flow even unto astonishment.*   I have already remarked upon the words implying this astonishment ; slaughter, or something like it, ought to be understood before the verb.   There is no doubt at all about the Prophet's meaning.   He says this slaughter should be like a continual shower, consuming the whole people.   He speaks of the people as astonished by their calamities, and deprived of all hope of escape from them ; for the slaughter shall flow forth upon the astonished people.

Meanwhile he shews how foolishly the Jews indulged in pride, and how fallaciously they flattered themselves in supposing the Almighty permanently attached and bound to themselves and their visible temple. *The slaughter shall flow forth even to consumption,* meaning, until the whole people should perish. He adds also another noun, *even to a determined end.* We have already unfolded the meaning of this noun. Here the Prophet explains the cause of that eternal distinction which the Almighty had determined and decreed to be irrevocable.

CHAPTER TENTH.

The tenth chapter now follows, which Daniel introduces as a preface to the eleventh and twelfth. He relates the manner in which he was affected, when the last vision was presented to him. This he briefly explains as referring to events about to occur until the advent of Christ; and then he extends it to the final day of the resurrection. God had previously predicted to his Prophet the future condition of the Church from its return from Babylon to the advent of Christ, but in the eleventh chapter he more distinctly and clearly points with the finger to every event, as we shall perceive in proceeding with our comments. In this chapter Daniel assures us that the prophecies which he is about to discuss are worthy of more than ordinary attention; when the angel appeared, he was immediately affected with sorrow and grief; then he was one moment astonished, and the next cast down by the secret instinct of the Spirit; he lay like a dead man, till he was restored again and again by the angel of God. We shall observe these points as we proceed. He first says,—

1. In the third year of Cyrus king of Persia a thing was revealed unto Daniel, whose name was called Belteshazzar; and the thing *was* true, but the time appointed *was* long: and he understood the thing, and had understanding of the vision.

1. Anno tertio Cyri regis Persarum sermo revelatus fuit Danieli, cujus nomen Beltsazar, et veritas sermo,[1] et tempus magnum,[2] et intellexit sermonem, et intelligentia ei fuit in visione.

[1] That is, the word itself was most true.—*Calvin.*

[2] That is, although the time of its fulfilment should be long.—*Calvin.*

We observe the Prophet by no means content with the usual method of address, for the purpose of stirring up the attention of the pious, and of assuring them how worthy of special notice are the prophecies which follow. He marks the time, the third year of King Cyrus, as the Jews were then forbidden by a new edict to build their temple, although liberty to do so had been previously granted to them. He says, " *a word" was made known to him*, and he adds, *the word was true*, although the time was long. The time is treated more at length in the next verse. By saying, *a word was manifested to him*, he is thought to distinguish this prophecy from others, as it was not offered to him by either a dream or a vision. He uses the word מראה, *merah*, a " vision," at the end of this verse, but I do not see why the noun " word" should be taken in so restricted a sense. Interpreters, again, seek for a reason why he mentions his own name as Belteshazzar; some think it celebrates some honour to which he was raised; others treat it as commending the superiority of his abilities, as the name implies—descended from heaven; while others bring forward various conjectures. I have no hesitation in stating Daniel's wish to erect some illustrious monument of his vocation among the Medes, Persians, and Chaldeans. There, most probably, he was usually called Belteshazzar, and the name Daniel was almost buried in oblivion, and so he wished to testify to his being no stranger to the people of God, although he suffered a foreign name to be imposed upon him; for we have already seen the impossibility of his avoiding it. I therefore think the Prophet had no other intention than to render this prophecy notorious throughout all those regions in which he was well known under the name of Belteshazzar. Besides this, he wished to testify to his fellow-countrymen that he was not entirely cut off from the Church through being called Belteshazzar by the Chaldees; for he was always the same, and while banished from his country, was endued with the Spirit of prophecy, as we have previously seen. As the name of Daniel was almost unknown in Chaldea, he wished to make known the existence of both his names.

It now follows, *And there is truth in the word.* Daniel

here commends the certainty of the prophecy, as if he had said, I bring nothing before you but what is firm and stable, and whose actual performance the faithful ought confidently to expect. *There is truth in the word,* says he ; meaning, there was no room for doubting his assertions, for he had been divinely instructed in events which should be fulfilled in their own time. I understand what follows to mean, although the time should be long. Some of the Rabbis take צבא, *tzeba,* for the angelic hosts, which is quite absurd in this place. The word signifies " army" as well as an appointed time, but the exposition which they thrust upon the passage cannot stand its ground. The particle "and," as I think, must here be taken adversatively, in the sense of "although." Thus the Prophet proclaims our need of calmness of mind, and patient endurance, until God shall really complete and perform what he has verbally announced. This feeling ought to be extended to all prophecies. We know how ardent are the dispositions of men, and how hastily they are carried away by their own desires. We are compelled, therefore, to curb our impetuosity, if we wish to make progress in the school of God, and we must admit this general principle : If a promise should tarry, wait for it ; for it will surely come, and will not delay. (Hab. ii. 3.) Here Daniel affirms in a special sense, *the time will be long ;* this would restrain the faithful from rushing headlong with too much haste ; they would command their feelings, and remain tranquil till the full maturity of the period should arrive.

He afterwards adds, *He understood the vision ;* by this assertion he confirms the prophecy which he is about to explain, and thus assures us of his not uttering anything either perplexed or obscure. He also induces all the pious to hope for the exercise of the same understanding as he had himself attained ; as if he had said, I know what God wished ; he has explained to me by his angel various events which I will now set forth in their own order ; let every one peruse these prophecies attentively and reverently, and may God grant him the same gift of understanding, and lead him to certain knowledge. The information conveyed by the Prophet belongs to all the pious, to deter them from sluggishness and

despair.   At the first glance this teaching may appear very
obscure, but they must seek from the Lord that light of
manifestation which he deigned to bestow upon the Prophet
himself.   It now follows,—•

2. In those days I Daniel was mourning three full weeks.	2. Diebus illis ego Daniel dedi me luctui tribus hebdomadibus dierum.
3. I ate no pleasant bread, neithei came flesh nor wine in my mouth, neither did I anoint myself at all, till three whole weeks were fulfilled.	3. Panem deliciarum[1] non comedi: et caro et vinum non intravit in os meum: et unguendo non fui unctus donec impletæ sunt tres hebdomades dierum.

We gather from this passage why the angel appeared to
the Prophet in the third year of Cyrus.   He says, *he was
then in the greatest sorrow ;* and what was the cause of it?
At that period we know an interruption of the work of re-
building the temple and city to have taken place.   Cyrus
was gone to a distance ; he had set out for Asia Minor, and
was carrying on war with the Scythians.   His son Cambyses
was corrupted by his courtiers, and forbade the Jews to proceed with the re-building of their city and temple.   The
freedom of the people might then seem in vain.   For God
had promised the Jews in glowing language a return to their
country with their standards unfurled.   Besides this, we
know the splendid language of the prophets respecting the
glory of the second temple.   (Isa. lii. 12 ; Hag. ii. 9, and
elsewhere.)   When thus deprived of all opportunity of re-
building their temple, what could the Jews determine except
that they had been deluded after returning to their country,
and God had made a shew of disappointing expectations
which had turned out a mere laughing-stock and deception?
This was the cause of the grief and anxiety which oppressed
the holy Prophet.   We now understand why he mentions
the third year of Cyrus, as the circumstances of that period,
even at this day, point out the reason of his abstinence from
all delicacies.

He says, *He was in affliction for three weeks of days.*   The
Hebrews often use the phrase weeks or times of days for
complete periods.   Very possibly, Daniel uses the word
"days" here, to prevent a mistake which might easily occur

[1] " Delicate ;" verbally, " of desires."—*Calvin.*

through his so lately speaking of weeks of years. The distinction is thus more clearly marked between the seventy weeks of years previously explained, and these three weeks of days here mentioned. And the angel appears to have dwelt purposely on the completion of these three weeks, as this was the third year of King Cyrus's reign. He says, *He did not eat delicate bread, and he abstained from flesh and wine*, implying his practice of uniting fasting with mourning. The holy Prophet is here represented as freely using flesh and other food, while the Church of God remained in a state of tranquillity ; but when there was danger, lest the few who had returned home should be diminished, and many were still suffering at Babylon those grievous calamities to which they were subject during their exile from neighbouring enemies, then the Prophet abstained from all delicacies. In the beginning of this book, he had stated the contentment of himself and his companions with bread, and pulse, and water for meat and drink. This statement is not contrary to the present passage. There is no necessity to fly to that refinement, which allows an old man to use wine, which he never touched in his youth and the flower of his age. This comment is far too frigid. We have shewn, how at the beginning of his exile the only reason for the Prophet's abstaining from the delicacies of the palace, was the desire of preserving himself free from all corruption. For what was the object of the king's designing shrewdness in commanding Daniel and his companions to be treated thus daintily and luxuriously ? He wished them to forget their nation by degrees, and to adopt the habits of the Chaldeans, and to be withdrawn by such enticements from the observance of the law, from the worship of God, and from the exercises of piety. When Daniel perceived the artful manner in which he and his companions were treated, he requested to be fed upon pulse, he refused to taste the king's wine, and despised all his dainties. His reason, therefore, concerned the exigencies of the times, as I then pointed out at full length. Meanwhile, we need not hesitate to suppose, that after giving this proof of his constancy, and escaping from these snares of the devil and of the Chaldean monarch, he lived rather freely than frugally, and made use of better bread, and flesh, and wine than before. This passage, then, though it asserts his abstinence from flesh and wine, need not imply actual fasting. Daniel's method of living was clearly after the common practice of the Chaldeans, and by no means implies the rejection of wine, or flesh, or viands of any kind. When he says, *he did not eat delicate bread*, this was a symbol of sorrow and mourning, like abstinence from flesh and wine. Daniel's object in rejecting delicate bread and wine during those three weeks, was not merely the promotion of temperance, but suppliantly to implore the Almighty not to permit a repetition of those sufferings to his Church under which it had previously laboured. But I cannot here treat at any length the object and use of fasting. I have done so elsewhere; even if I wished to do so, I have no time now. To-morrow, perhaps, I may say a few words on the subject, and then proceed with the rest of my observations.

PRAYER.

Grant, Almighty God, since thou settest before us so remarkable an example in thy holy Prophet, whom thou didst adorn in so many ways that he wrestled to even extreme old age with various and almost innumerable trials, and yet was never mentally broken down : Grant us to be endowed with the same untiring fortitude. May we proceed in the course of our holy calling without the slightest despondency through whatever may happen. When we see thy Church upon the brink of ruin, and its enemies plotting desperately for its destruction, may we constantly look for that liberty which thou hast promised. May we strive with unbroken courage, until at length we shall be discharged from our warfare, and gathered into that blessed rest which we know to be laid up for us in heaven, through Christ our Lord.—Amen.

Lecture Fifty-Third.

WE yesterday stated the reason why Daniel abstained from flesh and wine for three weeks. It was the sorrowful and depressed condition of the Church while the Jews were prohibited from building their Temple. We have stated the fallacious views of those who think him to have been always so abstemious in the flower of his age. Though he lived on bread and pulse, it was only for the purpose of remaining pure without any leaning towards the habits of the Chaldees, as it was the king's design to withdraw both himself and his companions from God's people, as if they had originally sprung from Chaldea. That, therefore, was but a temporary reason. But he now states, *He had not tasted delicate bread*, that is, made of fine flour, *and had not tasted either wine or flesh*, during the time in which the building of the Temple had been impeded. We must diligently notice this; for many celebrate fasting as if it were a principal part of the worship of God. They think it an act of obedience peculiarly pleasing to God. But this is a gross error, since fasting by itself ought to be treated as a matter unimportant and indifferent. It deserves no praise unless with reference to its object. Now the objects of fasting are various; the principal one is this, to enable the faithful suppliantly to deprecate God's wrath with the solemn testimony of their repentance, and to stimulate each other to more fervour in their prayers. Ordinary daily prayers do not require fasting; but when any great necessity presses upon us, that exercise is added by way of help, to increase the alertness and fervour of our minds in the pouring forth of prayer. For this reason the Scriptures often connect fasting with sorrow, and Daniel here follows the usual practice. We perceive then the reason of his rejecting all delicacies in meat and drink, through his desire to withdraw himself entirely from all hinderances, and to become more intent upon his prayers. I now touch but briefly upon fasting, because I cannot stop on casual passages like these. We should notice, however, how foolishly and absurdly fasting is observed in these days among the Papists, who think they have discharged that duty by eating but once in the day, and abstaining from flesh. The rule of fasting among the Papists is, to avoid flesh and not to partake of either supper or dinner. But real fasting requires something far different from this, namely, perfect abstinence from all delicacies. For Daniel extends this fasting even to bread. He says, *He did not taste wine*, meaning he abstained from all wine. Then, as to the word "flesh," he does not mean only that of oxen, or calves, or lambs, or fowls, or birds in general, but all food except bread is included under the term flesh. For Daniel did not trifle childishly with God, as the Papists do at this day, who feed without any religious scruple on the best and most exquisite viands, so long as they avoid flesh. This appears more clearly from the statement —*he did not eat pleasant bread*, that is, made of fine flour or the very best of the wheat. He was content with plain bread to satisfy his necessities. This abundantly proves the superstition of those who distinguish between flesh, and eggs, and fish. Now, fasting consists in this— the imposition of a bridle upon men's lusts, eating only sparingly and lightly what is absolutely necessary, and being content with black bread and water. We now understand how fasting in this and similar passages is not taken for that temperance which God recommends to us throughout the whole course of our lives. The faithful ought to be habitually temperate, and by frugality, to observe a continual fast; they ought not to indulge in immoderate food and drink, and in luxurious habits, lest they should debilitate the mind and weaken the body by such indulgences. As a mark of mourning and an exercise of humility, the faithful may impose upon themselves the law of fasting beyond their ordinary habits of sobriety, when they feel any sign of God's wrath, and desire to stimulate themselves to fervour in prayer, according to our former statements, and to confess themselves in the face of the whole world guilty before the tribunal of God. Such was Daniel's intention in not permitting himself to taste pleasant bread, or to drink wine, or to eat flesh. It now follows,—

4. And in the four and twentieth day of the first month, as I was by the side of the great river, which *is* Hiddekel.

4. Die vicessima quarta mensis primi, ego fui super ripam fluvii magni, nempe Hidekel.[1]

[1] The demonstrative pronoun is here used for the sake of explanation. —*Calvin.*

Daniel now narrates the acceptance of his prayers, because an angel appeared and instructed him in the future condition of the Church. Without the slightest doubt, the fasting already described was a preparation for prayer, as we have stated before, and as we may gather from many passages of Scripture, especially from the assertion of Christ, where he says, the demon could not be cast out except by prayer and fasting. (Matt. xvii. 21.) Daniel, therefore, did not abstain from all food, and wine, and luxuries, with the view of rendering any obedience to God, but of testifying his own grief: then he was anxious to rouse himself to prayer, and by that mark of humility, to prepare far better for repentance. He says now—*on the twenty-fourth day of the first month*—meaning March, the first month of the Jewish year—*he stood on the bank of the great river*, namely, the Tigris. The word דִּי, *yid*, is metaphorically used for the bank, and interpreters are agreed in identifying *Hidekel* with the Tigris. Geographers state the name of this river to be in some places, and especially near its fountain, *Digliton*, which answers to the common Hebrew name Hidekel. Without doubt, this river is called Phison by Moses, since the Tigris has three names among profane nations. Its usual name is Tigris, and in one part of its course it becomes the Hidekel, and has also the names of *Pasitigris* and *Phasis*, which is equivalent to Phison. The Prophet relates, *his standing on the bank of this great river.* It is uncertain whether he was then in that part of the world, or whether God set before him the prospect of the river, as we have seen elsewhere. I rather incline to the opinion of his being rapt in the prophetic spirit, and obtaining a vision of the river, and not to his being really there. Possibly, that province might have been placed under his government in the course of the great changes which took place in those times. While Belshazzar lived, he could not have been at Susan, and so we were compelled to explain his former language by the prophetic rapture. And as to the present passage, I shall not quarrel with the opinion of any one who supposes Daniel to have dwelt in that district, but, as I have stated before, I think it most probable, that this spectacle was offered to the holy Prophet when far distant from the river's bank, and only able to behold it in spirit. Very possibly, at the beginning of this month he commenced his abstinence from flesh, and food, and all pleasant viands, and then relaxed his fast for three weeks, as he here marks the date on the twenty-fourth day. But I leave this doubtful, through the impossibility of ascertaining the point with certainty. Let us now proceed,—

5. Then I lifted up mine eyes, and looked, and behold a certain man clothed in linen, whose loins *were* girded with fine gold of Uphaz:

6. His body also *was* like the beryl, and his face as the appearance of lightning, and his eyes as lamps of fire, and his arms and his feet like in colour to polished brass, and the voice of his words like the voice of a multitude.

5. Et levavi oculos meos, et vidi, et ecce vir unus indutus lineis, *vestibus scilicet,* et lumbi ejus accincti auro Uphaz.

6. Et corpus ejus sicut tharsis, et facies ejus quasi aspectus fulguris, et oculi ejus quasi lampades ignis: et brachia ejus, et pedes ejus quasi conspectus æris politi,[1] et vox sermonum ejus quasi vox multitudinis.[2]

As to the word *Uphaz,* some think it to be a pearl or precious stone, and they take the word כתם, *kethem,* which precedes it, for pure gold. Others take *uphaz* adjectively, for pure gold : I do not suppose it to be an epithet, but I rather subscribe to the view of those who understand it as the proper name of a place, because this view is in accordance with the phraseology of the tenth chapter of Jeremiah. There is another opinion which is unsuitable : Uphaz is said to be derived from the noun Phaz, and is called " pure," the letter Aleph being redundant. The above mentioned passage of Jeremiah is sufficient to prove my assertion, that it signifies a certain region ; and so some have translated it by ophir. The word תרשיש, *tharsis,* is thought to mean chrysolite : some think it denotes the colour of the sea, and then, by a figure of speech, take it generally for any sea. It is also said to mean sky-coloured.

Daniel now begins to relate the manner in which the vision was offered to him. He says, when he stood on the bank of the river a man appeared to him, different from the common order of men. He calls him a man, but shews him

---

[1] Some translate, burning brass.—*Calvin.*

[2] Some take חמון, *chemon,* for noise or tumult.—*Calvin.*

to be endued, or adorned with attributes which inspire full confidence in his celestial glory. We have elsewhere stated, how angels are called men, whenever God wished them to put on this outward form. The name of men is therefore used metaphorically whenever they assumed that form by God's command, and now Daniel speaks after the accustomed manner. Meanwhile, some absurdly imagine angels to have been really men, since they assumed this appearance, and were clothed in a human body. We ought not to believe them to be really men, because they appeared under a human form. Christ, indeed, was really man, in consequence of his springing from the seed of Abraham, David, and Adam. But as regards angels, God clothes them for a single day or a short period in bodies, for a distinct purpose and a special use. Wherefore, I assert the gross error of those who suppose angels to become men, as often as they are corporeally visible in a human form. Still they may be called men, because Scripture accommodates itself to our senses, as we know sufficiently well. Daniel therefore says, *he saw a man*, and afterwards distinguishes him from the human race, and shews fixed and conspicuous marks inscribed upon him, which discover him to be an angel sent down from heaven, and not a mere earthly mortal. Some philosophize with subtlety on the word *raised*, as if Daniel so raised his eyes upwards as to be unconscious of all earthly objects; but this does not appear to me sufficiently certain. The Prophet wishes to impress the certainty of the vision; not only was his mind composed and collected, but he applied all his senses to the one object before him— the attainment of some consolation from God. The Prophet, therefore, denotes the earnestness of his desire, for when he looked round he found himself subject to many cares and anxieties. Again, with reference to the marks by which Daniel might infer the object of his vision to be neither earthly nor mortal, he first says, *he was clothed in linen*. This kind of garment was common enough among the people of the East. Those regions are remarkably warm, and their inhabitants need not protect themselves against the cold, as we are necessarily compelled to do. They seldom wear woollen clothing. But on special occasions when they wish to use more splendid attire, they put on linen tunics, as we learn not only from many passages of Scripture, but also from profane writers. Hence I take this passage as if Daniel had said, the man appeared to him in splendid apparel. For בדּים, *bedim*, is supposed not to mean common linen, but a more exquisite kind of fabric.. This is one point.

He next says, *He was girt with pure gold;* that is, with a golden belt. The Orientals were formerly accustomed to gird themselves with belts or girdles, as their garments were long and reached almost down to the feet. Hence it became necessary for those who wished to move expeditiously to gird themselves with belts. When the angel appeared with raiment of this kind, the difference between himself and other men was displayed to the Prophet. Some refer the linen garment to the priesthood of Christ, and treat the girdle as an emblem of vigour. But these are mere refinements, and seem to me destitute of all reality. I therefore am content with the simple opinion on which I have touched, namely, this form of clothing distinguished the angel from ordinary mortals. But this will appear clearer from the following verse. For Daniel says, *His body was sky-coloured,* or like the precious stone called beryl, of a golden hue. Without doubt, the Prophet beheld something different from a human form, for the purpose of his clearly ascertaining the vision not to be a man, but an angel in the form of man. I leave the allegory here, although it proceeds through the whole verse. I am aware of the plausible nature of allegories, but when we reverently weigh the teachings of the Holy Spirit, those speculations which at first sight pleased us exceedingly, vanish from our view. I am not captivated by these enticements myself, and I wish all my hearers to be persuaded of this,—nothing can be better than a sober treatment of Scripture. We ought never to fetch from a distance subtle explanations, for the true sense will, as I have previously expressed it, flow naturally from a passage when it is weighed with maturer deliberation. He says, *His face was like the appearance of lightning.* This, again, assured

the Prophet of his being more than an earthly mortal.   His
eyes would lead to the same conclusion; they were *like
lamps of fire;* then *his arms and feet were like polished* or
burnished *brass;* lastly, *the voice of his words was the voice
of a tumult, or noise, or multitude.*   The sum of the whole
is this,—the angel, though clad in human form, possessed
certain conspicuous marks by which God separated him from
the common crowd of men.   Thus Daniel clearly perceived
the divine mission of the angel, and God wished to establish
the confidence and certainty of those prophecies which will
afterwards follow in the eleventh chapter.   Let us proceed:

7. And I Daniel alone saw the vision: for the men that were with me saw not the vision; but a great quaking fell upon them, so that they fled to hide themselves.

7. Et vidi ego Daniel solus visionem, et viri qui erant mecum, non viderunt visionem, imo[1] terror magnus irruit super eos, et fugerunt in latebras.[2]

He pursues his own narrative in which he appears prolix,
but not without design.   This prophecy required all kinds
of sanction for the purpose of inspiring unhesitating confidence in it, not only with the Jews of that generation, but
with all posterity.   Although the predictions of the eleventh
chapter have been fulfilled, yet their utility is manifest to us as
follows: first, we behold in them God's perpetual care of his
Church; secondly, we observe the pious never left destitute
of any necessary consolation; and lastly, we perceive, as in a
glass or in a living picture, the Spirit of God speaking in the
prophets, as I have observed before, and shall have occasion to
remark again.   Daniel, therefore, has good reasons for impressing us with the certainty of the vision, and with whatever
tends to prove its reality.   He says, *I alone saw the vision; but
the men who were with me did not see it;* just as the companions
of Paul did not hear Christ's voice, but only a confused sound:
they did not understand his language, as Paul alone was
permitted to comprehend it.   (Acts ix. 7.)   This is related
to promote belief in the prophecy.   Daniel's power of hearing was not superior to his companions', but God intended
to address him alone.   Thus the voice, although like the

[1] The word אבל, *abel,* " but," is put adversatively; it is not a simple
affirmation.— *Calvin.*
[2] Verbally, to hide themselves.—*Calvin.*

voice of a multitude, did not penetrate the ears of those who were with him. He alone was the recipient of these prophecies, as he alone was endued with the power of predicting future events, and of consoling and exhorting the pious to give them a knowledge of futurity even to the last day. Should any one inquire how he carried his companions with him while he was probably lying on his bed at a distance from the bank of the river, the answer is easy. He had his domestics with him ; the river's bank only existed in the vision, and he was carried completely out of himself, and thus his family would be acquainted with the ecstasy without being aware of the cause. Daniel then continued at his own home, and only visited the bank of the river during the vision ; although many witnesses were present, God struck them all with astonishment, while Daniel only perceived what is afterwards narrated. God deemed him worthy of this singular honour to fit him to become a teacher and instructor to others. *The men who were with me,* says he, *saw not the vision ; but a great terror fell upon them.* This distinction, as I have stated, shews Daniel to have been selected as the sole listener to the angel's voice, and as receiving the information which he was afterwards to convey to others. Meanwhile, God intended many witnesses to notice Daniel's entire freedom from any delusion through either a dream or a passing imagination. *His companions,* then, *were frightened.* This terror proves the Prophet to have been divinely instructed and not to have laboured under any delirium. *They fled,* therefore, *into hiding-places.* It afterwards follows :—

| 8. Therefore I was left alone, and saw this great vision, and there remained no strength in me: for my comeliness was turned in me into corruption, and I retained no strength. | 8. Et ego relictus fui solus, et vidi visionem magnam hanc, et non fuit residuum in me robur,[1] atque etiam decor[2] meus eversus fuit super me, *in me,* ad corruptionem,[3] et non retinui vigorem. |

This language all tends to the same purpose—to assure us that Daniel did not write his own comments with rashness, but was truly and clearly taught by the angel on all the

[1] Or, no vigour was left in me.—*Calvin.*
[2] Verbally, and comeliness.—*Calvin.*
[3] That is, to vanishing away.—*Calvin.*

points which he committed to writing, and thus all hesitation is removed as to our embracing what we shall afterwards perceive, as he is a faithful interpreter of God. He first states *he saw a vision.* He had said so before, but he repeats it to produce a due impression ; he calls the vision *great,* to arouse our attention to its importance. He adds, *he was deprived of all vigour ;* as if he had been rendered lifeless by the blast of the Spirit. Thus we gather the object of the exhibition of all these outward signs ; they not only bring before us God speaking by the mouth of his angel, but they prepared the Prophet himself, and trained him to reverence. God, however, does not terrify his sons, as if our disquiet was with him an object of delight, but solely because it is profitable for us ; for unless our carnal feelings were utterly subdued, we should never be fit to receive improvement. This necessarily requires violence, on account of our inborn perverseness; and this is the reason why the Prophet was reduced to this state of lifelessness. Even *my comeliness,* or beauty, or appearance, *was turned to corruption;* meaning, my deformity was similar to that induced by death. He adds lastly, *I did not retain my vigour.* He uses a variety of phrases to shew himself depressed by the heavenly blast, for but a slight amount of vitality remained, and he was scarcely preserved from actual death. We ought to learn to transfer this instruction to ourselves, not by the vanishing of our vigour or the changing of our appearance whenever God addresses us, but by all our resistance giving way, and all our pride and loftiness becoming prostrate before God. Finally, our carnal disposition ought to be completely reduced to nothing, as true docility will never be found in us until all our senses are completely mortified ; for we must always remember how hostile all our natural thoughts are to the will of God. It afterwards follows ;—but I cannot proceed further to-day ; I must delay my comment on the next verses till to-morrow.

PRAYER.

Grant, Almighty God, as thou didst formerly appear to Daniel thy holy servant, and to the other prophets, and by their doctrine didst render thy glory conspicuous to us at this day, that we may reverently approach and behold it. When we have become entirely devoted to thee, may those mysteries which it has pleased thee to offer by means of their hand and labours, receive from us their due estimation. May we be cast down in ourselves and be raised by hope and faith towards heaven; when prostrate before thy face, may we so conduct ourselves in the world, as in the interval to become free from all the depraved desires and passions of our flesh, and dwell mentally in heaven. Then at length may we be withdrawn from this earthly warfare, and arrive at that celestial rest which thou hast prepared for us, through the same Jesus Christ our Lord.—Amen.

Lecture Fifty=Fourth.

9. Yet heard I the voice of his words: and when I heard the voice of his words, then was I in a deep sleep on my face, and my face toward the ground.

10. And, behold, an hand touched me, which set me upon my knees and *upon* the palms of my hands.

9. Et audivi vocem sermonum ejus, et cum audirem vocem sermonum ejus, tunc ego fui sopitus super faciem meam,[1] et facies mea in terram, *projecta fuit scilicet.*

10. Et ecce manus tetigit me,[2] et movere me fecit super genua mea, et palmas, *aut volas,* manuum mearum.

In yesterday's Lecture Daniel confessed himself astonished at the sight of the angel, and deprived of all inward strength. He afterwards adds, *On hearing the sound of his words he threw himself on the ground;* for this is the sense of the ninth verse, as we have just read it. He represents himself as being *in a swoon,* and in the unconscious state which usually occurs when all our senses are paralyzed by excessive fear. While lying thus senselessly on the ground, *Behold,* he adds, *hands touched me, and placed me upon my knees and the palms of my hands.* He mentions his being partially raised by the angel, not only through the sound of his voice, but by the touch of his hand. He implies that he was not yet raised to either the standing or sitting posture; he was only placed upon his knees with his hands upon the ground, this posture being the sign of his dejection. Thus he was partially relieved, and fear no longer seized upon either his mind or his limbs. From this passage we should learn that when prostrated by the voice of God, we cannot be restored

---

[1] That is, I fell on my face as if asleep.—*Calvin.*

[2] Touched upon me; but the ב, *beth,* is superfluous.—*Calvin*

otherwise than by his strength. We know the hand to be
the symbol of strength. Unless God himself stretches out
his hand to us, we shall always remain apparently dead.
This is one lesson. The Prophet next adds the address of
the angel to him,—

11. And he said unto me, O Daniel, a man greatly beloved, understand the words that I speak unto thee, and stand upright: for unto thee am I now sent. And when he had spoken this word unto me, I stood trembling.	11. Et loquutus est ad me, Daniel vir desideriorum intellige, *attentus sis,* ad verba quæ loquor tecum et sta super stare tuum: quia nunc missus sum ad te. Et cum loqueretur mecum sermonem hunc, steti tremens, *vel, trepidus.*

He here relates how he was strengthened by the angel's
exhortation. He now begins to raise himself from his former position, and the angel now orders him to raise his
drooping spirits, and calls him *a man greatly beloved.* We
have previously discussed this word, which some refer to
Daniel's zeal, and take it passively, because he was inspired
with a most invincible ardour through anxiety for the common welfare of the Church. I rather incline to the opposite
view, thinking him so called through the force of his desires,
because he was dear and precious to God. By this epithet
the angel wished to animate the holy Prophet, and to calm
and quiet his mind for listening to what he so ardently expected. *Understand,* therefore, he says, or attend to, *the
words which I shall speak to thee, and stand upright.* Some
translate it, in thy station, but " station" does not refer to
the position of the body. I have already shewn how the
Prophet was not now quite prostrate; his face was towards
the earth, while he was supported by his hands and knees ;
and we now perceive him raised another step. This doctrine
is profitable to us, because many think themselves utterly'
neglected and deserted by God, unless they immediately re-
gain their mental vigour. But God does not all at once restore to life those whom he has rendered all but lifeless, but
he conveys new life by degrees, and inspires the dead with
fresh animation. We perceive this to have been done in
Daniel's case. Therefore I am never surprised when God
raises us gradually by distinct steps, and cures our infirmity
by degrees ; but if even a single drop of his virtue is supplied

to us, we should be content with this consolation, until he should complete what he has begun within us. Lastly, this passage unfolds to us how God works in his servants, by not rendering them perfect all at once, but allowing some infirmity to remain until the completion of his own work.

Daniel afterwards adds, *When he heard this address, he stood up.* We here observe the effect and fruit of the angel's exhortation, as Daniel no longer needed to support himself on his hands and knees. He could stand upright, although he adds, *he remained trembling.* Although thus erect in body, he was not entirely free from feelings of dread ; and, though he stood upon his feet, he was not yet relieved from all trepidation, even at the angel's command. This confirms my previous remark—God leaves in his servants some signs of fear, to remind them of their infirmity ; they venture to raise themselves by hope above the world, but they do not forget they are but dust and ashes, and so restrain themselves within the bounds of humility and modesty. It now follows :—

12. Then said he unto me, Fear not, Daniel ; for from the first day that thou didst set thine heart to understand, and to chasten thyself before thy God, thy words were heard, and I am come for thy words.	12. Et dixit ad me, Ne timeas Daniel, quia a die primo quo adjecisti cor tuum ad intelligendum, et affligendum te, *vel, humiliandum,* coram facie Dei tui, exaudita sunt verba tua : et ego veni in verbis tuis, *hoc est, propter verba tua.*

By the angel's commanding the Prophet to be of a serene and tranquil mind, we gather the continuance of his fright, and his being as yet unable to listen with composure. And yet this trembling improved his teachableness. Without the slightest doubt, God desired to prepare his servant in this way to render him more attentive to his disciples, and yet this very terror prevented Daniel from summoning all his senses to listen to the address of the angel. The remedy is exhibited in these words, *O Daniel, fear not.* The angel did not wish to remove all fear from the Prophet's mind, but rather to calm it, lest his trembling should prevent him from giving due attention to the prophecies which we shall soon discuss. I have already said enough on the subject of this address. As God knows fear to be useful to us, he does not wish us to be entirely free from it, as too great self-confidence would immediately produce slothfulness and pride. God, therefore, wishes our fears to restrain us like a bridle, but meanwhile he moderates this dread in his servants, lest their minds become stricken and disturbed, and thus disabled from approaching him with calmness.

The angel adds, *From the first day on which thou didst begin to apply thy mind to understanding, and to afflict thyself before God, thy prayers were heard.* This reason sufficiently shews in what sense and with what intention the angel forbade the Prophet's fears—*because*, says he, *thy prayers have been heard.* He was unwilling to banish all fear, but he offered some hope and consolation; and relying on this expectation, he might wait for the revelation which he so earnestly desired. He states *his prayers to have been heard from the time of his applying his mind to understanding, and from his afflicting himself before God.* These two points may be noticed: first, by the word "understanding" the angel informs us of God's being propitious to the prayers of his servant, because they were sincere and legitimate. For what spectacle did Daniel behold? He saw the condition of the Church entirely confused, and he desired the communication of some mark of favour, which might assure him of God's being still mindful of his covenant, and of his not despising those wretched Israelites whom he had adopted. As this was the object of the Prophet's prayer, he so far obtained his request, and the angel bears witness to God's being entreated by him. We are taught then by this passage, if we are anxious for our supplications to be both heard and approved by God, not to give way to those foolish lusts and appetites, which solicit and entice us. We ought to observe the rule here prescribed by the angel, and fashion our entreaties according to God's will. We know, says John, that if we ask anything according to his will, he will hear us. (1 John v. 14.) This is the first point. The second is the addition of penitence to fervour in devotion, when the angel says, *Daniel's mind was afflicted* or humbled. A second condition of true prayer is here set before us, when the faithful humble themselves before God, and being touched with

true penitence, pour out their groans before him.   The angel,
therefore, shews how Daniel obtained his requests, by suppliantly afflicting himself before God.   He did not utter
prayers for the Church in a mere formal manner, but as we
have previously seen, he united fasting with entreaty, and
abstained from all delicacies.   For this reason God did not
reject his petitions. He says, *before thy God ;* this expression
of the angel's implying that the Prophet's supplication sprang
from true faith.   The prayers of the impious, on the other
hand, always repel the Almighty, and they can never be
sure of his being propitious to them.   In consequence of the
hesitation and vacillation of unbelievers, this testimony to
true faith is set before Daniel—*he prayed to his own God.*
Whoever approaches God, says the Apostle, (Heb. xi. 6,)
ought to acknowledge his existence, and his being easily
entreated by all those who seek and invoke him.   We ought
diligently to notice this, as this fault is most manifest in all
ages,—men often pray to God, but yet through their hesitation they pour forth their petitions into the air.   They do
not realize God as their Father.   Another passage also reminds us how useless is the hope of obtaining anything by
prayer, if we are agitated and tossed about in our emotions.
(James i. 6, 7.)   Unless faith shine forth, we must not feel
surprise at those who call upon God losing all their labour
through their profanation of his name.   Lastly, by this expression, the angel shews us how Daniel's prayer was founded
on faith ; he had not sought God with rashness, but was
clearly persuaded of his being reckoned among the sons of
God. *He prayed,* therefore, *to his own God,* and for this
reason, his petitions were heard.   Then the angel adds, *he
came at his words ;* as it is said in the Psalms. (Ps. cxlv.
19.) God inclines with desire towards those who fear him ;
and in this sense the angel waits upon Daniel.   It now follows,—

13. But the prince of the king- dom of Persia withstood me one and twenty days: but, lo, Michael, one of the chief princes, came to help	13. Et Princeps regni Persarum stetit coram me, *vel, e regione,* viginti diebus et uno. Et ecce Michael unus principum primorum[1] venit ad opem

----

[1] That is, one of the chief leaders. — *Calvin.*

me; and I remained there with the   ferendam mihi,[1] et ego residuus[2] fui
kings of Persia.   apud reges Persarum, *vel, Persidis.*

The angel now assigns a reason why he did not appear at
once, and at the very first moment to the Prophet, who
might complain as follows,—"What treatment is this, to
suffer me to consume away through grief for so long a
period?" for Daniel had remained through three weeks in
succession in the severest affliction. God had heard him,
indeed, from the very first day ; how, then, could he still
behold this wretched man thus prostrate in mourning? why
did not God cause it to appear openly and really that he had
not prayed in vain? The angel now meets this objection,
and shews how he had been otherwise occupied in promoting
the Prophet's welfare. We ought carefully to notice this,
because delay often disturbs us when God does not immediately extend his help, and for a long time hides from us
the fruit of our prayers. Whenever our passions burst forth
with a strong impetuosity, and we easily manifest tokens of
impatience, we must notice this expression of the angel, for
our prayers may be already heard while God's favour and
mercy is concealed from us. The experience of Daniel is
daily fulfilled in every member of the Church, and without
the slightest doubt the same discipline is exercised towards
all the pious. This is our practical reflection. We must
notice, secondly, God's condescension in deigning to explain
himself by the angel to his own Prophet. He offers a reason
for the delay of the angel's return, and the cause of this
hinderance was, as I have already stated, his regard for the
safety of his elect people. The wonderful clemency of the
Almighty is here proved by his offering an excuse so
graciously to his Prophet, because he did not shew himself
easily entreated on the very day when prayer was offered to
him. But we ought to derive another practical benefit from
the passage,—God does not cease to regard us with favour
even while he may not please to make us conscious of it, for
he does not always place it before our eyes, but rather hides
it from our view. We infer from this, God's constant care

---

[1] Or, to strengthen me.— *Calvin.*
[2] That is, was left.—*Calvin.*

for our safety, although not exhibited exactly in the way which our minds may conceive and comprehend. God surpasses all our comprehension in the way in which he provides for our safety, as the angel here relates his mission in quite another direction, and yet in the service of the Church. It now appears how Daniel obtained an answer to his prayers from the very first day of their offering, and yet remained unconscious of it, until God sent him some consolation in the midst of his troubles. A very different interpretation of this verse has been proposed, for some expounders think the angel sent into Persia to protect that kingdom. There is some probability in this explanation, because the Israelites were still under the Persian monarchy, and God may have furnished some assistance to the kings of Persia for the sake of his own people. But I think the angel stood in direct opposition and conflict against Cambyses, to prevent him from raging more fiercely against God's people. He had promulgated a cruel edict, preventing the Jews from building their temple, and manifesting complete hostility to its restoration. He would not have been satisfied with this rigorous treatment, had not God restrained his cruelty by the aid and hand of the angel.

If we weigh these words judiciously, we shall readily conclude, that the angel fought rather against the king of the Persians than for him. *The prince*, says he, *of the kingdom of the Persians*, meaning Cambyses, with his father Cyrus, crossed over the sea and contended with the Scythians, as well as in Asia Minor. The prince of the kingdom of Persia was ranged against him, as if he had said,—He detained me from reaching you, but it was for the good of your race, for had not God used me in assisting you, his cruelty would have been aggravated, and your condition would have been utterly desperate. You perceive, then, how there has been no want of zeal on my part, for God was never deaf to your entreaties. *The prince of the kingdom of the Persians stood against me for twenty-one days ;* meaning, from the period of your beginning to pour forth your prayers before God, I have never flinched from any attack or assault, by which I might defend thy people. *The prince of the kingdom of the Per-*

sians stood against me: meaning, he was so hot against the Israelites, as to intend to pour forth the very dregs of his wrath, unless the help which I afforded you had been divinely interposed.

He adds next, *Behold! Michael, one of the chief leaders or princes, came to strengthen me.* Some think the word Michael represents Christ, and I do not object to this opinion. Clearly enough, if all angels keep watch over the faithful and elect, still Christ holds the first rank among them, because he is their head, and uses their ministry and assistance to defend all his people. But as this is not generally admitted, I leave it in doubt for the present, and shall say more on the subject in the twelfth chapter. From this passage we may clearly deduce the following conclusion,— angels contend for the Church of God both generally and for single members, just as their help may be needed. This we know to be a part of the occupation of angels, who protect the faithful according to Psalm xxxiv. (ver. 8.) They fix their camp in a circuit round them. God, therefore, plants his angels against all the endeavours of Satan, and all the fury of the impious who desire to destroy us, and are ever plotting for our complete ruin. If God were not to protect us in this way, we should be utterly undone. We are aware of Satan's horrible hatred to us, and of the mighty fury with which he assails us ; we know how skilfully and variously he contrives his artifices ; we know him as the prince of this world, dragging and hurrying the greater part of mankind along with him, while they impiously pour forth their threats against us. What prevents Satan from daily absorbing a hundred times over the whole Church both collectively and individually ? It clearly becomes necessary for God to oppose his fury, and this he does by angels. While they are contending for us and for our safety, we do not perceive this hidden malice, because they conceal it from us.

We may now treat this passage a little more in detail. The angel was stationed in Persia to repress the audacity and cruelty of Cambyses, who was not content with a single edict, but would have forcibly dragged the wretched Israelites back again to a fresh exile. And he must have succeeded, had

not first one angel and then another confronted him. The
angel now informs us how Michael, one of the chief leaders,
came up with the requisite supplies. The defence of one
angel might have been sufficient, for angels have no further
power than what is conferred upon them. But God is not
bound to any particular means, he is not limited to either
one or a thousand, as when Jehoshaphat speaks of a small
army, he states, It matters not before God, whether we be
few or many. (2 Chron. xiv. 11 ; 1 Sam. xiv. 6.) For God
can save his people by either a small force or a mighty one ;
and the same also is true of angels. But God is anxious to
testify to the care which he bestows upon the welfare of his
people, and to his singular loving-kindness towards the Israelites displayed by the mission of a second angel. He doubled
his re-inforcement to bear witness to his love towards these
wretched and innocent ones, who were oppressed by the
calumnies of their enemies, and by the tyranny of that impious king. Finally, the angel says, *he was left among the
Persian kings,* for the purpose of removing the numerous
obstacles in the way of the chosen people ; for, unless God
had withstood that deluge of weapons with his own shield,
the Jews would have been buried beneath it on the spot.
Let us proceed,—

14. Now I am come to make thee
understand what shall befall thy people in the latter days: for yet the
vision *is* for *many* days.

14. Et veni ut tibi patefacerem[1]
quod occurret populo tuo[2] in extre-
mitate dierum, *diebus postremis,* quia
adhuc visio ad dies.

The angel follows up the same sentiment. He states his
arrival for the purpose of predicting to Daniel coming events,
and those, too, for a long period of time. He further proves
the prayers of Daniel to have been neither vain nor fruitless,
as they produced this conflict with the kings of Persia, both
father and son. He now brings forward another proof of
this, because God wished his Prophet to be instructed in
patiently waiting for the arrival of the events, after being
made fully aware of the elect people being under God's care
and protection. This he would readily acknowledge from

[1] To make thee understand.—*Calvin.*
[2] That is, what shall happen to thy people.—*Calvin.*

the prophecies of the next chapter.   He next adds, *at the end of the days.*   By this expression the angel commends God's grace towards the Prophet, as he was its special minister.   His mission was not only to announce to him the occurrences of three or four years, or of any brief period, but he had to extend his predictions over many years, even to the extremity of the days.   I willingly refer this period to the renovation of the Church which happened at the advent of Christ.   The Scriptures in using the phrase, the last days, or times, always point to the manifestation of Christ, by which the face of the world was renewed.   It is exactly similar to the angel saying he would make Daniel fully acquainted with all future events, until the final redemption of the people, when Christ was exhibited for the salvation of his Church.   Hence the angel embraces the 490 years of which he had spoken.   For Christ's advent determined the fulness of times, and the subjoined reason suits the passage exceedingly well.   *The vision is yet for days,* says he ; thus frigidly some expounders take these words.   I feel persuaded that the angel intends to shew how God is now opening future events to his servant, and thus these prophecies become like a lamp ever shining in the Church.   The faithful complain in the 74th Psalm (ver. 9) of the absence of all signs, because no prophets are left.   We see no signs, say they, no Prophet exists among us.   This was an indication of God having rejected and deserted them.   However faintly the light of his doctrine may shine upon us, the slightest glimmer ought to be sufficient to produce patience and repose.   But when all the light of the Word is extinguished, we seem completely enveloped in tartarean darkness.   As the Israelites suffered so many afflictions for nearly 500 years, this remedy ought completely to restore them ; for when the angel testifies, *the vision is yet for days,* it means, although God permits his people to be miserably afflicted, yet by this very proof he shews that he had not entirely cast them off.   Some vision remained ; that is, by the light of prophecy he will always manifest his care for his chosen, and they may even anticipate a happy issue out of all their sorrows.   We now understand the angel's meaning when he says, *the vision is yet for days.* Prophecies, indeed, ceased soon afterwards, and God no longer sent other prophets to his people, yet their teaching always remained permanent like a finger-post, for in it was completed the whole series of times up to the advent of Christ. His children were never destitute of all necessary consolation; for although there were no prophets surviving who could instruct the people in God's commands by the living voice, yet Daniel's teaching flourished for nearly 500 years after his death. It also performed its part in supporting the courage of the pious, and shewing them the firmness of God's covenant notwithstanding all opposition. Although the Church was agitated in a variety of ways, yet God is consistent in all his promises, until the complete redemption of his Church by the advent of his only-begotten Son.

PRAYER.

Grant, Almighty God, as the weakness of our faith is such that it almost vanishes on the very least occasion: Grant, I say, that we may not hesitate to derive support from this remarkable and memorable example which thou wishest to propose to us in Daniel, although for a time thou hidest thy face from us, and we lie prostrate in darkness. Still do thou remain near us; and with undoubting hope may we be stedfast in our prayers and groanings, until at length the fruit of our prayers shall appear. Thus may we constantly make war with all kinds of trials, and persist unconquered until thou shalt stretch forth thine hand from heaven to us, and raise us to that blessed rest which is there laid up for us by Christ our Lord.—Amen.

Lecture Fifty-Fifth.

15. And when he had spoken such words unto me, I set my face toward the ground, and I became dumb.	15. Et cum loqueretur mecum secundum verba hæc, posui faciem meam in terram, et obmutui.

DANIEL again signifies by these words that he was so inspired by reverence for the angel as to be unable to stand. This tends to recommend the prophecy to our notice,—to shew us how the holy Prophet was not only instructed by the angel, but to confirm what he will afterwards record in the 11th chapter, and free it from all doubt. Lastly, he enables us to confide in the angel's words, which were not uttered in an ordinary way, but were so obviously divine as to cast Daniel headlong upon the earth. In my judgment those expounders of the phrase, *he became dumb,* are in error when they refer it to his repenting of his prophetic office, through supposing his prayers to have been disregarded. This is much too forced, because the Prophet expresses nothing more than his seizure by fear, causing both his feet and his tongue to refuse their usual duties. Thus he was apparently carried beyond himself. By becoming prostrate on the ground, he manifested his reverence, and by becoming dumb displayed his astonishment. I have already briefly explained the object of all these assertions—to prove to us how the angel was adorned with his own attributes, and what full authority should be assigned to his words. It follows :—

16. And, behold, *one* like the similitude of the sons of men touched my lips : then I opened my mouth, and spake, and said unto him that stood before me, O my lord, by the vision my sorrows are turned upon me, and I have retained no strength.

17. For how can the servant of this my lord talk with this my lord ? for as for me, straightway there remained no strength in me, neither is there breath left in me.

18. Then there came again and touched me *one* like the appearance of a man, and he strengthened me.

16. Et ecce secundum similitudinem filiorum hominis,[1] tetigit labia mea, et aperui os meum, et loquutus sum : et dixi ad eum qui stabat ad conspectum meum,[2] Domine, in visione conversi sunt dolores mei super me, et non continui robur.

17. Et quomodo poterit servus Domini mei hujus loqui cum Domino meo hoc ? Et exinde non stetit in me[3] robur ; Et anima, *halitus,* non fuit residuus in me.

18. Et addidit, *hoc est, secundo,* tetigit me secundum similitudinem[4] hominis, et roboravit me.

Daniel here narrates how the angel who inflicted the wound at the same time brought the remedy. Though he had been cast down by fear, yet the touch of the angel raised him up, not because there was any virtue in the mere touch, but the use of symbols we know to be freely encouraged by God, as we have previously observed. Thus the angel raised

[1] That is, some one wearing the form of the sons of man.—*Calvin.*
[2] That is, who stood opposite me, or at a distance from me.—*Calvin.*
[3] There is in the original the pleonasm of the words, "and I," of which the Latin language does not admit.— *Calvin.*
[4] That is, he who bore a human appearance.—*Calvin.*

the Prophet not only by his voice but by his touch. Whence we gather the oppressive nature of the terror from the difficulty with which he was roused from it. This ought to be referred to its own end, which was to stamp the prophecy with the impress of authority, and openly to proclaim Daniel's mission from God. We are aware, too, how Satan transforms himself into an angel of light, (2 Cor. xi. 14;) and hence God distinguishes this prediction, by fixed marks, from all the fallacies of Satan. Lastly, by all these circumstances the Prophet shews God to be the author of the prophecy to be afterwards uttered, as the angel brought with him trustworthy credentials, by which he procured for himself favour, and openly proved his mission to Daniel. He says he appeared *after the likeness of a man*, or of the sons of man. He seems here to be speaking of another angel; but as we proceed we shall perceive the angel to be the same as at first. He had formerly imposed upon him the name of a man; now, to distinguish him from men, and to prove him to be only human in form and not in nature, he says he bore the similitude of the sons of a man. Some restrict this to Christ, but I fear this is too forced; and when all points shall have been more accurately discussed, I have already anticipated the result, as most probably the same angel is here designated of whom Daniel has hitherto spoken. We have already stated him not to be the Christ, because this interpretation is better suited to that Michael who has been already mentioned, and will be again at the end of this chapter. Whence it is more simple to receive it thus: the angel *strengthened Daniel by touching his lips;* and the angel, formerly called a man, was only one in appearance, wearing the human figure and image, yet not partaking of our nature. For allowing God to have sent his angels clad frequently in human bodies, he never created them men in the sense in which Christ was made man; for this is the special difference between angels and Christ. We have formerly stated how Christ was depicted for us under this figure. And there is nothing surprising in this, because Christ assumed some form of human nature before he was manifested in flesh, and angels themselves have put on the human appearance.

He says afterwards, *he opened his mouth and spake.* By these words he explains more fully what we previously stated, for he was quite stupified by terror, and to all appearance was dead. Then he began to open his mouth, and was animated to confidence. No wonder, then, if men fall down and faint away, when God shews such signs of his glory; for when God puts forth his strength against us, what are we? At his appearance alone the mountains melt, at his voice alone the whole earth is shaken. (Ps. civ. 32.) How, then, can men stand upright who are only dust and ashes, when God appears in his glory? Daniel, then, was prostrate, but afterwards recovered his strength when God restored his courage. We ought to understand the certainty of our being compelled to vanish into nothing whenever God sets before us any sign of his power and majesty ; and yet he restores us again, and shews himself to be our father, and bears witness of his favour towards us by both words and other signs. The language of this clause might seem superfluous —*he opened his mouth, and spake, and said ;* but by this repetition he wished, as I have stated, to express plainly his own recovery of the use of speech after being refreshed by the angel's touch.

He says he spoke *to him who stood opposite.* This phrase enables us to conclude the angel here sent to be the same as the previous one ; and this will appear more clearly from the end of the chapter, and as we proceed with our subject. Then he says, *O my Lord, in the vision my distresses are turned upon me, and I have not retained my strength.* He here calls the angel "Lord," after the Hebrew custom. Paul's assertion was true under the law—there is but one Lord, (1 Cor. viii. 6,) but the Hebrews use the word promiscuously when they address any one by a title of respect. It was no less customary with them than with us to use this phrase in special cases. I confess it to be a weakness ; but as it was a common form of expression, the Prophet uses no ceremony in calling angels lords. The angel, then, is called *lord,* simply for the sake of respect, just as the title is applied to men who excel in dignity. *In the vision itself,* that is, before thou didst begin to speak, I was buried in grief and deprived of strength. How then, says he, am I able to speak now? Thou by thy very appearance hast depressed me; no wonder I was utterly dumb; and now if I open my mouth, I know not what to say, as the fright which thy presence occasioned me held all my senses completely spellbound. We perceive the Prophet to be but partially erect, being still subject to some degree of fear, and therefore unable to utter freely the thoughts of his mind. Therefore he adds, *And how shall the servant of this my Lord be able to speak with that my Lord?* The demonstrative זֶה, *zeh,* seems to be used by way of amplifying, according to the phrase common enough in our day, *with such a one.* Daniel does not simply point out the angel's presence, but wishes to express his rare and singular excellence. Dispute would be both superfluous and out of place should any one assert the unlawfulness of ascribing such authority to the angel. For, according to my previous remark, the Prophet uses the common language of the times. He never intended to detract in any way from the monarchy of God. He knew the existence of only one God, and Christ to be the only prince of the Church; meanwhile, he freely permitted himself to follow the common and popular form of speech. And truly we are too apt either to avoid or neglect religious ceremony in the use of words. Although we maintain that the Prophet followed the customary forms of expression, he detracted nothing from God by transferring it to the angel, as the Papists do when they manufacture · innumerable patron saints, and despoil Christ of his just honour. Daniel would not sanction this, but treated the angel with honour, as he would any remarkable and illustrious mortal, according to my previous assertion. He knew him to be an angel, but in his discourse with him he did not give way to any empty scruples. As he saw him under the form of a man, he conversed with him as such; and with reference to the certainty of the prophecy, he was clearly persuaded of the angel's mission as a heavenly instructor.

He next adds, *Henceforth my strength did not remain within me, and my breath was no longer left in me.* Some translate this in the future tense,—it will not stand; and certainly the verb יַעֲמֹד, *ignemed*, " shall stand," is in the future tense; but then the past tense follows when he says, *no breath was left in me.* Without doubt, this is but a repetition of what we observed before ; for Daniel was seized not only by fear, but also by stupor at the sight of the angel. Whence it appears how utterly destitute he was of both intellect and tongue, both to understand and express himself in reply to the angel. This is the full sense of the words. He adds, secondly, *he was strengthened by the touch of him who wore the likeness of a man ;* for *he touched me,* says he. By these words Daniel more clearly explains how he failed to recover his entire strength at the first touch, but was roused by degrees, and could only utter three or four words at first. We perceive, then, how impossible it is for those who are prostrated by God to collect all their strength at the first moment, and how they partially and gradually recover the powers which they had lost. Hence the necessity for a second touch, to enable Daniel to hear the angel speaking to him with a mind perfectly composed. And here again he inspires us with faith in the prophecy, as he was by no means in an ecstasy while the angel was discoursing concerning future events. If he had always lain prostrate, his attention could never have been given to the angel's message, and he could never have discharged towards us the duty of prophet and teacher. Thus God joined these two conditions—terror and a renewal of strength—to render it possible for Daniel to receive with calmness the angel's teaching, and to deliver faithfully to us what he had received from God through the hand of the angel. It follows :—

19. And said, O man greatly beloved, fear not : peace *be* unto thee; be strong, yea, be strong. And when he had spoken unto me, I was strengthened, and said, Let my lord speak ; for thou hast strengthened me.	19. Et dixit, Ne timeas vir desideriorum,[1] Pax tibi, confortare, et confortare.[2] Et cum loqueretur mecum, roboravi me : tunc dixi, Loquatur Dominus meus, quia roborasti me.

He first explains how he recovered his spirits at the angel's exhortation ; for he refers to this encouragement as a com-

---

[1] That is, to desire, as we said before.—*Calvin.*
[2] Some translate, " Act like a man and be strong." Both words are the same in the original.— *Calvin.* See the DISSERTATIONS on this chap.—*Ed.*

mand to be of good courage. *Fear not*, therefore, *O man of desires.* The angel here addresses Daniel soothingly, to calm his fears, for he needed some enticement when oppressed with fear at both the words and aspect of the angel. This is the reason why he calls him *a man to be desired.* He adds, *peace to thee*, a customary salutation with the Hebrews, who mean by the phrase the same as the Latin expression, May it be well with thee. Peace, as the Jews used it, means a state of prosperity, happiness, and quiet, and everything of this kind. *Peace*, therefore, *to thee*, meaning, May you prosper. By this word the angel declares his arrival in the Prophet's favour to bear witness to God's merciful feelings towards the Israelites, and to the reception of his own prayers. We ought diligently to notice this, because, as I have already remarked, whenever God puts forth any sign of his majesty, we necessarily become frightened. No other remedy is equal to the favour of God fully manifested towards us, and his testimony to his drawing near us as a father. The angel expresses this feeling by the phrase which he uses, shewing with what justice Daniel fell down lifeless through reverence for God's presence, and the necessity for his being calm and collected when he knew himself sent forth to bear witness to God's favour. *Peace*, therefore, *to thee.* He next adds, *Be strong, be strong.* By this repetition, the angel teaches how strong an effort was required to arouse the Prophet; if he had been but slightly terrified, one word would have been enough to recover him. But as he was carried beyond himself, and all his senses had failed him, the angel inculcates twice the same exhortation to be strong. *Be strong*, then, *be strong;* that is, recover your spirits; and if this cannot be done in a moment, persevere in recovering that alacrity which may render you a fitting disciple; for, while you thus remain astonished, I should address you in vain. There are two reasons why we must notice the Prophet's informing us again how dejected he was. First, it proves how free from ambiguity this revelation really was, and how clearly it was stamped with marks of genuineness. Secondly, we must learn how formidable God's presence is to us, unless we are persuaded of the exercise of his paternal love towards us.

Lastly, we must observe how, when once we are struck down, we cannot immediately and completely recover our spirits, but we must be satisfied if God gradually and successively inspires us with renewed strength.

Daniel afterwards says, *he was strengthened, and said, Let my lord speak, for thou hast made me strong.* By these words he indicates his peace of mind after the angel had roused him by touching him twice, and by giving him courage by means of his exhortation. It is very useful to us to take due notice of this mental tranquillity, because the Prophet ought first to become a diligent scholar to enable him afterwards to discharge for us the office of a faithful teacher. With the greatest propriety, he repeats his assertion about the recovery of his strength, which enabled him to address the angel with facility. It now follows:—

20. Then said he, Knowest thou wherefore I come unto thee? and now will I return to fight with the prince of Persia: and when I am gone forth, lo, the prince of Grecia shall come.	20. Et dixit, An cognoscis, *scisne,* quare venerim ad te, et nunc revertar ad pugnandum cum principe Persarum: et ego egrediens, *hoc est, ubi egressus fuero,* tunc ecce princeps Javan, *hoc est, Græcorum,* veniet.

The angel appears here to lead the Prophet in vain through a winding course; for he might directly and simply have told him why he had come. It was necessary to recall the Prophet to his senses, as he was at one time scarcely master of his actions. He was not indeed permanently injured in his mind, but the disturbance of feeling through which he had passed had temporarily disarranged the calmness of his thoughts. This event both occurred and is narrated for our advantage. This is the reason why the angel again uses this preface, *Dost thou know?* as if he wished to gather together the Prophet's senses which were formerly wandering and dispersed. He urges him to pay great attention. *And now,* says he, *I will return;* that is, after I shall have explained to thee what thou wilt afterwards hear, *I will return again to contend with the prince of the Persians.* Here the angel indicates the reason for the delay of his mission, not because God neglected the groans and prayers of his Prophet, but the fit time had not yet arrived. The angel had formerly stated how the Persian prince had stood before him; meaning, he

detained me, and I was obliged to enter into conflict with
him, for his cruelty to the people had become far more formidable and insolent.   This is the account which he gives of
his occupation.   But he now adds, *I will return to fight with
the prince of the Persians ;* implying, God sent me purposely
to unfold to thee future occurrences, but you now know how
far I was from being at leisure or shall be hereafter.   I now
come to be God's witness and herald of his good will towards
thyself and thy people.   In reality, I am the defender of thy
safety, since I have constantly to fight for thee with the
prince of the Persians.   He means Cambyses.   I follow my
former interpretation of an engagement between the angel
and the king of Persia, whom wicked men had stimulated to
cruelty ; for he had revoked the edict of his father.   The
angel resisted the king's fury, who was naturally very turbulent, and profane writers have described his character in a
similar way.

He now adds, *I will go to fight against the prince of the
Persians ;* for עִם, *gnem,* has the force of " against" here and
in many other passages.   He next adds, *And when I shall
depart,* that is, when I am gone, *then the prince of Greece
shall approach,* says he ; that is, God shall exercise him in
another way.   He does not mean this to refer to Cambyses,
but to other Persian kings, as we shall state in the proper
place.   It is quite correct to suppose the king of Macedon to
have arrived by God's permission ; but the angel simply
means to state the existence of various methods by which
God hinders the cruelty of kings whenever they attempt to
injure his people.   He shall send the prince of the Greeks,
says he.   God, therefore, thus restrained Cambyses by the
angel's assistance, and then he protected his people from the
cruelty exercised by Alexander, king of Macedon.   God is
always providing for the safety of his people, and always has
a variety of methods in operation.   The angel desired to
teach us this with all simplicity.   At length he adds :—

21. But I will shew thee that which is noted in the scripture of truth: and *there is* none that holdeth with me in these things, but Michael your prince.

21. Verum indicabo tibi quod exaratum est in Scriptura veraci : et non unus qui se roboret, *vel, qui viriliter agat,* mecum in his, nisi Michael princeps vester.

I omit the interpretation of those who say that after the departure of the angel the prince of the Greeks came forward, because God ceased to afford assistance to the kingdom of the Persians. This is altogether different from the Prophet's sense, and we must hold the explanation which I have adopted. The angel now adds the object of his mission—to make Daniel acquainted with what he will afterwards relate. He again attracts our confidence towards his message, not only for the sake of the Prophet privately, but to assure all the pious how free Daniel's writings were from any human delusion or invention, and how fully they were inspired from above. *I will announce*, therefore, *what has been engraven*, or ensculptured, *in the Scripture of truth*. By this phrase, " the Scripture of truth," he doubtless means the eternal and inviolable decree of God himself. God needs no books ; paper and books are but helps to our memory, which would otherwise easily let things slip ; but as he never suffers from forgetfulness, hence he needs no books. We are aware how often holy Scripture adopts forms of speech according to human customs. This clause implies the same as if the angel had said, he brought nothing but what God had already determined before, and thus the Prophet would expect a full and complete accomplishment.

He next adds, *There is no one who supports me in this duty except Michael*, whom he calls *prince of the elect people*. It is surprising why the angel and Michael alone fought for the safety of the people. It is written, Angels pitch their camp in a circuit around those who fear God, (Ps. xxxiv. 7,) and then but one Church existed in the world. Why, then, did not God commit this charge to more angels than one ? Why did he not send forth mighty forces ? We acknowledge that God does not confine himself to any fixed rule ; he can help us as well by many forces as by a single angel or by more. And he does not make use of angels as if he could not do without them. This is the reason of that variety which we observe : he is first content with one angel, and then joins more with him. He will give to one man a great army, as we read of Elisha, and as other passages in Scripture afford us examples. (2 Kings vi. 17.) The servant of Elisha

saw the air full of angels. Thus also Christ said, Can I not
ask my Father, and he will send me, not one angel only, but
a legion ? (Matt. xxvi. 53.) Again, the Spirit of God assigns many angels to each of the faithful. (Ps. xci. 11.)
Now, therefore, we understand why God sends more angels,
not always with the same purpose or intention, to inform us
that he is sufficient to afford us protection, even if no other
help should be supplied. He provides for our infirmities by
bringing us help by means of his angels, who act like hands
to execute his commands. But I have previously remarked
this is not an invariable practice, and we ought not to bind
him by any fixed conditions to supply our wants always in
the same manner. God seemed, at least for a time, to leave
his people without help, and afterwards two angels were sent
to contend for them ; first, a single one was sent to Daniel,
and then Michael, whom some think to be Christ. I do not
object to this view, for he calls him a prince of the Church,
and this title seems by no means to belong to any angels,
but to be peculiar to Christ. On the whole, the angel
signifies that God did not put forth his full strength in contending for his Church, but shews himself to be a servant to
promote its safety till the time of deliverance should arise.
He afterwards adds—for the next verse may be treated
shortly, and ought to be connected with this in one context.

CHAPTER ELEVENTH.

1. Also I, in the first year of
Darius the Mede, *even* I, stood to
confirm and to strengthen him.

1. Et ego anno primo Darii
Medi steti in roboratorem, et auxi-
lium illi.[1]

Interpreters explain this verse in various ways. Some
think the angel fought for the Persian king, and follow up
their opinion, because he did not for the first time begin
now to defend that monarchy in favour of the chosen people,
but had done so from the very beginning. Others refer this
to Michael, as the angel declares that he introduced the assistance of Michael. But that is forced and cold. I do not

[1] That is, I stood by to strengthen and assist him.—*Calvin.*

hesitate to state the argument to be from the greater to the less, and we have an instance of this in a tragedy of Ovid's. I have been able to preserve you; do you ask whether I can destroy you ? Thus the angel says, I have erected the Persian monarchy ; I have not the slightest doubt of my present power to restrain these kings, lest they should pour forth their fury upon the people. The full meaning is this, the king of the Persians is nothing, and can do nothing except through me. I was God's servant in transferring the monarchy of the Medes and Chaldeans to the Persians, as well as that of the Babylonians to the Medes. God, says he, entrusted me with that office, and so I placed Darius upon the throne. You now see how completely I have him in my power, and how I can prevent him from injuring my people should he be so inclined. When the angel boasts of *his standing forward to help Darius,* he claims nothing to himself, but speaks as it were in the person of God. For angels have no power distinct from God's when he uses their agency and assistance. There is no reason for any inquiry whether the angel ought to use this boastful language and claim anything for himself. For he does not claim anything as really his own, but he shews himself to have been an agent in the change of dynasty when Babylon was subdued by the Medes, and the empire transferred to Darius. For although, as we have previously shewn, Cyrus obtained the victory, yet he transferred the honours of government to his uncle Cyaxares. The Hebrews are accustomed to consider him as king for the first two years ; Cyrus began to reign after this period ; and now, when the angel appears to Daniel, the third year had arrived, as we saw at the beginning of the chapter.

PRAYER.

Grant, Almighty God, as thou daily and familiarly deignest to grant us the light of heavenly doctrine, that we may come to thy school with true humility and modesty. May our docility be really apparent; may we receive with reverence whatever proceeds from thy lips, and may thy majesty be conspicuous among us. May we taste of that goodness which thou dost manifest to us in thy word, and be enabled to rejoice in thee as our Father; may we never dread thy presence, but may we enjoy the sweet testimony of thy paternal grace and favour. May thy word be more precious to us than gold and worldly treasures, and, meanwhile, may we feed upon its sweetness, until we arrive at that full satiety which is laid up for us in heaven through Christ our Lord.—Amen.

Lecture Fifty=Sixth.

2. And now will I shew thee the truth. Behold, there shall stand up yet three kings in Persia; and the fourth shall be far richer than *they* all: and by his strength through his riches he shall stir up all against the realm of Grecia.	2. Et nunc veritatem annuntio tibi: Ecce adhuc tres reges stabunt in Perside, et quartus ditabitur opibus magnis,[1] præ omnibus et secundum fortitudinem suam, in, *inquam*, opibus suis,[2] excitabit omnes contra regnum Græcorum.

WE must now understand God's intention in thus informing his servant Daniel of future events. He was clearly unwilling to gratify a vain curiosity, and he enlarged upon events necessary to be known, thus enabling the Prophet not only privately to rely on God's grace, through this manifestation of his care for his Church, but also to exhort others to persevere in the faith. This chapter seems like a historical narrative under the form of an enigmatic description of events then future. The angel relates and places before his eyes occurrences yet to come to pass. We gather from this very clearly how God spoke through his prophets; and thus Daniel, in his prophetic character alone, is a clear proof to us of God's peculiar favour towards the Israelites. Here the angel discusses, not the general state of the world, but first the Persian kingdom, then the monarchy of Alexander, and afterwards the two kingdoms of Syria and Egypt. From this we clearly perceive how the whole discourse was directed to the faithful. God did not regard the welfare of other nations, but wished to benefit his Church, and principally to sustain the faithful under their approaching troubles. It was to assure them of God's never becoming forgetful of his covenant, and of his so moderating the convulsions then

---

[1] Or, he shall be rich with great opulence.—*Calvin.*
[2] Or. with his riches, that is, when he shall prevail.—*Calvin.*

taking place throughout the world, as to be ever protecting his people by his assistance.   But we shall have to repeat this again, and even more than once, as we proceed.

First of all, the angel states, *Three kings shall yet stand up in Persia.*   With respect to the clause, *Behold! I announce to you the truth,* I explained in yesterday's Lecture how frequently he confirmed his prophecy whenever he treated events of the greatest importance, which seemed almost incredible.   *I shall tell you the real truth; three kings shall stand up.*   The Jews are not only very ignorant of everything, but very stupid also : then they have no sense of shame, and are endued with a perverse audacity ; for they think there were only three kings of Persia, and they neglect all history, and mingle and confound things perfectly clear and completely distinct.   There were eight kings of Persia of whom no mention is made here.   Why, then, does the angel say, *three kings should stand up?*   This was the first year of Darius, as we saw before.   Hence, in their number of kings, Cyrus, the first monarch, is included, together with his son Cambyses.   When these two kings have been decided on, a new question will arise again ; for some add Smerdis to Cambyses, though he was only an impostor ; for the Magi falsely thrust him in as the son of Darius, for the purpose of acquiring the sovereignty to themselves.   Thus he was acknowledged as king for seven months ; but when the cheat was discovered he was slain by seven of the nobles, among whom was Darius the son of Hystaspes, and he, according to the common narrative, was created king by the consent of the others on the neighing of his horse.   The variations of interpreters might hinder us from reading them, and so we must gather the truth from the event.   For Smerdis, as I have stated, cannot be reckoned among the kings of Persia, as he was but an impostor.   I therefore exclude him, following the prudence of others who have considered the point with attention.

We must now observe why Daniel mentions four kings, *the fourth of whom,* he states, *should be very rich.*   Cambyses succeeded Cyrus, who was reigning when the prophecy was uttered.   He was always moving about to distant places ;

he scarcely allowed himself rest for a single year; he was exceedingly desirous of glory, insatiable in his ambition, and ever stirring up new wars. Cambyses, his son, who had slain his brother, died in Egypt, and yet added this country to the Persian empire. Darius, the son of Hystaspes, succeeded, and Xerxes followed him. They are deceived who think Darius, the son of Hystaspes, is the fourth king; without doubt the Prophet meant Xerxes, who crossed the sea with a mighty army. He led with him 900,000 men; and, however incredible this may appear, all historians constantly affirm it. He was so puffed up with pride that he said he came to put fetters upon the Hellespont, while his army covered all the neighbouring country. This is one point; the four kings were Cyrus, Cambyses, Darius the son of Hystaspes, and Xerxes, omitting Smerdis. We may now inquire why the angel limits the number to four, as the successor of Xerxes was Artaxerxes, or Darius Longimanus, the long-handed, and some others after him. This difficulty is solved by the following probable method,—Xerxes destroyed the power of the Persian empire by his rashness; he escaped with the greatest disgrace, and was scarcely saved by the baseness of his flight. He brought away but few companions with him hastily in a small boat, and could not obtain a single transport, although the Hellespont had been previously covered with his ships. His whole army was almost cut to pieces, first at Thermopylæ, then at Leuctra, and afterwards at other places. From that period the Persian empire declined, for when its warlike glory was annihilated, the people gave themselves up to sloth and idleness, according to the testimony of Xenophon. Some interpreters expound the phrase, *three kings stood up*, of the flourishing period of the Persian monarchy: they take the words "stood up" emphatically, since from that period the nation's power began to wane. For Xerxes on his return was hated by the whole people, first for his folly, then for his putting his brother to death, for his disgraceful conduct towards his sister, and for his other crimes; and as he was so loaded with infamy before his own people, he was slain by Artabanus, who reigned seven months. As the power of Persia was then almost en-

tirely destroyed, or at least was beginning to decline, some
interpreters state these three kings to stand up, and then
add Xerxes as the fourth and the most opulent. But suppose we take the word " stood up" relatively, with respect to
the Church ? For the angel states that the Persian prince,
Cambyses, stood before him, in an attitude of hostility and
conflict. The angel seems rather to hint *at the standing up
of four kings of Persia,* for the purpose of reminding the
Jews of the serious evils and the grievous troubles which
they must suffer under their sway. In this sense I interpret
the verb " to stand," referring it to the contests by which
God harassed the Church until the death of Xerxes. For at
that period, when the power of the Persians declined, a
longer period of rest and relaxation was afforded to the people
of God. This is the reason why the angel omits and passes
over in silence all the kings from Artabanus to Darius the
son of Arsaces ; for Arsaces was the last king but one, and
although Ochus reigned before him, we know from profane
historians how his posterity were reduced to the lowest rank
under the last Darius, whom Alexander conquered, as we
shall see by and bye. For this reason I think this to be the
genuine sense of the passage,—from Cyrus to Xerxes kings
of Persia should stand up against the Israelites, and during
the whole of that period the contests should be renewed, and
the Jews would almost perish through despair under that
continued series of evils. Some say, four kings should stand
forth until all the Jews were led out ; and we know this never
to have been completed, for a small portion only returned.
As to my own opinion, I am unwilling to contend with
others, yet I hesitate not to enforce the angel's wish to exhort all the pious to endurance, for he announced *the standing up of these four kings,* who should bring upon them
various tribulations. As to the fourth king, the statement
of this passage suits Xerxes exactly. *The fourth,* he says,
shall be enriched with wealth ; for the noun is of similar
meaning with the verb, as they both spring from the same
root. Truly enough Darius the son of Hystaspes determined
to carry on war with Greece ; he made the attempt but without success, especially at the battle of Marathon. He was

cut off by sudden death when his treasures were prepared
and many forces were collected. He thus left the material of
war for his son. Xerxes, in the flower of his age, saw every
preparation for war made ready to his hands ; he eagerly
embraced the occasion, and gave no heed to sound advice.
For, as we have already stated, he destroyed himself and the
whole monarchy, not by a single slaughter only, but by four.
And this power of raising an army of 900,000 men was no
ordinary occurrence. If he had only carried with him across
the sea 100,000 men, this would have been a large force.
But his power of feeding such large forces while he passed
through so many provinces, and then of passing them across
the sea, exceeds the ordinary bounds of our belief. We are
not surprised, then, at the angel's predicting the extreme
wealth of this king.

He adds, *In his fortitude and in his riches he shall stir
them all up against the realm of the Greeks.* This was not
accomplished by Darius the son of Hystaspes. According to
my former statement, he attacked certain Grecian cities, but
without producing confusion throughout the whole East, as
Xerxes his successor did. As to the phrase, the kingdom of
Javan, I willingly subscribe to their opinion who think the
word equivalent to the Greek word Ionia. For Javan went
forth in that direction, and dwelt there with his posterity in
the Grecian territory, whence almost the whole of Greece
obtained its present name. The whole Grecian nation is
often called " Chittim," and some see good reason for their
being termed " Machetæ," from Chittim the son of Javan,
and thus by the addition of a letter we arrive at the Macedonians. For the conjecture is probable that this people
were first called Maketæ, and afterwards Macedonians.
Without doubt, in this passage and in many others, Javan is
put for the whole of Greece, since Ionia was the portion of
the country most celebrated in Judea and throughout the
East generally. Xerxes then stirred up against the realm of
Javan—meaning Greece—all the people of the East ; for it is
very well known how his empire spread far and wide in every
direction. It follows :—

3. And a mighty king shall stand   3. Et stabit rex fortis, et domi-

up, that shall rule with great dominion, and do according to his will.	nabitur dominatione magna, et faciet secundum voluntatem suam.[1]

This refers to Alexander of Macedon. I have already shortly stated the reason why the angel passed over all the Persian kings from Artabanus to the last Darius,—they did not engage in any contests with the Jews up to Xerxes. But when Alexander invaded Asia, he struck the Jews with terror, as well as all other nations. He came like lightning, and it is by no means surprising that the Jews should be frightened at his arrival, because, as we formerly expressed it, he flew with amazing swiftness. Alexander then rose up, not only by the riches and might of his warlike preparations, but he necessarily inspired the Jews with trepidation when they perceived their inability to resist him, and thus he was deservedly hostile to them, because, from the very beginning, they had despised his empire. Josephus also informs us how he was moved at the sight of the high priest, and how he determined to mitigate his rage against the Jews. For when he was at home, before passing over into Asia, the vision of the high priest was offered to him, for God had sent his angel under that disguise.[2] Alexander supposed it to be some deity; but when the high priest met him in procession, the vision returned to his recollection, and he was struck as if he had seen God appearing to him from heaven. Whatever was the object of this occurrence, Alexander clearly came into Judea with the intention of utterly destroying the whole nation. This is the reason why the angel carefully predicts this change. *A brave king*, therefore, *shall stand up, and rule with extensive dominion, and do according to his pleasure;* that is, he shall succeed as if he had all the events of the war under his own hand and according to his own pleasure, as the event itself most fully proved. It follows:—

4. And when he shall stand up, his kingdom shall be broken, and	4. Et ubi constiterit, frangetur, *vel*, *conteretur*, regnum ejus, et dividetur

---

[1] That is, as he wishes, or according to his lust.—*Calvin.*

[2] There are various minor errors in the edition 1617, which are correct in the edition of 1571. For example, on folio 94, verse 3, *violavit* occurs for *volavit;* and on folio 95, verse 3, *non* begins the sentence instead of *nam.*—*Ed.*

shall be divided toward the four winds of heaven; and not to his posterity, nor according to his dominion which he ruled: for his kingdom shall be plucked up, even for others besides those.

in quatuor ventos cœlorum, *hoc est, in quatuor plagas mundi,* et non posteritati ejus, et non secundum dominationem ejus, qua dominatus fuerit: quia extirpabitur, *radicitus evelletur,* regnum ejus, et aliis absque illis.

This language is concise, but there is no ambiguity in the sense. First of all the angel says, After that brave king had stood up, his empire should be broken in pieces: for when Alexander had arrived at his height, he suddenly fell sick, and shortly afterwards died at Babylon. Ambassadors had assembled round him from every quarter. He was quite intoxicated by prosperity, and very probably poisoned himself. Historians, however, have viewed him as a remarkable example of singular valour, and so they have pretended and have related, because at least they thought so, that he was deceitfully poisoned by Cassander. But we all know how intemperately and immoderately he indulged in drinking; he almost buried himself in wine, and was seized with disease amidst his cups, and sank under it, because no remedy was found for him. This, then, was Alexander's poison. Whichever way we understand it, he fell suddenly, almost as soon as he began to stand. After conquering nearly the whole East, he came to Babylon, and was uncertain in his plans as to the employment of his forces, after he had procured peace for the whole East. He was then anxious to transfer his armies to either Europe or Africa. The angel says, *After he had stood up,* meaning, after he had acquired the monarchy of the whole East, *his kingdom should be broken up.* He uses this simile, because the whole power of Alexander was not so much extinguished as broken into separate parts. We know how the twelve chiefs who were his generals drew the spoils to themselves; every one took a portion of his kingdom, and divided it among themselves, as we have previously stated, just as if it were torn from their master's body. All consented in raising his brother Aridæus to the dignity of king, and they called him Philip, that, while his sons were young, the memory of his father might commend them to the world. But four kingdoms at length issued from Alexander's monarchy. It is unnecessary here to refer to what we may read at our leisure in the writings of historians.

The Prophet only touches shortly on those points which relate to the instruction of the Church ; he does not relate in order or in detail the events narrated in history ; he only says, *His empire shall be broken, and shall be divided,* says he, *towards the four winds of heaven.* The angel omits that partition which assigned the treasure to one, and gave the office of counsellor to Philip : Perdiccas was the guardian of his son, and he with others obtained a portion of his dominions. Seleucus obtained Syria, to whom his son Antiochus succeeded ; Antigonus became prefect of Asia Minor ; Cassander, the father of Antipater, seized the kingdom of Macedon for himself; Ptolemy, the son of Lagus, who had been a common soldier, possessed Egypt. These are the four kingdoms of which the angel now treats. For Egypt was situated to the south of Judea, and Syria to the north, as we shall afterwards have occasion to observe. Macedonia came afterwards, and then Asia Minor, both east and west. But the angel does not enter into any complicated details, but shortly enumerates whatever was necessary for the common instruction of the elect people. The common consent of all writers has handed down these facts,—four kingdoms were constituted at length out of many portions, after the chiefs had been so mutually slain by one another that four only survived, namely, Ptolemy, Seleucus, Antigonus, and Cassander. Afterwards the kingdom of Antiochus was extended when Antigonus was conquered ; for Antiochus added Asia Minor to the kingdom of Syria. But Antiochus stood only for a time, and hence the angel truly and properly states this empire to have been divided into four parts.

He next adds, *And not to his posterity.* No one could have guessed what the angel predicted so many years before Alexander's birth ; for he was not born till a hundred years after this period. Those who know the boldness of his warlike schemes, the rapidity of his movements, and the success of his measures, would never be persuaded of this result,—the complete destruction of all his posterity, and the utter extinction of his race.

Had Alexander lived quietly at home, he might have married, and have become the father of children who would have been his undisputed successors. He died young, soon after reaching the age of thirty ; still he might have married, and have had heirs to his throne. He had a brother, Aridæus, and other relations, among whom was his uncle Pyrrhus, king of Epirus, and a royal offspring might thus have been preserved, and a successor prepared for him. After he had subdued both upper and lower Asia, he became master of Syria, Egypt, and Judea, and extended his power to the Persian sea, while his fame extended over Africa and Europe. Since no one dared to raise a finger against him, as he possessed a most magnificent army, and all his generals were bound to him by most important benefits, and so many of his prefects were enriched by his extreme liberality, who would have thought that all his posterity and relations would be thus blotted out ? He left two sons, but they were slain as well as his brother Aridæus, while his wives and his mother, aged eighty years, shared the same fate. Nor did Cassander spare her, for she intrigued against him. At length, as if God would punish so many slaughters committed by Alexander, he wished his whole posterity to be extinguished. And yet, as I have stated, no foreign enemy was the agent in inflicting such heavy punishments. He had subjugated the whole East, and his bearing was such, as if the whole monarchy of that portion of the world had descended to him from his ancestors by hereditary right. As the world contained no enemy for him, his foes sprang from his own home ; they slew his mother, his wives, his children, and all his relatives, and utterly rooted out all his race. We observe, then, with what clearness and certainty the angel predicts events entirely concealed from that age, and for a hundred years afterwards, and such as would never be credited by mankind. There seems a great contrast in the language ; *his kingdom shall be broken, it shall be divided towards the four winds of heaven, and not to his posterity ;* that is, although the four kingdoms should spring up in the four quarters of the world, yet none of Alexander's posterity should remain in a single place, or obtain even the least por-

tion of his dominions.   This was a remarkable proof of God's
wrath against the cruelty of Alexander; not that he was
savage by nature, but ambition seized upon him, and made
him bloodthirsty, and indisposed him to desire any end to
his warfare.   God, therefore, avenged that grasping disposition of Alexander's, by allowing the whole of his race thus
to perish with disgrace and horrible cruelty.   On this account that pride of his which wished to be thought a son of
Jupiter, and which condemned to death all his friends and
followers who would not prostrate themselves before him as
a god ;—that pride, I say, never could secure a single descendant to reign in his place, or even to hold a single satrapy.
Not to his posterity, says the angel, *and not according to his
dominion.*

He passes to the four kings of which he had spoken: It
shall not break forth, he says, namely, from the four kings.
He had already stated their foreign extraction, not in any way
derived from the family of that king ; for none of the four
should equal his power, because his kingdom should be ex-
tirpated.   Here the angel seems to omit intervening events,
and speaks of an ultimate destruction.   We know how the
last king Perseus was conquered by the Romans, and how
the kingdom of Antiochus was partly destroyed by war, and
partly oppressed by fraud.   And the angel seems to mark
this.   We may interpret it more to the point, by considering
the cessation of Alexander's empire, with reference to his
own race, as if the angel had stated that none of his successors should acquire equal power with himself.   And why so ?
Not one of them could accomplish it.   Alexander acquired
so mighty a name that all people willingly submitted to his
sway, and no single successor could sustain the burden of
the whole.   Hence his kingdom, as far as it related to himself and his posterity, was divided, and no one succeeded to
his power and his opulence.   *And it shall be given to others.*
The angel here explains his meaning.   The destruction of
the kingdom ought not to be explained particularly of single
parts, for each seized his own portion for himself, and his
successors were all strangers.   And *to others besides those ;*
meaning, his kingdom shall be seized upon by others who

are not of his posterity; that is, strangers shall rush into Alexander's place, and no successor shall arise from his own kindred. It afterwards follows,—

5. And the king of the south shall be strong, and *one* of his princes; and he shall be strong above him, and have dominion; his dominion *shall be* a great dominion.	5. Et roborabitur rex austri, et ex principibus ejus, et roborabitur adversus eum, et dominabitur: dominatio magna, dominatio ejus.

Here the angel begins to treat of the kings of Egypt and of Syria. He does not mention the king of Syria yet, but will do so in the next verse; but he begins with the king of Egypt, the neighbouring monarchy to that of Israel. He says, the king of the south, meaning, the king of Egypt, would be brave. He next adds, *and one of his princes.* Many take this in one context; but I think the angel transfers his discourse to Antiochus the son of Seleucus. *And one of his princes,* he says, meaning, one of Alexander's princes, shall strengthen himself against him. For the letter ו, *vau,* is taken in the sense of opposing, and implies an opposition between Ptolemy the son of Lagus, and Antiochus king of Syria. Hence *the king of the south shall grow strong* —another of Alexander's chiefs shall grow strong against him, and shall have dominion. We know how much larger and more wealthy the kingdom of Syria was than that of Egypt, especially when Asia Minor was added to it. Without doubt, the angel was acquainted with the future superiority of Antiochus to Ptolemy, when these two kings are mutually compared. But the rest to-morrow.

PRAYER.

Grant, Almighty God, since thou not only deignedst to unfold future events to thy servant Daniel, and to the pious who waited for the advent of thine only-begotten Son, that they might be prepared for all sufferings, and might perceive the Church to repose under thy care and protection, but also wishedst these prophecies to profit us at this day, and to confirm us in the same doctrine: Grant us to learn how to cast all our cares and anxieties on thy paternal providence. May we never doubt thy oversight of the cares of thy Church in these days, and thy protection against the fury of the ungodly who try all means of destroying it. May we repose in peace under that guardianship which thou hast promised us, and struggle on under the standard of the cross; and possess our souls in patience, until at length thou shalt appear as our Redeemer with outstretched hand, at the manifestation of thy Son, when he returns to judge the world.—Amen.

Lecture Fifty-Seventh.

6. And in the end of years they shall join themselves together; for the king's daughter of the south shall come to the king of the north to make an agreement: but she shall not retain the power of the arm; neither shall he stand, nor his arm: but she shall be given up, and they that brought her, and he that begat her, and he that strengthened her in *these* times.

6. Et in fine annorum sociabuntur, *convenient inter se*, et filia regis austri veniet ad regem aquilonis ut faciat recta: et non retinebit vires brachii, et non stabit ipse, neque semen ejus, et dabitur ipsa, et qui adduxerit eam, et qui genuerit ipsam, et roborabit eam temporibus illis, *vel, roboraverit.*

As to the explanation of the words, the king of the south, we have stated to be the king of Egypt, and that of the north, of Syria. To do right things, means to make mutual peace; he shall not retain the strength of his arm, is, his arm shall not retain its strength; he shall not stand refers to his father Ptolemy, or Antiochus Theos, as we shall afterwards see. And then we must take the ו, *vau*, negatively, and read, nor his seed, which some translate his arm. She shall be delivered up, implies being given up to death, while some understand her parent, to be her mother or her nurse. Here, then, the angel prophesies the state of the kingdoms of Egypt and Syria; and still he has respect to the Church of God, as we stated yesterday, which was placed in the midst of these two nations. We must always strive to ascertain the intention of the Holy Spirit. He wished to support the pious under those convulsions by which they would be agitated and afflicted. Their confidence might have been utterly subverted unless they had been persuaded that nothing happens at random, since all these events were proclaimed beforehand. Again, God had sent his angel to Daniel, which proved both his power and his determination to defend his Church, and he would accomplish this, because he wished the faithful admonished beforehand neither rashly

nor yet without profit.   But we must first relate the history
—the angel says, *At the end of the times two kings should
enter into covenant and friendship.*   He had announced the
superiority of the king of Syria ; for when Antigonus was
conquered, and his son was dead, Seleucus the first king of
Syria far surpassed Ptolemy in his power and the magnitude
of his dominion.   But a mutual rivalry arose between them,
and there were some slight skirmishes on both sides, till the
condition of Ptolemy became weakened, and then Seleucus
rushed tumultuously, with the ferocity of a robber rather
than the magnanimity of a king.   After they had continued
the contest for some time, Berenice the daughter of the
second Ptolemy, named Philadelphus, was given in marriage
to Antiochus Theos.   She is also called Beronice and Ber-
nice.   He was so blinded with pride, as to take the name of
Theos, which means God ; he was the third of that name,
the former king being called Soter, meaning preserver.   For,
as Seleucus had acquired so many and such mighty possessions, his sons did not consider their authority fully established, and so they assumed these magnificent titles for the
sake of inspiring all nations with the terror of their name.
Hence the first Antiochus was called Soter, and the second
Theos.   Now the second Ptolemy, named Philadelphus, gave
his daughter in marriage to Antiochus Theos.   By this bond
peace and friendship were established between them, just as
at Rome, Pompey married Julia the daughter of Cæsar.
And we daily observe similar occurrences, for when one king
has in his power a daughter, or niece, or other relatives,
another king finds himself possessed of male and female relations, by whose intermarriage they confirm a treaty of
peace.   It was so in this case, although historians attribute some degree of craft to Philadelphus in bestowing his
daughter on Antiochus Theos.   He supposed this to be a
means by which he might ultimately acquire the dominion
over all Syria, and over the other provinces under the sway
of Antiochus.   Whether this really was so or not, profane
historians prove the fulfilment of the angel's prediction.
Without the slightest doubt, God, in his wonderful counsels,
dictated to these historians what we read at the present time,

and made them witnesses of his own truth. This thought, indeed, never entered their minds, but when God governs the minds and tongues of men, he wishes to establish clear and convincing testimony to this prophecy, for the purpose of shewing the real prediction of every occurrence. *At the end of the years,* says he, *they shall become united.*

He next states, *And the daughter of the king of the south,* meaning Berenice, whom we have mentioned, *shall come to the king of the north,* meaning the king of Syria, Antiochus Theos. This alliance was contracted in defiance of justice. For Antiochus repudiated his wife Laodice, who was the mother of two sons whom she had born to Antiochus; namely, Seleucus Callinicus, and Antiochus the younger, named Hierax, a hawk, on account of his rapacity. We perceive, then, how he contracted a second marriage, after an unjust and illegal divorce of his first wife. Hence it is not surprising if this alliance was cursed by the Almighty. It turned out unhappily for both the kings of Egypt and Syria. Ptolemy ought not to have thrust his daughter upon Antiochus, who was already married, nor yet to have allowed her to become a second wife, while the king's real wife was divorced. We perceive, then, how God became the avenger of these crimes, while the plans of Antiochus and Philadelphus turned out ill. Some think that Antiochus was fraudulently poisoned by his first wife, but as the point is doubtful, I pronounce no opinion. Whether it was so or not, Antiochus had a son by Berenice, and died immediately after being reconciled to his former wife. Some historians state, that after she had recovered her dignity and rank as queen, having once experienced her husband's fickleness and perfidy, she took sure means of preventing another repudiation. When Antiochus was dead, this woman was enflamed with vengeance, and in the perverseness of her disposition, she impelled her son to murder her rival, especially stimulating Seleucus Callinicus who succeeded to his father's throne. Hierax was then prefect of Asia Minor; hence she stimulated her son with fury to murder her rival. For, although Antiochus Theos had been reconciled to her yet some degree of rank and honour still attached to Berenice the daughter of Ptolemy. And her son perpetrated this murder with the greatest willingness, and with the basest cruelty and perfidy; for he persuaded her to entrust herself to his care, and then he murdered both her and her son.

The angel now says, *When the daughter of the king of the south shall come to the king of the north, his arm shall not retain his strength.* The language is metaphorical, as that marriage was like a common arm to both sides; for the king of Egypt stretched forth his hand to the king of Syria for mutual protection. *That arm,* then, *did not retain its strength;* for Berenice was most wickedly slain by her stepson, Seleucus Callinicus, as we have stated. He says, also, *she should come to make alliances.* Here, by way of concession, the angel calls that conjugal bond מישרים, *misrim,* " *rectitudines,*" " conditions of agreement," because at first all parties thought it would tend to that result. But Antiochus had already violated his marriage vow, and departed from his lawful alliance. Nothing, therefore, was right on his side. Without the slightest doubt he derived some advantage from the plan, as kings are always in the habit of doing. And with respect to Ptolemy, many historians, as we have already mentioned, suppose him to have longed for the kingdom of Syria. Whether or not this was so, their mutual transactions were not sincere, and so the word signifying "rectitude" is used, as we have said, only by concession. The angel does not speak in their praise, or excuse the perfidy of either, but he rather enlarges upon their crime, and from this we gather how they abused the sanctity both of marriage and of treaties, which God wished to be held sacred by all mankind. Hence, though the word is honourable in itself, yet it is used in a disgraceful sense, to shew us how the angel condemned King Ptolemy for this base prostitution of his daughter, and Antiochus for rejecting his wife, and marrying another who was not a real wife, but only a concubine. And, perhaps, God wished to use the lips of his angel to point out the tendency of all royal treaties. They always have the most specious appearances—national, quiet public peace, and similar objects which can be dexterously made prominent. For kings always court favour and praise for themselves from the foolish vulgar, whenever they make treaties of peace.   Thus all these alliances have no other tendency than to produce social deception, and at length they degenerate into mutual perfidy, when one party plots insidiously and wickedly against another.

The angel adds next, *He shall not stand;* using the masculine gender, and most probably referring to Antiochus, as well as to Ptolemy his father-in-law.   *Neither he nor his seed shall stand,* meaning his son by Berenice the daughter of Ptolemy.   I dare not translate it "arm," because in my opinion the letter ‫ו‬, *vau,* is needed in the word for "arm;" so I take it to denote "seed."   He afterwards adds, *And she shall be delivered up*—thus returning to Berenice—either by treachery or to death; *and those who led her forth*—meaning her companions.   Whenever any incestuous marriage is contracted, some persons of disgraceful character are sure to be concerned in bringing his new wife to the king. And very probably there were factions in the palace of Antiochus; one party being more attached to Seleucus and his brother, and his mother Laodice; while others desired a change of government, according to the usual state of affairs. The advisers of the marriage between Antiochus and Berenice were sent as a guard of honour to attend them to Syria, and the angel states all these to have been delivered up together with the queen.   He afterwards adds, *And those who were her parents.*   From the absence of a grammatical point under the letter ‫ה‬, *he,* many think the noun to be of the feminine gender.   And as it may mean mother, they treat it as if her nurse was intended, but I leave the question in doubt.   He now adds, *and those who strengthened her at those times.*   He, doubtless, intends to designate all those who wished to curry favour with the king, and thus took part in this marriage between him and the daughter of the king of Egypt.   The whole of that faction perished, when Berenice was slain by Seleucus Callinicus.   If, then, he did not spare his stepmother, much less would he spare the faction by which he was deprived of his hope of the kingdom, and through whom his mother Laodice had suffered the disgrace of a divorce. It now follows,—

7. But out of a branch of her roots shall *one* stand up in his estate, which shall come with an army, and shall enter into the fortress of the king of the north, and shall deal against them, and shall prevail;

7. Et stabit ex germine, *vel, surculo,* radicum ejus, *nempe Berenice,*[1] in gradu suo,[2] et veniet cum exercitu,[3] et veniet in munitionem regis Aquilonis, et faciet in illis,[4] et prævalebit.

The angel treats here of Ptolemy Euergetes, the third king of Egypt, who succeeded his father Philadelphus. He collected large forces to revenge the insult offered to his sister, and thus carried on the war with Seleucus Callinicus, who had become king after his father's death. The angel, therefore, now touches shortly on this war, by saying, *There shall stand up a shoot from the root of that queen.* Very possibly he was younger than his sister Berenice. He says, *He shall stand in his own degree,* meaning, in the royal rank. The interpretation of those who translate, He shall stand in his father's rank, is forced. What is it then? *He shall stand in his own rank;* that is, he shall arrive at his own rank by hereditary right. Although, therefore, at first all thought the death of Berenice would be unrevenged through her father being dead, here the angel announces that her brother should be like a branch, and become the avenger of this great wickedness. *He shall stand,* then, *in his* rank, meaning, he shall arrive at the royal throne, *from* the *branch* or germ *of her root,* namely, Berenice. *He shall come with an army against Callinicus.* Profane writers bear witness to this. *And he shall come even to the fortification of the king of the north.* He entered Syria, and caused so great a terror that many fortified cities surrendered themselves to him. During this war he drew to himself many cities which seemed impregnable; whence it is not surprising to find the angel stating his arrival at the fortifications. Some translate it "dwelling-place," but without reason, and thus injure the Prophet's meaning. *He shall come unto the very fortification,* meaning, he shall arrive in Syria, and shall possess many fortified cities.

---

[1] The relative article is in the feminine gender. — *Calvin.*

[2] Some translate, "in its degree;" but I see no reason for it. — *Calvin.*

[3] אל, *al,* is here used in the sense of "with;" yet some translate it literally, to his army; but the former exposition is preferable. — *Calvin.*

[4] That is, among the fortifications, or among the people. The number is changed, and it can only be referred to the people. — *Calvin.*

He next adds, *And he shall work on them,* meaning, he shall prosper ; for this word when used without any addition, implies in Hebrew performing great exploits. *He shall proceed* and acquire power over the greater part of Syria, *and shall prevail.* By this last word he explains how superior he should be to Callinicus. For this king sent for his younger brother whose fidelity he suspected, and thought it the safest course to treat with his enemy. But young Hierax, the hawk, determined to use that expedition to his own advantage. He was not content with his own province of Asia Minor, but he anticipated being his father's sole heir, especially as he had hired some troops from Gaul, who had invaded Asia Minor, Bithynia, and other provinces. He was greatly puffed up, and betrayed his own covetousness. Seleucus Callinicus preferred making peace with his enemy to fostering his brother's resources. At length Hierax more and more developed the perversity of his mind. For he openly declared war against his brother, to whose assistance he pretended to have come, after having been sent for according to agreement. His brother Seleucus had promised him a portion of Asia as far as Mount Taurus ; and when he saw himself the victim of his impious and disgraceful snares, he openly waged war with his brother. But he was conquered at length, and thus received the reward of his impiety. Thus Ptolemy Euergetes prevailed, while he departed from Syria after spoiling his enemy, according to what follows :—

8. And shall also carry captives into Egypt their gods, with their princes, *and* with their precious vessels of silver and of gold; and he shall continue *more* years than the king of the north.

8. Atque etiam deos ipsorum cum conflatilibus ipsorum, et cum vasis pretiosis ipsorum,[1] auri et argenti in captivitatem ducent in Ægyptum,[2] et ipse *pluribus* annis stabit quam rex aquilonis.

The angel explains more fully what he had already stated briefly, namely, Ptolemy should be the conqueror, and spoil the whole of Syria almost according to his pleasure. Profane writers also shew us the great number of images which were

[1] That is, with desirable vessels, as I formerly stated on this word.— *Calvin.*

[2] Or, they shall lead captive into Egypt their gods, together with their images and their desirable vessels of silver and gold.—*Calvin.*

taken away, and how Egypt recovered its gods of silver and gold which it had lost a long time ago. Thus the event proved the truth of the angel's prophecy. The particle ⫐ם, *gem*, is interposed for the sake of amplifying the subject, to inform us of the unequal condition of the peace, and how Ptolemy exercised the rights of a conqueror in spoiling the whole of Syria according to his lust. It is added, *He shall stand for more years than the king of the north.* Some restrict this to the duration of the life of each king, and others extend it farther. Probably the angel speaks of Ptolemy Euergetes, who reigned forty-six years. As God extended his life so long, we are not surprised at the angel's saying it should last longer than the king of Syria's. This explanation is applicable to the present case, for if he had died before, Callinicus might have recovered the effects of the war; but as Ptolemy survived, he dared not attempt anything, being assured of the utter fruitlessness of any effort against the king who had vanquished him. It follows :—

9. So the king of the south shall come into *his* kingdom, and shall return into his own land.

9. Et veniet in regnum rex austri, et redibit in terram suam.

This clause belongs to the former verse ; as if he had said, Ptolemy shall return by a peaceful march after this hostile invasion of Syria. For he might have some fears lest his enemy should not be completely prostrated. But as he departed as conqueror, the angel announces his safe arrival in his own land. The words " come" and " return" are used emphatically, implying the absence of all harass, fear, and danger.[1] He returned to his kingdom and his own land, since he could not trust to the quietness of the enemies whom he had laid prostrate. It follows :—

10. But his sons shall be stirred up, and shall assemble a multitude of great forces : and *one* shall certainly come, and overflow, and pass through; then shall he return, and be stirred up, *even* to his fortress.

10. Et filii ejus provocabuntur, et congregabunt multitudinem copiarum magnarum : et veniendo veniet, inundabit et transibit : revertetur et incitabitur usque ad munitionem ejus.

11. And the king of the south shall be moved with choler, and shall

11. Tum exacerbabitur rex austri, et egressus pugnabit adver-

The edition of 1617 has *modestia* incorrectly for *molestia.* The error is corrected in subsequent editions. The reader of the original must be prepared for many verbal inaccuracies in this edition.—*Ed.*

come forth and fight with him, *even* | sus eum, adversus regem aquilonis,
with the king of the north : and he | et stare faciet, *statuet*, multitudi-
shall set forth a great multitude ; | nem magnam, tradeturque multi-
but the multitude shall be given | tudo illa in manum ejus.
into his hand.

Here the angel passes to the third war, namely, that which
the son of Callinicus stirred up against Ptolemy Philopator.
After the death of Euergetes, the two sons of Callinicus
united their forces, and endeavoured to recover Syria, and
especially that part of it of which they had been deprived.
When they were already on their expedition, and their forces
were on their march, the elder Seleucus died, and his surviving brother was Antiochus, called the Great. Ptolemy,
called Philopator, which means a lover of his father, was
then alive. He was so called in consequence of the parricide of which he was guilty, having put to death both
parents, together with his brother. The word is used
by way of ridicule, and a sense the opposite to that expressed is implied by this epithet, which is honourable in
itself, and expresses the virtue of filial piety. But he slew
his father, mother, and brother, and on account of all these
impious murders, the name of Philopator was applied to him
as a mark of disgrace. As, therefore, he was so thoroughly
hated by his own people, the sons of Callinicus, namely,
Seleucus Ceraunus the elder, and Antiochus the Great,
thought the time had arrived for the recovery of the lost
cities of Syria. For he was detested and despised in consequence of his numerous crimes. They therefore anticipated
little trouble in recovering their possessions, when their
enemy was thus branded with infamy, and had many domestic foes. This is the reason why the angel says of the
sons of Callinicus, *They shall be provoked, and shall lead a
multitude of great armies ;* it may mean " great forces," as
some historians relate the collection of two very strong
armies. Unless I am mistaken, Antiochus the Great had
70,000 foot and 5000 horse. Ptolemy excelled in cavalry,
as he had 6000 horse but only 62,000 foot, as Polybius informs us in his fifth book.[1] They were nearly equal in

[1] Calvin quoting from memory has not stated the numbers accurately.
See Polyb., lib. v. p. 421, edit. Casaubon. Paris; also the DISSERTATIONS
at the end of this volume.—*Ed.*

forces, but the confidence of the two sons of Callinicus, of
whom alone the angel now speaks, was increased when they
beheld their wicked enemy so greatly detested in consequence
of his parricide. He afterwards says, *He shall come.* He
changes the number, since the elder brother, being the eldest
son of Callinicus, namely, Seleucus Ceraunus, died while they
were preparing for the war, and they say he was slain by his
attendants in passing through Asia Minor. Whether this
was so or not, all historians unite in stating that Antiochus
the Great alone carried on the war with Philopator. He
shall come so as *to overflow and pass through.* He recovered
that part of Syria which he had lost, and when he approached
Egypt, then Philopator met him. Profane historians state
him to have been a coward, and never to have obtained
power by open bravery, but by fraud alone. He was too
late in preparing his forces for resisting his enemy.

This is the reason why the angel says, *The king of Syria,*
or of the north, *should come, even to the citadels,* or fortifications ; for at length Philopator roused himself from slumber,
for he never put on his arms to repel an enemy except when
compelled by the direst necessity. Hence he adds, *The king
of the south shall be irritated,* or exasperated. He uses the
word " exasperated," because, as I have just said, he would
never have opposed himself to his enemy Antiochus except
he had perceived his own kingdom placed in great jeopardy.
He might have taken patiently the loss of Syria, so long as
Egypt had been safe ; but when his life and all his possessions were in danger, he became sufficiently exasperated to
attack his foe ; and yet he prevailed, as we shall afterwards
see. I cannot complete this subject to-day, and so I shall
draw to a close. Philopator became victorious, and yet he was
so sluggish that he distrusted his friends and foes alike, and
was forced by this very fear to make peace with his enemy,
although he was really the conqueror. Not only could he have
driven back his enemy whom he had vanquished, but he
might have taken possession of his territories ; but he did
not dare to do this : he was conscious of being a parricide,
and knew to his cost how hateful his name was among all
men. Hence, although superior in strength, and actually

the conqueror of his enemy in battle, he dared not proceed further.   But we will explain the remainder another time.

Grant, Almighty God, as thou hast deigned to set before our eyes as in a glass that peculiar providence of thine by which thou defendest thy Church: Grant, that being confirmed by these examples, we may learn to repose entirely upon thee.   Amidst the numerous disturbances by which the world is at this time agitated, may we remain quiet under thy protection.   May we so commit our safety to thee as never to hesitate, whatever may happen, as to our future safety and security.   Whatever we may suffer, may it all issue in our salvation, while we are protected by thy hand; thus will we call upon thy name with sincerity of mind, and thou wilt in return shew thyself as our Father in thine only-begotten Son.—Amen.

Lecture Fifty=Eighth.

In our last Lecture we explained why the angel mentions the exasperation of King Ptolemy.   Unless he had been dragged into the war, his disposition was so sluggish that he would have suffered many cities to be wrested from him, and he would never have been moved by either the disgrace or the loss.   But at length he took up arms, on seeing with what a stern and bold enemy he had to deal.   He afterwards adds, *He shall go out to battle against the king of the North,* meaning Antiochus king of Syria.   *And he shall set in array a large multitude.*   This may be referred to either of them, for Antiochus then brought into the field a large army ; he had 5000 horse and 70,000 foot.   Ptolemy was superior in his cavalry, which amounted to 6000 men.   This clause will suit the case of Antiochus.   *He shall bring into the field a great multitude, and the multitude shall be given into his hand,* meaning Ptolemy's.   The context seems thus to flow on more easily : yet if any one prefers considering it as applicable to Ptolemy himself, I will not contend the point.   It is not of much consequence, because the angel simply pronounces the superiority of Ptolemy in this battle, in which he conquered Antiochus the Great. Besides, we must notice, that he was not the conqueror by his own industry, or valour, or counsel, or military skill; but because the Lord, who regulates the events of battles, wished at that time to subdue the pride of Antiochus the Great. It now follows,—

12. *And* when he hath taken away the multitude, his heart shall be lifted up; and he shall cast down *many* ten thousands: but he shall not be strengthened *by it*.

12. Et tolletur multitudo illa, *hoc est, sese attollet*, et elevabitur cor ejus, et dejiciet myriades, *hoc est, magnas copias*, et non roborabitur.

The angel here marks the close of the war. Had Ptolemy's valour seconded his good fortune, he might easily have seized upon the whole kingdom of Syria, as profane historians report. But he was so given up to his own lusts, that he willingly entered into treaty with his enemy. On his return to his kingdom he slew his wife Eurydice, and was guilty of other enormities; he suffered a wicked woman, the sister of Agathocles, a victim of his passions, to rule over his kingdom, and lastly, he became a very foul example of a very cruel and degraded man. Therefore, the angel says at the beginning, *his army should raise him aloft; his heart should be elevated*, in consequence of his prosperity. He not only caused terror to Antiochus, but through all the neighbouring regions. Where he might have drawn to himself the whole power of the East, he then declined in his course. He subdued, indeed, a hostile army, and in this exploit he was in no slight degree assisted by his sister Arsinoe, as historians relate, but yet after great slaughters he did not retain his position. And what was the obstacle? His idleness and drunkenness, and his caring for nothing but banquets and debaucheries, and the most obscene pleasures. This caused his fall, after he had been raised even to the clouds by his victories. It afterwards follows,—

13. For the king of the north shall return, and shall set forth a multitude greater than the former, and shall certainly come after certain

13. Et redibit rex aquilonis, *rex Syriæ*, et statuet multitudinem magnam præut antea,[1] et circiter finem[2] temporum annorum, *ad*

[1] That is, he will collect a greater army than before.—*Calvin.*
[2] That is, at the close, at a fixed time, at the end.—*Calvin.*

years with a great army, and with
much riches.

14. And in those times there shall
many stand up against the king of
the south: also the robbers of thy
people shall exalt themselves to
establish the vision; but they shall
fall.

verbum, veniendo veniet cum exercitu magno, et cum opibus magnis.[1]

14. Et temporibus illis multi
stabunt contra regem Ægypti, et
filii dissipatores populi tui sese
attollent, ad stabiliendam visionem,
et corruent.

Here the angel prophesies of other wars. For he first
describes the war which was carried on by Antiochus against
the Egyptians, after the death of Philopater, who left as his
heir, a little son named Ptolemy Epiphanes. When, therefore, he perceived the land deprived of its king, he drew up
an army and invaded Egypt. As the Egyptians had no
strength to resist him, an embassy was sent to Rome ; and
we know how eager the Romans were to become involved
in all the business of the world. With the view of extending
their empire still further and wider, they sent immediately
to Antiochus the Great, and commanded him to desist from
the war; but after many trials he failed of success, until he
engaged in a very desperate battle with Scopas, and at
length obtained a victory. In the meantime, the Egyptians
were far from idle : although they hoped to be able to subdue
the empire of Antiochus by the assistance of the Senate, yet
they carefully fitted out an armament of their own under
their General Scopas, who was successful in many of his
plans, but was finally defeated in the borders of Judea. The
angel now describes this war. *The king of Syria shall
return,* he says; meaning, after the death of Ptolemy Philopator, he rested for a while, because he had been unsuccessful
with his forces, and they were so entirely disorganized that
he had no confidence in the success of any expedition. But
he thought Egypt would give him no trouble, as it had lost
its head and was like a lifeless corpse. Then he was elevated
with fresh confidence, and returned to Egypt. *And he shall
arrange a greater multitude than at the first.* He had a
large and powerful army, as we have said, and a noble armament of cavalry : he had 70,000 foot, and was still collecting
greater forces. The angel signifies the future arrival of the

[1] Or, "many," for there are two words in the original, "great and
many."—*Calvin.*

king of Syria, after the interval of a certain time. *At the end of the times of the years he shall surely come,* that is, he shall break forth. The angel seems to use this expression for the sake of increasing its certainty; for he at first despised the Romans in consequence of their great distance from him, and he had no fear of what afterwards occurred. He never supposed they had such boldness in them as to cross the sea against him.

He afterwards adds, *And in those times many shall stand against the king of the South,* or Egypt. The angel hints, that Antiochus the Great would not be his only enemy; and historians inform us of his treaty and alliance with Philip king of Macedon, for carrying on this war. Without doubt, the two kings stirred up the whole of Asia Minor, and they were so unitedly powerful, that many were excited to take part with them. It seemed to be all over with the kingdom of Egypt, and thus the angel says, *many should stand up against the king of the South.* He adds, *and his sons dissipating.* The Hebrews call " robbers" פריצים, *pheritzim.* The root of this word is פרץ, *pheretz,* which signifies to break or dissipate, and sometimes to destroy. Without doubt, the angel here uses the word to imply factious men, for the people had no other chance of standing, except by remaining quiet and united. The word then applies to those who violated that unity; for when any one attached himself to foreign monarchs, Judea became exposed as a prey to either the Syrians or Egyptians. Some interpreters apply this passage to the younger Onias, who seized on Heliopolis, and drew some exiles with him, and there built a temple, as we learn from Josephus and the Book of Maccabees. For he pretended to have the prophecy in Isaiah, chap. xix., on his side, where it is said, And there shall be an altar to God in the midst of Egypt, (v. 19.) Without doubt, the Prophet here predicts the enlargement of God's kingdom through the propagation of his religion throughout the whole world. As Egypt was to the last degree devoted to idolatry, Isaiah here shews how the pure and perfect worship of God should prevail in Egypt. As if he had said, Even the Egyptians who have hitherto endeavoured to abolish true and sincere piety, shall be added to God's people, and shall worship him acceptably. We know the Prophet to be here treating figuratively of the spiritual reign of Christ, and to be always bringing forward the shadows of his own time. By the word "altar" he simply means the worship of God. That impostor, Onias, when he erected his profane temple and polluted the sacred altar, boasted in his fulfilment of this prophecy of Isaiah.

This then is the meaning of the passage : *The sons—dissipators of thy people—shall exalt themselves to establish the vision ;* that is, under a fallacious pretext of fulfilling Isaiah's prediction, *and yet they shall fall.* It may also have an indefinite meaning, as if the angel declared that these multitudes should not come forth unless by God's secret counsel. We know how much this thought tends to lighten the sorrow of the pious, and how much consolation it brings, when we recognise all the tumults of the world as springing from the fixed counsel of God. Nothing then appears to happen at random, but mortals are agitated because God desires to inflict his punishments upon them, and the Church is often shaken because God wishes to prove and examine the patience of his people. We may, therefore, take this prophecy absolutely ; as if the angel had said : These apostates and dissipators never proposed to fulfil this prophecy of Isaiah's, and yet there was nothing confused, or out of order in all these events, as God was fulfilling what he had testified by his own Prophets. Wherefore we may receive this prediction simply, just as we do other similar ones scattered throughout the prophets. We have already heard how the Prophet was forewarned of the many distresses of the Church, on purpose to lead the faithful to acquiesce in the providence of God, when they saw things so disturbed throughout the world. It afterwards follows,—

15. So the king of the north shall come, and cast up a mount, and take the most fenced cities ; and the arms of the south shall not withstand,	15. Et veniet rex aquilonis et fundet aggerem,[1] et capiet urbem munitionum ; et brachia austri, *hoc est, Ægypti,* non

[1] That is, he shall build up a mound by casting up stones, and wood, and earth.—*Calvin.*

neither his chosen people, neither *shall there be any* strength to withstand.	stabunt, neque populus electorum ejus, neque virtus *erit* ad standum.

The angel follows up the same sentiment. He says, When Antiochus the Great shall burst forth, there shall be no valour in the Egyptians to resist him, for he shall take a fortified city. There is a change of number here, for he means fortified cities. For he should recover the cities which he had formerly lost, and should arrive at the city Raphia in Egypt. The explanation follows, *The arms of Egypt shall not stand, nor the people of its levies.* This relates to Scopas, who was sent forth with large forces : at first he prospered, but he was afterwards vanquished in the conflict, and had no courage to persevere in resistance. It afterwards follows,—

16. But he that cometh against him shall do according to his own will, and none shall stand before him ; and he shall stand in the glorious land, which by his hand shall be consumed.	16. Et faciet veniens ad eum pro beneplacito suo, *hoc est, pro suo libidine,* et nullus stabit coram facie ejus, et stabit in terra desiderabili, et consumetur, *alii nomen esse volunt, consumptio,* in manu ejus.

The angel proceeds with the same discourse. He says, Antiochus the Great should accomplish his wishes, and should spread the terror of his arms in every direction, and thus no one would dare to oppose him. *He shall do* therefore *according to his will,* he says, *and none shall stand before his face ; and he shall stand in the desirable land ;* meaning, he shall bring his victorious army into Judea, *and there shall be a great consumption under his hand,* or Judea shall be consumed and ruined under his hand. We originally stated, that the angel's mission did not authorize him to treat these events as military exploits are usually narrated by historians. Enough is revealed to lead the faithful to acknowledge God's continual regard for their safety. Experience also assures us of every occurrence being divinely foreseen, and thus they would acknowledge how everything tended to promote their welfare. God's predictions of future events were never in vain, and the angel now declares the future coming of Antiochus *to the desirable land.* We have previously given the reason for the use of this epithet as applied to Judea,—not through any natural excellence over other lands, but because God had chosen it for himself as his seat and dwelling-place.   The excellence of this land depended entirely on the gratuitous beneficence of God.   It might seem inconsistent to grant such license to an impious tyrant and robber, and to allow him to overrun Judea, which God had marked out with peculiar honour, in adopting it as his dwelling-place, and calling it his residence. (Psalm cxxxii. 14.)   But we know that the Church, while on its pilgrimage in this world, enjoys no freedom from many inflictions ; for it is profitable for the sons of God to be humbled under the cross, lest they should grow restive in the world, and give themselves up to luxuries, and sleep upon the desires of the flesh.   The angel, indeed, omits the reason why God suffered Antiochus thus cruelly to oppress the sacred land ; but the faithful had been taught by the Law and the Prophets how the Church was subject to various tribulations.   It is sufficient, then, to relate the event with simplicity : *and the pleasant land shall be consumed under his hand,* or there shall be a consumption.   It matters but little which way we read it as far as the sense is concerned. The angel here encourages Daniel and all others to the exercise of patience, lest they should faint under this divine scourge ; for he permitted Antiochus to wander about like a robber, and to exercise severe tyranny and cruelty against the Jews.   I need not discuss these events at greater length, as they are found in the Books of the Maccabees.   I will only touch on one point briefly ; Antiochus did not of his own accord harass the Jews by leading his army into their country, but he was stirred up by impious priests.   So great was their perfidy and barbarity that they willingly betrayed God's Temple, and exposed their nation to the most distressing calamities.   That was a severe trial : hence God consulted the interests of his own worshippers by predicting events which might weaken their confidence and cause them to indulge in despair.   It follows,—

17. He shall also set his face to enter with the strength of his whole

17. Et ponet faciem suam[1] ad veniendum cum potentia totius

[1] That is, he shall turn himself.—*Calvin.*

kingdom, and upright ones with him; thus shall he do: and he shall give him the daughter of women, corrupting her; but she shall not stand *on his side*, neither be for him.

regni, et rectitudines cum eo :[1] et faciet, et filiam mulierum dabit illi ad perdendum eam, sed non stabit ipsa, et non erit ipsa ei.[2]

He here describes the second war of Antiochus against Epiphanes, who was then growing old; and so he gave him his daughter Cleopatra in marriage, hoping in this way, by subtle contrivances, to subdue the kingdom of Egypt. For he thought his daughter would remain faithful to his interests ; but she rather preserved her conjugal fidelity to her husband, and hesitated not to espouse her husband's quarrel against her father. She faithfully adhered to her husband's interests according to her duty, and never listened to the cunning designs of Antiochus. Thus he was deprived of his expectation, and his daughter never became the means of his acquiring authority over Egypt. Before this marriage of his daughter with Ptolemy, he had tried the effect of war, but in this he failed ; and when he perceived the interposition of the Romans, he desisted from future hostilities, and consoled himself with the thought which we have already expressed, of receiving immediate assistance against Egypt through his daughter. *He turns*, therefore, *to come with the power of his whole kingdom ;* meaning, he collects all his forces to overwhelm Ptolemy Epiphanes, who was then but a young man, and had neither obtained any great authority, nor arrived at sound wisdom and discretion. When he perceived his want of success in the fortune of war, *he gave him the daughter of women*, referring to her beauty. This is the explanation of interpreters, who suppose the phrase to imply her remarkable beauty.

As to the next clause, those who translate it, *and the upright with him*, think the Jews are intended, for Antiochus had received them in surrender, and there were many who openly espoused his cause. They think the Jews so called as a mark of honour, and as upright with respect to

[1] Some translate, " the upright," pl., (*recti*) " with him." The copula may be superfluous, as we often find it in the Scriptures. We must read it in one context,—he shall make alliances with him, as we saw before.— *Calvin.*

[2] That is, she shall not obey his will, nor stand by him.—*Calvin.*

the worship of God. But this appears to me too forced. I hesitate not to suppose the angel to signify the superior character of the agreement between Antiochus and Ptolemy, when the former found the impossibility of obtaining his adversary's kingdom by open warfare. Although the Romans had not yet sent forth any armament, yet Antiochus began to fear them, and he preferred the use of cunning in providing for his own interests. Besides this, as we lately mentioned, he was longing for other booty, for he immediately transferred the war into Greece, as the angel will inform us. But he first announces, *his giving away his daughter to destroy her.* He here reproves the artifice of Antiochus the Great, in thus basely selling his daughter, as if she were a harlot. As far as he possibly could, he induced her to slay her husband either by poison or by other devices. Hence, *he gave up his daughter to destroy her, but she did not stand by him, and was not for him;* meaning, she did not assent to her father's impious desires, and was unwilling to favour such monstrous wickedness. We read in profane writers the fulfilment of these predictions of the angel, and thus it more clearly appears how God placed before the eyes of the pious, a mirror in which they might behold his providence in ruling and preserving his Church. It now follows,—

18. After this shall he turn his face unto the isles, and shall take many: but a prince for his own behalf shall cause the reproach offered by him to cease; without his own reproach he shall cause *it* to turn upon him.

18. Et vertet faciem suam ad insulas, et capiet multas, et quiescere faciet, *hoc est, retorquebit,* princeps opprobrium ejus apud ipsum. Ideo non torquebit opprobrium suum in ipsum.

There is some obscurity in these words, but the history will afterwards determine the angel's meaning. First, as to the word "islands," he doubtless means Asia Minor and the maritime coasts; also Greece, Cyprus, and all the islands of the Mediterranean Sea. It was a Jewish custom to call all places beyond the sea "islands," as they were not very well skilled in navigation. Therefore he says, *He will turn his face to the islands;* that is, he shall turn to the opposite regions of the world. The Mediterranean Sea is known to be

between Syria and Asia Minor ; Cilicia, too, is between them,
which was also under the dominion of Antiochus, although
the seat of his power was Syria.   Hence he calls Asia Minor,
and Greece, and the Mediterranean islands, all " isles," with
respect to Syria and Judea.   This occurred when the Ætolians
renewed ' he war after the defeat of Philip.   The Romans
were the originators of this war in Greece, and they had the
honourable pretext of liberating the whole of Greece after
Philip of Macedon had seized upon many cities most skilfully
fortified.   But the Ætolians were proud and puffed up with
the desire of superiority, as the event ultimately proved.
They boasted themselves to be the liberators of Greece ; they
used the help of the Romans, but professed to be the principal leaders in the war, and when they saw Chalcis and other
cities held by the Romans, the spirit of envy took possession
of them.   Titus Flaminius withdrew his garrisons from their
cities, but yet the Ætolians were not satisfied ; for they
wished for the sole pre-eminence and the entire departure of
the Romans.   With this view they sent their ambassadors
to Nabis the tyrant of the Lacedæmonians, to king Philip,
and also to Antiochus.   Thoas was the principal author of
this contention, for after stirring up the neighbouring
nations, he set out himself to Antiochus.   When the Ætolians were puffed up by the large promises which he brought
back, they expected to produce peace throughout Greece
without the slightest trouble.   Meanwhile Antiochus only
advanced as far as Asia Minor with but a small force.   He led
Hannibal with him, whose fame alone inspired the Romans
with dread ; and had he taken his advice, he would certainly
have had no difficulty in expelling the Romans.   But the flatterers of his court did not allow Hannibal's advice to prevail
with this foolish king.   Then Villius also cunningly rendered
Antiochus suspicious of his advice : for he had been sent as
ambassador into Asia Minor, had insinuated himself into his
favour, and had acquired his friendship, and was so engaged
in daily conference with him, that Antiochus suspected the
fidelity of Hannibal to his interests.   Hence he carried on
that war entirely without method, or plan, or perseverance.
When he arrived at Chalcis, he was smitten with the passion

for a damsel there, and celebrated a foolish marriage with her, as if he had been completely at peace. Thus he had a citizen of Chalcis for his father in-law, while he was a mighty monarch, unequalled by any throughout the world. Although he conducted himself thus inconsiderately, yet the celebrity of his fame rather than his personal exertions, enabled him at first to take many cities, not only in Asia Minor and on the coast of the Mediterranean Sea, but also in Greece itself. He recovered Chalcis and other cities which had been seized upon by the Romans. The angel relates this as if the event had already occurred, and yet we are aware of them all being as yet future.

He will turn his face to the islands, and will take many, and a general shall cause him to cease, and shall turn his reproach against himself. Antiochus often fought against the Romans, and always without success, although he sometimes thought himself superior ; but from the time when Attilius the prefect of the fleet intercepted his supplies, and thus stopped his progress, M. Acilius the consul began to gain the mastery by land, and his power became gradually more and more enfeebled. When conquered in a naval engagement by Livius the prætor, he suffered a severe loss, and then when too late he acknowledged his error in not obeying the counsels of Hannibal ; but he had lost the opportunity of renewing the war. Hence the angel here says, *A leader should make his reproach return upon himself.* This signifies how Antiochus should be puffed up with foolish pride, and how his insane boastings should rebound upon his own head, as he had vomited them forth with open mouth against the Romans. When he speaks here of *his disgrace,* I interpret it actively, as making his reproach remain ; for the word חרפת, *cherepheth,* means reproach, but there are two ways of interpreting it, actively and passively. But as I have already said, the angel more probably speaks of his foolish boasting, for he had despised the Romans with contempt and insult. We know how foolishly he insulted them by his ambassadors among all the assemblies of Greece. *A leader,* then, either Acilius or Lucius Scipio, who drove him beyond Mount Taurus, *made his disgrace rest upon himself,* and *he shall not turn away his own disgrace;* that is, Antiochus vomited forth his reproaches against the Romans with swollen cheeks, but with utter futility. All these disgraceful speeches came to nothing, and never injured the Romans in the least ; but *that leader,* either Lucius Scipio or Acilius, according to my statement, returned these reproaches upon himself by which he hoped to lay the Romans prostrate, but they turned out nothing but wind. The angel therefore derides the pride of Antiochus by saying, *A leader should come who should throw back these reproaches upon himself,* and prevent them from returning upon either this leader or the Romans. He takes the head as representing the whole body.

PRAYER.

Grant, Almighty God, since it pleases thee to exercise our confidence by not allowing us any fixed or stable rest upon earth, that we may learn to rest in thee while the world rolls over and over even a hundred times. May we never doubt either our protection under thy hand, or the perpetual issue of all things in our good. Although we are not beyond the reach of darts, yet may we know the impossibility of our suffering under any deadly wound, when thou puttest forth thy hand to shield us. May we have full confidence in thee, and never cease to march under thy standard with constant and invincible courage, until at length thou shalt gather us into that happy rest which is laid up for us in heaven, by Christ our Lord.—Amen. ˙

Lecture Fifty=Ninth.

19. Then he shall turn his face toward the fort of his own land : but he shall stumble, and fall, and not be found.	19. Et vertet faciem suam ad munitiones terræ suæ, et impinget, et cadet, neque invenietur.

HERE either the base end of Antiochus is denoted, who was slain in a popular tumult while spoiling the temple of Belus, or else the event of the war between him and the Romans is described. This war was conducted under the auspices of Lucius Scipio, because Cneius Scipio, the con-

queror of Africa, had offered himself as his brother's lieutenant-general, and after his death that province was committed to him.   But, as we have said, the resources of
Antiochus had been cut off before this.   He had lost the
cities of Asia, and if he had ceded them at first, he might
have quietly retained the greater part of Asia Minor.   But
as he extended his wings over Greece, and hoped by this
means to become completely master of the whole of Greece
and Macedonia, he could not be induced to withdraw his
garrisons from those cities, but at length was compelled to
give up Asia Minor.   In this way, then, the angel describes
the progress of the war by saying, *He will turn his face towards the fortifications of his own land ;* that is, when compelled to relinquish Greece, he will betake himself to fortified
places.   He was very safe there, and in a region sufficiently
at peace ; he had almost impregnable towns on all sides, and
appeared to be free from warfare.   Historians relate this to
have been done by the skill of Cneius Scipio.   For his son
was then a captive under Antiochus, and he knew him to
have greater authority than his brother, although he only
possessed the title of lieutenant-general.   They record his
persuading Antiochus not to try his fortune by any decisive
engagement.   However it was, it is quite evident that he
delayed fighting till he was compelled by a sense of shame,
as all men accused him of cowardice in not daring to try the
issue of an engagement when he possessed so large an army.
The Romans had scarcely ever taken the field against so
strong a force, and yet, according to the narrative of Titus
Livius, they never displayed less terror or concern.   The
extent of the forces of Antiochus is readily apparent from
the slaughter which occurred ; in one day 50,000 men
perished ; and this would be almost incredible, unless it
were borne out by numerous and trustworthy testimonies.
In this way the angel said, *Antiochus should return,* as he
did not go forth to meet Lucius Scipio, but suffered him to
pass on.   Had he given the least sign of resistance, without
doubt Philip had in his hand and power the whole force
of the Romans.   Many indeed pronounced the conduct of
L. Scipio to be rash, in daring to allow Philip such license,

as he had been lately conquered, and was still exasperated in consequence of the loss and disgrace which he had suffered. For if Antiochus had been on the alert to restrain the enemy, it would have been all over with the Roman army in those narrow and rugged defiles ; but, as we have stated, he kept his army in idleness and luxury among fortified towns. If another and a probable sense is preferred, the sentence applies to his base retreat to further Asia, where he fell, slain by the rustic population. *He shall fall, and shall not be found.* Antiochus in truth continued to reign from the period of the destruction of his army and of his acceptance of the conditions which the Romans imposed. He obtained peace, but not without the payment of a heavy fine while he retained the name of king. Although he united with the Romans in an honourable treaty, yet he was forced to retire beyond Mount Taurus, to pay a large sum of money on account of the expenses of the war, to give hostages, and to divide the ships equally with the Romans. In this latter case he was grossly and fraudulently deluded, for L. Scipio commanded all the ships to be cut to pieces, and delivered the materials to Antiochus, to whom they were utterly worthless. He knew the man to be deceptive and restless, and so he treated him with barbarity, according to his deserts. As far as the hostages are concerned, we find Antiochus and Demetrius his sons as hostages at Rome even after his death. He was left in peace indeed, but was deprived of the cities of Asia Minor, and was ordered to betake himself beyond Mount Taurus. Those ravines were the boundary of his empire ; a part of Asia was assigned to Eumenes, and many cities became independent. Antiochus, by way of concealing his disgrace, made a joke of it, saying he had managed cleverly, for the government of Asia Minor was a great trouble to him. He had another ample and opulent kingdom with which he might well be content : I have hitherto been but a steward in Asia, he used to say, and the Romans have relieved me of that encumbrance.

When, therefore, the angel says, *After his fall, he should be no longer king ;* this may be understood of his ignominious death which followed shortly afterwards. His avarice was

insatiable, and when compelled to pay a large tribute to the
Romans, he pretended to be reduced to extreme poverty ;
then he wished to spoil the temple of Jupiter Dodoneus, and
was slain there during a tumult.   This last word ought properly to be referred to this event, for King Antiochus was
not found, because these rustics slew him in the tumult which
arose.   Thus far concerning Antiochus the Great ; Seleucus
now follows, who was his first successor.   He had three sons,
Seleucus whom many call Ceraunus, then Antiochus Epiphanes, and Demetrius.   Concerning Seleucus the angel
speaks as follows,—

20. Then shall stand up in his estate a raiser of taxes *in* the glory of the kingdom: but within few days he shall be destroyed, neither in anger, nor in battle.	20. Et stabit super locum ejus transire faciens exactorem *in* honore regni,[1] et diebus paucis conteretur, idque non ira, neque in prælio.

Seleucus, it is well known, did not long survive his father,
for he was put to death either by poison, or by his domestics.
Suspicion fell upon his brother Antiochus, who was sent back
to his country after his father's death was known.   Demetrius alone was retained, who afterwards escaped by flight,
for he left the city under the pretence of hunting, and followed the bank of the Tiber as far as Ostia, where he em-
barked on a small vessel, preferring to run all risks to
remaining in perpetual banishment.   Concerning Seleucus,
the angel says, *he shall stand in his place,* meaning, he shall
succeed by hereditary right to the office of Antiochus the
Great.   Thus *he shall cause the exactor to pass over.*   Some
translate, He shall take away the exactor ; for the verb עבר,
gneber, in Hiphil, signifies to take away.   The Hebrews use
the verb of this clause in the sense of excluding.   Some
interpreters think this language implies the praise of Seleucus for lessening the tributes imposed by his father, but
historians shew this view to be false, and condemn his
avarice and rapacity.   In some points he was superior to
his brother Antiochus ; although both lustful and cruel to
those around him.   Through indulgence in great expenses,
he could not be moderate and lenient towards his subjects ;

[1] Some translate this word as if in opposition with the last,—" the
honour or glory of the realm."—*Calvin.*

for luxury and prodigality always draw with them cruelty
in the exaction of tribute. For he who is thus profuse,
must necessarily extract the very blood from his people. As
Seleucus was thus devoted to self-indulgence, this sense is
more appropriate—*he made the exactor to pass through,*
meaning, he laid new and fresh taxes on all his subjects.
Nothing but this is said of him, since he was immediately
put to death, as the second clause of the verse informs us.
If we prefer taking the words—the glory of the kingdom—
by way of opposition, Seleucus will be praised as an honour
and an ornament. But I think we must supply the letter
ל, *l*, and understand the passage thus,—*He who shall cause
the exactor to pass through shall stand in his place, and shall
be destroyed in a few days.* By the word "destroyed," he
signifies a bloody death. *But not in anger,* says he. I
wonder why some translate it "in mutual conflict," because
the Hebrews imply "anger" by this word; meaning, he
should not perish in open warfare, or in the course of a
battle, but by the hands of his domestics. Historians differ
as to the kind of death which he died, some saying he was
poisoned, and others, slain by the sword. But this difference
is of no consequence. Antiochus Epiphanes next succeeds
him.

21. And in his estate shall stand up a vile person, to whom they shall not give the honour of the kingdom: but he shall come in peaceably, and obtain the kingdom by flatteries.	21. Et stabit super locum ejus probrosus, et non dabunt ei[1] decorem regni,[2] et veniet cum pace, et apprehendet regnum per blanditias.

Historians agree in representing Antiochus Epiphanes to
have been of a very crafty disposition, and some state his
departure from Rome to have been by stealth. He was
most probably dismissed by the Romans, on the news of his
father's death, as they were content with his brother Demetrius. They had other hostages besides, who were among
the chief nobles of the land, as well as this third son of the
king. However this was, all are agreed in relating his cunning. He was so cruel and fierce, that Polybius says he was
called Epimanes by way of a nickname, and as he assumed

---

[1] That is, they shall not commit to him.—*Calvin.*
[2] That is, they shall not confer the glory of the kingdom.—*Calvin.*

the name of Illustrious, he was called the Madman, on account of his turbulent disposition. He was a monster puffed up with various vices; being of a slavish and flattering temperament, he endeavoured to acquire the favour of Rome by artifice, as we shall afterwards discover. But when he was not actuated by fear, his cruelty and ferocity were beyond all bounds. For this reason he is called *contemptible*. He was held in some esteem at Rome, and was received by a portion of his people with great applause. But he was not endued with any heroic or even regal qualities, for he always flattered the Romans, and insinuated himself into the favour of the citizens in this way, until he came to his kingdom as a suppliant; and then the angel calls him a contemptible or despicable person. Another reason equally probable may be brought forward, namely, his seizing upon the throne by fraud and wickedness, after setting aside the legitimate heir. For Seleucus left a successor whom this perfidious plotter deprived of his rights, and thus fraudulently acquired the kingdom for himself. We know of what importance God makes every one's calling, and how he restrains men from rashly arrogating anything to themselves, as they ought always to be satisfied with that station which is assigned them by God. As, therefore, Antiochus seized on the kingdom without any right to it, and drove out the lawful heir, he was contemptible before God, and would never have been king at all except by violence and tyranny on his part, as well as by deceit and cunning devices. I have no hesitation in stating that the angel here censures the perverse conduct of Antiochus, by calling him *despised* through the absence of all nobleness of feeling.

He next adds, *They shall not confer upon him the honour of royalty.* By these words he announces the injustice of his reign through not being chosen by the votes of the people. We have stated that the son of Seleucus ought to have reigned without any dispute, but the very person who should have been his nephew's guardian, wickedly deprived his ward of his paternal inheritance. Hence the angel speaks of him rather as a robber than as a king, because he seized upon the kingdom, and was not elected by the popular choice. It follows,—*he shall come in peace, and seize the kingdom by flatteries.* This is the explanation of the last clause. It might be asked, how did he deprive his nephew of his kingdom? the reply is—*he shall come peacefully*, meaning, he shall lay aside everything which he was agitating in his mind, and should not openly boast of his being king, but should deceitfully act in the character of guardian until he had the power of ruining his ward. *He shall come, then, peacefully, and shall seize the kingdom by flatteries.* Thus we see the angel's meaning in these words. Besides, although Daniel did not see all these things, nor even many of the chosen people, yet they tasted enough of these prophecies to satisfy them, and to banish anxiety from their minds. They were permitted to perceive God speaking through his angel, and experience taught them the truth of everything which is contained here, even if many events should be hidden from them. But it was God's object to support the spirits of the pious, even to the advent of Christ, and to retain them in tranquillity amidst the greatest disturbances. Thus they would acknowledge the value of the promise of the Redeemer, after he had been set forth, as will be mentioned at the close of the chapter. I will now proceed to the next words.

22. And with the arms of a flood shall they be overflown from before him, and shall be broken; yea, also the prince of the covenant.

22. Et brachia inundatione obruentur, *ad verbum, inundabuntur*, a conspectu ejus, et conterentur, atque etiam dux fœderis.

We may naturally conjecture that the dominions of Antiochus were not immediately at peace, because a portion of his court favoured the lawful heir. As it always happens in every change of government, there were many tumults in Syria before Antiochus could remove his adversaries out of his way. For although the kingdom of Egypt was then destitute of a head, as Ptolemy, called Philometor, was then only a boy, his counsellors were in favour of the son of Seleucus, and so by secret supplies afforded their aid to the faction opposed to Antiochus. He had much trouble not only with his own people, but also with the neighbouring nations. All pitied the lot of his ward, and his being quite undeserving of it, moved many to render him every possible help. The boy was aided by the favour of Egypt, and of other nations. Thus Antiochus was subject to many severe commotions, but the angel announces his final conquest. *The arms,* he says, *shall be inundated.* This is a metaphorical expression; for whatever aid the son of Seleucus acquired, was not by his own efforts, for he could use none, but by that of his friends. *The arms,* then, meaning, all the auxiliaries which should assist in the restoration of the son of Seleucus, *should be overwhelmed by an inundation.* This is another metaphor, signifying, they shall be drowned as by a deluge; and by this figure the angel hints not only at the victory of Antiochus, but at its great facility. It was like a deluge, not by its own strength, but because God wished to use the hand of this tyrant in afflicting the Israelites, as we shall afterwards see, and also in harassing both Egypt and Syria. Antiochus was in truth God's scourge, and is thus compared to a deluge. Hence he says, *out of his sight.* He shews the terror of Antiochus to be so great, that at his very appearance he should dispirit and prostrate his enemies, although he was without forces, and was neither a bold nor a persevering warrior.

And they shall be broken, says he, *and also the leader of the covenant;* meaning, Ptolemy shall take the part of his relative in vain. For the son of Seleucus was the cousin of Ptolemy Philometor, since, as we have said, Cleopatra had married Ptolemy Philopator, whence this Philometor was sprung, and Seleucus was the brother of Cleopatra. He, then, was the *leader of the covenant.* Ptolemy, indeed, who was but a boy, could neither undertake nor accomplish anything by his own counsel, but such was his dignity in the kingdom of Egypt, that he was deservedly called *leader of the covenant,* since all others followed the power of that king. The event fully proved with what ill success all who endeavoured to eject Antiochus from his possessions, contended against him. It now follows,—

23. And after the league *made* with him he shall work deceitfully: for he shall come up, and shall become strong with a small people.	23. Et a conjunctione cum eo faciet dolum, et ascendet, et prævalebit cum exigua gente, *vel, manu.*

The angel points out some interruption of the wars, because Antiochus would be content for a time with Syria, and would not make an attempt of Egypt. It was a great point to repel the attempts of all those who wished to recover the rights of his nephew. There is no doubt that the whole country was impoverished and exhausted with the continual expense of these wars ; for whenever fresh commotions arose, it was necessary to draw new levies from these provinces, and this occasioned very great expense. It is not surprising, then, if Antiochus, who was of a cunning disposition, negotiated a temporary peace with his nephew Ptolemy Philometor the king of Egypt. His sister Cleopatra still survived, and this was an honourable excuse. The angel, then, states first, the proposal of a truce leading to settled peace between the two sovereigns. He adds, however, the perfidious conduct of Antiochus in his friendships. *During*, or after *these agreements*, he *shall deal treacherously with him.* Although, therefore, he pretended to be the friend and ally of his nephew, yet he conducted himself deceitfully towards him. *And he shall ascend, and shall prevail by a small band;* meaning, he shall attack the boy suddenly. For when Ptolemy anticipated a lasting friendship with his uncle, Antiochus took the opportunity of fraudulently attacking some cities with a small force : He thus deceived his enemy, who thought all things would be tranquil with him ; and so when Ptolemy had no fear of his uncle, he suddenly lost some of his cities. The angel means this ; *he shall rise* by deceit, and *shall prevail without large forces,* because there shall be no suspicion of warfare. It is easy enough to oppress an enemy in a state of tranquillity, and in the absence of all fear. It is afterwards added,—

24. He shall enter peaceably even upon the fattest places of the province ; and he shall do *that* which his fathers have not done, nor his fathers' fathers : he shall scatter among them the prey, and spoil, and riches : *yea,* and he shall forecast his devices against the strong holds, even for a time.

24. In pace, et in pinguedinibus regionis, *aut provinciæ,* veniet, *hoc est, in deliciis,* et faciet quæ non fecerunt patres ejus, et patres patrum ejus : spolia et prædam, et substantiam illis dispertiet,[1] et super munitiones cogitabit cogitationes suas, idque ad tempus.

The history is here continued : The angel shews how An-

[1] Or, he shall disperse their property.—*Calvin.*

tiochus in a short time and with a small band should acquire
many cities, *as he should come in peace upon the fatness of
the province,* implying his oppressing them while sleeping in
security.   He shews also how he should become conqueror,
not by any hostile invasion of Egypt, but by cunning and
stealth he should deprive King Ptolemy of his cities when
he least expected it.   There should be no appearance of
war; hence he says, *he shall come in peace upon the fatness
of the land.*   The word "fatness" is used metaphorically for
"richness."   When the Egyptians supposed all danger to be
far removed, and were persuaded of the friendship of Antiochus towards them, and relied on him as an ally should
any adversity arise, they indulged themselves in luxuries
till Antiochus came suddenly and subdued them.   He next
adds, *He shall despise the spoil, and prey, and goods, which
belonged to them.*   Some take the words for spoil and prey
in the sense of "soldiers," and join it with the verb יבזור,
ibzor, "he shall disperse," meaning, he shall distribute their
possessions among his soldiers, to conciliate their good will,
and to prepare them for new wars, as we know how easily
soldiers are enticed when they receive the rewards of their
service; for they are actuated solely by covetousness and
avarice.   Some writers expound it in this way—Antiochus
shall divide the prey among his soldiers, but I prefer the
other sense—*he shall disperse the prey, and the spoil, and
the goods, of the Egyptians.*   After suddenly oppressing the
Egyptians, he shall proceed to spoil them like a robber.

He afterwards adds, *And against the fortifications shall he
devise machinations,* meaning, he shall lay his plans for
seizing the fortified cities.   For at first he penetrated as far
as certain cities, and occupied first Cœlo-Syria, and afterwards Phœnice, but could not quickly possess the fortified
towns; hence he deferred the execution of his plans to a
more suitable time.   Therefore, the angel says, *he shall
arrange his plans against the fortified cities, but only for the
time;* meaning, he shall not immediately bring forward his
intentions, hoping to oppress his nephew when off his guard.
Thus under the disguise of peace an access to these cities
would always be open to him, and he would reconcile to

himself all whom he could corrupt by either gifts or other devices. We perceive, then, how a summary is here presented to us of the arts and schemes by which Antiochus should deprive his nephew of a portion of his territory and its towns, how suddenly he should invade some of the weakest in a state of unsuspecting tranquillity; and how by degrees he should invent machinations for seizing upon the stronger towns as well as he could. He also says, *for the time.* The cunning and malice of Antiochus was always apparent throughout these transactions. He did not engage in open warfare, but was always endeavouring to add to his possessions by indirect frauds,—a course which was not without its success.

When it is said, *He shall do what neither his fathers nor his fathers' fathers did,* this must be restricted solely to Egypt. For Seleucus the first king of Syria enjoyed a wide extent of dominion : then he prospered in warfare, and his fame flourished even to a good old age, and though at last he was unsuccessful in battle, yet on the whole he was a superior and celebrated warrior. Besides this we know him to have been one of the chief generals of Alexander the Great. As to his son Antiochus, we have previously observed the wide extent of his dominion, and how highly he was esteemed for prudence and valour. The angel does not compare Antiochus Epiphanes generally with either his father, or grandfather, or great-grandfather, but only with respect to Egypt. For his ancestors always longed after Egypt, but their designs against it were entirely frustrated ; he, however, was more successful in his aggression where his ancestors had failed in their attempts. Hence it becomes manifest how God overrules the events of war, so that the conqueror and the triumphant hero is not the man who excels in counsel, or in prudence, or valour, but he who fights under the heavenly leader. It pleases God at one time to afflict nations, and at another to set over them kings who are really his servants. So he wished to punish Egypt by the hands of this robber. It afterwards follows,—

25. And he shall stir up his power and his courage against the king of the south

25. Et excitabit robur suum, et cor suum adversus regem

with a great army; and the king of the south shall be stirred up to battle with a very great and mighty army; but he shall not stand: for they shall forecast devices against him.

austri, cum exercitu magno: et rex austri irritabitur ad prælium cum exercitu magno, et robusto valde: et non stabit, quia cogitabunt contra eum cogitationes.[1]

The angel here announces how Antiochus Epiphanes after prevailing by fraud, should become bolder in his daring. He should venture to levy a hostile army and invade Egypt openly, without any further dissimulation. He therefore says, *at length he shall rouse his strength and his courage.* He had previously crept along through hiding-places and fastnesses, and had not roused either his strength or his courage when remaining quiet at home; meanwhile he obtained the possession of various towns by treachery and other artifices. This was only creeping on by burrowing underground. But he now openly declares war, and brings his forces into the field of battle, and thus *stirs up his strength and his courage.* As I have already said, his new method of warfare is here described as unusual with him, as his audacity, doubtless, gradually increased through that series of success which he had enjoyed, and by which he had become more powerful than his nephew, through the practice of deceit. He afterwards adds, *with a great army.* He had mentioned a small band, he now places opposite to it a large army; for it required a long space of time to collect extensive pecuniary resources for carrying on the war, and also for enlarging and extending his own boundaries. He was thus able to enrol fresh levies, while his prosperity induced many to become his auxiliaries. As he found himself in every way superior to his nephew, he collected a great army. *The king of the south also shall be irritated;* that is, he shall not dare to harass his own uncle Antiochus, but shall be forced to open warfare. *He shall come, then, with a great army,* very great, strong, and powerful, says he, *but he shall not stand, because they shall devise devices against him;* meaning, he shall be conquered by treachery. Here the angel signifies that Ptolemy should have sufficient courage to resist, had he not been betrayed by his adherents. We shall more clearly perceive this in the next verse to-morrow.

[1] That is, they shall agitate against him perfidious counsels.—*Calvin.*

PRAYER.

Grant, Almighty God, that we may remain quiet under thy shelter and protection, in the midst of those numerous disturbances which thou ever submittest to our eyes in this world. May we never lose our courage when an occasion is given to Satan and our enemies to oppress us, but may we remain secure under thy protection, and every hour and every moment may we fly to thy guardianship. Relying on thine unconquered power, may we never hesitate so to pass through all commotions, as to repose with quiet minds upon thy grace, till at length we are gathered into that happy and eternal rest which thou hast prepared for us in heaven, by Jesus Christ our Lord.—Amen.

Lecture Sixtieth.

26. Yea, they that feed of the portion of his meat shall destroy him, and his army shall overflow; and many shall fall down slain.

26. Et qui comedent portionem cibi ejus, conterent eum, et exercitus ejus obruetur, et cadent vulnerati multi.

THE angel predicted, yesterday, that Ptolemy should not stand forth in battle, through the treachery of his own adherents. He now expresses the kind of treachery, for his chief courtiers or counsellors should be the authors of this perfidy. He opposes the common soldiers to their leaders, for in the second clause, he shews how the soldiers should discharge their duty without sparing either their life or their blood. We now understand the Holy Spirit's intention in this verse, for he says the authors of this perfidy should not be ordinary men, but the chief among the counsellors. They are said to eat at the king's table, as in the first chapter we saw how a portion was given to Daniel, and to his companions, from the royal food at the king's table. Thus he shews how dishonourable this perfidy was, as they eat at his table, and were his intimate companions. *They shall destroy him,* says he, *and his army shall be overwhelmed.* He shews that many were prepared for this duty, who would boldly and freely expose their lives to danger for their king's safety and their country's defence, *but many should fall wounded.* He signifies that there should be a great slaughter in his army, and the issue of the battle would not be according to his wish, because his generals would not preserve their fidelity to their sovereign.   By this example the angel describes to us the ordinary situation of kings.   They choose their counsellors not by their honesty, but by the mere appearance of congeniality in their affections and tastes.   If a king is avaricious, or cunning, or cruel, or sensual, he desires to have friends and attendants who will not check either his avarice or his craftiness, his cruelty or his lust.   Hence they deserve the conduct which they receive, and experience treachery from those whom they ought not to treat with so much honour, if they considered themselves in duty bound to God and to their people.   It now follows,—

27. And both these kings' hearts *shall be* to do mischief, and they shall speak lies at one table; but it shall not prosper: for yet the end *shall be* at the time appointed.	27. Et duorum regum cor ipsorum, hoc est, et cor his duobus regibus, in malum: et in mensa eadem, *una,* mendacium loquentur, et non prospere eveniet, quia adhuc finis ad tempus statutum.

The angel here narrates that the close of this war should be by treaties and a hollow pretence of peace after the slaughter which Ptolemy had sustained.   Although Antiochus might have followed up his own good fortune, yet he durst not venture to push his advantage to the extremity, but according to his disposition, he thought it more to his interest to make peace with his enemy.   We have already alluded to his craftiness and his want of openness and integrity. The angel predicts the existence of bad faith in both these kings; the uncle and nephew will meet, says he, and sup together, and pretend the greatest friendship, *but they shall speak lies,* says he, *at the same table;* meaning, they shall plot against each other, and each shall act fraudulently for his own ends.   This prophecy indeed seems to be of little consequence to the faithful ; but it was needful to shew that in such a state of confusion they could not hold out without being furnished with all kinds of support.   If the angel had only said generally, first there shall be war, and then a temporary peace, this would not have been sufficient to sustain the minds of the pious ; but when the details are so clearly pointed out, a remarkable confirmation is afforded them.

Thus the faithful have no reason for doubting that God has spoken, when the angel predicts the future so exactly, and so openly narrates it, as if a matter of history.

He next adds, *Yet it shall not prosper, because the end is for the time,* says he. The angel recalls the faithful to the providence of God, as our minds always naturally rest in the midst of earthly things. We apprehend with our minds only as far as we see with our eyes. We always ask the reasons " why this happens" and " why that course of proceeding has not turned out well," entirely omitting the will of God. Hence the angel meets this fault and stupidity of men by saying, that whatever these kings were plotting should fail of success, *since the end was for the time;* meaning, God would hold many occurrences in suspense. While, therefore, we are considering only second causes, we perceive how the supreme power resides with God alone, and he governs by his will the mutual transactions of mankind. No slight advantage would result to the faithful from this instruction, because, while kings are devising many schemes, and using great cunning and all the perverse artifices of diplomacy, God still restrains their minds. He holds events by his secret bridle, and allows nothing to happen without his heavenly decree. Although we may gather this general instruction from this passage, yet the angel doubtless restricts what I have said to the historical events immediately before us. The end had not yet approached, yet the fitting time was fixed beforehand by God's secret counsel, so that Antiochus conquers at one period and retreats at another, as we shall see. It follows :—

28. Then shall he return into his land with great riches ; and his heart *shall be* against the holy covenant ; and he shall do *exploits,* and return to his own land.

28. Et revertetur in terram suam cum opibus magnis, et cor ejus ad fœdus sanctitatis, et faciet, et revertetur in terram suam.

Here the angel predicts the calamitous nature of that peace for the people of God, because Antiochus should turn his arms against Jerusalem and the whole Jewish people. It is said, *He shall return to his own land,* because he shall not possess Egypt. This return implies the victory of Antiochus, and yet his betaking himself within the boundaries of his own realm. When he adds, with great pomp, or *great riches*, he shews the source whence that wealth should be derived,—*his heart should be against the holy covenant.* He partially destroyed Jerusalem and the temple of God. He was compelled to leave the temple and many treasures, through either shame, or reverence, or a miracle, as we read in the 2d Book of Maccabees. (Chap. v. 2.) He would willingly have stripped the whole temple, but God then restrained him, while he had gathered for himself great wealth. Hence the angel joins the two events,—he should return to Syria with great wealth, and his heart should be against the holy covenant. Some refer this to persons, as if the angel meant the people who were in covenant with God. But the simpler sense pleases me better,—he should carry on war against God, because he was not enriched with such ample spoils as he had expected. We have mentioned his making peace with his enemy : lest, therefore, this expedition should be fruitless, he spoiled the temple of God. Thus *his heart was elated against God and against his holy covenant.* The other exposition is too cold and too forced.

And he shall do it and shall return to his own land. This return at the end of the verse is taken in a different sense from that at the beginning, as now he should use his own will as a conqueror, and no one should oppose his arrival in his own territories. These two expressions are to be read together,—*he shall do it and return to his own dominions.* The meaning of the word for " do" we have already explained. The angel signifies the absence of every obstacle which could prevent the destruction of the city and temple by Antiochus. This was a severe trial, and would cause the minds of the faithful to be disturbed and tossed about because God gave up his temple to this cruel tyrant, and permitted the sacred vessels and the hidden treasures to be carried off with the greatest ignominy. It was necessary, then, to inform the faithful beforehand of this grievous slaughter, lest its novelty should astonish them and overthrow the constancy of their faith. Hence we gather this practical instruction—God often predicts many sorrowful events for us, and yet this instruction ought not to imbitter our feelings ; for he wishes to fortify us against the trial which the novelty of the event must occasion. Thus the angel, while treating of occurrences by no means agreeable, was a useful herald of all the calamities which must happen, lest anything unusual or unexpected should fall upon the pious. Thus they would acknowledge the affliction to proceed from God's hand ; and while they were exposed to the lust of Antiochus, yet God by his certain and incomprehensible counsel allowed much license to this impious tyrant. It afterwards follows :—

29. At the time appointed he shall return, and come toward the south : but it shall not be as the former, or as the latter.

30. For the ships of Chittim shall come against him ; therefore he shall be grieved, and return, and have indignation against the holy covenant : so shall he do ; he shall even return, and have intelligence with them that forsake the holy covenant.

29. Ad tempus revertetur et veniet in Ægyptum : et non erit ut prius, ita posterius.[1]

30. Et venient contra eum naves Cithim, et debilitabitur,[2] et revertetur, et indignabitur adversus fœdus sanctitatis, et faciet, et revertetur, et intelliget,[3] ad desertores fœderis sanctitatis.

First of all, the angel says, Antiochus should return a short time afterwards and take possession of Egypt. This was the fruit of that pretended peace and perfidious friendship which has already been mentioned. For the uncle and nephew banqueted together in mutual distrust, as the angel has already stated, and as we found in the 27th verse of this chapter. This deception was shortly afterwards dissolved, when Antiochus, without any reasonable impulse, returned to Egypt. In this way he shewed his want of nothing but an opportunity for breaking the truce, and he only delayed it for a time, because he had no wish to oppress his nephew in haste. This, then, is one point. We may take the word מוֹעֵד, *mogned*, "time," for a period divinely predetermined ; but as this explanation may seem too forced, I am contented with the common one. *He shall return,* then, *for a time, and shall come,* says he, *to Egypt ; but the latter exposition*

---

[1] That is, the issue should be different, for the latter expedition should not succeed as the former one did.—*Calvin.*

[2] Or, he shall grieve, which sense I rather prefer. —*Calvin.*

[3] That is, he shall apply his mind.—*Calvin.*

shall not be like the former; for the whole preparation for war which had struck such terror into Egypt should lose its effect. He had seized on a portion of the kingdom, and King Ptolemy Philometor was besieged when Publius Popilius arrived, of whom the angel will presently speak. For the cause of his return is added,—*ships shall come from Chittim.* We have explained this word elsewhere. By comparing all the passages of Scripture in which the word occurs, we shall find all the Gentiles denoted by it, from Macedon through the whole of Greece, as far as Illyricum and Italy. The ancients used another term for the Macedonians; they call them *Maketæ,* and some think the letter M a useless addition. But whether this be so or not, the circumstances shew the Macedonians, and Greeks, and other transmarine nations, to have been called Chittim. If any one still disputes about this word, let us desist from all contention ; still, we cannot help observing what the perpetual tenor of Scripture enables us to discover,—that the Macedonians, Greeks, and Italians are included under this term. This passage is free from all doubt, because Antiochus was restrained not by the Greeks but by the Romans. Ambassadors were sent by them, not for this purpose alone, but to investigate the whole state of Greece and Asia Minor. The affairs of Greece were then very unsettled, and the Romans were turning their attention towards Achaia, for they thought the Achæan league would become too powerful. Among these ambassadors was P. Popilius, a stern man, as we may venture to conjecture, but austere and barbarous. When he met with Antiochus, who was then besieging Alexandria, and held the boy-king in captivity, he addressed him after his own manner. King Antiochus received him graciously, and mildly, and even blandly, and wished even to salute him, for, as we have already stated, his disposition was naturally servile. Popilius rejected all these advances, and ordered him to keep his familiarities for private intercourse ; for Antiochus had been intimate with him when a hostage at Rome, during his father's lifetime. He rejected all these acts of courtesy, and explained to him the commands of the Senate, and ordered him instantly to depart from Egypt. The king said he would consult with his friends. But he was unable to lay aside his accustomed sternness; he drew a circle with the wand which he held in his hand, and ordered the king to summon his counsellors, and to deliberate on the spot, otherwise he must declare war at once. When the king perceived this barbarian acting so decisively, he dared no longer to hesitate or dissemble, but threw himself at once into the power of the Senate, and suddenly retired from the country. This history is now described by the angel. All these events were as yet unperformed, but God set before the eyes of the pious what was then entirely concealed and contrary to the expectation of mankind. The angel therefore states the reason why that expedition of Antiochus should be quite unlike the last one. *There shall come against him*, says he, *ships of Chittim*, meaning Italy, *and he shall grieve and return ;* that is, he shall obey, although he shall feel indignant at such imperious treatment, and be compelled to retreat with every mark of disgrace. It was unworthy of a king to demean himself so humbly at the mere word of his adversary.

This accounts for his indignation : *But he shall return and be indignant against the covenant of holiness;* meaning, he shall turn his rage against the temple and city of God. This second return involved the Jews in a far longer period of slaughter than the former one. Antiochus was then unwilling to return home, unless laden with spoil, after pretending to establish peace; but now he was compelled to retreat with great disgrace, and this only exasperated and enraged him. Hence he acted most outrageously towards both the people and the temple of God. Thus the angel says, *He shall be indignant against the holy covenant, and shall do so and return.* He repeats the same language twice ; as if he had said, Antiochus should return to Syria without effecting his object, through obeying the Roman Senate, or rather his old friend whom he had known at Rome. We have already stated the reason, which we shall afterwards more fully explain, why the angel predicted the fury of the king as turned *against the holy covenant.* It is this,—the confidence of the pious would naturally be injured by observing the divine permission granted to the tyrant for spoiling the temple.

He next adds, *And he shall act with intelligence towards the forsakers of the holy covenant.* The angel here points out the manner in which secret agreements should take place between Antiochus and those apostates who should desert God's holy covenant. It is quite clear that he was summoned to Jerusalem, first, by Jason, and then by Menelaus. (2 Macc. iv. 19-23.) I shall touch but briefly events recorded in history. Profane authors inform us accurately of these occurrences, and besides this, a whole book of Maccabees gives us similar information, and places clearly before us what the angel here predicts. Every one who wishes to read these prophecies with profit, must make himself familiar with these books, and must try to remember the whole history. Onias the elder was a holy man ; his son has been previously mentioned. (2 Macc. iii. 1.) For, with the view of escaping from snares, he set out for Egypt and built a temple, as Josephus informs us, and pretended to fulfil that passage in Isaiah which says, There shall be an altar to God in Egypt. But Onias the elder, who discharged faithfully and sacredly the office of high priest, was put to flight, and eventually put to death. Then Jason, whom he had sent to appease Antiochus, assumed the high priesthood, and betrayed the temple and the whole nation, as well as the worship of God. (2 Macc. iv. 35-37 ; also 7.) He afterwards met with the reward which he deserved, for he was slain, and then Menelaus succeeded him, and conciliated the favour of Antiochus. (2 Macc. v. 9 ; iv. 27.) The authority of the priesthood prevailed so far as to enable him to draw with him a great portion of the people. Here, then, the angel predicts how Antiochus, on approaching the city, should have deserters and apostates as his companions. The words are, *He shall apply his mind to the forsakers of the holy covenant,* and the sense is by no means obscure. Antiochus should not make open war against the Jews, but one faction should go forth to meet him and ingratiate themselves with him. I run through these events briefly, because when I afterwards arrive at a general summary, it will be far more convenient to elicit the general improvement. The angel says next :—

31. And arms shall stand on his part, and they shall pollute the sanctuary of strength, and shall take away the daily *sacrifice*, and they shall place the abomination that maketh desolate.	31. Et brachia ab ipso stabunt, et profanabunt sanctuarium roboris, *aut virtutis*, et abolebunt juge, *sacrificium scilicet*, et ponent abominationem quæ obstupefaciet.[1]
32. And such as do wickedly against the covenant shall he corrupt by flatteries : but the people that do know their God shall be strong, and do *exploits*.	32. Et impie agentes contra fœdus abducet in errorem blanditiis,[2] et populus intelligentes[3] Deum suum roborabuntur et facient.

Here the angel describes the intestine evils of the Church, and more fully explains what he touched on in the last verse. He says, *The arms shall stand up for Antiochus.* Some explain this of the garrison which that tyrant imposed on Jerusalem. But this seems too far-fetched. I do not hesitate to suppose the angel to refer here to the apostates and forsakers of the Law. *Arms*, then, *shall stand up from him*, meaning, he shall not contend in his own strength, but shall rely upon the people's assistance. Many should offer themselves in obedience to him, and thus Antiochus would find a party devoted to himself at Jerusalem, which should willingly prostitute itself to his will. He afterwards adds, *They shall profane the sanctuary of strength.* The angel here joins together Antiochus and these impious apostates. (2 Macc. vi. 2.) To favour him, the temple is said to be polluted, and this was fulfilled when the statue of Jupiter Olympius was erected there. The tyranny and violence of Antiochus continued long afterwards, as we shall see in its own place. He brought the statue of the Olympian Jove into the temple, for the purpose of overthrowing the worship of God, and then he introduced other corruptions, which vitiated the purity of God's service. He might in one moment have overthrown the whole Law, but he first tried to mingle many superstitions with God's Law, and thus to estrange the Jews by degrees from true and sincere piety. The angel

---

[1] We have treated this word before.—*Calvin.*

[2] That is, he shall pervert them more and more by flatteries.—*Calvin.*

[3] That is, all the people who acknowledge.—*Calvin.*

speaks of *the sanctuary of power,* to shew the faithful that
Antiochus is not the conqueror of God, who was never deprived of his power, but continued the guardian and keeper
of his temple even unto the end.   He uses this epithet for
the temple, to assure the pious that God had not given way
to the violence of the tyrant.   His authority stood untouched
and untainted, although his temple was exposed to such foul
pollution.

Lastly, he wished the faithful to retain by this teaching a
sense of God's unconquered power in choosing that temple
for his dwelling-place, although for a time Antiochus was so
insulting, and was permitted to profane it with his impious
crew.   This instruction urged the pious to look upon God's
power with the eye of faith, although it was then hidden
from their view, and was trampled under foot by the impious
in the pride of their audacity.   Sorrowful indeed was the
spectacle of this statue erected within the temple, for God,
according to our previous statement, promised to be the defender of that sacred mountain.   When the impious were
raging thus insultingly, who would not have thought God to
be altogether conquered and unable to defend his residence
any longer?   The angel then here encourages the faithful
to cultivate far different thoughts from those suggested by
the prospect before them.   The temple, then, seemed weak
and deprived of every protection, and yet with respect to
God it was still a sanctuary of strength.   He next adds,
And they shall abolish the continual sacrifice, which really
occurred; but I pass it over shortly now, as I shall have
another opportunity of explaining it suitably and fully.
And they shall place, or set up, *that abomination which shall
cause astonishment.*   For who would not have been astonished
when he saw the temple deserted by the Almighty?   For if
God cared for the temple services, why did he not resist rage
like this?   Why did he suffer himself to be subjected to such
disgraceful indignity?   The angel meets such temptations
as these by saying, even if the very best men are astonished
at such disgrace, yet nothing happens by chance; for God
had already foreseen and decreed all things.   They would
not have been predicted, unless God had wished to prove

the people's faith, and to exact the penalty for their ingratitude. But I cannot complete the subject to-day.

PRAYER.

Grant, Almighty God, that as we are instructed by thy Spirit and
armed by thy sacred teaching, we may carry on the war bravely
with open enemies and with all who boldly oppose true religion.
May we also constantly despise all domestic foes and apostates,
and resist them manfully. May we never be disturbed, even if
various tumults should arise in thy Church. May we fix our
eyes upon thee, and always expect a happier issue than appears
possible at the time, until at length thou shalt fulfil thy promises.
And may all events which now seem contrary to us, issue in our
salvation, when thy Son our Redeemer shall appear.—Amen.

Lecture Sixty-First.

WE stated in the last Lecture, the seriousness of the test
by which God proved the faithfulness of his people, in
allowing Antiochus such unbounded liberty to pollute the
Temple, and to abolish, for a time, all the sacrifices and
services. He next set up in the midst of the Temple that
abomination which cast down the spirits of the pious; for
that prodigy could not be witnessed without the most profound astonishment. No one could suppose it possible,
that God would expose his own sanctuary to such dishonour,
as it was the only one which he had chosen in the whole
world. It now follows, *And he shall deceive the transgressors
of the covenant with blandishment, but a people knowing their
God will retain it firmly and practise it.* Here Daniel more
clearly expresses what he had previously said of the corruption and overthrow of God's worship, as Antiochus should
enticingly win over to himself a perfidious portion of those
who were nominally, at least, God's people. He thus repeats
what we observed before. These hypocrites were like the
arms of Antiochus; for had he captured the city by the
force of arms, still he would not have dared to offer these
insults to God's Temple, unless he had received assistance

from those apostates who rejected all fear of the Almighty, and whom ambition and avarice alone had impelled to unite with that impious tyrant, who was the avowed and professed enemy of their religion. The angel, then, here confirms what he had previously said, shewing how the wicked and impious despisers of the covenant should be tools in the hand of this robber. For the first word of verse 32 is derived from רשע, *reshegn,* " to do wickedly," and refers to that special act of sinfulness, their despising God's covenant. This refers to those intestine enemies who had previously boasted themselves to be sons of Abraham, and who were masked by circumcision, the sign of that covenant. He does not here point out any of the mere dregs of the people, but the impious priests, Menelaus, Jason, and others like them, as the passage has already been explained. He says then, *these should be deceived by the blandishments of Antiochus.* He doubtless offered to the priests and to others what he thought they would value most ; one he set over the Temple, another he deceived with vain and fallacious promises for a time, by distributing a variety of gifts among them. In this way he corrupted them all by his flatteries. To these the Prophet opposes the sincere worshippers of God, and the Hebrew copula ought to be understood here as implying this contrast. He had already spoken of many as deceived by vain promises, and had called them transgressors of the covenant : he now adds, *But the people who know God shall strengthen themselves and shall do it.* The angel means that the perfidy of those of whom he had spoken, should not prevail with the pious to lead them into the same alliance of wickedness, and to hurl them headlong into the same snares. Although such was the perfidy of these revolters, yet *all who know God,* says he, *shall strengthen themselves.*

This passage is specially worthy of notice, as experience teaches how very few stand their ground, when many fall away. The example of one often draws with it a hundred into the same ruin ; but the constancy of a hundred is scarcely sufficient to retain one in his position. In this case we behold the depth of our natural depravity. For we are not only moved, but shaken by the very slightest breezes,

and even when God sets before us a firm resting-place, still
we do not cease our vacillation. When an Apostle sets
before us the examples of the saints, he says, a cloud of witnesses is ever gazing upon us, with the view of retaining us
in the fear of God, and in the pure confession of our faith.
(Heb. xii. 1.) But that cloud vanishes too soon from our
view. Meanwhile, if any trifler whom we know to be a man
of no weight, and whom we have ourselves condemned,—if
such a one should decline even so little from the right way,
we think such an example sufficient to excuse us. Wherefore, I had good reason for stating how this passage lays
open to us our perverse and malignant disposition. We can
scarcely be attracted towards God by a multiplicity of
appliances, but we are easily dragged towards the devil to
our own destruction. Hence we ought diligently to meditate upon this passage, and continually to reflect upon the
Prophet's language. Although apostates may be deceived
by flatteries and reject God's worship, betray the Church
and throw off all semblance of piety, yet all the pious shall
stand fast in the faith. Let no one therefore quote the
example of the thoughtless to excuse his fault, if he imitates
the perfidious, the double-minded, and the hypocritical. The
angel here depicts to us a picture of the Church, by shewing
how many should prove backsliders ; but this levity, inconsistency, and perfidy ought never to be an obstacle to the
foes of God to impede their progress in faith and piety.

We should also notice the epithet which designates the
pious. *They are called a people knowing their God.* The
people may be supposed to mean the vulgar, but this is
forced. It may also be simply opposed to the profane Gentiles ; but I think there is here an implied contrast between
the true and genuine sons of Abraham, and the false Israelites, who boasted themselves to be members of the Church
when they had nothing but the empty title. For in the
prophets as in the writings of Moses, the name "people" is
often used in a favourable sense for that elect nation which
God had adopted as peculiarly his own. All the Israelites who
were descendants of Abraham after the flesh, used to boast
with much vanity in their being the elect people, and thus the

word was ever on their lips.   Wherefore the Prophet reproves
the foolish boasting of those who were accustomed to shelter
themselves under the name of God, and without having
anything real in themselves.   Hence *the people*, meaning
God's people, *shall strengthen themselves;* but, by way of
correcting any erroneous view, he adds, *who shall know God*,
as in the 73d Psalm, (ver. 1,) How good is the God of Israel
to those who are upright in heart!   Here the Prophet
restricts the name of Israel to the elect sons of Abraham
who cultivate piety seriously and heartily, as it had become
a prevalent habit carelessly to misuse this name of God.   So
here, *the people who shall know their God*, means his true
people—those whom he acknowledges as his elect.   The
angel here makes a distinction between the pious sons of
Abraham and the pious worshippers of God.   It is worthy
of careful observation, that the angel assigns their knowledge
of God as the cause and foundation of their constancy.   How
then, we may ask, does it come to pass, that some few are
left, when the apostates thus prostitute themselves?   Because their knowledge of God shall prevail, and enable them
to overcome these attacks, and bravely to repel them, and
to become superior to any temptations.   We see, then, the
source whence our own fortitude is derived—the knowledge
of God.   This acknowledgment is no vain and cold imagination, but springs from that faith which spreads its living
root in our hearts.   Hence it follows, we do not really
acknowledge God, unless we boldly contend when we are
put to the test, and remain firm and stable, although Satan
endeavours, by various machinations, to weaken our faithfulness.   And unless we persist in that firmness which is here
described, it is quite clear, that God has never been truly
and really acknowledged by us.   The relation too is not
without its weight in the phrase, *the people who shall know
their God*.   Here is a silent reproof, since God revealed
himself to the Israelites as far as was sufficient to retain
their allegiance.   No one, therefore, could offer any excuse
without being guilty of impiety, sacrilege, and perfidy, after
being so fully instructed by the Law and the prophets.

This instruction must now be applied to our own times.

We observe in these days how many fall off from the Church. Persecution sifts all those who profess to belong to Christ, and thus many are winnowed like chaff, and but a small portion remain steadfast.   Their backsliding ought not to overthrow our faithfulness when they so carelessly forsake all piety, either through being enticed by the allurements of Satan, or deceived by the conduct of the ungodly.   Let us bear in mind the assertion of the angel, and thus the true knowledge of God will reign supreme in our hearts, and we shall still proceed in the course we have pursued.   And to shew how consistently the faithful progress in the teaching of the Law and the Gospel, he says, *they shall strengthen themselves and shall do it.*   Here the word "to do" is taken in the sense of to " execute"—" exploicter," as we say in France ; meaning, they shall summon their courage to discharge their duty ; for the word " to do," or " to execute," is referred to the vocation of the pious ; they should not be sluggish or slothful in the discharge of their duty, says the Prophet, but should gather courage for these contests.   And whence ? from the acknowledgment of God.   We observe, too, that faith is no idle feeling or cold imagination, lying suffocated in our minds, but an energizing principle.   For we may say that from faith springs strength, and from strength execution, and thus we avoid all slothfulness in our calling. It follows,—

33. And they that understand among the people shall instruct many; yet they shall fall by the sword, and by flame, by captivity, and by spoil, *many* days.	33. Et intelligentes populi docebunt multos, et cadent in gladio, et flamma, et exilio, *vel, captivitate,* et direptione, diebus multis.
34. Now, when they shall fall, they shall be holpen with a little help : but many shall cleave to them with flatteries.	34. Et in cadendo,[1] juvabuntur auxilio[2] modico : et adjungent se illis multi in blanditiis.

With reference to the words, they mean, *those who shall be taught among the people shall make many understand.*   Some take the first word of the verse transitively, as " those who shall instruct," but this is wrong ; and they shew their

[1] When they shall fall.—*Calvin.*
[2] These two words spring from the same root; as " they shall be fortified," comes from " fortitude," so " they shall be assisted," from " assistance."—*Calvin.*

ignorance by supposing the relative pronoun understood before the next verb, as if it were, "and those who shall teach." The simple sense is, "Those who shall be wise among the people shall teach many." Here the Prophet, under the angel's guidance, predicts the multitude of apostates as well as the existence of some of an opposite character, who should retain the people within the pure worship and fear of God. Without doubt, he speaks specially of the priests. The greater part were defaulters, and they implicated the foolish vulgar in their wickedness. We observe similar effects at this day in the Papacy, as they corrupt the whole world by their sacrifices. At that time the priests laid snares for the people, and drew them almost all with them into the same impiety. The angel here allows the existence of some wise men among the people; I do not restrict this entirely to the priests, although I suppose the angel to begin with them. A small portion of them taught the truth, and God joined a party with them, but yet the angel predicts the existence of another remnant. Yet afterwards, in the second place, he embraces others who were truly proficients in God's law, and although the obligations of the priesthood did not bind them, yet they laboured to recall the wandering into the way of salvation. He says, then, *Whosoever should be skilful should teach many.* There is also here a tacit contrast between the honest servants of God and those fictitious teachers who pride themselves on their titles; as we observe an instance of this in these days in the Papacy. For bishops and cardinals, abbots and pretenders of this kind, strut about with insolence and stupify the miserable vulgar. What? do not we represent the Church? Is not judgment with us, as well as the interpretation of the Law and of Scripture? As, therefore, in these times these impostors arrogate to themselves all knowledge and wish to be thought equal to the angels, so we know it came to pass among the ancient people. The Prophet, therefore, here chastises that foolish confidence by saying, *Those who shall be understanding among the people;* meaning, the truly wise. As if he had said, those masked hypocrites acquire reputation for themselves, but without the slightest reason. God considers those only intelligent who remain in the pure doctrine of his Law, and practise piety with simplicity and sincerity. Hence he calls these, *the intelligent among the people.* He repeats the word "people," in the same sense as before, implying that all who use this name are not true Israelites before God, as true knowledge of him is required. What kind of knowledge or skill is meant, we easily ascertain from the next verse. For all knowledge which men think they possess without this acquaintance with God, is nothing but vanity. These, therefore, *shall teach many.* This prediction of the angel not only asserts the existence of some among the people who should remain constant amidst such grievous assaults, and should preserve the integrity of their faith, but says they should be the directors of others ; as if he had said, God will grant to each of his elect, not only the power of a bold resistance and of preserving himself pure and uncontaminated amidst every corruption, but at the same time he will render these good men the supporters of others, either in preventing their decline, or if they have fallen off, in bringing them back into the right path.

Lastly, the angel signifies how small a seed God should preserve in his Church as the teachers and rulers of others, though but few in number ; as Isaiah says, God shall consume his people, but that consumption should leave some remnant, and then it shall flow forth. (Chap. x. 22.) The sentiment of this passage is the same ; even if many should degenerate and depart from the faith, and this spirit should extend to the whole people, yet some few should stand firm —perhaps ten in a thousand—and these should be God's ministers in gathering together a new Church ; and thus the land which was formerly sterile, should profit by this irrigation and produce new seed. *Those,* therefore, *who shall be wise among the people shall teach many.* While the angel is here predicting the future, we ought to take to ourselves this admonition : the more each of us becomes a proficient in the faith, the more he ought to exert his utmost endeavours to teach his rude and ignorant neighbours according to this exhortation of the angel. God does not stretch forth his hand to us to lead each of us to follow his own course, but to assist others and to advance their spiritual progress. We read therefore here, a condemnation of the slothfulness of those on whom God has bestowed much knowledge and faith, when they fail to use the trust committed to them for the edification of their brethren. This prediction of the angel ought to influence each of us, as a law and rule, to seek the profit of his brethren according to the measure of his intelligence. The angel adds,—these should not be teachers of shadows, who prescribe men's duty at their ease, and dispute without inconvenience, danger, or personal trouble, about what is right in itself and pleasing to God, but they should be strenuous warriors for the truth. Here, therefore, the angel joins instruction with fortitude, as by this measure it would overcome all dangers, anxieties, and terrors. The passage becomes, in this way, most useful to us in these days, if we only learn to reflect upon what God delivers to us by his angel and his prophet. In conclusion then, the angel demonstrates how God never approves of any teachers as true and legitimate, unless they deliver their message as if ready to defend it, and prepared to seal it with their blood whenever it shall be necessary. We must read the two clauses together, *Those who teach many the worship of God shall fall by the sword and the flame;* meaning, they would rather fall or perish a hundred times by the sword and the flame than desist from their office of teaching. Besides, the angel here mentions the various kinds of death, for the sake of exhortation ; for, had he mentioned only *the sword,* he would not have fully expressed the usefulness of this instruction. Whatever teachers God sets over his Church, they are not fully proved in the discharge of their duty by overcoming a single form of temptation, but they must contend with foes on the right hand and on the left, and must not allow the variety of their perils to weaken either their constancy or their fortitude. If the sword threaten them on one side, and fire on the other,—if they must suffer the spoiling of their goods and banishment from home, nevertheless these teachers must persevere in their course. We observe, then, the multiplicity of conflicts here enumerated by the angel, to teach us the strength of the grace of the Spirit in supporting the teachers and rulers of the Church, and in preventing them from yielding to any temptations while contending even with the sword, and fire, and exile, and the spoiling of their goods.

He adds, *And that too for many days.* This circumstance possesses great weight, as we observe many endure for a time with a manly and intrepid courage, who afterwards languish, and then vanish away and become utterly unlike their former selves. The angel, however, here promises to those who should be sustained by the Spirit of God an invincible constancy. They should gather fresh courage for fresh conflicts, not only for a single day, or month, or year, but it should never fail them. He adds next, *And when they shall fall,* or shall have fallen, *they shall be strengthened,* or assisted, *with a small help.* Without the slightest doubt, the angel here speaks of the Maccabees, by whose assistance the faithful were gathered together and completely separated from those apostates who had betrayed God's temple and worship. He calls the help *small,* and truly it was so. For what could the Maccabees do to resist Antiochus ? The powerful influence of this king is well known ; and what was Judea when compared with Syria ? The Jews indeed had destroyed their own power ; we have already seen how they violated treaties, and corrupted the majority of their own people : there was neither skill, nor plan, nor concert among them. *The help,* then, *was small,* which God sent them. But then the angel shews how God would afford succour to his people when in distress, and allow them some alleviation from the cruelty of the tyrant.

He adds next, *Many shall join themselves to them by flatteries.* Even from this small number the angel cuts off the greater part, and informs them of the miserable condition of the Church, because very few should dare to oppose the madness of the tyrant, and out of these few many should be hypocrites. The whole of this chapter must be interpreted of Antiochus, and yet doubtless God wishes to promote our improvement by these prophecies. They belong equally to us ; for as God governs his Church in a variety of ways, so he always sustains it under its various crosses and trials.

Besides this, the old enemy the devil, who formerly opposed the Church, is equally troublesome to us. He assails us partly by enemies without and partly by enemies within. Such teaching as this was useful, not only to the ancients, but to us also in the present day. First of all, the angel predicts the assistance to be received by the faithful as *small*. Let us learn, then, when God wishes to succour and to help us, —that he does not always exert the fulness of his power. He does not thunder from heaven and overthrow our enemies by the first stroke of his lightning ; but he enables us to contend successfully with our cross, and thus we are far separated from the reprobate by our firmness in resistance. Again, from the second clause we must notice the absolute certainty of many hypocrites being found mingled with the sons of God, and when God purges his Church, but a small portion will remain sincere, just as in these days the very counterpart of this prophecy is exhibited before our eyes. The whole Papacy is called the Church of God ; we are but few in number, and yet what a mixture exists even among us ? How many in these days profess attachment to the Gospel, in whom there is nothing either solid or sincere ! If God should search narrowly into small Churches, still among these few, some would be found deceivers. It never has been otherwise, or shall be different until the end of the world. Here, then, we are admonished to desire, as far as lies in our power, the purity of the Church, and to avoid all impurity, because, in desiring auxiliaries too eagerly on the pressure of any urgent necessity, we shall be certain to become sprinkled with many stains which may ultimately cover us with confusion. The angel doubtless here reproves a fault in the conduct of the Maccabees. Although God stirred them up to afford some consolation to his Church, their proceedings are not to be approved ; for it does not follow that all their actions were praiseworthy because their cause was pious and holy. But I must defer this subject till to-morrow.

PRAYER.

Grant, Almighty God, as at this day thou dost try the faith of thy
people by many tests, that they may obtain strength from the
unconquered fortitude of thy Holy Spirit. May we constantly
march under thy standard, even to the end, and never succumb
to any temptation. May we there join intelligence with zeal in
building up thy Church : as each of us is endowed with superior
gifts, so may he strive for the edification of his brethren with
greater boldness, manliness, and fervour, while he endeavours to
add numbers to the cause. And should the number of those
who are professed members of thy Church diminish, yet may some
seed always remain, until abundant produce shall flow forth from
it, and such fruitfulness arise as shall cause thy name to be
glorified throughout the whole world, in Jesus Christ our Lord.
—Amen.

Lecture Sixty-Second.

WE began yesterday to explain what the angel said about
the future persecution of the Church, and its subsequent
consolation. He first shewed how all the intelligent among
the people should be subject to the cruelty of their enemies,
in consequence of their manly perseverance in teaching
others. We have shewn how inefficient those teachers whom
God has set over his Church would be, if they discharged
their duties at ease and in the shade, and were unprepared
to undergo all contests, and intrepidly to expose their lives
to a variety of dangers. This, then, is a living and efficacious method of teaching, when we do not cease to discharge
our duties in the midst of sword and flame. But, on the
other hand, we must notice how much this instruction is
sought for when these fatal conflicts arise. Many in these
days listen to our instruction concerning Christ ; only they
must continue without injury or annoyance. We observe
many greedily drinking in the evangelical doctrines ; but
yet when anything disperses the crowd they flee immediately,
and with as little consideration as when they first joined the
assembly. That conduct which we daily observe was equally
common in former times. Clearly enough this fault has

been rampant throughout all ages, and it is innate in men not only to escape the cross and all things vexatious, but especially to disclose their own infirmities, because they are unwilling to undergo any danger for the worship of God and the free confession of the truth.   This passage, then, must be noticed, since the Prophet not only exhorts the learned and the wise to instruct others, but he prescribes a rule for the infirm and unlearned, urging them to strengthen themselves against all temptations, when they see all things in confusion, and Satan plotting for the complete annihilation of piety.   As this is the angel's language, we must diligently notice the circumstances of the times, for he was not here instituting a peaceful school, and discoursing like philosophers at their ease concerning virtue without any practical contest; but he enforces the duty of both learning and teaching, even if a variety of deaths should be placed before our eyes.   He speaks next, as I have lately stated, the language of consolation.   God shews how he would afford help to his elect, although it might possibly seem of no consequence to them.   For he dwells on *the smallness of the assistance*—which literally happened.   Without doubt the angel referred to Mattathias and his sons, usually called the Maccabees.   (1 Macc. ii. 1.)   A restriction is put upon that help by an allusion to the members who should prove hypocritical out of that small band.   We are fully aware how the Church would be reduced in its extent, for all would not prove sound in the faith, but the greater part would be drawn aside by those fallacies which the angel here calls *blandishments*.   This was a very grievous trial to the faithful when they perceived their own fewness and weakness in the face of their enemies.   Besides, they dared not trust those allies who had pledged their faith to them and made wonderful promises, since many were deceived by these flatteries, and abandoned the cause through want of sincerity of mind.

We have already adverted to the usefulness of such instruction for our own times; for we ought to apply it personally to ourselves, as our circumstances are similar to those of the ancients.   Out of the great multitude of those who wish to be esteemed Christians, we observe how very

few retain the pure and uncorrupted worship of God. The
Papists treat their own community, which is defiled with
filth of all kinds, as the only Church ; there piety is utterly
subverted or else contaminated with the multitude of superstitions. And even in that small company which has withdrawn itself from the Papal idolatries, the greater part is
full of perfidy and deceit. They pretend to remarkable zeal,
but if you thoroughly examine them, you will find them full
of deception. For if God should probe his Church to the
quick, as he did some years ago in Germany, and as he may
do shortly in our own case, in all these serious conflicts, and
amidst these persecutions, many will boast in the bravery
of their championship, and yet their zeal will quickly ooze
away. When the Lord, therefore, exercises us by methods
similar to those by which he proved the ancient Church, this
instruction ought always to occur to our remembrance, lest
our minds should grow dull and languid.

This passage may lead us to inquire whether the angel
approved of all the exploits of the Maccabees. We may
reply to the question in two opposite ways. First of all, if
any one persists in contending from the angel's words for
God's approval of every action of the Maccabees, this view
is by no means correct. God might use the Maccabees in
succouring the wretched Israelites, and yet it does not follow
that they conducted the good cause properly and lawfully.
It very often occurs, when the faithful offer their services to
God, and have one object set before them, that they fail
either through inconsiderate zeal, or through partial ignorance. Whether we take this view or not, our object is often
good when our manner of proceeding is objectionable. And
thus it was with the Maccabees ; God, doubtless, stirred up
Mattathias to collect the dispersed remnant of the people, to
restore his worship, and to purge his temple from the abominations which Antiochus had set up. Yet in the troublous
times which occurred, his sons, doubtless, failed in many
points of duty. The cause which they undertook was just,
while particular actions of theirs cannot be approved by us.
It now follows,—

35. And *some* of them of under-   35. Et ex intelligentibus cadent

standing shall fall, to try them, and to purge, and to make *them* white, *even* to the time of the end: because *it is* yet for a time appointed.

ad probandum[1] in ipsis,[2] et mundandos,[3] et dealbandos usque ad tempus finis, *id est, finitum,* quoniam adhuc usque ad præfixum tempus.

The angel pursues the same sentiment as before; shewing us how the children of God, in their eagerness to defend the cause of piety, should be subject to many grievous persecutions. *Some of the learned shall fall;* meaning, that calamity shall not be for a single moment only; for those who earnestly desired to defend the true worship of God should perish by the sword, and by fire, and by other methods of destruction, and their successors, too, should suffer the same calamities. The phrase, *the learned should fall,* implies the perishing of the very flower of the Church. There will always be much refuse among a people, and the greater part of it flies off and revolts when their religion requires of them the sacrifice of their life. A few remain, here called intelligent, who, as we stated yesterday, are not wise after the flesh. Making provision for the flesh, implies taking care of themselves, and of their own interests, running no risks, and avoiding all troubles; while those are called intelligent, who, forgetful of their own lives, offer themselves in sacrifice to God. They do not hesitate to incur universal hatred, and are prepared to meet death with fortitude. The angel, therefore, predicts the perishing of the flower of the Church. For who could have expected the name of God to have existed upon earth when all his sincere worshippers were thus murdered with impunity? The severity of the despotism of Antiochus is notorious, no one dared to utter a word, all the sacred books were burnt, and he thought the worship of God entirely abolished. Women with their children were promiscuously seized for burning, and the satellites of this tyrant did not spare the mothers with infants hanging on their breasts. (1 Macc. i.) During the progress of such atrocious cruelty, who would not have thought the whole seed of God to have been extinct? But the angel here shews the true result to have been different, namely, *that the sons*

---

[1] Or, to be tried; the word properly signifies to pour out.— *Calvin.*

[2] That is, to purify them.—*Calvin.*

[3] Or, to purge them again.—*Calvin.*

of God should be purged, cleansed, and whitened. He signifies that all events should not prove so destructive, but should rather promote their salvation. This passage unfolds to us the nature of true prudence in the sight of God ; for we ought to be prepared for death, rather than be turned aside from the free and ingenuous profession of the heavenly doctrine, and from the true worship of God. For this necessity is imposed on the sons of God—to fall either by the sword or by fire, and to suffer the spoiling of their goods, and banishment from their homes. The angel points out from the result how persecutions which seem to issue in the destruction of the Church, are yet profitable and salutary to the sons of God, as this is the method of their being *purified, and cleansed, and whitened.* But we must always remember how some defiling dregs, which require clearing out, remain in the elect, nay, even among the holy Martyrs. The angel does not here treat of hypocrites, or of ordinary believers, but of whatever is most conspicuous and most perfect in the Church, and yet asserts their need of purification. None, therefore, he concludes, possess such sanctity and purity as to prevent the remnant of some pollution which requires to be removed. Hence it becomes necessary for them to pass through the furnace, and to be purified like gold and silver. This is extended to all God's martyrs.

This reminds us of the great folly of the Papists, in imagining the merits of saints to be transferred to us, as if they had more than they required for themselves. Indulgences, as they call them, depend upon this error, according to the following reasoning,—had Peter lived to the ordinary period of human life, he would have proved faithful to the end, and then would have merited the crown of the heavenly kingdom ; but when he went beyond this, and poured out his blood in martyrdom, some merits were superabundant ; these ought not to be lost, and hence the blood of Peter and Paul profit us at this day for the remission of sins. This is the Papal theology, and these miserable sophists are not ashamed of these gross blasphemies, while they vomit forth such foul sacrilege. But the angel's teaching is far different ;—the martyrs themselves are benefited by meeting death for their adherence to the truth, because God *purges, and cleanses,* and refines, *and whitens them.* The angel would not have said this except some admixture of dross still defiled the purity of the saints. But this doctrine ought to be more than enough to animate us to undergo all dangers, when we see ourselves stained and polluted with hidden dross ; besides this, we ought certainly to determine that death would be profitable in this sense, as God will then purge us from those vices by which we are both infected and defiled. Whence the value of the repetition here ; the angel does not simply say *to purge* them, but adds, *to cleanse and whiten them.* Whatever holiness may shine forth in the best of men, yet many stains and much defilement lie concealed within them ; and thus in consequence of their many failings, persecution was always useful to them.

The angel mitigates whatever might seem exceedingly bitter, by saying, *until the time of an end,* meaning, a fixed and definite time. These words imply the merciful character of God, in not urging his people beyond their strength, as Paul also states his faithfulness in granting them a happy issue out of their trials, and in not pressing us beyond the measure of that strength and fortitude which he has conferred upon us. (1 Cor. x. 13.) The angel predicts an end to these evils, and confirms this opinion by saying, *even to a determined time.* In the last clause he signified the temporary nature of the persecutions of which he had spoken ; for they should not cease directly, nor yet for two or three years. By the words, *as yet even to a time determined,* he urges the sons of God to prepare themselves for new contests, as they should not reach the goal for the space of a year. But if God wished to humble them for three, or ten, or a hundred years, they should not despond, but wait for the time divinely predetermined, without depending on their own will. This is the substance of the instruction conveyed. It now follows,—

36. And the king shall do according to his will; and he shall exalt himself, and magnify himself above every god, and shall speak marvellous things against the God of gods,

36. Et faciet secundum voluntatem suam, *vel, libidinem,* rex : et extollet se, et magnificabit se supra omnem Deum, et contra Deum deorum loquetur mirabilia, et prospere aget

and shall prosper till the indignation be accomplished: for that that is determined shall be done.

usque ad consummationem iræ, quoniam decisio facta est, *vel decisa est*, *nempe consumptio.*

This passage is very obscure, and has consequently been explained in very opposite ways by interpreters. And whatever is obscure, is usually doubtful, and there would be little utility and no termination, if I were to narrate the opinions of them all. I shall therefore follow another method, and omitting all superfluous labour, I shall simply inquire the angel's meaning. I must, however, refer briefly to opinions received by the consent of the majority, because they occupy the minds of many, and thus close the door to the correct interpretation. The Jews, for instance, are not agreed among themselves, and their difference of opinion only serves to produce and perpetuate darkness, rather than to diffuse the clearness of light. Some explain it of Antiochus, and others of the Romans, but in a manner different to that which I shall afterwards state. The Christian expositors present much variety, but the greater number incline towards Antichrist as fulfilling the prophecy. Others, again, use greater moderation by supposing Antichrist to be here obliquely hinted at, while they do not exclude Antiochus as the type and image of Antichrist. This last opinion has great probability, but I do not approve of it, and can easily refute it. Antiochus did not long survive the pollution of the Temple, and then the following events by no means suit the occurrences of his time. Nor can his sons be fairly substituted in his place, and hence we must pass on to some other king, distinct from Antiochus and his heirs. As I have already stated, some of the Rabbis explain this of the Romans, but without judgment, for they first apply the passage to Vespasian, and Titus his son, and then extend it to the present times, which is utterly without reason, as they chatter foolishly, according to their usual custom. Those who explain it of Antichrist, have some colour of reason for their view, but there is no soundness in their conclusion, and we shall perceive this better in the progress of our exposition. We must now discover what king the angel here designates. First of all, I apply it entirely to the Roman Empire, but I do not[1] consider it to begin at the reign of the Cæsars, for this would be unsuitable and out of date, as we shall see. By the word "king" I do not think a single person indicated, but an empire, whatever be its government, whether by a senate, or by consuls, or by proconsuls. This need not appear either harsh or absurd, as the Prophet had previously discussed the four monarchies, and when treating of the Romans he calls their power a kingdom, as if they had but a single ruler over them. And when he spoke of the Persian monarchy, he did not refer to a single ruler, but included them all, from Cyrus to the last Darius, who was conquered by Alexander. This method of speech is already very familiar to us, as the word "king" often means "kingdom." The angel, then, when saying, *a king shall do* anything, does not allude to Antiochus, for all history refutes this. Again, he does not mean any single individual, for where shall we find one who exalted himself against all gods? who oppressed God's Church, and fixed his palace between two seas, and seized upon the whole East? The Romans alone did this. I intend to shew more clearly to-morrow how beautifully and appositely everything related by the angel applies to the Roman empire; and if anything should appear either obscure or doubtful, a continued interpretation will bring it to light and confirm it.

We lay this down at once; the angel did not prophesy of Antiochus, or any single monarch, but of a new empire, meaning, the Roman. We have the reason at hand why the angel passes directly from Antiochus to the Romans. God desired to support the spirits of the pious, lest they should be overwhelmed by the number and weight of the massacres which awaited them and the whole Church even to the advent of Christ. It was not sufficient to predict the occurrences under the tyranny of Antiochus; for after his time, the Jewish religion was more and more injured, not only by foreign enemies, but by their own priesthood. Nothing remained unpolluted, since their avarice and ambition had arrived at such a pitch, that they trode under foot the whole

[1] The edit. of 1617 has *nunc* instead of *non*, which is the correct reading. — *Ed.*

glory of God, and the law itself. The faithful required to
be fortified against such numerous temptations, until Christ
came, and then God renewed the condition of his Church.
The time, therefore, which intervened between the Maccabees
and the manifestation of Christ ought not to be omitted.
The reason is now clear enough why the angel passes at once
from Antiochus to the Romans.

We must next ascertain how the Romans became connected with the elect people of God. Had their dominion
been limited to Europe alone, the allusion to them would
have been useless and out of place. But from the period of
the kings of Syria being oppressed by many and constant
devastations in war, both at home and abroad, they were
unable to injure the Jews as they had previously done ; then
new troubles sprang up through the Romans. We know,
indeed, when many of the kings of Syria were indulging in
arrogance, how the Romans interposed their authority, and
that, too, with bad faith, for the purpose of subjecting the
east to themselves. Then when Attalus made the Roman
people his heir, the whole of Asia Minor became absorbed
by them. They became masters of Syria by the will of this
foolish king, who defrauded his legal heirs, thinking by this
conduct to acquire some regard for his memory after his
death. From that period, when the Romans first acquired
a taste of the wealth of these regions, they never failed to
find some cause for warfare. At length Pompey subdued
Syria, and Lucullus, who had previously carried on war with
Mithridates, restored the kingdom to Tigranes. Pompey,
as I have already remarked, subjected Syria to the Romans.
He left, indeed, the Temple untouched, but we may conjecture the cruelty which he exercised towards the Jews by
the ordinary practice of this people. The clemency of the
Romans towards the nations which they subdued is notorious
enough. After Crassus, the most rapacious of all men, had
heard much of the wealth of the Jews, he desired that province as his own. We know, too, how Pompey and Cæsar,
while they were friends, partitioned the whole world among
themselves. Gaul and Italy were assigned entirely to Cæsar ;
Pompey obtained Spain, and part of Africa and Sicily ;

while Crassus obtained Syria and the regions of the east, where he miserably perished, and his head, filled with gold, was carried about in mockery from place to place. A second calamity occurred during that incursion of Crassus, and from this time the Jews were harassed by many and continual wars. Before this period, they had entered into an alliance with the Romans, as we are informed by the books of the Maccabees, as well as by profane writers. Therefore, when they granted liberty to the Jews, (1 Macc. viii. and xiv.,) it was said,[1] they were generous at the expense of others. This was their ordinary and usual practice ; at first they received with friendship all who sought their alliance by treaty, and then they treated them with the utmost cruelty. The wretched Jews were treated in this way. The angel then alludes to them first, and afterwards speaks of Antiochus. All these points, thus briefly mentioned, we must bear in mind, to enable us to understand the context, and to shew the impossibility of interpreting the prophecy otherwise than of the Romans.

I now proceed to the words, *The king shall do according to his will.* I have stated that we need not restrict this expression to a single person, as the angel prophesies of the continued course of the Roman monarchy. *He shall raise himself, and magnify himself*, says he, *above every god.* This will be explained by and bye, where the king is said to be a despiser of all deities. But with reference to the present passage, although impiety and contempt of God spread throughout the whole world, we know how peculiarly this may be said of the Romans, because their pride led them to pass an opinion upon the right of each deity to be worshipped. And, therefore, the angel will use an epithet for God, meaning fortitudes and munitions, מעזים, *megnezim*, as in verse 38. That passage, I shall shew you to-morrow, has been badly explained ; for interpreters, as we shall discover, are utterly " at sea" as to its meaning.[2] But here the angel, by attributing contempt of the one God and of all deities to

---

[1] The Latin is " *ille dicebat*," the French has " *un quidam disoit*,"—a curious mixture which implies uncertainty. Can it be Crassus?—*Ed.*

[2] See the DISSERTATIONS at the end of this volume.

the Romans, implies their intense pride and haughtiness, in which they surpassed other profane nations. And, truly, they did not preserve even a superstitious fear of God ; and while they vauntingly paraded the superior piety of both their ancestors and themselves, yet an accurate perusal of their writings will disclose what they really thought. They made a laughingstock of all divinities, and ridiculed the very name and appearance of piety, and used it only for the purpose of retaining their subjects in obedience. The angel then says most truly of this empire, *it shall magnify itself against all deities ;* and *it shall speak wonderful things against the God of gods,* by which the Jewish religion is intended. For before they had passed into Asia Minor, and penetrated beyond Mount Taurus, they were ignorant of the law of God, and had never heard of the name of Moses. They then began to take notice of the worship of some peculiar god by that nation, and of the form of their piety being distinct from that of all other people. From the period of the knowledge of the peculiarities of the Jewish religion being spread among the Romans, they began to vomit forth their blasphemies against *the God of gods.* We need not gather together the proof of this from their histories ; but Cicero in his oration for Flaccus, (sec. 28,) tears most contemptuously to pieces the name of the true God; and that impure slanderer—for he deserves the name—so blurts out his calumnies, as if the God who had revealed himself to his elect people by his law, was unworthy of being reckoned with Venus or Bacchus, or their other idols. Lastly, he treats the numerous massacres to which the Jews were exposed, as a proof of their religion being hated by all the deities ; and this he thinks ought to be a sufficient sign of the detestable character of their religion. The angel then has every reason to declare the Romans puffed up with pride and haughtiness, as they did not hesitate to treat the name of the true God with such marked contempt.

He shall utter, says he, *remarkable things against the God of gods.* The angel seems to refer to a single individual, but we have stated his reference to be to this empire. He adds next, *And he shall prosper until the consumption,* or completion, or consummation *of the indignation, since the determination has been made.*   Here also the angel treats of a long succession and series of victories, which prevent the application of the passage to Antiochus.   For he died immediately after he had spoiled the Temple ; all his offspring perished by each other's hands ; and the Romans, to their great disgrace, acquired possession of Syria and that portion of the East.   We must necessarily explain this of the Romans, as they notoriously prospered in their wars, especially on the continent of Asia.   And if they were sometimes in difficulties, as we shall see to-morrow when treating the words which the angel will then use, they soon recovered their usual success.   The angel here says, *This king shall prosper till the end of the indignation ;* meaning, until God should punish the hypocrites, and thus humble his Church. I refer this to God, as I shall explain more at length to-morrow.

PRAYER.

Grant, Almighty God, as in these days the affairs of the world are in a state of disturbance, and as wherever we turn our eyes we see nothing but horrible confusion : Grant, I pray, that we may be attentive to thy teaching.   May we never wander after our own imaginations, never be drawn aside by any cares, and never turn aside from our stated course.   May we remain fixed in thy word, always seeking thee and always relying on thy providence. May we never hesitate concerning our safety, as thou hast undertaken to be the guardian of our salvation, but ever call upon thee in the name of thine only-begotten Son.—Amen.

Lecture Sixty=Third.

WE yesterday commenced an explanation of the prophecy, in which the angel begins to treat of the Roman Empire.   I then shewed the impossibility of applying any other exposition to the passage, as it would have been absurd to pass by the point most necessary to be known.   At the very beginning, we stated that God did not inform Daniel of other occurrences for the purpose of pandering to the foolish and vain curiosity of the many, but to fortify his servants, and to prevent their falling away in the midst of these most grievous contests. But after the death of Antiochus, we know by what various and grievous machinations Satan had endeavoured to overthrow the faith of all the pious. For this reason their courage required propping up. If the whole of this period had been passed over in silence, God would have appeared to have neglected his servants. Therefore either our yesterday's subject of comment would have been useless, or else this clause ought to be added, lest the prophecy should appear either defective or mutilated. And we previously observed, while the angel was predicting future changes, there was no omission of the Roman Empire, which is again introduced here. Let us remember, then, that the angel is not now speaking of Antiochus, nor does he make a leap forwards to Antichrist, as some think, but he means a perpetual series. Thus the faithful would be prepared for all assaults which might be made upon their faith, if this rampart had not been interposed. The remainder of the verse now remains to be explained, *Even to the end of the wrath, because the decision has been made.* The angel had narrated the perverseness of this king in not sparing the living God, but in darting his calumnies against him. He now adds, *He shall prosper even to the end of the wrath.* The angel doubtless here meets that trial which might utterly overwhelm the faithful, unless they hoped for some termination to it. By *wrath* he does not mean the rage of those who were sent as proconsuls into Asia and the East, or even the bitterness and rigour of the Roman people and Senate, but the word refers to God. We must remember, then, what I have previously impressed, namely, the sons of God are called upon to examine their faults, to humble themselves before God, without either murmuring or complaining when chastised by his rods. We know how impatient human nature is in bearing adversity, and how grudgingly men submit to the cross, not only stubbornly refusing it, but openly rebelling against God. Hence those who are oppressed by his hand are always outrageous, unless he displays himself as their judge. The angel then here presents us with a rea-

son why God did not rashly expose his Church to the lust
of the impious ; he only wished to exact the punishment due
to their sins ; and judgment ought always to begin at the
house of God, as we learn from another prophet. (Isa. x. 12 ;
Jer. xxv. 29 ; 1 Peter iv. 17.)

In conclusion, then, the angel, in the first place, exhorts
the pious to repentance, and shews them how deservedly God
laid his hand upon them, because it was absolutely necessary.
He then mitigates what would otherwise have been too
severe, by adding, *till the end,* or completion. The word
signifies both consumption and end, but it here means end,
or completion. The explanation next follows, *since the determination,* or decision, *has been made,* says he. This means,
God will not pursue his children to extremities without
moderation, but will bring their punishment to an end after
they have been humbled. As we read in the 40th chapter
of Isaiah, the time of their warfare was completed, when God
pitied his Church, and freed it from the tyranny of its
enemies. (Ver. 2.) Isaiah there speaks in the person of
God ; the Church had received double, meaning, sufficient
punishment had been exacted. It almost implies his being
displeased with himself for having been too severe against
his Church, as we are familiar with the indulgence with
which he usually treated his children. He says, then, in
this passage, *Even to the end of the wrath ;* meaning, the
punishment should be but temporary, as God had prescribed
a certain termination which should put an end to all their
troubles and anxieties. It follows :—

37. Neither shall he regard
the God of his fathers, nor the
desire of women, nor regard any
god : for he shall magnify himself
above all.

37. Et ad deos patrum suorum
non attendet, et ad desiderium, *vel,*
amorem, mulierum, et ad ullum Deum
non attendet, quia super omne, *super*
omnia, sese magnificabit.

I do not wonder at those who explain this prophecy of
Antiochus, experiencing some trouble with these words ; for
they cannot satisfy themselves, because this prediction of
the angel's was never accomplished by Antiochus, who did
neither neglect all deities nor the god of his fathers. Then,
with regard to the love of women, this will not suit this
person. But it is easy to prove by other reasons already

mentioned, the absence of all allusion here to Antiochus. Some refer this prophecy to the Pope and to Mahomet, and the phrase, the love of women, seems to give probability to this view. For Mahomet allowed to men the brutal liberty of chastising their wives, and thus he corrupted that conjugal love and fidelity which binds the husband to the wife. Unless every man is content with a single wife, there can be no love, because there can be no conjugal happiness whenever rivalry exists between the inferior wives. As, therefore, Mahomet allowed full scope to various lusts, by permitting a man to have a number of wives, this seems like an explanation of his being inattentive to the love of women. Those who think the Pope to be intended here remind us of their enforcing celibacy, by means of which the honour of marriage is trodden under foot. We know with what foulness the Roman Pontiffs bark when marriage is hinted to them, as we may see in the decrees of Pope Siricius, in the seventh chapter of the first volume of the Councils.[1] They quote the passage, Those who are in the flesh cannot please God; and thus compare marriage with fornication, thereby disgracefully and reproachfully throwing scorn upon an ordinance sanctioned by God. We observe, then, some slight correspondence, but the remaining points will not suit this idea. Some assert that as Mahomet invented a new form of religion, so did the Pope ; true indeed, but neither of them are intended here, and the reason is, because God wished to sustain the spirits of his people until the first coming of Christ. Hence he predicts by his angel the sufferings to be endured by the Church until Christ was manifest in the flesh. We must now come to the Romans, of whom we began to explain the passage.

The angel says, *The king shall pay no regard to the gods of his fathers.* The application of this clause is at first sight obscure ; but if we come to reflect upon the outrageous pride and barbarity of the Romans, we shall no longer doubt the meaning of the Prophet's words. The angel states two circumstances ; this king should be a despiser of all deities, and

---

[1] The French edition altogether omits this reference to the *Concilia.* —*Ed.*

yet he should worship one god, while the singular and magnificent pomp displayed should exceed all common practices. These two points, so apparently opposite, were found united in the Romans. Our explanation will appear clearer by adding the following verses,

38. But in his estate shall he honour the God of forces: and a god whom his fathers knew not shall he honour with gold, and silver, and with precious stones, and pleasant things.

39. Thus shall he do in the most strong holds with a strange god, whom he shall acknowledge *and* increase with glory: and he shall cause them to rule over many, and shall divide the land for gain.

38. Et Deum fortitudinum, *vel,* munitionum, in loco suo honorabit: et Deum quem non cognoverunt patres ejus honorabit cum auro, et argento, et lapide pretioso, et desiderabilibus,[1] *hoc est, rebus omnibus pretiosis.*

39. Et faciet adversus munitiones fortitudinum cum Deo alieno, quem agnoverit, multiplicabit gloriam, et dominari faciet eos in multis, et terram dividet pretio.

As I have already hinted, at the first glance these statements seem opposed to each other; the king of whom we are now treating shall despise all deities, and yet shall worship a certain god in no ordinary way. This agrees very well with the Romans, if we study their dispositions and manners. As they treated the worship of their deities simply as a matter of business, they were evidently destitute of any perception of the divinity, and were only pretenders to religion. Although other profane nations groped their way in darkness, yet they offered a superstitious worship to some divinities. The Romans, however, were not subject to either error or ignorance, but they manifested a gross contempt of God, while they maintained the appearance of piety. We gather this opinion from a review of their whole conduct. For although they fetched many deities from every quarter of the world, and worshipped in common with other nations Minerva, Apollo, Mercury, and others, yet we observe how they treated all other rites as worthless. They considered Jupiter as the supreme deity. But what was Jupiter to them in his own country? Did they value him a single farthing, or the Olympian deity? Nay, they derided both his worshippers and himself. What then really was their supreme god? why the glory of the Capitol; without the additional title of Lord of the Capitol, he was nobody at all. That title dis-

[1] That is, with all precious things.—*Calvin.*

tinguished him as specially bound to themselves. For this reason the Prophet calls this Roman Jupiter *a god of bulwarks,* or of powers. The Romans could never be persuaded that any other Jupiter or Juno were worthy of worship; they relied upon their own inherent strength, considered themselves of more importance than the gods, and claimed Jupiter as theirs alone. Because his seat was in their capital, he was more to them than a hundred heavenly rulers, for their pride had centred the whole power of the deity in their own capital. They thought themselves beyond the reach of all changes of fortune, and such was their audacity, that every one fashioned new deities according to his pleasure. There was a temple dedicated to fortune on horseback; for this gratified the vanity of the general who had made good use of his cavalry, and obtained a victory by their means; and in building a temple to equestrian fortune, he wished the multitude to esteem himself as a deity. Then Jupiter Stator was a god, and why? because this pleased somebody else; and thus Rome became full of temples. One erected an image of fortune, another of virtue, a third of prudence, and a fourth of any other divinity, and every one dared to set up his own idols according to his fancy, till Rome was completely filled with them. In this way Romulus was deified; and what claim had he to this honour? If any one object here —other nations did the same—we admit it, but we also know in what a foolish, brutal, and barbarous state of antiquity they continued. But the Romans, as I have already intimated, were not instigated to this manufacture of idols by either error or superstition, but by an arrogant vanity which elevated themselves to the first rank among mankind, and claimed superiority over all deities. For instance, they allowed a temple to be erected to themselves in Asia, and sacrifices to be offered, and the name of deity to be applied to them. What pride is here! Is this a proof of belief in the existence of either one god or many? Rome is surely the only deity—and she must be reverently worshipped before all others!

We observe then how the expression of this verse is very applicable to the Romans; *they worshipped the god of bul-*

warks, meaning, they claimed a divine power as their own, and only granted to their gods what they thought useful for their own purposes. With the view of claiming certain virtues as their own, they invented all kinds of deities according to their taste. I omit the testimony of Plutarch as not quite applicable to the present subject. He says in his problems, it was unlawful to utter the name of any deity under whose protection and guardianship the Roman State was placed. He tells us how Valerius Soranus was carried off for foolishly uttering that deity's name, whether male or female. These are his very words. And he adds as the reason, their practice of using magical incantations in worshipping their unknown divinity. Again, we know in what remarkable honour they esteemed "the good goddess." The male sex were entirely ignorant of her nature, and none but females entered the house of the high priest, and there celebrated her orgies. And for what purpose ? What was that " good goddess ?" Surely there always existed this *god of bulwarks, since* the Romans acknowledged no deity but their own selves. They erected altars to themselves, and sacrificed all kinds of victims to their own success and good fortune ; and in this way they reduced all deities within their own sway, while they offered them only the specious and deceptive picture of reverence. There is nothing forced in the expression of the angel,—*he will pay no attention to the gods of his fathers ;* meaning, he will not follow the usual custom of all nations in retaining superstitious ceremonies with error and ignorance. For although the Greeks were very acute, yet they did not dare to make any movement, or propose any discussions on religious matters. One thing we know to be fixed among them, to worship the gods which had been handed down by their fathers. But the Romans dared to insult all religions with freedom and petulance, and to promote atheism as far as they possibly could. Therefore the angel says, *he should pay no attention to the god of his fathers.* And why ? They will have regard to themselves, and acknowledge no deity except their own confidence in their peculiar fortitude. I interpret the phrase, *the desire of women,* as denoting by that figure of speech which puts a

part for the whole, the barbarity of their manners. The love
of women is a scriptural phrase for very peculiar affection ;
and God has instilled this mutual affection into the sexes to
cause them to remain united together as long as they retain
any spark of humanity.   Thus David is said to have loved
Jonathan beyond or surpassing the love of women.   (2 Sam.
i. 26.)   No fault is there found with this agreement, otherwise the love of David towards Jonathan would be marked
with disgrace.   We know how sacred his feelings were
towards him, but "the love of women" is here used *par*
excellence, implying the exceeding strength of this affection.
As therefore God has appointed this very stringent bond of
affection between the sexes as a natural bond of union
throughout the human race, it is not surprising if all the
duties of humanity are comprehended under this word by a
figure of speech.   It is just as if the angel had said ; this
king of whom he prophesies should be impious and sacrilegious, in thus daring to despise all deities ; then he should
be so evil, as to be utterly devoid of every feeling of charity.
We observe then how completely the Romans were without
natural affection, loving neither their wives nor the female
sex.   I need not refer to even a few examples by which this
assertion may be proved.   But throughout the whole nation
such extreme barbarity existed, that it ought really to fill us
with horror.   None can obtain an adequate idea of this,
without becoming thoroughly versed in their histories ; but
whoever will study their exploits, will behold as in a mirror
the angel's meaning.   This king, then, should cultivate
neither piety nor humanity.

And he shall not pay attention to other gods, because he
shall magnify himself against them all.   The cause is here
assigned why this king should be a gross despiser of all
deities, and fierce and barbarous against all mortals, *because*
he should magnify himself above them all.   That pride so
blinded the Romans, as to cause them to forget both piety
and humanity ; and so this intolerable self-confidence of
theirs was the reason why they paid no honour to any deity,
and trampled all mortals under foot.   Humility is certainly
the beginning of all true piety ; and this seed of religion is

implanted in the heart of man, causing them whether they will or not to acknowledge some deity. But the Romans were so puffed up by self-consequence, as to exalt themselves above every object of adoration, and to treat all religions with contemptuous scorn ; and in thus despising all celestial beings, they necessarily looked down on all mankind, which was literally and notoriously the fact. Now, the second clause is opposed to this, *He shall worship* or honour *the god of fortitudes.* He had previously used this word of the Temple, but this explanation does not seem suitable here, because the angel had before expressed the unity of God, while he now enumerates many gods. But the angel uses the word " fortitudes," or " munitions," for that perverse confidence by which the Romans were puffed up, and were induced to treat both God and men as nothing in comparison to themselves. How then did these two points agree—the contempt of all deities among the Romans, and yet the existence of some worship ? First, they despised all tradition respecting the gods, but afterwards they raised themselves above every celestial object, and becoming ashamed of their barbarous impiety, they pretended to honour their deities. But where did they seek those deities, as Jupiter for instance, to whom all the tribe of them were subject ? why, in their own capitol. Their deities were the offspring of their own imaginations, and nothing was esteemed divine but what pleased themselves. Hence it is said, *He shall honour him in his own place.* Here the angel removes all doubt, by mentioning the place in which this god of fortitudes should be honoured. The Romans venerated other deities wherever they met with them, but this was mere outward pretence. Without doubt they limited Jupiter to his own capitol and city ; and whatever they professed respecting other divinities, there was no true religion in them, because they adored themselves in preference to those fictitious beings. Hence *he shall worship the god of ramparts in his place, and shall honour a strange god whom his fathers knew not.*[1]

---

[1] The word " Mahuzzim " has occasioned a great variety of translations. See Wintle *in loco,* and the DISSERTATION on this passage at the end of this volume.

Again, *He shall honour him in gold, and silver, and precious stones, and all desirable things;* meaning, he shall worship his own deity magnificently and with remarkable pomp. And we know how the riches of the whole world were heaped together to ornament their temples. For as soon as any one purposed to erect any temple, he was compelled to seize all things in every direction, and so to spoil all provinces to enrich their own temples. Rome, too, did not originate this splendour for the sake of superstition, but only to raise itself and to become the admiration of all nations; and thus we observe how well this prophecy is explained by the course of subsequent events. Some nations, in truth, were superstitious in the worship of their idols, but the Romans were superior to all the rest. When first they became masters of Sicily, we know what an amount of wealth they abstracted from a single city. For if ever any temples were adorned with great and copious splendour and much riches, surely they would confess the extreme excellence of those of Sicily. But Marcellus stripped almost all temples to enrich Rome and to ornament the shrines of their false deities. And why so? Was it because Jupiter, and Juno, and Apollo, and Mercury, were better at Rome than elsewhere? By no means; but because he wished to enrich the city, and to turn all sorts of deities into a laughingstock, and to lead them in triumph, to shew that there was no other deity or excellence except at Rome, the mistress of the world. He afterwards adds, *He shall perform.* Here, again, the angel seems to speak of prosperity. Without doubt he would here supply courage to the pious, who would otherwise vacillate and become backsliders when they observed such continued and incredible success, in a nation so impious and sacrilegious, and remarkable for such barbarous cruelty. Hence he states how the Romans should obtain their ends in whatever they attempted, as their fortitude should prevail, as if it were their deity. Although they should despise all deities, and only fabricate a god for themselves through a spirit of ambition; yet even this should bring them success. This is now called a *foreign deity.* Scripture uses this word to distinguish between fictitious idols and the one true

God.   The angel seems to say nothing which applies especially to the Romans.   For the Athenians and Spartans, the
Persians and the Asiatics, as well as all other nations, worshipped strange gods.   What, then, is the meaning of the
name? for clearly the angel did not speak after the ordinary
manner.   He calls him *strange*, as he was not handed down
from one to another; for while they boasted vainly in their
veneration of the idols received from their ancestors, together
with all their sacred institutions and their inviolable rites,
yet they inwardly derided them, and did not esteem them
worth a straw, but only wished to retain some fallacious form
of religion through a sense of shame.   We remember the
saying of Cato concerning the augurs, "I wonder when one
meets another how he can refrain from laughing!" thus
shewing how he ridiculed them.   If any one had asked
Cato either in the senate or privately, What think you of the
augurs and all our religion? he would reply, "Ah! let the
whole world perish before the augurs; for these constitute
the very safety of the people and of the whole republic: we
received them from our ancestors, therefore let us keep them
for ever!"   Thus that crafty fellow would have spoken, and
thus also would all others.   But while they prated thus to
each other, they were not ashamed to deny the existence of
a Deity, and so to ridicule whatever had been believed from
the very beginning, as entirely to reduce to nothing the traditions received from their forefathers.   It does not surprise
us to find the angel speaking of a *strange god* which was
worshipped at Rome, not, as I have said, through superstition or mistake, but only to prevent their barbarity from
becoming abominable throughout the world.   *That God*, says
he, *whom he had acknowledged:* great weight is attached to
this word.   The angel means, that the whole divinity rested
on the opinion and will of the sovereign people, because it was
agreeable to its inclination, and promoted its private interest.
As the plan of worshipping any gods would be approved,
and they would pride themselves in their own pleasure, they
should boast with great confidence, that there could be no
piety but at Rome.   But why so?   Because they acknowledge strange gods, and determine and decree the form of

worship which was to be preserved. The angel thus places the whole of the religion of Rome in lust, and shews them to be impure despisers of God.

He afterwards says, *He shall multiply the glory.* This may be referred to God, but I rather approve of a different interpretation. The Romans should acquire great wealth for themselves, and should increase wonderfully in opulence, in the magnitude of their empire, and in all other sources of strength. Therefore *they shall multiply the glory*, meaning, they shall acquire new territories, and increase their power, and accumulate a multitude of treasures. This explanation fits in very well with the close of the verse, where he adds, *he shall make them rule far and wide.* This is a portion of that glory which this king shall heap upon himself, for he should be superior to the kings over many lands, and should distribute the booty which he had acquired, and that, too, *for a price.* He says, therefore, *he shall make them rule over many ;* for the relative is without a subject, which is a frequent practice of the Hebrews. Whom, then, should the Roman king, or the Roman empire, thus cause to have dominion ? Whoever rendered them any assistance should receive his reward from a stranger, as we know Eumenes to have been enriched by the booty and spoil of Antiochus. The provinces also were distributed according to their will. The island was given up to the Rhodians, while a kingdom was wrested from another, and the Ætolians enlarged their dominions. As each party laboured hard for their benefit, and incurred large expenses, so the Romans conferred riches upon them. After conquering Antiochus, they became the more liberal towards Attalus and Eumenes, and thus they became masters of the greater part of Asia. Again, when they had deprived Nabis, the tyrant of Sparta, of the greater part of his territories, those who had taken care to gratify the Romans, were favoured with the spoils they had seized from him. We have another instance in the favours conferred upon Massinissa after the conquest of Carthage ; for after being expelled from his own kingdom, his dominion extended far and wide throughout the continent of Africa : after being deprived of his paternal sovereignty, he had not a spot in the world on which to plant his foot until they bestowed upon him what they had seized from the Carthaginians. And how did they manage this? *They shall divide the soil for a price*, says the angel; thus obliquely reproving the cunning of the senate and Roman people, because they did not give away these ample dominions gratuitously; they would willingly have devoured whatever they had acquired, but they found it better policy to sell them than to retain them. They did not sell at any fixed price—for the word "price" here need not be restricted to a definite sum of money—but displayed their avarice, and sold and distributed for the sake of gain, just as much as if all these territories had been immediately reduced into provinces of their empire. They had need of great resources; it was objectionable to continue their garrison in perpetuity in the cities of Greece, and hence they proclaim perfect freedom through them all. But what sort of liberty was this? Each state might choose its senate according to the pleasure of the Romans, and thus as each acquired rank and honour in his own nation, he would become attached and enslaved to the Roman people. And then, in this condition of affairs, if any war should spring up, they sought aid from these friends and allies. For had they been only confederate, the Romans would never have dared to exact so much from each tributary state. Let us take the case of the Carthaginians. After being reduced by many exactions to the lowest pitch of poverty, yet when the Romans made war against Philip and Macedon, and against Antiochus, they demanded ships from these allies. They demanded besides, as a subsidy, an immense quantity of gold, silver, provisions, garments, and armour, till at length these wretched Carthaginians, whose very life-blood the Romans had drained, still sent for the war whatever gold they had remaining, and all they could scrape together. Thus Philip king of Macedon is compelled to destroy himself, by plunging his own sword into his body; for every state of Greece was forced to contribute its own portion of the expenses of the war.

We perceive, then, how *the lands were divided for a price*, each with regard to its own utility, not by fixing a certain

defined money value, but according to the standard of political expediency. And what kind of bargaining did they
afterwards mutually execute? We have an instance of it in
the prevalence of proscription among the Romans, by which
they turned their rapacity against their own vitals. They
had previously confiscated the goods of their enemies.
Philip, for instance, was forced to pay a large sum of money
to repurchase the name of king and the portion of territory
which remained his own. Antiochus and the Carthaginians
were subject to the same hardship. The Romans, in short,
never conquered any one without exhausting both the
monarch and his dominions to satisfy their insatiable avarice
and cupidity. We now perceive *how they divided the lands
for a price,* holding all kings in subjection to themselves,
and bestowing largesses upon one from the property of
another.

We now perceive the angel's meaning throughout this
verse, *The king should be so powerful as to bestow dominion
on whomsoever he pleased in many* and ample territories, but
not gratuitously. We have had examples of some despoiled
of their royal dignity and power, and of others restored to
the authority of which they had been deprived. Lucullus,
for instance, chose to eject one king from his dominions,
while another general restored him to his possessions. A
single Roman citizen could thus create a great monarch; and
thus it often happened. Claudius proposed to the people to
proscribe the king of Cyprus, although he was of the royal
race; his father had been the friend and ally of the Roman
people, he had committed no crime against the Roman empire, and there was no reason for declaring war against him.
Meanwhile he remained in security at home, while none of
those ceremonies by which war is usually declared took place.
He was proscribed in the market-place by a few vagabonds,
and Cato is immediately sent to ravage the whole island.
He took possession of it for the Romans, and this wretched
man is compelled to cast himself into the sea in a fit of
despair. We observe, then, how this prediction of the angel
was by no means in vain; the Roman proconsuls distributed
kingdoms and provinces, *but yet for a price,* for they seized

everything in the world, and drew all riches, all treasures, and every particle of value into the whirlpool of their unsatisfied covetousness. We shall put off the remainder.

PRAYER.

Grant, Almighty God, as in all ages the blindness of mankind has been so great as to lead them to worship thee erroneously and superstitiously, and since they manifest such duplicity and pride as to despise thy name, and also the very idols which they have fashioned for themselves: Grant, I pray thee, that true piety may be deeply rooted in our hearts. May the fear of thy name be so engraven within us, that we may be sincerely and unreservedly devoted to thee. May each of us heartily desire to glorify thy name, and may we endeavour to lead our brethren in the same course. Do thou purge us more and more from all dissimulation, until at length we arrive at that perfect purity which is laid up for us in heaven, through Jesus Christ our Lord.—Amen.

Lecture Sixty-Fourth.

40. And at the time of the end shall the king of the south push at him: and the king of the north shall come against him like a whirlwind, with chariots, and with horsemen, and with many ships; and he shall enter into the countries, and shall overflow and pass over.

40. Et in tempore finis confliget cum eo rex austri, et tanquam turbo irruet rex aquilonis, cum curru et equitibus, et navibus multis: et veniet in terras, et exundabit, et transibit, *pervadet*.

As to the time here mentioned, it is a certain or predetermined period: the kings of the south and the north we have already shewn to refer to Egypt and Syria, such being their position with respect to Judea. The word נגח, *negech*, *confliget*, is literally he shall "push with the horns," while the word translated, "he shall rush as a whirlwind," is deduced from שער, *segner*, "to be stormy." The angel here predicts the numerous victories by means of which the Romans should extend their empire far and wide, although not without great difficulties and dangers. He states, *The king of the south should carry on war with the Romans for a definite period.* I dare not fix the precise time intended by the angel. So great was the power of Egypt, that had the kings of that country relied upon their native resources, they might have summoned courage to make war upon the Romans. Gabinius the proconsul led his army there for the sake of restoring Ptolemy. He expelled Archelaus without much trouble, and then like a mercenary he risked his life and his fame there, as well as his army. Cæsar was in danger there, after vanquishing Pompey; then Antony next made war upon Augustus, assisted by the forces of Cleopatra ; then Egypt put forth all her strength, and at his failure was reduced herself to a province of Rome. The angel did not propose to mark a continued series of times, but only briefly to admonish the faithful to stand firm amidst those most grievous concussions which were then at hand. Whatever be the precise meaning, the angel doubtless signified the difficult nature of the struggle between the Romans and the Egyptians. I have already stated the witness of history to the fact, that the Egyptians never made war against the Romans in their own name ; sometimes events were so confused that the Egyptians coalesced with the Syrians, and then we must read the words conjointly—thus the king of the south, assisted by the king of the north, should carry on war with the Romans. The angel thus shews us how the king of Syria should furnish greater forces and supplies than the Egyptian monarch, and this really happened at the beginning of the triumvirate. He states next, *The king of the south* should come *with chariots and horses and many ships.* Nor is it necessary here to indicate the precise period, since the Romans carried on many wars in the east, during which they occupied Asia, while a part of Lybia fell to them by the will of its king without arms or force of any kind.

With reference to these two kingdoms which have been so frequently mentioned, many chiefs ruled over Syria within a short period. First one of the natives was raised to the throne and then another, till the people grew tired of them, and transferred the sovereignty to strangers. Then Alexander rose gradually to power, and ultimately acquired very great fame : he was not of noble birth, for his father was of unknown origin. This man sprang from an obscure family, and at one period possessed neither authority nor re-

sources. He was made king of Syria, because he pretended
to be the son of Seleucus, and was slain immediately, while
his immediate successor reigned for but a short period. Thus
Syria passed over to the Romans on the death of this Seleucus. Tigranes the king of Armenia was then sent for, and
he was made ruler over Syria till Lucullus conquered him,
and Syria was reduced to a province. The vilest of men
reigned over Egypt. Physcon, who was restrained by the
Romans when attempting to wrest Syria from the power of
its sovereign, was exceedingly depraved both in body and
mind : and hence he obtained this disgraceful appellation.
For the word is a Greek one, equivalent to the French *andou-
ille ;* for *physce* means that thicker intestine into which the
others are usually inserted.   This deformity gave rise to his
usual name, signifying " pot-bellied," implying both bodily
deformity and likeness to the brutes, while he was not endowed with either intellect or ingenuity.   The last king who
made the Romans his son's guardians, received the name of
Auletes, and Cicero uses this epithet of " flute-player," because he was immoderately fond of this musical instrument.
In each kingdom then there was horrible deformity, since
those who exercised the royal authority were more like dogs
or swine than mankind.   Tigranes, it is well known, gave
the Romans much trouble.   On the other side, Mithridates
occupied their attention for a very long period, and with various and opposite success.   The Romans throughout all Asia
were at one period put to the sword, and when a close engagement was fought, Mithridates was often superior, and he
afterwards united his forces with those of Tigranes, his father-
in-law.   When Tigranes held Armenia, he was a king of
other kings, and afterwards added to his dominions a portion
of Syria.   At length when the last Antiochus was set over
the kingdom of Syria by Lucullus, he was removed from his
command by the orders of Pompey, and then, as we have
stated, Syria became a province of Rome.   Pompey crossed
the sea, and subdued the whole of Judea as well as Syria :
he afterwards entered the Temple, and took away some part
of its possessions, but spared the sacred treasures.   Crassus
succeeded him—an insatiable whirlpool, who longed for this

province for no other reason than his unbounded eagerness for wealth. He despoiled the Temple at Jerusalem; and lastly, after Cleopatra was conquered, Egypt lost its royal race, and passed into a Roman province. If the Romans had conquered a hundred other provinces, the angel would not have mentioned them here; for I have previously noticed his special regard to the chosen people. Therefore he dwells only on those slaughters which had more or less relation to the wretched Jews. First of all he predicts the great contest which should arise between the kings of Egypt and Syria, *who should come on like a whirlwind,* while the Romans *should rush upon the lands like a deluge, and pass over them.* He compares the king of Syria to a whirlwind, for at first he should rush on impetuously, filling both land and sea with his forces. Thus he should possess a well-manned fleet, and thus excite fresh terrors, and yet vanish away rapidly like a whirlwind. But the Romans are compared to a deluge. The new king of whom he had spoken *should come,* says he, *and overflow,* burying all the forces of both Egypt and Syria; implying the whole foundations of both realms should be swept away when the Romans passed over them. *He shall pass over,* he says; meaning, wherever they come, the way shall be open for them and nothing closed against them. He will repeat this idea in another form. He does not speak now of one region only, but says, *they should come over the lands,* implying a wide-spread desolation, while no one should dare to oppose them by resisting their fury.

41. He shall enter also into the glorious land, and many *countries* shall be overthrown: but these shall escape out of his hand, *even* Edom, and Moab, and the chief of the children of Ammon.

42. He shall stretch forth his hand also upon the countries; and the land of Egypt shall not escape.

41. Et veniet in terram desiderii, et multæ, *regiones scilicet,* cadent, et hæ evadent e manu ejus, Edom, Moab, et principium filiorum Ammon.

42. Et mittet, *hoc est, extendet,* manum suam in terras, et terra Ægypti non erit in evasionem.[1]

The land of Judea is called the pleasant or desirable land, because God thought it worthy of his peculiar favour. He chose it for his dwelling-place, called it his resting-place, and

[1] That is, "shall not escape," or "snatch itself away."—*Calvin.*

caused his blessing to remain in it.   In this verse also, regions are treated, and not merely cities, as the regions of
Edom and of Moab.   After the angel had briefly predicted
the occurrence of the most grievous wars with the Romans, he
now adds what he had briefly commenced in the last verse,—
namely, their becoming conquerors of all nations.   *They
shall come,* he says, *into the desirable land.*   This is the reason why the angel prophesies of the Roman empire, for he
was not sent to explain to Daniel the history of the whole
world, but to retain the faithful in their allegiance, and to
persuade them under the most harassing convulsions to remain under the protection and guardianship of God.   For
this reason he states,—*they shall come into the desirable
land.*   This would be a dreadful temptation, and might overthrow all feelings of piety, as the Jews would be harassed on
all sides, first by the Syrians and then by the Egyptians.   And
we know with what cruelty Antiochus endeavoured not only
to oppress but utterly to blot out the whole nation.   Neither
the Syrians nor the Egyptians spared them.   The Romans
came almost from the other side of the globe ; at first they
made an alliance with these states, and then entered Judea
as enemies.   Who would have supposed that region under
God's protection, when it was so exposed to all attacks of
robbery and oppression ?   Hence it was necessary to admonish the faithful not to fall away through this utter confusion.

They shall come, then, *into the desirable land, and many
regions shall fall ;* meaning, no hope should remain for the
Jews after the arrival of the Romans, as victory was already
prepared to their hand.   The angel's setting before the faithful this material for despair was not likely to induce confidence and comfort, but as they were aware of these divine
predictions, they knew also that the remedy was prepared
by the same God who had admonished them by means of the
angel.   It was in his power to save his Church from a hundred
deaths.   This prophecy became an inestimable treasury, inspiring the faithful with the hope of the promised deliverance.
The angel will afterwards add the promise intended to support and strengthen and revive their drooping spirits.   But
he here announces that God's aid should not immediately ap-

pear, because he would give the Romans full permission to exercise a cruel sway, tyranny, and robbery, throughout the whole of Asia and the East. He says, *The lands of Edom, Moab, and a portion of Ammon should escape from their slaughter.* This trial would in no slight degree affect the minds of the pious: What does he mean? He suffers the land that he promised should be at rest, to be now seized and laid waste by its enemies! The land of Moab is at peace and enjoys the greatest tranquillity, and the condition of the sons of Ammon is prosperous! We should here bear in mind what the prophets say of these lands: Esau was banished into the rugged mountains, and God assigned to the Moabites a territory beyond the borders of the land of blessings. (Malachi i. 3.) The Jews alone had any peculiar right and privilege to claim that territory in which the Lord had promised them perfect repose. Now, when Judea is laid waste and their foes according to their pleasure not only seize upon everything valuable in the city and the country, but seem to have a special permission to ravage the land at their will, what could the Jews conjecture? The angel therefore meets this objection, and alleviates these feelings of anxiety to which the faithful could be subject from such slaughters. He states that the territories of *Edom* and *Moab,* and of the *children of Ammon,* should be tranquil and safe from those calamities. By the expression, *to the beginning of the children of Ammon,* he most probably refers to that retreat whence the Ammonites originated. For doubtless the Romans would not have spared the Ammonites unless they had been concealed among the mountains, for every district in the neighbourhood of Judea was subject to the same distress. Those who interpret this passage of Antichrist, suppose safety to be extended only to that portion of the faithful who shall escape from the world and take refuge in the deserts. But there is no reason in this opinion, and it is sufficient to retain the sense already proposed as the genuine one. He afterwards adds, *The Romans should send their army into the land, and even in the land of Egypt, they should not escape.* The angel without doubt here treats of the numerous victories which the Romans should obtain in a short time. They carried on war with Mithridates for a long period, and then Asia was almost lost ; but they soon afterwards began to extend their power, first over all Asia Minor, and then over Syria ; Armenia was next added to their sway, and Egypt after that : meanwhile this was but a moderate addition, till at length they ruled over the Persians, and thus their power became formidable. Wherefore this prophecy was fulfilled by *their extending their power over many regions,* and *by the land of Egypt becoming a portion of their booty.* It follows :

43. But he shall have power over the treasures of gold and of silver, and over all the precious things [1] of Egypt : and the Libyans and the Ethiopians *shall be* at his steps.

43. Et dominabitur thesauris auri, et argenti, et omnibus desiderabilibus [1] Ægypti, et Lybiæ, et Æthiopiæ ingressibus suis.

I have previously stated that though the language applies to a single king, yet a kingdom is to be understood, and our former observations are here confirmed. Although many nations should endeavour to resist the Romans, they should yet be completely victorious, and finally acquire immense booty.   Their avarice and covetousness were perfectly astonishing ; for he says, *they should acquire dominion over the treasures of gold and silver, and should draw to themselves all the precious things of Egypt, Lybia, and Ethiopia ; and that, too, in their footsteps.* In these words he more clearly explains our previous remarks upon the emblem of the deluge.   All lands should be laid open to them ; although the cities were fortified, and would thus resist them by their closed gates, yet the way should be open to them, and none should hinder them from bursting forth over the whole east, and subduing at the same time cities, towns, and villages.   This we know to have been actually accomplished. Hence there is nothing forced in the whole of this context, and the prophecy is fairly interpreted by the history.   He afterwards adds,—

44. But tidings out of the east and out of the north shall trouble him : therefore he shall go forth with great fury to destroy, and utterly to make away many.

44. Rumores vero, [2] terrebunt eum ab oriente, et ab aquilone : egredieturque cum ira magna, ut perdat et internecione deleat multos.

[1] That is, over all precious things.—*Calvin.*
[2] Probably "reports" or " statements" which should be heard.—*Calvin.*

The angel's narrative seems here to differ somewhat from the preceding one, as the Romans should not succeed so completely as to avoid being arrested in the midst of their victorious course. He says, *they shall be frightened by rumours,* and the events suit this case, for although the Romans subdued the whole east with scarcely any trouble, and in a few years, yet they were afterwards checked by adversity. For Crassus perished miserably after spoiling the temple, and destroyed himself and the flower of the Roman army; he was conquered at Carræ, near Babylon, in an important engagement, through betrayal by a spy in whom he had placed too much confidence. Antony, again, after dividing the world into three parts between himself, and Octavius, and Lepidus, suffered miserably in the same neighbourhood against the Parthians. We are not surprised at the angel's saying, *The Romans should be frightened from the east and the north,* as this really came to pass. Then he adds, *they should come in great wrath;* meaning, although they should lose many troops, yet this severe massacre should not depress their spirits. When their circumstances were desperate, they were excited to fury like savage beasts of prey, until they rushed upon their own destruction. This came to pass more especially under the reign of Augustus; for a short period he contended successfully with the Parthians, and compelled them to surrender. He then imposed upon them conditions of peace; and as the Roman eagles had been carried into Persia, much to their disgrace, he compelled this people to return them. By this compulsion he blotted out the disgrace which they had suffered under Antony. We see, then, how exceedingly well this suits the context,—*the Romans shall come with great wrath to destroy many;* as the Parthians expected to enjoy tranquillity for many ages, and to be perfectly free from any future attempt or attack from the Romans. It now follows,—

45. And he shall plant the tabernacles of his palaces between the seas in the glorious holy mountain: yet he shall come to his end, and none shall help him.

45. Et figet tabernacula palatii sui inter maria ad montem desiderii sanctitatis, et veniet ad finem suum, et non auxiliator ei.

The angel at length concludes with the settled sway of

the Romans in Asia Minor and the regions of the east, as well as in Syria, Judea, and Persia. We have already shewn how everything here predicted is related by profane historians, and each event is well known to all who are moderately versed in the knowledge of those times. We must now notice the phrase, The Roman king *should fix the tents of his palace.* This expression signifies not only the carrying on of the war by the Romans in the east, but their being lords of the whole of that region. When he had said they should fix their tents according to the usual practice of warfare, he might have been content with the usual method of speech, but he contrasts the word "palace" with frequent migrations, and signifies their not measuring their camp according to the usage of warfare, but their occupying a fixed station for a permanence. Why then does he speak of tents? Because Asia was not the seat of their empire; for they were careful in not attributing more dignity to any place than was expedient for themselves. For this reason the proconsuls took with them numerous attendants, to avoid the necessity of any fixed palace: they had their own tents, and often remained in such temporary dwellings as they found on their road. This language of the angel—*they shall fix the tents of their palace*—will suit the Romans exceedingly well, because they reigned there in tranquillity after the east was subdued ; and yet they had no fixed habitation, because they did not wish any place to become strong enough to rebel against them. When he says, *between the seas,* some think the Dead Sea intended, and the Lake of Asphalt, as opposed to the Mediterranean Sea. I do not hesitate to think the Persian Sea is intended by the angel. He does not say the Romans should become masters of all the lands lying between the two seas, but he only says *they should fix the tents of their palace between the seas ;* and we know this to have been done when they held the dominion between the Euxine and the Persian Gulf. The extent of the sway of Mithridates is well known, for historians record twenty-two nations as subject to his power. Afterwards, on one side stood Asia Minor, which consisted of many nations, according to our statement elsewhere, and Armenia became theirs after Tigranes was conquered, while Cilicia, though only a part of a province, was a very extensive and wealthy region. It had many deserts and many stony and uncultivated mountains, while there were in Cilicia many rich cities, though it did not form a single province, like Syria and Judea, so that it is not surprising when the angel says the Romans *should fix their tents between the seas,* for their habitation was beyond the Mediterranean Sea. They first passed over into Sicily and then into Spain; thirdly, they began to extend their power into Greece and Asia Minor against Antiochus, and then they seized upon the whole east. On the one shore was Asia Minor and many other nations; and on the other side was the Syrian Sea, including Judea as far as the Egyptian Sea. We observe, then, the tranquillity of the Roman empire *between the seas,* and yet it had no permanent seat there, because the proconsuls spent their time as foreigners in the midst of a strange country.

At length he adds, *They should come to the mountain of the desire of holiness.* I have already expressed the reason why this prophecy was uttered; it was to prevent the novelty of these events from disturbing the minds of the pious, when they saw so barbarous and distant a nation trampling upon them, and ruling with pride, insolence, and cruelty. When, therefore, so sorrowful a spectacle was set before the eyes of the pious, they required no ordinary supports lest they should yield to the pressure of despair. The angel therefore predicts future events, to produce the acknowledgment of nothing really happening by chance; and next, to shew how all these turbulent motions throughout the world are governed by a divine power. The consolation follows, *they shall come at length to their end, and no one shall bring them help.* This was not fulfilled immediately, for after Crassus had despoiled the temple, and had suffered in an adverse engagement against the Parthians, the Romans did not fail all at once, but their monarchy flourished even more and more under Augustus. The city was then razed to the ground by Titus, and the very name and existence of the Jewish nation all but annihilated. Then, after this, the Romans suffered disgraceful defeats; they were cast out of nearly the whole east, and

CHAP. XII. 1.   COMMENTARIES ON DANIEL.   367

compelled to treat with the Parthians, the Persians, and other nations, till their empire was entirely ruined. If we study the history of the next hundred years, no nation will be found to have suffered such severe punishments as the Romans, and no monarchy was ever overthrown with greater disgrace. God then poured such fury upon that nation as to render them the gazing-stock of the world. The angel's words are not in vain, *their own end should soon come;* after they had devastated and depopulated all lands, and penetrated and pervaded everywhere, and all the world had given themselves up to their power, then the Romans became utterly ruined and swept away. *They should have none to help them.* Without doubt this prophecy may be here extended to the promulgation of the gospel; for although Christ was born about one age before the preaching of the gospel, yet he truly shone forth to the world by means of that promulgation. The angel therefore brought up his prophecy to that point of time. He now subjoins,—

CHAPTER TWELFTH.

1. And at that time shall Michael stand up, the great prince which standeth for the children of thy people; and there shall be a time of trouble, such as never was since there was a nation *even* to that same time: and at that time thy people shall be delivered, every one *that shall be* found written in the book.

1. Et tempore illo stabit Michael princeps, magnus stans pro filiis populi tui, et erit tempus afflictionis, quale non fuit abesse gentem, *hoc est, ex quo cœperunt esse gentes,* ad tempus illud usque: et tempore illo servabitur populus tuus quicunque inventus fuerit scriptus in libro.

The angel no longer relates future occurrences specially, but proclaims God to be in general the guardian of his Church, so as to preserve it wonderfully amidst many difficulties and dreadful commotions, as well as in the profound darkness of disaster and death. This is the meaning of this sentence. This verse consists of two parts: the first relates to that most wretched period which should be full of various and almost numberless calamities; and the second assures us of God's never-failing protection and preservation of his Church by his own innate power. In this second part the promise is restricted to the elect, and thus a third clause may be distinguished, but it is only an addition to the second just mentioned. At the close of the verse, the angel presents us with a definition of the Church, as many professed to be God's people who were not really so. He says, *Michael, the prince of the people, should stand up.* Then he states the reason, *The calamities of that period should be such as were never witnessed from the beginning of the world.* As he addresses Daniel, he says, *sons of thy people;* for he was one of the sons of Abraham, and the nation from which Daniel sprang was in that sense "his." From this it follows that the calamities of which he will by and bye treat, belong to the true Church, and not to the profane nations. The singular aid of Michael would not have been needed, unless the Church had been oppressed with the most disastrous distresses. We perceive, then, the angel's meaning to be according to my explanation. The Church should be subject to most numerous and grievous calamities until the advent of Christ, but yet it should feel God's propitious disposition, ensuring its own safety under his aid and protection. By Michael many agree in understanding Christ as the head of the Church. But if it seems better to understand Michael as the archangel, this sense will prove suitable, for under Christ as the head, angels are the guardians of the Church. Whichever be the true meaning, God was the preserver of his Church by the hand of his only-begotten Son, and because the angels are under the government of Christ, he might entrust this duty to Michael. That foul hypocrite, Servetus, has dared to appropriate this passage to himself; for he has inscribed it as a frontispiece on his horrible comments, because he was called Michael! We observe what diabolic fury has seized him, as he dared to claim as his own what is here said of the singular aid afforded by Christ to his Church. He was a man of the most impure feelings, as we have already sufficiently made known. But this was a proof of his impudence and sacrilegious madness—to adorn himself with this epithet of Christ without blushing, and to elevate himself into Christ's place, by boasting himself to be Michael, the guardian of the Church, and the mighty prince of the people !   This fact is well known, for I have the book at hand should any one distrust my word.

PRAYER.

Grant, Almighty God, since we are placed in similar distresses to those of which thou dost wish to warn us by thy angel, as well as thine ancient people, that thy light may shine upon us by means of thy only-begotten Son.   May we feel ourselves always in safety under his invincible power.   May we dwell securely under his shadow, and contend earnestly and boldly unto the end, against Satan and all his impious crew.   And when all our warfare is over, may we arrive at last at that blessed rest where the fruit of our victory awaits us, in the same Christ our Lord.—Amen.

Lecture Sixty-Five.

THE twelfth chapter commenced, as we stated in yesterday's Lecture, with the angel's prediction as to the future state of the Church after the manifestation of Christ.   It was to be subject to many miseries, and hence this passage would soothe the sorrow of Daniel, and of all the pious, as he still promises safety to the Church through the help of God.   Daniel therefore represented Michael as the guardian of the Church, and God had enjoined this duty upon Christ, as we learn from the 10th chapter of John, (ver. 28, 29.) As we stated yesterday, Michael may mean an angel ; but I embrace the opinion of those who refer this to the person of Christ, because it suits the subject best to represent him as standing forward for the defence of his elect people.   He is called the *mighty prince*, because he naturally opposed the unconquered fortitude of God to those dangers to which the angel represents the Church to be subject.   We well know the very slight causes for which terror often seizes our minds, and when we begin to tremble, nothing can calm our tumult and agitation.   The angel then in treating of very grievous contests, and of the imminent danger of the Church, calls *Michael the mighty prince*.   As if he had said, Michael should be the guardian and protector of the elect people, he should exercise immense power, and he alone without the slightest doubt should be sufficient for their protection.   Christ confirms the same assertion, as we just now saw, in the 10th chapter of John. He says all his elect were given him by his father, and none of them should perish, because his father was greater than all ; no one, says he, shall pluck my sheep out of my hand. My father, who gave them me, is greater than all ; meaning, God possesses infinite power, and displays it for the safety of those whom he has chosen before the creation of the world, and he has committed it to me, or has deposited it in my hands. We now perceive the reason of this epithet, which designates *Michael as the great prince.* For in consequence of the magnitude of the contest, we ought to enjoy the offer of insuperable strength, to enable us to attain tranquillity in the midst of the greatest commotions. It was in no degree superfluous for the angel to predict such great calamities as impending over the Church, and in the present day the same expressions are most useful to us. We perceive then how the Jews imagined a state of happiness under Christ, and the same error was adopted by the Apostles, who, when Christ discoursed on the destruction of the temple and the city, thought the end of the world was at hand, and this they connected with their own glory and triumph.   (Matth. xxiv. 3.)   The Prophet then is here instructed by the angel how God should direct the course of his Church when he should manifest to them his only-begotten Son. Still the severity of distress awaited all the pious ; as if he had said, The time of your triumph is not yet arrived ; you must still continue your warfare, which will prove both laborious and harassing. The condition of the new people is here compared with that of the ancient one, who suffered many perils and afflictions at God's hands. The angel therefore says, even although the faithful suffered very severely under the law and the prophets, yet a more oppressive season was at hand, during which God would treat his Church far more strictly than before, and submit it to far more excruciating trials. This is the meaning of the passage, *a season full of afflictions should arise, such as the nations had never seen*

since they began to exist. This may refer to the creation of
the world, and if we refer it to the people themselves, the exposition will prove correct ; for although the Church had in
former periods been wretched, yet after the appearance of
Christ, it should suffer far more calamities than before.   We
remember the language of the Psalmist : The impious have
often opposed me from my youth ; they have drawn the
plough across my back. (Ps. cxxix. 1-3.) Through all ages
then God subjected his Church to many evils and disasters.
But a comparison is here instituted between two different
states of the Church, and the angel shews how after Christ's
appearance it should be far from either quietness or happiness.   As it should be oppressed with heavier afflictions, it is
not surprising that the fathers should wish us to be conformed to the image of his only-begotten Son. (Rom. viii. 29.)
Since the period of Christ's resurrection, even if a more
harassing warfare awaits us, we ought to bear it with great
equanimity, because the glory of heaven is placed before
our eyes far more clearly than it was before theirs.

At length he adds, *At that time thy people shall be preserved.* By this expression the angel points out to us the
great importance of the protection of Michael.   He promises
certain salvation to his elect people, as if he had said,
although the Church should be exposed to the greatest
dangers, yet with respect to God himself, it should always
be safe and victorious in all contests, because Michael should
be superior to every enemy. The angel then, in thus exhorting the faithful to bear their cross, shews how free they
should be from all doubt as to the event, and the absolute
certainty of their victory.   Although at first sight this prophecy might inspire us with fear and dismay, yet this comfort ought to be sufficient for us : " We shall be conquerors
amidst fire and sword, and amidst many deaths we are sure
of life."   As perfect safety is here set before us, we ought to
feel secure, and to enter with alacrity into every engagement.   We are in truth obliged to fight, but Christ has conquered for us, as he says himself, Trust in me, I have overcome the world. (John xvi. 33.) But the angel restricts
what he had said generally by way of correction. Many pro-

fessed to belong to the people of God, and every one naturally sprung from the stock of Israel boasted of being the off-spring of divine seed. As all wished promiscuously to belong to God's people, the angel restricts his expression by a limiting phrase, *all people*, says he, *who were found written in the book*. This clause does not mean all Israel after " the flesh," (Rom. ix: 6-8,) but such as God esteems to be real Israelites according to gratuitous election alone. He here distinguishes between the carnal and spiritual children of Abraham, between the outward Church and that inward and true community which the Almighty approves. Upon what then does the difference depend between those who boast of being Abraham's children, while they are rejected by God, and those who are really and truly his sons? On the mere grace and favour of God. He declares his election when he regenerates his elect by his Holy Spirit, and thus inscribes them with a certain mark, while they prove the reality of this sonship by the whole course of their lives, and confirm their own adoption. Meanwhile we are compelled to go to the fountain at once; God alone by his gratuitous election distinguishes the outward Church, which has nothing but the title, from the true Church, which can never either perish or fall away. Thus we observe in how many passages of Scripture hypocrites are rejected in the midst of their swelling pride, as they have nothing in common with the sons of God but the external symbols of profession.

We ought to notice this restriction, which assures us of the utter uselessness of outward pomp, and of the unprofit-able nature of even a high station in the outward Church, unless we are truly among God's people. This is expressed fully in Ps. xv. and xxiv., while Ps. lxxiii. confirms the same sentiments. How good is God to Israel, especially to the upright in heart! In these passages of the Psalms the cause is not stated to be the secret election of God, but the out-ward testimony of the conduct; and this although inferior in degree, is not contrary to the first cause which produces it. This has its proper place, but God's election is always superior. The word *book* refers to that eternal counsel of God, whereby he elected us and adopted us as his sons before the foundation of the world, as we read in the first chapter of Ephesians, (ver. 4.) In the same sense Ezekiel inveighs against the false prophets who deceived the people of Israel, (xiii. 9.) My hand, says God, shall be upon those prophets who deceive my people: they shall not therefore be in the secret assembly of my people, nor shall they be found in the roll of the house of Israel. The word signifying to write is used here,—they shall not be written in the enrolment of the house of Israel. The word book is here used in the same sense, and yet we need not adopt the gross idea, that the Almighty has any need of a book. His book is that eternal counsel which predestinates us to himself, and elects us to the hope of eternal salvation. We now understand the full sense of this instruction, as the Church shall remain in safety amidst many deaths, and even in the last stage of despair it shall escape through the mercy and help of God. We must also remember this definition of a church, because many boast of being God's sons, who are complete strangers to him. This leads us to consider the subject of election, as our salvation flows from that fountain. Our calling, which is his outward testimony to it, follows that gratuitous adoption which is hidden within himself; and thus God when regenerating us by his Spirit, inscribes upon us his marks and signs, whence he is able to acknowledge us as his real children. It follows,—

2. And many of them that sleep in the dust of the earth shall awake, some to everlasting life, and some to shame *and* everlasting contempt.	2. Et multi ex dormientibus in terra pulvere, evigilabunt hi in vitam seculi, *hoc est, perpetuo,* hi vero in opprobium et in abominationem perpetuam.

As to the translation of the first words, it is literally many who sleep in the earth of dust, or who are in earth and dust; for the genitive is used as an epithet, though it may be read as if in opposition with the former word sleep, meaning those who are reduced to earth and dust.

The angel seems here to mark a transition from the commencement of the preaching of the gospel, to the final day of the resurrection, without sufficient occasion for it. For why does he pass over the intermediate time during which many events might be the subject of prophecy? He

unites these two subjects very fitly and properly, connecting
the salvation of the Church with the final resurrection and
with the second coming of Christ. Wheresoever we may
look around us, we never meet with any source of salvation
on earth. The angel announces the salvation of all the
elect. They are most miserably oppressed on all sides, and
wherever they turn their eyes, they perceive nothing but
confusion. Hence the hope of the promised salvation could
not be conceived by man before the elect raise their minds
to the second coming of Christ. It is just as if the angel
had said, God will be the constant preserver of his Church,
even unto the end; but the manner in which he will preserve it must not be taken in a carnal sense, as the Church
will be like a dead body until it shall rise again. We here
perceive the angel teaching the same truth as Paul delivers
in other words, namely, we are dead, and our life is hidden
with Christ; it shall then be made manifest when he shall
appear in the heavens. (Col. iii. 3.) We must hold this first
of all, God is sufficiently powerful to defend us, and we need
not hesitate in feeling ourselves safe under his hand and protection. Meanwhile it is necessary to add this second point;
as long as we fix our eyes only on this present state of things,
and dwell upon what the world offers us, we shall always be
like the dead. And why so? Our life ought to be hid with
Christ in God. Our salvation is secure, but we still hope for
it, as Paul says in another passage. (Rom. viii. 23, 24.)
What is hoped for is not seen, says he. This shews us how
completely seasonable is the transition from this doctrine
respecting God's elect to the last advent of Christ. This
then is enough with respect to the context. The word *many*
seems here clearly put for all, and this is not to be considered
as at all absurd, for the angel does not use the word in contrast with all or few, but only with one. Some of the Jews
strain this expression to mean the restoration of the Church
in this world under themselves, which is perfectly frivolous.
In this case the following language would not be correct,—
Some shall rise to life, and others to disgrace and contempt.
Hence if this concerned none but the Church of God, certainly none would rise to disgrace and condemnation. This

shews the angel to be treating of the last resurrection, which is common to all, and allows of no exceptions. I have lately explained why he calls our attention to the advent of Christ. Since all things in the world will be constantly confused, our minds must necessarily be raised upwards, and gain the victory over what we observe with our eyes, and comprehend with our outward senses.

Those who sleep in the earth and the dust; meaning, wherever the earth and dust exist, nevertheless they shall rise, implying the hope of a resurrection not founded on natural causes, but depending upon the inestimable power of God, which surpasses all our senses. Hence, although the elect as well as the wicked shall be reduced to earth and dust, this shall by no means form an obstacle to God's raising them up again. He uses *earth and dust.* In my judgment אדמת, *admeth,* "of the earth," is the genus, and עפר, *gnepher,* "dust," is the species, meaning, although they are only putrid carcases, yet they shall be reduced to dust, which is minute particles of earth. God, then, is endued with sufficient power to call forth the dead to newness of life. This passage is worthy of especial notice, because the prophets do not contain any clearer testimony than this to the last resurrection, particularly as the angel distinctly asserts the future rising again of both the righteous and the wicked. Eternity is here opposed to those temporal miseries to which we are now subjected. Here we may notice the admonition of Paul, that those momentary afflictions by which God tries us, cannot be compared with that eternal glory which never shall cease. (Rom. viii. 18.) This, therefore, is the reason why the angel so clearly expresses, that eternal life awaits the elect, and eternal disgrace and condemnation will be the lot of the ungodly. He afterwards subjoins,—

3. And they that be wise shall shine as the brightness of the firmament; and they that turn many to righteousness as the stars for ever and ever.

3. Et prudentes fulgebunt quasi fulgor expansionis,[1] et qui justificant multos,[2] sicut stellæ in seculum et seculum, *id est, in perpetuum.*

The word "prudent" means endued with intellect. Some take it transitively, and in this passage their opinion is pro-

---

[1] Of the heavens, meaning the firmament.—*Calvin.*

[2] That is, those who justified many.—*Calvin.*

bably correct, because the office of justifying will soon be
assigned to these prudent ones. But the former sense suits
chapter xi. better, and in verse 10 it will be put absolutely.
Hence it means those who are endued with understanding.
The angel here confirms what I have lately expressed concerning the final resurrection, and shews how we shall enjoy
its fruits, because eternal glory is laid up for us in heaven.
We ought not to complain of being treated unworthily,
whenever we seem to suffer harshness at God's hands, because we ought to be satisfied with the glory of heaven, and
with the perpetual existence of that life which has been
promised to us. He says then, *the teachers*, or those who
excel in understanding, *shall shine forth as the light of
heaven.* If the word "teachers" is thought preferable, there
will be a figure of speech, a part being put for the whole,
and, therefore, I follow the usual explanation. He applies
the phrase, "endued with understanding," to those who do
not depart from the true and pure knowledge of God, as will
be afterwards explained more fully. For the angel contrasts
the profane who proudly and contemptuously rage against
God, and the faithful whose whole wisdom is to submit
themselves to God, and to worship him with the purest
affection of their minds. We shall say more on this subject
to-morrow. But he now says, those who retained sincere
piety should be like *the light of the firmament ;* meaning,
they shall be heirs of the kingdom of heaven, where they
shall enjoy that glory which surpasses all the splendour of the
world. No doubt, the angel here uses figures to explain what
is incomprehensible, implying, nothing can possibly be found
in the world which answers to the glory of the elect people.

And those who shall justify many shall be *like stars*, says
he. He repeats the same thing in other words, and now
speaks of *stars*, having formerly used the phrase, *the brightness of the firmament*, in the same sense ; and instead of
"those who are endued with understanding," he says,
those who shall have justified. Without doubt, the angel
here especially denotes the teachers of the truth, but in my
opinion he embraces also all the pious worshippers of God.
No one of God's children ought to confine their attention

privately to themselves, but as far as possible, every one ought to interest himself in the welfare of his brethren. God has deposited the teaching of his salvation with us, not for the purpose of our privately keeping it to ourselves, but of our pointing out the way of salvation to all mankind. This, therefore, is the common duty of the children of God, —to promote the salvation of their brethren. By this word "justifying," the angel means, not that it is in the power of one man to justify another, but the property of God is here transferred to his ministers. Meanwhile, we are as clearly justified by any teaching which brings faith within our reach, as we are justified by the faith which springs from the teaching. Why is our justification ever ascribed to faith? Because our faith directs us to Christ in whom is the complete perfection of justification, and thus our justification may be ascribed equally to the faith taught and the doctrine which teaches it. And those who bring before us this teaching are the ministers of our justification. The assertion of the angel, in other words, is this,—The sons of God, who being devoted entirely to God and ruled by the spirit of prudence, point out the way of life to others, shall not only be saved themselves, but shall possess surpassing glory far beyond anything which exists in this world. This is the complete explanation. Hence, we gather the nature of true prudence to consist in submitting ourselves to God in simple teachableness, and in manifesting the additional quality of carefully promoting the salvation of our brethren. The effect of this our labour ought to increase our courage and alacrity. For "how great is the honour conferred upon us by our Heavenly Father, when he wishes us to be the ministers of his righteousness? As James says, We preserve those about to perish if we bring them back into the right way. (Chap. v. 19.) James calls us preservers, just as the angel calls us justifiers; neither the angel nor the apostle wish to detract from the glory of God, but by these forms of speech the Spirit represents us as ministers of justification and salvation, when we unite in the same bonds with ourselves all those who have need of our assistance and exertions. It follows next :—

4. But thou, O Daniel, shut up the words, and seal the book, *even* to the time of the end: many shall run to and fro, and knowledge shall be increased.

4. Et tu Daniel, claude, *vel, obsera* verba, *sermones,* et obsigna librum ad tempus finis; discurrent multi, et augebitur scientia.

We have already explained "the time of the end" as a period previously fixed on by God, and settled by his own counsel. The following word refers to tracing out and running to and fro, but not necessarily in a bad sense, while it also signifies to investigate. Interpreters explain the angel's meaning, as if many should be unworthy to receive this prophecy from Daniel; and hence it was to be closed up and only enigmatically delivered to a few, because scarcely one in a hundred would attend to what he had delivered. I think the Holy Spirit has a different intention here. The angel's advice is this, There is no reason why this prophecy should cause despondency or dismay, because few should receive it. Although it should be universally despised and ridiculed, *nevertheless shut it up* like a precious treasure. Isaiah has a passage nearly similar, (chap. viii. 16,) Close up my law, seal the testimony among my disciples. Isaiah's spirit would be broken when he perceived himself an object of universal derision, and God's sacred oracles trodden under foot; thus he might lose all courage and decline the office of a teacher. But God affords him comfort: Close up, says he, my law among my disciples, and do not notice this profane crew; although they all despise thy teaching, do not suppose thy voice deserves their ridicule; close it up, close it up among my disciples, says he; how few soever may embrace thy teaching, yet let it remain sacred and laid up in the hearts of the pious. The Prophet afterwards says, Behold my children with me. Here he boasts in his contentment with very few, and thus triumphs over the impious and insolent multitude. Thus at the present time in the Papacy and throughout the whole world, impiety prevails so extensively that there is scarcely a single corner in which the majority agree in true obedience to God. As God foresaw how very few would embrace this prophecy with becoming reverence, the angel desired to animate the Prophet, lest he should grow weary, and esteem this prophecy as of little value, in consequence of its failing to command the applause of the whole world.

Close up the book, then ! but what does the phrase imply ? Not to hide it from all men, but to satisfy the Prophet when he saw but few reverently embracing the teaching so plainly laid before him by the angel. This is not properly a command ; the angel simply tells Daniel to hide or seal up this book and these words, offering him at the same time much consolation. If all men despise thy doctrine, and reject what thou dost set before them,—if the majority pass it by contemptuously, *shut it up and seal it,* not treating it as valueless, but preserving it as a treasure. I deposit it with thee, do thou lay it up among my disciples. *Thou, Daniel ;* here the Prophet's name is mentioned. If thou thinkest thyself to be alone, yet companions shall be afterwards added to thee who shall treat this prophecy with true piety. *Shut up,* then, *and seal it, even till the time of the end ;* for God will prove by the event that he has not spoken in vain, and experience will shew me to have been sent by him, as every occurrence has been previously predicted. It now follows,—

Many shall investigate, and knowledge shall increase. Some writers take this second clause in a contrary sense, as if many erratic spirits should run about with vague speculations, and wander from the truth. But this is too forced. I do not hesitate to suppose the angel to promise the arrival of a period when God should collect many disciples to himself, although at the beginning they should be very few and insignificant. *Many,* then, *shall investigate ;* meaning, though they are most careless and slothful, while boasting themselves God's people, yet God should gather to himself a great multitude from other quarters. Small indeed and insignificant is the apparent number of the faithful who care for the truth of God, and who shew any eagerness to learn it, but let not this scantiness move thee. The sons of God shall soon become increased. *Many shall investigate, and knowledge shall increase.* This prophecy shall not always be buried in obscurity ; the Lord will at length cause many to embrace it to their own salvation. This event really came to pass. Before Christ's coming, this doctrine was not esteemed according to its value. The extreme ignorance and grossness of the people is notorious, while their religion was nearly overthrown till God afterwards increased his Church. And at the present time any one who will carefully consider this prediction will experience its utility. This can scarcely be fully expressed in words ; for, unless this prophecy had been preserved and laid up like an inestimable treasure, much of our faith would have passed away. This divine assistance affords us strength, and enables us to overcome all the attacks of the world and of the devil.

PRAYER.

Grant, Almighty God, as we have to engage in battle through the whole course of our lives, and our strength is liable to fail in various ways, that we may be supported by thy power and thus persevere unto the end. May we never grow weary, but learn to overcome the whole world, and to look forward to that happy eternity to which thou invitest us. May we never hesitate while Christ thy Son fights for us, in whose hand and power our victory is placed, and may he ever admit us into alliance with himself in that conquest which he has procured for us, until at length he shall gather us at the last day into the enjoyment of that triumph in which he has gone before us.—Amen.

Lecture Sixty-Sixth.

5. Then I Daniel looked, and, behold, there stood other two, the one on this side of the bank of the river, and the other on that side of the bank of the river.

6. And one said to the man clothed in linen, which was upon the waters of the river, How long shall it be to the end of these wonders ?

7. And I heard the man clothed in linen, which was upon the waters of the river, when he held up his right hand and his left hand unto heaven, and sware by him that liveth

5. Et aspexi ego Daniel, et ecce duo alii stantes, unus hac ad ripam fluminis, et unus, id est, alter, illac ad ripam fluminis.[1]

6. Et dixit ad virum qui indutus erat lineis, vestibus subaudiendum est, qui erat supra aquas fluminis,[2] Quousque finis mirabilium ?

7. Et audivi virum indutum lineis, qui erat supra aquas fluvii, et sustulit dextram suam, et sinistram suam versus cœlos, et juravit per viventem in æternum, quod ad tempus

[1] That is, one on one side, and the other on the opposite.—Calvin.
[2] That is, stood above the bank.—Calvin.

for ever, that *it shall be* for a time, times, and an half; and when he shall have accomplished to scatter the power of the holy people, all these *things* shall be finished.

præfixum, tempora præfixa, et dimidium : et ut consumpserint, *vel,* compleverint, dispersionem, *vel, contritionem,* manus populi sancti, complebuntur omnia hæc.

Daniel here relates his vision of other angels standing on each bank of the river. He alludes to the Tigris which he had previously mentioned, as the vision was offered to him there. He says, *One asked the other, How long will it be to the end ?* He who was asked, swore, with hands upraised to heaven, by the living God, that no single prediction was in vain, since the truth would be evident in its own period, and men must wait for *the time, times, and half a time.* This is a summary of the passage. When he says *he beheld,* he commends to our notice the certainty of the vision. Unless he had been attentive, and had applied his mind seriously to these mysteries, his narrative would have failed to produce confidence. But as his mind was completely calm, and he was desirous of receiving the instruction conveyed by God through his angel, not the slightest doubt can be thrown upon what he so faithfully delivers to us. He speaks of angels as if they were men, for the reason previously assigned. He does not imply their being really men, but uses that expression in consequence of their outward appearance, for as they had a human face, they were called men. I do not assert their bodies to be merely imaginary, nor will I say Daniel saw only spectral forms and human shapes, for God might have clothed his angels in real bodies for the time, and yet they would not on that account become men. For Christ took upon Him our flesh and was truly man, while He was God manifest in flesh. (1 Tim. iii. 16.) But this is not true of angels, who received only a temporary body while performing the duties of their office. There is no doubt of this assertion,—the name of " men" cannot properly belong to angels, but it suits very well the human form or likeness which they sometimes wore.

It does not surprise us to find one angel questioning another. When Paul is extolling the mystery of the calling of the Gentiles, which had been hidden from the preceding ages, he adds,—it was an object of wonder to angels, as they had never hoped for it, and so it had not been revealed to them. (Eph. iii. 10.) So wonderfully does God work in his Church, that he causes admiration among the angels in heaven, by leaving many things unknown to them, as Christ testifies concerning the last day. (Matt. xxiv. 36.) This is the reason why the angel uses the interrogation, *How long is it to the end of these wonders ?* God doubtless here urged the angel to inquire into an event veiled in obscurity, for the purpose of waking up our attention. Absurd indeed would it be for us to pass by these things with inattention, when angels themselves display such anxiety by their questions, while they perceive traces of the secret power of God. Unless we are remarkably stupid, this doubt of the angel ought to stir us up to greater diligence and attention. This also is the force of the word פְלָאוֹת, *phlaoth*, " wonderful things ;" for the angel calls everything which he did not understand, *wonderful*. If the comparison be allowable, how great would be our ingratitude not to give our whole attention to the consideration of these mysteries which angels are compelled to confess to be beyond their grasp ! The angel, as if he were astonished, calls those things " wonderful" which were hidden not only from the minds of men, but also from himself and his companions. *But the other answers ;* whence some difference, although not a perpetual one, exists between the angels. The philosophy of Dionysius ought not to be admitted here, who speculates too cunningly, or rather too profanely, when treating the order of angels. But I only state the existence of some difference, because God assigns various duties to certain angels, and he dispenses to each a certain measure of grace and revelation, according to his pleasure. We know there is but one teacher of men and angels,—the Son of God, who is his eternal wisdom and truth. This passage may be referred to Christ, but as I cannot make any positive assertion, I am content with the simple statement already made. He states *this angel's clothing to have been linen garments*, implying splendour. Linen garments were then of great value; hence an ornament and decoration is here applied to angels, as God separates them from the common herd of men. Thus Daniel would the more easily comprehend these persons not to be earth-born mortals, but angels clad by God for a short period in the human form.

He says, *This angel raised up his hands to heaven.* Those who consider this action as a symbol of power are mistaken, for without doubt the Prophet intended to manifest the usual method of swearing. They usually raised the right hand, according to the testimony of numerous passages of Scripture. I have raised my hand towards God. (Gen. xiv. 22.) Here the angel raises both his hands, wishing by this action to express the importance of the subject. Thus to raise both hands, as if doubling the oath, is stronger than raising the right hand after the ordinary manner. We must consider then the use of both hands as intended to confirm the oath, as the subject was one of great importance. It follows, *for a time, times, and half a time.* I have stated my objection to the opinion of those who think one year, and two, and a half, to be here intended. I confess the passage ought to be understood of that pollution of the Temple which the Prophet has already treated. History clearly assures us that the Temple was not cleansed till the close of the third year, and seven or eight months afterwards. That explanation may suit its own passage, but with reference to the doctrine here delivered, its meaning is very simple, *time* means a long period, *times*, a longer period, and *a half* means the end or closing period. The sum of the whole is this : many years must elapse before God fulfils what his Prophet had declared. *Time* therefore signifies a long period ; *times*, double this period ; as if he had said, While the sons of God are kept in suspense so long without obtaining an answer to their petitions, the time will be prolonged, nay, even doubled. We see then that a time does not mean precisely one year, nor do times signify two years, but an indefinite period. With respect to the *half of a time,* this is added for the comfort of the pious, to prevent their sinking under the delay, because God does not accomplish their desire. Thus they rest patiently until this " time" as well as " the times" pass away. Besides, the issue is set before them by the words *half a time,* to prevent them from despairing through excessive weariness. I admit the allusion to years, but the words are not to be understood literally but metaphorically, signifying, as I have already stated, an indefinite period.

He afterwards adds, *And in the complement* or consumption of *the dispersion* or contrition *of the hand of God's people, all these things shall be fulfilled :* first, the time must pass away, next, the times must be added, then the half time must follow ; all these things must arrive at their accomplishment, and when they are thoroughly completed, says he, then will come *the contrition of the hand of the holy people.* The angel again proclaims how the Church of God should be oppressed by many calamities ; and thus the whole of this verse contains an exhortation to endurance, to prevent the faithful from becoming utterly hopeless, and completely losing their spirits, in consequence of their suffering severe and multiplied cares, not for a few months merely, but for a lengthened duration.   He uses this phrase, *the wearing down of the hand of the holy people*—if you please to read it so—metaphorically, meaning, the holy people should be deprived of strength, just as if their hands were completely worn down. Whatever agility men possess is usually shewn in the hands, and they were given to men by God for the special purpose of being extended to all parts of the body, and for executing the ordinary operations of mankind.   This metaphor is now very suitable, as the people were so mutilated, as to be deprived of all strength and vigour.   This is a slight sketch of the meaning of the clause.

If we read "dispersion" according to the common signification, it will suit very well, since the hand of the holy people should be dispersed ; meaning, the Church should be a stranger in the world, and be dispersed throughout it.   This was continually fulfilled from that day to the present.   How sad is the dispersion of the Church in these days !   God indeed defends it by His power, but this is beyond human expectation.   For how does the body of the Church now appear to us ? how has it appeared throughout all ages ? surely it has ever been torn in pieces and dispersed.   Hence the angel's prediction is not in vain, if we adopt the interpretation—the hand of the holy people should be dispersed— but yet the end should be prosperous, as he had previously announced, when treating of its resurrection and final salvation.   It now follows :

8. And I heard, but I understood not : then said I, O my Lord, what *shall be* the end of these *things ?*	8. Et ego audivi, et non intellexi : et dixi, Domine mi, quod posstremum horum?[1]

Now Daniel begins to ask questions in accordance with the angel's example.   He had first heard one angel inquiring of the other ; he next summons up courage, and becomes desirous of information, and asks what should be the end or issue ?   He says, *he heard without understanding.*   By the word " hearing," he bears witness to the absence of ignorance, slothfulness, or contempt.   Many depart without any perception of a subject, although it may be very well explained, because they were not attentive to it.   But here the Prophet asserts that he heard ; implying, it would be no fault of his diligence if he did not understand, because he was desirous of learning, and had exerted all his powers, as we formerly intimated, and yet he confesses *he did not understand.* Daniel does not mean to profess utter stupidity, but restricts his ignorance to the subject of this interrogation.   Of what then was Daniel ignorant ?   Of the final issue.   He could not attain unto the meaning of these predictions, which were so extremely obscure, and this was needful to their full and thorough comprehension.   It is quite clear that God never utters his word without expecting fruit ; as it is said in Isaiah, I have not spoken unintelligibly, nor have I said to the seed of Jacob, seek ye me in vain.   (Chap. xlv. 19.)   God was unwilling to leave his Prophet in this perplexity of hearing without understanding, but we are aware of distinct degrees of proficiency in the school of God.   Again, sufficient revelation was notoriously conferred upon the prophets for the discharge of their office, and yet none of them ever perfectly understood the predictions they delivered.   We know, too, what Peter says, They ministered more for our times than for their own.   (1 Peter i. 12.)   They were by no means useless to their own age, but when our age is compared with theirs, certainly the instruction and discipline of

[1] That is, what shall be the end of these things ?— *Calvin.*

the prophets is more useful to us, and produces richer and riper fruit in our age than in theirs. We are not surprised, then, at Daniel confessing *he did not understand*, so long as we restrict the words to this single instance. It now follows :—

9. And he said, Go thy way, Daniel: for the words *are* closed up and sealed till the time of the end.	9. Et dixit, Vade Daniel, quia clausi sunt, et obsignati sermones ad tempus finis.[1]

Although Daniel was not induced by any foolish curiosity to inquire of the angel the issue of these wonderful events, yet he did not obtain his request. God wished some of his predictions to be partially understood, and the rest to remain concealed until the full period of the complete revelation should arrive. This is the reason why the angel did not reply to Daniel. The wish in truth was pious, and, as we have previously stated, it did not contain anything unlawful ; but God, knowing what was good for him, did not grant his request. He is dismissed by the angel, *because the words were shut up and sealed.* The angel uses this expression in a sense different from the former one. For he ordered Daniel to close and seal the words like precious treasures, as they would be set at nought by many disbelievers, and by almost the whole people. Here then, he says, *the words were closed up and sealed,* as there was no fitting occasion for revealing them. As if he had said, nothing has been predicted either vainly or rashly, but the full blaze of light has not yet been thrown upon the prediction : hence we must wait until the truth itself is proved by the event, and thus the divine utterance of the angel is made manifest. This is the summary. He then says, *until the time of the end.* Some one might possibly object ; then for what purpose was this prediction delivered ? For Daniel himself, who was instructed by the angel, could not thoroughly comprehend his own message, and the rest of the faithful, although versed in these prophetic studies, felt themselves in a labyrinth here. The answer is at hand, *until the time of the end ;* and we must also remember that neither Daniel nor the rest of the faith-

---

[1] That is, the prefixed time, as we have formerly explained it.—*Calvin.*

ful were deprived of all the advantage of this prophecy, for God explained to them whatever was sufficient for the necessities of their own times. I must pass over some points slightly, with the view of finishing to-day. It follows:—

10. Many shall be purified, and made white, and tried; but the wicked shall do wickedly: and none of the wicked shall understand; but the wise shall understand.	10. Mundabuntur, et dealbabuntur, et fundentur multi,[1] et impie se gerent impii: et non intelligent omnes impii, et prudentes intelligent.

Again, the angel mentions the persecutions which were at hand for the purpose of arming the faithful for the approaching conflicts. We know from other sources how tender and weak our minds naturally are, for as soon as any cause for fear arises, before it comes to blows, we fall down lifeless through terror. As, therefore, our natural imbecility is so great, we necessarily require many stimulants to patience, and to urge us to contend with earnestness, and never to yield to any temptations. This is the reason why the angel announces the necessity for such multiplied purifications, *to cleanse them,* as wheat from chaff; *to whiten them,* as cloth by the fuller; and *to melt them,* as metal to be separated from dross. First of all, as I have previously explained, he admonishes Daniel and all the pious of the future state of the Church, to lead them to prepare and gird themselves for battle, and to gather up their unconquered fortitude, since the condition of life set before them is that of forcing their way through the midst of troubles. This is one point. Again, the angel shews the practical utility of this kind of life, which might otherwise seem too bitter. We naturally refuse the cross because we feel it contrary to our disposition, while God shews the pious that nothing can be more profitable to them than a variety of afflictions. This is a second point. But afflictions by themselves might possibly consume us, and hence we are cast into a furnace. How, then, could we expect these sufferings to promote our salvation, except God changed their nature in some wonderful way, as their

---

[1] Or, "shall be melted by fire;" the word means originally "to pour out," but is here taken transitively for to purify.—*Calvin.* Wintle's explanation of the allusion in these three verbs is most satisfactory.—*Ed.*

natural tendency is to effect our destruction ?   But while we are *melted down, and whitened, and cleansed,* we perceive how God consults for our welfare by pressing us with his cross and causing us to submit to adversity.   Now, thirdly, the angel shews the insufficiency of one single act of cleansing, and our need of many more.   This is the object of this numerous heaping together of words, *they shall be cleansed, and whitened, and melted down,* or poured forth.   He might have embraced the whole idea in a single word ; but, as through our whole lives God never ceases to test us in various ways, the angel heaps together these three words to shew the faithful their need of continual cleansing as long as they are clothed in flesh ; just as garments which are in daily use have need of continual washing.   However snowy a mantle may be, it becomes soiled immediately when used for even a single day ; requiring constant ablution to restore it to its original purity.   Thus we are brought in contact with the defilements of sin ; and as long as we are pilgrims in this world, we necessarily become subject to constant pollution. And as the faithful also are infected with the contagion of numerous iniquities, they require daily purifications in different ways.   We ought, then, diligently to notice these three distinct processes.

The angel afterwards adds, *The impious will act impiously, and will never understand anything ; but the prudent will be ever endued with intelligence.*   Here he wishes to fortify the pious against a stumblingblock in their way, when they see the profane despisers of God exulting in every direction, and defying God to his face.   When the faithful see the world so full of the impious, they seem to be indulging so freely in lust as if there were no God in heaven.: hence they are naturally subject to grievous sorrow and distress.   To prevent this trial from agitating their minds, the angel announces how *the impious should conduct themselves impiously ;* implying,—there is no reason why thou, O Daniel, or the rest of the righteous, should depend upon the example of others ; Satan will cunningly set before you whatever obstacles may draw you into the contempt of God, and the abyss of impiety, unless you are remarkably cautious ; but let not the conduct of the impious cause either you or the rest of the pious to stumble. Howsoever they conduct themselves, do you stand invincible. He afterwards assigns a reason for their behaviour—*they understand nothing*, they are perfectly blinded. But what is the source of this blindness? Their being given over to a reprobate sense. If any one should see a blind man fall, and should cast himself down after this blind man, would he be excusable? Surely his blindness was the cause of his perishing so miserably, but why does the other person destroy himself willingly? Whenever we see the impious rushing furiously on to their destruction, while God is admonishing them that their blindness proceeds from Satan, and that they are given over to a reprobate mind, are we not doubly mad if we willingly follow them? The cause then of this impious behaviour on the part of the wicked, is added with good reason; namely, they understand nothing. Meanwhile, the faithful are recalled to the true remedy, and the angel subjoins, *But the prudent shall understand*, meaning they shall not permit themselves to be implicated in the errors of those whom they see entirely devoted to their own destruction. Lastly, the angel points out to us the true remedy which will prevent Satan from drawing us off towards impiety, and the impious from infecting us with their evil examples, if we earnestly apply ourselves to the pursuit of heavenly doctrine. If, therefore, we heartily desire to be taught by God and to become his true disciples, the instruction which we derive from him will snatch us from destruction. This is the true sense of the passage. It afterwards follows,—

11. And from the time *that* the daily *sacrifice* shall be taken away, and the abomination that maketh desolate set up, *there shall be* a thousand two hundred and ninety days.

12. Blessed *is* he that waiteth, and cometh to the thousand three hundred and five and thirty days.

11. Et a tempore quo ablatum fuerit juge, *nempe sacrificium*, et posita fuerit abominatio obstupefaciens,[1] erunt dies mille ducenti et nonaginta.

12. Beatus qui expectaverit, et attigerit usque ad dies mille trecentos et triginta quinque.

In consequence of the obscurity of this passage it has

---

[1] We have translated it so before; some translate, "of desolation." The word signifies "to be desolate," but the other sense suits better here.— *Calvin.*

been twisted in a variety of ways. At the end of the ninth chapter I have shewn the impossibility of its referring to the profanation of the Temple which occurred under the tyranny of Antiochus; on this occasion the angel bears witness to such a complete destruction of the Temple, as to leave no room for the hope of its repair and restoration. Then the circumstances of the time convinces us of this. For he then said, Christ shall confirm the covenant with many for one week, and shall cause the sacrifices and oblation to cease. *Afterwards, the abomination that stupifieth shall be added*, and desolation or stupor, and then death will distil, says he, upon the astonished or stupified one. The angel, therefore, there treats of the perpetual devastation of the Temple. So in this passage, without doubt, he treats of the period after the destruction of the Temple; there could be no hope of restoration, as the law with all its ceremonies would then arrive at its termination. With this view Christ quotes this passage in Matthew xxiv., where he admonishes his hearers diligently to attend to it. Let him who reads, understand, says he. We have stated this prophecy to be obscure, and hence it requires no ordinary degree of the closest attention. First of all, we must hold this point; the time now treated by the angel begins at the last destruction of the Temple. That devastation happened as soon as the gospel began to be promulgated. God then deserted his Temple, because it was only founded for a time, and was but a shadow, until the Jews so completely violated the whole covenant that no sanctity remained in either the Temple, the nation, or the land itself. Some restrict this to those standards which Tiberius erected on the very highest pinnacle of the Temple, and others to the statue of Caligula, but I have already stated my view of these opinions as too forced. I have no hesitation in referring this language of the angel to that profanation of the Temple which happened after the manifestation of Christ, when sacrifices ceased, and the shadows of the law were abolished. *From the time*, therefore, *at which the sacrifice really ceased to be offered;* this refers to the period at which Christ by his advent should abolish the shadows of the law, thus making all offering of sacrifices to

God totally valueless. *From that time*, therefore. Next, *from the time at which the stupifying abomination shall have been set up.* God's wrath followed the profanation of the Temple. The Jews never anticipated the final cessation of their ceremonies, and always boasted in their peculiar external worship, and unless God had openly demonstrated it before their eyes, they would never have renounced their sacrifices and rites as mere shadowy representations. Hence Jerusalem and their Temple were exposed to the vengeance of the Gentiles. This, therefore, was the setting up of this stupifying abomination ; it was a clear testimony to the wrath of God, exhorting the Jews in their confusion to boast no longer in their Temple and its holiness.

Therefore, from that period there shall be 1290 *days.* These days make up three years and a half. I have no hesitation in supposing the angel to speak metaphorically. As he previously put one year, or two years, and half a year, for a long duration of time, and a happy issue, so he now puts 1290 *days.* And for what reason ? To shew us what must happen when anxieties and troubles oppress us. If a man should fall sick, he will not say, Here I have already been one month, but I have a year before me—he will not say, Here I have been three days, but now I languish wretchedly for thirty or sixty. The angel, then, purposely puts days for years, implying—although that time may seem immeasurably prolonged, and may frighten us by its duration, and completely prostrate the spirits of the pious, yet it must be endured. The number of days then is 1290, yet there is no reason why the sons of God should despair in consequence of this number, because they ought always to return to this principle—if those afflictions await us for a time and times, the half time will follow afterwards.

Then he adds, *Happy is he who shall have waited and endured until the* 1335 *days.* In numerical calculations I am no conjurer, and those who expound this passage with too great subtlety, only trifle in their own speculations, and detract from the authority of the prophecy. Some think the days should be understood as years, and thus make the number of years 2600. The time which elapsed from this prophecy to the advent of Christ was about 600 years. From this advent 2000 years remain, and they think this is the assigned period until the end of the world, as the law also flourished about 2000 years from the date of its promulgation to its fulfilment at Christ's advent. Hence they fix upon this sense. But they are quite wrong in separating the 1290 days from the 1335, for they clearly refer to the same period, with a slight exception. It is as if the angel had said, although half the time should be prorogued, yet the faithful ought constantly to persist in the hope of deliverance. For he adds, about two months, or a month and a half, or thereabouts. By half a time, we said, the issue was pointed out, as Christ informs us in Matt. xxiv. 22. Unless those days had been shortened, no flesh would have been safe. Reference is clearly made here to that abbreviation of the time for the Church's sake. But the angel now adds forty-five days, which make a month and a half, implying—God will put off the deliverance of his Church beyond six months, and yet ye must be strong and of good courage, and persevere in your watchfulness. God at length will not disappoint you—he will succour you in all your woes, and gather you to his blessed rest. Hence, the next clause of the prophecy is this,—

13. But go thou thy way till the end be: for thou shalt rest, and stand in thy lot at the end of the days.

13. Et tu vade ad finem, et quiesces, et stabis in sorte tua ad finem dierum.

Here the angel repeats what he had said before, the full time of perfect light had not yet arrived, because God wished to hold the minds of his people in suspense until the manifestation of Christ. The angel, therefore, dismisses the Prophet, and in commanding him to depart, says—Be content with thy lot, for God wishes to put off the complete manifestation of this prophecy to another time, which he himself knows to be the fitting one. He afterwards adds, *And thou shalt rest and shalt stand.* Others translate it, *rest and stand;* but the angel does not seem to me to command or order what he wishes to be done, but to announce future events, as if he had said,—Thou shalt rest, meaning, thou shalt die, and then thou shalt stand; meaning, thy death shall not be complete destruction. For God shall cause thee to stand in thy lot with the rest of the elect; *and that, too, at the end of the days, in thy lot;* that is, after God has sufficiently proved the patience of his people, and by long and numerous, nay, infinite contests, has humbled his Church, and purged it, until the end shall arrive. *At that final period thou shalt stand in thine own lot,* although a time of repose must necessarily intervene.

PRAYER.

Grant, Almighty God, since thou proposest to us no other end than that of constant warfare during our whole life, and subjectest us to many cares until we arrive at the goal of this temporary race-course: Grant, I pray thee, that we may never grow fatigued. May we ever be armed and equipped for battle, and whatever the trials by which thou dost prove us, may we never be found deficient. May we always aspire towards heaven with upright souls, and strive with all our endeavours to attain that blessed rest which is laid up for us in heaven, in Jesus Christ our Lord. —Amen.

Praise be to God.

END OF THE COMMENTARIES ON THE BOOK OF THE PROPHET DANIEL.

AN INDEX OF THE SCRIPTURAL PASSAGES QUOTED IN THESE LECTURES.

INDEX OF THE HEBREW WORDS ILLUSTRATED.

THE ORDER OF THE PAGING HAS BEEN OBSERVED UNDER EACH LETTER.

VOL. I.

VOL. II.

A LIST OF AUTHORS, SACRED AND PROFANE, QUOTED IN THESE VOLUMES.

SACRED.

	VOL.	PAGE
Augustin, Ep. clxvi. adv. Donat., . . .	i.	245
Augustin, adv. Pelag., ...	ii.	189, 207
Jerome, ...	i. 258, ii.	207
Origen, ...	i. 258, ii.	207
Tertullian, ...	ii.	41, 207
Irenæus, ...	ii.	41
Luther, ...	ii.	119
Hippolytus, ...	ii.	207
Nicolaus de Lyra, ...	ii.	207
Apollinaris, ...	ii.	207, 208
Œcolampadius, ...	ii.	208
Eusebius, ...	ii.	207
Melancthon, ...	ii.	209, 210
Concilia, Decret., vol. i. chap. vii., . . .	ii.	346

PROFANE.

	VOL.	PAGE
Cicero, De Divinat., lib. i., ii., . . .	i.	119, 207
Cicero, De Legibus, ...	i.	207
Homer, Iliad, i., ...	i.	119
Virgil, Æneid, ...	i.	207
Juvenal, Sat. i., ...	i.	239
Herodotus, lib. i., ...	i.	306, 327
Xenophon, lib. iv., ...	i.	307
Ovid, Traj., ...	ii.	267
Ovid, Ar. Am., ...	i.	311
Terence, Andr., ...	ii.	163
Polybius, lib. v., ...	ii.	287
Cicero, pro Flacc., ...	ii.	342
Plutarch, ...	ii.	349

COPIOUS INDEX OF THE CHIEF WORDS AND SUBJECTS TREATED OF IN THESE VOLUMES.

THE END.